GATEWAYS
TO DEMOCRACY

AN INTRODUCTION TO
AMERICAN GOVERNMENT
THE ESSENTIALS

JOHN G.
GEER
VANDERBILT UNIVERSITY

WENDY J.
SCHILLER
BROWN UNIVERSITY

JEFFREY A.
SEGAL
STONY BROOK UNIVERSITY

DANA K.
GLENCROSS
OKLAHOMA CITY COMMUNITY
COLLEGE

WADSWORTH
CENGAGE Learning™

Australia • Brazil • Japan • Korea • Mexico • Singapore • Spain • United Kingdom • United States

WADSWORTH
CENGAGE Learning™

Gateways to Democracy: An Introduction
to American Government, The Essentials
John G. Geer, Wendy J. Schiller,
Jeffrey A. Segal, and Dana K. Glencross

Publisher: Suzanne Jeans

Executive Editor: Carolyn Merrill

Managing Development Editor: Jeff Greene

Developmental Editor: Ohlinger Publishing
    Services

Assistant Editor: Laura Ross

Editorial Assistant: Nina Wasserman

Media Editor: Laura Hildebrand

Marketing Manager: Lydia LeStar

Marketing Communications Manager:
    Heather Baxley

Production Manager: Suzanne St. Clair

Art Director: Linda Helcher

Print Buyer: Fola Orekoya

Printer: RRD Crawfordsville

Rights Acquisition Specialist, Image:
    Jennifer Meyer Dare

Rights Acquisition Specialist, Text:
    Katie Huha

Text Researcher: Sarah D'Stair

Production Service: MPS Limited,
    a Macmillan Company

Text Designer: RDHD

Photo Researcher: Stacey Dong

Copy Editor: Beth Chapple

Cover and Interior Designer: RHDG

Cover Image:
    Front Cover: © Marjorie Kamys Cotera;
    Kenn Stilger/Shutterstock; Photo
    courtesy of George Tarbay, University
    Relations, Northern Illinois University;
    Courtesy of the University Science and
    Arts of Oklahoma; Courtesy of the
    College of the Redwoods, Eureka
    Back Cover (Student Edition): © 2010
    Carlos Gotay/Getty Images;
    DianeRicePhotos.com; © Bob Kalmbach/
    University of Michigan Photo Services—
    ALL RIGHTS RESERVED

Compositor: MPS Limited, a Macmillan
    Company

For product information and technology assistance, contact us at
Cengage Learning Customer & Sales Support, 1-800-354-9706.

For permission to use material from this text or product,
submit all requests online at **www.cengage.com/permissions**.
Further permissions questions can be e-mailed to
permissionrequest@cengage.com.

Library of Congress Control Number: 2010935368

Student Edition:

ISBN-13: 978-0-495-90619-3

ISBN-10: 0-495-90619-0

Wadsworth
20 Channel Center Street
Boston, MA 02210
USA

Cengage Learning is a leading provider of customized learning solutions
with office locations around the globe, including Singapore, the United
Kingdom, Australia, Mexico, Brazil, and Japan. Locate your local office at
www.cengage.com/global.

Cengage Learning products are represented in Canada by
Nelson Education, Ltd.

To learn more about Wadsworth, visit **www.cengage.com/Wadsworth**.

Purchase any of our products at your local college store or at our
preferred online store **www.cengagebrain.com**.

Printed in the United States of America
1 2 3 4 5 6 7 14 13 12 11 10

BRIEF CONTENTS

FEATURES

Supreme Court Cases

Other Places

Policy

CONTENTS

3 FEDERALISM 72

4 CIVIL LIBERTIES 106

7 THE NEWS MEDIA AND THE INTERNET 210

10 ELECTIONS, CAMPAIGNS, AND VOTING 318

PART III The Institutions of American Government

11 CONGRESS 360

14 THE JUDICIARY 492

PREFACE

Our book begins with a simple question: How does anyone exert political influence in a country of more than 308 million people? We know that students in American government classrooms across the country are grappling with this question as they develop an appreciation of their role in American public life. In our own classrooms, students ask us, What is my responsibility? Can I make a difference? Does my participation matter? How can I get my opinions represented? These are gateway questions that probe the opportunities and limits on citizen involvement in a democracy.

Although the size and complexity of the American constitutional system is daunting, it is imperative to prepare students for the demands of democratic citizenship. As teachers and scholars of American government, we have come together to write a textbook that explains the theoretical and structural foundations of American democracy and the resulting political process that demands an active and informed citizenry. To help students understand American democracy and see how they can be involved in their government, we peel back the layers of the political system to expose its inner workings and to examine how competing interests can both facilitate and block the people's will. In doing so, we use the conceptual framework of gateways. We contend that there are gates—formal and informal—that present obstacles to participation and empowerment. But there are also gateways that give students a chance to influence the process and to overcome the obstacles.

The gateways framework helps students conceptualize participation and civic engagement—even democracy itself—with reference to access. Our book is both realistic and optimistic, contending that the American system can be open to the influence of students and responsive to their hopes and dreams—if they have information about how the system works. But we avoid cheerleading by also pointing out the many gates that undermine the workings of government.

We use the gateways theme to encourage students to develop critical thinking skills. We employ concrete examples of political activism and engagement, from a teenager to the president of the United States, inviting students to enter a conversation about the workings of American democracy. This textbook digs below the surface of standard descriptions of democracy by asking students to consider how democratic we are as a nation. We pose questions: Does equality require equal opportunity, or does it require equal outcomes? How responsive and accountable is American government? And we challenge students to figure out their own standards for the society in which they want to live in the twenty-first century. Questions like these encourage students to think about the meaning of self-government, and they constitute a sustained analytical component of this textbook.

Organization of the Textbook

We begin with student engagement. Chapter 1 describes the demands of democratic citizenship and asks students to judge American democracy. In the next three parts, we examine the foundations of the American constitutional system, the means of citizen access and influence in a democratic society, and the institutions of American government.

Chapter 1, Gateways to American Democracy: Judging the Democratic Experiment, provides the rationale and road map for citizen engagement in self-government. We describe the Constitution as a gatekeeper, protecting liberty and order but also facilitating representation. The dimensions of representation are set forth as ideological, economic, and partisan. The chapter's overall goal is to establish the nature of democracy, the need for an informed citizenry, and the framework we employ on this intellectual journey.

The chapter also encourages students to assess how they might navigate the gateways to become effective citizens. In doing so, we want to provide students with tools and incentives to assess the quality of their current political institutions. We point out that how one assesses the American political system depends very much on where one sits. Further, the standards one brings to bear shape the answers one develops. There will always be a gap between the ideals and the realities of government, but that is a good thing, for it provides the reason to improve government and bring the nation closer to its ideals.

We include in this chapter a special section that describes the policy-making process as a foundation for policy coverage throughout the book. We view policy as central to understanding American democracy. As a result, we do not isolate the discussion of policy in chapters at the end of the book. Instead, we integrate policy into each of the substantive chapters, situating it as a central part of understanding American politics. By so doing, we underscore the importance of the topic and give students a better understanding of American government.

Part I, Building a System of Government, includes chapters on the Constitution, federalism, civil liberties, and civil rights that discuss the major issues the Framers confronted when they created a representative government. This section examines why the Framers made particular choices and what the intended and unintended consequences of their decisions have been over time. Students will understand that the ideals expressed in the Declaration of Independence have only slowly been realized and are still evolving. This section of the textbook provides basic information about the operation of American government—the separation of powers, unitary president, lifetime appointments for judges, staggered elections, divided legislature, state and local government, and geographic apportionment—and helps students assess whether the foundations of American government ensure responsiveness and equality.

Part II, Citizen Gateways in a Democracy, includes chapters on public opinion, the news media, interest groups, political parties, elections, campaigns, and voting and participation. Together these chapters address the question of how a single individual's opinions are formed, expressed, and included in the policy-making process at all levels of government. These matters are essential to our approach. If students are to be part of the political process, they need to understand how to make the best use of the avenues for representation that exist in the American political system. We begin with basic data about how much people know about American government, where they get their information, to whom they listen, and to what extent their opinions change over time. By starting with individual opinion, we help students assess their own opinions about politics and analyze the sources of those opinions.

We continue with the nature of communication among citizens by addressing the impact of the news media on American politics. The news media are important sources of information for the public, politicians, and policy elites. They do more than just report the news; they frequently construct the news. We talk about the role of the news media not only historically but also in the context of the rise of cable news networks, the growth of the Internet, the decline of newspapers, and the potential of social networking. Does the immediacy of the modern media environment have an empowering or a detrimental effect on our democratic system? Does the intense and sometimes intrusive media scrutiny enhance or restrict government's responsiveness to the needs of its citizenry? These are the kinds of questions we address to get students thinking about the political environment in which twenty-first-century government has to function.

We then turn to interest groups as a means by which individual opinions are aggregated and given voice in a democracy, but in markedly different ways and to varying degrees of success. Community or grassroots efforts, from environmental movements to religious organizations to public interest groups, are often a satisfying and empowering form of civic participation. The conventional wisdom is that powerful "special interests" can trounce small citizens' groups when competing for government benefits, but we counter that the increasing number of interest groups means that more people are represented in the formulation of public policy and that improved communication has given small citizens' groups a new gateway for influence.

We next examine how political parties evolved and their crucial and controversial roles in the functioning of government. From the first debates over the ratification of the Constitution to the recent Tea Party movement, this chapter delves into the reasons why the United States remains a predominantly two-party political system. We also address the nature of partisan identification, realignment, modern party organizations, and the nature of party accountability in government. A fundamental theme of the chapter is whether parties have the potential to serve as instruments for engaging and channeling citizens' efforts to elicit responsiveness from government.

The last chapter in this part looks directly at the most basic form of participation in a democracy—elections, campaigns, and voting. When politicians seek elective office, they strive to appear as responsive as possible. Can voters make informed decisions and hold their elected officials accountable? We grapple with the difficult question of whether or how much campaigns as political institutions shape our government. Campaigns tend to be associated with "dirty politics" and candidates who are willing to say anything to get elected. But such perceptions miss the fact that campaigns are also gateways connecting the public and politicians. We argue that political campaigns provide voters with the information they need to make good choices and to hold public officials accountable. We also provide comprehensive analyses of the accuracy and type of information presented in campaigns, the strategic framing of campaign issues, and the factors that ultimately determine the outcomes of elections.

This chapter also looks at voting, the most straightforward and least costly form of participation in American democracy. It is also the simplest way for individuals to influence their elected officials. But students are often skeptical about the power of the vote. Given the size of the country, do all votes even count? If they do, are they counted equally? The election of 2000 serves as a sharp illustration of why and how individual votes can matter, and we also look at the 2008 election that sparked great interest and attention. We discuss other types of civic participation, such as membership in religious and community-based organizations, not-for-profit organizations, and Internet blogging. We use this chapter in part to illustrate how the gateways to involvement in twenty-first-century American life are wider and more direct than they have been in the past.

Part III, The Institutions of American Government, provides an in-depth description and explanation of Congress, the presidency, the bureaucracy, and the judiciary. In the Institutions chapters, we describe the fundamental components of Congress, the presidency, and the judiciary, as well as the ways each interacts with the other two. We ask students to examine the behavior and outputs of government by responsiveness and equality. For example, does having term limits weaken the president relative to Congress, which does not have term limits? Does the bicameral structure of Congress give the legislative branch an advantage when dealing with the executive branch? We also focus students' attention on how party politics creates a governing dynamic that changes depending on the balance of control of these branches. For the judicial branch, we contend that the courts provide an important gateway for influencing the process and also for advancing the cause of equality. Yet courts are not electorally accountable to citizens, and federal judges hold life tenure. Do the courts mete out equal justice to all citizens, regardless of race and income? If they do not, are there means beyond elections by which Congress and the president can help hold courts accountable?

In the chapter on the bureaucracy, our aim is to show students how policy making and the bureaucracy affect day-to-day life. We examine the layers of bureaucratic decision making to demonstrate that the decisions made at each level of an agency or cabinet department can have a profound impact on how laws affect individuals. We discuss decision making in the areas of economic policy, budget policy, entitlement spending for the elderly and the disadvantaged, health care policy, education policy, and environmental policy, all in the context of the dynamics of policy implementation within agencies and the departments that oversee them. In these discussions, we highlight the areas of public policy that students may experience firsthand.

Additional Online Chapter

The United States as a Global Partner examines how the United States will navigate the changing global economic and political environment of the twenty-first century. In this online chapter we look at the compatibility of American democratic ideals, values, and institutions with other forms of government and ask whether the United States can forge working relationships with governments that are different from it. This chapter looks at the global footprint of the United States in the areas of trade and economic development, arms control and human rights, and health, energy consumption, and climate change.

Special Instructional Features

Special instructional features facilitate a comprehensive introduction to American government that also takes the demands of citizenship seriously.

Participation. A goal of the book is to encourage participation in public life by helping students recognize their own self-interest and a broader civic interest. The book makes the case that democracies demand citizen participation and that citizenship is a serious responsibility.

Critical thinking. We also want to facilitate critical thinking by asking students to evaluate American democracy through the measures of government responsiveness and citizen equality. This emphasis sharpens students' analytical skills and gives them greater competence and additional confidence to become involved in public life. We devote special sections in each chapter to fundamental types of information that we believe students need to navigate the political process. We also add pedagogical tools to help both instructors and students identify key concepts and terms.

Constitutional and legal setting. For instructors, the book provides strong support for the institutional foundations of American government. The first section of every chapter is an overview of the constitutional and legal setting of the chapter's subject. This essential, basic information helps ensure that students are equipped with what they need to know to understand the process, limits, and safeguards of democracy.

Public policy. We believe public policy is much too important to be relegated to separate chapters at the back of the book. Students cannot take their place as active citizens in American democracy unless they understand how the policy process works. We bring policy applications into our consideration of every aspect of American government by incorporating the policy process and specific policy examples in a dedicated section in every chapter. Attention to a series of specific issues in a variety of contexts helps students understand the political process. And, indeed, specific policies are often the best incentives for getting them engaged.

Student engagement. In the opening of every chapter we focus on people who were young when they got their start in political and civic life to encourage students and show them reasons and ways to become involved.

Comparative feature. A box in many of the chapters examines a particular topic with reference to political practice in other countries. Additional comparative content is available online.

Supreme Court feature. To buttress the book's attention to the legal and constitutional context in which American government operates, most chapters feature a relevant Supreme Court case, stating the facts and the decision, with an analysis of its impact.

Pedagogical Tools for Conceptual Reinforcement

An array of pedagogical tools supports the textbook's purpose and aids in student learning.

Focus questions. Focus questions at the beginning of each chapter encourage students to think about the chapter topic in terms of government's responsiveness, the people's equality, and the gates and gateways to access. These questions are revisited in the chapter's final section, where we offer interpretive responses.

Margin questions and cues. Brief questions in the margins provoke students to think about the big issues even as they are reading about the details of American government. These questions keep students thinking critically about the information they are absorbing, serve as prompts for class discussions, and aid in chapter review.

Key terms. Terms important to know for an understanding of American government are boldfaced in the text and defined on the page for ease of understanding and review.

Gateways to Learning. A special "Gateways to Learning" section at the end of each chapter includes a ten-point list of main ideas for review and learning. Lists of key terms, exercises, review questions, and resources are also included in this section or on the book's website.

To access additional course materials and companion resources, please visit www.cengagebrain.com/shop/ISBN/0495906190 or visit www.cengage brain.com and search on the ISBN of this book.

Supplements

PowerLecture DVD with JoinIn™ and ExamView®
ISBN-10: 0495906255 | ISBN-13: 9780495906254

This DVD includes two sets of PowerPoint slides—a book-specific set and a media-enhanced set; a test bank in both Microsoft Word and Exam View formats; an Instructor Manual; JoinIn clicker questions; and a Resource Integration Guide.

- **Interactive, book-specific PowerPoint® lectures** make it easy for you to assemble, edit, publish, and present book-specific lectures for your course. You will have access to outlines specific to each chapter of the text as well as photos, figures, and tables found in the text.
- **Media-enhanced PowerPoint slides** can be used on their own or easily integrated with the book-specific PowerPoint outlines. Look for audio and video clips depicting both historic and current events; animated learning modules illustrating key concepts; tables, statistical charts, and graphs; and photos from both the book and outside sources, provided at the appropriate places in the chapter.
- **Test bank in Microsoft® Word and ExamView® computerized testing** offers a large array of well-crafted multiple-choice and essay questions, along with their answers and page references.
- **Instructor's Manual** includes learning objectives, chapter outlines, discussion questions, suggestions for stimulating class activities and projects, tips on integrating media into your class (including step-by-step instructions on how to create your own podcasts), suggested readings and Web resources, and a section specially designed to help teaching assistants and adjunct instructors.

- **JoinIn™ "clicker" questions** test and track student comprehension of key concepts.
- **The Resource Integration Guide** outlines the rich collection of resources available to instructors and students within the chapter-by-chapter framework of the book, suggesting how and when each supplement can be used to optimize learning.

CourseMate

Text + CourseMate Printed Access Card:
ISBN-10: 0538793112 | ISBN-13: 9780538793117

This media-rich website offers a variety of rich online learning resources designed to enhance the student learning experience. These resources include video activities, audio summaries, critical thinking exercises, simulations, animated learning modules, interactive timelines, primary source quizzes, flashcards, learning objectives, glossaries, and crossword puzzles. Chapter resources are correlated to key chapter learning concepts, and users can browse or search for content in a variety of ways.

NewsNow is a new asset available in CourseMate. It is a combination of weekly news stories from the Associated Press and videos and images that bring current events to life for the student. For instructors, NewsNow includes an additional set of multimedia-rich PowerPoint slides posted each week to the password-protected area of the text's instructor companion website. Instructors may use these slides to take a class poll or trigger a lively debate about the events that are shaping the world right now.

The **Engagement Tracker** assesses student preparation and engagement. Use the tracking tools to see progress for the class as a whole or for individual students. Identify students at risk early in the course. Uncover which concepts are most difficult for your class. Monitor time on task. Keep your students engaged.

Coursemate also features an **interactive eBook** that has highlighting and search capabilities along with links to simulations, animated PowerPoints that illustrate concepts, interactive timelines, video activities, primary source quizzes, and flashcards.

Go to cengagebrain.com/shop/ISBN/0495906190 to access your Political Science CourseMate resources.

American Government CourseReader

Text + CourseReader Printed Access Card:
ISBN-10: 111147995X | ISBN-13: 9781111479954

The CourseReader allows instructors to create a customized reader using a database of hundreds of documents, readings, and videos. Instructors can search by various criteria or browse the collection, to preview and then select a customized collection to assign to their students. The sources are edited to an appropriate length and include pedagogical support—a headnote describing the document and critical-thinking and multiple-choice questions to verify that the student has read and understood the selection. Students can take notes, highlight, and print content. The CourseReader allows the instructor to select exactly what students will be assigned with an easy-to-use interface and also provides an easily used assessment tool. The sources can be delivered online or in print format.

Aplia (available for Fall 2011 classes)

Text + Aplia Printed Access Card: ISBN-10: 1111300801 | ISBN-13: 9781111300807

Aplia is dedicated to improving students' learning by increasing their engagement with your American Government course through premium, automatically graded assignments. Aplia saves instructors valuable time they'd otherwise spend on routine grading, while giving students an easy way to stay on top of coursework with regularly scheduled assignments.

Organized by specific chapters of their textbook, immediate, detailed explanations are supplied to students for every answer they input. Grades are automatically recorded in the instructor's Aplia gradebook.

Instructor Companion Website

The instructor companion site includes the Instructor's Manual, text-specific PowerPoint slides containing lecture outlines, photos, and figures, and News-Now PowerPoint slides.

WebTutor on WebCT or Blackboard

Text + WebCT Printed Access Card:
ISBN-10: 0538793155 | ISBN-13: 9780538793155

Text + Blackboard Printed Access Card:
ISBN-10: 0538793139 | ISBN-13: 9780538793131

Rich with content for your American government course, this Web-based teaching and learning tool includes course management, study/mastery, and communication tools. Use WebTutor™ to provide virtual office hours, post your syllabus, and track student progress with WebTutor's quizzing material.

CourseCare

Available exclusively to Cengage Learning, CourseCare is a revolutionary program designed to provide you and your students with an unparalleled user experience with your Cengage Learning digital solution.

CourseCare connects you with a team of training, service, and support experts to help you implement your Cengage Learning Digital Solution. You'll find real people dedicated to you, your students, and your course from the first day of class through final exams.

Political Theatre 2.0

ISBN-10: 0495793604 | ISBN-13: 9780495793601

Bring politics home to students with Political Theatre 2.0, up-to-date through the 2008 election season. This is the second edition of this 3 DVD series and includes real video clips that show American political thought throughout the public sector. Clips include both classic and contemporary political advertisements, speeches, interviews, and more.

JoinIn™ on Turning Point®
for Political Theatre

ISBN-10: 0495798290 | ISBN-13: 9780495798293

For even more interaction, combine Political Theatre with the innovative teaching tool of a classroom response system through JoinIn™. Poll your students with questions created for you or create your own questions.

The Wadsworth News Videos
for American Government 2012 DVD

ISBN-10: 1111346143 | ISBN-13: 9781111346140

This collection of three- to six-minute video clips on relevant political issues serves as a great lecture or discussion launcher.

Great Speeches Collection

Throughout the ages, great orators have stepped up to the podium and used their communication skills to persuade, inform, and inspire their audiences. Studying these speeches can provide tremendous insight into historical, political, and cultural events. The Great Speeches Collection includes the full text of over sixty memorable orations for you to incorporate into your course. Speeches can be collated in a printed reader to supplement your existing course materials or bound into a core textbook.

ABC Video: Speeches by President Barack Obama

ISBN-10: 1439082472 | ISBN-13: 9781439082478

DVD of nine famous speeches by President Barack Obama, from 2004 through his inauguration, including his speech at the 2004 Democratic National Convention; his 2008 speech on race, "A More Perfect Union"; and his 2009 inaugural address. Speeches are divided into short video segments for easy, time-efficient viewing. This instructor supplement also features critical-thinking questions and answers for each speech, designed to spark classroom discussion.

Election 2010: An American Government Supplement

Text + Election 2010 supplement: ISBN-10: 1111341788 | ISBN-13: 9781111341787

Written by John Clark and Brian Schaffner, this booklet addresses the 2010 congressional and gubernatorial races, with both real-time analysis and references.

Latino American Politics Supplement

Text + Latino American Politics supplement: ISBN-10: 1111344817 | ISBN-13: 9781111344818

This 32-page supplement uses real examples to detail politics related to Latino Americans.

Instructor's Guide to YouTube for Political Science

Instructors have access to the Instructor's Guide to YouTube, which shows American government instructors where to find videos on the Internet that can be used as learning tools in class. Organized by fifteen topics, the guide follows the sequence of a typical American government course and includes a preface with tips on how to use Internet videos in class.

Acknowledgments

Writing the first edition of an introductory textbook requires a dedicated and professional publishing team, and we were extremely fortunate to work with a number of excellent people at Wadsworth Publishing/Cengage Learning. Our development editor, Ann Hofstra Grogg, has been outstanding; she was an essential part of translating our ideas about encouraging students to participate in American politics into an organized and comprehensive textbook. Although our sponsoring editor, Edwin Hill, did not see this project to its completion, he was an integral part of it, and we thank him for all his guidance. We thank Matthew DiGangi for his time and energy. We want to extend a special note of thanks to Carolyn Merrill, who has been so supportive of this project. Joshua Allen, Stacey Dong, Jeffrey Greene, Suzanne Jeans, Monica Ohlinger, and Sybil Sosin all provided key support on format, photos, and production of this book. We also would like to thank Amy Whitaker, Lydia Lestar, and the entire sales force at Wadsworth Publishing for their tireless efforts to promote the book. In addition, we thank Traci Mueller for her early support of this project.

By definition, an American politics textbook is a sweeping endeavor, and it was not possible to succeed without our reviewers. They provided truly constructive input throughout the writing process. We list their names below, and we are grateful to them for their contributions to the development of this textbook.

Each of us would also like to thank the individuals who supported us throughout the project.

John G. Geer: I wish to thank Corey Bike and Mason Moseley for able research assistance. I also want to express deep appreciation to my daughter, Megan Geer, and my cousin, William Geer Masalehdan, for reading early drafts of my chapters and providing helpful comments. A special note of thanks goes to Cyndi Keen, who twenty years ago recommended that I write a textbook; I hope that this text was worth the wait. Finally, I want to thank my coauthors, Wendy and Jeff. When I pulled this team together, I knew that Jeff and Wendy were good people and gifted scholars. Having worked with them over the last few years, I now realize that judgment underestimated their many talents. It has been an honor for me to be part of this collaboration.

Wendy J. Schiller: I would also like to express my appreciation for the opportunity to work with John and Jeff—two excellent scholars and supportive colleagues. I would like to thank Mary Jane April, Ilene Berman, Matthew Corritore, Lucy Drotning, Helen Guler, Curtis Kelley, Fiona McGillivray, Molly Phee, Marsha Pripstein Posusney, Jessica Breese Schiller, Jordana Schwartz, Alastair Smith, Tiffany Trigg, Miriam Wugmeister, and Alan Zuckerman for all their support and assistance with this project. A special thanks goes to Roger Cobb, with whom I teach introduction to American politics at Brown, for all his help. Lastly, I would like to thank my husband, Robert Kalunian, who provided an endless supply of patience, support, and perspective.

Jeffrey A. Segal: I would like to thank my family—Christine, Michelle, and Paul—for allowing me the time to work on this project as needed. I also have special gratitude for my coauthors, who made working on the book as pleasant as possible. Writing the book coincided with difficult medical news, and John, Wendy, and everyone involved at Wadsworth/Cengage stepped up, no questions asked. I cannot overstate my appreciation on this score. I also thank several people for research assistance, including Nasser Javaid, Roland Kappe, Ellen Key, Magen Knuth, Maxwell Mak, Andrew O'Geen, Christopher Parker, and Shannon Stagman, plus my colleagues in the Department of Political Science at Stony Brook University, who readily answered the questions I asked them. It is nearly impossible to imagine a more supportive work environment.

Dana K. Glencross: I must thank a great cadre of people. First, to this trio of great authors, I sincerely thank you for this opportunity. To my first government teacher, Phyllis Davis, thank you for beginning my life-long quest of civic engagement. Thanks to my students with whom I share teaching and learning. For your patience and support, thank you to my husband Carl and my parents, Betty and Franklin Delano Baker, and Reagan, the basset hound, who tirelessly waited for the computer to go dark. Mendy Barr, your insights were of terrific assistance. Lisa Davis, thanks for your dedication. Finally, to all who capture this book's passion to make government more responsive to those in need, thank you for understanding that the democratic lesson endures through its freedom keepers.

Reviewers and Contributors

We would like to thank the following faculty for leading us through the many gateways we encountered in creating this new textbook. Some participated in focus groups, others answered surveys, and still others provided valuable feedback on the drafts of the manuscript. The people whose names are in boldface reviewed the manuscript.

Yishaiya Abosch, California State University–Fresno
Martin Adamian, California State University Los Angeles
Grace Adams-Square, Towson University
Noe Alexander Aguado, University of North Alabama
Gary Aguiar, South Dakota State University
Philip Aka, Chicago State University
Craig W. Allin, Cornell College
Davida Alperin, University of Wisconsin–River Falls
Rodney Anderson, California State University Fresno
Warren Anderson, North Harris College
Louis Andolino, Monroe Community College
Steve Anthony, Georgia State University
Andrew Aoki, Augsburg College
Phillip Ardoin, Appalachian State University

Leighton Armitage, College of San Mateo
Ruth Arnell, Idaho State University
Ross Baker, Rutgers University
Thomas Baldino, Wilkes University
Evelyn Ballard, Houston Community College Southeast
Jodi Balma, Fullerton College
Chris Banks, Kent State
Michael Baranowski, Northern Kentucky University
Lance Bardsley, Gainesville State College
Kedron Bardwell, Simpson College
Mary Barnes-Tilley, Blinn College
Tim Barnett, Jacksonville State University
Joyce Baugh, Central Michigan University
Chris Baxter, University of Tennessee at Martin
Kris Beck, Gordon College
Jenna Bednar, University of Michigan
James Belpedio, Becker College
Robert E. Bence, Massachusetts College of Liberal Arts
Philip Benesch, Lebanon Valley College
John Berg, Suffolk University
Justin Bezis, West Hills College
Amanda Bigelow, Illinois Valley Community College
Robert Bilodeau, South Plains College, Levelland
Richard Bilsker, College of Southern Maryland
William Binning, Youngstown State University
Bethany Blackstone, University of North Texas
Ted Blair, Diablo Valley College
John Blakeman, University of Wisconsin–Stevens Point
Jeff Blankenship, University of South Alabama
Leon Blevins, El Paso Community College
Richard Blisker, College of Southern Maryland
Julio Borquez, University of Michigan–Dearborn
Janet M. Box-Steffensmeier, Ohio State University
Matthew Bradley, Indiana University-Kokomo
Todd Bradley, Indiana University-Kokomo
Stephen Bragaw, Sweet Briar College
Lynn Brink, North Lake College
Andreas Broscheid, James Madison University
Lee Brown, Reedley College
Ronald Brown, Wayne State University–Detroit
Martin Brownstein, Ithaca College
Jane Bryant, John A. Logan College

Richard Buckner, Santa Fe Community College, Gainesville
Laurie Buonnano, Buffalo State College, SUNY
Randi Buslik, Northeastern Illinois University
Jennifer Byrne, James Madison University
Rachel Bzostek, California State University Bakersfield
Joseph Cammarano, Providence College
Michelle Camou, College of Wooster
Mary Caravelis, Barry University
James Carlson, Providence College
Jamie Carson, The University of Georgia
Monica Carter, Chaffey College
Terrence Casey, Rose-Hulman Institute of Technology
Marn Cha, California State University–Fresno
James Chalmers, Wayne State University
Van Chaney, El Camino College
Elsa Chen, Santa Clara University
Alade Chester, San Bernardino Valley College
Wendy Cho, University of Illinois
John Clark, Western Michigan University
Michael Clark, St. Xavier University
Kurt Cline, California State University–Fresno
Jean Clouatre, Manchester Community College
Michael Cobb, North Carolina State University
Carolyn Cocca, SUNY College at Old Westbury
Jeff Colbert, Elon University
Annie Cole, Los Angeles City College
Kathleen Colihan, American River College
Paul Collins, University of North Texas
Todd Collins, Western Carolina University
Frank Colucci, Purdue University–Calumet
David Connelly, Utah Valley University
George Connor, Missouri State University–Springfield
Joseph Corrado, Clayton College and State University
Thomas Costa, Florida Community College–Jacksonville
Michael Coulter, Grove City College
Albert Cover, Stony Brook University
Leland Coxe, University of Texas at Brownsville
Robert Craig, The College of St. Scholastica
William Cunion, Mount Union College
Dyron Keith Dabney, Albion College
Alison Dagnes, Shippensburg University
Nicholas D'Arecca, Temple University

Peter Davies, California State University–Sacramento
Paul Davis, Truckee Meadows Community College
Wartyna Davis, William Paterson University
Derek Davis, Austin Community College
Frank De Caria, West Virginia Northern Community College
Laura De La Cruz, El Paso Community College
Robert DeLuna, St. Phillips College
Iva Deutchman, Hobart and William Smith Colleges
Jeff Diamond, Skyline College
Brian Dillie, Odessa College
Richardson Dilworth, Drexel University
Thomas Dolan, Columbus State University
Jay Dow, University of Missouri–Columbia
Alan Draper, St. Lawrence University
Mary Drinan, Palomar College
Bryan Dubin, Oakland Community College
Patricia Dunham, Duquesne University
Cecile Durish, Austin Community College
Diana Dwyre, California State University–Chico
Joshua Dyck, University of Buffalo–SUNY
Stanley Dyck, Colorado Christian University
Victor Edo-Aikhionbare, Palm Beach State College
Kathryn Edwards, Ashland Community and Technical College
Sheryl Edwards, University of Michigan–Dearborn
Matthew Eshbaugh-Soha, University of North Texas
Andrew Ewoh, Kennesaw State University
Hyacinth Ezeamii, Albany State University
Vallye Ezell, Richland College
Traci Fahimi, Irvine Valley College
Frank Fato, Westchester Community College–SUNY
Henry Fearnley, College of Marin
William Felix, Rutgers University
Therese Filicko, Ohio State University–Newark Campus
Glen Findley, Odessa College
Mark Fish, Dallas Christian College
Patrick Fisher, Seton Hall University
Sam Fisher, University of South Alabama
Michael Fisher, John Jay College of Criminal Justice–CUNY
Richard Flanagan, College of Staten Island–CUNY
Brian Fletcher, Truckeee Meadows Community College
Julianne Flowers, DePaul University
Michael Frank, Anderson University

Steve Frank, St. Cloud State University

Bill Franklin, San Bernardino Valley College

Rodd Freitag, University of Wisconsin–Eau Claire

Barry Friedman, North Georgia College and University

George Gallo, Albertus Magnus College

Hoyt Gardner, Columbia State Community College

Steve Garrison, Midwestern State University

Yolanda Garza-Hake, South Texas College

Michael Gattis, Gulf Coast Community College

Eddie Genna, Phoenix College

Mitch Gerber, Southeast Missouri University

Jeffrey Gerson, University of Massachusetts–Lowell

Chris Gilbert, Gustavus Adolphus College

James Gleason, Purdue University

Dana Glencross, Oklahoma City Community College

Herbert Gooch, California Lutheran University

Martha Good, Miami University (Ohio)

Robert Green, St. Phillips College

Steven Greene, North Carolina State University

Gloria Guevara, Oxnard College / California State University Northridge

Max Guirguis, Shepherd University

Rhonda Gunter, Maryland Community College

Jose Angel Gutierrez, University of Texas–Arlington

Michael A. Haas, University of North Carolina–Wilmington

Anna Liesl Haas, California State University–Long Beach

Lori Han, Chapman University

Roger Handberg, University of Central Florida

Cathy Hanks, University of Nevada–Las Vegas

Sally Hansen, Daytona State

Richard Harris, Rutgers University

Edward Hasecke, Wittenberg University

Lori Hausegger, Boise State University

David Head, John Tyler Community College

Stacy Hunter Hecht, Bethel University

Robert Heineman, Alfred University

Diane Heith, St. John's University

Joann Hendricks, City College of San Francisco

John Hermann, Trinity University

Jeffrey Hernandez, East Los Angeles College

Richard Herrera, Arizona State University

John Heyrman, Berea College

Kenneth Hicks, Rogers State University

Marti Hill, Southwest Texas Junior College–Uvalde
Jefferey Hill, Northeastern Illinois University
James Hite, Portland State University and Mt. Hood Community College
John Hitt, North Lake College
James Holland, University of Akron
Suzanne Homer, City College of San Francisco
Jennifer Hora, Valparaiso University
Randolph Horn, Samford University
Melody Huckaby, Cameron University
Elizabeth Huffman, Consumnes River College
Scott Huffmon, Winthrop University
Patrick Hughes, Camden Community College
Gregg Ivers, American University
David Jackson, Bowling Green State University
Robert Jackson, Florida State University
Winsome Jackson, Sierra College
Lloyd Jansen, Green River Community College / University of Washington
Amy Jasperson, University of Texas at San Antonio
Mark Jendrysik, University of North Dakota
Terri Jett, Butler University
Alana Jeydel, American River College
Richard Johnson, Oklahoma City University
Scott Johnson, Frostburg State University
Susan Johnson, University of Wisconsin–Whitewater
Jean-Gabriel Jolivet, Southwestern College
Oliver Jones, Palo Alto College
Rebecca Jones, Widener University
James Joseph, Fresno City College
Andrew Karch, University of Texas at Austin
Mary Kazmierczak, Marquette University
Gina Keel, SUNY College at Oneonta
Michael Kelley, Pittsburg State University
Sean Kelly, California State University–Channel Islands
John Kemanski, Oakland University
Alyson Kennedy, University of Mississippi
Linda Kennedy, Lassen Community College
Stephen Kerbow, Southwest Texas Junior College
Brian Kessel, Columbia College
Jeffery Key, Hardin-Simmons University
Soleiman Kiasatpour, Western Kentucky University
Richard Kiefer, Wabaunsee Community College

Bill Klein, St. Petersburg College
Daniel Klinghard, College of the Holy Cross
Elizabeth Kloss, Oklahoma State University
Helen Knowles, SUNY Oswego
Katie Knutson, Gustavus Adolphus College
Jonathan Krasno, Binghamton University
Stephen Krason, Franciscan University
Dina Krois, Lansing Community College
William Kubik, Hanover College
Ashlyn Kuersten, Western Michigan University
Brian Kupfer, Tallahassee Community College
John Kuzenski, North Carolina Central University
Jeffrey Lantis, College of Wooster
Roger Larocca, Oakland University
Maria Perez Laubhan, Lake County
Lisa Laverty, Eastern Michigan University
Russell Lawson, Bacone College
Celeste Lay, Tulane University
Roger D. Lee, Salt Lake Community College
Wayne Lesperance, New England College
Tal Levy, Marygrove College
Angela Lewis, University of Alabama
Steven Lichtman, Shippensburg University
Nancy Lind, Illinois State University
Matt Lindstrom, St. John's University
John Lipinski, Robert Morris University
Brad Lockerbie, East Carolina University
Fred Lokken, Truckee Meadows Community College
Kenneth Long, Saint Joseph College
Claude Louishomme, University of Nebraska at Kearney
James Lutz, Indiana University Purdue
Edy Macdonald, University of Central Florida
Shari MacLachlan, Palm Beach State College
Donald Mac-Thompson, Winston Salem State University
Tony Madonna, University of Georgia
Richard Maiman, University of Southern Maine
Gary Lee Malecha, University of Portland
Lorie Maltby, Henderson Community College
Joseph Mancos, Lenoir-Rhyne University
William Mangun, East Carolina University
David Mann, College of Charleston
Magdaleno Manzanarez, Western New Mexico University

Nancy Marion, University of Akron
Bobby Martinez, Northwest Vista College
Nancy Martorano, University of Dayton
Asher Matathias, St. John's University (Queens Campus)
Derek Maxfield, Capital Community College
Terry Mays, The Citadel
Colette Mazzucelli, Molloy College
Heather Mbaye, University of West Georgia
Scott Mcclurg, Southern Illinois University
Tera McCown, University of Charleston
Adam McGlynn, The University of Texas-Pan American
Patrick McKinlay, Morningside College
Bryan McQuide, University of Idaho
R. Michael Mcsweeney, Bunker Hill Community College
Scott R. Meinke, Bucknell University
Nathan Melton, Utah Valley University
Joseph Melusky, Saint Francis University
John Mercurio, San Diego State University, San Diego City College, Grossmont College
Mark Milewicz, Gordon College
Melissa Miller, Bowling Green State University
Alexander Moon, Ithaca College
Martin Morales, Consumnes River College
Lucas Morel, Washington and Lee University
Eric Moskowitz, College of Wooster
Joanna Mosser, Drake University
Benjamin Muego, Bowling Green State University
Melinda Mueller, Eastern Illinois University
Lanette Mullins, Ivy Tech Community College
Philip Mundo, Drew University
Leah Murray, Weber State University
Mark Robert Murray, South Texas College
Christopher Muste, University of Montana
Jason Mycoff, University of Delaware
Carolyn Myers, Southwestern Illinois College
Trevor Nakagawa, Merritt College
Blaine Nelson, El Paso Community College
Steven E. Nelson, Northern Michigan University
James Newman, Idaho State University–Pocatello
William L. Niemi, Western State College of Colorado
Douglas Nilson, Idaho State University–Pocatello
Barbara Norrander, University of Arizona

Timothy O' Neill, Southwestern University

Al Ortiz, San Joaquin Delta College

James Owens, Oakton Community College

Richard Pacelle, Georgia Southern University

Steven Parker, University of Nevada–Las Vegas

David Penna, Gallaudet University

Mark Peplowski, Southern Nevada Community College

Gerhard Peters, Citrus College

Geoff Peterson, University of Wisconsin–Eau Claire

Joyce Pigge, Bethany College

Jamie Pimlott, Niagara College

Daniel Ponder, Drury University

Barbara Poole, Eastern Illinois University

Robert Porter, Ventura College

David Price, Santa Fe Community College

Narges Rabii, Santiago Canyon College / Orange Coast College / Saddleback College

Chapman Rackaway, Fort Hays State University

Daniel Reagan, Ball State University

Renford Reese, Cal Poly Pomona

Keith Reeves, Swarthmore College

B. Jeffrey Reno, College of the Holy Cross

Tim Reynolds, Alvin Community College

Patricia Bayer Richard, Ohio University

Christopher Riley, Big Bend Community College

Delbert Ringquist, Central Michigan University

Hank Rischel, Macomb Community College Center Campus

Kent Rissmiller, Worcester Polytechnic Institute

Chase Ritenauer, University of Akron

Laurie Robertstad, Navarro College

John Robey, University of Texas–Brownsville

Karin Robinson, Hood College

Rob Robinson, University of Alabama–Birmingham

Richard Robyn, Kent State

Sheri Rogers, Calvin College

Joe Romance, Drew University

Tom Rotnem, Southern Polytechnic State University

Donald Roy, Ferris State University

Ted Rueter, University of Wisconsin–Oshkosh

Mark Rush, Washington and Lee University

Patricia Ryan, Fairmont State University

Robert C. Sahr, Oregon State University

Bart Salisbury, Green River Community College
William Salka, Eastern Connecticut State University
Arthur Sanders, Drake University
Eric Sands, Berry College
Stephanie Sapiie, Suffolk Community College
Robert Saunders, Farmingdale State College
Todd M. Schaefer, Central Washington University
Michael Scheib, Lewis University
Steven E. Schier, Carleton College
Diane Schmidt, California State University–Chico
Michael Schnall, Pace University
Monica Schneider, Miami University (Ohio)
B. Schrader, Rowan University
Deron Schreck, Moraine Valley Community College
Ronnee Schrieber, San Diego State University
Vann Scott, Snead State Community College
Margaret Scranton, University of Arkansas at Little Rock
Michael Semler, Oxnard College / California State University Northridge
Stanley Serwatka, El Paso Community College
Allen Settle, Cal Polytechnic
Mark Setzler, High Point University
William Shafer, Purdue University
David Shafie, Chapman University
Edward Sharkey, Columbia College
Maurice Sheppard, Madison Area Technical College
John Shively, Longview Community College
Chris Shortell, Portland State University
Stephen Shulman, Southern Illinois Carbondale
Sanford Silverburg, Catawba College
Leigh Sink, University of North Carolina–Greensboro
Michael Slattery, Campbell University
Candy Stevens Smith, Texarkana College
James Smith, Indiana University
Karl Smith, Delaware Technical and Community College
Keith Smith, University of the Pacific
Ron Smith, Hanover College
Sandra Smith, Indiana University Northwest
Udi Sommer, University at Albany–SUNY
David Sousa, University of Puget Sound
Jeff Spanbauer, Illinois Valley Community College
June Sager Speakman, Roger Williams University
Scott Spitzer, California State University Bakersfield

John Squibb, Lincoln Land Community College
Marcus Stadelman, University of Texas at Tyler
Barry Steiner, California State University–Long Beach
Robert Sterken, University of Texas–Tyler
Janet Stevens, Madison Area Technical College
Willard Stouffer, Southwest Texas State University
Ginny Stowitts-Traina, Palo Alto College
Mark Stratton, Indiana University–Purdue
Ryane Straus, College of Saint Rose
Robert A. Strong, Washington and Lee University
Tamir Sukkary, American River College
Julie A. Sullivan, San Diego State University
John Swain, Governors State University
Regina Swopes, College of DuPage
John Szmer, University of North Carolina–Charlotte
Tressa Tabares, American River College
Barry Tadlock, Ohio University
Edwin Taylor, Portland State University
Jami Taylor, Ohio State University
Dange Tedla, Sacramento City College
Frank Thames, Texas Tech
John Theilman, Converse College
Michael Thompson, William and Patterson University
Alec Thomson, Schoolcraft College
Trevor Thrall, University of Michigan Dearborn
Jim Thurman, Central Wyoming College
Daniel Tichenor, University of Oregon
Terri Towner, Oakland University
Joe Trachtenberg, Clayton College and State University
Cathy Trecek, Iowa Western Community College
Margaret Tseng, Marymount University
David Tully, De Anza College
Bill Turini, Reedley College
Cindi Unmack, American River College
Richard Valelly, Swarthmore College
Jeff VanDerWerff, Northwestern College
Pamela Van Zwaluwenburg, Modesto Junior College
John Vento, Antelope Valley College
William Vogele, Pine Manor College
Mathis Waddell, Galveston College
Kevin Wagner, Florida Atlantic University
Scott Wallace, Indiana University–Purdue

Dana Waller, Front Range College
George Waller, University of Wisconsin–Fox Valley
Howard Warshawsky, Roanoke College
Andrew Jackson Waskey, Dalton State College
Rick Whisonant, York Technical College
Eric Whitaker, Western Washington University
Lois Duke Whitaker, Georgia Southern University
James A. White, Concord University
Elizabeth Williams, Santa Fe College
Kenneth Williams, Michigan State University
Jon Winburn, University of Mississippi
Michael Wiseman, Ashford University
Tony Wohlers, Cameron University
Christina Wolbrecht, University of Notre Dame
Robert (Bo) Wood, University of North Dakota
Gordon Vurusic, Grand Rapids Community College
Peter Yacobucci, Walsh University
Brad Young, Ocean Community College
Melanie Young, University of Nevada Las Vegas
Jay Zarowitz, Muskegon Community College
Noah Zerbe, Humboldt State University
Martha Zingo, Oakland University

GATEWAYS
TO DEMOCRACY

AN INTRODUCTION TO
AMERICAN GOVERNMENT
THE ESSENTIALS

1

GATEWAYS TO AMERICAN DEMOCRACY: JUDGING THE DEMOCRATIC EXPERIMENT

> *Being there is half the battle. What can happen from there is because you are involved in the process.*

On a hot August day in 2006, a 20-year-old college student was doing the summer job he had volunteered to do. Working for the Senate campaign of Democrat Jim Webb, S. R. ("Sid") Sidarth was videotaping Webb's Republican opponent, Senator George Allen, who was seeking reelection in what was assumed would be an easy win. Allen, with solid conservative credentials, had been a popular governor of Virginia and in his first Senate race had beaten longtime Virginia Senator Chuck Robb. Some were comparing Allen to Ronald Reagan, and he seemed to be on his way not only to winning his second Senate race but also to running for president in 2008.

Sidarth, a computer engineering and American government major at the University of Virginia, had long been interested in politics. It was a family tradition. He had been an intern on Capitol Hill and a volunteer on John Kerry's presidential campaign and in the Virginia governor's race. This summer, before his senior year in college, he had volunteered for Webb. At first, he worked behind the scenes at Webb's campaign headquarters in Arlington, helping set up field offices around the state and doing odd jobs. Then, on August 7, the campaign gave him a digital camcorder and asked him to follow Allen on his "Listening Tour" of Virginia, taping the candidate's appearances in a routine campaign practice known as tracking. Sidarth drove off alone. The work was mostly solitary. At campaign stops, he chatted with Allen's aides, and once the senator had walked up to him,

CourseMate

Visit http://www.cengagebrain
  .com/shop/ISBN/0495906190
  for interactive tools including:

- Quizzes
- Flashcards
- Videos
- Animated PowerPoint slides,
  Podcast summaries, and more

S. R. Sidarth ▶

Bernard Annebicque/CORBIS SYGMA

Rich Lipski/The Washington Post/Getty Images

shook his hand, and asked his name. "I'm following you around," said Sidarth, and he knew Allen understood what that meant.

On August 11, the Allen campaign held a meet-and-greet picnic at Breaks Interstate Park, in far southwest Virginia, near the Kentucky border. Allen picked up his microphone and Sidarth picked up his camcorder. During the speech, however, Allen paused and pointed: "This fellow here, over here with the yellow shirt, macaca, or whatever his name is. He's with my opponent. He's following us everywhere." As his supporters began to laugh, Allen continued, "Let's give a welcome to macaca, here. Welcome to America and the real world of Virginia."

Sidarth recorded it all. The episode, posted on YouTube, led to a furor. Within a week, more than two hundred thousand had watched the clip, and as major newspapers across the country picked up the story, Allen's campaign was in trouble. He had poked fun at Sidarth by using a pejorative term with strong racial overtones. "The kid has a name," said Webb communications director Kristian Denny Todd. "This is trying to demean him, to minimize him as a person." The irony was that Allen, born and raised in California, had come to Virginia only as a college student, whereas Sidarth had been a Virginian all his life. It was Allen who appeared out of touch with the increasing diversity of the state he was representing.

Allen's lead disappeared, and on election day, out of more than 2.3 million ballots cast in Virginia, he lost by just over seven thousand votes. With this narrow defeat, Allen's presidential hopes died as well. When asked about his role in this dramatic turn of events, Sidarth chose his words carefully. "I was just doing my job, and I got sort of pulled into this," he said. "I was the only person of color there, and it was useful for him [Allen] in inciting his audience. I was annoyed that he would use my race in a political context." Later, after the election, Sidarth wrote in the *Washington Post,* "I am proud to be a second-generation Indian American and a practicing Hindu," but "I would not wish the scrutiny on anyone." Still, he reflected, "Webb's victory last week gives me hope that Virginia will not tolerate playing the race card. . . . The politics of division just don't work anymore. Nothing made me happier on election night than finding out the results from Dickenson County, where Allen and I had our encounter. Webb won there, in what I can only hope was a vote to deal the race card out of American politics once and for all."[1]

It does not often happen that a summer volunteer alters political careers and changes the composition of the U.S. Senate, but that it did happen points to the power of the individual in a democracy. In a democracy, citizens have the right, and the responsibility, to be involved in the public sphere and to take part in governing themselves. In this case, the impact of Sidarth's story was magnified by the Internet, but the ability of citizens to influence the political process does not depend on new technologies.

Since the nation's beginnings 230 years ago, the actions of citizens have shaped the country's development. We open each chapter of this textbook with the story of one of them. Some of these individuals are ordinary, some are extraordinary, and most are college students. Each used one of the many gateways to participation in government that American democracy provides, because at its core, American government is about individuals and self-governance. Even though the size of American government is daunting, individuals can make real changes. What often appear to be small and localized efforts can produce big shifts. Elections, for example, offer the chance to transform the system. Citizens can hold government accountable by voting legislators and presidents in and out of office. They can make their opinions known more directly because the right to speak out and to join with others in promoting causes is protected by the Constitution. A free press and the Internet allow information and opinion to be widely spread and shared. Courts hear cases brought by citizens, and citizen juries determine the outcome. Citizens can—and have—changed the Constitution through amendments. Elections, protest marches, blogs, the courts, and the constitutional amendment process are each gateways of influence. So are interest groups and political parties, and even Congress itself, for they represent the views of citizens, especially those who are active and engaged.

This textbook, *Gateways to Democracy,* explains how citizen involvement has expanded American democracy and how each of you, too, can influence the political system. We call the avenues of influence *gateways*. This book serves as kind of a handbook for democratic citizenship by peeling back the layers of American government to reveal the ways you can get involved and to explain the reasons you should do so. The American political system is complicated, it is large, and it can be frustrating. As the term *gateways* implies, there are also gates—obstacles to influence, institutional controls that limit access, and powerful interests—that seem to

Four out of five young people do volunteer work in high school and college, and, according to the Harvard University Institute of Politics, 94 percent believe that volunteer service is an effective way to deal with challenges in their local communities. In 2008, college students from around the country spent their spring break as volunteers in New Orleans, painting houses that had been damaged in Hurricane Katrina.

AP Photo/Bill Haber

Founders: *Those who were involved in establishing the United States, whether at the time of the Declaration of Independence or the writing of the Constitution.*

block the people's will. James Madison, Thomas Jefferson, John Adams, and the other **Founders** had read many of the great political theorists. They drew, for example, on the ideas of the British political philosophers Thomas Hobbes and John Locke in perceiving the relationship between government and the governed as a **social contract**. If people lived in what these philosophers called a state of nature, without the rule of law, conflict would be unending and the strong would destroy the weak. Thomas Jefferson understood the connection between the people and their government as a social contract; if a government did not serve the people, the people should end it. He speaks of revolution as a right of self-governing men in the Declaration of Independence:

> We hold these truths to be self-evident, that all men are created equal, that they are endowed by their Creator with certain unalienable Rights, that among these are Life, Liberty and the pursuit of Happiness.—That to secure these rights, Governments are instituted among Men, deriving their just powers from the consent of the governed,—That whenever any Form of Government becomes destructive of these ends, it is the Right of the People to alter or to abolish it, and to institute new Government, laying its foundation on such principles and organizing its powers in such form, as to them shall seem most likely to effect their Safety and Happiness.

Immediately, Jefferson goes on to say that if government is not responsive to the governed, then the people have the right "to alter or abolish it." In other words, it is the people's right—and responsibility—to ensure that the gateways to democracy are always open and available to them in their pursuit of life, liberty, and happiness. Jefferson (and the other Founders), in effect, sought to replace the British Crown and build effective and meaningful gateways whereby the people of the new nation could enjoy a responsive government while retaining their individual freedoms. These themes of the Declaration of Independence—*equality* and *responsiveness*—were present at the creation of the new government. They continue to shape our government, as each generation of Americans have sought to make them a reality.

Through citizen involvement, American democracy has achieved many successes:

- The nation and its institutions are amazingly stable. The United States has the oldest written constitution in the world.
- The government has weathered severe economic crises, a civil war, two world wars, and yet it still maintains peaceful transitions of power from one set of leaders to the next.
- Citizens are able to petition the government and to criticize it. They can assemble and protest the government's policies.
- Americans enjoy substantial freedom and are protected from the abuse of power by the government.
- The American economy has created an excellent standard of living, among the highest in the world.
- Americans exhibit more commitment to civic duty than do citizens in nearly all other major democracies.[2]
- Americans show a great deal more tolerance for wide-ranging political views than citizens in other major democracies.[3]

These successes do not mean there are not problems:

- Inequality persists, and government is sometimes slow to respond.
- Even with the election of President Barack Obama in 2008, racial tensions continue to haunt the country.
- The imbalance of wealth in this country continues to grow, with increasing numbers of people living in poverty.[4]
- The public's trust in the institutions of government has eroded in recent years.[5]
- The rate of turnout in our elections is among the lowest of the major democracies.
- Despite a high level of religious tolerance, there is also persistent distrust of some religious minorities, such as Muslims.[6]

John Moore/Getty Images

Social scientists have been measuring the gap between the rich and the poor since the 1930s, and in the past few decades it has grown to the point that the income of the richest 5 percent is now six times greater than that of the poorest 20 percent. Reports in 2007 indicated that the top 300,000 Americans enjoyed the same total income as the bottom 150 million Americans. Following job losses in the 2008 recession, this Wilmington, Ohio, family is living in a homeless shelter.

social contract: *Theory that government has only the authority accorded it by the consent of the governed.*

FOCUS QUESTIONS

- How can you get yourself and your opinions represented in government?

- How can you make government more responsive, and responsible, to citizens?

- How can you make American democracy better?

- Political polarization is now so extensive that members of Congress often attack one another on personal as well as political grounds. Some members have even taken to yelling at the president.
- The American military is stretched thin by two wars in the Middle East and a global war against terrorism.

To solve these and other problems and achieve the "more perfect union" promised in the Constitution, the nation's citizens must be vigilant and engaged. We have framed our book with the goal of demonstrating the demands and rewards of democratic citizenship. As we explore the American political system, we place special emphasis on the multiple and varied connections among citizenship, participation, institutions, and public policy.

democracy: *System of government in which the supreme power is vested in the people and exercised by them either directly or indirectly through elected representatives.*

self-government: *Goal of democracy, whereby average people have control of the institutions of government.*

majority rule: *Idea that a numerical majority of a group should hold the power to make decisions binding on the whole group; a simple majority.*

mob rule: *Government by a mob or mass of people with no formal authority whatsoever.*

liberty: *Political value that cherishes freedom from an arbitrary exercise of power that constricts individual choice.*

order: *Political value in which the rule of law is followed and does not permit actions that infringe on the well-being of others.*

Democracy and the American Constitutional System

Today, democracy is presumed to be a good form of government, and some would say the best form. Indeed, democracy is the kind of government to which the people of many nations aspire. But it has not always been so. Only in the last two centuries—partly through the example of the United States—has democracy gained favor. Let us sketch some of the fundamental aspects of American democracy.

Liberty and Order

Literally and most simply, **democracy** is rule by the people, or **self-government**. In a democracy, the citizens hold political authority, and they develop the means to govern themselves. In practice, that means rule by the majority. In the years before American independence, **majority rule** had little appeal. In 1644, John Cotton, a leading clergyman of the colonial period, declared democracy "the meanest and worst of all forms of government."[7] Even after American independence, Edmund Burke, a British political philosopher and politician, wrote that a "perfect democracy is . . . the most shameless thing in the world."[8] At the time, democracy was associated with **mob rule**, and mobs were large, passionate, ignorant, and dangerous. If the mob ruled, the people would suffer. There would be no **liberty** or safety; there would be no **order**. Eighteenth-century mobs destroyed private property, burned effigies of those they detested, tarred and feathered their enemies, and threatened those who disagreed with them. In fact, such events occurred in the protests against British rule in the American colonies, and they were fresh in the minds of those who wrote the Declaration of Independence and the Constitution.

John Adams, a signer of the Declaration of Independence and later the nation's second president (1797–1801), was not a champion of this kind of democracy. "Democracy," he wrote, "while it lasts is more bloody than either aristocracy or monarchy. Remember, democracy never lasts long. It soon wastes, exhausts, and murders itself. There is never a democracy that did not commit suicide."[9] Adams knew about mobs and their effects firsthand. As a young lawyer before the Revolution, he agreed to defend British soldiers who had been charged with murder for firing on protesters in the streets of Boston. The soldiers' cause was unpopular, for the people of Boston detested the British military presence. But Adams believed that, following British law, the soldiers had a right to counsel (a lawyer to defend them) and to a fair trial. In later years, he considered his defense of these British soldiers "one of the best pieces of service I ever rendered my country."[10]

Why? In defending the soldiers, Adams was standing up for the **rule of law**, the principle that could prevent mob rule and keep a political or popular majority under control so it could not trample on **minority rights**. An ancient British legal principle, the rule of law holds that all are equal before the law, all are subject to the law, and no one is above it. Adams and the others who wrote America's founding documents believed in a **constitutional system**, in which the people set up and agreed on the basic rules and procedures that will govern them. A constitutional system is a government of laws, not of men. Without a constitution and rule of law, an unchecked majority could act to promote the welfare of some over the welfare of others, and society would be torn apart.

The American constitutional system, therefore, serves to protect both liberty and order. The Constitution sets up a governmental structure with built-in constraints on power (gates) and multiple points of access to power (gateways). It also has a built-in means for altering the basic rules and procedures of governance through amendments to the Constitution. As you might expect, however, the procedure for passing amendments comes with its own set of gates and gateways.

The Constitution as Gatekeeper

James Madison and the other **Framers** of the Constitution recognized that the government they were designing had to be strong enough to rule but not strong enough to take away the people's rights. In other words, the

rule of law: *Legal system with known rules that are enforced equally against all people.*

minority rights: *Idea that the majority should not be able to take certain fundamental rights away from those in the minority.*

constitutional system: *System of government in which people set up and agree on the basic rules and procedures that will govern them.*

Framers: *Those who were involved in writing the Constitution.*

Constitution had to serve as a gatekeeper, allowing and limiting access to power at the same time. Thus, to secure order and safety, individuals come together to form a government and agree to live by its rules. In return, government agrees to protect life, liberty, and property. The right to life, liberty, and property, said Locke, are **natural rights**, rights so fundamental that government cannot take them away.

But these ideas about government as a social contract were still just theories when Madison and others began to write the Constitution. The closest actual model for self-government was ancient Athens, where the people had governed themselves in a **direct democracy**. In Athens, citizens had met together to debate and to vote. That was possible because the number of citizens (property-owning males) was small and had similar interests and concerns.[11]

But the new United States was nothing like the old city-state of Athens. It was an alliance of thirteen states—former colonies—with nearly 4 million people spread across some 360,000 square miles. Direct democracy was impractical for such a large and diverse country, so those who wrote the Constitution created a **representative democracy** in which the people elect representatives who govern in their name. Some observers, including the Framers, call this arrangement a **republic**, a form of government in which power derives from the citizens but their representatives make policy and govern according to existing law.

But could a republic work? No one knew, and certainly not the Framers. The government they instituted was something of an experiment, and they developed their own theories about how it would work. Madison, for example, rejected the conventional view that a democracy had to be small and homogeneous, so as to minimize conflict. He argued instead that size and diversity were assets, because competing interests in a large country would balance and control—or check—one another and prevent an abuse of power. Madison called these competing interests **factions**, and he believed that the most enduring source of faction was "the various and unequal distribution of property." "Those who hold and those who are without property have ever formed distinct interests in society," he wrote. "Those who are creditors, and those who are debtors, fall under a like discrimination. A landed interest, a manufacturing interest, a mercantile interest, a moneyed interest, with many lesser interests, grow up of necessity in civilized nations, and divide them into different classes, actuated by different sentiments and views" (see *Federalist* 10 in the Appendix).

In a pure democracy, where the people ruled directly, Madison expected that passions would outweigh judgments as to the common good. Each individual would look out for himself, for his **self-interest**, and not necessarily for the interests of society as a whole, what we might call **civic interest**. In a republic, however, the people's representatives would of necessity have a broader view. Moreover, they would, Madison assumed, come from the better

natural rights: *Natural (or unalienable) rights that government cannot take away.*

direct democracy: *Form of democracy in which political power is exercised directly by citizens.*

representative democracy: *Form of democracy in which citizens elect public officials to make political decisions and formulate laws on their behalf.*

republic: *Form of government in which power derives from citizens, but public officials make policy and govern according to existing law.*

faction: *Defined by Madison as any group that places its own interests above the aggregate interests of society.*

self-interest: *Concern for one's own advantage and well-being.*

civic interest: *Concern for the well-being of society and the nation as a whole.*

educated, a natural elite. The larger the republic, the larger the districts from which the representatives would be chosen, and thus the more likely that they would be civic-minded leaders of the highest quality. More important, in a large republic, it would be less likely that any one faction could form a majority. In a small seaside republic, for example, it would be possible for fishing interests to form a majority that could pass laws to the detriment of non-fishing interests. Or in another small republic, a religious sect could form a majority. But in a large and diverse republic, such narrow-minded majorities would not be possible. Interests would balance each other out, and selfish interests would actually be checked by majority rule.

Balance, control, order: these values were as important to the Framers as liberty. So while the Constitution vested political authority in the people, it also set up a governing system designed to prevent any set of individuals, any political majority, or even the government itself, from becoming too powerful. The Framers purposely set up barriers and gates that blocked the excesses associated with mob rule.

Consequently, although the ultimate power lies with the people, the Constitution divides power both vertically and horizontally. Within the federal government, power is channeled into three different branches—the **legislature** (Congress), which makes the laws; the **executive** (the president and the government departments, or bureaucracy), which executes the laws; and the **judiciary** (the Supreme Court and the federal courts), which interprets the law. This vertical division of power is referred to as the **separation of powers** (see Figure 1.1). To minimize the chance that one branch will become so strong that it can abuse its power and harm the citizenry, each branch has some power over the other two in a system known as **checks and balances**. The Constitution also divides power horizontally, into layers, between the national government and the state governments. This arrangement is known as **federalism**. In a further division of powers, state governments create local governments.

legislative branch: *Makes the laws.*

executive branch: *Enforces the laws.*

judicial branch: *Interprets the laws.*

separation of powers: *Government structure in which authority is divided among branches (executive, legislative, and judicial), with each holding separate and independent powers and areas of responsibility.*

checks and balances: *Government structure that authorizes each branch of government (executive, legislative, and judicial) to share powers with the other branches, thereby holding some scrutiny of and control over the other branches.*

federalism: *System of government in which sovereignty is constitutionally divided between national and state governments.*

The Three Branches of Government

Legislative Branch	Executive Branch	Judicial Branch
Makes the laws	Executes the laws	Interprets the laws

FIGURE 1.1 The Separation of Powers.

Thirteenth (1865): Prohibits slavery in the United States

Fourteenth (1868): Makes all persons born in the United States citizens of the United States, and prohibits each states from denying persons within its jurisdiction the privileges or immunities of citizens, the due process of law, or equal protection of the laws; apportionment by whole persons

Fifteenth (1870): Prohibits states from denying the right to vote on account of race

Seventeenth (1913): Gives the people (instead of state legislatures) the right to choose U.S. senators directly

Nineteenth (1920): Guarantees women the right to vote

Twenty-Third (1961): Grants residents of the District of Columbia votes in the Electoral College

Twenty-Fourth (1964): Prohibits poll taxes

Twenty-Sixth (1971): Guarantees 18-year-olds the right to vote

FIGURE 1.2 Amendments That Opened Gateways to Participation.

Today, after more than 230 years, the Constitution and the government it established are largely intact. There are still three branches of government. Though the power of each has expanded enormously, they still check and balance each other, as the Framers had hoped they would. There have been just twenty-seven amendments to the Constitution, most of which have expanded liberties, such as freedom of speech, or opened gateways to participation—by African Americans (the Thirteenth, Fourteenth, and Fifteenth Amendments), by women (the Nineteenth Amendment), by poor people (the Twenty-Fourth Amendment), and by young adults (the Twenty-Sixth Amendment). The Seventeenth Amendment further enhanced democracy by providing for the direct election of senators (see Figure 1.2). Arguably, the only amendment to restrict rights was the Eighteenth Amendment, which prohibited the manufacture, sale, and transportation of alcohol within the United States, but the Twenty-First Amendment repealed that.

With the Constitution and its amendments, the nation has not only survived but prospered. The success of the United States would surely be welcome news for any of the Founders and Framers. But has the nation met their expectations? As we address this question, it is important to point out that these early leaders were not of one mind. They were talented individuals with a range of perspectives about what constituted good government. A useful way to organize their many perspectives is to consider again two perspectives that first battled during the administration of George Washington (1789–97): the **Jeffersonian view** and the **Hamiltonian view**.

Jeffersonian and Hamiltonian views: *Two political schools of thought or perspectives on what constituted good government.*

The *Jeffersonian* view had the following major tenets:

1. Believed in the fundamental equality of all people and held that the American Revolution set into motion forces that would give rise to greater equality. Even though the rights of African Americans and women were not recognized in the 1787 Constitution, the system was set up to be flexible enough to incorporate future generations of citizens into political life.
2. Worried that any form of government could be corrupted and feared a strong executive in particular.
3. Wanted the states, not the federal government, to have power, in the belief that citizens could keep better watch over the government that was closest to them.
4. Assumed the United States would be an agrarian nation not involved in world affairs and argued that the closer the people were to their own land, the stronger would be their interest in preserving their political and social way of life.
5. Regarded expanding gateways of influence as a good thing, confident that the people would check the power of government and ensure individual liberty.

The *Hamiltonian* view had the following major tenets:

1. Preferred that elites should govern the nation, especially at its inception, and took some degree of inequality as inevitable, as some people have more ability and motivation than others.
2. Believed a successful government demanded a strong executive.
3. Viewed a strong national government as a way to unify the many competing interests of the thirteen former colonies.
4. Hoped that the United States would become more industrial and a military power that would play a major role in international affairs.
5. Regarded restrictions on the gateways to influence as a good thing, because educated and experienced elites would be better at governing than common citizens.

These two schools of thought anticipated some of the many changes that have unfolded over 230 years. The Jeffersonians correctly recognized that the American Revolution would give rise to greater demands for equality. In terms of political equality, those demands have been largely met, as all citizens over age 18 (except those in prison) now have a gateway to political power through the ballot box. In terms of economic equality, the Hamiltonians' assumption that there would always be inequality among citizens, even in a democracy, has also proven true, given the nation's income disparities.[12]

The Jeffersonians' assumption that the United States would remain an agrarian nation, with limited involvement in world affairs, has proved incorrect. Although farming expanded with the nation's boundaries, the Hamiltonians correctly foresaw that the United States would be an industrial power with significant influence in world affairs. Yet, that both agriculture and industry have flourished is evidence of just how strongly these two views reflected the fundamentals of the U.S. economy from the beginning.

Some of the other differences in the two schools of thought reflect competing political values. The Jeffersonians wanted strong states, a limited national government, and a weak chief executive. The Hamiltonians held no loyalty to states and viewed the national government, under a strong leader, as best able to bring prosperity and military power. Commerce, rather than agriculture, would assure the continuity and stability in government essential for success. It is clear, again, that the Hamiltonians' view more closely resembles the modern United States, but there is still a deep strain among the American people that favors the Jeffersonian ideal of limited government and an isolationist international posture.

All in all, the Hamiltonians had a clearer understanding of America's future than the Jeffersonians, and they probably would be happier with the outcome. Even so, the Jeffersonians' faith in equality and in the capabilities of the people has been vindicated. Jefferson himself would be stunned by the size of twenty-first-century government, the trappings of the American presidency, and the military might of the nation. But he would be pleased to see the expansion of fundamental rights and the increase in the number of gateways to influence. Hamilton would, frankly, be worried by such power for average people. Perhaps today's wide access to education would ease his concerns, but Jefferson was, by nature, more optimistic about the ability of citizens to govern themselves.

The American constitutional system thus simultaneously provides gateways for access and gates that limit access. The people govern themselves, but indirectly and through a system that disperses power among many competing interests. This textbook explores both the gateways and the gates that channel and block the influence of citizens.

American Political Culture

As an experiment, the American republic has been open to change in the course of the nation's history. Despite their theorizing, the Framers could not have anticipated exactly how it would develop. Madison was, however, right about the enduring influence of factions. The people quickly divided themselves into competing interests and shortly into competing **political parties**, groups organized to win elections. The process by which competing interests determine who gets what, when, and how, is what we call **politics**.[13]

Madison was right, too, about the sources of division, often centering in the unequal distribution of property and how far government should go to

political parties: *Broad coalitions of interests organized to win elections in order to enact a commonly supported set of public policies.*

politics: *Process by which people make decisions about who gets what, when, and how.*

political ideology: *Set of consistent political beliefs.*

liberals: *Individuals who have faith in government to improve people's lives, believing that private efforts are insufficient. In the social sphere, liberals usually support diverse lifestyles and tend to oppose any government action that seeks to shape personal choices.*

reduce inequality. Public opinion about such matters is sometimes described as falling on a scale that ranges from left to right, and when people have a fairly consistent set of views over a range of policy choices, they are said to have a **political ideology**. Toward the left end of the scale are **liberals**, who favor government efforts to increase equality, including higher taxes on the wealthy than on the poor and the provision of social benefits, such as health care, unemployment insurance, and welfare payments to support the poor. **Conservatives**, on the right, believe that lower taxes will prompt greater economic growth that will ultimately benefit everyone, including the poor. Thus, liberals support a large and active government that would regulate the economy, while conservatives fear that such a government will suppress individual liberty and create a dependency that actually harms those it aims to help.

The left-right division is not just about economics, however. For social issues, liberals generally favor less government interference, while conservatives favor rules that will uphold traditional moral values (see Figure 1.3). Conservatives are, therefore, more likely to support laws that ban abortion and same-sex marriage, while liberals are more likely to favor a woman's right to make decisions over private matters as well as the right of same-sex couples to wed.

Although terms such as *conservative* and *liberal* are often used to label American political attitudes, most Americans are not very ideological in their orientation to politics. They are likely to take independent positions on various issues, leaning left on some, right on others. In fact, most Americans are **moderates**, not seeing themselves on one end of the scale or the other. A sizable number of Americans also describe themselves as **libertarians**, believing that government should not interfere either in economic matters or in social matters. Others take a **populist** perspective, opposing concentrated wealth and adhering to traditional moral values.

Despite its many perspectives, American **political culture** as a whole generally favors **individualism** over communal approaches to property and poverty, especially in comparison to the industrialized democracies of Europe and elsewhere in the world. The United States spends less on government programs to help the less well off than many other countries, and it has historically refrained from assuming control of business enterprises, such as railroads and banks, except in times of crisis. The United States tends to favor **capitalism**, an economic system in which business enterprises and key industries are privately owned, as opposed to **socialism**, in which they are owned by government. Yet, to prevent the worst abuses of capitalism, which can arise as businesses pursue profit to the detriment of citizens, Congress has passed laws that regulate privately owned businesses and industries. Government monitors banks and financial markets, for example, ensures airline safety, and protects workers from injury on the job.

conservatives: *Individuals who distrust government, believing that private efforts are more likely to improve people's lives. In the social sphere, conservatives usually support traditional lifestyles and tend to believe government can play a valuable role in shaping personal choices.*

moderates: *Individuals who are in the middle of the ideological spectrum and do not hold consistently strong views about whether government should be involved in people's lives.*

libertarians: *Those who generally believe that government should refrain from acting to regulate either the economy or moral values.*

populists: *Those who oppose concentrated wealth and adhere to traditional moral values.*

political culture: *Set of beliefs common to a group of people.*

individualism: *Set of beliefs holding that people, and not government, are responsible for their own well-being.*

capitalism: *Economic system in which businesses and key industries are privately owned and in which individuals, acting on their own or with others, are free to create businesses.*

socialism: *Economic system in which the government owns major industries.*

FIGURE 1.3 **American Political Ideology.**

Political ideology has been described in many ways. In one version, political thought is plotted on a continuum between left (liberal) and right (conservative). The terms left and right derive from the seating arrangements for political parties in the Assembly during the French Revolution.

LEFT (LIBERAL):
Greater faith in a large and active government to promote equality.

RIGHT (CONSERVATIVE):
Greater preference for a small and limited government to encourage economic growth.

But this version is somewhat simplistic. A more fully developed version plots a graph that shows where liberals and conservatives stand on both economic and social issues. Liberals favor government regulation of the economy; conservatives do not. Conservatives favor government regulation of traditional moral values; liberals do not.

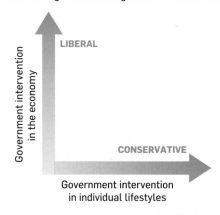

In a third version, the ideological spectrum is further complicated by the inclusion of libertarians, who favor no government intervention in either the economy or society, and populists, who favor government intervention in both the economy and society.

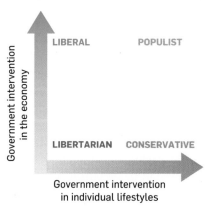

The truth is, however, that Americans are not really very ideological. Most Americans describe themselves as moderates or as independent thinkers who might lean left on some issues and right on others. Americans generally look to government to be active in some areas of life, but they differ on which areas.

These regulations tend to moderate vast inequalities in wealth as well. Though prizing individualism, American political culture also has a long-standing **egalitarian** tradition. This greater equality produced a political culture that values each individual's ability to achieve wealth and social status through hard work, not inheritance, and supports a free enterprise economic system, within limits.

egalitarianism: *Belief in human equality that disdains inherited titles of nobility and even inherited wealth.*

Public Policy under a Constitutional System

The laws that regulate the American economy, as well as the tax rates, exemptions, and subsidies that help direct it, are examples of **public policy**—the intentional action by government to achieve some goal. It is in the arena of public policy—in determining who gets what, when, and how, and with what result—that we can see whether the constitutional system created by Madison and the Framers really works. Can the people pursue policies that advance their own interests? Can the people's representatives, while pursuing policies that advance their constituents' interests, produce a nation that looks out for the civic interest generally, for the common good and for the welfare of all the people?

With a government deliberately designed to constrain power and the popular will, and a citizenry divided into factions and prizing individualism, the

public policy: *Intentional actions of government designed to achieve some goal*

JEFF HAYNES/AFP/Getty Images

Government policy is just one cause of decay in Detroit. The decline of the auto industry is a major explanation for the condition of this city, which since the 1950s has lost half its population. Policy makers are now developing plans to turn some of its 40 square miles of abandoned properties into farms—a new kind of urban agriculture that is commercial rather than community based.

problem identification: *First stage in the policy-making process, in which a problem in politics, the economy, or society is recognized as warranting government action*

policy agenda: *Stage in the policy-making process in which a problem gets the attention of policy makers.*

interest groups: *Group of citizens who share a common interest—a political opinion, religious or ideological belief, social goal, or economic characteristic—and try to influence public policy to benefit themselves.*

development of public policy has never been easy. In some ways, it has tended to cycle. One argument gains favor, driving policy in one direction. But new problems arise, calling for a redirection of policy. The development of good public policy is always difficult and complex. A policy, for example, of providing tax benefits to homeowners, which would spur home ownership, sounds like a good thing. It would help homeowners, support the home construction industry, and create jobs, building more stable communities. But what sounds simple rarely is that simple, because there are usually unintended consequences. A policy of tax benefits for homeowners can also encourage sprawl that turns agricultural land into suburbs, thus decreasing crop yields and altering food production, while leaving cities with vacant housing and declining tax bases. Subsequently, government responds to these new problems by developing additional policies to revitalize both agriculture and urban infrastructure.

With so many competing interests and the high potential for unintended negative consequences, government seeks to pursue policy making that maximizes benefits and minimizes costs. This is not easy. Political scientists—those who study politics and the processes of government—have, however, categorized the steps in policy making to make the process more understandable.

The first step is **identification** of the problem. For example, constituents might complain to members of Congress that the cost of college is too high. The second step is that the cost of higher education must make it to the agenda of policy makers.[14] That is, of all the problems that government might be able to solve, only a small fraction can receive attention at any one time. Those that get on the **policy agenda** get the attention of Congress, the president, the executive branch agency that deals with the issue, the courts, political parties, **interest groups**, and interested citizens. Third, these **stakeholders** attempt to **formulate** a policy that will solve the problem (see Figure 1.4). In this example, which got on the policy agenda in 2009,

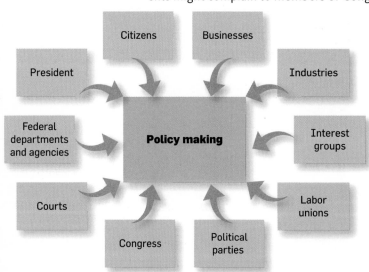

FIGURE 1.4 Stakeholders in the Policy-Making Process. One reason policy making is difficult and complex in America is that so many citizens, businesses, industries, labor unions, interest groups, political parties, Congress, the president, federal agencies, the courts, and others have a stake in policy outcomes. For emphasis, we will repeat this figure in discussions of policy making throughout this textbook, with the various stakeholders identified.

the stakeholder network considered direct federal loans to college students, promoting private loans by paying banks the interest on student loans while the student is in college, and guaranteeing the loans if a student is unable to repay. In a fourth step, **policy enactment**, the legislative branch passes a law that enacts one or more of those proposals, as Congress did regarding student loans in 2010. Following passage, the legislature grants an executive branch department the authority to **implement the program**. In this case, the Department of Education was given the authority to direct the student loan program. In a few years, Congress might revisit the new student loan program to see if it is producing the outcomes that were intended. Following **policy evaluation**, the cycle of policy making might begin again, with new legislation to adjust the program to make it work better (see Figure 1.5).

In a republic, policy making should reflect the will of the people, expressed through their elected representatives and interest groups. Madison envisioned that the people's representatives managing the policy-making process would be an elite consisting of well-educated people of "merit." But if the people divided into different classes, as Madison also envisioned, there is a danger to democracy if the people's representatives are an elite who represented only their own interests, and not civic-minded leaders who would consider the common good. In the 1950s, the sociologist C. Wright Mills in fact wrote of a narrow **power elite** from corporations, government, and the military that controlled the gates and gateways to power. But in the 1960s, the political scientist Robert Dahl took issue with Mills and argued that policy making has a more **pluralist** basis, with authority held by different groups in different areas. In this view, coal companies, as stakeholders, have a large say in coal policy and farmers, as stakeholders, have a large say in farm policy, rather than a single power elite controlling both policy areas. And while it is still true, for example, that the coal industry pursues its interests vigorously, so do other industries. Elected representatives seek to balance these various interests even as they seek to do what is best for their constituents. The fact that no one group has a monopoly on power suggests that a more **majoritarian** policy-making process is in the making, in which those with a numerical majority hold the authority.

Responsiveness and Equality: Does American Democracy Work?

Does American democracy work? That is a question we will be asking in every chapter of this book, and we invite you now to start working on an answer. As citizens, you have both a right and a responsibility to judge the government—because it is *your* government.

stakeholders: *Participants in the policy-making system who each seek to influence the content and direction of legislation.*

policy formulation: *Stage in the policy-making process in which those with a stake in the policy area propose and develop solutions to the problem that has been identified.*

policy enactment: *Stage in the policy-making process in which Congress passes a law that authorizes a specific governmental response to a problem.*

policy implementation: *Stage in the policy-making process in which the executive branch develops the rules that will put a policy into action.*

policy evaluation: *Stage in the policy-making process in which a policy is evaluated for its effectiveness and efficiency; if changes are needed, the issue is placed back on the policy agenda.*

power elite: *Small handful of decision makers who hold authority over a large set of issues.*

pluralism: *System of policy making in which competing interests hold authority over issues most important to them.*

majoritarian: *System of policy making in which those with a numerical majority hold authority.*

FIGURE 1.5 **The Policy-Making Process.**

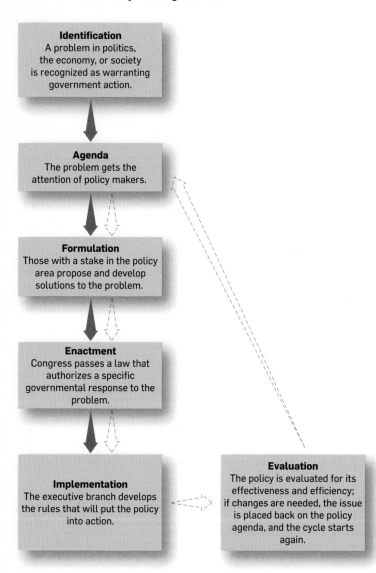

Identification
A problem in politics, the economy, or society is recognized as warranting government action.

Agenda
The problem gets the attention of policy makers.

Formulation
Those with a stake in the policy area propose and develop solutions to the problem.

Enactment
Congress passes a law that authorizes a specific governmental response to the problem.

Implementation
The executive branch develops the rules that will put the policy into action.

Evaluation
The policy is evaluated for its effectiveness and efficiency; if changes are needed, the issue is placed back on the policy agenda, and the cycle starts again.

responsiveness: *Idea that government should implement laws and policies that reflect the wishes of the public and any changes in those wishes.*

To guide your thinking, we will focus on two basic themes, **responsiveness** and **equality**. Is government responsive to the needs of its citizens? And do all citizens have an equal chance to make their voices heard? We ask you to keep these themes in mind as you learn about the U.S. political system. To give you a basis for making a judgment, we inform you of the findings of political scientists who have been asking and answering these questions for decades. Throughout this textbook, we present the latest data that speak to these broad issues. It is important to remember that we are not offering you our opinions about government; instead, we are putting forward the most important evidence and theories, from a variety of perspectives, over the last fifty or so years. It is up to you to consider them, forming your own conclusions.

One way to begin to evaluate American democracy, and to appreciate it, is to look, briefly, at alternative models of government. In **autocracy**, **oligarchy**, or **monarchy**, a single person or a small elite rules society. Such rulers have little need to be responsive to the people. They hold most of the power and are not generally accountable to those they rule. They may try to satisfy the people with programs that meet basic needs for food and safety, but they do so to ensure submission. These rulers have a low regard for the people and do not want them to be engaged in public life. In these systems, rulers are excessively wealthy while the people are likely to be impoverished. To maintain order, rulers typically rely on a strong army or secret police force, which keeps the people in line through fear and intimidation. Rulers in such systems are overthrown when dissatisfaction rises to a level at which citizens are willing to risk their lives in open revolt, or when the army or police conspire to replace one ruler with another.

In contrast, a democracy asks that the citizens be actively engaged in their own governance, for the benefit of all. As the preamble to the Constitution states, the people create government (agree to a social contract) to "establish Justice, insure domestic Tranquility, provide for the common defense, promote the general Welfare, and secure the Blessings of Liberty to ourselves and our Posterity." The American system of government fundamentally provides protection from foreign enemies and from internal disorder; it also strives to meet the common needs of all its citizens.

To promote the general welfare, government develops public policy, as we have seen. Through incentives, it can alter the actions of individuals that lead collectively to bad outcomes. Consider the following example. If everyone drives to work, pollution increases and more resources are consumed. If a few people then decide to take the bus, those decisions, while admirable, do not yield a cleaner environment or save many resources. But if government incentives, such as a tax on cars, encourage many people to take the bus, the result is a cleaner environment and a saving of resources.

The government often has a stake in pursuing what economists call **public goods**: goods that everyone benefits from. The core idea is that no one can be excluded. We all get the benefits of clean air, even if we have been driving a car and not taking a bus. **Private goods**, by contrast, can be extended to some individuals and denied to others. When a government awards a contract to build a new library, the firm that wins the contract gets private goods (that is, money) from the government. The firms that lost the bid are denied that chance.

Who determines what goods, whether private or public, the government should provide, at what levels, and how they will be paid for? These are core public policy problems. There are competing interests at every point in determining who gets what, when, and how. Politics is the process by which the people determine how government will respond. And it is in evaluating the basic fairness of government's response, and the basic equality of the people's general welfare that is thus secured, that we see whether American democracy is working.

For a representative democracy to succeed, there must be a constant interaction between the people and the government. But should representatives act as **trustees** who exercise independent judgment about what they believe is best for the people, or act as **delegates** who do exactly as the

equality: *Idea that all individuals are equal in their moral worth and so must be equal in treatment under the law and have equal access to the decision-making process.*

autocracy: *System of government in which the power to govern is concentrated in the hands of one individual ruler.*

oligarchy: *System of government in which the power to govern is concentrated in the hands of a powerful few, usually wealthy individuals.*

monarchy: *System of government that assigns power to a single person who inherits that position and rules until death.*

public goods: *Goods or benefits provided by government from which everyone benefits and from which no one can be excluded.*

private goods: *Goods or benefits provided by government; most of the benefit falls to the individuals or families receiving them.*

trustee: *Idea of representation that says elected officials should do what they think best, even if the public disagrees, and elections allow the public to render a judgment on their decisions.*

delegate: *Idea of representation that says elected officials should do what the public wants and not exercise independent judgment.*

people wish? This is a question that has been long debated. In the end, the government must be responsive to the needs and opinions of the people, and the people must find ways to hold government accountable. Those who are unresponsive to the people need to be removed from office. Elections provide the most common way to remove elected officials and are the primary mechanism for forging responsiveness. But unelected officials are also responsive to the public. Justices to the Supreme Court are appointed by the president, with the advice and consent of the Senate, and they generally issue judgments that are consistent with public opinion. The bureaucrats who are hired to work in government departments carry out laws that the people's representatives have passed and the president has signed. In addition, work in government is always subject to review and investigation by other branches of government, by the media, or by citizen watchdog groups.

For a government to respond fairly to citizens, all citizens must have an equal opportunity to participate in government. Each citizen must have a chance to have his or her voice heard, either by voting or by participating in the political process and public life. These ideas form the basis of **political equality**. If citizens are not treated equally, with the same degree of fairness, then the foundation of democratic government is weakened. The notion of equality was enshrined in the Declaration of Independence: "We hold these truths to be self-evident, that all men are created equal, that they are endowed by their Creator with certain unalienable Rights, that among these are Life, Liberty and the pursuit of Happiness." But this ringing statement did not announce an enforceable right, and government under the Constitution has in the course of the nation's history involved profound inequalities, most notably permitting slavery and a severe restriction of the civil rights of the African American minority for nearly two centuries. The American constitutional system was nearly a century and a half old before it guaranteed women the right to vote. Other racial and ethnic minorities have had to challenge the system to secure their rights, and, as the next chapters will demonstrate, civil rights are still evolving. One way to evaluate American democracy is to evaluate the degree to which political equality has been achieved.

There are other aspects of equality, however. **Equality of opportunity** is one aspect—the expectation that citizens will be treated equally before the law and have an equal opportunity to participate in government. Does equality of opportunity also mean that citizens have an equal opportunity to participate in the economy (to get a job, to get rich) and in social life (to join a club, to eat at a restaurant)? And what about **equality of outcome**, the expectation that incomes will level out or that standards of living will be roughly the same for all citizens? In the United States, equality of outcome, or results, might entail the proportional representation of groups

political equality: *Idea that holds people should have equal amounts of influence in the political system*

equality of opportunity: *Expectation that citizens may not be discriminated against on account of race, gender, or national background, and that every citizen should have an equal chance to succeed in life*

equality of outcome: *Expectation that equality is achieved if results are comparable for all citizens regardless of race, gender, or national background, or that such groups are proportionally represented in measures of success in life*

that have experienced discrimination in the past; that is, for full equality of outcome in Congress or on corporate boards, the number of African Americans would have to be equal to their proportion in the overall population, about 13 percent. What can, or should, government do to ensure equality of opportunity, or equality of outcome? These questions are hotly contested, especially efforts to forge equality of outcome. As you will see, we raise these issues in the final section of this introductory chapter.

"I stand here today humbled by the task before us," said President Obama as he began his inaugural address in January 2009, "grateful for the trust you have bestowed, mindful of the sacrifices borne by our ancestors." Those "ancestors" include the millions of Americans who over more than two centuries have worked to make American democracy more responsive and to make America more equal. We challenge you to join them. This textbook will give you the information you need to understand the way American government works, to recognize the gates and the gateways. We also invite you to think critically about our American democracy, to engage in a classwide and nationwide conversation about how well it is working, to offer ideas for making it work better, to influence the decision makers who make public policy, and even to become one of them.

When Barack Obama took the presidential oath of office on the steps of the Capitol on January 20, 2009, a record crowd (1.8 million, according to the *Washington Post*) turned out to see this historic transition of power.

The Demands of Democratic Citizenship

If you were born in the United States or have been naturalized, you are a citizen, and it is important for you to know what that entails. To begin, citizenship is not a spectator sport. It does not mean choosing sides and rooting for your "team" from the sidelines, or from the comfort of your living room. It requires more than being a fan: you need to get into the game. But politics is more than a game. It shapes your life on a day-to-day basis. Citizenship, as a result, carries with it both rights and responsibilities. While the specific reasons to be involved in public life may vary, the need to participate does not.

Self-Interest and Civic Interest

The first reason to be involved is self-interest. You want government to serve your needs. Those "needs," of course, range widely, depending on one's stage of life, personal circumstances, and values. Some citizens will prefer that the government stay as much out of people's lives as possible, but others will prefer governmental assistance for the causes they hold dear. As a student, you may want the government to invest more in higher education and job creation; as a parent, you may want more aid for child care and school construction; as a working person, you may view job security as the most important government responsibility. Whatever way you define your self-interest, by getting involved you send signals to elected officials, and if enough people agree with you, the government will likely act.

The second reason, what we call civic interest, is more complex. The idea is that citizens get involved in the process because they want to be part of the voluntary organizations of **civil society** that enable communities to flourish. They want to help others, improve their neighborhoods, and make this an even better country. Groups of interested people can accomplish things that individuals, acting alone, cannot. As gains in civic interest lead to broader public involvement, they also advance equality. In a democracy, the power of individual acts can be amplified, as the actions of Sidarth demonstrate. Sometimes this amplification takes place through the courts, because lawsuits arising from an alleged injustice experienced by just one person can result in broad rulings that affect a great many. There are spillover effects to citizen activism that can benefit everyone.

civil society: *Voluntary organizations that allow communities to flourish.*

Today's college students—you—are more likely to be civic-minded than previous generations. If you were born between 1982 and 2003, you are the generation that social science researchers have identified as the *Millennials*. In reaction to the idealist and ideological baby boomers, the generation born between 1946 and 1964, and the cynical Generation X, born between 1964 and 1982, Millennials are more likely to be optimistic and practical, to value consensus and community building, to solve problems through compromise, to be committed to political involvement, to be concerned for the welfare of others, and to want to strengthen the political system.[15]

Participation in the public sphere serves the larger civic interest. Voting is only the most obvious political act. In addition, people also express their views and ideas to public officials by volunteering in political campaigns, attending rallies, writing letters, and organizing meetings. E-mail, websites, blogs, social networking, text messaging, and uploading of videos on YouTube offer additional means of joining the debate about politics and having an influence on government. Those who control the levers of power need to know your views so they can respond. With all the new technologies, the interface between people and politicians is now easier than ever.

Politics and the Public Sphere

Your generation has the power to shape the future in which you will live. The following issues are just a small sample of the concerns that confront this nation, and they are reason enough to take part in the nation's civic life.

Terrorism and Civil Liberties.
U.S. efforts to defeat terrorism involve a long-term military and ideological commitment against an opponent that defies traditional state boundaries. In response to the danger of international terrorism, and specifically to the attacks on the United States on September 11, 2001, Congress and the president curtailed basic civil liberties to help protect the nation's borders. So, for example, the Federal Bureau of Investigation (FBI) can more easily tap phones than it was able to prior to 9/11. The FBI and other intelligence agencies have argued that access to private phone conversations will help prevent another terrorist attack. That seems important. But given the background of the 9/11 attackers, government wiretaps have more frequently targeted Muslims than evangelical Christians. Such action does not treat all citizens equally. If the Constitution protects freedom of religion, should people who worship differently be treated differently? The answer, it turns out, is not simple. There is often an inverse relationship between liberty and order. At times, protecting the safety of the public generally requires that the civil liberties of some people be curtailed. On the issue of terrorism and civil liberties, some say curtailment is essential; others say it has gone too far. It is your responsibility to forge informed opinions on such matters and to create the kind of society in which you want to live.

AP Photo/Carmen Taylor

When terrorists hijacked planes and crashed them into the World Trade Towers in New York City on September 11, 2001, most Americans said their lives changed forever. The nation seemed vulnerable: a very few people intent on harming the United States could do a great deal of damage, and the victims were innocents. How can the government protect the nation against such attacks?

Political Polarization and the Media.
Over the past few decades, the U.S. political system has become highly polarized, as the gulf between the Democratic and Republican parties has widened. This polarization plays out not only in the halls of Congress but also on the streets of Middle America. Politicians question each other in harsh and nasty tones, and people describe one another with labels that can be equally harsh and nasty.

Many believe the current news media, with the decline of newspapers and the growth of cable TV and blogging, have intensified this polarization. Certainly, individuals with extreme views do have many more opportunities to broadcast them widely today. The news media are no longer centralized and hierarchal, and their transformation has given rise to the citizen-journalist,

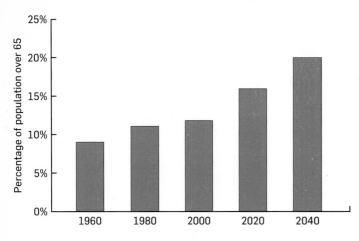

FIGURE 1.6 The Graying of America.
Source: Data from U.S. Census.

someone like Sidarth who posts videos on the web to provide firsthand reports of what public officials are doing and saying. The Internet now enables information to move from the bottom up as well as from the top down, and it is available 24-7. The new media promote equality, but do they promote responsiveness in government? Is there too much information? Is it now too easy for biased assessments to circulate and distort? The Internet is certainly a gateway to citizen involvement in a democracy, but it may be creating new gates as well.

Social Security and Entitlement Programs.   As a nation, we are aging. As Figure 1.6 shows, by 2040 citizens over 65 will constitute 20 percent of the population, doubling in just twenty-five years. This "graying of America" affects the kinds of policies that the nation pursues, because older citizens tend to vote in great numbers and thus get the attention of elected officials. They want to protect their Social Security payments and the Medicare program, which pays for part of their medical bills. Yet these entitlements are so costly that they will determine what else can and cannot be done with the federal budget (see Figure 1.7). Over the next twenty-five years, the cost of Social Security benefits will increase at a rate greater than economic growth, saddling the nation with a greater burden that has implications for all of you.[16] This issue is more than just self-interest. It also involves civic interest. How does a government respond fairly, to secure the welfare of all the people, equally? Should all people, regardless of age, have access to a decent standard of living? These are tough questions with no easy answers.

Immigration and Diversity.   Another policy that matters is immigration, not only the rise of undocumented workers but the larger pattern of legal immigration as well. This development has a major effect on the nation. The data in Figure 1.8 show that within thirty or so years, nearly 25 percent of the population will be Hispanic. The proportion of Asian Americans will triple in this time frame. These gains mean the relative proportion of the Anglo population is declining, while the African American community is holding steady at about 13 percent of the population. The United States is indeed becoming more and more diverse, and diversity will have implications for elections, political parties, and the policies they produce. The question for students of American politics in the twenty-first century is how to manage all the competing interests from these different sectors of society. But you may have your own questions: How much does ethnic background matter to you personally, or to politics generally? As Americans, are we becoming more diverse, or more integrated? Do you see your future as determined by competition among groups for government response, or by a decline in the importance of racial and ethnic categories? Is diversity making America more, or less, equal?

Education. Education policy is another, surely more immediate, concern. Each of you, for example, knows that the cost of college is rising and outstripping the general rate of inflation. Over a recent ten-year period, tuition at public universities has increased 72 percent and 99 percent at private schools.[17] Beyond your own ability to pay for your education, what impact

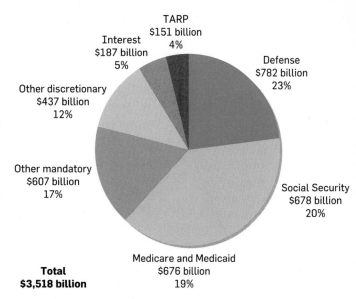

Total $3,518 billion

FIGURE 1.7 U.S. Budget, 2009. Social Security payments accounted for 20 percent of U.S. federal spending in 2009, and Medicare accounted for 13 percent (shown here in combination with Medicaid, the program that provides medical benefits to the poor). That means that about one-third of all federal spending goes for benefits to senior citizens.
Source: OMB, 2011 Budget.

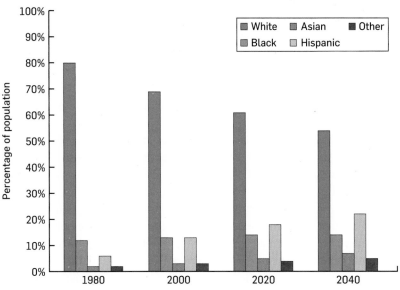

FIGURE 1.8 The Changing Ethnic Composition of America.
Source: Data from U.S. Census.

will decreased access to education have for American democracy as a whole? Is education an equalizer? Does education offer equality of opportunity? Can it ensure an equality of outcome? Do American schools make Americans more, or less, equal? What should and will government do to respond to problems in education? These are serious questions that warrant careful debate. Yet Americans do not hear much discussion about education in the press. A recent study by the Brookings Institution indicates that, in 2009, only 1.4 percent of coverage by television, websites, and radio dealt with education.[18] This lack of attention poses additional barriers to forging a helpful solution to this pressing problem.

These five issues just discussed are only a small sample of the many problems that confront America. How you and your fellow citizens choose to participate will affect their resolution.

Evaluating the American Political System

The views of the Founders and Framers provide some context for judging the American political system, but the central question is whether most Americans are satisfied with the core institutions of government. Individuals may be unhappy with particular leaders, but these opinions reflect partisan assessments, not assessments of the overall political system. If you ask Americans whether they are proud of the country, or patriotic, there is near consensus. Pollsters do not even ask people if they favor replacing the Constitution. Why bother? Almost no one holds such an opinion.

How you judge American politics depends in large part on where you sit. If you are financially well off, you are likely to see the merits of the American system. But what if you are poor? Homeless? Out of work? Context and perspective are critical.

The same is true for American politics: your interpretation will be shaped by where you sit. Consider the American Recovery and Reinvestment Act of 2009. This so-called Stimulus Bill authorized $787 billion of spending and tax cuts to revitalize the sagging economy. If you are sitting in the committee rooms and on the floor of Congress as the legislation is drafted, your story will be about contest and compromise—the hallmark of legislative policy making in the American political system. Legislators try to get advantages for their constituents because that will help them get reelected. At the same time, there are cross-pressures on the legislative process, from competition among staffers, to the influence of lobbyists representing competing interests, to the urgency for quick action expressed by the president. A close-up view of this process would not be pretty and would not necessarily build faith in the political system.

With a bit more distance, one can see that the compromises bring progress, and the process looks more democratic. When the political parties disagree on how best to write a bill, it is in large part because they are reflecting the concerns of their members, the rank-and-file voters. Citizens disagree fundamentally on more tax cuts or more federal spending, and Congress typically reflects those concerns. On top of that, the nation's separation of powers system gives the president an important say in the content of legislation. In early 2009, it was the Democratic majorities in each house along with a Democratic president that made passage of the Stimulus Bill possible. Remember that the Democrats had just won the 2008 elections, where the public was calling for change. The Democrats were trying to institute that change. So, from this *vantage point*, Congress and the president are striving to be responsive to the wishes of the public. It may not be democratic in the sense that the people directly rule, but it looks more democratic than what was reported from the political trenches in Congress.

The real lessons here are twofold. First, we always need to remember that the accuracy of any interpretation of the American political process depends on where you sit. Disagreement about an interpretation is due, in part, to differences in perspective. Second, there is no single or correct interpretation of the American political system. If you disagree with someone about the policy outcomes that the American system produces, look to see if one of you sits on the sidelines while the other plays in the game. If so, then you may be able to better understand each other. It is not that you will agree about things, but at least you will see where the other person is coming from.

Many perspectives exist. The standards you bring to bear on your judgment of the American system matter a great deal. We turn to them next.

Defining Standards of Evaluation

When deciding whether America is democratic or not, we must grapple with the very definition of democracy, and the definition itself is contested. As stated previously, "In a democracy, the citizens hold political authority, and they develop the means to govern themselves. In practice, that means rule by the majority." But not all subscribe to this definition, because if the majority can make all the decisions, it can also block minority rights. Since democracy also has to ensure liberty for all citizens, it does so through the rule of law: "all are equal before the law, all are subject to the law, and no one is above it." In some sense, the Constitution sought to balance these competing views, by giving the majority a chance to have its say while ensuring that the minority, too, could advance its interests.

If one adopts the "pure" definition that democracy is "rule by the people," it is difficult to conclude that America is democratic. There are many gateways in the American constitutional system, but there are gates, too. The Electoral College is one example, where majority rule can be thwarted as it was in the 2000 presidential election, in which the candidate with the most votes, Al Gore, lost the election. The U.S. Senate is another example, where the 500,000 citizens of Wyoming have the same number of senators as the 22.8 million of Texas.[19] These two examples underscore that the American system is complicated, and we do not have rules consistent with a direct democracy. That might lead you to question the fairness of American government's responsiveness to its citizens and even the equality of its citizens, given their differing opportunities for influence. The standard of equality is indeed contested. If we focus on equality of *outcome*, then there is reason to think America comes up short. The nation tolerates huge income inequalities: some people have multiple homes and private jets; others have no place to sleep and not enough to eat. If we focus on equality of *opportunity*, the United States fares better. Many people celebrated President Obama's election, even if they did not vote for him, because it validated the idea of equal opportunity. Of course, the nation still faces problems with racial, ethnic, and religious discrimination (to name only a few). Even so, Americans do enjoy equality in civil liberties (see Chapter 4), including rights such as freedom of expression, of association, of religion, and of speech. These are not absolutes, but the United States fares well by these measures. Compared to the rest of the world on these matters of freedom, it is in the very top tier.[20]

The conversation about whether America is democratic is a good thing in and of itself. It is a powerful reminder that when evaluating whether a political system is democratic or not, standards of judgment are not fixed. Indeed, they are dynamic, and they evolve over time. The Founders, for example, were revolutionary for their day, asserting that "all men are created equal" and daring to create a government based on "the consent of the governed" at a time when all other nations were monarchies or authoritarian regimes.

It is important to understand that there will always be a gap between the people's ideals and the institutional response. When Americans reform their institutions to bring them closer to their ideals, there is progress. But ideals are not static; they are constantly reshaped. New standards for equality evolve all the time. In the early 1900s, the debate was about women's right to vote with little discussion about the rights of homosexuals. Today, these rights are debated. Sometimes technology forces new debates. Right-to-die issues are current today because people live longer, and more technological ways to keep people alive exist that were not possible in the nineteenth century. The gap between ideals and institutions, or ideals and the law, may be frustrating for some, but it is the constant motivator of reform.

In short, you can be pessimistic or optimistic about the future of the American political system. We encourage you to make use of the information we have provided to make your own judgment. As authors of this textbook, we do not have a stake in the direction you take or the conclusion you reach, so long as you reach one. The nation as a whole benefits when more people weigh in. The more people participate, the better the policy outcomes. Chances for equality increase, and government's responsiveness is more likely.

A Gateway to American Democracy

The gateways to American democracy have opened wider over the last 230 years. For example:

- Citizens, not state legislatures, now vote for the president and U.S. senators.
- Initiatives and referenda allow many citizens a direct say in policy making in the states.
- Equal suffrage has been extended to all Americans.
- New media have opened new avenues of communication between citizens and elected leaders.
- Scientific polling has deepened understanding of public opinion.
- Increased educational opportunities have made it possible for more citizens to be better informed about government and policy debates.

Have any new gates arisen? Are there new hurdles that block access to the American political system? The answers are less clear. Some changes in American politics have proved to be both gateways and gates, depending on where one sits.

Consider the size of the federal government. The vast bureaucracy in Washington serves as a gateway for people to secure responsiveness on some matters of interest to them. But sheer size can impede efficiency.

The population of the country has also increased, and here again, size may prove to be a gate. With the 2000 census, each congressional district served roughly 650,000, and that figure will likely increase to over 700,000 after the 2010 census. In 1789, the typical congressional district held around 30,000 people. That means that, today, a member of the House represents more than twenty times as many people as representatives in the First Congress. To deal with this population increase, the size of congressional staff has grown. Additional staff should make it possible for House members to continue to be responsive to the needs of their constituents, but they also create a gate between constituents and their member of Congress or senator. In the nineteenth century, each senator had just one clerk and much more time to meet voters in session.

Technology has advanced beyond what the Founders could have imagined. E-mail, blogs, and cell phones can serve as gateways for increased participation. But what is the nature of that participation? Technology often reduces direct human interaction. If people do not have to gather in the same room to communicate, do the bonds of civic association decrease? Can these new modes of communication fuel disassociation and apathy? This is another recent development that can be both a gateway and a gate.

The growth of interest groups has the same dual outcome. Interest groups increase the number of voices in the political system, but they can also create inequality among those new voices. And if the voices of the less powerful cannot be heard as well as those with more power and money, what are the consequences for equality? Moreover, interest groups interpose themselves between elected officials and citizens, serving as gates against direct citizen influence even as they operate as gateways. Again, any assessment of the impact of interest groups depends on one's vantage point. The contradictory consequences of all reforms and changes in the American political system need to be considered in any evaluation of it.

The existence of an overall increase in the number of gateways to American democracy is clear. Whether there are also new gates is less clear, but any judgment of the American democratic experiment will have to take the possibility into account.

We have written this book to give you the information you need to understand your government—its gates and gateways. We hope it will also push you to evaluate whether government is working for you, and for all the nation's citizens. How democratic are we? How can we be better? One thing is certain: we will not be better unless you are involved. The only way to make American democracy more responsive and more equal is by your participation.

Each chapter will conclude with two pages of review materials that will help you study and learn. In other chapters there will be exercises that will help you apply what you have learned in the classroom to American civic life. For this chapter, we offer a ten-point summary, review questions, a list of key terms, and resources. Visit the book's website—www.cengagebrain.com/shop/ISBN/0495906190—for more.

To help you get started thinking about whether American democracy works, we also include here a series of "advance questions" to keep in mind as you read the book. They will help you judge the democratic experiment.

Top Ten to Take Away

1. American democracy offers many gateways to participation because, at its core, American government is about individuals and self-governance. (pp. 5–7)

2. There are also gates against public participation—obstacles to influence, institutional controls that limit access, and powerful interests that seem to block the people's will. (pp. 7–8)

3. To be an engaged and productive citizen, you need to take advantage of the gateways but also know how to navigate around the gates. (pp. 7–8)

4. Democracy is self-government. In the American constitutional system, the people establish and agree on the basic rules and procedures that will govern them. (pp. 8–9)

5. The American constitutional system works to protect both liberty and order. The Constitution sets up a governmental structure with built-in constraints on power (*gates*) and multiple points of access to power (*gateways*). (pp. 9–14)

6. In American government, power is divided among three branches (executive, legislative, and judicial) and between the national government and the states. (p. 11)

7. American political culture favors individualism and the U.S. economic system favors capitalism. (pp. 14–17)

8. American citizens may lean conservative or liberal, but most are moderates. (pp. 15–16)

9. With a government designed to constrain power and the popular will, and a citizenry divided into different perspectives and prizing individualism, the development of public policy is difficult and complex. (pp. 17–19, 25–28)

10. One way to evaluate whether public policy is serving the people of the United States and to judge whether American democracy is working is to measure government responsiveness and citizen equality. (pp. 19–23)

A full narrative summary of the chapter is on the book's website.

Ten to Test Yourself

1. What did the nation's Founders think about democracy?

2. How is government thought of as a social contract?

3. What is the difference between a direct democracy and a representative democracy?

4. How do checks and balances, and the separation of powers, work?

5. What are the most important American political values?

6. What are the stages in the making of public policy?

7. How should public policy be evaluated?

8. What are various meanings of equality?

9. How can citizens hold government accountable? How can citizens make government responsive?

10. What does it mean to be a citizen?

More review questions and answers and chapter quizzes are on the book's website.

GATEWAYS TO LEARNING

Terms to Know and Use

autocracy (pp. 20, 21)
capitalism (p. 15)
checks and balances (p. 11)
civic interest (p. 10)
civil society (p. 24)
conservatives (p. 15)
constitutional system (p. 9)
delegate (p. 21)
democracy (p. 8)
direct democracy (p. 10)
egalitarianism (p. 17)
equality (pp. 20, 21)
equality of opportunity (p. 22)
equality of outcome (p. 22)
executive branch (p. 11)
faction (p. 10)
federalism (p. 11)
Founders (p. 6)
Framers (p. 9)
individualism (p. 15)
interest groups (p. 18)
Jeffersonian and Hamiltonian
  views (p. 12)

judicial branch (p. 11)
legislative branch (p. 11)
liberals (pp. 14, 15)
libertarians (p. 15)
liberty (p. 8)
majoritarian (p. 19)
majority rule (p. 8)
minority rights (p. 9)
mob rule (p. 8)
moderates (p. 15)
monarchy (pp. 20, 21)
natural rights (p. 10)
oligarchy (pp. 20, 21)
order (p. 8)
pluralism (p. 19)
policy agenda (p. 18)
policy enactment (p. 19)
policy evaluation (p. 19)
policy formulation (pp. 18, 19)
policy implementation (p. 19)
political culture (p. 15)
political equality (p. 22)
political ideology (pp. 14, 15)

political parties (p. 14)
politics (p. 14)
populists (p. 15)
power elite (p. 19)
private goods (p. 21)
problem identification (p. 18)
public goods (p. 21)
public policy (p. 17)
representative democracy (p. 10)
republic (p. 10)
responsiveness (p. 20)
rule of law (p. 9)
self-government (p. 8)
self-interest (p. 10)
separation of powers (p. 11)
social contract (pp. 6, 7)
socialism (p. 15)
stakeholders (pp. 18, 19)
trustee (p. 21)

Use the vocabulary flash cards on the book's website.

Advance Questions

Use these questions to guide your reading of this textbook and your learning in this course.

1. Does American democracy work? How can you evaluate it?

2. How democratic was the constitutional system of 1787? How democratic is the United States today?

3. What are the pros and cons of a system in which state governments and a national government share power?

4. What should be the balance between liberty and order? How has the U.S. government balanced the two? What liberty versus order questions do citizens face today?

5. Why is equality important in a democracy? What role does, or should, government play in ensuring equality? What kinds of equality can, or should, government ensure? What should be the balance between equality and liberty?

6. What role does public opinion play in government responsiveness? How responsive should government officials be to public opinion?

7. Describe the role of the press, or more generally, the media, in a democracy. Is the media today working to make government better, or to make governing more difficult?

8. What is the role of interest groups in a democracy? How do they serve citizens? Are they working today to make government better, or to make governing more difficult?

9. What is the role of political parties in the American electorate? In government? Are they working today to make government better, or to make governing more difficult?

10. Why are elections important? Are they fair? Do political campaigns ensure that voters' ideas and wishes are represented?

11. Voting is the most fundamental action a citizen can take. Does voting matter? Is voting fair? What other ways can citizens influence public policy, besides voting?

12. The Framers thought that Congress would be the most powerful branch of government: is it? How effective is Congress as a legislative body? What gates limit its effectiveness?

13. The presidency grew in power in the twenty-first century. Is it now too powerful? What are the checks on presidential power? What are the necessities for presidential power?

14. The bureaucracy is often under attack for inefficiency and unresponsiveness. Describe the purpose of the bureaucracy. Which parts of it function well? Which do not? Why not?

15. The pediment above the main entrance to the Supreme Court proclaims: "Equal Justice under Law." What does that mean? How do the courts ensure equality? Is the judiciary responsive?

16. How do you judge the American democratic experiment?

17. What are the dangers to democratic government in the twenty-first century?

18. Why do you think the United States has survived as a representative democracy for more than two centuries? What has been the experience of other democracies?

19. How easy, or hard, is it to influence public policy? What types of people have had the greatest influence—politicians, corporate executives, military leaders, grassroots organizers?

20. How do cultural similarity and diversity work to help or impede the operations of American democracy?

21. How can you get yourself and your opinions represented in government?

22. How can you make government more responsive, and responsible, to its citizens?

23. How equal are America's citizens? How equal should they be? What kinds of opportunities do American citizens have? Are the outcomes equitable?

24. What can you do, as an active citizen, to make American democracy better?

2

THE CONSTITUTION

YE SHALL KNOW THE TRUTH AND THE TRUTH SHALL MAKE YOU FREE

▲ **University of Texas at Austin**

> *An active and engaged citizen must have the ability to pressure politicians for a long period of time and have plenty of resources available.*

Gregory Watson, a sophomore economics major at the University of Texas at Austin, had a term paper to write for a government class. It was 1982, the year in which the proposed equal rights amendment to the U.S. Constitution would expire unless three more states ratified it, and Watson decided to investigate the failure of this amendment, which would have prevented the United States or any state from denying equality of rights on account of sex. Congress had passed it in 1972, setting a seven-year time frame for ratification by the states, following the two-step course established in the Constitution for the passage of amendments. The proposed amendment got off to a quick start, with twenty-two of the thirty-eight states necessary to pass the amendment approving it. Momentum slowed, however, as opposition to the amendment mobilized, and even though Congress extended the deadline for three more years, no more states ratified the amendment. It was the legality of this extension—an "odd process," Watson called it, that fascinated him.

While researching that issue, Watson discovered another unratified amendment, one that dated back to 1789. This amendment, proposed by James Madison, would prohibit any congressional pay raise from

Chapter Topics

CourseMate

Visit http://www.cengagebrain
  .com/shop/ISBN/0495906190
  for interactive tools including:
- Quizzes
- Flashcards
- Videos
- Animated PowerPoint slides,
  Podcast summaries, and more

Gregory Watson

taking effect until after an ensuing election. In essence, it prevented members of Congress from awarding themselves pay raises within sessions; if they did vote an increase, they would have to stand for election before it went into effect. Six states ratified this amendment between 1789 and 1791, but no other state approved it until Ohio in 1873. Then, in 1978, Wyoming approved it. By that time, it would have needed the approval of thirty-eight states to go into effect, but it seems there was no deadline. Watson switched the topic of his paper to argue that the Constitution does not put time limits on ratification, that the congressional pay raise amendment was still pending, and that it should be passed, for it would help protect members of Congress against charges of corruption.

Watson got a C on the paper. "The professor told me this amendment could not pass. I was disgusted," he later told *USA Today*, and he set out to prove her wrong. Using $6,000 of his own money and voter anger over congressional pay raises, he launched a letter-writing campaign to targeted states. In 1983, Maine ratified the amendment, and other states followed. In 1992, Alabama became the thirty-eighth state to approve the amendment, and on May 14 of that year, the archivist of the United States declared it the Twenty-Seventh Amendment. It states: "No law, varying the compensation for the services of the senators and representatives, shall take effect, until an election of representatives shall have intervened."

Watson's professor never changed his grade, but Watson pursued his interest in politics as an aide in the Texas legislature and continued to research the status of other amendments.[1]

In this chapter, we will examine the governing documents prior to the Constitution, particularly the Articles of Confederation and its deficiencies. We will also track the debates at the Constitutional Convention and afterward, as the people of the United States decided whether to ratify the new Constitution. They did ratify it, but almost immediately they amended it. After we examine the structure and philosophy behind the new Constitution, we consider the responsiveness of the Constitution, through both amendment and less formal procedures, to changing times.

FOCUS QUESTIONS

- In what ways did the Constitution ensure that government would be responsive to the people? How has government become more responsive since 1787?

- In what ways did the Constitution seek to control the popular will and ensure order?

- In what ways did the Constitution seek to control government itself?

- In what ways did the nation's founding documents promote equality? In what ways did they fail to promote equality?

- Is the Constitution a gate or a gateway to American democracy? Is it a gatekeeper? Explain.

Before the Constitution

From the beginning, Great Britain accorded the American colonists, as British subjects, a certain amount of self-rule. When the colonists perceived that Parliament and the king were blocking their participation in government, they moved toward independence from Britain. They established a new national government under documents that included state constitutions and a national Articles of Confederation. In this section, we trace that process.

What Is a Constitution?

A **constitution** is the fundamental law undergirding the structure of government. In modern democracies, a constitution sets forth the basic rules and procedures for how the people shall be governed, including the powers and structure of the government, as well as the rights retained by the people.

constitution: Document or set of documents that sets forth the basic rules and procedures for how a society shall be governed.

Toward Independence

The American colonists believed they had all the rights of British subjects. Thus they objected when, following the French and Indian War (1754–63), Great Britain tried to recoup some of the costs of defending the colonies by imposing regulations and taxes on them. The Sugar Act of 1764 set forth a long list of items that could be exported only to Great Britain, thus limiting competition for the colonists' goods. The Stamp Act of 1765 established a tax on virtually all forms of paper used by the colonists. Although Britain had previously levied import and export taxes on the colonies, this was the first direct tax by Britain on the colonists for products made and sold in America.

The colonists reacted angrily, forming trade associations to boycott, or refuse to buy, British goods. They also published pamphlets denouncing the loss of liberty. Led by Patrick Henry, they challenged not just the taxes themselves, but Parliament's authority to pass such measures. "Give me liberty," proclaimed Henry in the Virginia House of Burgesses, "or give me death." Soon enough, riots broke out against Stamp Act collectors, making enforcement impossible.

Britain repealed the Stamp Act in 1766, replacing it with the Townshend Acts, which imposed taxes on various imports. Having successfully fought off the direct, internal taxes on paper, colonists mobilized against the new external (importation) taxes. Led by Samuel Adams, the Massachusetts legislature issued a letter declaring the Townshend Acts unconstitutional because they violated the principle of "no taxation without representation." The colonists thus began to insist that they had the right to participate in the political decisions that affected them, rights they believed they held as British subjects.

The British, however, had a more limited view of both participation and representation. At the time, only about one in six British adult males had the right to vote for Parliament, whereas two-thirds of free American adult males could vote for their colonial representatives.[2] Women and children could not vote anywhere; males, as heads of the family, were assumed to be able to represent them. Moreover, while most British cities did have representation in Parliament, some—just like the colonies—did not. Rather, representation in Parliament was based on historic population centers, so large new cities such as Manchester and Birmingham sent no representatives to Parliament, while the town of Dunwich continued to send a representative even though storms and erosion had swept the town into the North Sea centuries earlier.

As for towns such as Manchester and Birmingham, the British justified their lack of representation by claiming that all English citizens were virtually represented by all members of Parliament, who purportedly acted in the common good. As Edmund Burke wrote, "Parliament is a *deliberative* assembly of *one* nation, with *one* interest, that of the whole."[3] The colonists, however, rejected the view that their interests were one with Britain's, or that Parliament could represent those interests.

How does the American view of representation differ from the British view?

Aggrieved by taxation without representation, the colonists continued to resist the Townshend Acts. Britain responded by dissolving the Massachusetts legislature and seizing a ship belonging to John Hancock, one of the leaders of the resistance. Britain also sent troops to quell the resistance, but the presence of soldiers during peacetime only aggravated tensions. British soldiers fired on a threatening crowd in 1770, killing five colonists and wounding six others in what became known as the "Boston Massacre."

With boycotts of British goods costing Britain far more than the taxes raised, Parliament rescinded all of the Townshend Act taxes except for that on tea. In 1773, Parliament granted the East India Company the exclusive right to sell tea to the colonies, which then granted local monopolies in the colonies. Angered by both the tax and the monopoly, colonists once again took action. Disguised as Indians, they dumped a shipload of tea into Boston Harbor. Britain responded to the **Boston Tea Party** in 1774, with the Coercive Acts, which, among other things, gave the royal governor the right to select the upper house of the Massachusetts legislature. The Coercive Acts also denied Massachusetts the right to try British officials charged with capital offenses. The Quartering Acts required colonists to quarter British soldiers in their private homes, even during times of peace.[4] These acts convinced many colonists that their liberty was at stake, and that rebellion and independence were the only alternatives to British tyranny.

In an attempt to present a united front about colonial grievances, Benjamin Franklin proposed a **Continental Congress**. The first Congress, with delegates chosen by the colonial legislatures, met in Philadelphia in 1774.

Boston Tea Party (1774): *Protest in which colonists dressed as Indians boarded vessels in Boston Harbor and threw chests of tea overboard to express anger at Britain's tax policies and commercial regulations.*

How is the Boston Tea Party like, and not like, the Tea Party protests of 2009?

Continental Congress (First, 1774; Second, 1775–81): *Initial governing authority over the Revolutionary War and other common affairs of the thirteen independent states.*

The Congress rejected a reconciliation plan with England and instead sent King George III a list of grievances. It also adopted a very successful compact among the colonies not to import any English goods. Finally, it agreed to meet again as the Second Continental Congress in May 1775. This Second Continental Congress acted as the common government of the states between 1775 and 1781.

In April 1775, following skirmishes with British troops in Lexington and Concord, outside of Boston, the Second Continental Congress named George Washington commander of a new Continental Army. In 1776, with battles raging throughout the colonies, Thomas Paine penned his influential pamphlet *Common Sense*, which called for independence from Britain.[5] *Common Sense* was the most widely distributed pamphlet of its time and helped convince many Americans that independence was the only way they could secure their right to self-government.

Was the American Revolution really about taxation, or was it about something else?

The Declaration of Independence

In June 1776, the Continental Congress debated an independence resolution, but postponed a vote until July. Meanwhile, it instructed Thomas Jefferson and others to draft a **Declaration of Independence**. Congress approved the Declaration of Independence on July 4. Jefferson's Declaration relied in part on the writings of John Locke in asserting that people had certain natural (or unalienable) rights that government could not take away, including the right to life and liberty (see Chapter 1). For Locke's reference to property, Jefferson substituted "the pursuit of Happiness."

The Declaration that Jefferson penned was a radical document. It declared the right of the people to alter or abolish governments that do not meet the needs of the people; it declared the colonies independent from Britain; it contained a stirring call for equality, human rights, and public participation in government that, though not at the time legally enforceable, served as inspiration for generations of Americans seeking to make these ideas a reality.

Declaration of Independence (1776): *Document declaring American independence from Great Britain and calling for equality, human rights, and public participation.*

What has the Declaration of Independence's statement on equality meant to Americans? How are Americans equal, and not equal, today?

> *We hold these truths to be self evident, that all men are created equal, that they are endowed by their Creator with certain unalienable Rights, that among these are Life, Liberty, and the pursuit of Happiness.—That to secure these rights, Governments are instituted among Men, deriving their just powers from the consent of the governed. That whenever any Form of Government becomes destructive of these ends, it is the Right of the People to alter or to abolish it, and to institute new Government, laying its foundation on such principles and organizing its powers in such form, as to them shall seem most likely to effect their Safety and Happiness.*

The Declaration went on to list grievances against King George III, including the suspension of popularly elected colonial legislatures, taxing without representation, and trials without juries. It then declared the united colonies to be thirteen "free and independent states." (The full text of the Declaration of Independence is in this book's Appendix.)

Even before the Declaration, the Continental Congress advised the colonies to adopt new constitutions "under the authority of the people." Reacting against the limitation on rights imposed by the British monarch and by royal governors in the colonies, these new state constitutions severely limited executive power but barely limited legislative authority. At the same time, Americans made little effort to establish a national political authority, as most Americans considered themselves primarily citizens of the states in which they lived. Nevertheless, the Continental Congress needed legal authority for its actions and proposed the **Articles of Confederation** in 1777.

Members of the Second Continental Congress voted to approve the Declaration of Independence on July 4, 1776, though only John Hancock, president of the Congress, signed it that day. John Trumbull, *Declaration of Independence*, 1817.

Articles of Confederation: *Initial governing authority of the United States, 1781–88.*

The Articles of Confederation

The Articles were not approved until 1781, just a few months before American victory in the Revolutionary War. They formally established "the United States of America," in contrast to the Declaration, which was a pronouncement of "thirteen united States of America." According to the Declaration, each of the thirteen independent states had the authority to do "all Acts and Things which independent States may of right do," such as waging war, establishing alliances, and concluding peace. These were thirteen independent states united in a war of independence. With the Articles, the states became one nation with centralized control over making war and foreign affairs. But due to the belief that Great Britain had violated fundamental liberties, the Articles emphasized freedom from national authority at the expense of order. Thus the states retained all powers not expressly granted to Congress under the Articles.

Moreover, those expressly granted powers were extremely limited. Congress had full authority over foreign, military, and Indian affairs. It could decide boundary and other disputes between the states, coin money, and establish post offices. But Congress did not have the authority to regulate commerce, or indeed, any authority to operate directly over citizens of the United States.

For example, Congress could not tax citizens or products (such as imports) directly; it could only request (but not command) revenues from the states.

In addition to the limited powers granted under the Articles, the structure of the Articles made governing difficult. Each state had one vote in Congress, with the consent of nine of the thirteen required for most important matters, including borrowing and spending money. Amending the Articles required the unanimous consent of the states. In 1781, tiny Rhode Island, blocking an amendment that would have set a 5 percent tax on imports, denied the entire nation desperately needed revenue. Moreover, the Articles established no judicial branch, with the minor exception that Congress could establish judicial panels on an ad hoc basis to hear appeals involving disputes between states and to hear cases involving crimes on the high seas. There was no separate executive branch, but Congress had the authority to establish an executive committee along with a rotating president who would manage the general affairs of the United States when Congress was not in session.[6]

These deficiencies in the Articles led to predictable problems. With insufficient funds, the nation's debts went unpaid, hampering its credit. Even obligations to pay salaries owed to the Revolutionary War troops went unfulfilled. Without a centralized authority to regulate commerce, states taxed imports from other states, stunting economic growth. Lack of military power allowed Spain to block commercial access to the Mississippi River. Barbary pirates off the shores of Tripoli captured American ships and held their crews for ransom.

With the United States in desperate financial straits, Madison proposed a convention of states to consider granting the national government the power to tax and to regulate trade. Only five states showed up at this 1786 Annapolis Convention, preventing them from accomplishing anything.

As the Annapolis Convention took place, word spread of a revolt in western Massachusetts that made the weakness of the national government all too clear. Revolutionary War hero Daniel Shays and several thousand distressed farmers forced courts to close and threatened federal arsenals. Not until February 1787 did Massachusetts put down **Shays's Rebellion**. The revolt helped convince the states that, on top of the Articles' other problems, there was too much freedom and not enough order, which neither the federal nor the state governments could ensure. The Annapolis Convention thus issued an invitation to all thirteen states to meet in Philadelphia in May 1787, to consider revising the Articles of Confederation. Only Rhode Island declined.

The Constitutional Convention

The delegates chosen for the Constitutional Convention were charged with amending the Articles of Confederation so that the national government could work more effectively. Almost immediately, however, they moved beyond that

Why didn't the Articles of Confederation work as a governing document?

Shays's Rebellion (1786–87): *Revolt by Massachusetts farmers against heavy debts; helped convince states that neither the state nor federal governments were functioning properly.*

Were the delegates to the Constitutional Convention more concerned about liberty or about order?

© Bettmann/CORBIS

charge and began debating a brand new constitution. To complete that newly proposed constitution, the delegates needed to reach compromises between large and small states over representation, between northern and southern states over issues related to slavery, and between those who favored a strong national government and those who favored strong state governments in the balance of power between the two. That constitution, which was then sent to the states for ratification, is, with subsequent amendments, the same Constitution Americans live by today. It is printed in the Appendix to this book.

The Delegates

The fifty-five delegates to the **Constitutional Convention** of 1787 represented large (Virginia) and small (Delaware) states. They represented states in the South with large slave populations (South Carolina, 43 percent), states in the north with small slave populations (Connecticut, 1 percent), but only one state, Massachusetts, with no slaves.[7] Not all the delegates were rich, but none were poor. All were white and all were male. Most were in their thirties or forties, and a majority had legal training.[8] Not surprisingly, the delegates' behavior at the Convention substantially reflected their interests and the statewide interests they represented.[9]

The Convention's rules granted each state one vote, regardless of the size of the state or the number of delegates it sent. To secure the assent of all states represented at the Convention, compromises had to be reached that would satisfy the various interests represented there. To keep the gateways to compromise open, the delegates voted to keep their deliberations secret until they completed their work. This decision also created a gate that limited popular influence.

Large versus Small States

Upon the opening of the Philadelphia Convention in May 1787, Edmund Randolph of Virginia presented the delegates with James Madison's radical proposal for a new government. Known as the **Virginia Plan**, Madison's proposal included a strong central government that could act directly on the citizens of the United States without the states acting as an intermediary. The legislative branch would consist of two chambers: a lower chamber elected by the people and an upper chamber elected by the lower chamber. Each chamber would

Daniel Shays led a protest movement of debt-ridden farmers facing foreclosures on their homes and farms. Demanding lower taxes and an issuance of paper money, they engaged in mob violence to force Massachusetts courts to close.

Constitutional Convention (1787): *Meeting by twelve states to revise the Articles of Confederation; ended up proposing an entirely new Constitution.*

What compromises made the Constitution possible? Is compromise, as a political strategy, good or bad for democracy? Do politicians use compromise as a strategy today?

Virginia Plan: *Madison's proposal at the Constitutional Convention to radically strengthen the national government.*

FRAMERS

FOUNDERS

John Jay (1745–1829) of New York was a delegate to the First Continental Congress and president of the Second, though he was not present when the Declaration of Independence was signed. He was U.S. minister to Spain from 1780 to 1782 and a negotiator of the peace treaty with Britain in 1783. He was an author of the *Federalist Papers* and the first chief justice of the Supreme Court.
The Granger Collection, New York

John Adams (1735–1826) of Massachusetts was a delegate to the First and Second Continental Congresses and, with his cousin Samuel, a Signer of the Declaration of Independence. He was a diplomat to France in 1778–79, a negotiator of the peace treaty with Britain in 1783, and U.S. minister to Britain in 1785–88. He was vice president under George Washington and president from 1797 to 1801.
Réunion des Musées Nationaux / Art Resource, NY

Thomas Jefferson (1743–1826) of Virginia, was a delegate to the Second Continental Congress and drafted the Declaration of Independence. He was U.S. minister to France in 1785–89, vice president under John Adams, and president from 1801 to 1809.
© Corbis

Benjamin Franklin (1706–90) was born in Boston but moved to Philadelphia. He was a delegate to the Second Continental Congress and helped draft the Declaration of Independence. He was a diplomat to France in 1776–85 and a negotiator of the peace treaty with Britain in 1783. He was a member of the Constitutional Convention.
National Portrait Gallery, Smithsonian Institution / Art Resource, NY

James Madison (1751–1836) of Virginia was a delegate to the Second Continental Congress. He was an influential member of the Constitutional Convention and an author of the *Federalist Papers*, and he was instrumental in drafting the Bill of Rights. He was president from 1809 to 1817.
The White House Historical Association (White House Collection)

George Washington (1732–99) of Virginia was a delegate to the First and Second Continental Congresses and was commander of the Continental Army. He presided over the Constitutional Convention and was president from 1789 to 1797.
© Bequest of Mrs. Benjamin Ogle Tayloe; Collection of The Corcoran Gallery of Art

Alexander Hamilton (1755–1804) who was born in the West Indies but attended college in New York, served on General Washington's staff during the Revolution. At the Constitutional Convention, he advocated a strong central government. He was an author of the *Federalist Papers* and the first secretary of the treasury.
The Granger Collection, New York.

FIGURE 2.1 Founders and Framers. The Founders are the leaders of the American Revolution and the new United States. The Framers, more specifically, are those who wrote the Constitution. All Framers are Founders, but not all Founders are Framers. Only some of the Founders are Signers, those who signed the Declaration of Independence.

have **proportional representation**, representation proportional to the population of the state: the larger the population, the more representatives a state would have. The legislature would have a general authority to pass laws that would "promote the harmony" of the United States and could veto laws passed by the states. The Virginia Plan proposed a national executive and national judiciary, both chosen by the legislature. A council of revision, composed of the executive and judicial members, would have final approval over all legislative acts.

Madison's proposals astonished many of the delegates from the smaller states, and some from the larger states as well. To counter them, on June 15 William Patterson of New Jersey presented the Convention with the so-called **New Jersey Plan**, which strengthened the Articles by providing Congress the authority to regulate commerce and to directly tax imports and paper items. It also proposed a national executive chosen by the legislature, and a national judiciary chosen by the executive.[10] Each state would retain equal representation in Congress.

proportional representation: *System of legislative districting in which larger states receive more representatives than smaller states.*

New Jersey Plan: *Counterproposal to the Virginia Plan, aimed to strengthen the Articles of Confederation but leave the basic workings of the Articles intact.*

Connecticut
Compromise: *Compromise
on legislative representation
whereby the lower chamber is
based on population and the
upper chamber provides equal
representation of the states.*

If you were an "at-large" delegate to the Constitutional Convention and could design your own plan, what elements would you include in your Constitution and why?

enumerated powers:
*Powers of Congress listed
in Article I, Section 8 of
the Constitution, such as
regulating commerce and
coining money.*

The convention debated these measures, with enormous controversy over proportional versus equal representation. With Madison insisting that proportional representation of both chambers was the only fair system and the small states insisting that they would walk out if they lost their equal vote, Roger Sherman of Connecticut proposed what became known as the **Connecticut Compromise**. The lower chamber, the House of Representatives, would be proportional to population, but the upper chamber, the Senate, would represent each state equally.

Nation versus State

While the question of representation threatened the Convention, there was substantial agreement over the nationalist platform that Madison supported. The delegates rejected the New Jersey Plan, which would have continued government under the Articles, by a 7 to 3 vote, with Maryland divided and New Hampshire absent.

The delegates did not approve the Virginia Plan in full, yet it substantially influenced the proposed Constitution. Under the new Constitution, the government had the authority to act directly on the citizens of the United States. Congress was not granted a general legislative power, but rather **enumerated powers**; that is, a list of powers in which it could engage. Among its enumerated powers were the authority to tax to provide for the general welfare; to regulate commerce among the states and with foreign nations; to borrow money; to declare war, raise armies, and maintain a navy; and to make all laws "necessary and proper for carrying into Execution the foregoing Powers." The tax and commerce powers, of course, were among those missing from the Articles.

Congress did not receive the authority to veto state laws, but the Constitution declared that national law would be supreme over state law, bound state judges to that decision, and created a national judiciary that would help ensure such rulings. Moreover, the Convention set explicit limits on state authority, prohibiting the states from carrying on foreign relations, coining money, and impairing certain rights. Finally, the Convention approved a national executive (that is, the president), someone who could serve as a unifying force throughout the land. Table 2.1 presents the components of the Virginia Plan, the New Jersey Plan, and the proposed Constitution.

North versus South

Resolving the question of nation versus state proved less difficult than the question of representation. More difficult than either were questions related to slavery. Although slavery existed in every state except Massachusetts, the overwhelming majority of slaves, nearly 95 percent, were in the southern states, from Maryland to Georgia.[11] Not all northern delegates at the Convention opposed slavery, but those who were abolitionists wanted an immediate

TABLE 2.1 **The Virginia and New Jersey Plans Compared to the Constitution**

Issue	Virginia Plan	New Jersey Plan	Constitution
Operation	Directly on people	Through the states	Directly on people
Legislative Structure	Bicameral and proportional	Unicameral and equal	Bicameral, with lower chamber proportional and upper chamber equal
Legislative Authority	General: power to promote the harmony of the United States	Strict enumerated powers of the Articles of Confederation, plus power to regulate commerce and limited power to tax	Broad enumerated powers
Check on Legislative Authority	Council of revision	None	Presidential veto, with possibility of a two-thirds override
Executive	Unitary national executive chosen by legislature	Plural national executive chosen by legislature	Unitary national executive chosen by Electoral College
Judiciary	National judiciary chosen by legislature	National judiciary chosen by executive	National judiciary chosen by president with advice and consent of Senate

ban on importing slaves from Africa, prohibitions against the expansion of slavery into the western territories, and the adoption of a plan for the gradual freeing of slaves. Delegates from Georgia and South Carolina, whose states would never accept the Constitution on these terms, wanted guaranteed protections for slavery and the slave trade, and no restrictions on slavery in the territories. To secure a proposed Constitution, compromises were necessary. A slave trade compromise prohibited Congress from stopping the slave trade until 1808. This compromise also resulted in a ban on the taxing of exports, a substantial benefit to the export-driven economies of the southern states. A second compromise involved how slaves should be counted when calculating population for purposes of representation. Under the Articles, taxes requested of the states were based on the population of each state, with five slaves counting as three people. The Convention agreed to use this **three-fifths** formula not just for representation, but also for whatever direct or population taxes the national government might choose to levy. This compromise had a significant impact on representation in the House of Representatives.[12]

Were the delegates right or wrong to compromise on slavery?

three-fifths compromise: *Compromise over slavery at the Constitutional Convention that granted states extra representation in the House of Representatives based on their number of slaves at the ratio of three-fifths.*

A third compromise involved slavery in the western territories, and it came not from the Convention but from the government under the Articles, which passed the Northwest Ordinance in July 1787. This ordinance, which established the means for governing the western lands north of the Ohio River (eventually the states of Ohio, Indiana, Illinois, Michigan, Wisconsin, and parts of Minnesota), prohibited slavery in this territory but also provided that fugitive slaves who escaped to the territory would be returned to their owners. The Constitution repeated these provisions.

With the precedent of prohibiting slavery in the Northwest Territory established in the Northwest Ordinance, the Convention gave Congress the right to regulate the territories of the United States without mentioning whether slavery could be allowed or prohibited.

Gates against Popular Influence

Compared to the British constitutional system, the 1787 Constitution provided direct and indirect gateways for popular involvement. Nevertheless, the Framers did not trust the people to have complete control over choosing the government. In two important ways—the election of the president and the election of the Senate—popular control was limited. One of these gates against the people's participation—the election of the president through the **Electoral College**—remains in effect today.

Rather than directly electing the president through a popular vote, the Constitution establishes an Electoral College, in which electors actually choose the president. Each state receives a number of electors equal to its number of representatives plus senators, and each state legislature chooses the manner for selecting the electors from its state—by popular vote, legislative selection, or some other mechanism. Today, each state legislature allows the people of the state to choose that state's electors, but in the early days of the republic, many state legislatures kept that right for themselves. See Chapter 10 (Elections, Campaigns, and Voting) for a full discussion of the Electoral College and its consequences for presidential elections and campaigns.

Until 1913, state legislatures also selected U.S. senators. The Framers feared that a Congress elected directly by the people would be too responsive to popular will. Popularly elected state legislatures often passed unjust and confusing laws. The indirect election of senators was thus intended to serve as a check on the popular will. In 1913, the Seventeenth Amendment granted the people the right to elect senators directly.

The Ratification Process

With agreements reached on representation in Congress, federal or national power, and slavery, the delegates made a few final decisions. First, despite

Why did the delegates set up gates against citizen participation? Whose participation did they not even consider at all?

Electoral College: *The presidential electors, selected to represent the votes of their respective states, who meet every four years to cast the electoral votes for president and vice president.*

the urging of George Mason of Virginia, the delegates chose not to include a **Bill of Rights**—a listing of rights retained by the people that Congress did not have the authority to take away, such as freedom of speech or freedom of religion. Because Congress only had enumerated powers, and because the authority to regulate speech, religion, and other freedoms were not among the powers granted to Congress, delegates believed there was no need to prohibit Congress from abridging such rights.

Second, the delegates needed a method for *ratifying*, or granting final approval of, the Constitution. Fortunately, the states had already established a precedent for ratifying constitutions. In the early years of independence, state legislatures passed bills that established what were essentially state constitutions, setting up the branches of the state government or declaring the fundamental rights that their state citizens possessed. But with no special mechanism for approving such fundamental laws, what one legislature passed, another could simply repeal. Giving relative permanence to these fundamental laws required an extra step. Thus many states had moved to have their constitutions approved and enshrined in state ratifying conventions. The people's representatives at these conventions therefore had the exclusive authority to establish constitutions.

Similarly, the delegates at the Philadelphia Convention chose to send the proposed Constitution to the states for approval via special ratifying conventions to be chosen by the people. The Constitution would take effect among those states approving it when ratified by nine of the thirteen states. The Articles had required unanimity of state delegations for amendment, but the Constitutional Convention sought approval from a higher authority: the people of the United States. This process for ratification followed the statement in the Declaration of Independence that "it is the Right of the People . . . to institute new Government." Hence, the Constitution's preamble establishes the Constitution in the name of "We the People of the United States."

In September 1787, with these final steps taken, the Convention voted on the final document. Some of the delegates had left by September, but thirty-nine signed the document, with only three refusing to sign. Crucially, given Convention rules, a majority of the delegates from each of the states voted yes.

Bill of Rights: *First ten amendments to the Constitution, which provide basic political rights.*

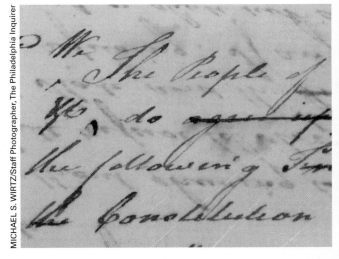

MICHAEL S. WIRTZ/Staff Photographer, The Philadelphia Inquirer

This draft of the Constitution, written by Pennsylvania delegate James Wilson, was rediscovered in 2010 in Wilson's papers in Philadelphia. At the start of the Constitution the delegates adopted a rule of secrecy that has limited access to the delegates' thoughts and daily deliberations ever since. Researchers are still uncovering the history of the Convention.

Government under the Constitution

The final document sent to the states for ratification laid out a structure of democratic government and proposed mechanisms whereby the Constitution could be amended. It also reflected the Framers' attempt to establish a government powerful enough to ensure public order yet containing enough gateways to guarantee individual liberty.

The Structure of Government

The Constitution established three branches of government—the legislative, the executive, and the judicial.

The Legislative Branch. The legislative branch, as explained in Chapter 1, makes the laws. The Constitution established a **bicameral** Congress, consisting of two chambers. The lower chamber, the House of Representatives, is proportioned by population (until the Civil War, the slave population was added to the free population according to the three-fifths formula described above).

bicameral: *Two-chamber legislature, as the House and the Senate.*

The upper chamber, the Senate, consists of two senators from each state, regardless of size. Designed to serve as a check on popular will, which would be expressed in the House of Representatives, senators were chosen by their respective state legislatures until the Seventeenth Amendment granted the people of each state the exclusive right to choose senators. Bills to levy taxes have to originate in the House, but other bills may originate in either chamber. To become law, any bill has to pass each chamber in identical form. It is then presented to the president for his signature. If the president signs the bill, it becomes law, but if he disapproves, he can **veto** the bill. Congress can then **override** the veto by a two-thirds majority in each chamber.

veto: *Authority of the president to block legislation passed by Congress. Congress can override vetoes by two-thirds majority in each chamber.*

override: *Congress's power to overturn a presidential veto with a two-thirds vote in each chamber.*

Article I, Section 8 of the Constitution limits Congress's authority to a listing, or enumeration, of certain powers in eighteen paragraphs. The first paragraph grants Congress the authority "to tax . . . to pay the debts and provide for the common defense and general welfare of the United States." Paragraphs 2 through 17 grant additional powers such as borrowing and coining money, regulating commerce, and raising an army. Then paragraph 18 grants Congress the authority to pass all laws "necessary and proper for carrying into execution the foregoing powers."

Additionally, the Constitution gives the House the authority to **impeach**—to bring charges against—the president and other federal officials. The Senate has the sole authority to try cases of impeachment, with a two-thirds vote

impeach: *Authority of the House of Representatives to bring charges against the president and other federal officials.*

required for removal from office. The Senate also has sole authority to ratify treaties, which also requires a two-thirds vote, and by majority vote to confirm executive and judicial branch appointments.

The Executive Branch.   The executive branch of government consists of a single president, chosen for a four-year term by an Electoral College. The Electoral College itself is chosen in a manner set by the legislatures of each state. Eventually, every state gave the people the power to vote for its electors. Each state receives the number of electors equal to its number of representatives plus senators. If no person receives a majority of the Electoral College vote, then the election goes to the House of Representatives, where each state gets one vote. The Electoral College also chooses a vice president who presides over the Senate, casting votes in case of a tie. The vice president becomes president following the death, resignation, removal, or disability of the president.

Because the Framers believed that the legislative branch would naturally be stronger than the executive branch, they did not feel the need to enumerate the executive power as they did with the legislative power. Recall that Congress does not have a general legislative authority, but only those legislative powers granted under the Constitution. In contrast, the Constitution provides the president with a general grant of "the executive power" and, in addition, certain specific powers, including the right to veto legislation and grant pardons. The president also is commander in chief of the armed forces. With the advice and consent of the Senate, the president makes treaties and appoints ambassadors, judges, and other public officials. The president leads the executive branch of government, being charged with taking care that the laws are faithfully executed.

The Judicial Branch.   The Constitution vests the judicial authority of the United States in one Supreme Court and other inferior courts that Congress might choose to establish. The president appoints judges with the advice and consent of the Senate. They serve during "good behavior," which, short of impeachment, means a life term.

The Constitution extends the authority of the federal courts to hear cases to certain classes of parties to a suit—cases involving the United States, ambassadors and other public ministers, suits between two or more states or citizens from different states—and to certain classes of cases, most notably cases arising under the Constitution, laws, and treaties of the United States. In the historic case *Marbury v. Madison* (1803), the Supreme Court took this authority to hear cases arising under the Constitution of the United States to establish the power of **judicial review**, the authority of the Court to strike down any law passed by Congress if the Court believes the law violates the Constitution[13] (see Supreme Court Cases: *Marbury v. Madison*).

judicial review: *Authority of courts to declare laws passed by Congress and acts of the executive branch to be unconstitutional.*

supremecourtcases

Marbury v. Madison (1803)

QUESTION: Does Congress have the authority to expand the Supreme Court's original jurisdiction beyond that granted by the Constitution?

ORAL ARGUMENT: February 10, 1803

DECISION: February 23, 1803

OUTCOME: No, thus establishing the power of judicial review (4–0).

It is hard to imagine a more momentous decision resulting from what the historian John A. Garraty called this "trivial squabble over a few petty political plums."* In the closing days of President John Adams's administration, the Federalist Adams nominated William Marbury to the position of justice of the peace for the District of Columbia, and the Federalist Senate confirmed the nomination. But in the hectic final hours of Adams's administration, Secretary of State John Marshall forgot to deliver the commission. When Democratic-Republican Thomas Jefferson became president, his new secretary of state, James Madison, refused to deliver the commission, thus keeping Marbury from assuming his office.

Marbury filed suit at the Supreme Court, believing that the Judiciary Act of 1789 expanded the Court's original jurisdiction to give the Court the authority to hear cases involving writs of *mandamus* (orders to government officials to undertake a specific act) as an original matter, that is, as a trial, and not just as an appeal.

The Supreme Court declared that, because the Constitution precisely specified which types of cases the Supreme Court could hear as an original matter, the section of the Judiciary Act that expanded the Court's original jurisdiction conflicted with the Constitution. Moreover, if a law conflicts with the Constitution, either the law is supreme over the Constitution, or the Constitution is supreme over the law. The Court ruled that it must be the case that the Constitution is supreme over the law. Finally, the Court declared that the judiciary would decide such issues. "It is emphatically the province and duty of the judicial department to say what the law is," wrote Marshall, by this time chief justice of the Supreme Court. The Court in this decision thus granted itself the momentous authority of judicial review, the power to strike down laws passed by Congress on the grounds that those laws violate the Constitution.

- **How does judicial review provide a gateway to participation in the political system?**

* Quotation from John A. Garraty, "*Marbury v. Madison: The Case of the 'Missing' Commissions,*" in *Quarrels That Have Shaped the Constitution,* ed. John Garraty (New York: Harper and Row, 1964), 13.

The Amendment Process

The Constitution provides two paths for changing the constitution, or **amendment**. The first path requires a two-thirds vote in each chamber of Congress, followed by the approval of three-fourths of the states. That state-wide approval can be attained either through the state legislatures or through state ratifying conventions, as directed by Congress. The second path allows two-thirds of the states to request a national constitutional convention that could propose amendments that would go into effect when approved by three-fourths of the states (see Figure 2.2). Again, this approval could be through state legislatures or through state ratifying conventions. Additionally, the Constitution prohibits amendments that would deny any state an equal vote in the Senate, or any amendment that would have allowed a banning of the foreign slave trade prior to 1808.

amendment: *Formal process of changing the Constitution.*

Why did the delegates make it hard to amend the Constitution?

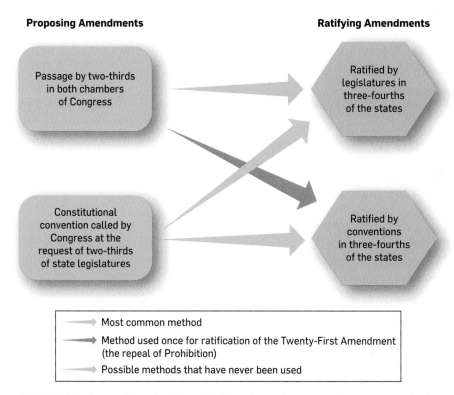

FIGURE 2.2 Amending the Constitution. Amendments can be proposed by two-thirds of each chamber of Congress or by a constitutional convention called by two-thirds of state legislatures. Either way, for ratification, three-quarters of the states must approve. Why do you think the methods indicated by the blue arrows have never been used?

Both paths for amending the Constitution are complex and difficult, and that has kept the Constitution from being modified over popular but short-lived issues. The states have never called a constitutional convention to amend the 1787 Constitution, but Congress has sent thirty-three proposed amendments to the states for ratification. Congress sent the Twenty-First Amendment (the repeal of Prohibition) to state ratifying conventions, but all other proposed amendments went directly to the state legislatures. Of the thirty-three amendments that Congress proposed, twenty-seven received the required assent of three-fourths of the states. These include the Bill of Rights (the First Amendment through the Tenth Amendment), which passed within two years of the adoption of the Constitution, and three Civil War amendments (the Thirteenth Amendment through the Fifteenth Amendment) that abolished slavery and attempted to protect the rights of former slaves. The equal rights amendment that interested Gregory Watson did not pass, nor did a proposed 1978 amendment granting the District of Columbia representation in Congress, but the Twenty-Seventh Amendment, which Watson revived, did. We further discuss these and other amendments to the Constitution later in this chapter.

The Partition of Power

In attempting to explain and justify the constitutional structure, James Madison wrote of "the necessary partition of power among the several departments as laid down in the Constitution" (see *Federalist* 51 in the Appendix). He acknowledged that "a dependence on the people is, no doubt, the primary control on the government," and thus elections serve as the primary means of ensuring that government is responsive to the wishes of the people. If it is not, the people can vote for a new government. Under the Constitution, the people have direct authority to elect the House of Representatives. But to prevent the majority from imposing oppressive laws on the minority, the rest of the government was chosen indirectly: the Senate by the state legislatures, the president by the Electoral College, and judges by the president, with the advice and consent of the Senate.

Lest the people not be sufficient to keep government under control, however, the Constitution had built-in "auxiliary precautions," as Madison called them, to make sure that government could not concentrate power. Thus, **federalism** splits power between nation and state, **separation of powers** divides those powers that remained with the national government among the three branches of government, and **checks and balances** gives each branch some authority over the powers of the other branches. Even after all this, the Constitution places additional limits on both federal and state powers.

Federalist **51:** *Written by James Madison, discusses the needs for checks and balances in government.*

Why does the Constitution divide and separate power?

federalism: *System of government in which sovereignty is constitutionally divided between national and state governments.*

separation of powers: *Government structure in which authority is divided among branches (executive, legislative, and judicial), with each holding separate and independent powers and areas of responsibility.*

checks and balances: *Government structure that authorizes each branch of government (executive, legislative, and judicial) to share powers with the other branches, thereby holding some scrutiny of and control over the other branches.*

Federalism.   The first means of preventing a concentration of power was to divide authority between the national and state governments. Rather than provide Congress with a general power to legislate in the national interest, the Constitution granted Congress enumerated powers. All powers not granted to Congress remained with the states. This division of power is made explicit in the Tenth Amendment to the Constitution: "The powers not delegated to the United States by the Constitution, nor prohibited by it to the States, are reserved to the States respectively, or to the people."

Has the division of power between the national government and the states been good or bad for democracy?

Separation of Powers.   Madison believed that "the accumulation of all powers, legislative, executive, and judiciary, in the same hands, whether of one, a few, or many, and whether hereditary, self-appointed, or elective, may justly be pronounced the very definition of tyranny."[14] Thus, after dividing power between the national and state governments, the Constitution separates those powers that it grants to the national government among the three branches. Moreover, because the "legislative authority necessarily predominates" in a republican government (*Federalist 51*), legislative power was further separated into two distinct chambers—a House and a Senate—each with different manners of election and terms of office.

Checks and Balances.   Under the Constitution, balance among the branches was achieved by giving each one some authority to counteract, or check, the authority of the other two (see Figure 2.3). Thus the president has the authority to propose legislation to Congress and to veto bills passed by Congress; Congress, however, can override that veto by two-thirds majority of each chamber. The president has the authority to pardon people convicted of crimes. The president also nominates federal judges, subject to the advice and consent of the Senate. The Senate also advises and consents to high-ranking executive branch appointments, such as ambassadors and cabinet officials. The House can impeach executive and judicial appointees, and the Senate can convict and remove impeached officials from office by a two-thirds majority. Congress, subject to presidential veto, has the authority to establish lower courts and set their jurisdiction (decide what cases they can hear). It also has the authority to set the Supreme Court's appellate jurisdiction. This appellate jurisdiction is the Supreme Court's authority to hear cases on appeal from lower courts and is the heart of the Supreme Court's judicial power. Congress has this authority over the courts; the courts, on the other hand, can decide the constitutionality of laws passed by Congress. While this power of judicial review is not explicitly granted courts by the Constitution, it has been largely unchallenged since announced by the Supreme Court in *Marbury v. Madison*. The courts also have the authority to review the legality of actions taken by executive branch officials and can decide in any term which cases are argued before it.

What is the purpose of checks and balances?

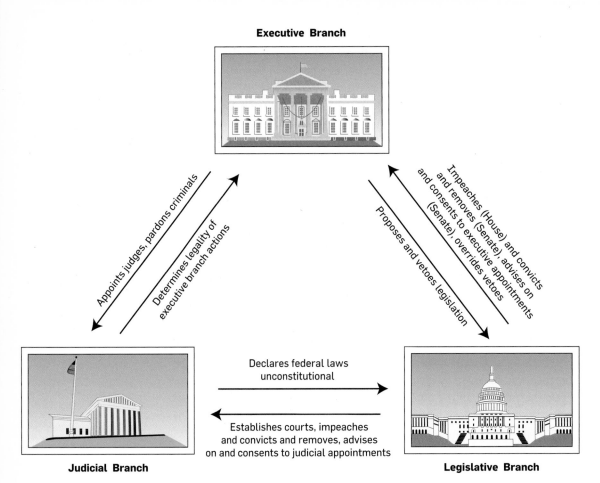

Executive Branch

Appoints judges, pardons criminals

Determines legality of executive branch actions

Impeaches (House) and convicts and removes (Senate), advises on and consents to executive appointments (Senate), overrides vetoes

Proposes and vetoes legislation

Declares federal laws unconstitutional

Establishes courts, impeaches and convicts and removes, advises on and consents to judicial appointments

Judicial Branch

Legislative Branch

FIGURE 2.3 **Checks and Balances.**

Limits on Powers.

The delegation of powers to Congress, and the reservation of all remaining powers to the states, would have left states with the same authority they had to pass oppressive laws under the Articles. To prevent that, the Constitution limits state authority in several ways. First, it makes federal law supreme over state law. Second, it guarantees that the states provide a republican form of government. Third, the Constitution sets limits on the sort of legislation states can pass. Not only are states prohibited from coining money or engaging in foreign affairs, they cannot pass bills of attainder (legislative acts declaring people guilty of a crime) or prosecute individuals under *ex post facto* laws that have made behavior illegal only after the individuals have engaged in it. The Constitution also prohibits states from passing laws that would allow individuals to disregard the obligation of contracts, such as laws negating debts.

The Constitution also expressly limits the authority of Congress. Like the states, Congress can pass neither bills of attainder nor *ex post facto* laws. It also cannot suspend the **writ of *habeas corpus***—a guarantee that incarcerated people can go before a judge to have the legality of their confinement determined—except in cases of invasion or rebellion. Also like the states, Congress cannot grant titles of nobility.

writ of *habeas corpus*: *Right of individuals who have been arrested and jailed to go before a judge who determines if their imprisonment is legal.*

The Ratification Debates

With the proposed Constitution to be accepted or rejected by the people of the various states, state ratification debates largely ignored the question of representation that led to the Connecticut Compromise. So too, little debate took place about the questions involving slavery. Instead, most of the debate concerned the extent of national power under the Constitution, including a feared consolidation of federal authority over the states, the scope of executive and legislative power, and the lack of a bill of rights.

Federalists and Antifederalists

By the time the state ratifying conventions started meeting, two distinct camps had formed. Those who supported the Constitution cleverly named themselves **Federalists**, even though they were really more nationalist than federalist. ("Federal," according to Madison, meant "a confederacy of sovereign states,"[15] which better described the Articles of Confederation, or even the New Jersey Plan, than the new Constitution.) Those who opposed the Constitution, whose leaders included the outspoken Revolutionary leader Patrick Henry of Virginia, became known as the **Antifederalists**.

Madison, along with John Jay, who later became the first chief justice of the United States, and Alexander Hamilton, who later founded the Federalist Party and served as first secretary of the treasury, wrote eighty-five essays, today known as the *Federalist Papers*, that attempted to convince the citizens of New York to ratify the Constitution. They wrote anonymously, under the pen name "Publius," from an early leader in the ancient Roman Republic. Madison's essays, especially, are still read today as a leading source for understanding the Constitution. Two of the most famous essays, numbers 10 and 51, are in this book's Appendix. The Antifederalists published their attacks under anonymous pen names as well, most notably "Brutus"—another leader of the ancient Roman Republic—and "Old Whig," named after the English political party that opposed the monarchy.

Federalists: *Initially, those who supported the Constitution during the ratification period; later, the name of the political party established by supporters of Alexander Hamilton.*

Were the Antifederalists more concerned about liberty or about order?

Antifederalists: *Those who opposed the newly proposed Constitution during the ratification period.*

Federalist Papers: *Series of essays written by James Madison, Alexander Hamilton, and John Jay arguing for the ratification of the Constitution; today a leading source for understanding the Constitution.*

Consolidation of Federal Authority

The Antifederalists found much to disapprove of in the proposed Constitution. They argued that the Constitutional Convention had violated the Articles by moving beyond mere amendment and proposing a new government, one that did not require the unanimous consent of the states. They worried that because sovereignty, the ultimate lawmaking authority, could not be split, and because national law was supreme over state law, a national government under the Constitution would inevitably consolidate its authority over the state governments.

The Federalists answered both of these charges by claiming that sovereignty rested not in the legislature, as had typically been believed, but in the people, as the preamble to the Constitution suggested. Therefore the people could propose any new form of government they wished. And if the people were sovereign, they could split their grant of lawmaking authority between the national and state governments as they saw fit.

The Scope of Executive Authority

Other concerns centered on the scope of executive authority. With no term limits on the executive in the original Constitution, the Antifederalists feared that the president would turn into a monarch. George Mason, who attended the Convention but was one of three delegates not to sign the proposed Constitution, also worried that "the President of the United States has the unrestrained Power of granting Pardon," which could be used to instigate crimes and then cover them up by pardoning his criminal partners. Alexander Hamilton responded in *Federalist* 69 with an explanation of the limits on the executive: elections, whereby the president could be voted out of office; impeachment, whereby the president could be removed from office for "high crimes and misdemeanors"; and the limited veto power, which could be overridden. The president of the United States, Hamilton concluded, was much closer in power to the governor of New York than to the king of England.

Why were the Antifederalists opposed to a strong executive?

general welfare clause (Article I, Section 8): *Gives Congress the power to tax to provide for the general welfare.*

necessary and proper clause (Article I, Section 8): *Gives Congress the power to pass all laws necessary and proper to the powers enumerated in Section 8.*

The Scope of Legislative Authority

Two provisions in Article I, Section 8 of the Constitution, which specified the powers of Congress, particularly alarmed the Antifederalists: the **general welfare clause** and the **necessary and proper clause**. This section of the Constitution begins by stating that "Congress shall have Power To lay and Collect Taxes . . . to . . . provide for . . . the general Welfare of the United States." It concludes by stating that Congress has the power "to make all Laws which shall be necessary and proper for carrying into Execution the foregoing Powers." The Antifederalist "Brutus" contended that "the legislature under this constitution may pass any law which they may think proper."[16] Brutus further wrote that the necessary and proper clause, labeled "the sweeping clause" by the Antifederalists, granted the government "absolute and uncontroulable power, legislative, executive and judicial."[17] James Monroe, who would later serve as the fifth president (1817–25), told the Virginia ratifying convention that the sweeping clause gave Congress "a general power . . . to make all laws that will enable them to carry their powers into effect. There are no limits pointed out. They are not restrained or controlled from making any law, however oppressive in its operation, which they may think necessary to carry their powers into effect."[18] Madison responded in *Federalist* 41 that the power to tax "to provide for the general welfare" was not a general grant of power to tax for any purpose whatsoever but, rather, a power to tax for the enumerated powers that followed.

What elements of the Antifederalist argument do you detect in political arguments today?

Similarly, the Federalists argued that the necessary and proper clause was not a general grant of authority to pass all laws that were necessary and proper, but rather, as the clause explicitly stated, the authority to pass all laws that were "necessary and proper for carrying into execution the foregoing [that is, previously listed] powers." Thus, if a law is necessary and proper for borrowing money, or raising an army, or establishing a post office, Congress may do so, for those powers are among the "foregoing powers" granted Congress. This explicit restriction of the necessary and proper clause to the other powers was absent, however, in the general welfare clause. To Madison, the restriction was obviously implied; to the Antifederalists, it was a threat to limited government.

Nevertheless, to clarify that the Constitution did not provide general powers to Congress, the Federalists agreed to an amendment to the Constitution that declared that "The powers not delegated to the United States by the Constitution, nor prohibited by it to the States, are reserved to the States respectively, or to the people." Interestingly, the amendment parallels a similar provision from the Articles, which declared that the states retained all powers not "expressly delegated" to the national government. By limiting congressional authority to those powers delegated to it, rather than the stricter standard of those powers expressly delegated to it, the Constitution creates a somewhat greater authority for **implied powers**. What elements of the Antifederalist argument do you detect in political arguments today?

implied powers: *Powers not explicitly granted to Congress but added through the necessary and proper clause.*

The Lack of a Bill of Rights

The most serious charge against the Constitution was that it did not contain a bill of rights. The Federalists argued that a bill of rights was not necessary because Congress had only those powers granted by the Constitution. If Congress was not granted the authority to, say, abridge freedom of the press, then it was unnecessary to say that Congress could not abridge freedom of

Was the Bill of Rights necessary in 1787? Is it necessary today?

the press. The Federalists went further to claim that a bill of rights could even be dangerous, because if certain rights were listed but not others, the implication could be that those rights not listed could be abridged.

Consider two documents. The first one states that Congress has the right to regulate commerce between the states, to tax to provide for the general welfare, and to raise armies.

Under this document, does Congress have the right to abridge the right to assemble? The Federalist answer was no, because Congress only has enumerated powers, and the right to limit freedom of assembly is not one of them. The Antifederalist answer was yes, because the power was not prohibited.

Now consider a second document, which states that Congress has the right to regulate commerce between the states, to tax to provide for the general welfare, and to raise armies. In addition, it states that Congress may not abridge freedom of the press.

Now, may Congress abridge the right to assemble? The Federalists argued that the potential for Congress to regulate the right to assemble is greater in the second document than in the first. That is, in the second case, Congress could say "we are prohibited from abridging freedom of the press, but we are not prohibited from abridging the right to assemble, so we are allowed to do that." By listing certain rights, the Constitution could be interpreted to allow Congress to limit those freedoms not listed.

It is hard to imagine people concluding from the Federalist argument that rights would be safer without a bill of rights. Not only is this is a complicated argument, but the broad powers granted Congress under the Constitution—such as regulating interstate commerce and taxing to provide for the general welfare—combined with the necessary and proper clause, probably mean that Congress could have found ways to pass laws abridging freedom of assembly, freedom of speech, and other freedoms. The Federalists eventually gave in to the Antifederalist argument, agreeing that amending the Constitution to provide a bill of rights would be among the first items of business under a newly ratified Constitution. And to prevent the listing of certain rights to create an assumption that Congress could abridge other rights not listed, among the Bill of Rights was the Ninth Amendment: "The enumeration in the Constitution, of certain rights, shall not be construed to deny or disparage others retained by the people."

Despite the Antifederalist arguments about excessive national power, the lack of a bill of rights, and a too-powerful executive, states began ratifying the new Constitution. By June 1788, ten states had ratified, one more than needed to establish the new Constitution. New York then followed, but North Carolina and Rhode Island did not ratify until after George Washington was elected president.

What would have happened if the Constitution had not been ratified?

The Responsive Constitution

The government the Framers devised has lasted more than two hundred years. As in 1787, it still has three branches of government, Congress still consists of two chambers, and the Electoral College still chooses the president. But other parts of the U.S. constitutional system have changed substantially, some to fix flaws and some to respond to new circumstances and developing ideas about the nature of equality. Some of these changes, such as the Bill of Rights, came through the formal amendment process. Others were the result of changing interpretation by the Supreme Court as to what the Constitution means. Still others are what some call "extraconstitutional." That is, they affect the way the constitutional system operates even though the Constitution itself has not been amended to reflect them. Most prominent is the development of political parties.

The Bill of Rights

As part of the fight over ratification, the Federalists agreed that they would propose a bill of rights once the new Constitution was ratified, and some state ratifying conventions forwarded proposals for specific amendments. Madison, elected as a member of Congress from Virginia, quickly selected twelve proposed amendments, among them the congressional pay raise amendment that Gregory Watson revived nearly two hundred years later. The states then ratified ten of the amendments in 1791, as a Bill of Rights that became part of the Constitution.

The First Amendment guarantees major political rights, including freedom of speech, press, assembly, and the free exercise of religion. It also prohibits establishing a national religion, or more precisely, any law "respecting an establishment of religion." The Second Amendment protects the right to bear arms; the Third Amendment prohibits the quartering of soldiers in one's home in times of peace. The Fourth, Fifth, Sixth, and Eighth Amendments protect rights relating to criminal procedure, including the right at trial to the assistance of an attorney and the right to trial by jury (Sixth). (The Seventh Amendment protects the right to a trial by jury in civil cases over twenty dollars.)

How has the Constitution changed, and why?

The Civil War Amendments

Following the Civil War, Congress and the states ratified three amendments. The Thirteenth Amendment prohibits slavery. The Fourteenth Amendment, aimed at protecting the newly emancipated slaves, makes all people born in the United States citizens of the United States. It also prohibits states from denying anyone due process of law, the equal protection of the law, or the privileges and immunities of citizens of the United States. The Fifteenth Amendment prohibits states from denying anyone the right to vote on account of race or prior status as slaves. All three amendments give Congress the authority to enforce its measures by appropriate legislation, thus adding to Congress's enumerated powers. These amendments radically changed the structure of the federal government by giving the national government authority over internal matters of the states.

Amendments That Expand Public Participation

Other amendments have further extended the gateways to public participation in government by giving the people the right to vote for their senators directly (Seventeenth), guaranteeing women the right to vote (Nineteenth, 1920), allowing residents of the District of Columbia to vote in presidential elections (Twenty-Third, 1961), prohibiting states from setting poll taxes as a requirement of voting in federal elections (Twenty-Fourth, 1964), and guaranteeing the right to vote for those age 18 or older (Twenty-Sixth, 1971). For a summary of all the amendments, see Figure 2.4.

Constitutional Interpretation

The Constitution has also changed through interpretation by the Supreme Court. Following the explicit establishment of judicial review in *Marbury v. Madison,* the Court has exercised authority to determine what the Constitution means, and under that authority, the powers of Congress have grown enormously. During the Great Depression of the 1930s, the Court began to interpret Congress's power to tax to provide for the general welfare as extending beyond the enumerated powers. Rather, in line with the interpretation of the general welfare clause that the Antifederalists feared, the Court now holds that Congress can tax and spend for virtually any purpose that is not expressly prohibited. Additionally, Congress's authority to regulate commerce between the states is now so grand that it covers virtually all commercial activity. This is an authority that even the Federalists hardly could have imagined.

What is the significance of judicial review?

This growth of national authority confirms that the Antifederalists were correct to insist on a bill of rights. Although Congress has not been granted the explicit right to abridge freedom of speech or freedom of the press, it would have the authority to do so under current readings of the commerce, taxing, and various other clauses, were it not for the Bill of Rights.

Future Amendments

Many of the formal changes in the Constitution since the Bill of Rights have centered on greater direct participation—direct voting for the Senate; no poll

FIGURE 2.4 The Amendments to the Constitution.

Following the specific protections of the first eight amendments to the Constitution, many subsequent amendments have corrected structural problems in the operation of government. Others have expanded participation and equality.

Color Code :

Criminal procedure   Participation   Equality   Structure   Miscellaneous

First (1791): Prohibits abridging freedoms of religion, speech, press, assembly, and petition

Second (1791): Prohibits abridging the right to bear arms

Third (1791): Prohibits involuntary quartering of soldiers in one's home during peacetime

Fourth (1791): Prohibits unreasonable searches and seizures

Fifth (1791): Affirms the right to indictment by a grand jury and the right to due process; protects against double jeopardy, self-incrimination, and taking of property without just compensation

Sixth (1791): Affirms rights to speedy and public trial, to confront witnesses, and to counsel

Seventh (1791): Affirms right to jury trials in civil suits over $20

Eighth (1791): Prohibits excessive bail, excessive fines, and cruel and unusual punishments

Ninth (1791): Declares that the enumeration of certain rights does not limit other rights retained by the people

Tenth (1791): Reserves the powers not granted to the national government to the states or to the people

Eleventh (1798): Prevents citizens from one state from suing another state in federal court

Twelfth (1804): Requires that electors cast separate votes for president and vice president and specifies requirements for vice presidential candidates

Thirteenth (1865): Prohibits slavery in the United States

Fourteenth (1868): Makes all persons born in the United States citizens of the United States, and prohibits states from denying persons within its jurisdiction the privileges or immunities of citizens, the due process of law, and equal protection of the laws; apportionment by whole persons

Fifteenth (1870): Prohibits states from denying the right to vote on account of race

Sixteenth (1913): Grants Congress the power to tax income derived from any source

Seventeenth (1913): Gives the people (instead of state legislatures) the right to choose U.S. senators directly

Eighteenth (1919): Prohibits the manufacture, sale, or transportation of intoxicating liquors

Nineteenth (1920): Guarantees women the right to vote

Twentieth (1933): Declares that the presidential term begins on January 20 (instead of March 4)

Twenty-First (1933): Repeals the Eighteenth Amendment

Twenty-Second (1951): Limits presidents to two terms

Twenty-Third (1961): Grants Electoral College votes to residents of the District of Columbia

Twenty-Fourth (1964): Prohibits poll taxes

Twenty-Fifth (1967): Specifies replacement of the vice president and establishes the position of acting president during a president's disability

Twenty-Sixth (1971): Guarantees 18-year-olds the right to vote

Twenty-Seventh (1992): Sets limits on congressional pay raises

taxes; no abridgements of rights to vote on account of race, sex, or age so long as one is 18; and residents of the District of Columbia are no longer excluded from voting for president. District residents do not have actual voting representation in Congress, however, because the Constitution gives Congress "exclusive legislation" authority over "the Seat of Government of the United States." It is unlikely that three-quarters of the states would approve granting District residents representation in Congress, given the partisan consequences of such a change.

Another perennial suggestion is the replacement of the Electoral College with some form of popular vote. Calls for this reform by Democrats revived after George W. Bush became president in 2000 despite losing the popular vote. But Bush was not the first to win the electoral vote without winning a popular majority. John Quincy Adams in 1824, Rutherford B. Hayes in 1876, and Benjamin Harrison in 1888 won the presidency without popular majorities, and the election of 1960 was so close that John F. Kennedy, too, might have become president though losing the popular vote.[19] Nevertheless, expanding participation through the direct election of the president remains unlikely given the difficulties of amending the Constitution and the influence of small states.

What amendments to the Constitution would you like to see pass?

Other Changes

Not all changes to the Constitution occur via amendment or interpretation. Fundamental changes to the U.S. constitutional system have occurred through the establishment of new institutions, most notably **political parties**. They began to emerge during Washington's first term as president. When Secretary of the Treasury Hamilton pushed for aggressive use of the "sweeping clause" to allow the national government to regulate the economy, Madison and Jefferson rose in opposition (see Chapter 9, Political Parties). These early divisions between political elites laid the groundwork for the emergence of the first set of opposing political parties.

political parties: *Broad coalitions of individuals who organize to win elections in order to enact a commonly supported set of public policies.*

The rise of political parties has meant that the president and vice president run as members of a political party, not as individuals. In Congress, representatives and senators organize themselves by parties, with members of the majority party having most of the power. The struggle that Madison envisioned between the different branches of government, with Congress and the president checking each other, really exists only when the president and the majority party in Congress represent different parties, a situation known as **divided government**. When Congress and the president are of the same party, checks by Congress are curtailed. Members of the president's party in Congress are more likely to be loyal to the president than they are to their own branch of government.[20]

divided government: *Situation when one party controls the executive branch and the other party controls the legislative branch.*

Political parties also allow for greater responsiveness of politicians to the national welfare. With political parties, however, voters can hold their representatives of the party in power accountable not just for the job that the representative is doing for the district, but for the job that the government is doing for the nation. Thus the representatives of the people are more likely to be responsive to the interests of the people.

Policy Making in a Constitutional System: The Death Penalty

The decisions the Framers made in constructing the constitutional system have profound implications for public policy making. The U.S. constitutional system imposes separation of powers, but that separation is limited by a system of checks and balances that adds complexity to the policy-making process. Additionally, the federalism component adds a level of inconsistency by allowing each state, within the bounds of the Constitution, to pursue its own policies. This inconsistency generates an inequality in the application of the death penalty, which we will examine as an example.

Checks and Balances

Although the separation of powers established under the Constitution means that it is generally true that the legislature makes laws, the executive enforces laws, and the judiciary interprets the law, the checks and balances established in the Constitution complicate the process, granting all three branches a say in policy making. The president can set the legislative agenda and veto legislation. If the legislation passes, implementing the law is up to the executive branch, and because laws cannot cover every circumstance, the laws typically leave discretion to the executive branch in carrying them out. For example, if state or federal law allows for the death penalty in certain types of cases, state or federal prosecutors in their respective executive branches must decide whether to seek the death penalty in an appropriate case. If the executive branch has little discretion in carrying out a law, such as deciding the amount of Social Security checks, there is little policy making done while doing so. But where discretion is substantial, such as the death penalty example, the executive branch becomes a key player in policy making.

Another notable feature of checks and balances is that the judiciary can strike down laws passed by the legislative branch if it believes that those laws violate the Constitution. Similarly, the judiciary can also nullify actions the executive branch takes, if those actions violate constitutional provisions. Thus, under the U.S. constitutional system, all three branches of government can have a say in policy making.

Federalism

The fact that states each have their own separate governments and sets of laws further complicates the policy-making process. The Constitution, particularly as interpreted by the Supreme Court, leaves some policies in exclusive federal control, some (though as Chapter 3 shows, a shrinking number) under exclusive state control, and many others under both state and federal control. States, for example, may generally establish their own criminal justice systems, but those systems must abide by guarantees found in the Constitution.

Does the federal system make government more responsive or less? Does it make citizens more or less equal?

The Death Penalty

This balancing act among the branches of the federal government and between nation and state affects a wide range of policy issues, including the imposition of the death penalty, also known as capital punishment. The Constitution contains some degree of ambiguity about the death penalty. In several places, it seems to allow capital punishment. The Fourteenth Amendment's due process clause says that states may not deprive people of life, liberty, or property without due process of law, thus suggesting that life, liberty, and property may be taken so long as the states follow due process. Similarly, the Fifth Amendment's declarations that no person shall be held for a capital crime without indictment by a grand jury similarly suggests that a person can be held for a capital crime with indictment by a grand jury.

Alternatively, the Eighth Amendment prohibits "cruel and unusual" punishments.

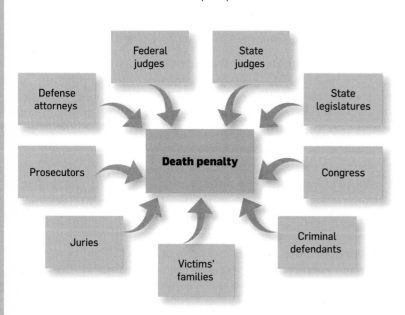

The Supreme Court interprets that clause to mean that the constitutionality of punishments are to be subject to evolving standards of justice and that the death penalty might violate those standards.

Prior to 1972, most states allowed capital punishment and did so by declaring crimes for which capital punishment could be imposed (usually murder, but sometimes rape) and then leaving it up to the jury in such cases to decide whether capital punishment should be inflicted. Then in 1972, the Supreme Court put a temporary halt to capital punishment, declaring that this process of complete jury discretion was cruel and unusual in that it led to such an arbitrary and unequal imposition of the death penalty.[21] According to one of the Court opinions in this heavily divided case, who received the death penalty and who did not was as arbitrary as who gets hit by lightning.

Various states responded to this decision by requiring that juries follow certain guidelines before they impose the death penalty (see Figure 2.5 for fluctuations in the number of executions per year). In 1976, the Supreme Court ruled 7–2 that the death penalty with guidelines did not constitute cruel and unusual punishment under the Constitution.[22] Currently, thirty-five states permit capital punishment in their state criminal statutes.[23] Given strong public

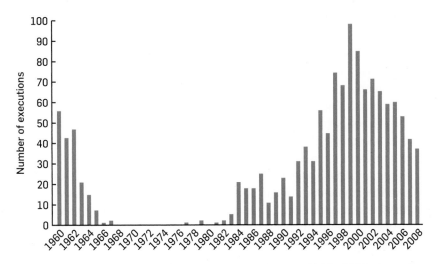

FIGURE 2.5 **Annual Executions in the United States, 1960–2008.** Annual executions dropped significantly in the years prior to the Supreme Court's temporary halt of capital punishment in 1972. After the Court reinstated capital punishment in 1976, executions rose as public support for capital punishment remained high. The number later dipped, as DNA evidence revealing that some death row inmates had been wrongly convicted made the public wary about the death penalty.
Source: Death Penalty Information Center, http://deathpenaltyinfo.org/executions-us-1608-2002-espy-file and http://deathpenaltyinfo.org/executions-united-states.

approval for the death penalty, Congress allows it for certain federal crimes, including terrorist acts that result in death, murder for hire, kidnappings that result in murder, and running a large-scale illegal drug enterprise.[24] The federal death penalty can be imposed throughout the country, even in states that do not allow the death penalty for violations of state law.

Though the Supreme Court has attempted to limit the unequal application of the death penalty, one clear finding from studies of the death penalty is the effect of the race of the victim: juries are far more likely to impose the death penalty when the victim is white than when the victim is black.[25] The Supreme Court ruled, however, that even if this were the case overall, someone challenging a death sentence based on such statistics would have to prove that the jury intentionally discriminated in the particular case.[26]

Although the Supreme Court has ruled the use of the death penalty to be constitutional, it has put prohibitions on who can receive it as punishment. These include offenders who were under the age of 18 when their crimes were committed[27] and those convicted of rape, even when the rape victim is a child.[28]

Do you think the death penalty is constitutional?

In addition to the Court's steps in limiting states' powers to use the death penalty, some states have begun to limit their own use of this punishment. The Innocence Project, a group dedicated to reversing convictions of people who truly were innocent, reports 218 death penalty cases in which DNA testing demonstrated that the wrong person was convicted of the crime.[29] This finding has led many states to reduce the number of death penalty sentences. It has also led many, but not all, states to allow convicted criminals access to DNA evidence, though the Supreme Court does not require them to do so.[30]

In considering how well policy making works in the constitutional system, it is worth noting the inconsistent use of the death penalty across states. If two individuals commit the same crime but in different states, one criminal might be put to death, but the other allowed to live. Should states have their own policies on capital punishment as they see fit, or should the federal government be allowed to impose one uniform policy on the use of the death penalty in every state? The inconsistent use of the death penalty raises questions about equality under the constitutional system and serves as one of the most important examples of the unintended consequences of constitutional design.

The Constitution and Democracy

Government under the 1787 Constitution would today be considered severely lacking in both democracy and equality. The government allowed some of the people, mostly white males with property, to choose one chamber of the legislative branch of their government, but did not grant the people a direct vote for the other chamber of the legislature or for the chief executive. And needless to say, a government that allowed slavery would be a pariah, an outcast, among the nations of the world.

Moreover, in 1787, the right to vote was regulated by the states. Slaves were not allowed to vote, but states differed as to whether free blacks, women, and those without property could vote. In 1790, Georgia, South Carolina, and Virginia prohibited free blacks from voting. South Carolina also required voters to believe in God, heaven, and hell. Only New Jersey granted women the right to vote, a right that lasted only until 1807. Every state except Vermont required some form of tax payment for voter eligibility.[31]

Yet, compared to the despots and monarchs that had long ruled other countries, the government of 1787 allowed for a remarkable degree of participation by the common person. With a direct say in their state legislatures, and at least indirect influence in all branches of the national government, the 1787 Constitution was a striking break with the past, even if it did not live up to the Declaration's statement that "All men are created equal."

Of course, today participation is much more widespread than in 1787. Although the Electoral College remains in effect, every state allows the people to choose their electors. And those electors exert no independent influence on who shall be president. In addition to these changing practices, amendments to the Constitution have widened the gateways to democracy. Due to the Seventeenth Amendment, the people today directly choose their senators, making that body directly responsive to public wishes. Moreover, voting equality is guaranteed in various ways: poll taxes are illegal (Twenty-Fourth Amendment), and voting rights, which are now guaranteed to those 18 years old or older (Twenty-Sixth Amendment), may not be abridged on account of race (Fifteenth Amendment) or sex (Nineteenth Amendment).

Although the 1787 Constitution allowed the national government to exercise direct control over the citizenry, its tiny size left the people with far more control over their daily lives than they have today. But it is also the case that today the people have more control over the government. In addition to new constitutional gateways, opportunities for participation are greater than ever, with the Internet relaying information virtually instantly. It is much easier for representatives to be responsive to their constituents' desires when representatives can easily learn what their constituents believe, and constituents can readily learn what their representatives have done.

FOCUS QUESTIONS

- In what ways did the Constitution ensure that government would be responsive to the people? How has government become more responsive since 1787?

- In what ways did the Constitution seek to control the popular will and ensure order?

- In what ways did the Constitution seek to control government itself?

- In what ways did the nation's founding documents promote equality? In what ways did they fail to promote equality?

- Is the Constitution a gate or a gateway to American democracy? Is it a gatekeeper? Explain.

GATEWAYS TO LEARNING

Top Ten to Take Away

1. The colonists declared independence from Britain because they believed that the British Parliament and king were denying their rights as British subjects. (pp. 39–41)

2. Congress's powers under the Articles of Confederation were limited, and the structure the Articles established made governing difficult. (pp. 42–43)

3. In 1787, delegates from twelve states met in Philadelphia to amend the Articles; instead, they wrote a new Constitution. (pp. 43–48)

4. To secure the assent of all states represented at the Constitutional Convention, the delegates reached compromises between large and small states over representation, between northern and southern states over issues related to slavery, and between those who favored a strong national government and those who favored strong state governments in the balance of power between the two. (pp. 44–48)

5. This newly proposed Constitution was then sent to the states for ratification, and it is, with subsequent amendments, the same Constitution Americans live by today. (pp. 48–50)

A full narrative summary of the chapter is on the book's website.

6. The Constitution lays out the structure of democratic government and the means by which the Constitution can be amended. It reflects the Framers' attempt to establish a government powerful enough to ensure public order yet restrained enough to guarantee individual liberty. (pp. 50–57)

7. Debates over the ratification of the Constitution centered on a fear of consolidated federal authority over the states, the scope of executive and legislative power, and the lack of a bill of rights. (pp. 57–61)

8. To achieve ratification, the Federalists gave in to Antifederalist demands for the Bill of Rights, passed as the first ten amendments to the Constitution. (pp. 59–61)

9. Subsequent amendments ended slavery, protected the rights of African Americans, and generally extended public participation in government while also expanding federal authority over the states. (pp. 61–62)

10. The constitutional system established in 1787 has also been changed by constitutional interpretation and its operation altered by the development of political parties and the growth of the executive branch. (pp. 62–65)

Ten to Test Yourself

1. How did English and colonial notions of representation differ?

2. What were the deficiencies of the Articles of Confederation?

3. Overall, how did slave and antislave interests fare at the Constitutional Convention?

4. In what ways did the proposed Constitution more closely resemble the Virginia Plan, and in what ways did it more closely resemble the New Jersey Plan?

5. In what ways was power divided under the Constitution?

6. What powers did the legislative, executive, and judicial branches receive from the 1787 Constitution?

7. What are the checks that each branch has over the other branches?

8. How has the extent of public participation expanded since colonial times?

9. What were the Antifederalists' fears about the Constitution? How justified were these fears?

10. Describe the complications (gates) to policy making in the U.S. constitutional system.

More review questions and answers and chapter quizzes are on the book's website.

Terms to Know and Use

amendment (p. 53)

Antifederalists (p. 57)

Articles of Confederation (p. 42)

bicameral (p. 50)

Bill of Rights (p. 49)

Boston Tea Party (p. 40)

checks and balances (p. 54)

Connecticut Compromise (p. 46)

constitution (p. 39)

Constitutional Convention
  (p. 44)

Continental Congress (p. 40)

Declaration of Independence (p. 41)

divided government (p. 64)

Electoral College (p. 48)

enumerated powers (p. 46)

federalism (p. 54)

Federalist 51 (p. 54)

Federalist Papers (p. 57)

Federalists (p. 57)

general welfare clause (p. 58)

impeach (p. 50)

implied powers (p. 59)

judicial review (p. 51)

necessary and proper clause (p. 58)

New Jersey Plan (p. 45)

override (p. 50)

political parties (p. 64)

proportional representation (p. 45)

separation of powers (p. 54)

Shays's Rebellion (p. 43)

three-fifths compromise (p. 47)

Virginia Plan (p. 44)

veto (p. 50)

writ of *habeas corpus* (p. 57)

Use the vocabulary flashcards on the book's website.

3 FEDERALISM

▲ Brown University, Providence Rhode Island

> *As I grew up, my mom and dad taught me the values that attracted them to this country, and they instilled in me an immigrant's wonder at the greatness of America.*

In 1992, when Bobby Jindal was a senior at Brown University in Rhode Island, he had a lot of choices to make. As an honors student in biology and public policy, he had been accepted to law school and medical school at both Harvard and Yale. He was also selected as a Rhodes Scholar, and he decided to accept the scholarship to study politics at Oxford. At Brown, his conservative views had put him in the minority, and he had founded the university's first Republican Club, later serving as its president and of the College Republican Federation of Rhode Island. Once Jindal decided on a career in politics, his rise was meteoric. By 2007, he was governor of Louisiana. Though swift, his career path was a zigzag, not a straight line, reflecting the separate and overlapping state and national authorities built into America's federal system.

Following study at Oxford, Jindal returned to his native Louisiana and got his crucial start in politics, at age 24, as head of the Louisiana Health and Hospitals Department. State hospital administration in Louisiana, as in all fifty states, is a mix of both national and state monies and regulations. The department is among the most important in

Bobby Jindal ▶

CourseMate

Visit http://www.cengagebrain
.com/shop/ISBN/0495906190
for interactive tools including:
• **Quizzes**
• **Flashcards**
• **Videos**
• **Animated PowerPoint slides, Podcast summaries, and more**

Douglas Graham/Congressional Quarterly/Getty Images

Joy Brown/Shutterstock.com

Louisiana, accounting for about 40 percent of the state budget. Its responsibilities include programs such as Medicaid, a joint state-federal program that provides free health care to poor people. When Jindal took over in 1996, the department was running a $400 million deficit. Jindal wiped out the deficit and returned a substantial surplus to the state. A few years later, he moved to Washington to become an assistant secretary in the U.S. Department of Health and Human Services.

After a few more years, Jindal, now age 32, resigned his federal position and went back to Louisiana to run for governor. He lost that 2003 race but then quickly decided to run for a House seat in Louisiana's First Congressional District. Jindal received the Republican Party endorsement in the conservative district and won the 2004 race with 78 percent of the vote. Back in Washington, Jindal served on House committees that worked with national issues (Homeland Security) and traditionally local issues (Resources and Education). He won reelection in November 2006, but in January 2007, he announced that he would again run for governor. This time, against three other candidates, Jindal won with 54 percent of the vote. At age 36, Jindal became the nation's youngest governor and the nation's first governor with South Asian heritage.[1]

In this chapter, we examine the federal system of government, including the authority of the national and state governments, how that authority has shifted over time, and how federalism can both enhance and detract from American democracy.

FOCUS QUESTIONS

- How does federalism affect government's responsiveness? To what and to whom are federal systems accountable?

- What does it mean for citizen equality when different states are allowed to have different laws on certain subjects?

- How does a federal system make it easier for citizens to have an influence in government?

- What has been the relationship between federalism and the push for equality in the United States?

- Does federalism prove to be a gate or a gateway to democracy? Explain.

Why Federalism?

The delegates to the 1787 Constitutional Convention in Philadelphia recognized that the system of government established by the Articles of Confederation was failing. If the delegates could not fix the problems caused by the Articles, James Madison and others feared that the union could disintegrate.[2] All the steps taken toward union since 1774 would be reversed (see Chapter 2).

Why Unify?

The Constitution established itself in the name of "We the People of the United States." Thus, in this action, the colonies, now states, chose to unify.

They need not have taken this path. Federalism presupposes some form of union, so the answer to the question "why federalism?" first requires an answer to the question "why unify?" The primary answer is that some form of union allows smaller political entities to pool their resources to fight a common enemy.

Beyond military necessity, the colonists considered themselves to be part of a common nation with Americans in the other states. A **nation** exists when people in a country have a sense of common identity due to a common origin, history, or ancestry, all of which the colonists shared. This sense of common identity made some form of union not only a military necessity but a political advantage. The American people, however, also had a strong loyalty to their states, an attachment that would have made eliminating states politically impossible. How strong the national government would be was the subject of heated debate at the Constitutional Convention.

nation: *Political unit whose people share a sense of common identity.*

Today the people of the United States no longer share a common origin, history, or ancestry. Does it matter?

Confederal, Unitary, and Federal Systems

Because splitting up was an unattractive option, one of the forms of union available to the colonists was to continue but strengthen the **confederal system** that existed under the Articles of Confederation. In a confederal system, independent states grant limited powers to a national government to rule for the common good in certain limited areas such as defense. The independent states that make up the confederation usually have an equal vote, and the confederation might require unanimous consent or other supermajorities (for example, two-thirds or three-quarters) to pass legislation. The confederal organization usually acts through the states that constitute it rather than acting directly on the citizens of those states.

confederal system: *System of government in which ultimate authority rests with the regional (for example, state) governments.*

But the Framers who met in Philadelphia in 1787 were not inclined to continue the confederal system. A majority of the delegates believed that the New Jersey Plan, which would have strengthened the Articles but still granted each state one vote and still required a supermajority to pass most important issues, did not go far enough. They knew that the United States needed a stronger national government.

If a confederal system gives hardly any power to the national government, a **unitary system** of government gives it virtually every power. State or regional governments might still exist under a unitary system, but their powers, and in fact their very existence, are entirely up to the national government. The authority of state or regional governments in a pure unitary system is similar to the relationship between state governments today and the cities and counties that exist under the state's

unitary system: *System of government in which ultimate authority rests with the national government.*

jurisdiction. Counties can make local decisions, but they exist only because their state established that county, and a county has only the authority that the state grants to it. A confederal system was too weak for the United States, and an overly strong central government would pose its own set of problems. The Framers particularly feared that too much power in any government could lead to tyranny. Freedom would be better guaranteed by dividing governmental powers, rather than concentrating them in a central government.

federalism: *System of government in which sovereignty is constitutionally divided between national and state governments.*

The Framers thus established a new system of government, **federalism**. A federal system, like that of the United States, mixes features of confederal and unitary governments. The Constitution created one legislative chamber chosen by the people, based on population and another chosen by the states based on equal representation. Within the states' areas of authority—those areas not granted to the national government—their decisions are final and cannot be overturned by the national government. Moreover, the existence of states in a federal system does not depend on the national government; rather, the states derive their authority directly from the people. Nevertheless, within areas of authority granted to the national government, or areas of authority shared by both the states and the national government, the national government reigns supreme. The political scientist William Riker defines federalism as a system of government in which there exists "a government of the federation [that is, a national government] and a set of governments of the member units [that is, the states] in which both kinds of governments rule over the same territory and people and each kind has the authority to make some decisions independently of the other"[3] (see Figure 3.1).

Which government has the biggest impact on you—the federal government or your state government?

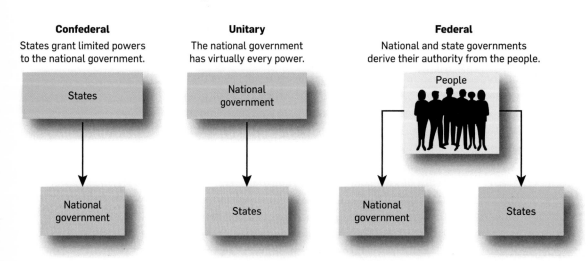

Confederal
States grant limited powers to the national government.

Unitary
The national government has virtually every power.

Federal
National and state governments derive their authority from the people.

States → National government

National government → States

People → National government · States

FIGURE 3.1 Confederal, Unitary, and Federal Systems of Government.

A federal system, besides lessening the risks of tyranny, promotes self-government. While any representative democracy involves **self-government**, or government by the people, self-government is enhanced when the decisions that affect the citizens' lives are made by representatives who are local, closer to them, and more similar to them, rather than by representatives who live far away and are dissimilar. The Framers' choice of a federal system of government was innovative, as virtually all the world's governments at the time were either unitary or confederal. The American system was an experiment, and its evolution has been shaped by the tensions, even conflicts, inherent in a system in which power is both divided and shared. Since 1787, about two dozen other nations have ordered themselves as federal systems (see Other Places: Federal Political Systems).

self-government: *Rule by the people.*

In addition to federalism, in what other ways was the Constitution of 1787 innovative, even experimental?

Constitutional Framework

The Constitution lays out the framework of the U.S. federal system in a variety of ways. First, the Constitution grants specified powers to the national government, reserving all remaining powers to the states or the people. Second, the Constitution sets limits on both the powers granted the federal government and the powers reserved to the states. Third, the Constitution lays out the relationships among the several states as well as between the states and the federal government.

Grants of Power

The Constitution lists the grants of power to Congress in Article I, Section 8. These **enumerated powers** include several powers that could only lie in a national government. These are raising armies, declaring war, and establishing rules for citizenship. The enumerated powers also grant powers that the central government under the Articles of Confederation did not have, including the power to tax to provide for the general welfare, to borrow money, and to regulate interstate and foreign commerce. To the list of powers in Article I, Section 8, the Framers added one final power that would substantially strengthen the national government: the power to make all laws that are "necessary and proper" for carrying out the enumerated powers. This **necessary and proper clause** does not grant Congress the authority to pass any law that it desires. Rather, the clause requires that the law be necessary and proper to one of the listed powers, such as collecting taxes or regulating commerce.

The original Constitution does not list the powers of the state governments, as the states retained all powers that were not prohibited by the Constitution. The Tenth Amendment declares that "the powers not

enumerated powers: *Powers expressly granted to Congress by the Constitution.*

necessary and proper clause (Article I, Section 8): *Gives Congress the power to pass all laws necessary and proper to the powers enumerated in Section 8.*

otherplaces

Federal Political Systems

Only a small percentage of the world's nations are federalist systems, but the tendency of larger nations to rely on federalism means that they cover most of the world's landmass. Of the world's largest countries—Russia, Canada, the United States, China, Australia, and Brazil—only China is not federalist. Of the world's most populous countries—China, India, the United States, Indonesia, and Brazil—all but China and Indonesia are federalist. Note that federalist does not necessarily mean democratic (as in Russia), and democratic does not necessarily mean federalist (as in the United Kingdom).

With the recent devolution of power to Scotland, Wales, and Northern Ireland, however, the United Kingdom is not quite so unitary as it once was. India, a multilingual nation, has a federal system, with twenty-eight states and seven territories. Its federal system has a stronger national government as compared with the United States, with reserve powers belonging to the national government and the states' powers enumerated. South Africa is also a federal system and a multilingual nation. The constitution divides the country into nine provinces. It delegates certain powers

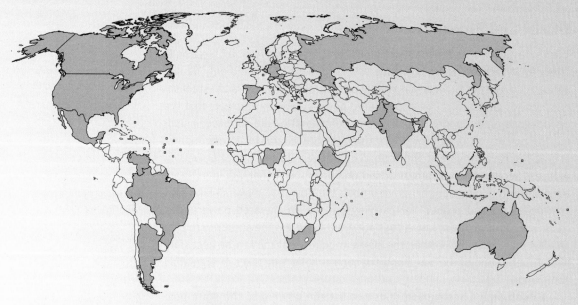

Countries with Federal Political System.
Source: Forum of Federations, "Federalism by Country."

to the national government, others to the provincial governments. Unlike the United States, the provinces do not retain reserve powers. Mexico is a federal system, with thirty-one states plus a federal district. The Mexican Constitution limits the form of those state governments in ways that the U.S. Constitution does not.

In short, within federal political systems as a type, there are many variations, as multilingual and multiethnic nations around the globe feel a greater need to provide the local autonomy that comes with federalism.

- **Why have certain nations chosen a federal system?**
- **Why have most nations not chosen a federal system?**

Source: Data from Forum of Federations, "Federalism by Country," http://www.forumfed.org/en/federalism/by_country/index.php.

delegated to the United States by the Constitution, nor prohibited by it to the States, are reserved to the States respectively, or to the people" (see Figure 3.2 for the amendments that pertain to federalism). The **reserve powers** of the states, sometimes referred to as the **police powers**, include the powers to protect the safety, health, and welfare of its citizens, though the federal government now regulates many of these activities. Marriage and divorce laws, insurance regulations, and professional

reserve powers: *Powers retained by the states under the Constitution.*

police powers: *Authority of the states to protect the health, safety, and welfare of their citizens.*

FIGURE 3.2 Constitutional Amendments That Pertain to Federalism.

Color Code :
Criminal procedure   Participation   Equality   Structure   Miscellaneous

Fifth (1791): Affirms the right to indictment by a grand jury and right to due process; protects against double jeopardy, self-incrimination, and taking of property without just compensation

Tenth (1791): Reserves the powers not granted to the national government to the states or to the people

Eleventh (1798): Prevents citizens from one state from suing another state in federal court

Thirteenth (1865): Prohibits slavery in the United States

Fourteenth (1868): Makes all persons born in the United States citizens of the United States, and prohibits states from denying persons within its jurisdiction the privileges or immunities of citizens, the due process of law, and equal protection of the laws; apportionment by whole persons

Fifteenth (1870): Prohibits states from denying the right to vote on account of race

Sixteenth (1913): Grants Congress the power to tax income derived from any source

Seventeenth (1913): Gives the people (instead of state legislatures) the right to choose U.S. senators directly

National
Regulating interstate commerce
Raising armies
Declaring war
Coining money

Shared
Taxing
Borrowing
Spending
Regulating health*
Regulating education*
Setting time, place, and manner
　of congressional elections*

State
Regulating intrastate commerce
Regulating family law
Licensing
Handling most criminal law

*These were once reserved powers of the states, but the growth of federal authority means that they are now regulated by both.

FIGURE 3.3 Examples of National, State, and Shared Powers.

licensing (of teachers and electricians, for example), however, remain almost exclusively within state authority. States have authority to define and prosecute most crimes, but the federal government may do so, too, with the most prominent examples including federal laws relating to guns, drugs, and terrorism.

Many powers belong to both the state and national governments. These **concurrent powers** include taxing, borrowing and spending money, making and enforcing laws, establishing court systems, and regulating elections. Many areas that were once exclusively within state authority, such as health care and education, are now regulated by both state and federal governments (see Figure 3.3).

concurrent powers:
Powers held by both the national and state governments in a federal system.

Limits on Power

The Constitution grants only specified powers to the national government, but even those powers are limited. The Constitution prohibits Congress from suspending the **writ of *habeas corpus***, the right of individuals who have been arrested and jailed to go before a judge who determines if their imprisonment is legal. Also prohibited is the passage of any law that declares an individual guilty of a crime (bills of attainder), or any law that makes an act illegal after the fact (*ex post facto* laws).

Following concerns expressed by Antifederalists during the state ratification debates that the proposed Constitution granted the national

writ of *habeas corpus*:
Right of individuals who have been arrested and jailed to go before a judge who determines if their imprisonment is legal.

government too much power, one of the first orders of business for the First Congress was a proposed Bill of Rights. These amendments created associational freedoms (speech, press, assembly, and religion) that Congress could not abridge; limited the authority of governmental prosecutions against alleged criminals by restricting searches and seizures and guaranteeing the right to counsel and to public trials; and protected certain additional rights, including the right to bear arms and the right to jury trials in civil suits over twenty dollars (see Chapter 4 for more details on these rights). The Bill of Rights originally applied only to the national government, not to the states.

The Constitution contains its own set of limits on the state governments. Like the national government, states cannot pass bills of attainder or *ex post facto* laws, or create titles of nobility. Moreover, states cannot enter into any treaty or alliance with foreign nations. The Constitution also limits the authority of states to tax imports and exports.

The **guarantee clause** of the Constitution (Article IV, Section 4) guarantees that states shall have a "Republican Form of Government." In Federalist 39, Madison defined a republican form of government as one that "derives all its powers directly or indirectly from the great body of the people; and is administered by persons holding their offices during pleasure, for a limited period, or during good behavior."[4] That is, as long as the persons who run the government are selected directly (as in the House of Representatives) or indirectly (as in the Electoral College) by the people, and those officeholders either have limited terms of office (as do the president and members of Congress) or can be removed for not meeting the standards of "good behavior" (as in the judiciary), the government can be considered republican. The Supreme Court has declared that the question of whether a state has a republican form of government is one that Congress must decide, not the federal courts.[5]

States are, however, limited by the Fourteenth (1868) and Fifteenth Amendments (1870). The Fourteenth Amendment prohibits the states from denying "any person" due process of law and the equal protection of the laws, and the Fifteenth Amendment prohibits states from denying voting rights on account of race, color, or previous condition of servitude. The Supreme Court later used the **due process clause** of the Fourteenth Amendment to require the states to follow most of the provisions of the Bill of Rights (see Chapter 4). Thus states must protect the same liberties as the federal government, resulting in a nationalizing of the nation's most basic rights. Both the Supreme Court and Congress have used the Fifteenth Amendment to protect equal voting rights in the states and the **equal protection clause** of the Fourteenth Amendment to protect other civil rights (see Chapter 5).

guarantee clause (Article IV, Section 4): *Provides a federal government guarantee that the states will have a republican form of government.*

due process clause: *Prevents the federal government (Fifth Amendment) and the state governments (Fourteenth Amendment) from denying any person due process of law.*

equal protection clause (Fourteenth Amendment): *Prevents the states from denying any person the equal protection of the law.*

Groundwork for Relationships

In the U.S. federal system, where both the states and the federal governments have final say over different matters, the Constitution lays out not only the powers of the national government and restrictions on the powers of both the national and state governments, but also the groundwork for the relationship between the national government and state governments, and relationships among state governments.

Relationships between the Nation and the States.
The Constitution regulates the relationship between the national government and the states through three main clauses: the supremacy clause, the Tenth Amendment, and the sovereign immunity provision of the Eleventh Amendment.

supremacy clause (Article VI): *Makes federal law supreme over state laws.*

The **supremacy clause** (Article VI) makes the Constitution of the United States, plus all laws and treaties made under the Constitution, supreme over state law. Thus, if federal law conflicts with state law, the federal law (assuming it is within the powers of Congress) is supreme. Moreover, because state and federal courts might differ about whether state and federal law actually conflict with each other in a particular case, the ultimate decision rests with the U.S. Supreme Court.[6]

preemption: *Doctrine by which extensive federal regulation can prevent regulation by the states.*

The supremacy clause also allows for the **preemption** of state laws. If Congress and the states both seek to regulate an area of concurrent authority, such as pollution control or the minimum wage, the supremacy clause requires states to meet national standards if national standards are higher than state standards. But there are two exceptions. First, Congress can declare that it has preempted state legislation in that area, meaning only Congress can legislate on the topic. For example, Congress preempted state regulation of warnings on cigarette packages, prohibiting the states from adding their own warnings. Second, even if Congress has not explicitly declared that it has preempted state activity, the Supreme Court can rule that Congress's regulation is so thorough that Congress must have intended to "occupy the field," thus disallowing state regulations. The Supreme Court struck down state regulations of Communist activities under this exception.[7]

As noted, the Tenth Amendment states that all powers not delegated to the national government under the Constitution are reserved to the states, or to the people. The Articles of Confederation had a similar clause, but it included the word *expressly* before the word *delegated*. Because the Tenth Amendment omits the word expressly, the implication is that the national government retains the sort of **implied powers** granted by the necessary and proper clause.

implied powers: *Powers not expressly granted to Congress but added through the necessary and proper clause.*

If the government illegally harms an individual or seizes his or her property, the person might be inclined to sue the government. The doctrine of

sovereign immunity, however, means that a government cannot be sued without its permission. The Eleventh Amendment prohibits federal courts from hearing suits against a state by citizens of another state. However, the Eleventh Amendment is not absolute: Congress can allow suits based on provisions in constitutional amendments passed after the Eleventh, such as the due process or equal protection clauses of the Fourteenth Amendment.

Relationships among the States.   One of the many problems of governance under the Articles of Confederation was that the states could establish trade barriers against one another, thus limiting economic growth. Therefore, in the **commerce clause** (Article I, Section 8) the Constitution established Congress's exclusive authority to regulate commerce among the states. Thus states may not regulate interstate commerce and cannot establish trade barriers against goods from other states. States may tax goods from other states equal to the amount that they tax goods produced in their own states, but they cannot charge extra taxes to goods that are made out of state. Congress cannot establish trade barriers in interstate commerce either, because Article I, Section 9 prohibits Congress from taxing exports from any state.

The Constitution also requires that agreements between two or more states must receive the approval of Congress. States that share rivers, lakes, or other natural resources frequently make agreements over the use of their shared resources so that no one state overuses or overpollutes those resources.[8]

Article IV of the Constitution establishes additional rules that guide relationships among the states. The **full faith and credit clause** generally requires states to accept court decisions made in other states. Couples who are married (or divorced) in Las Vegas, Nevada, are married (or divorced) throughout the United States. This seemingly simple constitutional rule has recently become controversial, as some states have recognized same-sex marriages as valid. Under the full faith and credit clause, same-sex marriage performed in Massachusetts would presumably be valid throughout the nation. But the clause allows Congress to create exceptions. Congress passed and President Bill Clinton (1993–2001) signed one such exception into law with the Defense of Marriage Act (1996), which relieves states of the obligation of accepting the validity of same-sex marriages performed in other states. Another general exception to the full faith and credit clause concerns child custody decisions. Because the best interests of a child may change over time, if a child is moved from one state to another, the courts in the new state need not accept the child custody determinations made by the previous state.

sovereign immunity: *Doctrine holding that states cannot be sued without their permission.*

commerce clause (Article I, Section 8): *Gives Congress the power to regulate commerce with foreign nations, with Indian tribes, and among the various states.*

full faith and credit clause (Article IV, Section 1): *Requires states to accept civil proceedings from other states.*

Should all states be required to recognize same-sex marriages valid in one state?

Justin Sullivan/Getty Images

Article IV also requires, through its **privileges and immunities clause**, that states treat people from other states equally to its own residents. Thus states may not limit the right to practice law to residents, nor may they require people to live in the state for a set amount of time to receive welfare benefits. The courts, however, have allowed certain exceptions to this constitutional guarantee, the most notable being the higher tuition that out-of-state residents pay at state universities.

Same-sex marriage is a contentious federalism issue. Regulating family law has been a state power, but as some states have approved same-sex marriage, the federal Defense of Marriage Act (1996) affirms that other states have the option of not recognizing these marriages. A challenge regarding the status of same-sex marriage is likely to reach the Supreme Court.

privileges and immunities clause (Article IV, Section 2): *Requires states to treat nonresidents equally to residents.*

Should out-of-state students pay higher tuition at state universities? Why or why not?

The Changing Nature of American Federalism

The ratification of the Constitution pitted the state-centered Antifederalists against the nation-centered Federalists, and pro-state and pro-nation interests have contested the relative balance between the two ever since. Because a federal system presupposes separate states with guaranteed rights, tension between the layers of government is built-in and inevitable. Those who believe in relatively more national power contend that the national government does not derive its powers from the states, but from the people. They cite as evidence the fact that the Constitution was established by "We, the People of the United States" (Preamble). Others believe in greater state power, a view that considers the national government to be an agreement by thirteen independent states (the original colonies) to delegate certain limited powers that they had held to a national government.

Americans might have sincere preferences about the relative authority between the national and state governments, but it is also the case that politicians can use federalism arguments to mask substantive concerns. For example, while Republicans in recent years have generally supported state authority more often than Democrats, Democrats will support state authority when states support liberal policies and Republicans will be particularly supportive of state authority when states support conservative policies.

Nationalization in the Founding Generation

In the 1789 and 1792 elections, every elector cast a vote for George Washington. Washington did not run as the candidate of any political party, and his administration had no organized opposition. Within his administration, however, divisions over the extent of the authority of the national government split Secretary of the Treasury Alexander Hamilton and his allies from Secretary of State Thomas Jefferson and his allies. Hamilton favored a **nation-centered federalism**. He sought expansive federal power and, in 1790, proposed that Congress establish a national Bank of the United States under a broad reading of the necessary and proper clause. Jefferson, who favored a **state-centered federalism**, unsuccessfully opposed the bank, which Congress created with a twenty-year charter. Jefferson's allies, however, were able to limit Hamilton's plan to promote manufacturing through subsidies to producers and taxes on imports. The split between Hamilton and Jefferson over federal authority and other issues led to the development of the first party system in the United States, with the pro-national Hamiltonians labeling themselves the Federalist Party and the Jeffersonian supporters of **states' rights** labeling themselves the Democratic-Republicans (see Chapter 7).

In 1798, when the Federalist administration of John Adams (1797–1801) passed the Sedition Act (see Chapter 4), making criticism of the government illegal, Jefferson wrote a resolution adopted by the Kentucky legislature that declared the act void, claiming that states could decide for themselves which national laws to obey. James Madison authored a similar resolution that the Virginia legislature passed. Known as the Virginia and Kentucky Resolutions, these acts argued for **nullification**, the right of states to nullify, or reject, national laws that went beyond the powers granted in the Constitution. Though the Virginia and Kentucky Resolutions met with little approval outside their home states, the doctrine of nullification has reappeared when pro-state forces have questioned national authority.

The debate over national authority to establish a bank resurfaced after the first National Bank charter expired and Congress chartered a Second National Bank. The Supreme Court resolved this issue in *McCulloch v. Maryland* (1819), in an opinion written by Federalist Chief Justice John Marshall.[9] Marshall noted that Congress had the explicit authority to coin money and collect taxes, and declared that the creation of a bank helped reach those goals. Thus creating a bank was an implied power that fell within the scope of authority granted by the necessary and proper clause (see Supreme Court Cases: *McCulloch v. Maryland*).

Five years later the Court, in another opinion by Marshall, established a **broad construction**, or interpretation, of one of Congress's enumerated powers: to regulate interstate commerce. In *Gibbons v. Ogden* (1824) the Court ruled that Congress's authority to regulate commerce among the states gave it, rather than the states, the authority to manage the licensing of steamboats traveling between New York and New Jersey. Marshall further declared that the authority of Congress to regulate commerce between the states did not begin or end at state boundaries, but necessarily included commercial

nation-centered federalism: *View that the Constitution and the federal government derive from the people, not from the states.*

state-centered federalism: *View that the states created the Constitution and the federal government.*

states' rights: *View that states have strong independent authority to resist federal rules under the Constitution.*

nullification: *Right of states to invalidate acts of Congress they believe to be illegal.*

McCulloch v. Maryland (1819): *Supreme Court decision upholding the right of Congress to create a bank.*

broad construction: *Interpretation of the Constitution that goes beyond the plain meaning of the specific words used.*

Gibbons v. Ogden (1824): *Supreme Court decision giving broad latitude to Congress under the commerce clause.*

supremecourtcases
McCulloch v. Maryland (1819)

QUESTION: May the federal government establish a bank? If so, does a state have the right to tax that bank?

ORAL ARGUMENT: February 22, 1819

DECISION: March 6, 1819 (read at http://caselaw.lp.findlaw.com/cgi-bin/getcase.pl?court=us&vol=17&invol=316)

OUTCOME: The bank is constitutional, and Maryland may not tax it (6–0).

Following the decision of Congress to establish the Second National Bank, the state of Maryland imposed a tax on the Maryland branch. The bank manager, James McCulloch, refused to pay the tax, and Maryland brought suit. The Maryland Supreme Court ruled that the bank was unconstitutional because the Constitution does not grant Congress the specific authority to create a bank. McCulloch appealed to the Supreme Court.

McCulloch's attorney, Daniel Webster, who had served in the House and would later serve in the Senate and as secretary of state, represented McCulloch before the Supreme Court. Among the most famed litigators of his day, he also represented the nationalist position before the Supreme Court in the District of Columbia lottery case and the New York steamboat case.

The Supreme Court's decision, written by Chief Justice John Marshall, began by accepting the nation-centered view of the Constitution's founding: rather than a compact of states, the government established by the Constitution "proceeds directly from the people; is 'ordained and established,' in the name of the people."

Regarding the power to establish a bank, Marshall noted that while the Constitution makes no reference to a bank, it does provide for the coining and borrowing of money, paying government debts, and levying taxes. It also allows Congress to pass all laws that are "necessary and proper" to any of the enumerated powers. Declaring that "necessary and proper" does not mean "absolutely necessary," Marshall read the necessary and proper clause to mean "ordinary and appropriate."

In explaining the scope of the necessary and proper clause, Marshall declared, "Let the end be legitimate, let it be within the scope of the constitution, and all means which are appropriate, which are plainly adapted to that end, which are not prohibited, but consist with the letter and spirit of the constitution, are constitutional." Thus, creating a bank was an appropriate means toward legitimate ends: regulating money and collecting taxes.

As for state taxation of the bank, Marshall based his response on the supremacy clause, observing that "the power to tax involves the power to destroy." Because states cannot destroy creations of the federal government, neither can they tax them.

The McCulloch decision created a broad scope to implied powers under the Constitution, powers that are not explicitly in the Constitution but are related to those powers that are. Without this broad set of implied powers, Congress could not establish criminal laws for offenses, investigate executive wrongdoing, provide student loans, establish administrative agencies, or conduct many of the other activities it routinely engages in today.

- If Congress does not have the express authority to establish a national bank, by what authority may it do so?

- What is the harm to federalism if a state can tax a national bank?

activities interior to each state.[10] Between the decisions in *McCulloch* and *Gibbons*, the Supreme Court under Marshall supported the Federalist Party position of a strong national government with expansive powers.

The Revolt against National Authority: Nullification, Slavery, and the Civil War

Because nothing in the Constitution suggested that Congress had the power to limit slavery in the states, the most heated contests over congressional authority to regulate slavery involved the territories. This debate split abolitionists who wanted to ban slavery in the territories, states' rights supporters such as John C. Calhoun who thought that slave owners had the right to take their slaves into any territory, and those who favored compromises that would allow slavery in some territories but not others. In 1857, the Supreme Court sided with the states' rights supporters, declaring in **Dred Scott v. Sandford** that Congress had no authority to regulate slavery in the territories[11] (see Chapter 4). When Abraham Lincoln (1861–65), who favored federal efforts to prohibit slavery in the territories, won the presidential election of 1860, southern states seceded.

Dred Scott v. Sandford **(1857):** *Supreme Court decision prohibiting Congress from regulating slavery in the territories.*

During the Civil War, Lincoln used his power as commander in chief to issue the Emancipation Proclamation, which prohibited slavery in states under rebellion, as slave labor was an asset to the Confederate army. Even during the war, few believed that the national government could end slavery in the four slave states—the so-called border states of Delaware, Kentucky, Maryland, and Missouri—that had remained in the union. Slavery in some of these states did not end until the states ratified the Thirteenth Amendment (1865), which prohibited slavery throughout the nation.

The Congresses that followed the Civil War tried to exert federal power over the *states* to promote equality between freedmen and whites, but President Andrew Johnson (1865–69) vetoed a civil rights bill, claiming it represented a trend toward "centralization and the concentration of all legislative power in the National Government."[12] The bill granted former slaves the rights to make contracts, sue, give evidence, and to inherit, purchase, lease, and convey real and personal property; in 1866, Congress passed it over Johnson's veto. But as part of the effort to ensure that all such laws would be constitutional, Congress proposed and the states ratified the Fourteenth Amendment (1868) and the Fifteenth Amendment (1870). These greatly expanded the authority of the national government over the states. The Fourteenth Amendment requires states to provide each person due process of law (see Chapter 4) and the equal protection of the laws (see Chapter 5). The Fifteenth Amendment prevents states from abridging the right to vote on account of race. Like the Thirteenth Amendment, the Fourteenth and Fifteenth Amendments

Civil Rights Cases (1883):
*Limited congressional
authority to prohibit private
discrimination under the
Fourteenth Amendment.*

granted Congress the authority to enforce their provisions by appropriate legislation, thus adding to Congress's enumerated powers. In 1883, however, the Supreme Court decided in the *Civil Rights Cases* to keep Congress's powers within the words of the amendments: Congress could prevent states from denying people equality, but it could not prevent private businesses or individuals from doing so, for example, by refusing to hire former slaves or to serve them at inns or restaurants. The Court thus invalidated Congress's Civil Rights Act of 1875, which had prohibited this type of private discrimination. This era, covering the period before and after the Civil War, saw the defeat of the most strident (secessionist) state-centered views, but with the Supreme Court's interpretation of the Civil War amendments, state authority remained strong.

Dual Federalism

dual federalism: *Doctrine holding that states and federal governments have almost completely separate functions.*

Although the supporters of state-centered federalism lost the Civil War, the viewpoint of a national government with limited powers did not disappear. A new viewpoint, **dual federalism**, recognized that, while the national government was supreme in some spheres, the state governments remained supreme in others, with layers of authority separate from one another, an arrangement that political scientists later compared to a "layer cake."[13] Thus the national government would be supreme over issues such as foreign affairs and interstate commerce, and the states would be supreme in matters concerning intrastate commerce and police powers. Given that the Constitution does not specifically define the difference between interstate commerce and intrastate commerce, this division worked out well as long as Congress made little effort to regulate any form of commerce.

A countertrend later emerged, however. In 1913, Congress passed and the states ratified the Sixteenth Amendment, which granted Congress the power to tax income from whatever source derived, giving the national government access to millions (and later billions and even trillions) of dollars in revenue. The increase in federal authority over areas once left to the states was aided that same year by the ratification of the Seventeenth Amendment, which took the selection of U.S. senators out of the hands of state legislatures and required that they be directly elected by the people of each state. Prior to 1914, state legislatures could count on senators being responsive to the needs of the states, but with direct elections, senators had to be responsive to the needs of the people.[14]

Cooperative Federalism: The New Deal and Civil Rights

With the onset of the Great Depression following the stock market crash of 1929, the people wanted national action to aid the economy. Nation-centered federalism, signaled by the Sixteenth and Seventeenth Amendments as well as passage of the New Deal legislation, strengthened considerably.

After President Franklin D. Roosevelt's failed attempt at increasing the size of the Supreme Court, in response to the Court striking down a number of New Deal provisions, the Court began to accept a broad authority of Congress to regulate the economy. On taxing and spending, the Court accepted the view that virtually any taxing or spending plan that Congress believed supported the general welfare would be acceptable.

On commerce, the Court began by accepting the regulation of a giant steel company with operations throughout the United States as an appropriate regulation of interstate commerce.[15] Congress could also use the commerce clause to regulate employment conditions, said the Court, rejecting the Tenth Amendment as a limit on federal power.[16] The Court's definition of what constituted interstate commerce grew to include anything that affected interstate commerce, whether over several states or confined to one state.

© Cengage Learning,

Layer cake

Marble cake

With federal intervention in manufacturing, farming, and other areas traditionally governed by the states, Roosevelt's nation-centered federalism was said by political scientists to more closely resemble a "marble cake," with specific powers under both national and state authority, than the layer-cake structure of dual federalism.[17]

Nation-centered federalism continued to dominate over dual federalism through World War II and beyond. Indeed, President Lyndon Johnson's (1963–69) Great Society program expanded national authority even further, with federal aid to public schools—traditionally a state duty—and health care coverage to the poor (Medicaid) and elderly (Medicare). The Johnson administration also expanded national power to ensure greater equality, pushing for passage of the **Civil Rights Act** (1964), which prohibited job discrimination and segregation in public accommodations, and the **Voting Rights Act** (1965), which regulated voting rules that had largely been left to the states since the adoption of the Constitution (see Chapter 5).

State-centered federalism gained some favor, though, in opposition to the push toward equality and civil rights. In 1954, in *Brown v. Board* of Education, the Supreme Court struck down school segregation,[18] which had been legally mandated or permitted in twenty states plus the District of Columbia. The Supreme Court decision helped put the federal government at the forefront of the fight for equality.

Dual Federalism and Cooperative Federalism. Dual federalism has been likened to a layer cake (left), and cooperative federalism has been likened to a marble cake (right). © Cengage Learning, *Source:* LAITS

Civil Rights Act (1964): *Prohibits discrimination in employment, education, and places of public accommodation.*

Voting Rights Act (1965): *Gives the federal government the right to prevent discrimination in voting rights.*

The New Federalism

Presidents, Congress, and the New Federalism.   The Nixon administration (1969–74) began the trend, labeled **New Federalism**, of shifting powers back to the states.[19] While the Democratic Johnson administration gave money to the states in **categorical grants**, that is, money to the states for what the national government wanted, the Republican Nixon administration began a **general revenue sharing** program that gave the states greater leeway as to how funds the national government provided could be spent. The main idea behind Nixon's federalism was that states could more efficiently spend governmental resources than the enormous federal bureaucracy could.

Republican President Ronald Reagan (1981–89) sought to reduce the power of government in general and, as an avid supporter of the New Federalism, of the federal government in particular. In his first inaugural address, he declared, "Government is not the solution to our problem; government is the problem."[20] He thus cut back on categorical grants, replacing them with fewer, more flexible **block grants**, which set fewer restrictions on how the money could be spent. He also eliminated general revenue sharing (see Table 3.1).

New Federalism: *Shifting of power back to the states beginning with the Nixon administration.*

categorical grants: *Money from Congress to the states that has to be spent in specific categories.*

general revenue sharing: *Money from Congress to the states that could be spent however the states wanted.*

block grants: *Money from Congress to the states that had to be spent in broad, rather than specific, categories.*

TABLE 3.1 Annual Percent Change in Federal Aid to State and Local Governments, in Constant Dollars

President	Percent Change
Lyndon Johnson (1963–68)	11.7%
Richard Nixon (1969–74)	9.0%
Gerald Ford (1974–77)	8.7%
Jimmy Carter (1977–81)	−1.0%
Ronald Reagan (1981–89)	−1.3%
George H. W. Bush (1989–93)	8.4%
Bill Clinton (1993–2001)	4.2%
George W. Bush (2001–9)	3.9%
Barack Obama (2009–)	18.5*%

*2009–10 only. This increase is largely due to added stimulus spending as a result of the 2008–2009 recession.

Source: GPO Access, U.S. Budget for Fiscal Year 2009, 2010, Historical Tables, Table 12.1.

President Bill Clinton (1993–2001) did not have strong views on federalism, but one of his early proposals was a plan for national health insurance for all Americans, traditionally an area that had been left to private parties such as businesses and individuals, or to the states. Opposition to Clinton's plan led both to the plan's defeat and a Republican platform in the 1994 congressional elections, called the **Contract with America**, which included limits on the powers of the federal government. Voters that year chose Republican majorities in both the House and the Senate, believing, by 47 percent to 6 percent, that the federal government had too much power as compared to the state governments.[21] Similarly, in 2010 the Republicans' Pledge to America, calling for a repeal of federal health care legislation, helped them regain the House.

Following the Republican victories, Clinton shifted gears and worked with the Republicans on a **devolution** of power from the national government to the states, declaring, "The era of big government is over."[22] During the Clinton administration, Congress moved to shift the balance of power toward the states in several ways. First, it limited unfunded **mandates**—legal requirements Congress imposes on the states (for example, to provide clean air, disability access, or health benefits to poor people under Medicaid) without supplying the resources to accomplish those activities. Congress did not eliminate such mandates, but it did make them harder to impose. Second, Clinton and Congress overhauled the federal welfare system, ending the federal guarantee of welfare to families with poor children. Third, Congress abandoned national speed limits that had been established at the time of the 1973 Arab oil embargo and allowed states to set whatever speed limits they desired.

Although since the New Deal Republicans have typically supported state authority over that of the national government, President George W. Bush oversaw an administration that strengthened national authority, sometimes at the expense of the states.[23] His most prominent actions in this regard include the No Child Left Behind Act (2002), which increased federal involvement in public education, and his prescription drug plan for Medicare.[24] Following the terrorist attacks of September 11, 2001, Congress and the Bush administration expanded national power in various ways, including the establishment of national standards for driver's licenses. Though Bush was a Republican and a former governor—two factors that might ordinarily indicate greater support for the states over the federal government, his administration was, concluded two political scientists, "routinely dismissive of federalism concerns."[25]

On the other hand, two early decisions by the Obama administration signal support for state-centered federalism, at least where the policies support Democratic Party positions: support for permitting states to set higher standards than the federal government on fuel economy and tailpipe emissions[26] and a reversal of the Bush administration's crackdown on state medical

Was Reagan right in stating, "Government is the problem"?

Contract with America: *Campaign proposal containing ten legislative initiatives used by Republicans running for the House of Representatives in 1994.*

devolution: *Shifting of power from the national government to the states.*

mandates: *Congressional requirements on the states to undertake particular activities; states object particularly to unfunded mandates.*

Do you tend to support nation-centered federalism, or state-centered federalism? Which is more responsive? Which ensures citizen equality?

The La Brea Collective medical marijuana dispensary in Los Angeles displays varieties of marijuana in canning jars. Fourteen states including California have legalized medical marijuana. Elsewhere in the United States, marijuana cannot be sold or used for medical purposes, although cancer patients report that it relieves nausea and vomiting during chemotherapy, and others claim a variety of additional medical benefits. In November 2010 Californians rejected an initiative to legalize marijuana use for any purpose.

Should guns be allowed near or in schools? Who should decide?

AP Photo/Reed Saxon

marijuana programs.[27] Additionally, the stimulus package of 2009 directed more than $100 billion in federal revenue to the states.[28]

The Supreme Court and the New Federalism.

President Reagan was supportive of state-centered federalism, and in 1986, by nominating Justice William Rehnquist to be chief justice, Reagan hoped to move the Court toward greater judicial respect toward the states. He was not disappointed. As an associate justice (1971–86), Rehnquist had pressed, often alone on the Court, for greater judicial respect toward the states. As chief justice, Rehnquist (1986–2005) further advanced New Federalism, now aided by a Republican-nominated bloc that rose to seven justices. The Rehnquist Court put together pro-state majorities in two series of decisions: interstate commerce and sovereign immunity.

Concerning interstate commerce, for the first time since 1937 the Court decided national laws were beyond Congress's authority to regulate under the commerce clause. In one case, the Court struck down congressional legislation banning the possession of guns near schools, declaring that the possession of a gun near a school is not an economic activity.[29] Similarly, the Court rejected a central provision of the Violence against Women Act, which gave victims of gender-based violence the right to sue their attackers in federal court. A Virginia Tech student who had allegedly been raped by members of the football team sued her attackers and Virginia Tech, a state university, in federal court after the state chose not to bring criminal charges. The Court rejected congressional findings on the effect of such violence on commerce and ruled that the section of the act that allowed the lawsuits was beyond Congress's authority either under the commerce clause or under its authority to enforce the equal protection of the laws under the Fourteenth Amendment.[30]

The Rehnquist Court also limited national authority over the states through the doctrine of sovereign immunity. Although the Eleventh Amendment prevents citizens of one state from suing a different state in federal court, the Court ruled that the amendment limits the rights of citizens to sue their own states in federal court. The Court thus prevented citizens from suing their own states for violations of federal labor law,[31] for harm to businesses by unfair competition, for infringements of patents or copyrights by state universities,[32] or for otherwise illegal discrimination against a breast cancer victim by her employer, the Alabama State University system. According to the Court in the Alabama case, "the ultimate guarantee of the Eleventh Amendment is that nonconsenting States may not be sued by private individuals in federal court."[33]

While these decisions stand in contrast to the decidedly pro-national decisions of the Court since the New Deal, most questions of federal authority still are decided in favor of the national government. The Court, for example, did not permit states to allow medical marijuana.[34] Indeed, it routinely continues to uphold Congress's authority to regulate commercial activity; there has been no return to the pre–New Deal distinction between commerce and manufacturing.

Summing Up: Were the Antifederalists Correct?

In sum, the people of the United States ratified the Constitution over the protests of Antifederalists who claimed that the Constitution gave virtually unlimited powers to the national government. Nevertheless, until the New Deal, the powers exercised by the national government were clearly limited. Today, however, between the popular belief in the need to regulate a complex economy and the Supreme Court's interpretation of the Constitution, Congress has vast powers. The fact that Congress can regulate commerce, that Congress can spend money on virtually anything as long as it is not specifically prohibited by the Constitution, and that the necessary and proper clause means "ordinary and appropriate," leads to the conclusion that, as far as the powers of the national government are concerned, the Antifederalists were correct: The federal government's powers have few limits. But as more recent events demonstrate, if the people believe that the national government has too much power, they can vote for parties and issues limiting that power.

Should states or the federal government regulate medical marijuana? Small amounts of marijuana for "recreational use?"

What do you think? Were the Antifederalists right to fear the power of the national government?

State and Local Governments

The Constitution requires that the states maintain a republican form of government, and all have done so by patterning their structure after the national government, with separate legislative, judicial, and executive branches. With the exception of procedures that allow citizens to place proposed laws directly on the ballot, the state governments look remarkably similar to the federal government. Local governments, however, use a greater range of organizational options.

State Governments

All fifty states have separate legislative and executive branches, and all fifty states choose the head of the executive branch by direct election. Most states have four-year gubernatorial terms, limit their governor to two consecutive terms, and provide for succession by the lieutenant governor.

The governors of all fifty states have the authority to veto laws subject to override by the state legislatures. Most states further grant their governors a **line-item veto**, the ability to veto certain parts of spending bills without vetoing the entire bill. The president does not have this power, so when Congress passes spending bills, it usually does so by combining tens of thousands of separate spending items together in **omnibus bills**. The president's choice is to sign the entire bill or veto it; he cannot veto only those appropriations of which he disapproves. Governors in forty-two states do have that authority, however, giving them a much stronger tool to control spending than the president has.

In addition to the line-item veto, some states grant governors special budgetary authority to limit spending. West Virginia's constitution does not allow the legislature to increase spending on any item over the amount proposed by the governor. New York's governor has sole authority over the language in spending bills. The legislature can increase or decrease the amounts, but it cannot add provisions not in the governor's budget, nor can it change formulas for distributing aid contained in spending bills.[36] Every state except Vermont requires a balanced budget. Unlike the federal government, which can borrow money to pay for spending programs, states typically have to match popular spending increases with typically unpopular tax increases. Governors generally seek less spending than legislators, especially when the governor is facing a tough election.[37]

On the legislative side, forty-nine of the fifty states have bicameral (two-chamber) legislative branches; Nebraska has only a single chamber. Nebraska also has nonpartisan elections, meaning that candidates for election are not listed under a party banner. Most states have four-year terms for their upper chambers and two-year terms for their lower chambers. While there are no term limits for members of Congress, fifteen states mandate term limits for state legislators, with limits ranging between six and twelve years in those states. Such limits spread power more equally throughout government, preventing any given legislator from amassing too much power over time.

The greatest differences between national and state governments appear at the judicial level. Federal judges are nominated by the president

line-item veto: *Power given to some governors to veto parts of appropriations bills.*

omnibus bill: *One very large bill that encompasses many separate bills, to help ensure passage.*

What would happen if the president had a line-item veto?

and confirmed by the Senate. States have various procedures for selecting judges: nearly half use an appointment process for judges on their highest court, while the rest use elections. For states that use appointments, most grant the governor the right to make appointments (usually with the consent of the state senate).

While federal judges serve during good behavior, which essentially means life terms, only Rhode Island does that at the state level, with Massachusetts and New Hampshire judges serving until age 70. In the rest of the states, judges have set terms. For example, in the widely copied **Missouri Plan** for selecting judges, also know as the merit plan, a board of experts recommends candidates to the governor for selection. The selected judges are then subject to **retention elections**: when a judge's term expires, voters get to vote yes or no on retaining the judge.

Missouri Plan: *Process for selecting state judges whereby the original nomination is by appointment and subsequent retention is by a retention election.*

retention election: *Election in which voters determine whether a state judge, originally appointed under a merit plan, should be retained in the state court system.*

Local Governments

Local governments are far more diverse in function and design than state governments. First, there can be several different layers of local governments, with residents regulated by villages, cities, and towns at the most local level, and counties above that. Some local governments run all local services, including police, schools, and sanitation. Many states, however, delegate specialized activities to special jurisdiction governments, such as school boards, water districts, fire districts, library districts, and sewer districts. Overall in the United States, there are tens of thousands of special jurisdiction governments and about 500,000 local elected officials, plus another 100,000 who serve on school boards.[38] These local governments provide a ready gateway for citizen involvement in public affairs.

© Tribune Media Services, Inc. All Rights Reserved Reprinted with Permission

Second, local governments, unlike the state governments, do not necessarily have three separate branches of government. One reason is that criminal and civil trials are usually handled in state courts, leaving little need for a local community to have its own judicial branch. Many local governments have an elected leader of the executive branch—mayors for villages and cities, county executives for counties, and supervisors for townships—but many use a **city-manager system** in which the legislative branch appoints a professional administrator to run the executive branch.

city-manager system: *Local government system in which the legislative branch hires a manager to run the executive branch.*

What impact does your local government have on you?

Direct Democracy

recall: *Process whereby citizens can remove state officials prior to the end of their elected term of office.*

initiative: *Process by which citizens place a proposed law on the ballot for public approval.*

referendum: *Process by which public approval is required before states can pass certain laws.*

Examples of direct gateways to democracy in American federalism include use of recall, the initiative, and referenda (see Figure 3.4). **Recall** allows citizens, if they gather enough petition signatures, an opportunity to hold a special vote to remove state or local elected officials before their terms expire. Permitted in eighteen states, recall allowed California voters to remove its unpopular Governor Gray Davis in 2003, who was then replaced in a special election by actor Arnold Schwarzenegger. **Initiative** is a process that allows citizens who collect the required number of petition signatures to place proposed laws directly on the ballot for the state's citizens to vote on. **Referendum** is a process that allows legislatures to put certain issues on the ballot for citizen approval

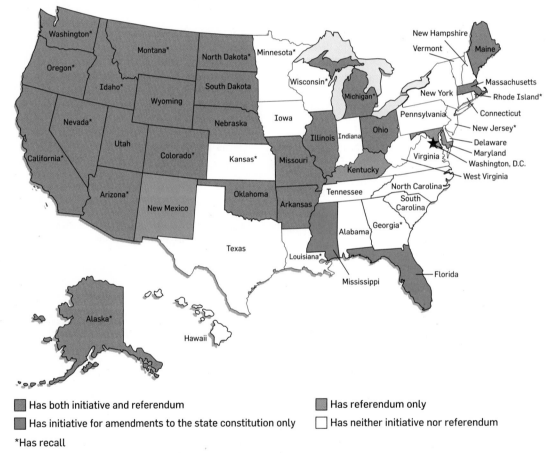

■ Has both initiative and referendum
■ Has initiative for amendments to the state constitution only
*Has recall

■ Has referendum only
□ Has neither initiative nor referendum

FIGURE 3.4 States That Allow Recall, Initiative, and Referendum.
Source: Council of State Governments, *The Book of the States.*

and requires legislatures to seek citizen approval for certain actions by the legislature. Depending on the state, these actions could be proposals to borrow money, increase taxes, or approve constitutional amendments. All fifty states require referenda on some issues. Only twenty-four states allow initiative.[39] Both procedures allow well-organized citizens to bypass the elected representatives in their state. The U.S. Constitution, in setting specific terms for the House, Senate, and president, prohibits recall for federal officials, and in granting all legislative powers to Congress, similarly prohibits initiative and referendum at the national level.

The number and importance of initiatives have grown in recent years. California's Proposition 13 famously slashed property taxes in 1978. Ward Connerly, chair of the American Civil Rights Institute, has put initiatives banning **affirmative action** (the use of racial preferences in hiring and university admissions) on the ballot in California, Michigan, Colorado, and Nebraska, with bans passing in California, Michigan, and Nebraska (see Chapter 14). In 2008, voters across the United States faced fifty-nine initiatives, approving twenty-four of them, including bans on gay marriage in Arizona, California, and Florida.[40]

Direct democracy is not without its critics, however. Like other aspects of American government, money heavily influences initiatives. Although socialists and populists originally pushed for direct democracy to expand the influence of ordinary citizens, the cost of gathering enough signatures to get on the ballot means that such initiatives are limited largely to those with great financial resources. In 1998, California Indian tribes spent $66 million in support of a successful California proposition that would allow them to expand casino gambling on Indian reservations. Fearful of losing business, Las Vegas casinos spent $26 million in opposition to the proposal. In the 2008 California vote banning gay marriage, contributions totaled over $72 million, with the money nearly evenly split between the supporters and opponents of the successful ban (see Figure 3.5).

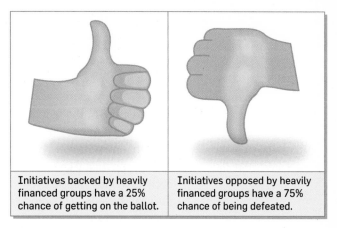

| Initiatives backed by heavily financed groups have a 25% chance of getting on the ballot. | Initiatives opposed by heavily financed groups have a 75% chance of being defeated. |

FIGURE 3.5 Initiative Spending. Large interest groups with abundant funds have a powerful influence on initiatives. Most initiatives have no chance at all of getting on the ballot, but money makes a difference. The influence of money in initiatives calls into question their reputation for direct democracy.
Source: Thomas E. Cronin, *Direct Democracy: The Politics of Initiative, Referendum, and Recall* (Cambridge, Mass.: Harvard University Press, 1989).

The last time you voted, were there any initiatives or referenda on the ballot? Were you well enough informed about them to make a choice?

affirmative action: *Policies that grant racial or gender preferences in hiring, education, or contracting.*

direct democracy: *Form of democracy in which political power is exercised directly by citizens.*

Federalism and Public Policy: Education

The structure of the federal system has a profound effect on public policy. It allows states to copy policies from one another but sometimes forces them into competition with one another. Many state policies involve issues in which the national government does not get involved, whereas in other areas, such as welfare policies, federal mandates and incentives push the states to do what the federal government wants. In this section, we examine education policy as an example.

Federal Aid to the States

intergovernmental lobby: *Set of lobbies that represent the interests of state and local governments.*

Through the supremacy clause, Congress has final say on many issues, but an **intergovernmental lobby**, made up of groups such as the National Governors Association, the National Conference of State Legislatures, and the National League of Cities, pressures Congress to limit mandates and provide funding for state and local needs.

Federal aid to the states is influenced by a large number of factors, including equal representation in the Senate.[41] The fact that small states have the same number of senators as large states means that small states receive a disproportionate amount of federal aid. For example, in 2007, Wyoming and Alaska received the most aid per capita.[42] These states even get more antiterrorism aid per capita than do terrorist targets such as New York.[43] As the president is particularly responsive to the people and party who elected him, it is hardly surprising that states that heavily supported an incumbent president in the previous election and states whose governors are of the same party as the president get more federal aid than other states.[44]

Where does your state rank in the amount of federal aid it receives? Should federal aid be equally distributed among all states?

Policy Diffusion

In a 1932 opinion, Supreme Court Justice Louis Brandeis wrote, "It is one of the happy incidents of the federal system that a single courageous State may, if its citizens choose, serve as a laboratory; and try novel social and economic experiments without risk to the rest of the country."[45] As far back as the Revolutionary era, New Jersey experimented with women's suffrage, as did several western states at the end of the nineteenth century. Nebraska has experimented with a unicameral legislature, Wisconsin experimented in the 1920s with an unemployment insurance program, and

Oregon and Washington are currently experimenting with the nation's first physician-assisted suicide laws.

The main benefit of states serving as "laboratories of change" is that other states can learn about successful programs and copy them, or likewise learn what not to do if an experimental program fails. This takes place through a process known as **policy diffusion**, and it typically starts with states that border one another. Examples are numerous, including the Children's Health Insurance Program,[46] school choice plans (allowing students to choose which school in a district to attend),[47] health care reform,[48] and Indian gambling casinos.[49] States learn not only from neighboring states but also from their local governments. Such was the case with antismoking ordinances, which cities and towns successfully adopted before states did.[50]

The Race to the Bottom

If diffusion is the good side of policy making in a federal system, the **race to the bottom** can, depending on one's point of view, potentially involve negative consequences. A race to the bottom exists when states compete against each other to lower taxes, environmental protections, or welfare benefits in order to create incentives for businesses to come to the state or disincentives for poor people to come. For example, lower tax rates draw people to a state, yet to keep people there, the state cannot raise taxes even when the public might otherwise desire more spending.[51] When states are economic competitors with one another, if one state decreases environmental enforcement, a neighboring state may be forced to do so as well.[52] In terms of welfare benefits, individuals seeking benefits move to the most generous states. This situation led states to establish residency requirements for welfare. The Supreme Court, however, prohibits such residency requirements.[53] Consequently, states that want to increase welfare benefits for their own citizens hesitate to do so unless neighboring states also do so, lest they attract an overload of recipients from those other states.[54]

Education Policy

The Founders considered an educated citizenry essential to the survival of the democracy, believing that an educated people will be able to hold their leaders accountable and pay attention to the overall responsiveness of their government.

Yet, despite the fact that federally elected politicians talk frequently about the importance of education, the federal government itself only funds 8 percent of all elementary and secondary education spending.[55] The primary reason for this minimal federal funding for education is the federal

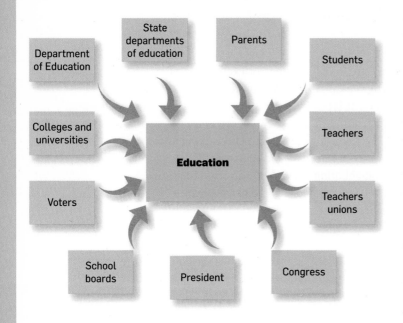

Department of Education

State departments of education

Parents

Students

Colleges and universities

Teachers

Education

Voters

Teachers unions

School boards

President

Congress

structure. With education among the reserved powers left to the states, state and local governments developed the responsibility for educating the populace. Originally, states set education policy that local communities then implemented through locally elected school boards, or "Ten Thousand Democracies," as one book called them.[56] Depending on the state, local school boards had differing amounts of power to establish the curriculum, support extracurricular activities, hire and fire teachers, negotiate salaries for school district employees, and set standards for graduation. Over time, funding for elementary and secondary education became based on local property taxes, with some additional assistance from state governments. Just as the overall wealth of local communities and states varies, so does the amount of funding available for education. As a result, there are vast disparities in the quality of education provided by elementary and secondary schools across the country. In addition, the legacy of racial segregation and other forms of discrimination has compounded the regional inequalities in education.

Congress originally played almost no role in public school (K–12) education, but as in health care and many other areas, Congress's role has increased after World War II. In 1944 it passed the GI Bill, which provided educational benefits for veterans. Then in 1958 it passed the National Defense Education Act, which provided grant money for increased math and science education in elementary and secondary schools. In 1965 it passed the Elementary and Secondary Education Act and the Higher Education Act.[57] Each of these programs widened the gateway of access to quality education by increasing the federal responsibility to fund specific programs, ranging from remedial reading and writing for elementary school children to subsidized loan programs for college and graduate school. Each of these programs is reauthorized by Congress about every five years, so Congress and the president have a chance to revise them according to the changing needs of education over time.

Should the federal government make sure funding for public education is equal, the same amount per child in every state?

Like the general trends on federalism covered in this chapter, part of the initial impetus for federal regulation came because of segregation and the denial of equality in educational opportunity by the states. The Civil Rights Act of 1964 put Congress into the role of regulating education. Title IV of the act grants the attorney general the authority to file suits on behalf of the United States to end school segregation. Title VI prohibits schools that receive federal funds from discriminating on account of race. The act left enforcement to the Department of Health, Education, and Welfare (HEW; today there is a separate Department of Education). The importance of the funding provision increased when the Elementary and Secondary Education Act of 1965 vastly increased federal spending on education. This act gave HEW a powerful tool to fight segregation. According to one analysis of school desegregation, "Districts under HEW enforcement were significantly less segregated than court-ordered districts."[58]

Today the federal government has numerous programs to provide equal access to education across income level, race, and level of disability. These programs are under the jurisdiction of a variety of agencies. For example, the Department of Health and Human Services oversees the Head Start and Early Head Start programs for low-income children, while the Department of Education has programs for homeless children and remedial education for disadvantaged children, and it also implements programs for children with disabilities under the Individuals with Disabilities Education Act. These are all programs that serve those who have historically not had access to a high-quality education because of low income or disability.[59] All these programs remain the foundation of the federal role in education policy, albeit in different forms from the original programs. For example, most people know the Elementary and Secondary Education Act as No Child Left Behind, President George W. Bush's effort to revamp the program to impose stricter performance and accountability standards for education. The controversy surrounding this effort has been that the federal government mandated a number of changes for states and localities to implement without providing the federal funds necessary to accomplish these goals. President Obama (2009–) seeks to change the No Child Left Behind program by setting higher standards that will measure U.S. students against their peers worldwide but also allow states and schools to have more flexibility in achieving goals.[60]

At the higher education level, a number of federally funded financial aid programs are available to undergraduate and graduate students. These programs include need-based grants, need-based loans, subsidized and unsubsidized loans, and work-study programs.[61] Under the previous loan system, the federal government contracted with banks and private

On March 30, 2010, President Obama approved the Student Aid and Fiscal Responsibility Act at Northern Virginia Community College in Alexandria. He was introduced by Dr. Jill Biden, (far left) the vice president's wife, who teaches English on the campus. In her remarks she said, "I have seen the power of community colleges to change lives and serve as a gateway to opportunity for students at all stages of their lives and careers."

LUKE SHARRETT/The New York Times/Redux Pictures

lenders, which would then lend money to students, and the government paid the interest on loans while the students were in school. However, in March 2010, Congress passed the Student Aid and Fiscal Responsibility Act (SAFRA) as part of the Health Care and Education Reconciliation Act. SAFRA ended the federally guaranteed student loan program and created a new program that authorizes the federal government to do 100 percent of the lending for student loan programs directly.[62] The new arrangement means that students applying for loans now deal directly with the federal government instead of with banks. In addition, SAFRA increased spending for Pell Grants, increased funding for community colleges by $2 billion over four years, and increased spending for historically black colleges.[63] SAFRA represents a major extension of the role of the federal government in financing higher education and in expanding equality of educational opportunity. Despite the stronger federal role, however, education under a federal system still permits inequality by allowing a vast disparity in how much states and local communities choose to spend on education.

Federalism and Democracy

A federal system has more gateways to influence than confederal or unitary systems. In confederal systems, citizens can influence their local governments, but there is little value in influencing the national government given its limited scope. Alternatively, in unitary systems, the national level has a lot of authority, but citizens cannot work their way through more localized structures to influence it. Although federal systems create multiple gateways to influence, they also make it less clear who is responsible if policies are not well run.

Under a unitary system, there is little doubt who is responsible if a policy fails. A unitary system, however, would mean that the diversity in state laws would be replaced with one set of laws on issues such as medical marijuana, gay marriage, divorce, and gun control. A unitary system also increases **conformity costs** by increasing the number of people who disagree with the policies of the government. These costs are not financial; they represent the dissatisfaction that people feel when they live under laws that they do not like.

Citizens in states with conservative majorities can obtain conservative government through the election of conservative representatives, as can liberals in states with liberal majorities. These citizens can also obtain results they desire through direct governing procedures such as the initiative and referendum. Although initiative procedures presumably provide for greater democratic responsiveness than the filtering of preferences through elected representatives, initiatives may be too responsive to citizen desires. Madison, though not referring to initiative itself, feared direct democracy, believing that citizens were prone to factions that would put self-interest over the best interests of society. Thus Madison and the Framers preferred a large-scale republic over local democracies, fearful that local majorities would infringe the rights of local minorities (see *Federalist* 10, in the Appendix). One disadvantage of federalism in the United States has been that those opposed to equality for blacks have used arguments about states' rights to protect slavery and limit civil rights. Alternatively, the nation-centric view of federalism has been used in the United States to create a more equal society for minorities subject to discrimination.

Overall, though, federalism enhances democracy by enabling more people to live under laws that are made locally, rather than forcing everyone in a nation to live under all of the same rules. State experiments with direct democracy procedures such as initiative and referendum give citizens a gateway to influence that they do not have with the national government.

FOCUS QUESTIONS

- How does federalism affect government's responsiveness? To what and to whom are federal systems accountable?

- What does it mean for citizen equality when different states are allowed to have different laws on certain subjects?

- How does a federal system make it easier for citizens to have an influence in government?

- What has been the relationship between federalism and the push for equality in the United States?

- Does federalism prove to be a gate or a gateway to democracy? Explain.

conformity costs: *Cost of democracy borne by those people in the minority, who on one or more issues live under the rules set by the majority.*

GATEWAYS TO LEARNING

Top Ten to Take Away

1. The American colonies joined together as a nation to pool their resources in fighting for their independence from Britain, but they also shared a common identity—origin, history, and ancestry. (p. 75)

2. In writing a new Constitution in 1787, the Framers established a new system of government—federalism—in which state and national governments share power. (pp. 75–77)

3. The Constitution grants specified powers to the national government, reserving all remaining powers to the states and to the people. It also limits both federal and state powers and lays out the relationships among the states and between the states and the federal government. (pp. 77–81)

4. The American system was an experiment, and its evolution has been shaped by the tensions, even conflicts, inherent in a system in which power is both divided and shared. From the beginning, nation- and state-centered interests have been pitted against each other. (pp. 82–84)

5. One recurring substantive theme in the federalism debate has involved slavery, race, and equality, with nation-centered federalism used generally to advance equality for minorities subject to discrimination. (pp. 87–88)

6. Over the years nation-centered federalism has generally expanded through legislation and court interpretation, though there have been eras in which the Court held Congress back and elections in which the people indicated they thought the national government had too much power. (pp. 84–93)

7. All fifty states have separate legislative, executive, and judicial branches that look remarkably similar to the federal government, while local governments use a greater range of organizational options. (pp. 93–96)

8. The structure of the federal system has a profound effect on public policy, allowing states to learn from each other but sometimes forcing them into competition with each other. (pp. 98–99)

9. The federal system also allows for vast disparities among the states, particularly in the quality of elementary and secondary education. (pp. 99–102)

10. Benefits of federalism include multiple gateways to influence, including methods of direct democracy such as the initiative and referendum. Federalism also enhances democracy by enabling more people to live under laws that are made locally, rather than forcing nationwide conformity. (pp. 96–98)

A full narrative summary of the chapter is on the book's website.

Ten to Test Yourself

1. What distinguishes confederal, unitary, and federal systems?

2. What are the advantages and disadvantages of each system?

3. Why was the United States allowed to create a national bank?

4. What is nullification?

5. What are the different types of aid that Congress provides the states?

6. What is the New Federalism?

7. How have states served as laboratories of change?

8. How do state governments differ from the federal government?

9. How do local governments differ from federal or state governments?

10. Describe the concurrent powers over education.

More review questions and answers and chapter quizzes are on the book's website.

Terms to Know and Use

affirmative action (p. 97)

block grants (p. 90)

broad construction (p. 85)

categorical grants (p. 90)

city-manager system (p. 95)

Civil Rights Act (1964) (p. 89)

Civil Rights Cases (p. 88)

commerce clause (p. 83)

concurrent powers (p. 80)

confederal system (p. 75)

conformity costs (p. 103)

Contract with America (p. 91)

devolution (p. 91)

direct democracy (p. 97)

Dred Scott v. Sandford (p. 87)

dual federalism (p. 88)

due process clause (p. 81)

enumerated powers (p. 77)

equal protection clause (p. 81)

federalism (p. 76)

full faith and credit clause (p. 83)

general revenue sharing (p. 90)

Gibbons v. Ogden (p. 85)

guarantee clause (p. 81)

initiative (p. 96)

implied powers (p. 82)

intergovernmental lobby (p. 98)

line-item veto (p. 94)

mandates (p. 91)

McCulloch v. Maryland (p. 85)

Missouri Plan (p. 95)

nation (p. 75)

nation-centered federalism
  (p. 85)

necessary and proper clause (p. 77)

New Federalism (p. 90)

nullification (p. 85)

omnibus bill (p. 94)

police powers (p. 79)

policy diffusion (p. 99)

preemption (p. 82)

privileges and immunities
  clause (p. 84)

race to the bottom (p. 99)

recall (p. 96)

referendum (p. 96)

reserve powers (p. 79)

retention election (p. 95)

self-government (p. 77)

sovereign immunity (p. 83)

state-centered federalism
  (p. 85)

states' rights (p. 85)

supremacy clause (p. 82)

unitary system (p. 75)

Voting Rights Act (p. 89)

writ of *habeas corpus* (p. 80)

Use the vocabulary flash cards on the book's website.

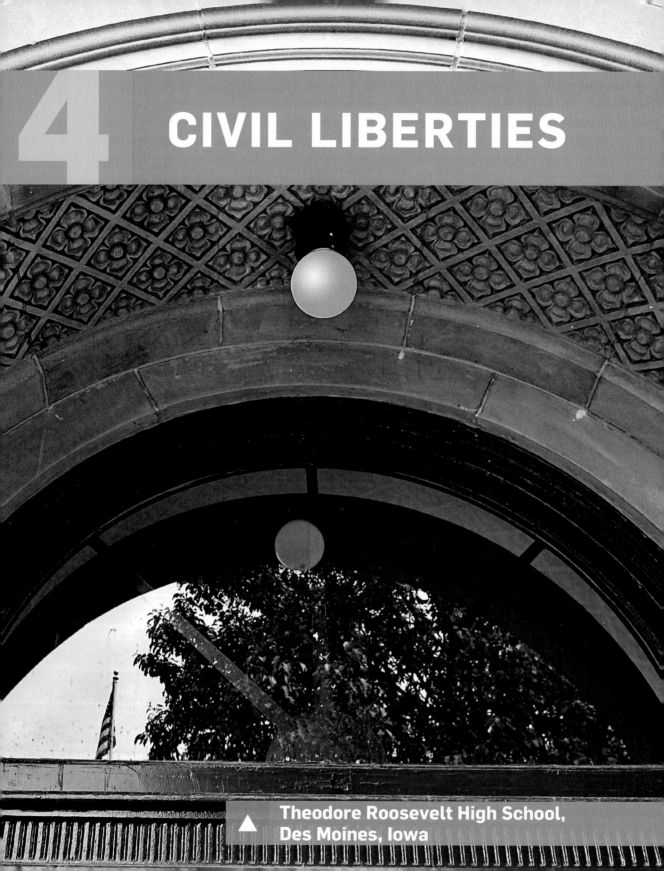

4 CIVIL LIBERTIES

▲ Theodore Roosevelt High School, Des Moines, Iowa

> *It's not only important for citizens to stand up for what they believe in, but it makes life really interesting and meaningful.*

In November 1965, Mary Beth Tinker, age 13, listened intently to the stories she heard from her mother and brother older John on their return from a peace march in Washington, D.C. Her father was a Methodist minister "who put the values of love, brotherhood, and democracy into action," she later recalled, and "showed us that being a citizen-activist could be a good way of life." These family values, together with the images of the Vietnam War on television—of "children and soldiers being burned and killed," Mary Beth said— convinced her and her brother that they should do something in Des Moines, to continue to stand up for peace. With their friend Chris Eckhardt, who had also been at the Washington peace march, they decided to wear black armbands to school. As word of their planned protest got out, the school administrators banned the wearing of armbands, perhaps because they believed that the armbands would disrupt educational activities, or more likely because they opposed antiwar activities. As the school board president declared, "Our leaders have decided on a course of action and we should support them."

Despite the prohibition, Mary Beth and Chris wore the armbands, leading the district to suspend them. The Iowa Civil Liberties Union, an interest group that supports civil rights and liberties, brought suit against the school board on behalf of the Tinkers and Eckhardt, claiming that school students, equal to other Americans, retain freedom of speech

CourseMate

Visit http://www.cengagebrain .com/shop/ISBN/0495906190 for interactive tools including:
- Quizzes
- Flashcards
- Videos
- Animated PowerPoint slides, Podcast summaries, and more

Mary Beth Tinker and John Tinker ▶

Ikonix Studio

Bettmann/CORBIS

rights granted by the First Amendment. The federal trial court ruled in favor of the school board, and the court of appeals upheld the trial court. The students then appealed to the Supreme Court, which agreed to hear their case, *Tinker v. Des Moines School District*.

At the Supreme Court, the Des Moines School Board claimed that it banned the armbands due to a fear of disruption, but no disruption in fact occurred. Because the board allowed students to wear other political symbols, such as the German iron cross, the Supreme Court concluded that the board's main reason for opposing the armbands was the antiwar message they conveyed. This or other forms of "viewpoint discrimination" are not sufficient justification for limiting speech, declared the Court, creating a landmark decision guaranteeing First Amendment rights to students in schools. The Court ruled that the gates that keep unwanted intruders away from schools cannot also be used to keep out unwanted ideas: "It can hardly be argued that either students or teachers shed their constitutional rights to freedom of speech or expression at the schoolhouse gate."[1]

Today Mary Beth Tinker is a registered nurse, but she regularly gives invited lectures about freedom of speech, urging ordinary citizens like her to "speak up, shake things up and create change that makes the world a better place."[2]

Students today have the right to express their viewpoints because of the Tinkers. They and their lawyers used the gateway of the courts to secure this right. In recent years, lower courts have upheld the right of a student to wear a T-shirt making fun of President George W. Bush,[3] the right of a student to give a speech critical of homosexuality,[4] and the right of students who wore black armbands—as had the Tinkers—to protest the school's dress code.[5]

Disagreements about politics, particularly in wartime, test people's willingness to tolerate differences in opinion. Even outside of wartime, the tension between liberty, the desire to say or do what one wants, and order, the need for rules necessary for society to function, divide society. Americans want their homes to be secure against police intrusions but they also want the police to be able to find evidence of crimes committed by others. They want freedom

FOCUS QUESTIONS

- What is government's role with regard to civil liberties? How responsive can, or should, it be to the people's will?

- What is the proper balance between liberty and order?

- Under what circumstances should civil liberties be restrained?

- What happens when rights clash? Are restrictions of civil liberties justified if they promote equality?

- In what ways does the guarantee of civil liberties promote democracy? Or does it pose challenges for democratic government that can be considered gates?

to follow their personal religious beliefs but they do not want illegal practices to be allowed just because one religion might endorse them. In this chapter, we examine the balance and tension between liberty and order, with particular attention to those liberties guaranteed in the U.S. Constitution.

What Are Civil Liberties?

In 1787, the most powerful argument of the Antifederalists against the proposed constitution was that it did not protect fundamental liberties. The Antifederalist who wrote under the name "Brutus" declared that these liberties, including the rights of conscience and the right of accused criminals to hear the charges against them, needed to be explicitly stated.[6] As we saw in Chapter 2, the Federalists eventually agreed, and to secure ratification of the Constitution, promised to amend it immediately.

Civil Liberties and Civil Rights

The **civil liberties** that were then written into the Constitution as the first ten amendments, or **Bill of Rights**, were freedoms that Americans held to be so fundamental that government may not legitimately take them away. This placed into law some of the **natural** or **unalienable rights** that Jefferson spoke about in the Declaration of Independence. These include, among others, freedom of speech and religious belief. Civil liberties are outside government's authority, whereas **civil rights** are rights that government is obliged to protect. These are based on the expectation of equality under the law and relate to the duties of citizenship and to the opportunities for full participation in civic life. They are the subject of the next chapter.

Balancing Liberty and Order

The protection of civil liberties requires a governmental system designed to do so. James Madison noted in *Federalist* 10 (see the Appendix) that a representative democracy will be able to keep a minority from abridging the rights of others but it may not be able to hold back a majority. Yet civil liberties, by their very nature, are so basic that they cannot be taken away regardless of whether it is a minority or a majority that might wish to do so. Thus if a majority wishes to abridge rights, it often falls to the judiciary, which is not designed to be responsive to public desires, to protect those rights.

While maximizing individual liberty might seem like a great idea, complete liberty could lead to a breakdown of order. As Supreme Court Justice Oliver Wendell Holmes wrote in a World War I speech case, *Schenck v. United*

civil liberties: *Those rights, such as freedom of speech or religion, that are so fundamental that they are outside the authority of government to regulate.*

Bill of Rights: *First ten amendments to the Constitution.*

natural (unalienable) rights: *Rights that every individual has and that government cannot legitimately take away.*

civil rights: *Set of rights, centered around the concept of equal treatment, that government is obliged to protect.*

anarchy: *State of society without governmental authority, in which everyone does as he or she pleases.*

tyranny: *Government that severely limits liberty.*

Which is more important to you, liberty or order?

States, freedom of speech does not mean that an individual has the right to falsely shout "Fire!" in a crowded theater, and cause a panic.[7] Nor can liberty completely protect people from police investigations when criminal activity is suspected. Too much freedom can lead to **anarchy**, a state in which everyone does as he or she chooses without regard to others. Alternatively, too much order can lead to **tyranny**, a state in which the people are not free to make decisions about the private aspects of their lives. Protecting civil liberties thus requires a balance between individual liberty and public order.

The freedom obtained through civil liberties can conflict not only with order, but with equality as well. In fact, civil liberties and civil rights sometimes conflict with each other. As we shall see in Chapter 5, government's attempts to ensure the equality of some can limit the freedoms of others.

Constitutional Rights

The main sources of civil liberties are the Constitution and the Bill of Rights. The Constitution protects the right of *habeas corpus*, the right of individuals to be brought before a judge to have the legality of their imprisonment determined. It also prohibits *ex post facto* **laws**, which make something a crime after the act was committed, and **bills of attainder**, legislative acts that declare individuals guilty of a crime. The Constitution also guarantees the right to trial by jury.

writ of *habeas corpus*: *Right of individuals who have been arrested and jailed to go before a judge, who determines if their detention is legal.*

ex post facto laws: *Laws that make something a crime after the act was committed.*

bills of attainder: *Legislative acts that declare individuals guilty of a crime.*

The Bill of Rights, ratified in 1791, protects various rights surrounding freedom of expression and criminal procedure, plus a few additional rights (see Figure 4.1). The expression-based freedoms are each included in the First Amendment; they are the rights to freedom of speech, freedom of the press, freedom of assembly, freedom to petition the government, and the free exercise of religion. The criminal justice provisions of the Bill of Rights protect individuals accused of crimes by directing how the government may investigate crimes (Fourth and Fifth Amendments), conduct trials (Fifth and Sixth Amendments), and punish those convicted (Eighth Amendment). The Fifth Amendment also protects certain economic and property rights: individuals cannot be deprived of their property without due process of law, and if the government takes private property for public purposes, such as building a highway or park, it must provide just compensation. The Second Amendment protects a very particular property right: the right to keep and bear arms. Finally, starting in the 1960s, the Supreme Court has interpreted the Ninth Amendment to include a very general right, the right to privacy.

The Bill of Rights and the States

As originally written, the Bill of Rights limited the activities of the national government, not the state governments. Only at the end of the nineteenth

FIGURE 4.1 Constitutional Amendments That Pertain to Civil Liberties.

Color Code :

Criminal procedure   Participation   Equality   Structure   Miscellaneous

First (1791): Prohibits abridging freedoms of religion, speech, press, assembly, and petition

Second (1791): Prohibits abridging the right to bear arms

Third (1791): Prohibits the involuntary quartering of soldiers in a person's home during peacetime

Fourth (1791): Prohibits unreasonable searches and seizures

Fifth (1791): Affirms the right to indictment by a grand jury and right to due process; protects against double jeopardy, self-incrimination, and taking of property without just compensation

Sixth (1791): Affirms rights to speedy and public trial, to confront witnesses, and to counsel

Seventh (1791): Affirms right to jury trials in civil suits over $20

Eighth (1791): Prohibits excessive bail, excessive fines, and cruel and unusual punishments

Ninth (1791): Declares that the enumeration of certain rights does not limit other rights retained by the people

Tenth (1791): Reserves the powers not granted to the national government to the states or to the people

Fourteenth (1868): Makes all persons born in the United States citizens of the United States, and prohibits states from denying persons within its jurisdiction the privileges or immunities of citizens, the due process of law, and equal protection of the laws; apportionment by whole persons

century did the Supreme Court slowly begin to apply, or **incorporate**, the provisions of the Bill of Rights to the states.

The First Amendment is explicit about its application to the national government as it forbids certain actions by Congress. But other amendments are not explicitly tied to the national government. Thus the Fifth Amendment prohibits taking private property without just compensation. Was this a protection of citizens only against actions by the federal government, or against their state governments as well?

The original answer, given by the Supreme Court in *Barron v. Baltimore* (1833) was no. Under the *Barron* decision, state governments could abridge freedom of speech, press, and religion, could conduct unreasonable searches and seizures, and so forth, without violating the Constitution. State constitutions might protect such rights, but often they did not.

incorporate: *Process of applying provisions of the Bill of Rights to the states.*

Which government are citizens more likely to need a gate against—national or state?

***Barron v. Baltimore* (1833):** *Supreme Court decision declaring that the Bill of Rights was not binding on the states, slowly reversed in the twentieth century.*

due process clause:
Prevents the federal government (Fifth Amendment) and the state governments (Fourteenth Amendment) from denying any person due process of law.

selective incorporation:
Doctrine used by the Supreme Court to make those provisions of the Bill of Rights that are fundamental rights binding on the states.

fundamental rights:
Those rights deemed by the Court to be essential to liberty.

grand jury: *Special jury charged with determining whether people should be put on trial.*

test: *Standard used by courts to determine whether a law or a right has been violated across a range of cases.*

compelling interest test:
Standard frequently used by the Supreme Court in civil liberties cases to determine if a state has a compelling interest for infringing on a right and if the law is narrowly drawn to meet that interest.

The potential for the application of the Bill of Rights to the states began with the passage of the Fourteenth Amendment (1868), which adds several restrictions on what the states can do. One section declares, "No State shall make or enforce any law which shall abridge the privileges or immunities of citizens of the United States; nor shall any State deprive any person of life, liberty, or property, without due process of law." Some of those who wrote this amendment stated that one of its purposes was to overturn the *Barron v. Baltimore* decision and make the entire Bill of Rights applicable to the states.[8]

Beginning in 1897, the Supreme Court slowly began to use the protection of "life, liberty or property" in the Fourteenth Amendment's **due process clause** to incorporate *some* of the provisions of the Bill of Rights as binding on the states. In 1925, the Court assumed that the protection of "liberty" in the due process clause prevented states from abridging freedom of speech, a right similarly protected by the First Amendment.[9] By 1937, the Court had settled on a process of **selective incorporation**, using the due process clause to bind the states to those provisions of the Bill of Rights that it deems to be **fundamental rights**.[10] This process helps equalize the protection of rights across the United States.

Today, almost all of the provisions of the First, Fourth, Fifth, Sixth, and Eighth Amendments have been incorporated, with the exception of grand jury indictment and excessive bail (see Table 4.1). Thus, states can indict people, or bring them up on charges, through the decision of judges, though charges in federal courts need the approval of a **grand jury**, a special jury whose sole duty is to determine whether an individual should be put on trial. The Second Amendment's right to keep and bear arms has not been incorporated, nor has the Third Amendment's protection against the quartering of soldiers in one's home during peacetime, a practice that angered the colonists but is not likely to be used today. Nor are states required, as the Seventh Amendment commands, to provide jury trials in civil suits over $20.

The fact that a right has been incorporated does not answer how the Court will determine whether that right has been violated. Generally speaking, rather than rule on each case purely on its own, the Court adopts a **test** to guide its decision and applies the test to the case at hand to determine whether a particular limitation on rights is acceptable. For the political rights in the Bill of Rights, such as freedom of speech, the Court most commonly uses variations of the **compelling interest test**. Under the compelling interest test, the federal government or a state can limit rights only if the Supreme Court decides: (1) that the government has a compelling interest in passing the law (for example, the law is necessary for the functioning

TABLE 4.1 Incorporated and Not Incorporated Provisions of the First through Eighth Amendments

Amendment	Incorporated Provisions	Not Incorporated Provisions
First	Religion, speech, press, assembly, petition	
Second	Bear arms	
Third		Quarter soldiers
Fourth	No unreasonable searches and seizures	
Fifth	Double jeopardy, self-incrimination, due process, taking of property without just compensation	Grand jury indictment
Sixth	Speedy and public trial, confront witnesses, right to counsel	
Seventh		Jury trials in civil suits over $20
Eighth	Cruel and unusual punishments, excessive fines	Excessive bail

of government), and (2) that the law is narrowly drawn to meet that interest. In the *Tinker* case, the Des Moines School Board did not convince the Court that there was sufficient justification for suppression of nondisruptive speech.

Civil Liberties in Times of Crisis

In some regard, the effort to censor the Tinkers fits a pattern in American politics: attempts to limit civil liberties are more frequent in wartime or during other threats, given the government's increased concern for order and citizens' increased concern about security. Popular support for civil liberties usually rebounds once the crisis ends.

Do tests ensure that judicial decisions are uniform and equal? What responsibility does the judicial branch have to ensure equality?

Sedition Acts: *Laws passed in 1798 and 1918 (and later repealed) that made it a crime to criticize the government.*

The World Wars

During World War I, Congress passed the Espionage Act of 1917, which made it a crime to obstruct military recruiting, and amendments known as the **Sedition Act** of 1918, which banned "disloyal, profane, scurrilous or abusive language" about the Constitution or government of the United States, as well as speech that interfered with the war effort. Subsequently, juries convicted antiwar activist Charles Schenck for circulating a flyer to draftees that compared the draft to the "involuntary servitude" prohibited by the Thirteenth Amendment, and Socialist presidential candidate Eugene V. Debs for giving a speech criticizing the war. The Supreme Court upheld both convictions, noting that greater restrictions on speech could be allowed in wartime.[11]

After the war, Congress repealed the Sedition Act and President Warren G. Harding (1921–23) pardoned Debs. In no subsequent wars has the government restricted speech as it did with the Sedition Acts of 1798 or 1918.

© Bettmann/CORBIS

Speaking in Canton, Ohio, on June 16, 1918, Eugene V. Debs, labor organizer and three-time Socialist candidate for president, criticized the government for restricting free speech during wartime and declared, "If war is right let it be declared by the people." Charged with sedition, he was convicted and sentenced to prison. While in jail, he ran for president once again and received more than 900,000 votes, about 3.4 percent of votes cast.

Other liberties, however, continue to be restricted during the dangers of wartime. One event during World War II raised the question of procedural rights for enemy combatants, an issue that is also relevant in the world since the terrorist attacks of September 11, 2001. In the summer of 1942, teams of German saboteurs landed at Amagansett, New York, and Ponte Vedra, Florida. President Franklin Roosevelt (1933–45) ordered that they be tried by **military tribunals** rather than in criminal courts. The accused saboteurs nevertheless filed *habeas corpus* petitions. The Supreme Court agreed to review the case, but according to Justice Owen Roberts, Roosevelt's attorney general told him before the Supreme Court hearing that, with the nation at war, Roosevelt planned to have the saboteurs executed no matter what the Court ruled.[12] The Supreme Court eventually denied the *habeas* petitions, and the government eventually executed several of the saboteurs. Unlike antiwar speech, where views soften after the crisis has passed, planned attacks on American soil generally do not meet with later forgiveness.

The War on Terror

After 9/11, Congress passed the USA PATRIOT Act, which allowed greater sharing of intelligence information and enhancing law enforcement's ability to tap telephone and e-mail communications. The act also regulated financial transactions with overseas entities and eased the deportation of immigrants suspected of terrorist activities. Beyond the act, President Bush claimed the right, as commander in chief, to indefinitely detain alleged enemy combatants, whether U.S. citizens or foreign nationals. Thus Bush declared Jose Padilla, an American allegedly involved in a plan to detonate a radioactive bomb in the United States, an "enemy combatant" and transferred him from civilian to military authority, where he would have few if any procedural rights. The government kept Padilla in complete isolation for more than three and a half years. Unique among those declared enemy combatants, Padilla had not been captured on the field of battle but on American soil, and, born in Brooklyn, he was an American citizen. Thus his claims of procedural legal protections were stronger than those of the two other American citizens, Yaser Hamdi and John Walker Lindh, captured while allegedly fighting American forces in Afghanistan, or those of thousands of foreigners captured during the war in Afghanistan.

In June 2004, when the Supreme Court ruled that Hamdi could not be held indefinitely as an enemy combatant, it became clear that Padilla could not either. So, in November 2005, the Justice Department removed Padilla from military custody and charged him under federal criminal law with providing material support to terrorist organizations. The government did not charge him with attempting to detonate a radioactive bomb in the United States or with conspiring to commit any terrorist acts in the United States, suggesting that the original claims against him might not have held up in a court of law. His trial in Miami, with the full set of constitutional rights, required that Padilla be represented by counsel, that he be allowed to cross-examine witnesses, and that the government prove its case beyond a reasonable doubt. The government proved its case, and a jury quickly determined that Padilla was guilty of conspiring to kill people overseas. The judge then sentenced him to seventeen years in prison.

Although fewer rights exist for enemy combatants who are not U.S. citizens,[13] the Supreme Court has ruled that Congress must authorize hearings to determine the legality of the detention of even foreign enemy combatants. Such hearings must be consistent with the 1949 **Geneva Conventions**, an international treaty that protects the rights of prisoners of war.[14]

Beyond the enemy combatant cases, President Bush ordered warrantless wiretapping of conversations and interception of e-mails between American citizens and suspected foreign terrorists; normally, wiretapping

How free should you be to criticize the government? Should you be less free in wartime? Or since 9/11?

military tribunal: *Specially authorized court that determines the innocence or guilt of enemy combatants.*

Should enemy combatants have the same procedural safeguards as American citizens? What if the enemy combatant is an American citizen?

Are alleged terrorists enemy combatants?

Geneva Conventions: *Set of treaties that define lawful military combat and protect the rights of prisoners of war.*

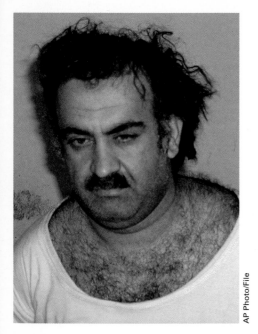

This widely circulated photograph of Khalid Sheikh Mohammed was taken on March 1, 2003, shortly after his capture during a raid in Pakistan. He is accused of masterminding the September 11, 2001, terrorist attacks on the United States and is being held at Guantanamo Bay, Cuba, awaiting trial.

warrant: *Legal document authorizing a search or a seizure.*

probable cause: *Determination by a neutral official that specific evidence is likely to be found in a place to be searched, or that an individual to be seized has likely committed a crime.*

AP Photo/File

requires a **warrant** signed by a judge or magistrate backed by **probable cause** that a crime is being committed. No court decisions exist on the wiretapping, though Congress did endorse aspects of the president's plan after the *New York Times* published stories about the then-secret program. The Obama administration has not made public a decision to continue or discontinue the program, but in 2009, it moved on national security grounds to block a lawsuit over the wiretapping.[15] The executive branch, with the most direct responsibility over national security, is more likely to support restrictions on civil liberties during times of crisis than either the legislative or judicial branches.

Civil Liberties and American Values

As these examples have demonstrated, in times of crisis, Congress and the president, often with public support, limit civil liberties to secure order. The courts, however, being less responsive to public pressure, can push back against these efforts. Thus, the courts forced the government to try Padilla in civilian courts, knowing that if the evidence fell short of the "guilty beyond a reasonable doubt" standard required for conviction, the result could have been that an alleged terrorist went free. The courts have also blocked efforts to censor newspapers even when the government believes that the publication of certain reports will benefit wartime enemies. Nevertheless, in wartime or other times of crisis, concerns about order are at their highest and protections for civil liberties by national and state governments typically decline. Following the emergency, a political culture that favors freedom means that public support for civil liberties, as well as the government's protections of those liberties, generally rebound.

The First Amendment and Freedom of Expression

The civil liberties most at risk during times of crisis are those protected by the First Amendment—freedom of speech, freedom of the press, and freedom of association. In this section, we examine each of these freedoms of expression individually. The scope of these freedoms has expanded over time, despite the occasional scaling back during wartime.

Freedom of Speech

While the First Amendment declares that "Congress shall pass no law . . . abridging the freedom of speech," the Court has never taken the phrase "no law" to literally mean "no law." Today the Court allows limits on advocacy of unlawful activities, the use of fighting words, symbolic speech, and campaign spending.

Advocacy of Unlawful Activities.

When Justice Holmes wrote in the opinion in the case of Charles Schenck that free speech does not mean one can falsely shout "Fire!" in a theater, he went on to explain that words spoken in wartime may have a different impact than they would in peacetime. "The question in every case," he continued, "is whether the words used are used in such circumstances and are of such a nature as to create a clear and present danger that they will bring about the substantive evils that Congress has a right to prevent." From this statement, the Court adopted the **clear and present danger test**. The Court shifted standards in subsequent decades, at one point allowing states to limit speech that merely had a tendency to cause unlawful acts. But in 1969 the Court moved back toward a stricter protection of civil liberties, ruling in *Brandenburg v. Ohio* (see Supreme Court Cases) that speech cannot be banned unless it leads to "imminent lawless action."

Fighting Words and Hate Speech.

Besides speech that incites unlawful activities, the Supreme Court also allows restrictions on the basis of what is called the **fighting words doctrine**. "Fighting words" are phrases that might lead the individual to whom they are directed to respond with a punch. Today, hateful racial epithets would be the leading examples of fighting words, but when the Supreme Court first developed the doctrine, many milder types of words offended people. Thus, in 1942, the Court used the fighting words doctrine to uphold the conviction of a defendant for calling a town marshal a "G__-damned racketeer" and a "damned Fascist."[16]

Related to fighting words is **hate speech**, speech that attacks or demeans a group, rather than a particular individual. Over the past thirty years, as we noted earlier, more than 350 public colleges and universities have attempted to provide equal, nonhostile educational environments through speech codes that tell students what they are and are not allowed to say.[17] For example, the University of Wisconsin prohibited any speech that created "an intimidating, hostile, or demeaning environment for education (or) university-related work."[18] The University of Connecticut's speech code banned "inappropriately directed laughter" and purposefully excluding people from conversations.[19] Tufts University established three separate free speech zones: public areas, where speech could not be prohibited; classrooms and libraries, where derogatory and demeaning speech could be punished;

Should the United States exemplify fair treatment to the world? Should it obey the Geneva Conventions?

clear and present danger test: *First Amendment test that requires the state to prove that there was a high likelihood that the speech in question would lead to a danger that Congress has a right to prevent.*

Brandenburg v. Ohio (1969): *Supreme Court decision requiring imminent lawless action before speech can be banned.*

fighting words doctrine: *Doctrine allowing speech to be banned if the likely response would be a punch.*

How can you distinguish between fighting words and hate speech?

hate speech: *Speech that attacks or demeans a group, rather than a particular individual.*

supremecourtcases
Brandenburg v. Ohio (1969)

QUESTION: Can states prevent racist speech that advocates illegal action but falls short of inciting a riot?

ORAL ARGUMENT: February 27, 1969 (listen at http://www.oyez.org/cases/)

DECISION: June 9, 1969 (read at http://www.findlaw.com/CaseCode/supreme.html)

OUTCOME: Brandenburg's conviction is overturned, establishing a broad right to freedom of speech (8–0)

Clarence Brandenburg headed an Ohio branch of the Ku Klux Klan. The Klan, formed following the Civil War, was an avowedly racist organization that revived and grew in the 1920s, when it opposed Catholic immigration to the United States, and in the 1950s and 1960s, when it opposed the civil rights movement. Seeking publicity for his group, Brandenburg invited a Cincinnati reporter and camera crew to film his speeches. At one speech, he threatened, "We're not a revengent organization, but if our President, our Congress, our Supreme Court, continues to suppress the white, Caucasian race, it's possible there might have to be some revengeance taken." In another speech, he declared, "Personally I believe the n* should be returned to Africa, and the Jew returned to Israel." The state of Ohio tried and convicted Brandenburg for violating its criminal syndicalism law, which made it a crime to advocate "the duty, necessity, or propriety of crime, sabotage, violence, or unlawful methods of terrorism as a means of accomplishing . . . political reform."

The Supreme Court unanimously reversed Brandenburg's conviction, declaring that the First Amendment protection of freedom of speech means that states cannot prohibit speech advocating the use of force "except where such advocacy is directed to inciting or producing imminent lawless action and is likely to incite or produce such action." Because Brandenburg's speech may have been "mere advocacy" of lawless action, as opposed to the "incitement of imminent lawless action," it was protected by the First Amendment.

- **Does "hate speech" deserve the same constitutional protection as other forms of speech?**

- **Should the government have the right to ban speech that advocates violence even if the violence would not be imminent (immediate)?**

*Offensive expletive deleted.

and dorms, where the university placed the strictest restrictions on speech. Whereas students at many universities accepted speech codes, students at Tufts debated the issue, held public forums about freedom of speech, and physically marked off "free speech" from "non–free speech" zones.[20] Under this pressure, Tufts, a private university not legally bound by the Bill of Rights, rescinded the code.

The University of Michigan's speech code prohibited any speech that "stigmatizes or victimizes individuals or groups on the basis of race, ethnicity, religion, sex, sexual orientation, creed, national origin, ancestry, age, marital status, handicap, or Vietnam-era veteran status." In addition to the regulations, the university created guidelines that gave examples of actionable conduct. These examples include stating in class that women are not as good as men in a particular field; not inviting someone to a party because she is a lesbian; excluding someone from a study group because of race or sex; displaying a Confederate flag; telling jokes about gays or lesbians; laughing at jokes about people who stutter; or commenting in a derogatory way about a particular person's physical appearance.[21]

A graduate student in psychology was concerned that Michigan's code would prevent class discussions of theories that claimed biological differences between sexes and races, and he brought suit against the code in federal court. The court struck down the code as violating the First Amendment.[22] Two years later, a federal court struck down the University of Wisconsin's speech code.[23] Thus the courts have made it clear that while state universities may encourage the goal of equality, they cannot do so by limiting First Amendment rights. Note that the First Amendment applies to these schools because they are state universities. The Bill of Rights limits the national government and, through the selective incorporation doctrine, also limits state governments and thus state universities. Private colleges, though subject to certain federal regulations, are not subject to the Bill of Rights.

Symbolic Speech. The armbands that Mary Beth and John Tinker wore to protest the Vietnam War were not pure speech, because the Tinkers voiced no opinions while wearing them. Rather, the armbands were considered **symbolic speech**, like other nonverbal activities that convey a political message, such as saluting the flag, burning the flag, or burning draft cards—the latter two actions also undertaken by anti–Vietnam War protesters.

David McNew/Getty Images

California State University, Long Beach, posts a sign designating its free-speech zone.

Does your college have a speech code? Should your college regulate what you can and cannot say?

What is more important—freedom of speech or an equal and nonhostile educational environment?

symbolic speech: *Expressive communication, such as wearing armbands, that is not verbally communicated.*

Clay Good/ZUMA

In 2002, high school student Joseph Frederick unfurled this banner while his class watched the Olympic Torch relay pass through Juneau, Alaska. When the principal suspended Frederick for the banner's message about drugs, Frederick sued, saying his free speech rights had been violated. The court of appeals, relying on the *Tinker* case, reversed the suspension, but in 2007 the Supreme Court upheld it, saying a student's free speech rights did not extend to the promotion of illegal drugs.

Should the Tinkers have been suspended for wearing armbands to school to protest the Vietnam War?

The Court has allowed prohibitions on the burning of draft cards, because Congress has a **content neutral** justification for requiring that draft-eligible citizens be in possession of their draft cards. That is, draft cards are essential to the smooth running of the draft,[24] and prohibiting their destruction is not intended to suppress the views of those who burn them. States also have a neutral justification for banning cross burning, a terrorist tactic historically used by the white supremacist Ku Klux Klan to intimidate African Americans.[25] But the Court has overturned laws that require flag salutes, as they do intend to instill a political viewpoint.[26] Similarly, the Court has overturned laws prohibiting flag burning, as they are based almost entirely on opposition to the idea being delivered by flag burning.[27] Of course, flag burners can be arrested on whatever charges would apply to anyone who starts a fire in public. On the other hand, the content-neutral rule, like most constitutional rules, is not absolute. Some messages can be regulated solely because of opposition to the message, as when the Supreme Court upheld a student's suspension for unfurling a banner at a parade that declared "Bong Hits 4 Jesus," because of the banner's promotion of drug use.[28] It is easy for the Court to formulate simple rules, such as a prohibition on content-based regulations, but harder for the Court to apply those rules consistently in the unusual cases that come before it.

Campaign Finance. Another attempt to advance equality by restricting expression involves laws that try to level the playing field in elections by limiting campaign contributions. Without such limits, supporters of campaign finance reform claim that the wealthy will have a disproportionate influence on elections. Nevertheless, the Supreme Court has consistently ruled that campaign contributions are a form of speech protected by the First Amendment and that laws restricting campaign contributions or campaign activities must pass the compelling interest test (see Chapters 6 and 8).

Time, Place, and Manner Regulations.

The fact that the First Amendment protects freedom of speech does not mean that there is a right to speak wherever one wants, whenever one wants. Regulations of the time, place, and manner of speech, such as when or where protests may take place, are generally valid as long as they are neutral or equal, that is, they do not favor one side or another of a controversy. Thus states can prohibit protests near school grounds that interfere with school activities as there is no indication that such bans favor one side of any controversy over any other side.[29] Nevertheless, the Court has upheld bans on protests near abortion clinics, even though the protesters there are almost always anti-abortion, given concerns over the welfare of women seeking abortions.[30]

Freedom of the Press

Thomas Jefferson, among other Founders, thought freedom of the press crucial to a free society, because the press keeps the public informed about the government's activities. Though when the Bill of Rights was written the press meant newspapers, today it covers not only the large companies that own television and radio stations but also individually run blogs or Internet sites that anyone can create. While freedom of the press once belonged to those who owned one, today it belongs to everyone.

Like freedom of speech, however, freedom of the press is not absolute. In extraordinarily extreme cases, the government can censor items before they are published. This practice is known as **prior restraint**. In other situations, the government can punish people after the fact for what they publish.

Prior Restraint.

Following English law, "freedom of the press" in the colonies and in the early years of the United States meant freedom from prior censorship;[31] today, an *extraordinary burden of proof of imminent harm* is needed before the courts will shut down a newspaper before a story is printed. Even when the *New York Times* began publishing excerpts from a top secret Pentagon analysis of U.S. involvement in the Vietnam War, the courts refused to stop the presses. The story of this case, *New York Times v. United States* (1971),[32] is told in more detail in Chapter 7. One case in which the courts said the government had met the extraordinary burden standard involved the publication of instructions on how to build a hydrogen bomb,[33] but generally, court approval of censorship by prior restraint has been so difficult to achieve that since the 1970s the federal government has not sought it.

First Amendment law protects the Internet and blogs from government censorship in much the same way that it protects newspapers, but the technology of the Internet makes censorship far more difficult. This was the lesson

Should Americans be required to salute the flag? Prevented from burning the flag?

content neutral: *Free speech doctrine that allows certain types of regulation of speech, as long as the restriction does not favor one side or another of a controversy.*

prior restraint: *Government restrictions on freedom of the press that prevent material from being published.*

learned in 2008 by a federal judge who tried to censor the Wikileaks website,[34] which specializes in publishing confidential documents from government, business, and religious organizations. Though the judge ordered the Wikileaks .org domain name disabled, Wikileaks already had mirror sites set up all over the world. Facing a barrage of criticism from bloggers and mainstream media groups, and the ineffectiveness of his original decision, the judge reversed himself. But while many will support the right of Wikileaks to publish allegations of money laundering by a Swiss bank, as in this case, what happens when Wikileaks publishes, as it has, a diagram of the first atomic bomb?[35]

What information on the web should the government censor?

Subsequent Punishment.   In certain instances, the government can engage in **subsequent punishment**, punishing writers and publishers with fines and/or imprisonment after the fact for what they publish. Examples here include penalties for libel and for publishing obscenity, incitement to acts of violence, and secret military information.

subsequent punishment: *Restrictions on freedom of the press that occur after material is published.*

libel: *Publishing false and damaging statements about another.*

The standards for convicting in a case of **libel**—the publishing of false and damaging statements about another person—vary according to whether that person is a public figure. The Supreme Court has made it harder for public figures to sue for libel than for ordinary individuals, because public figures have access to the media and can more readily defend themselves without lawsuits. For public figures to sue, the materials must be false, damaging, and the writer or publisher must have acted with **actual malice**, that is, with knowledge that the material was false or reckless disregard of whether it was true or false (see Supreme Court Cases: *New York Times v. Sullivan* in Chapter 7). For private figures to sue for libel, the material must be false, damaging, and there must be some degree of negligence, but the actual malice test does not apply.

actual malice test: *Supreme Court test for libel of a public figure, in which the plaintiff must prove that the publisher knew the material was false or acted with "reckless disregard" of whether it was true or false.*

Prior to the Internet, only those who published printed materials could libel someone, but even then, the damage would largely be limited to those who subscribed to the publication. With the Internet, anyone can libel anyone else, and the whole world can see it. At Yale University, for example, anonymous contributors to a popular law school message board wrote derogatory references about several female law students, including fabricated statements about their mental capacity and sexual activities. Because anyone, including potential employers, can see such statements, the potential for harm is enormous.[36] Given the anonymous nature of the posts, there is little that the victims can do. There is no easy solution to protecting privacy in the internet age when freedom of speech is a fundamental right.

How can you protect yourself from what others may say about you on the web?

Today, the government can seek subsequent punishment against individuals who publish military secrets or obscene materials. Note that pornographic material is not necessarily obscene, and that pornography that falls short of the legal definition of "obscenity" receives First Amendment protection. Specifically, for materials to be obscene, they must pass all three parts of what has become known as the **Miller test**:[37]

Miller test: *Supreme Court test for determining whether material is obscene.*

1. To the average person, applying contemporary community standards as established by the relevant state, the work, taken as a whole (not just isolated passages), appeals to the prurient (sexual) interest.
2. The work depicts in an offensive way sexual conduct specifically defined by the state law.
3. The work lacks serious literary, artistic, political, or scientific value.

Under the Miller test, only "hard-core" materials could be banned.[38] The government has much greater leeway to prohibit "kiddie porn" that uses actual children,[39] but not "virtual child pornography," which uses computer-simulated children.[40] Nor can the government's desire to protect children from indecent materials be used as a justification for prohibiting pornography that does not reach the level of obscenity from the Internet.[41]

The Miller test reversed a trend toward greater protection of pornography that the liberal Warren Court (1954–69) had instituted and stands opposed to the general trend of greater rights of the press to publish without fear of prosecution by the state.

The Right of Association

The First Amendment's protections include the right of the people to peaceably assemble. This means the right to associate with whom one wants, as well as the right not to associate with those with whom one does not want to be. As we observed earlier, here a civil liberty can conflict with a civil right, as when a restaurant owner might choose, for example, not to serve people of a certain race. This dilemma was resolved by the Civil Rights Act and subsequent court challenges in the 1960s, so far as businesses that serve the public are concerned (see Chapter 5). But for private clubs and groups, Supreme Court's rulings indicate that states can enforce antidiscrimination laws as long as those groups do not engage in speech-related or expressive activities. But if the group does engage in expressive activities and association with certain groups that violate the views thus expressed, the group has a First Amendment **right of association** that overrides state laws banning discrimination.

New Jersey's law prohibiting private groups from discriminating against homosexuals did not override the Boy Scouts' stated belief that homosexuality is inconsistent with the group's values. The Court thus allowed the Scouts to prohibit homosexuals from being members.[42]

Which is more important to you—freedom of association or laws banning discrimination?

right of association: *Right to freely associate with others and form groups, protected by the First Amendment.*

Religious Freedom

The First Amendment sets forth two distinct protections about religion. Congress (and now the states) generally may not prevent people from practicing their religious beliefs. They also cannot pass laws that establish an official religion or even favor one religion over another.

Free Exercise

Many of the first settlers in the American colonies came because of restrictions on their religious beliefs in England, where the Anglican Church was established as the official religion.

In 1786, however, the Virginia General Assembly passed Thomas Jefferson's Statute for Religious Freedom, which declared freedom of religious conscience to be a natural right of mankind that governments could not abridge. Five years later, this right was affirmed in the **free exercise clause** of the Bill of Rights. While it is taken for granted by Americans today, it is still not protected throughout much of the world.

free exercise clause (First Amendment): *Protects the free exercise of religion.*

Under the First Amendment, the government cannot criminalize an individual's private religious beliefs. Nor can the government ban specific religious activities just because they are based on religious beliefs. For example, the Supreme Court struck down a ban on religious-based animal sacrifices because killing animals for other reasons was not prohibited.[43] But not all religious-based activities are protected, and states are generally free to pass laws that restrict religious practices as long as such laws have a **valid secular** (nonreligious) **purpose**. For example, states can ban polygamy, even though marriage with multiple wives is a central belief to some religions.[44] In the 1960s, however, the Court ruled that states must have a compelling interest before they could abridge people's religious practices, even if the law had a valid secular purpose. Thus even though the government has a valid secular purpose in conducting a military draft, members of religious groups that oppose warfare, such as Quakers, may be exempt. In the case of Muslim boxing champion Muhammad Ali, who argued that he could only fight wars declared by Allah or the Prophet, the Court overturned a conviction for draft evasion.[45]

valid secular purpose: *Supreme Court test that allows states to ban activities that infringe on religious practices as long as the state has a nonreligious rationale for prohibiting the behavior.*

One case that demonstrates the contest between the branches over what constitutes free exercise concerns the use of the hallucinogenic drug peyote in religious rituals. In 1990, when two Native American drug counselors who used peyote were fired from their jobs and denied unemployment compensation, the Supreme Court used the valid secular purpose test to uphold Oregon's decision to deny this compensation.[46] Members of Congress overwhelmingly disapproved, however, and passed legislation stating that the Supreme Court must use the compelling interest test in deciding free exercise cases. The Supreme Court responded by declaring that law unconstitutional, repeating the statement from *Marbury v. Madison*: "It is emphatically the province and duty of the judicial department to say what the law is." Congress does have the authority, however, to declare the religious use of peyote to be legal, and it has done so. But generally, states need only have a valid secular purpose to pass laws that also happen to restrict religious practices.

The Establishment of Religion

The **establishment clause** of the First Amendment prevents Congress from recognizing one church by law as the nation's official church, as Britain had done with the Anglican (Episcopal) Church. Originally, states were free to establish state religions, if they chose, and when the Constitution was adopted, nearly half the states had done so.[47] In 1802, Jefferson called for a "wall of separation" between church and state. The Supreme Court adopted that phrase in 1947, but declared in that case that providing taxpayer funds to provide public transportation to parochial schools did not breach the wall.[48]

The establishment clause literally prohibits not just the establishment of religion, but also *"any law respecting an establishment of religion."* The Supreme Court has taken this phrase to mean that steps by the government that favor one religion over another, or even religion over no religion, cannot be taken, even if those steps fall far short of an official establishment of religion.

The Supreme Court's test for determining whether laws violate the establishment clause is known as the **Lemon test**, named after a litigant in a 1971 case.[49] Under this test, challenged laws must be shown to have a secular (nonreligious) legislative purpose and a primary effect that neither advances nor inhibits religion. The law must also avoid an excessive entanglement between church and state, such as a strict monitoring of church activities. Using these standards, the Supreme Court has banned organized school prayers (*Engel v. Vitale*) and devotional Bible readings (*Abington School District v. Schempp*).[50] The Bible can be read as part of a comparative religion course, however, and students can always pray silently. The Supreme Court has also used this test to strike down laws that prohibited the

establishment clause (First Amendment): *Prohibits governmental establishment of religion.*

Lemon test: *Test for determining whether aid to religion violates the establishment clause.*

Universal Press Syndicate, Tom Toles The Washington Post 3-3-05

BUT MAYBE THIS ISN'T THE MOST APPROPRIATE PLACE FOR IT.

The Ten Amendments Monument

I SEPARATION OF CHURCH AND STATE
II
III
IV
V
VI
VII
VIII
IX
X

THE GOVERNMENT DOESN'T WANT IT EITHER.

UNIVERSAL PRESS SYND. © 2005 THE WASHINGTON POST

3·3·05

teaching of evolution[51] as well as laws granting equal time for creation science—the position that evidence supports the Biblical view of creation—if evolution is taught.[52] In 2005, a district court judge in Pennsylvania ruled that "intelligent design"—a view that claims that the world is too complex to have resulted from evolution and that thus there must have been a purposeful designer of the universe (that is, God)—was nothing more than a renamed creation science. Whether creation science or intelligent design, courts have ruled that these are religious doctrines that cannot be taught as part of the science curriculum in public schools.

It is often difficult to understand why some activities violate the establishment clause whereas others do not. **Separationists** believe, with Jefferson, that there should be a strict wall between church and state. **Accommodationists**, on the other hand, believe that as long as the state does not favor one religion over another, it can generally pass laws that support religion. The Supreme Court's decisions, on these grounds, have been mixed, with conservative justices typically supporting the accommodationist position and liberal justices typically supporting the separationist view (see Chapter 14 on ideology and the Supreme Court). The end result has been a fair amount of confusion: the Court allows short religious prayers by clergy at high school graduation ceremonies as long as students are not compelled to participate,[53] but not by students at high school football games.[54] States may provide textbooks for secular subjects in parochial schools,[55] but not instructional aids like charts and maps.[56]

The Right to Keep and Bear Arms

While many if not most Americans agree about the fundamental aims of the various First Amendment rights, no such agreement exists about the fundamental aims of the Second Amendment. The amendment declares, "A well regulated militia being necessary to the security of a free state, the right of the people to keep and bear arms shall not be infringed." Supporters of gun rights view the amendment as providing an individual right of the people to keep and bear arms, while opponents view the "well regulated militia" clause as limiting this right to those in organized militias.

At the time of the amendment's passage, the term *militia* meant all free, able-bodied, adult males, who could be called upon to protect their states or communities from external military threats. The Founders favored citizen militias, which could be called on in moments of crisis, over standing armies, which could pose a threat to liberty.

separationists: *Those who believe that the Establishment Clause requires a wall of separation between church and state.*

accommodationists: *Those who believe that as long as the government does not favor one religion over another, it may generally support religious practices.*

Should prayers in school be allowed? Under what circumstances? What type of prayer? Is saying a prayer the same as wearing an armband?

Not until the 1934 National Firearms Act did the federal government attempt to regulate gun ownership. In 1939, the Supreme Court upheld a conviction under the act for possession of a sawed-off shotgun against a Second Amendment challenge, unanimously ruling that as such weapons had never been used by any militia, they did not receive Second Amendment protection. The Court sidestepped the question as to whether there was an individual right to bear arms.

The Supreme Court finally decided that issue in 2008, ruling that there is an individual right to possess a gun, at least for self-defense in one's home.[57] The case involved a law prohibiting the private possession of firearms by the District of Columbia, which is a "federal enclave" and, for constitutional purposes, considered part of the federal government rather than a state. The Court's 5–4 decision split along ideological lines, with the five most conservative justices supporting an individual right to keep and bear arms for self-defense. That right can be regulated but cannot be denied. The four most liberal justices dissented, arguing that the well-regulated militia clause limits whatever right of gun ownership exists to military purposes.

The conclusion that the Second Amendment protects an individual right to bear arms does not answer whether that amendment is also binding on the states. The Supreme Court answered that question in 2010, declaring that the right is incorporated.[58]

What are the arguments for and against gun control? What is your position?

Criminal Procedure

Provisions in the Fourth, Fifth, Sixth, and Eighth Amendments contain the heart of the protections afforded people against arbitrary police and law enforcement tactics. They protect the manner in which the police conduct investigations, the procedures used at trial, and the punishments that may be given following conviction. The liberal Warren Court of the 1960s and 1970s greatly expanded the rights of accused criminals, but more conservative courts since then have trimmed these rights.

Investigations

The major limits on investigating crimes involve the authority to search for physical evidence and the warnings that must be given prior to questioning a suspect.

Searches and Seizures. The English practice of issuing writs of assistance, general warrants that allow searches of any person or place with no expiration until the death of the king, was among the causes that led to the Revolution. Thus, the Fourth Amendment prohibits unreasonable searches and seizures. Though the amendment does not specify what makes a search unreasonable, it does specify that warrants must be backed by probable cause.

The Supreme Court has never interpreted the amendment to require warrants for all searches or seizures. If the police see illegal goods in plain view, they may seize them without a warrant. Similarly, if they observe a crime, they do not have to get a warrant before they arrest the individual. Following an arrest, the Supreme Court has also established a broad right to search, incident to that arrest, the person and the area within his or her control.

expectation of privacy test: *Supreme Court test for whether Fourth Amendment protections apply.*

The areas over which individuals have Fourth Amendment protections are those in which there is an **expectation of privacy**. According to the Supreme Court, there are no Fourth Amendment rights in areas over which there is no expectation of privacy, such as discarded garbage, someone else's home, a hotel room once one has checked out, or at international borders. The Supreme Court has not ruled on the issue, but several state supreme courts have upheld the right of schools to search lockers used by students, because students have a diminished expectation of privacy over their lockers. While students at public universities do have an expectation of privacy in their college dorm rooms, many schools require that students waive their Fourth Amendment rights when they sign their dorm contracts. (Like the First Amendment, the Fourth Amendment does not limit private parties, such as private universities.) More generally, people waive their Fourth Amendment rights whenever they grant permission for the police to search, as long as the police request is not coercive.[59]

For areas over which there is an expectation of privacy, the degree of Fourth Amendment protection depends on the level of that expectation, as determined by the Supreme Court. For example, the Court has ruled that individuals have the highest expectation of privacy in their homes, nearly as much in their places of business, but substantially less in their cars.[60] There is no expectation of privacy in what is exposed in plain view, even if, like a marijuana patch on private property, it requires a low-flying plane to view it.[61] There is no expectation of privacy over smells, allowing police to use drug-sniffing dogs to establish probable cause. There is, however, an expectation of privacy over the thermal (heat) signals given off by homes, thus prohibiting the police from using heat monitors to establish probable cause for indoor marijuana growing.[62]

Searches of homes almost always require a warrant (and thus probable cause). Searches of businesses usually do, but the Court allows warrantless searches of businesses that are subject to health, safety, or administrative regulations, such as restaurants, construction sites, or banks. For example, restaurant kitchens suspected of health violations may be searched without a warrant. The police may establish, without probable cause, roadblocks to stop all cars on a road to check for licenses and registration, or for drunk drivers. They may, of course, pull over any car for an observed violation and may search the car incident to arrest if they choose to arrest the person for that violation.[63] The Court also allows drug testing without probable cause in "special needs" cases, such as student athletes[64] and people applying for jobs at the U.S. Customs Office,[65] but not of politicians seeking elective office.[66]

If the police conduct a search later found to be in violation of the Fourth Amendment, the **exclusionary rule** holds that such evidence cannot be used in trial. Defenders support the rule, which is not explicitly in the Constitution, as the only means of making sure that the police follow the Fourth Amendment. Police will have less incentive to violate the Fourth Amendment if they know that the evidence from illegal searches cannot be used in court. Critics complain that excluding such evidence allows guilty people to go free simply because the police made a mistake.[67] The Supreme Court has backtracked a bit on the rule, establishing a **good faith exception** on the part of the police, which allows evidence to be used if the police obtain a warrant but the warrant is later found to lack probable cause.

Interrogations. The Fifth Amendment protects the right against **self-incrimination**, being forced to give testimony against oneself during criminal investigations or at criminal trials. The Supreme Court originally interpreted the self-incrimination clause to prohibit coerced confessions because they are inherently unreliable. But in the famous 1966 decision, *Miranda v. Arizona*,[68] the Court declared that the right against self-incrimination would be protected regardless of whether there was any evidence of coercion. Rather, prior to police interrogation of subjects who are in custody, the subjects must be told that: (1) they have the right to remain silent; (2) anything they say may be used against them; and (3) they have the right to an attorney, free if they cannot afford one. Police strenuously objected to these requirements at first, fearing that they would drastically curtail legitimate confessions. But, in 2000, the Court upheld the *Miranda* decision, noting that its requirements had become so embedded in routine police practice that they had become part of the national culture.[69]

Trial Procedures

The trial protections of the Bill of Rights include the right to indictment by a grand jury (Fifth Amendment), the **right to counsel** and an impartial jury (both Sixth Amendment), and the right against self-incrimination (Fifth Amendment), which, as noted, applies to trials as well as investigations.

To prevent the government from bringing people to trial without sufficient cause, the Fifth Amendment requires indictment by a grand jury, which

exclusionary rule: *Supreme Court rule declaring that evidence found in violation of the Fourth Amendment cannot be used at trial.*

good faith exception: *Limit on exclusionary rule that allows evidence to be used if the police obtain a warrant but the warrant is later found to lack probable cause.*

self-incrimination: *Fifth Amendment prohibition against being forced to give testimony against oneself.*

Miranda v. Arizona (1966): *Supreme Court decision requiring that suspects be informed of their rights before questioning.*

right to counsel: *Sixth Amendment right that now includes appointed counsel if the suspect cannot afford an attorney.*

decides by majority vote. This right has not been incorporated so it only applies to the federal government, which prosecutes only a small percentage of total criminal cases, as criminal law is mostly under the authority of the states.

The Sixth Amendment's right to counsel originally meant that defendants could have an attorney represent them if they could afford one. In *Powell v. Alabama* (1932), a case involving undoubtedly false allegations of rape filed against several black youths, the Supreme Court ruled that, in death penalty cases where the defendants were ignorant, illiterate, or the like, the government must provide an attorney if defendants cannot afford one.[70] In 1942, the Supreme Court chose not to guarantee poor people a right to counsel in all felony cases, usually defined as crimes where possible imprisonment exceeds one year.[71] In 1963, the Court, recognizing how crucial counsel is in even simple cases, overruled the 1942 decision in the landmark *Gideon v. Wainwright* case.[72] Today, that rule applies to any case in which a defendant receives even one day of jail time.[73]

The application of the self-incrimination clause to trials means that defendants cannot be compelled to be a witness against themselves. That is, they have an absolute right not to testify, and the prosecution cannot even tell the jury that the defendant chose not to testify.

The Right to Privacy

Although a number of constitutional provisions bear on privacy, such as search and seizure, self-incrimination, and First Amendment freedoms, none explicitly grants a general **right to privacy**. Nevertheless, the Ninth Amendment demands that the listing of certain rights, such as speech and religion, should not be understood as invalidating rights not listed. Since 1965, the Supreme Court has used the Ninth Amendment, the due process clause of the Fourteenth Amendment, and other privacy-related amendments to establish a general right to privacy. Subsequently the Court has faced decisions as to whether to expand this privacy right to include abortion, homosexual behavior, and the right to die.

Birth Control and Abortion

In 1873, Anthony Comstock, a crusader for traditional morality, lobbied Congress to pass a law prohibiting the transportation in interstate commerce of both pornography and birth control. Many states, including Connecticut, passed their own Comstock Laws, which prohibited the use of birth control, even among married couples. In 1961, Estelle Griswold, executive director of the Planned Parenthood League of Connecticut, opened a birth control clinic

Powell v. Alabama (1932): *Supreme Court decision creating a right to appointed counsel in exceptional cases.*

Gideon v. Wainwright (1963): *Supreme Court decision creating a right to appointed counsel in all felony cases.*

Where would you draw the line in searches? Should government be allowed to search your home, your car, your bank account? Under what conditions?

right to privacy: *Constitutional right inferred by the Court that has been used to protect unlisted rights such as sexual privacy, reproductive rights, and the right to end life-sustaining medical treatment.*

in order to get arrested or fined so that she could challenge the constitution-ality of the law. Her $100 fine, upheld by the Connecticut Supreme Court, allowed her to appeal to the U.S. Supreme Court. In *Griswold v. Connecticut* (1965), the Court voided what one justice called "an uncommonly silly law" that made it a crime for any person—including married couples—to use birth control.[74] The case established a right to privacy (see Figure 4.2), and the Court soon expanded this decision to cover the right of unmarried people to use birth control.[75]

Griswold v. Connecticut **(1965):** *Supreme Court case establishing the right to privacy.*

No Soldier shall, in time of peace be quartered in any house, without the consent of the Owner. ...

Third Amendment

Congress shall make no law ... abridging ... the right of the people peaceably to assemble. ...

First Amendment

The right of the people to be secure in their persons, houses, papers, and effects, against unreasonable searches and seizures, shall not be violated. ...

Fourth Amendment

The enumeration in the Constitution, of certain rights, shall not be construed to deny or disparage others retained by the people.

Ninth Amendment

No person ... shall be compelled in any criminal case to be a witness against himself. ...

Fifth Amendment

... nor shall any State deprive any person of life, liberty, or property, without due process of law. ...

Fourteenth Amendment (section 1)

In 1965, in *Griswold v. Connecticut*, the Supreme Court overturned a Connecticut law that madeit a crime for any person, including married couples, to use birth control. This landmark case drew on guarantees in the First, Third, Fourth, Fifth, Ninth, and Fourteenth Amendments to establish a general right to privacy. These guarantees are the right of association, the prohibition against quartering soldiers, the protection against unreasonable searches, the protection against self-incrimination, the rights retained by the people, and the due process of law. Justice William O. Douglas, who wrote the opinion, explained the justification with reference to "penumbras," or "zones": "Specific guarantees in the Bill of Rights have penumbras formed by emanations from those guarantees that help give them life and substance." He also stated the justifi cation more bluntly: "Would we allow the police to search the sacred precincts of marital bedrooms for the tell-tale signs of the use of contraceptives? The very idea is repulsive."

FIGURE 4.2 The Right to Privacy.

In 1973, the Supreme Court decided *Roe v. Wade*, which established a national right to abortion.[75] Using the compelling interest test, the Court declared that states had a compelling interest in *preventing* abortion in the third trimester, when the fetus could live on its own, and a compelling interest in *regulating* abortion during the second trimester, to protect the health of the woman seeking the procedure. The state had no interest in regulating or preventing abortion in the first trimester. The Court's ruling took the issue out of state politics, where it had been located, and situated it in national politics, where it has become a perennial controversy, with presidential candidates regularly vowing to nominate Supreme Court justices who would either uphold or strike down *Roe v. Wade*. Since that time, states have sought to regulate and limit the procedure, and in the past twenty years abortion rates have slowly declined.

Following years of debate about *Roe v. Wade*, the Court reconsidered the decision in 1992.[77] That decision upheld the basic right to abortion established in *Roe v. Wade*, but replaced the compelling interest/trimester framework, declaring that states could regulate abortion prior to viability as long as those regulations did not constitute an **undue burden** on a woman's right to terminate her pregnancy. According to the Court, spousal notification constitutes an undue burden, but requiring doctors to provide the woman with information about the risks of abortion and a twenty-four-hour waiting period does not. Parental consent for minors is not an undue burden as long as the minor has an option of seeking a judge's approval if she cannot obtain a parent's consent.

undue burden: *Current test used by the Court to determine if abortion regulations are allowable.*

What are the arguments for and against the right of privacy in relation to abortion? What is your opinion—pro-life or pro-choice?

Perhaps the most controversial abortion procedures are those conducted late in a pregnancy. The Supreme Court struck down Nebraska's ban of these so-called partial-birth abortions in 2000, in a 5–4 decision, because the state law did not contain an exception for the woman's health. Congress responded with national legislation banning late-term abortions, and the Court upheld the statute by a 5–4 vote in 2007. The difference: the replacement of Justice Sandra Day O'Connor, who voted to strike the statute in 2000, with Justice Samuel Alito, who voted to uphold the statute in 2007.

Abortion remains a salient issue in national politics, with the Supreme Court's role front and center. At confirmation hearings for Supreme Court nominees (see Chapter 14), senators ask more questions about *Roe v. Wade* than about any other case.[78]

Homosexual Behavior

As of 1961, every state had laws prohibiting sodomy, and these laws were broad enough to cover virtually all sexual conduct between people of the same sex. In the next decades, some states decriminalized sodomy, and by

AP Photo/Topeka Capital-Journal, Anthony S. Bush, file

What happens when rights clash? In 2009, the Supreme Court agreed to hear a case involving the Westboro Church of Topeka and Albert Snyder of York, Pennsylvania. Westboro members claim freedom of speech permits them to protest at military funerals, which they do to assert that the deaths of military personnel are God's punishment for the tolerance of homosexuality. Snyder claims that their protest at his son's funeral was an invasion of privacy causing emotional distress.

1986, only twenty-four states continued to outlaw sodomy between consenting adults. Georgia, one of the states that continued such laws, authorized twenty-four years of imprisonment for a single act of consensual sexual behavior that fell under its sodomy laws. In a case challenging this law, the Supreme Court declared that the right to privacy did not cover homosexual behavior.[79] At the time, over 80 percent of Americans thought that homosexual behavior was "always" or "almost always" wrong.[80] But by 2003, with the percentage of Americans with this belief down more than 20 percentage points, the Supreme Court reversed itself, declaring in *Lawrence v. Texas* that "the liberty protected by the Constitution allows homosexual persons the right to choose to enter upon relationships in the confines of their homes and their own private lives."[81]

The Right to Die

As part of the right to privacy, the Supreme Court has held that that people who make their wishes clearly known have a constitutional right to terminate life-sustaining care, such as artificial feeding or breathing tubes.[82] This right does not, however, include the right to assisted suicide, when physicians or family provide ill people with pills or other means of ending life.[83]

Lawrence v. Texas **(2003):** *Supreme Court case extending the right to privacy to homosexual behavior.*

Civil Liberties and Public Policy: Private Property and Public Use

Civil liberties include not only political rights but also economic rights, particularly the right of property, which is explicitly protected in the Constitution. While the Fifth and Fourteenth Amendments, respectively, prevent the federal and state governments from denying people life, liberty, or property without due process of law, the strongest protection of private property is the Fifth Amendment's **takings clause**, which prohibits the government from using its power of **eminent domain**, the taking of private property for **public use** without providing **just compensation**. The takings clause requires compensation not just for wholesale seizures of private property but also for changes in economic regulations that severely limit the economic value of private property.

takings clause (Fifth Amendment): *Requires just compensation when the government seizes private property for a public purpose.*

eminent domain: *Right of the government to seize private property for public use.*

public use: *Requirement of the takings clause that once meant that the use of seized property had to be beneficial to all citizens, such as the building of roads or parks, and not just to private parties.*

just compensation: *Payment by the government of fair market value for seized property.*

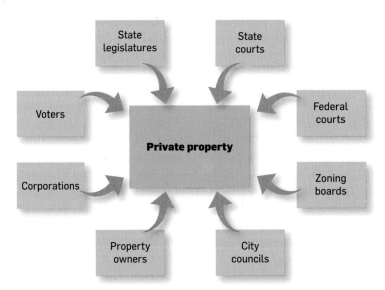

Civil Liberties and Democracy

Supreme Court Justice Robert Jackson wrote in 1943, in a case striking down a state requirement that children salute the flag in school, "If there is any fixed star in our constitutional constellation, it is that no official, high or petty, can prescribe what shall be orthodox in politics, nationalism, religion, or other matters of opinion or force citizens to confess by word or act their faith therein."[84] By this, Jackson meant that the Constitution prohibits the government from interfering in what individuals say or think.

But what if elected officials do so anyway? Jackson responded that it was then the Court's job to protect such rights: "The very purpose of a Bill of Rights was to withdraw certain subjects from . . . political controversy, to place them beyond the reach of majorities and officials and to establish them as legal principles to be applied by the courts. One's . . . fundamental rights may not be submitted to vote; they depend on the outcome of no elections."[85]

Judicial decisions do not exist in a vacuum. Over the long run, if the Court is unresponsive to the people, new presidents will appoint new judges who better represent the people's preferences.[86] And while the Supreme Court is not accountable to the electorate in the same way that Congress and the president are, Congress and the president do have means at their disposal to try to hold the Court accountable. Additionally, the Court cannot stand alone in protecting civil liberties if popular support is not behind it. One of the difficulties of protecting civil liberties in a democracy is that although it is easy to feel sympathy for teenagers who wear black armbands to protest war, most litigants whose cases set precedents that protect all the nation's freedoms are not as wholesome, and the causes they espouse may be racist, sexist, or violent.[87]

Unlimited liberties can also harm social order, particularly in times of crisis. Note, however, that in the period following 9/11, Congress made no attempt to criminalize antiwar speech, as it had during World War I; there was little public demand for such restrictions, as tolerance of opposing viewpoints among Americans has increased dramatically over the years. **Political tolerance**, the willingness of people to put up with ideas with which they disagree, is essential to both the marketplace of ideas and democratic stability.[88] A current example of this conflict is occurring currently next to the site of the 9/11 World Trade Center bombing as a Muslim community center or mosque is proposed to be built but has been the subject of court challenges.

Similarly, the appointment process furthers responsiveness. Although critics have attacked the Supreme Court for establishing a right to privacy that is not explicitly in the Constitution, this decision remains highly popular, with 98 percent of Americans considering the right essential or important.[89] But if the public loses its concern over civil liberties, sooner or later, the Supreme Court will as well.

political tolerance: *Willingness of people to put up with ideas with which they disagree.*

FOCUS QUESTIONS

- What is government's role with regard to civil liberties? How responsive can, or should, it be to the people's will?

- What is the proper balance between liberty and order?

- Under what circumstances should civil liberties be restrained?

- What happens when rights clash? Are restrictions of civil liberties justified if they promote equality?

- In what ways does the guarantee of civil liberties promote democracy? Or does it pose challenges for democratic government that can be considered gates?

Top Ten to Take Away

1. Civil liberties are freedoms so fundamental that they are outside the authority of government to regulate. It often falls to the judiciary to protect them. (pp. 109–110)

2. They include, among others, rights surrounding freedom of expression and criminal procedure, and were written into the Constitution in 1791 as the first ten amendments, or Bill of Rights. (pp. 110–112)

3. Although these protections of individual freedoms at first applied only to the federal government, Supreme Court decisions have gradually applied many of them also to the states. (pp. 112–113)

4. Attempts to limit civil liberties are more frequent in wartime or during other threats, given increased government need for order and increased citizen concern about security. But support for the protection of civil liberties usually rebounds after the crisis ends. (pp. 113–116)

5. The scope of First Amendment freedoms of expression has generally expanded, although during wartime they are likely to be curtailed. (pp. 116–123)

6. Even in wartime, the courts have almost always protected the press from government censorship, but the government can prosecute newspapers for publishing obscenity, secret military information, and articles that incite violence. (pp. 121–123)

7. The First Amendment also protects freedom of religious practice and prevents the government from establishing one religion over all the others. (pp. 123–126)

8. Provisions in the Fourth, Fifth, Sixth, and Eighth Amendments protect individuals accused of crimes in police investigations, trial procedures, and types of punishments. (pp. 127–130)

9. Although the Constitution and its amendments do not explicitly grant a general right to privacy, the Supreme Court has used various constitutional provisions to establish this right, leading to one of the most contentious areas of constitutional law and interpretation. (pp. 130–134)

10. While in the short run the Supreme Court can protect liberties without public approval, in the long run procedures relating to the presidential appointment and Senate approval of justices keeps the Court responsive to the people. (pp. 134–135)

A full narrative summary is on the book's website.

Ten to Test Yourself

1. How have civil liberties fared during times of war or other crises?

2. Why does it fall to the judicial branch to protect civil liberties?

3. What is the selective incorporation doctrine?

4. What is the compelling interest test?

5. What types of speech receive more or less protection by the Supreme Court?

6. In what ways is the concept of "neutrality" important to First Amendment rights?

7. How has the Supreme Court applied the *Lemon* test?

8. What constitutional rights do criminal defendants have during investigations? At trial? During sentencing?

9. What is the constitutional basis for the right to privacy?

10. What rights related to private property are protected by the Constitution?

More review questions and answers and chapter quizzes are on the book's website.

Terms to Know and Use

accommodationists (p. 126)
actual malice test (p. 122)
anarchy (p. 110)
Barron v. Baltimore (p. 111)
Bill of Rights (p. 109)
bills of attainder (p. 110)
Brandenburg v. Ohio (p. 117)
civil liberties (p. 109)
civil rights (p. 109)
clear and present danger test (p. 117)
compelling interest test (p. 112)
content neutral (pp. 120, 121)
due process clause (p. 112)
eminent domain (p. 134)
establishment clause (p. 125)
ex post facto laws (p. 110)
exclusionary rule (p. 129)
expectation of privacy test (p. 128)
fighting words doctrine (p. 117)

free exercise clause (p. 124)
fundamental rights (p. 112)
Geneva Conventions (p. 115)
Gideon v. Wainwright (p. 130)
good faith exception (p. 129)
grand jury (p. 112)
Griswold v. Connecticut (p. 131)
hate speech (p. 117)
incorporate (p. 111)
just compensation (p. 134)
Lawrence v. Texas (p. 133)
Lemon test (p. 125)
libel (p. 122)
Miller test (p. 122)
military tribunal (pp. 114, 115)
Miranda v. Arizona (p. 129)
natural (unalienable) rights (p. 109)
political tolerance (p. 135)
Powell v. Alabama (p. 130)

prior restraint (p. 121)
probable cause (p. 116)
public use (p. 134)
right of association (p. 123)
right to counsel (p. 129)
right to privacy (p. 130)
Roe v. Wade (p. 132)
Sedition Acts (p. 114)
selective incorporation (p. 112)
self-incrimination (p. 129)
separationists (p. 126)
subsequent punishment (p. 122)
symbolic speech (p. 119)
takings clause (p. 134)
test (p. 112)
tyranny (p. 110)
undue burden (p. 132)
valid secular purpose (p. 124)
warrant (p. 116)
writ of *habeas corpus* (p. 110)

Use the vocabulary flash cards on the book's website.

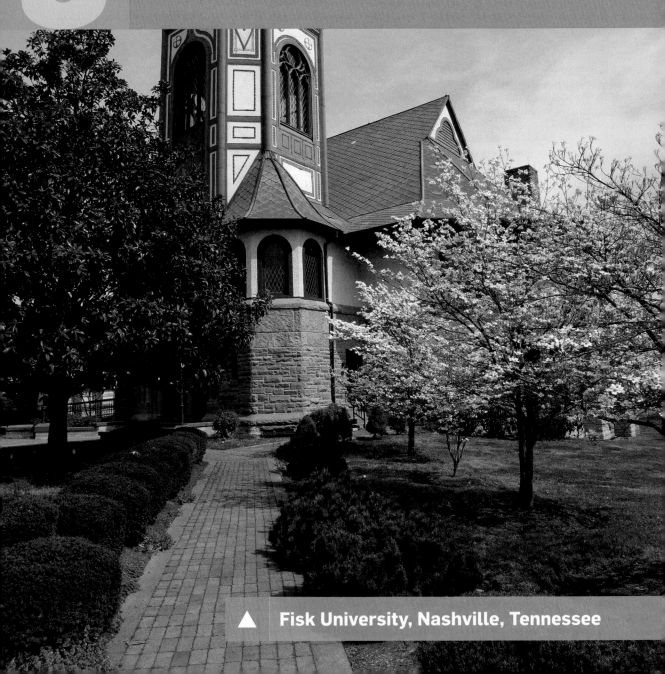

▲ Fisk University, Nashville, Tennessee

> *I think it's really important to realize that each individual shoulders a great deal of responsibility, and that's the way the movement in the 1960s was accomplished.*

In 1956, when Diane Nash went to college, she first chose Howard University in Washington, D.C., where she enrolled as an English major. But she soon transferred to Fisk University, in Nashville, Tennessee. Attending school in the segregated South was something of a shock for this Chicago native. "I understood the facts," she later recalled, but "when I went south and saw the signs that said 'white' and 'colored,' and I actually could not drink out of that water fountain or go to that ladies' room, I had a real emotional reaction." Nashville was more of a shock than Washington, and humiliation turned to outrage.

But the ethic of service that Howard and Fisk promoted in African American students was familiar to Nash, who had grown up in a Catholic family and considered becoming a nun. Instead, while at Fisk, she began attending workshops in social change and Christian nonviolence led by John Lawson, a graduate student in theology at nearby Vanderbilt University, and at the Highlander Folk School, where civil rights leaders such as Rosa Parks and Martin Luther King had received training. When in February 1960 four African American college students in Greensboro, North Carolina, launched a sit-in movement to integrate lunch counters, Diane Nash was ready.

Quickly, Nash organized and trained local students to carry out nonviolent protests at downtown

Diane Nash ▶

CourseMate

Visit http://www.cengagebrain .com/shop/ISBN/0495906190 for interactive tools including:
- Quizzes
- Flashcards
- Videos
- Animated PowerPoint slides, Podcast summaries, and more

lunch counters. Arrested, she spoke eloquently of injustice to the judge. Confronting the mayor of Nashville, she turned his plea for praying together into a case for eating together, and the mayor caved in. After the lunch counters were desegregated, Nash organized college students to replace Freedom Riders who had been beaten while testing the enforcement of desegregation orders on buses and in bus stations across the South. A founding member of the Student Nonviolent Coordinating Committee (SNCC), she left Fisk to become a full-time activist, leading civic education and voting rights campaigns in Mississippi and Alabama.

Twenty years later, reflecting on her role in the civil rights movement, Nash was astonished at her own courage. "I remember realizing that with what we were doing, trying to abolish segregation, we were coming up against governors of seven states, judges, politicians, businessmen, and I remember thinking, 'I'm only 22 years old. What do I know? What am I doing?'" But she also felt "the power of an idea whose time had come." "The movement had a way of reaching inside me and bringing out things that I never knew were there," she continued. "Like courage, and love for people." "I think it's really important," she concluded, "that young people today understand that the movement of the sixties was really a people's movement. . . . Young people should realize that it was people just like them, their age, that formulated the goals and strategies, and actually developed the movement. When they look around now, and see things that need to be changed, they should say: 'What can I do? What can my roommate and I do to effect that change?'"[1]

Fifty years after Nash and young people throughout the South risked their lives for the right to drink at a water fountain, to eat at a lunch counter, and to vote and participate in American civic life, Barack Hussein Obama, the child of a white mother and an African father, was elected president of the United States. An African American president could scarcely have been imagined at the time, but the gateways that civil rights activists like Nash forced open changed American law and politics forever. In this chapter, we examine the changing concept of equality from

FOCUS QUESTIONS

- What is the meaning of equality? How has its meaning changed since the Constitution was written in 1787?

- What role has government played with regard to equality in the past? What role does it assume today?

- What means have various groups used to secure their civil rights? What means has government used to respond?

- What is the effect on a democracy if some of its people lack civil rights?

- Are civil rights a gate or a gateway to democracy? Explain.

exclusive to inclusive and track the changing response and responsibilities of government.

What Are Civil Rights?

Although the Declaration of Independence declared that "All men are created equal," the 1787 Constitution had little to say about equality, at least as the concept is understood today. The Antifederalists insisted on a Bill of Rights that would protect fundamental liberties, but they did not argue for equality. Today equality is a hallowed principle of American political culture, but the notion and the reality evolved slowly, over two centuries.

Civil Rights and Civil Liberties

Civil rights are rights related to the duties of citizenship and the opportunities for participation in civic life that the government is obliged to protect. These rights are based on the expectation of equality under the law. The most important is the right to vote. In contrast to civil rights are **civil liberties**, freedoms so fundamental that government may not legitimately take them away. They are the subject of Chapter 4.

Civil rights also differ from civil liberties in that while government is the only authority that could suppress liberties, for example by suppressing freedom of speech or forbidding a certain religious belief, both government and individuals have the capacity to engage in **discrimination** by treating people unequally: the government through laws that discriminate and individuals or businesses through actions that discriminate.

The government can thus take three different roles when it comes to civil rights. It can engage in state-sponsored or **public discrimination** by actively discriminating against people. It can treat people equally but permit **private discrimination** by allowing individuals or businesses to discriminate. Finally, it can try, as it has since the 1960s, both to treat people equally and to prevent individuals or businesses from discriminating. Thus it falls to government to protect individuals against unequal treatment and to citizens to ensure that the government itself is not discriminating against individuals or groups. In a democracy, the majority rules, but the gateways for minorities must also be kept open.

The Constitution and Civil Rights

Despite the wording in the Declaration of Independence, the role of the government with regard to ensuring equality was not written into the Constitution, and in fact, the United States has a bleak history on civil rights. The

civil rights: *Set of rights, centered around the concept of equal treatment, that government is obliged to protect.*

civil liberties: *Those rights, such as freedom of speech or religion, that are so fundamental that they are outside the authority of government to regulate.*

discrimination: *Favoring one person over another, usually on irrelevant grounds such as race or gender.*

public discrimination: *Discrimination by national, state, or local governments.*

private discrimination: *Discrimination by private individuals or businesses.*

Founders were not much concerned with equality as it is understood today. Many of them owned slaves, and they did not see a contradiction between their doing so and the Declaration's statement on equality. Though the words *slave* and *slavery* do not appear in the Constitution, it endorsed the slave system by requiring states to return runaway slaves and prohibiting any ban on importing slaves from Africa until 1808. The Constitution also gave the states authority over voting, and most states restricted the right to vote to free males with a certain amount of property. Slaves could not vote and, in a few states, free African Americans could not either. Neither could women (except in New Jersey), Native Americans, or, in many states, men without property.[2] During the nation's first century and even thereafter, state laws and the national government actively discriminated against people on the basis of race, gender, and ethnic background.

Following the Civil War, the Thirteenth Amendment ended slavery, and the Fourteenth Amendment forbade states to deny any person "the equal protection of the laws." Nevertheless, the equality of African Americans was not thereby guaranteed. Some who wrote the Fourteenth Amendment believed equality was limited to "the right to go and come; the right to enforce contracts; the right to convey his property; the right to buy property" and little more.[3] The courts agreed, and during the nation's second century, the federal government made little effort to ensure equal treatment.

During these years, however, women won the right to vote (1920) but not the right to full participation in public life. American Indians became citizens (1924), but not until the civil rights and women's movements of the 1950s and 1960s did legal discrimination against African Americans, women, and ethnic minorities end. Today, the government actively aims to treat individuals and groups as equals before the law and to use its authority to prevent state and local governments and individuals and businesses from discriminating.

In the last half-century, the meaning of "all men are created equal" has been expanded to include women and all people subject to the jurisdiction of the United States. Americans now look to the government to protect equality and enforce equal treatment under the law. But they still debate the meaning of equality. Should, or can, the government ensure **equality of opportunity** for all people? Should, or can, it engineer **equality of outcome**? That is, is it enough for society to provide equality of opportunity by prohibiting discrimination? What if that still leaves members of groups that have historically been discriminated against, such as women and minorities, with fewer advanced degrees and lower incomes? As it has throughout the course of the nation's history, the meaning of equality continues to evolve.

In the next sections, we will see how, as the idea of equality expanded, the federal government moved from actively treating different groups unequally

What did equality mean to the Founders?

equality of opportunity: *Expectation that citizens may not be discriminated against on account of race, gender, or national background, and that every citizen should have an equal chance to succeed in life.*

equality of outcome: *Expectation that equality is achieved if results are comparable for all citizens regardless of race, gender, or national background, or that such groups are proportionally represented in measures of success in life.*

What is your idea of equality—equality of opportunity or equality of outcome?

under the law, to asserting equality under the law but doing little to protect it, to actively enforcing it. Equality of rights is now a central feature of the Constitution and the Court's interpretation of it.[4]

Legal Restrictions on Civil Rights

Slavery split the United States from the founding of the nation through the Civil War. Following the Civil War, the Constitution prohibited slavery. It also prohibited the states from denying equality, but many states continued to discriminate. Both Congress and the Supreme Court had the authority to enforce equality, but neither took action to do so. Women as well as African Americans suffered under unequal laws, with denial of the right to vote and laws that limited their full participation in labor markets, professions, and public life. Discriminatory laws also affected Asians, as laws prohibited those who were not born in the United States from becoming citizens and later prevented them from immigrating to the United States altogether. As exemplified by the internment of Japanese Americans during World War II, government restrictions on the civil rights of ethnic minorities are far more likely during wartime.

Slavery

The compromises made at the Constitutional Convention allowed the United States to form, but they also allowed slavery to grow and spread. By 1808, when Congress banned the further importation of slaves from Africa, the slave population had reached one million and continued growing thereafter through natural increase. With neither slave nor free forces dominant politically, Congress continued the path of compromise: the **Missouri Compromise** (1820) banned slavery in the territories that were north of the southern border of Missouri, thus keeping most of the vast lands in the Louisiana Purchase free; the Compromise of 1850 allowed territories captured in the Mexican War to decide for themselves whether to be free or slave-holding and denied alleged fugitive slaves the right to a jury trial; the Kansas-Nebraska Act (1854) undid the Missouri Compromise by allowing each territory to vote whether to allow slavery or not. The Supreme Court further extended the reach of slavery in *Dred Scott v. Sandford* (1857).[5]

Dred Scott, a slave who had moved with his master from the slave state of Missouri to the free Wisconsin Territory and then back to Missouri, sued in federal court for his freedom based on his extended stay in free territory. The Supreme Court's decision in the case, written by Chief Justice

Missouri Compromise (1820): *Prohibited slavery in territories north of the southern border of Missouri.*

Dred Scott v. Sandford (1857): *Supreme Court decision declaring that blacks could not be citizens and Congress could not ban slavery in the territories.*

What is the role of compromise in American politics?

In 1846, Dred Scott, a black slave and household servant, sued for his freedom, claiming that since his owner had taken him to a free territory, he should be free. The Supreme Court said no, and went further to say that Scott, as an African American, had no standing to sue, and that Congress could not prohibit slavery in any territory. The ruling, handed down in 1857, pleased southerners but infuriated northerners.

Emancipation Proclamation (1863): *Lincoln's order ending slavery in states in rebellion.*

Roger Taney, a former slave owner, declared: (1) that no black—slave or free—could be an American citizen, and thus could not sue in a federal court; (2) that blacks were "beings of an inferior order" who had "no rights which the white man was bound to respect"; (3) that the Declaration's statement that "all men are created equal" did not include those of African heritage; (4) that Congress's authority to "make all needful Rules and Regulations respecting the Territory . . . of the United States" did not include the right to prohibit slavery in those territories; and (5) that slaves were the property of their owners, so freeing Scott would violate his owner's Fifth Amendment right against being deprived of his property without due process of law. With this decision, the regulation of slavery was out of the national hands of Congress and into the local hands of states and territories.

The 1860 election of Abraham Lincoln (1861–65), who opposed the extension of slavery, prompted southern states to secede from the union. During the ensuing Civil War, Lincoln issued the **Emancipation Proclamation**, which made slavery illegal in those states in rebellion as of January 1, 1863. Slavery was finally ended in the United States following Union victory and ratification of the Thirteenth Amendment in 1865 (see Figure 5.1).

Racial Segregation and Discrimination

The end of slavery did not, however, make former slaves equal citizens. Immediately after the war, southern states wrote new constitutions that severely limited the civil and political rights of freedmen. These so-called **black codes** prevented freedmen from voting, owning land, or leaving their plantations. Congress responded with the Civil Rights Act of 1866, which guaranteed the right of freedmen to make contracts, sue in court if those contracts were violated, and own property. Congress also established military rule over the former Confederate states, which would end when a state passed a new state constitution that guaranteed black suffrage and when it ratified the Fourteenth Amendment. With former Confederates barred from voting, blacks constituted a majority of the electorate in several states, and more than 600 freedmen served in state legislatures during **Reconstruction**.

The Fourteenth Amendment (1868), in addition to guaranteeing that no state shall deny any person due process of law (see Chapter 4), prohibits

FIGURE 5.1 **Constitutional Amendments That Pertain to Civil Rights.**

Color Code :

Criminal procedure   Participation   Equality

Thirteenth (1865): Prohibits slavery in the United States

Fourteenth (1868): Makes all persons born in the United States citizens of the United States, and prohibits states from denying persons within its jurisdiction the privileges or immunities of citizens, the due process of law, and equal protection of the laws; apportionment by whole persons

Fifteenth (1870): Prohibits states from denying the right to vote on account of race

Nineteenth (1920): Guarantees women the right to vote

Twenty-Fourth (1964): Prohibits poll taxes

states from denying any person the equal protection of the law. It also makes all people born in the United States citizens of the United States, overturning the Supreme Court's ruling in the *Dred Scott* case that blacks could not be U.S. citizens. In an attempt to prevent states from rescinding the right of black suffrage, the Fifteenth Amendment (1870) declared that the right to vote could not be abridged on account of race.

Opponents of freedmen rights turned to violence. In 1866, Confederate veterans formed the **Ku Klux Klan** (KKK), a terrorist organization aimed at restoring white supremacy. In 1873, white supremacists massacred more than 100 blacks in Colfax, Louisiana, as part of an ongoing election dispute. The federal government brought charges against three of the perpetrators, but the Supreme Court reversed their conviction, arguing that the Fourteenth Amendment gave Congress the authority to act only against states that violated civil rights (public discrimination), not against individuals who did so (private discrimination).[6]

Reconstruction ended with a deal over the 1876 election. A close and contested race between Republican Rutherford B. Hayes and Democrat Samuel Tilden was resolved when southern Democrats in Congress agreed to Hayes becoming president in return for the withdrawal of federal troops from the South.

Freed from military rule, white supremacist groups such as the Klan embarked on a campaign of lynching and other forms of terrorism against blacks. State governments were not responsive to the victims of this terrorist campaign, because despite the Fifteenth Amendment, southern politicians established a set of rules that kept blacks from voting. **Poll taxes** limited the voting of poor blacks (as well as poor whites). The **white primary** took advantage of the fact that, with the Republican Party negatively associated with Lincoln and the Civil War, the Democratic Party completely dominated

black codes: *Southern laws that prohibited freedmen from voting, owning land, or leaving their plantations.*

Reconstruction (1865–77): *Period in which the former Confederate states gained readmission to the Union and the federal government passed laws to help the emancipated slaves.*

After ratification of the Fifteenth Amendment, who could not vote?

Ku Klux Klan: *White supremacist terrorist organization.*

poll taxes: *Tax on voting, prohibited by the Twenty-Fourth Amendment (1964).*

white primary: *Election rules that prohibited blacks from voting in Democratic primaries.*

South Carolina Dept. of Archives and History

In segregated school systems, the schools for black children and for white children were almost never equal. These insurance photographs show Liberty Hill Colored School and Summerton Graded School in Clarendon County, South Carolina, 1948. They were used as evidence in *Briggs v. Elliott,* one of the five school segregation cases decided with *Brown v. Board of Education* (1954).

southern politics. Therefore whoever won the local Democratic primary for any office was sure to win in the general election. Excluding blacks from Democratic primaries meant that blacks had no effective vote at all. Even so, states used **literacy tests** to disqualify voters. These involved reading and interpreting difficult passages. To avoid thereby disqualifying white voters as well, **grandfather clauses** gave exemptions to those whose grandfathers had been eligible to vote. Those who received these exemptions were, of course, always white.

These legal strategies effectively disfranchised black men. In addition, state and local laws, called **Jim Crow laws**, enforced segregation of whites and blacks in all public places. When a New Orleans civil rights organization challenged a Louisiana law requiring segregated railway cars by having Homer Plessy, who was one-eighth black, sit in the whites-only section, the Supreme Court upheld the segregation.[7] *Plessy v. Ferguson* (1896)[8] established the **separate-but-equal doctrine**, which held that states could segregate the races without violating the equal protection clause of the Fourteenth Amendment as long as the separate facilities were equal. Southern states segregated schools, libraries, and other public institutions, and required the segregation of restaurants, inns, and other places of public accommodation. The facilities were almost never equal. In northern states, African Americans often experienced discrimination in hiring, housing, hotels, and restaurants, though segregation was not enforced by law. African Americans could serve in the military, but generally in segregated units under white officers. During the late nineteenth and early twentieth centuries, discrimination was state-sponsored in the South; elsewhere in the nation, people engaged in private discrimination without challenge.

Other ethnic groups besides blacks suffered discrimination, too. California's 1879 Constitution prohibited Chinese from voting or employment in state or local government. Three years later, the **Chinese Exclusion Act** prohibited Chinese immigration. In 1913, California prohibited Japanese immigrants from purchasing farmland.[9] Segregation in the South often placed Hispanics in the same position as African Americans. Segregation also existed in the West. Phoenix, Arizona, ran separate schools for blacks, Indians, and Mexicans.[10] California ran separate schools for Asians as well as Mexicans,[11] while Texas kept Mexican Americans in separate classrooms.[12]

Women's Suffrage

By law and by custom, women were also excluded from public life, from the earliest days of the nation. Neither the Declaration nor the Constitution made any provision for women's rights. Rather, the states continued the English policy of **coverture**, which granted married women no rights independent of their husbands. They could not own property, keep their own wages, or sign contracts. As for voting, each state set its own rules. In 1789, only New Jersey allowed women the right to vote (provided the women met the state's property requirements), a right it rescinded in 1807.[13]

In 1848, leaders of the **women's suffrage** movement met in Seneca Falls, New York, to organize for the right to vote. They prepared a "Declaration of Sentiments" that used the language of the Declaration of Independence to assert that "all men and women are created equal," but little in the way of results came from this meeting. Then, in 1869, Susan B. Anthony and Elizabeth Cady Stanton formed the National Woman Suffrage Association (NWSA), which lobbied for the right of women to vote and unsuccessfully opposed the Fifteenth Amendment unless it was changed to include women's suffrage. With the NWSA focused on gaining national suffrage through constitutional amendment, an alternative organization, the American Woman Suffrage Association (AWSA), formed to press for state-by-state suffrage rights.

In 1872, a Missouri voting registrar prohibited suffragist Virginia Minor from registering to vote. Minor sued, alleging that the privileges of citizenship, as guaranteed by the Fourteenth Amendment, included the right to vote. The Supreme Court ruled, however, that citizenship does not imply a right to vote.[14] With the courts rejecting a gateway to voting through the Fourteenth Amendment, suffragists focused on the legislative arena.

While state control of voting gave southern states the power to disenfranchise blacks, it also gave western states the power to experiment with women's suffrage. The territory of Wyoming granted women's suffrage in 1869, which continued upon statehood in 1890. Males in Colorado voted for

literacy tests: *Tests requiring reading and interpretation skills in order to vote.*

grandfather clauses: *Election rules that exempted people from difficult literacy and interpretation tests for voting if their grandfathers had been eligible to vote.*

Jim Crow laws: *Southern laws that established strict segregation of the races.*

Plessy v. Ferguson (1896): *Supreme Court case that upheld validity of segregation.*

separate-but-equal doctrine: *Supreme Court doctrine that upheld segregation as long as there were equivalent facilities for blacks.*

Chinese Exclusion Act (1882): *Barred immigration of Chinese to America.*

coverture: *Legal doctrine that grants married women no rights independent of their husbands.*

women's suffrage: *Movement to grant women the right to vote.*

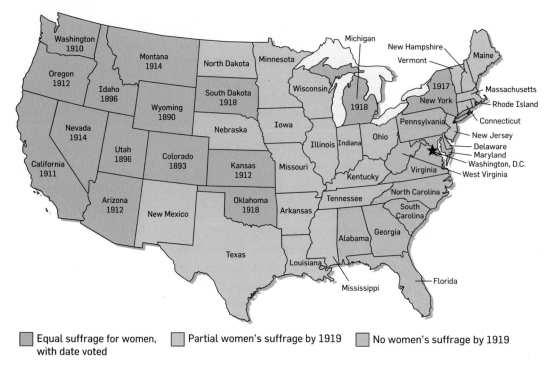

FIGURE 5.2 **Women's Suffrage by States, 1890–1919.** Because states control voting laws, women's suffrage advocates campaigned at the state level, and before the Nineteenth Amendment was ratified in 1920 women could vote in some elections in most states. The Nineteenth Amendment superseded state law, stating that the right to vote could not be denied or abridged by the United States, or by any state, on account of sex.
Source: Sandra Opdycke, *The Routledge Historical Atlas of Women* (New York: Routledge, 2000), 82.

women's suffrage in 1893. Utah granted women the right to vote in 1895. In 1913, Illinois granted women the right to vote for president, but not other national offices. In 1916, the people of Montana elected the first woman to serve in the U.S. House of Representatives, Jeannette Rankin (see Figure 5.2).

Suffragist amendments failed numerous times in Congress before receiving the necessary two-thirds vote in both chambers in 1919.[15] By August 1920, with effective lobbying by suffragist groups, three-quarters of the states ratified the Nineteenth Amendment, guaranteeing women the right to vote in the November 1920 presidential election.

Continued Gender Discrimination

Nevertheless, public law and private attitudes continued to block women from full participation in the nation's public life. Radical feminists pushed for an equal rights amendment, which would have overturned protective legislation and other laws that treated men and women differently, but though introduced in Congress in 1923 and every year thereafter, it was not taken seriously. Even as late as 1945, only a minority of white males thought that women should be able to take jobs outside the home.[16]

Should there be an equal rights amendment?

Not surprisingly, the federal and state governments were responsive to these sorts of views. As late as 1972, eleven states continued to enforce coverture laws.[17] Louisiana law, for example, gave a husband "as 'head and master' of property jointly owned with his wife," the complete right to dispose of such property without his wife's consent.[18] Teachers were commonly forced to "retire" if they got married.[19] Outside of coverture laws, Social Security provided survivors benefits for children whose working fathers died, but not if their working mothers died. It similarly provided unemployment benefits to children of unemployed fathers, but not to children of unemployed mothers. Because women were treated differently than men under the law, many laws also discriminated against men. Colorado allowed females to drink beer at age 18; males had to wait until 21. California, like many states, made it a crime for males of any age to have sexual relations with females under the age of 18, but had no corresponding penalty for females having sexual relations with underage males. Many of these laws were based on an implicit assumption that women, viewed as the weaker sex, needed special protection from the government.[20] As late as 1961, the Supreme Court exempted women from jury duty because they were "the center of home and family life."[21]

Restrictions on Citizenship

In the case of both African Americans and women, the status of **citizenship** did not guarantee the right to vote or serve on juries. Yet, on the basis of ethnic background some groups were denied even the status of citizenship and the privileges it entailed. For example, under the Fourteenth Amendment's **privileges or immunities clause**, state laws curtailed rights that other citizens held.

citizenship: *Full-fledged membership in a nation.*

privileges or immunities clause (Fourteenth Amendment): *Prohibits states from abridging certain fundamental rights.*

Citizenship in the Constitution. The Constitution was not explicit on birthright citizenship, but the clause requiring that presidents be **natural-born citizens** seemingly implies that people born in the United States would be citizens.[22] But the *Dred Scott* ruling, until overturned by the Fourteenth Amendment, belied that assumption, as did the status of American Indians.

natural-born citizens: *People who are citizens in a nation from birth, usually by being born there.*

In 1823, the Supreme Court declared that Indians were merely inhabitants, "an inferior race of people, without the privileges of citizens."[23] The Fourteenth Amendment's citizenship clause did not remedy this situation: the

Court ruled in 1884 that the clause did not provide citizenship to Native Americans born on reservations because reservations are not fully under the jurisdiction of the United States.[24] Not until the Indian Citizenship Act of 1924 did Congress provide natural-born citizenship to Native Americans born on reservations.

Should all citizens have the right to vote? Are there any citizens who should not have this right?

Naturalization. The Constitution explicitly allows those not born in the United States to become citizens through **naturalization** by granting Congress the authority "to establish a uniform rule of naturalization."

naturalization: *Acquired citizenship through formal application procedures.*

Congress's first such law, the Naturalization Act of 1790, restricted citizenship to "free white persons" who had lived in the United States for two years, swore allegiance to the United States, and had "good character." Though restrictive on race, the act allowed Catholics, Jews, and other "free white persons" to become naturalized citizens, rights that most European nations did not allow. The act also declared people born overseas to parents of U.S. citizens to be natural-born citizens.

Congress first allowed nonwhites to become naturalized citizens in 1870, when it extended naturalization to "persons of African descent." Asians, however, still could not become naturalized citizens. Indeed, fear of Chinese immigrants led to an 1882 prohibition on the immigration of Chinese to America. That ban was the first significant restriction on immigration to the United States. Congress extended this ban to all Asians in 1921. The ban stayed in effect until 1943, when Congress allowed an annual quota of 105 immigrants from China, a World War II ally. The 1943 act also allowed Chinese to become naturalized citizens, but did not allow other Asians to do so. Congress ended this restriction on Asian naturalization in 1952, but kept strict limits on the number of Asian immigrants until 1965.

Who should be a citizen?

The Immigration Act of 1924 placed quotas for ethnic groups based on the proportion of Americans from each nationality resident in 1890, thereby severely limiting the number of whites considered to be of "lower race," that is, those from southern and eastern Europe.[25] Under the act, the quota for Italy, for example, dropped more than 90 percent.[26]

In 1952, President Harry Truman (1945–53), claiming that such quotas were un-American, vetoed a bill that continued the national quota system, but Congress overrode his veto. With the Immigration and Nationality Act of 1965, Congress rescinded the quota system and the especially severe restrictions on Asian immigration. Today, to apply for citizenship, one must have had legal permanent residence for five years, or three years if married to a U.S. citizen. Applicants also must be of good moral character and be able to pass a test on questions such as "who elects the president?" (Table 5.1, see if you can pass it).

What restrictions, if any, should there be on immigration?

TABLE 5.1 Questions on the Citizenship Test

The U.S. Bureau of Citizenship and Immigration Services administers a citizenship test to applicants for naturalization. Here is a sampling of the questions from the "American Government" section of the test. There is also a section on "American History" and a section on "Integrated Civics."

1. What is the supreme law of the land?

2. What does the Constitution do?

3. The idea of self-government is in the first three words of the Constitution. What are these words?

4. What is an amendment?

5. What do we call the first ten amendments to the Constitution?

6. What is one right or freedom from the First Amendment?

7. How many amendments does the Constitution have?

8. What did the Declaration of Independence do?

9. What are two rights in the Declaration of Independence?

10. What is freedom of religion?

Source: More questions plus the answers at http://usgovinfo.about.com/library/blinstst_new.htm.

Restraints during Wartime

As noted in Chapter 4, civil liberties suffer during wartime because the balance between freedom and order pushes toward order when survival is at stake. When the wartime enemy is racially or ethnically distinct from the majority of the American people, civil rights are also likely to suffer.

Two months after the Japanese attack on Pearl Harbor, President Franklin Roosevelt (1933–45) issued an executive order for the evacuation of all 110,000 people of Japanese ancestry who resided west of the Rocky Mountains—whether citizen (most of them) or alien—and their placement in relocation camps. Congress ratified the president's order, and in 1944 the Supreme Court endorsed it in *Korematsu v. United States*, ruling that the authority for relocation was within the war power of the United States.[27]

Although the government justified the program on the grounds of military necessity as opposed to racial animosity, it did not attempt wholesale roundups of German Americans despite the existence of the German American Bund, a pro-Nazi association that before the war had about 20,000 members. That the government even rounded up Japanese American children from orphanages suggests racial animosity was more important than security

Korematsu v. United States (1944): Supreme Court decision upholding the detention of Japanese Americans during World War II.

concerns.[28] The program remained in effect through the war years, although the government filed no charges of disloyalty or subversion against any person of Japanese ancestry. Indeed, many Japanese Americans valiantly served the United States during the war in segregated military units.

After the terrorist attacks of September 11, 2001, which were carried out by Muslim Arabs, other Arabs and Muslims in the United States came under suspicion. The government immediately rounded up and detained more than 5,000 immigrants, most from Muslim or Middle Eastern countries. Of these detainees, three were convicted of terrorism-related crimes unrelated to 9/11, but two of those had their convictions overturned.[29] None of the other detainees had terrorism-related charges brought against them.

The Expansion of Equal Protection

Today the public discrimination documented in the previous section has been ended by acts of Congress, constitutional amendments, and court decisions, and no clause has been so powerful in this effort as the **equal protection clause** of the Fourteenth Amendment, which prohibits states from denying any person the equal protection of the law. The amendment then gives Congress the authority to enforce its provisions by appropriate legislation, adding to Congress's enumerated powers by allowing Congress to pass laws that prevent states from discriminating. Additionally, the Supreme Court, through the power of judicial review, retains the authority to strike down state laws that violate equal protection. Thus the federal government has a crucial role in the push for equality. This brief section pauses to examine equal protection before we continue the account of how the U.S. government shifted from engaging in discrimination to protecting against it.

The Changing Meaning of Equality

Equality had a very different meaning in 1776 than it does today. With the civil rights movement following World War II came a push to end state-sponsored segregation and then private discrimination in businesses and public accommodations. The equality of opportunity goal of that era has been superseded, among civil rights activists, to a goal for an equality of outcome, wherein economic well-being should be roughly equal and various sectors of the professions should be roughly proportional to each group's proportion of the population.

State Action

Shortly after the passage of the Fourteenth Amendment, Congress tried banning private discrimination at inns, public conveyances, theaters, and other public places. The Supreme Court rejected congressional authority to do so

Does military necessity overrule civil rights? If so, under what circumstances?

equal protection clause (Fourteenth Amendment): *Prevents states from denying any person the equal protection of the laws.*

in the *Civil Rights Cases* (1883), ruling that the Fourteenth Amendment only prohibited public discrimination by the states, not private discrimination by business or individuals.

In 1948, however, the Court ruled that private discrimination can be prohibited if it involves significant **state action**. The case at issue involved housing. A group of homeowners signed a contract pledging never to sell their homes to blacks, but one of the homeowners did so. The neighbors sued to prevent the new owners from taking possession of the house, and the state supreme court ruled in favor of the neighbors. The U.S. Supreme Court reversed the state supreme court, ruling that judicial enforcement of the discriminatory private contract constitutes state action and thus is prohibited by the Fourteenth Amendment.[30]

Judicial Review

While the state-action doctrine allowed the Supreme Court to prohibit limited types of private discrimination, the equal protection clause of the Fourteenth Amendment is better suited to fighting public discrimination. In the next two decades, the Supreme Court actively applied the equal protection clause of the Fourteenth Amendment to do so. Congress also has the authority to enforce the equal protection clause, but democratically elected legislatures and executives are not necessarily designed to be responsive to minority groups, for they are chosen by a majority of voters. Thus civil rights organizations such as the **National Association for the Advancement of Colored People** (NAACP) turned to the judiciary, whose members are not elected and thus do not directly depend on majority support, for assistance in establishing legal equality. Congress later wrote protections of civil rights into law.

As with civil liberties issues, for which the Court uses the standard of **compelling interest** (see Chapter 4), in civil rights cases the Court has constructed **tests** to determine whether laws violate the equal protection clause. Depending upon the group whose right has been violated, the Court sets different standards of how closely it will scrutinize the law alleged to violate equal protection. There are at least three levels. The Court reserves the toughest standard of review, **strict scrutiny**, for laws alleged to discriminate on account of race, ethnicity, religion, or status as an alien. It uses mid-level or **heightened scrutiny** for laws that discriminate on account of sex, and the lowest level of scrutiny, **rational basis**, for general claims of discrimination (see Table 5.2).

We now turn to an examination of how grassroots movements pressured the courts to be the protector of civil rights as well as civil liberties, and how Congress enforced court rulings with legislation. As with civil liberties (see Chapter 4), however, finding the right balance of rights

Civil Rights Cases (1883): *Limited congressional authority to prohibit private discrimination under the Fourteenth Amendment.*

state action: *Action by a state, as opposed to a private person, that constitutes discrimination and therefore is an equal protection violation.*

National Association for the Advancement of Colored People (NAACP): *Civil rights organization dedicated to helping African Americans.*

compelling interest test: *Standard frequently used by the Supreme Court in civil rights cases to determine if a state has a sufficient justification for making distinctions on account of race, ethnicity, religion, or citizenship status.*

tests: *Standards used by the courts to determine whether a law or right has been violated across a range of cases.*

strict scrutiny: *Toughest standard of review, used when laws discriminate on account of race, ethnicity, religion, or alienage.*

heightened scrutiny: *Standard of review used when laws discriminate on account of sex.*

rational basis: *Lowest standard of review, used when laws discriminate against groups that do not receive strict or heightened scrutiny.*

TABLE 5.2 Supreme Court Scrutiny in Equal Protection Cases

Claim of Discrimination	Standard of Review	Test
Unprotected Category	Lowest	Rational basis to achieve a legitimate governmental objective
Sex	Heightened	Exceedingly persuasive justification; use of sex as a governmental category must be substantially related to important governmental objectives
Race, Ethnicity, Religion, and Alienage	Strict	Most rigid scrutiny; use of race as a governmental category must be precisely tailored to meet a compelling governmental interest

to provide minority groups frequently divides members of society from one another, and democratically responsive legislatures from lifetime-appointed judges.

The End of Legal Restrictions on Civil Rights

It is important to understand that the course of events that brought about the government's shift from enforcing discrimination to protecting against it did not begin with the government. It began with pressure from groups that were discriminated against mobilizing on their own behalf. This gateway of public pressure generally involves the use of civil liberties such as freedom of speech and of assembly to engage in protests and other activities aside from voting, because minority groups, by definition, do not have the numbers to change policies through the ballot box alone.

The African American soldiers and sailors who fought for freedom in World War II against totalitarian regimes in Nazi Germany, fascist Italy, and imperial Japan often returned uneasily to hometowns, particularly in the South, where segregation remained the law. The three largest legal barriers African Americans faced in the post–World War II era were state-sponsored segregation of "separate-but-equal" public facilities, such as schools and buses; the legal right of private businesses to discriminate, that is, the right not to serve customers or hire people on account of race; and effective pro-hibitions on the right to vote, such as discriminatorily enforced literacy tests. These gates blocking full civic participation existed throughout the United States, but most prevalently in the former slave states. After we trace the

African American struggle for equal rights, we turn to the women's movement, which likewise pressured the government to dismantle gender-based discrimination.

What gateways did citizens use to end segregation?

Dismantling Public Discrimination Based on Race

Among the most consequential forms of segregation from the Jim Crow era was the mandatory separation of schools for whites and blacks. Beginning in 1935, the NAACP's Legal Defense Fund embarked on a legal campaign—led by Thurgood Marshall, who would later become the first African American to serve on the Supreme Court—to dismantle the system of separate-but-equal schools in southern and border states that were always separate but rarely equal. After a series of cases in which the Supreme Court struck down specific segregated schools because they were not equal,[31] the Court ruled more generally in *Brown v. Board of Education* (1954) that separate schools were inherently unequal, even should facilities be essentially similar (see Supreme Court Cases: *Brown v. Board of Education*). Segregation in schools violated the equal protection clause of the Fourteenth Amendment. The Fourteenth Amendment only requires that states provide equal protection of the laws, but on the same day as the *Brown* decision, the Supreme Court used the due process clause of the Fifth Amendment to prohibit the national government from denying equal protection.[32]

Brown v. Board of Education (1954): *Supreme Court decision striking down segregated schools.*

As historic as the *Brown* decision was, the case by itself did little to desegregate southern schools. Part of the problem was that the Court allowed local circumstances to influence the rate of integration, ambiguously requiring that local districts desegregate "with all deliberate speed."[33] Further, southern segregationists launched a plan of massive resistance to the *Brown* decision. This campaign included "The Southern Manifesto," a document signed by 101 southern members of Congress deploring the *Brown* decision; the denial of state funds to any integrated school; and tuition grants for white students to attend segregated private schools. In addition, unruly segregationist mobs threatened black students seeking to integrate previously white schools. While neither the Supreme Court nor the Eisenhower administration (1953–61) could prevent every school disruption by segregationist mobs, both intervened in Little Rock, Arkansas. Eisenhower federalized the Arkansas National Guard and sent in the 101st Airborne to protect the black students seeking to integrate Central High School, while the Supreme Court, declaring that it had the final say on what the Constitution means, rejected the threat of violence as a justification for delaying segregation.[34]

Chapter 3 asked what has been the relationship between federalism and the push for equality. What was your answer?

At the college level, President John Kennedy (1961–63) had to send 25,000 federal troops to ensure the enrollment of one black man, James Meredith, at the University of Mississippi in 1962. The following year, segregationist Governor George Wallace of Alabama famously "stood at the schoolhouse"

supremecourtcases
Brown v. Board of Education (1954)

QUESTION: Can states provide segregated schools for black and white schoolchildren?

ORAL ARGUMENT: December 7–9, 1953

DECISION: May 17, 1954 (read at http://www.findlaw.com/CaseCode/supreme.html)

OUTCOME: No, separate educational facilities are inherently unequal (9–0).

Linda Brown lived seven blocks from Sumner Elementary School, but the state of Kansas would not let her go to school there, as Sumner was for whites only. Because Linda was black, the state decreed that she go to Monroe School, which was about a mile away. Linda had to leave her house by 7:40 a.m. to reach the bus stop by 8:00, crossing dangerous railroad yards along the way. When Linda was in third grade, her father, with the help of the NAACP, brought a suit against the Topeka school board for refusing to allow Linda to attend the local school that white children in Brown's neighborhood attended.

The Supreme Court's 1896 decision dealing with segregation declared that the Fourteenth Amendment, which prohibits states from denying any person "the equal protection of the laws," did not prohibit the states from establishing "separate-but-equal" facilities for whites and blacks.* The Court did not really begin to look at whether the facilities were equal or not until 1938, however, when it held that Missouri's paying for blacks to go to law school out of state was not the same as providing facilities within the

state that were equal to its white law school.** A pair of 1950 cases declared, first, that admitting a black to an all-white school but forcing him to sit in a separate row and dine at a separate table was unconstitutional,† and second, that the equality of separate schools had to be compared on both objective factors that could be measured, such as the number of faculty, and subjective factors that could not be, such as the reputation of the faculty.††

The *Brown* case came to the Supreme Court with similar desegregation cases from South Carolina, Virginia, Delaware, and Washington, D.C. Thurgood Marshall, who headed legal strategy for the NAACP and would later become the first African American to serve on the Supreme Court, argued the case for Brown. John W. Davis, a West Virginian who ran unsuccessfully as the Democratic candidate for president in 1924, represented two of the states fighting desegregation. Marshall readily admitted that the schools in Linda Brown's case were roughly equal in objective characteristics but argued that segregation in and of itself denied black students the equal protection of the laws, because it created the feeling of inferiority among black schoolchildren.

The Supreme Court's preliminary vote following the arguments showed a majority for striking down segregation, with two or three dissenters. Chief Justice Earl Warren, however, thought that a decision that

---

* *Plessy v. Ferguson*, 163 U.S. 537 (1896).

** *Missouri ex rel. Gaines v. Canada*, 305 U.S. 337 (1938).

† *McLaurin v. Oklahoma*, 339 U.S. 637 (1950).

†† *Sweatt v. Painter*, 339 U.S. 629 (1950).

was bound to be met with resistance in the South should be unanimous if at all possible. Following several months of bargaining and persuasion, he eventually got every member of the Court to agree that the Court should strike down school segregation.

Based on the precedent established in *Brown*, the Supreme Court later struck down mandated segregation in all state or local government activities.

- **Can separate schools ever be equal?**
- **Why were the courts more likely to be responsive to the problems of segregated schools than the legislature?**

door to prevent two black students from registering at the University of Alabama. He stepped aside only when Kennedy again sent troops to enforce integration.

Nevertheless, with few blacks able to vote, there was little need for southern politicians or school board officials to be responsive to their concerns, especially given massive opposition to desegregation by those who could vote. Only when the federal government took action did states respond. After Congress cut off federal aid to segregated schools in 1964, many districts began to integrate.[35] The rate of integration increased further in the late 1960s, when the Supreme Court ended the "all deliberate speed" era and required an immediate end to segregated schools, thus pushing open the gateways to greater equality.[36]

Outside of schools, civil rights activists fought segregation in public facilities. The first grassroots action to receive nationwide attention was a bus boycott in Montgomery, Alabama. On December 1, 1955, police arrested Rosa Parks, a 42-year-old black seamstress and active member of the NAACP, for refusing to give her seat to a white person. In response, the black community, led by a 26-year-old Baptist minister, Martin Luther King, Jr., launched a boycott of city buses. Blacks walked, bicycled, and shared rides to avoid using the Montgomery bus system. Although the city arrested boycotters and terrorists firebombed King's home, the boycotters held firm for over a year. The Supreme Court then declared Montogomery's segregated bus system unconstitutional.[37] A new ordinance allowing blacks to sit anywhere on any bus ended the boycott. King became one of the national leaders of the emerging **civil rights movement**, and Rosa Parks its first heroine.

With the *Brown* precedent in hand, the Supreme Court struck down state-mandated segregation not only in public transportation but also in other public facilities, such as beaches and city auditoriums. Given the massive

AP Photo/Montgomery County Sheriff's office

When Rosa Parks was arrested, the black community of Montgomery quickly mobilized to plan a boycott of city buses.

civil rights movement:
Movement following World War II to gain equal rights for African Americans, later expanded to end discrimination on account of race, gender, sexual preference, and disability status.

opposition to the *Brown* decision, however, the Court refused to hear the appeal by a black woman sentenced to prison for the crime of marrying a white man.[38] As one justice reportedly said when the Court rejected another interracial marriage case, "One bombshell at a time is enough."[39] Not until 1967, in **Loving v. Virginia** did the Court strike down **miscegenation**,[40] finding no compelling interest in a law that prohibited interracial marriage.

Dismantling Private Discrimination Based on Race

The decisions of businesses over whether to serve customers or hire workers on account of their race (or sex) was largely beyond judicial authority, because the Fourteenth Amendment's equal protection clause only prevents states from discriminating; it does not bar private discrimination. Thus, if a restaurant chose not to serve blacks, or an employer chose not to hire them, there was little a court could do unless Congress passed legislation forbidding such actions. The effort to dismantle private discrimination thus took two tracks: protests to pressure businesses into serving blacks, and lobbying to pressure Congress into passing legislation that would make private discrimination in commercial matters illegal.

The grassroots protests began when four African American freshmen at North Carolina Agricultural and Technical College sat down at the whites-only counter at Woolworth's, asked for coffee, and refused to leave when not served. Within weeks, the sit-ins spread to dozens of other cities, with Diane Nash leading Nashville's protests. Tens of thousands participated in sit-ins, and thousands were arrested.[41] Nash and other young participants in these protests formed the Student Nonviolent Coordinating Committee (SNCC).

In the spring of 1963, Martin Luther King's Southern Christian Leadership Conference (SCLC) led demonstrations in Birmingham, Alabama, to bring about the integration of downtown businesses. The police met demonstrators with fire hoses, police dogs, and cattle prods. Police arrested hundreds of protesters, including King. When white clergymen questioned why King, an outsider, had come to Birmingham, King answered in his famous letter from Birmingham Jail, "I am in Birmingham because injustice is here."[42] Rejecting violence, King insisted that peaceful **civil disobedience** was the only gateway to negotiation. Those negotiations ended with Birmingham businesses agreeing to integrate lunch counters and hire more blacks. Nevertheless, or perhaps because of this, KKK members exploded a bomb at a local black church on a Sunday morning, murdering four girls.

Earlier that summer, King had led 200,000 protesters at the March on Washington. It was there that King delivered his historic "I Have a Dream" speech, in which he declared

Loving v. Virginia (1967): *Supreme Court case striking down laws that prohibit racial intermarriage.*

miscegenation: *Interracial marriage and/or sexual intercourse, often forbidden by state law until* Loving v. Virginia.

What is more important—equality or freedom of association?

civil disobedience: *Peaceful protests in violation of a law believed to be unjust or immoral.*

If a law is immoral, are you right or wrong to disobey it? What is the remedy?

I have a dream that one day this nation will rise up and live out the true meaning of its creed: "We hold these truths to be self-evident: that all men are created equal." I have a dream that one day on the red hills of Georgia the sons of former slaves and the sons of former slave owners will be able to sit down together at the table of brotherhood. I have a dream that one day even the state of Mississippi, a state sweltering with the heat of injustice, sweltering with the heat of oppression, will be transformed into an oasis of freedom and justice. I have a dream that my four little children will one day live in a nation where they will not be judged by the color of their skin but by the content of their character.[43]

Civil Rights Act (1964): *Prohibits discrimination in employment, education, and places of public accommodation.*

disparate impact: *Job tests that differentially affect minority groups, even if there is no intent to discriminate.*

President Kennedy proposed a civil rights bill that would have banned discrimination in public accommodations, such as restaurants and hotels. Five days following Kennedy's assassination in 1963, President Lyndon Johnson (1963–69) told Congress that nothing could better honor Kennedy than passage of this bill. The next year, Congress passed the **Civil Rights Act**, which significantly strengthened Kennedy's original bill by also prohibiting employment discrimination on account of "race, color, religion, sex, or national origin."

Because the Fourteenth Amendment's equal protection clause only applies to state-sponsored discrimination, the Supreme Court upheld Congress's authority to ban private discrimination under the interstate commerce clause. Given the

Jack Corn/The Tennessean

Court's broad interpretation of interstate commerce (see Chapter 3), the Court ruled that even small inns and restaurants had to abide by the act.[44]

In 1971, the Supreme Court interpreted the Civil Rights Act to limit job qualification requirements that had a **disparate impact** on whites and blacks.[45] For example, if more whites receive high school diplomas than blacks, then requiring a high school diploma for a job would be more harmful to blacks than to whites. A business seeking to establish job requirements that have a disparate impact would have to prove that the requirement is necessary to the job. In the late 1970s and through the 1980s, a more conservative Supreme Court reached a series of decisions that restricted civil rights protections, for example, making disparate impact more difficult to prove and ruling that discrimination against pregnant women was not a form of sex discrimination under the Civil Rights Act.[46] Passing new laws,

In the spring of 1960, following a wave of sit-in protests, Diane Nash and a thousand other participants marched to the courthouse square in Nashville. On the way, some of them sang "We Shall Overcome," a gospel song that became the anthem of the civil rights movement. Confronting the mayor on the courthouse steps, the protesters forced him to admit that segregation was morally wrong.

Congress overturned these Court decisions plus several others, thus demonstrating widespread support for the continued protection of civil rights. The new rules, for example, make it easier to find that job tests have a disparate impact, but leave it to the courts to determine whether disparate impact, by taking race into account, conflicts with the equal treatment obligation of the Civil Rights Act.[47]

Dismantling Voting Barriers Based on Race

As noted previously, the end of Reconstruction left black men in the South with a constitutional right to vote, but a hostile social and legal environment that made it extremely difficult for them to do so. The Supreme Court pushed things along, striking down grandfather clauses (1915)[48] and white primaries (1944),[49] the latter in a suit filed by the NAACP. Congress and the states pushed things along further, outlawing poll taxes with the Twenty-Fourth Amendment (1964).

On August 28, 1963, more than 200,000 gathered on the Washington Mall in a March for Jobs and Freedom. Among them were seventy-five members of Congress who were working to pass a civil rights bill that had President Kennedy's support. Folk singer Joan Baez led the crowd in singing "We Shall Overcome," but the day belonged to Martin Luther King, whose "I Have a Dream" speech still challenges Americans to work for equality.

Which branch of government has been more powerful in ensuring equality—Congress or the courts? Why?

During the summer of 1964, voting rights supporters from around the country, many of them college students, moved south to help with voter registration drives. Klansmen murdered three of the volunteers in Philadelphia, Mississippi, that June. In March 1965, King organized a voting rights march from Selma to Montgomery. With national news media on hand, Alabama police, under the authority of Governor George Wallace, beat the marchers with whips, nightsticks, and cattle prods. Selma natives murdered two more voting rights activists.

A week later, President Johnson addressed a joint session of Congress, calling for passage of the strictest possible voting rights legislation. He ended the speech by adopting a line from the civil rights movement, telling Congress and the nation, "we shall overcome."[50] Congress responded with the **Voting Rights Act**, passed in August 1965. The act banned literacy, interpretation, and other such tests for voting. It required states with low voter registration levels, essentially seven southern states plus Alaska, to receive Justice Department approval for any changes to its voting laws. It also established new criminal penalties for those who sought to keep people from voting on account of race. The law was an enormous success. By 2008, blacks and whites voted at essentially the same rate nationwide,[51] and at slightly higher rates in some southern states[52] (see Figure 5.3).

Dismantling Discrimination Based on Gender

The success of the civil rights movement for African Americans inspired other groups, most notably women, to put pressure on the political system to obtain equal rights under the law. Women active in the civil rights movement easily shifted the movement's strategies to promoting rights for women, particularly after the publica-

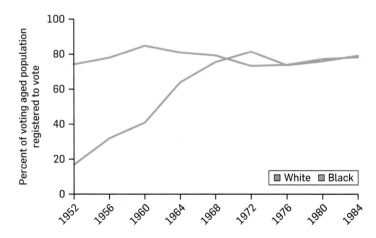

AP Photo/File

tion of Betty Friedan's *The Feminine Mystique* (1963), a book considered by many to have launched the American feminist movement. Based on a survey Friedan sent to her Smith College classmates in advance of their fifteenth reunion, the book broadcast the sense of dissatisfaction that many American women had in their roles as wives and mothers. About the same time, the Kennedy administration's President's Commission on the Status of Women,

In 1965, civil rights leaders turned their focus to voting rights, planning a five-day march from Selma to Montgomery. The first marchers were beaten back by local police and state troopers. Regrouping, and with reinforcements from all over the nation, the march began again two weeks later. As it reached Montgomery, King spoke from the steps of the state capitol, saying, "The end we seek is a society at peace with itself."

Voting Rights Act (1965): *Gives the federal government the power to prevent discrimination in voting rights.*

The Feminine Mystique (1963): *Book by Betty Friedan considered by many to have launched the modern feminist movement.*

FIGURE 5.3 White and Black Southern Voter Registration, 1952–1984. Dramatic increases in black voter registration preceded passage of the Voting Rights Act in 1965, but substantial equality between whites and blacks did not occur until after its passage.
Source: Harold W. Stanley, *Voter Mobilization and the Politics of Race* (New York: Praeger 1987).

Prohibits different pay for males and females for the same work.

Why, in U.S. history, have women's rights movements followed, rather than preceded, movements to remove racial barriers?

National Organization for Women: *Organized interest group devoted to securing equal rights for women.*

Equal Rights Amendment (ERA): *Proposed amendment that would have banned federal and state governments from discriminating on account of sex.*

American Civil Liberties Union (ACLU): *Interest group devoted to freedom of expression, criminal due process, civil rights, and reproductive rights.*

Women's Rights Project: *Litigation group for women's rights formed by the ACLU.*

charged with making recommendations for overcoming sex discrimination, urged passage of the **Equal Pay Act**. Passed by Congress in 1963, the act prohibits employers from paying different wages for the same job on account of sex. Although the act did not prohibit discrimination in hiring of male and female workers, that prohibition came with the Civil Rights Act of 1964.

Following passage of the Civil Rights Act, Friedan helped found the **National Organization for Women** (NOW), which advocates for women's rights through education and litigation. NOW protested airline policies that forced stewardesses to retire at marriage or age 32, "help wanted" ads that listed jobs by gender, as well as protective legislation. NOW also supported abortion rights and a proposed **Equal Rights Amendment** (ERA), which would have prohibited the federal government and the states from discriminating on account of sex.

In 1972, the **American Civil Liberties Union** established the **Women's Rights Project** (WRP), which worked to eliminate discriminatory laws. The first WRP director, future Supreme Court Justice Ruth Bader Ginsburg, developed a litigation strategy for ending gender-based discrimination. Prior to Ginsburg's work, the Court had rejected equal protection claims for women. Ginsburg first persuaded the Court to strike down laws based on the rational-basis standard, and then got the Court to approve a heightened-scrutiny standard. This is a step below the strict scrutiny used in cases discriminating on account of race, but it is a tough enough standard that the Court usually strikes down laws that discriminate according to sex.

Meanwhile, the ERA, passed by Congress and sent to the states for ratification in 1972, began to falter. An anti-ERA movement led by political activist Phyllis Schlafly reversed the momentum by arguing that an Equal Rights Amendment would remove special privileges women enjoyed with regard to protective legislation, Social Security benefits, and draft exemption. Ironically, another argument against the ERA was that it was unnecessary because the Supreme Court was striking down most laws that discriminated on account of sex anyway. Despite an extension of the deadline to 1982, the ERA ultimately fell three states short of the three-quarters majority needed to pass an amendment (see Figure 5.4).

Frontiers in Civil Rights

Many of the civil rights battles against legal discrimination have been won: governments cannot discriminate on account of race or sex, and businesses cannot discriminate in whom they hire as employees or serve as customers. But the expanded notion of equality promoted by the civil rights and women's rights movements inspired other groups, such as homosexuals and the disabled, to demand full access to equality. At the same time, as the fight over

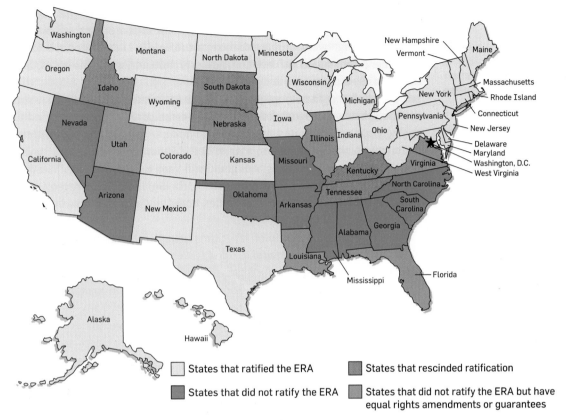

States that ratified the ERA
States that did not ratify the ERA
States that rescinded ratification
States that did not ratify the ERA but have equal rights amendments or guarantees

FIGURE 5.4 States Approving the Equal Rights Amendment. Passed by Congress in 1972 and sent to the states for ratification, the Equal Rights Amendment got a quick start, then faltered, as opposition materialized and grew. In 1979 Congress extended the deadline for ratification to 1982, but in 1982 the amendment expired. Thirty-five states had voted to ratify it (of the thirty-eight needed to make three-quarters), and five states had voted to rescind ratification.

the ERA made clear, the extension of rights for some may involve a loss of privileges for others, and sometimes rights clash. Congress and the courts have sought to define the meaning and limits of rights as new areas of conflict emerge over such issues as racial and religious profiling, the voting rights of felons, and the civil rights of illegal immigrants. Whatever the new issues, however, the trend in the United States has been for a broader meaning of equality and greater support for civil rights.

Sexual Preference and Same-Sex Marriage

The movement to protect the rights of homosexuals first came to widespread public attention in 1969, when a police raid on the Stonewall Inn, a gay bar in New York City, turned into a riot by the patrons at the bar and gay rights supporters who lived in the area. The **Stonewall riots** became the signature

Is the era of civil rights over? Have all the battles been fought and won?

Stonewall riots (1969): *Street protest by gay patrons against police raid at a gay bar in New York, considered to have launched the gay rights movement.*

event of a growing gay rights movement. Activists soon formed the Gay Liberation Front, which established branch organizations around the world. By the 1990s, the movement had expanded into the LGBT movement, a broader movement seeking to protect the rights of lesbians, gays, bisexuals, and transgendered persons.

At the time of the Stonewall riots, all states banned sodomy, which would include virtually all sexual activity between same-sexed couples.[53] In the following years several states decriminalized homosexual activity, but as noted in Chapter 4, the Supreme Court ruled in 1986 that homosexual activity was not a fundamental right, so states could still keep such activity illegal if they so chose. Then, in *Lawrence v. Texas* (2003), the Supreme Court reversed the 1986 decision and declared that states could not prohibit sexual activity between people of the same sex.[54]

Nevertheless, a majority of Americans believe that homosexual conduct is always or almost always wrong,[55] and issues related to homosexual rights have been fraught with conflict. Under President Bill Clinton (1993–2001), Congress enacted a **don't ask, don't tell** policy for the military. Prior to this policy, simply having homosexual tendencies, without any evidence of homosexual activities, was sufficient grounds for discharge. Under the policy, sexual preference alone is not a ground for discharge, but lesbians, gays, or bisexuals can still be discharged for engaging in homosexual relationships or for discussing their sexual orientation. President Obama has asked Congress to change the policy so that lesbians, gays, and bisexuals can serve openly.

More controversial has been the issue of same-sex marriage. State laws typically govern family matters, including marriage, divorce, child custody, and wills, and in most states, marriage is limited to members of the opposite sex. While each state can set its own rules for such proceedings, the full faith and credit clause of the Constitution generally requires each state to accept the status granted by other states. Thus, opposite-sex couples who get married in Las Vegas under Nevada law are recognized as married throughout the United States. However, thousands of citizens in same-sex partnerships want to be married but are not eligible for that legally recognized status, which brings advantages with regard to visitation rights at hospitals, the right to make health-care decisions for a spouse, inheritance rights, and tax benefits.

When the Hawaii Supreme Court ruled in 1993 that, under the state constitution, Hawaii would have to show a compelling interest in its prohibition of same-sex marriages, opponents feared that same-sex marriages performed in Hawaii would have legal recognition throughout the United States. In 1996, Congress passed and President Clinton signed the **Defense of Marriage Act**, which defines marriage, for the purpose of federal law, as between a man and a woman and declares that states do not have to recognize same-sex

Do court decisions follow public opinion? Do they lead public opinion? What should be the relationship?

don't ask, don't tell: *Policy allowing gays to serve in the military if they do not discuss their sexual preferences.*

Defense of Marriage Act (1996): *Federal law exempting states from any requirement to recognize same-sex marriages performed in other states.*

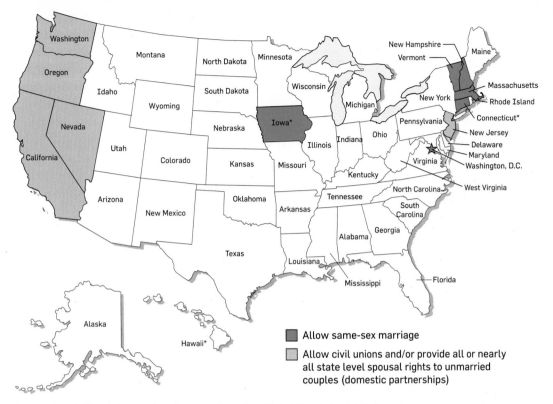

Allow same-sex marriage

Allow civil unions and/or provide all or nearly all state level spousal rights to unmarried couples (domestic partnerships)

*In October 2008 the Connecticut Supreme Court invalidated the state statute banning same-sex marriage.
†In April 2009 the Iowa Supreme Court invalidated the state statute banning same sex marriage.
‡Hawaii's constitution was amended in 1998 to read "The Legislature shall have the power to reserve marriage to opposite-sex couples." The Hawaii legislature subsequently passed a law prohibiting marriage for same-sex couples.

FIGURE 5.5 States Approving Same-Sex Marriage, 2010.
Source: Data from National Conference of State Legislatures.

marriages performed in other states. Later that year, the Hawaii Supreme Court ruled that the state did not have a compelling interest in prohibiting same-sex marriages, but voters then approved a state constitutional amendment allowing the state legislature to ban same-sex marriage. Since that time, courts, legislatures, and citizen initiatives have battled over same-sex marriage, with judicial protection sometimes overridden by popular opposition, as in California (2009) and Maine (2009) (see Figure 5.5).

National public opinion remains mixed on the matter of same-sex marriage (see Figure 5.6). While a majority of Americans favor some form of legal recognition for same-sex couples, only four states and the District of Columbia have legally recognized same-sex marriage; another five recognize **civil unions**. Even the major political parties remain internally divided on the issue of gay marriage;

What government (state or federal) or branch of government (executive, legislative, judicial) should have the power to decide if same-sex marriage is legal?

civil unions: *State laws that provide the benefits of marriage to same-sex couples without using the term marriage.*

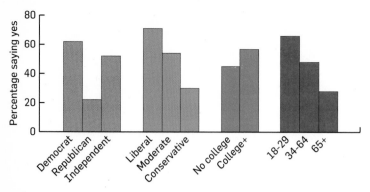

FIGURE 5.6 Changing Views on Same-Sex Marriage, 2006–2009.
Source: Jennifer Agiesta, "Behind the Numbers: On Gay Marriage, a New Even Split," *Washington Post*, April 30, 2009.

while Democrats are typically more supportive of same-sex marriage than Republicans, President Barack Obama, a Democrat, opposes federal recognition of same-sex marriage, yet Republican former Vice President Dick Cheney supports it. Because support for same-sex marriage is much greater among younger Americans than among older Americans, the legality of same-sex marriage may increase over time.

Affirmative Action

Almost as controversial as issues relating to gay rights are matters relating to remedies for overcoming the effects of centuries-long discrimination. Known as **affirmative action**, these programs grant preferences to African Americans, minorities, and/or women in employment, education, or contracting. They not only aim to ensure equality of opportunity but actually move toward promoting equality of outcome.

But do the effects of unequal treatment in the past justify potential unequal treatment in the present? Is fear of causing inequality in the present sufficiently compelling not to correct the inequalities of the past? The Supreme Court has struggled to find the right balance between these positions. Today affirmative action programs by private businesses must comport with the Supreme Court's interpretation of the nondiscrimination clauses of the Civil Rights Act; affirmative action programs by national, state, and local governments also must comport with constitutional requirements of equal protection.

Higher Education.   As colleges and universities actively sought racial and gender balances in their student bodies, several controversial cases arose. The Supreme Court first confronted college affirmative action plans in 1978. The medical school at the University of California, Davis, had eighty-four seats in each entering class for which anyone could apply and sixteen seats set aside for minority candidates only. Allan Bakke, a white male, was denied admission although he had a 3.5 grade point average (GPA) and a Medical College Admission Test (MCAT) score in the 90th percentile, whereas the average scores for the sixteen minority seats were a 2.6 GPA and an MCAT score in the 20th percentile. Bakke sued, and a split Court decreed in *Bakke v. California* that this sort of quota system violated the equal protection

affirmative action:
Policies that grant racial or gender preferences in hiring, education, or contracting.

Bakke v. California **(1978):** *Supreme Court decision upholding affirmative action at colleges as long as there are no quotas.*

clause. Nevertheless, the Court held that other sorts of affirmative action plans, where race is a "plus" in an applicant's overall file, did meet the state's compelling interest in establishing a diverse student body.[57]

The Supreme Court revisited the *Bakke* decision in a pair of 2003 cases that are discussed more extensively in Chapter 14 (The Judiciary). In those cases, the Supreme Court upheld the affirmative action program at the University of Michigan Law School, because the law school considered race as one part of an entire file.[58] On the other hand, the Court struck down the program at the University of Michigan's undergraduate college, where race automatically created a set number of points toward admissions, without any individualized consideration of how particular individuals who are minorities might contribute to the school's diversity.[59]

In the law school case, the opinion of Justice Sandra Day O'Connor, the first woman to serve on the Court, expressed the belief that the Constitution required that affirmative action programs be only a temporary solution, and the hope that by 2028 they would no longer be necessary. Opponents of affirmative action, such as Ward Connerly, chair of the American Civil Rights Institute, hope that such plans will not last that long. Connerly has launched state-level referenda in California, Washington, Michigan, Nebraska, and Colorado to let the voters decide whether such programs should be allowed. Voters have rejected affirmative action in all those states except Colorado.

Should race or sex be a factor in college admissions?

Disability Rights

Advocates for the rights of the disabled, encouraged by the civil rights, women's rights, and other movements, successfully lobbied for the Rehabilitation Act of 1973, which prohibits discrimination against the disabled by any federal agency or by any private program or activity that receives federal funds. The landmark **Americans with Disabilities Act** (ADA) (1990) goes further, requiring public and private employers to make "reasonable accommodations" to known physical and mental limitations of employees with disabilities and, if possible, to modify performance standards to accommodate an employee's disability.

Americans with Disabilities Act (1990): *Requires businesses and government to make reasonable accommodations for employees with known physical or mental limitations.*

To comply with the act, public transportation authorities have made buses and trains accessible to those in wheelchairs. Public accommodations, such as restaurants, hotels, movie theaters, and doctors' offices, must also meet ADA accessibility standards, within reason, removing barriers from existing structures. Related legislation, the Individuals with Disabilities Education Act (1990, updated 2004) requires states to provide a free public education to all children with disabilities in the least restrictive environment as appropriate to their particular needs.

Congress does not provide a full list of disabilities covered under the ADA, but rather covers any disability that "substantially limits a major life activity." Thus, a trucking company need not make accommodations to drivers who can only see clearly out of one eye, even if the disability did not affect driving skills, because the disability is not one that substantially limits major life activities. On the other hand, the ADA does protect people who have HIV or AIDS. It even protects people with drug and alcohol problems, provided the drug use in question is not illegal.[60]

Racial and Religious Profiling

profiling: *Practice of using racial or ethnic characteristics to determine whether to investigate.*

Profiling, the use by police of certain racial, ethnic, or religious characteristics in determining whom to investigate for particular kinds of crimes, has become controversial because evidence has mounted that profiling entails unequal treatment under the law. For example, along the Interstate 95 corridor north of Baltimore, a team of observers found that about 17 percent of cars had black drivers and nearly 76 percent had white drivers, and the drivers observed traffic laws in similar proportions. Nevertheless, of those cars that the Maryland State Police stopped and searched, over 80 percent were driven by blacks or Hispanics, whereas cars driven by whites constituted less than 20 percent of the searches.[61] So much more likely were blacks to be pulled over than whites that the phrase "driving while black" came to signify the near criminal status many African Americans felt they risked on the highway. In 2008, the Maryland State Police agreed to pay more than $400,000 to settle racial profiling suits. Litigation in eight other states continues.[62] State and federal courts have specifically prohibited the use of race as a factor in "drug courier profiles."[63]

Following the terrorist attacks of 9/11, profiling of Arabs and Muslims increased, particularly in matters of airline security. In efforts to screen potential terrorists, mistakes are often made. In 2007, for example, police detained six Arabs, a few of whom were American citizens returning from a stint training Marines about Iraqi culture, when an airline passenger became worried after hearing the men speak in Arabic. Where issues of security are at stake, profiling is especially controversial.

Should profiling be used to protect American citizens against terrorist plots?

Illegal Immigrants

The Fourteenth Amendment's equal protection clause prohibits states from denying to any person—in other words, not just citizens—equal protection under the law. Thus even illegal immigrants receive some degree of legal protection in the United States. The level of that protection is deeply controversial, especially as the number of illegal immigrants, estimated to be about 12 million, has skyrocketed in recent years.

Should children of illegal immigrants who are born on American soil be U.S. citizens?

Congress has been considering a number of actions, including creating easier paths to citizenship for illegal immigrants or, alternatively, denying natural-born citizenship to U.S.-born children of illegal immigrants. By a 49 percent to 45 percent margin, Americans do not believe such children should automatically become citizens, but the constitutionality of a law that would deny them citizenship, given the Fourteenth Amendment's citizenship clause, remains unclear.[64]

By Clay Bennett. Reproduced with permission from the March 28, 2006 issue of The Christian Science Monitor (www.CSMonitor. com). © 2006 The Christian Science Monitor

Whereas the Court reviews laws that discriminate against legal immigrants under its strictest level of scrutiny, it reviews laws that discriminate against illegal immigrants under the easier rational basis standard. Yet, the Court has held that states may not deny public education to illegal immigrants,[65] and federal law requires hospitals to provide emergency care to illegal immigrants through Medicaid, the federal program that supports health care to poor people. The growth of civil rights to cover illegal immigrants is surely one of the most controversial of the frontiers examined.

Civil Rights and Public Policy: Workplace Equality

Although national legislation and constitutional amendments define civil rights policy, and the Supreme Court interprets such laws, deciding whether they are constitutional, and if so, what they mean, the day-to-day protection of civil rights now falls to two separate executive branch agencies. One is the Civil Rights Division of the Department of Justice, with sections on educational opportunity, employment, housing, voting, and disability rights. The other is the Equal Employment Opportunity Commission, which protects against sexual harassment in the workplace and promotes gender equity.

The Equal Employment Opportunity Commission

Equal Employment Opportunity Commission (EEOC): *Independent federal agency charged with protecting equal employment rights.*

The **Equal Employment Opportunity Commission** (EEOC) is an independent agency, with its commissioners selected for five-year fixed terms; unlike heads of government departments, they cannot be removed by the president. They are thus thought to be shielded from political pressures, but fixed terms also limit responsiveness to the president, who is chief executive of the United States.

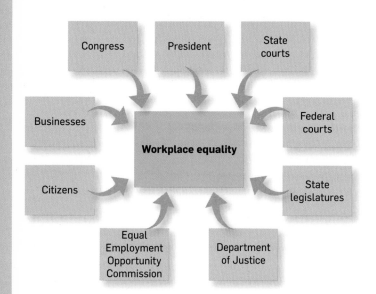

Congress established the EEOC as part of the Civil Rights Act of 1964. The original EEOC could receive and investigate complaints of discrimination on the basis of race, sex, religion, and national origin (Congress later added age and disability status). As one of the compromises that allowed the act to pass, however, the EEOC originally had no enforcement power. Rather, it could refer cases in which there were patterns or practices of discrimination to the Justice Department. In 1972, Congress provided the commission with the right to file lawsuits against companies that discriminate.

Although Congress passed the basic law declaring discrimination based on race or sex to be illegal, the EEOC established the guidelines that prohibited discrimination against hiring married women, pregnant women, or mothers. The commission also allowed companies to establish affirmative action plans that include quotas for hiring and promoting women and minorities if those companies had previously engaged in discriminatory practices.

Sexual Harassment

The problem of discrimination on account of sex can take many forms, and one of the most prevalent in the workplace is sexual harassment. Survey data reveal that nearly 60 percent of women report potentially harassing behaviors at work.[66] The EEOC receives more than 12,000 sexual harassment complaints per year.[67] The commission first set regulations against sexual harassment in 1980, stating that such harassment was a form of sex discrimination prohibited by the Civil Rights Act. The Supreme Court agreed with the EEOC's interpretation of the act in 1986, upholding the lawsuit of a woman who claimed that her boss coerced her into having sex with him and then she was fired from her job.[68] (See Chapter 14 [The Judiciary] on the sexual harassment allegation against Supreme Court nominee and former EEOC chair Clarence Thomas.)

The Supreme Court recognizes two distinct types of sexual harassment. Some harassment takes *quid pro quo* form, in which supervisors link the benefits of employment to sexual favors. But harassment does not have to be linked to benefits or threats. Sexual harassment can take place whenever one or more employees establish, on account of sex, a hostile work environment, one that interferes with a worker's ability to do his or her job.

Gender Equality in the Workplace

From a policy standpoint, the underlying principle of equal pay simply means that two people who are employed in the same job and do the same quality of work should be paid the same wage. Achieving gender equality in the workplace means that there are no barriers to advancement or hiring based on gender, and that gender plays no role in how employees are treated or compensated. Unfortunately, true pay equity has not been achieved in the American workplace. Census statistics from 2008 show that, in 2007, women earned only 77.8 percent of what men earned. For African American and Latina women, this percentage was even lower: African American women earned only 68.7 percent, and Latinas earned only 59 percent, of what men made.[69]

Though the Equal Pay Act is supposed to guarantee equal pay for the same work, and the Civil Rights Act aims to protect against any form of employment discrimination on account of sex, the judicial branch has also played a pivotal role. A recent set of Supreme Court decisions has prompted changes in the laws governing discrimination, harassment, and pay equity in the workplace. In one case, the Supreme Court ruled in favor of a woman who was suspended without pay for more than a month and was reassigned to a less desirable position after she claimed sex discrimination in the workplace. The Court decided that an indefinite suspension without pay is retaliation that would reasonably deter any employee from making a discrimination complaint, and that it was therefore illegal.[70]

But the Court's 2007 ruling in *Ledbetter v. Goodyear Tire and Rubber Co.* had the greatest impact on public policy.[71] In 1998, Lilly Ledbetter filed a

Should laws regarding the behavior of women in the workplace be different from laws regarding the behavior of men? Do women need or warrant added protection?

complaint with the EEOC that she had consistently received poor job performance evaluations because of her gender, and that over the nineteen years she had worked at the Goodyear Tire plant her pay had fallen well below that of her male colleagues who did the same type of job. Her employer countered that, even if that were true in the past, she did not file her complaint within the 180 days required by the Civil Rights Act. The Court ruled in favor of Goodyear, stating that Ledbetter's claims alleging forms of sex discrimination were time-barred because the discriminatory decisions relating to pay had been made more than 180 days prior to the day she filed the charge with the EEOC. In her dissent, Justice Ruth Bader Ginsburg wrote that the effect of this ruling would allow "any annual pay decision not contested immediately (within 180 days) . . . [to become] grandfathered, a *fait accompli* beyond the province of Title VII ever to repair."[72] Basically, a company could pay a woman less on the basis of gender, and as long as she did not contest the discriminatory wage within 180 days, the discriminatory wage would be acceptable.

In 2009 Congress reversed the court ruling by passing the Lilly Ledbetter Fair Pay Act, which President Obama signed into law. The act restarts the clock each time an employee receives a paycheck that has been compromised by discriminatory practices.[73] Many equal pay advocates think this new law will be helpful, but not nearly helpful enough to close the salary gap between men and women.

Why do women still earn less than men for performing the same job? Do women warrant equality of opportunity or equality of results?

Lilly Ledbetter's pay discrimination suit went all the way to the Supreme Court. After the Court ruled against her, Ledbetter spoke at the 2008 Democratic National Convention. "How fitting," she said, "that I speak to you on Women's Equality Day, when we celebrate ratification of the amendment that gave women the right to vote. Even as we celebrate, let's also remind ourselves: the fight for equality is not over." The next year Congress reversed the impact of the decision by passing the Lilly Ledbetter Fair Pay Act.

Mark Wilson/Getty Images

Civil Rights and Democracy

The core demand of civil rights is equal opportunity under the law. When laws discriminate or allow discrimination, people are effectively excluded from civic life. The demands for equal opportunity are often made to government, which alone has the authority to prohibit discrimination.

While a democratic system of government works to be responsive to its citizens, responsiveness to minorities is harder to obtain when majorities seek to limit minority rights. But when factions form on the basis of majority group versus minority group, such as white versus black, heterosexual versus gay or lesbian, or native versus immigrant, responsiveness to minority preferences has been achieved through the gateways of lawsuits, protests, and other forms of civic engagement by the minority group. In response, the government has struck down laws that discriminated and passed laws that prevented other people from discriminating.

Out of all the activities by groups seeking equal rights, voting might be key. With the vote, declared King in 1965, comes accountability. Blacks could "vote out of office public officials who bar the doorway to decent housing, public safety, jobs, and decent integrated education. It is now obvious that the basic elements so vital to Negro advancement can only be achieved by seeking redress from government . . . To do this, the vote is essential."[74]

While voting rights provide accountability by allowing citizens to remove incompetent officials from office, they also provide responsiveness. A minority group's elected opponents are not as forceful once a group has the right to vote. The voting patterns of southern House and Senate members on issues related to civil rights have moderated over the past forty years, proving that King was certainly correct about the value of the ballot.[75]

The frontiers of civil rights will continue to evolve. Some Americans believe that equal opportunity is not enough, that the government must take stronger measures to ensure a greater equality of outcome. A case currently moving through the court system of note in this regard is a class action lawsuit potentially involving more than 1.5 million women against Walmart. The case is currently the largest employment discrimination lawsuit in the history of the United States. These women allege they were not given equal pay raises when compared to men and had far fewer opportunities for promotion.[76] However, because there is no constitutional right to equal results, the ultimate battle over this meaning of equality may be fought primarily in democratically elected legislatures.

FOCUS QUESTIONS

- What is the meaning of equality? How has its meaning changed since the Constitution was written in 1787?

- What role has government played with regard to equality in the past? What role does it assume today?

- What means have various groups used to secure their civil rights? What means has government used to respond?

- What is the effect on a democracy if some of its people lack civil rights?

- Are civil rights a gate or a gateway to democracy? Explain.

GATEWAYS TO LEARNING

Top Ten to Take Away

1. Civil rights are rights related to the duties of citizenship and the opportunities for participation in civil life that the government is obliged to protect. These rights are based on the expectation of equality under the law. The most important is the right to vote. (pp. 141–143)

2. The government can take three different roles when it comes to civil rights: engage in state-sponsored or public discrimination; treat people equally but permit private discrimination; or try, as it has since the 1960s, both to treat people equally and to prevent individuals or businesses from discriminating. (p. 141)

3. Thus it falls to government to protect individuals against unequal treatment and to citizens to ensure that government itself is not discriminating against individuals or groups. (p. 141)

4. During the nation's first century and even thereafter, state laws and the national government actively discriminated against people on the basis of race, gender, and ethnic background. (pp. 143–144; 147–148)

5. During the nation's second century, discrimination was state-sponsored in the South; elsewhere in the nation private discrimination was practiced without challenge. (pp. 144–147; 148–149)

6. Today public discrimination has been ended by constitutional amendments and the courts, largely through the Fourteenth Amendment's equal protection clause, which prohibits states from denying any person the equal protection of the law, gives Congress the authority to enforce its provisions by appropriate legislation, and gives the Supreme Court the authority to strike down state laws that violate equal protection. (pp. 152–154)

7. Beginning in the 1950s, litigation by the NAACP and grass-roots protests by African Americans forced a response by the federal government that ended segregation and secured voting rights for African Americans. Only when the federal government took action did states respond. Following a similar model, a resurgent women's movement ended limits to women's full participation in public life, including politics, work, and the professions. (pp. 154–162)

8. The expanded notion of equality promoted by the civil rights and women's rights movements inspired other groups, such as homosexuals and the disabled, to demand full access to equality. (pp. 162–168)

9. At the same time, the extension of rights for some may involve a loss of privileges for others, and sometimes rights clash. Congress and the courts have sought to define the meaning and limits of rights as new areas of conflict emerge over such issues as racial and religious profiling and the civil rights of illegal immigrants. (pp. 168–169)

10. Whatever the new issues, however, the trend in the United States has been for a broader meaning of equality and greater support for civil rights. (p. 173)

A full narrative summary of the chapter is on the book's website.

Ten to Test Yourself

1. What are civil rights?

2. What did the *Dred Scott* case decide?

3. What rights are protected by the Thirteenth, Fourteenth, and Fifteenth Amendments?

4. Why is the distinction between public (governmental) and private (individual and business) discrimination important?

5. How have immigration and naturalization laws tied in to the public mood?

6. In what ways were women second-class citizens? Homosexuals?

7. What are the tests the Supreme Court uses to determine the validity of laws alleged to discriminate?

8. What are the major pieces of legislation that protect civil rights?

9. What is the difference between equality of opportunity and equality of outcome?

10. How does government try to ensure workplace equality?

More review questions and answers and chapter quizzes are on the book's website.

Terms **to Know and Use**

affirmative action (p. 166)
American Civil Liberties
  Union (p. 162)
Americans with Disabilities
  Act (p. 167)
Bakke v. California (p. 166)
black codes (pp. 144, 145)
Brown v. Board of Education (p. 155)
Chinese Exclusion Act (p. 147)
citizenship (p. 149)
civil disobedience (p. 158)
civil liberties (p. 141)
civil rights (p. 141)
Civil Rights Act (p. 159)
Civil Rights Cases (p. 153)
civil rights movement
  (p. 157)
civil unions (p. 165)
compelling interest test (p. 153)
coverture (p. 147)
Defense of Marriage Act (p. 164)
discrimination (p. 141)
disparate impact (p. 159)
don't ask, don't tell (p. 164)

Dred Scott v. Sandford (p. 143)
Emancipation Proclamation (p. 144)
Equal Employment Opportunity
  Commission (p. 170)
Equal Pay Act (p. 162)
equal protection clause (p. 152)
Equal Rights Amendment (p. 162)
equality of opportunity (p. 142)
equality of outcome (p. 142)
grandfather clauses
  (pp. 146, 147)
heightened scrutiny (p. 153)
Jim Crow laws (pp. 146, 147)
Korematsu v. United States (p. 151)
Ku Klux Klan (p. 145)
literacy tests (pp. 146, 147)
Loving v. Virginia (p. 158)
miscegenation (p. 158)
Missouri Compromise (p. 143)
National Association for the
Advancement of Colored
  People (p. 153)
National Organization
  for Women (p. 162)

natural-born citizens (p. 149)
naturalization (p. 150)
Plessy v. Ferguson (pp. 146, 147)
poll taxes (p. 145)
private discrimination
  (p. 141)
privileges or immunities
  clause (p. 149)
profiling (p. 168)
public discrimination (p. 141)
rational basis (p. 153)
Reconstruction (pp. 144, 145)
separate-but-equal doctrine
  (pp. 146, 147)
state action (p. 153)
Stonewall riots (p. 163)
strict scrutiny (p. 153)
The Feminine Mystique (p. 161)
tests (p. 153)
Voting Rights Act (pp. 160, 161)
white primary (p. 145)
Women's Rights Project
  (p. 162)
women's suffrage (p. 147)

Use the vocabulary flash cards on the book's website.

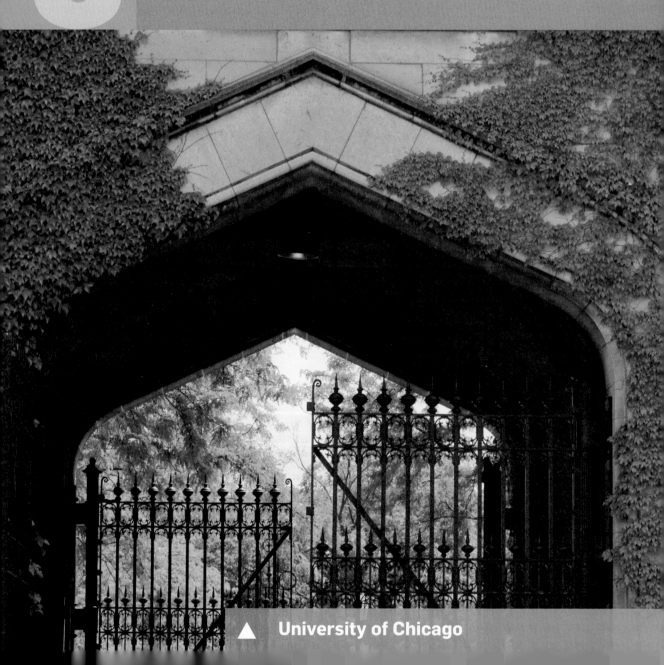

6 PUBLIC OPINION

University of Chicago

> *Entire states may change hands as a result of motivating the youth vote, particularly in the South . . . and the West . . . where young voters are abundant.*

At the University of Chicago, Nate Silver was an economics major. He might have studied math or statistics, given his love of numbers. His father recalls that Nate would start counting when they dropped him off at preschool. "When we picked him up two and a half hours later, he was 'Two thousand one hundred and twenty-two, two thousand one hundred and twenty-three . . .'."

After college, Silver worked as an economic consultant for an accounting firm in Chicago. But the work was boring. For fun, he started a website called the Burrito Bracket, rating Mexican restaurants in the Wicker Park neighborhood. Adopting the Chicago White Sox and the Cubs as his home teams, he began using statistics to predict player performance. His system generated a huge amount of attention within the baseball world. In 2004, he sold his PECOTA projection system to Baseball Prospectus and joined its staff, writing books and articles forecasting team and player performance.

Three years later, Silver turned his forecasting skills to politics. He began by writing a political blog for Daily Kos under the pseudonym "Poblano." Frustrated by sloppy polling and reporting, in March 2008 he established his own blog, FiveThirtyEight (the total number of electoral votes in a presidential election),

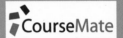
CourseMate

Nate Silver ▶

Beth Rooney/The New York Times/Redux

© Bob Krist/Corbis

which tracked and predicted the outcome of presidential primaries so accurately that it got attention from pundits and commentators. FiveThirtyEight became a daily staple of political junkies and political observers of all stripes. At 9:46 P.M. on November 4, 2008, he called the election for Barack Obama, whom he had forecast as the winner way back in March. Silver's rise "from obscurity to quotable authority" was compared to Obama's, the candidate he had supported all along. "Not only," said *Vanity Fair*, "did his disciplined models and microfine data mining command respect, his prognostications hit the Zen mark on Election Day."[1]

Nate Silver's gateway to participation in the American political system came by doing what he loved—working with numbers—and applying those skills to politics. He still runs FiveThirtyEight and now writes a monthly column of political analysis for *Esquire*. It has also highlighted the importance of public opinion in a democracy. In fact, without the expression of the public will, there would be no democracy. For politicians, knowing which way the public leans or what citizens think is an avenue to power. For citizens, being able to express an opinion and know it is being heard is a gateway to influence. But reading public opinion correctly is not easy. Polls are a great help, but they can be flawed. Even if well measured, public opinion does not always produce a sound direction for the country. A sound direction requires an informed citizenry. In this chapter, we investigate the contours, sources, and impact of public opinion.

FOCUS QUESTIONS

- How does public opinion influence public policy?

- In what ways are elected officials responsive to public opinion? How responsive should they be?

- Is every citizen voice equal, or are some people more influential? Why?

- How well does polling capture public opinion? Should polls direct public policy?

- Does public opinion provide a gateway or a gate to democracy?

The Power of Public Opinion

"Our government rests on public opinion," claimed Abraham Lincoln (1861–65). "Public sentiment is everything. With public sentiment, nothing can fail. Without it, nothing can succeed."[2] Knowing what the public is thinking and having public support are a powerful combination. Perhaps no one appreciates the power of public opinion more keenly than former President George W. Bush (2001–2009).

The Power of Presidential Approval

George W. Bush came to office in 2001 following a contested election in which more than half the electorate had voted against him. However, following the terrorist attacks on September 11 of that year, the country rallied to his side.[3] Bush enjoyed the approval of 90 percent of the public. No president ever scored higher—not Ronald Reagan (1981–89), not John Kennedy (1961–63), not Franklin Roosevelt (1933–45). With this unprecedented level of public support, President Bush was able to get Congress to go along with nearly everything he wanted. It passed the Patriot Act, which expanded the powers of the federal government in the area of national security, and it approved his call for a new cabinet-level Department of Homeland Security.

When President Bush launched the Iraq War in March 2003, his **approval rating** was over 70 percent. Then it began to drift downward. In 2004, he won reelection in a tight race, but the increasing unpopularity of the Iraq War undermined his support among the American people and his influence with Congress. Even on the heels of his successful reelection, he could not convince Congress to reform Social Security. Then the inadequate federal response to Hurricane Katrina, which devastated the Gulf Coast, further eroded Bush's standing with the public. By 2007, Bush's public approval rating hovered around 35 percent, and he faced a Democratic Congress—the consequence of the "thumping," as he put it, that the Republicans took in the 2006 midterm elections.

In 2007, when the immigration reform bill he backed was defeated, Bush visited Congress personally in an effort to revive it, but even this unusual move had little effect. In fact, Bush was rebuked by his own party when Senator Jeff Sessions (R-Ala.) stated that the president "needs to back off."[4] By the time of Barack Obama's (2009–) election in November 2008, Bush's approval stood in the mid-20s, and the CBS/*New York Times* poll suggested that he had become the most unpopular president since the start of scientific polling in the 1930s.[5]

Bush's political roller coaster reveals the power of the public. The views of average citizens can humble the most experienced statesman and elevate a novice to great influence. During 2009 alone, President Obama started out with high ratings from the public, but by the end of the year, his approval rating had sunk below 50 percent. Like Bush, Obama faced a struggling economy and an unpopular war—in this case Afghanistan.[6]

What Is Public Opinion?

Public opinion is recognized for its power, but it is ever changing, hard to measure, harder to predict, and nearly impossible to control. **Public opinion** is the aggregate of individual attitudes or beliefs about certain issues or officials, and it is the foundation of any democracy.

Of course, the electorate expresses its opinion primarily through voting, and elections are the most visible means by which citizens hold elected officials accountable. But a system that claims to be democratic should not rely

How did public opinion influence public policy during the George W. Bush administration?

approval rating: *Job performance evaluation for the president, Congress, or other public official or institution; generated by public opinion polls and typically reported as a percentage.*

public opinion: *Aggregate of individual attitudes or beliefs about certain issues or officials.*

just on elections to ensure politicians are doing the people's will. Elections are not held very often. Further, elections give signals, but not directions. Voters can only indicate whether they like one candidate more than the other; they cannot convey the reasons for their vote. So legislators and elected executives who want to stay in power expend considerable energy trying to find out what the public wishes and respond accordingly. Because public opinion plays such an important role in forging responsiveness, it is central to understanding U.S. politics.

polls: *Methods for measuring public opinion.*

Today's surveys of public opinion, or **polls**, are the most reliable indicator of what the public is thinking. But polls are not the only source of public opinion. In one recent Supreme Court case, the justices sought to gauge public opinion on what constituted "cruel and unusual punishment" by looking at laws passed by state legislatures (see Supreme Court Cases: *Roper v. Simmons*). Other sources of public opinion are attendance at rallies and protests, the tone of letters sent to elected officials or newspapers, the amount of money given to particular causes or candidates, the content of newspaper editorials, and information gleaned from day-to-day conversations with average Americans.

The Public's Support of Government

The health and stability of a democracy rests with the public. Just as government must respond to what the people want, so citizens must view the system as legitimate and want to be part of it. If the public withdraws its support, the government collapses. For these reasons, political scientists have sought to measure the public's faith in the political system. Two of the most common efforts involve assessing whether the people trust their government and whether they believe their participation in government matters. Political scientists call the latter **efficacy**—the extent to which people believe their actions affect the course of government. **Political trust** is the extent to which people believe the government acts in their best interests. Political trust has generally declined over the last fifty years, with a steeper decline since the Iraq War began in 2003 and the financial collapse that began in 2008. One estimate, made in February 2010, suggests just 19 percent of the public trusts "the government in Washington to do what is right."[7] This is a very low rating by historical standards.[8]

efficacy: *Extent to which people believe their actions can have an impact on public affairs and the actions of government.*

political trust: *Extent to which people believe the government acts in their best interests.*

Efficacy has also declined. It stood at over 70 percent in 1960; by 1994, it had fallen by half. In other words, only one-third of Americans felt their opinions mattered to government. The figure rebounded to 60 percent by 2002, but then declined again, with the Iraq War and financial crisis. There is little doubt, as President Barack Obama said in his 2009 inaugural address, that there has been a "sapping of confidence across our land."

What does a decline in efficacy and public trust mean for American democracy?

supremecourtcases

Roper v. Simmons (2005)

QUESTION: Does the cruel and unusual punishment clause of the Constitution prevent states from executing people who were minors at the time of their crime?

ORAL ARGUMENT: October 13, 2004 (listen at http://www.oyez.org/cases/)

DECISION: March 1, 2005 (read at http://www.findlaw.com/CaseCode/supreme.html)

OUTCOME: States may not execute people who were minors at the time of their crime (5–4).

While only 17 years of age, Christopher Simmons plotted a murder, believing he could "get away with it" because he was a minor. Simmons and another minor burglarized the house of Shirley Cook, tied her up, and threw her off a bridge into a river. A jury found Simmons guilty of first-degree murder and sentenced him to death. Simmons challenged the death sentence on the grounds that executing a person who is a minor at the time of the crime constitutes cruel and unusual punishment, which is prohibited by the Eighth Amendment.

The U.S. Supreme Court's decisions on the Eighth Amendment consider sentences to be cruel and unusual if they violate society's "evolving standards of decency." This makes the Court's Eighth Amendment decisions, alone among constitutional clauses, explicitly dependent on public opinion.

The Court's use of public opinion, however, is not based on public opinion polls but rather on the actions of the democratically elected legislative branches. The Court assumes that the legislatures are responsive to the wishes of the people. They thus represent the "clearest and most reliable objective evidence of contemporary values."

In 1989, the Supreme Court declared in a 5–4 decision that executing minors did not violate evolving standards of decency because twenty-five of the thirty-seven states that allowed the death penalty allowed the execution of 17-year-olds, and twenty-two of those states allowed the execution of 16-year-olds.

By the time the Simmons case reached the U.S. Supreme Court, the states had shifted away from the execution of minors, with four more state legislatures prohibiting the practice. Although recognizing that this change was not dramatic, it was enough to tip the Court majority against allowing the execution of minors.

Polls of public opinion, which the Court finds to be a less reliable indicator of public values than legislative decisions, show that a majority of Americans do in fact oppose the death penalty for those who are minors when they committed the crime. Typically, the percentage of people opposed falls in the mid-50s, whereas the percentage of supporters is in the mid-30s.

- **Which branch of government is most likely to be responsive to "evolving standards of decency"? Which would be least responsive? Why?**

- **Do different state standards on the death penalty violate democratic principles of equality? Explain.**

Public Opinion Polls

Polls make it possible to gauge the public's thinking on a variety of issues or officials, but they have been scientifically conducted only since the 1930s. Even today, a poorly designed or executed poll can produce misleading results. Moreover, there is so much information available from surveys that it is important to know which findings warrant attention and which warrant caution. Poll results can be biased, contradictory, and confusing, and that is why Nate Silver's clear assessments of them during the 2008 presidential race proved so popular.

Scientific Polling and the Growth of Survey Research

straw polls: *Ballot polls by nineteenth-century newspapers to predict the outcome of elections.*

random sample: *Method of selection that gives everyone who might be selected to participate in a poll an equal chance to be included.*

Gallup Poll: *Most well-known and perhaps most respected polling firm in the United States, founded by George Gallup.*

scientific polling: *Method of polling that provides a fairly precise reading of public opinion by using random sampling.*

census: *Constitutionally mandated count of the population every ten years.*

sample: *Subset of a population from which information is collected and analyzed to learn more about the population as a whole. The norm for an accurate sample size is around one thousand people.*

In the 1800s, newspapers and other organizations polled the people to assess public opinion, but these "polls" were of limited help because it was unclear who was being surveyed. So-called **straw polls**, for example, sought to predict the outcome of elections. During the presidential campaign of 1824, the *Harrisburg Pennsylvanian* canvassed the opinion of newspaper readers and concluded that Andrew Jackson would get 63 percent of the vote and be an easy winner.[9] As it turned out, Jackson received only about 40 percent of the popular vote.

Though straw polls were often inaccurate, newspapers and magazines continued to poll readers' opinions well into the twentieth century. During the 1936 presidential campaign, the *Literary Digest* conducted a poll that predicted Republican Alf Landon would win the election by 57 percent over President Franklin Roosevelt. Just the reverse happened: Roosevelt won with a landslide 61 percent of the vote.

But George Gallup, who had founded the American Institute of Public Opinion in 1935, correctly predicted the outcome of the 1936 election by using the idea of a **random sample** to generate a way to select people to participate in surveys. He made his sample representative of the American public by giving, in effect, every American an equal chance to be part of it. The end product was a sample of five thousand, which was far smaller than the *Literary Digest*'s but far more representative of average Americans. As a result of his innovative approach, Gallup is often considered the father of modern polling, and the best-known name in polling today remains **Gallup**. His **scientific polling** and survey research techniques have been refined over the years.

The advent of scientific polling made it possible to assess the opinions of the public with some degree of ease and accuracy. Scientific polling also permitted greater equality in assessing public opinion, because these polls had the ability to tap the opinions of all Americans. George Gallup understood this aspect of polling—that scientific polls democratized the measurement of public opinion.[10]

Types of Polls

In a nation of more than 200 million adults, gathering opinions from everyone is not practical. Even the U.S. **census**, a count of the population required by the Constitution every ten years, has trouble reaching every adult.[11] So polls draw a **sample** from a larger population. But first the **population** must be defined. It might be all adults over age 18, or only voters, or only voters who contributed to Republican candidates in 2008.

The typical size of a sample survey is one thousand people, though it can vary between five hundred and about one thousand five hundred. Size does not matter as much as whether the sample is representative of the population being assessed. A **representative sample** means, in effect, that everyone in that population has an equal chance of being asked to participate in the poll. If a random thousand people are asked to be part of the survey, they should be representative of the population generally—in wealth, ethnicity, or educational attainment, for example. The key to a representative sample is the randomness. It should be much like drawing numbered balls for a lottery: each ball has the same chance of being chosen. The collection of information has evolved with technology from in-person interviews to telephone polls to Internet polls.

Presidential elections are awash in polls. In the heat of the fall campaign, nightly polls gauge changes in voters' preferences for the major contenders. These surveys are called **tracking polls**. Another type of survey involving elections is the **exit poll**, conducted as voters leave the polling booth. The goal here is to learn about the reasoning behind the votes citizens just cast, but, more important, to predict the outcome of the election before all the ballots are formally counted.

The most famous and consequential exit poll took place in Florida during the 2000 presidential elections, fueling one of the most controversial electoral struggles of all time. The major networks used an exit poll to predict that the Sunshine state would go to then Vice President Al Gore (1993–2001). With Florida in the Democratic column, Gore was the apparent winner of the presidency. Florida's electoral votes would put him over

In the 1930s, George Gallup developed a scientific approach to polling, greatly increasing its accuracy and authority.

population: *Group the poll is to represent.*

representative sample: *Polling sample that is not biased, in which all members of the population have an equal chance of being included.*

tracking polls: *Polls that seek to gauge the change of opinion of the same sample size over a period of time, common during the closing months of presidential elections.*

exit polls: *Polls that survey a sample of voters immediately after exiting the voting booth, to predict the outcome of the election before the ballots are officially counted.*

Sequential editions of the *Orlando Sentinel* following election day 2000 testify to the confusion wrought by news media calling the election on the basis of exit polls and early returns, which for Florida were confusing.

AP Photo/Peter Cosgrove

the 270 needed. These predictions started to roll in at 8 P.M. election night. The campaign of Republican George W. Bush protested, saying it was too early to call the state and that the race was still too close to know who won. By 10 P.M., that forecast was withdrawn, making the outcome of the presidential election unclear. By 2 A.M. the next morning, Fox News called the election for Bush, with the other major networks soon following. Just two hours later, however, the Bush "win" was retracted. There followed a long battle over which candidate actually won in Florida. It was not settled until the U.S. Supreme Court halted the Florida recount, and Governor Bush became president.

Many have wanted to blame exit polls for the confusion that election night, but the polls were not as big a problem as the news media's use of them. The networks feel real pressure to make early calls, and that pressure sometimes leads them to go beyond what the data support. So while CBS was making that first call around 8 P.M., its polling experts behind the scene were urging caution.[12]

A final kind of election poll is actually a campaign strategy. **Push polls** are conducted by interest groups or candidates who try to affect the opinions of respondents by priming them with biased information. During the 2000 presidential primary in South Carolina, John McCain claimed that

Do polls make sure the people's voices are heard?

push polls: *Polls that are designed to manipulate the opinions of those being polled.*

George W. Bush ran a push poll against him. Interviewers called people to ask if they knew that McCain was a "cheat" and a "liar." The question was not designed to get information but to turn people against McCain.[13] These polls, therefore, seek to shift public opinion, not measure it.

Error in Polls

Pollsters do everything they can to ensure that their samples are representative. Even if the sample is drawn properly, however, there is still a chance for error. To capture this uncertainty, all poll numbers come with a **confidence interval**. The poll produces a single estimate for the public's thinking, but the best way to think of that estimate is as a range of possible estimates. For a sample of six hundred respondents, the **sampling error** is about 4 percent. That 4 percent generates the confidence interval. Assume, for example, that 65 percent of those sampled support the efforts of Congress to reform the campaign finance laws. With a sampling error of 4 percent, the best way to think of the proportion is that, with 95 percent certainty, the actual amount of public support is somewhere between 61 percent and 69 percent. This range is the confidence interval. Note, however, that there is still a 1 in 20 chance (5 percent) that the true proportion is above or below that 8-point confidence interval. Hence, caution is always required when interpreting poll data.

In addition to sampling error, the wording of the question can introduce error. The controversial issue of abortion offers a vivid example. What the public thinks about this issue depends a great deal on the way the question is asked. In November 2003, an NBC News/*Wall Street Journal* poll asked a representative sample of Americans the following question: *Which of the following best represents your views about abortion—the choice on abortion should be left up to the woman and her doctor, abortion should be legal only in cases when pregnancy results from rape or incest or when the life of the woman is at risk, or abortion should be illegal in all circumstances?*

The answers show that 53 percent of the public felt abortion was a decision best left up to the woman and her doctor. Only 15 percent of Americans felt it should be illegal in all circumstances, with 29 percent wanting to have exceptions. In short, a majority of the public appears to support abortion rights for women. That is an important finding.

But is it true? Consider the following question asked earlier that year, in July, by Fox News/Opinion Dynamics: *Once a woman is pregnant, do you believe the unborn baby or fetus should have all the same rights as a newborn baby?* The answers tell a different story. Nearly 60 percent of the public said yes, the unborn fetus should have the same rights as a newborn baby. Only

confidence interval: *Statistical range, with a given probability, that takes random error into account.*

sampling error: *Measure of the accuracy of a public opinion poll, reported as a percentage.*

Should public officials be influenced by polls?

nonattitudes: *Sources of error in public opinion polls in which individuals feel obliged to give an opinion on something when, in reality, they are unaware of the issue or have no opinion on it.*

response rate: *Proportion of the public who respond to inquiries from pollsters to do surveys.*

_____.

YOU DECIDE

U.S. officials say Iran is about a year from being nuclear-bomb capable, a timeline that has been predicted for 10 years. What should the U.S. do now?

○ Nothing. Israel will deal with it.

○ Use our own missiles to bring an end to the program

○ Work on tougher sanctions with the U.N. and other nations

○ Overthrow the Islamic regime by helping democratic forces on the ground

[**Vote**]   View Results

Screencapture courtesy of FOXnews.com

Quick vote

Was the Supreme Court right to overturn the ban on animal cruelty videos?

○ Yes   ○ No

[VOTE] or view results

Screen capture courtesy of cnn.com

Many websites, especially of news organizations, invite participation in polls. How reliable do you think the results are?

26 percent said no. According to this poll, a strong majority wants to protect the rights of the unborn and, therefore, to limit abortion rights for women.

So what is American public opinion on abortion? Clearly, the answer depends on the wording of the question, specifically on whether respondents are asked to focus on the rights of women or the rights of the unborn. This same dynamic applies to other controversial issues, such as attitudes toward homosexuality and race. Although interviewers are trained to be neutral in their questioning, respondents sometimes try to give the response that they think the questioner wants to hear. A final source of error in polls involves what political scientists call **nonattitudes**. When asked, many people feel compelled to answer, even if they do not have an opinion or know much about the question. They do not want to seem uninformed, but their responses create error in the survey.

The Future of Polls

Today, polling is facing a transition. Representative sampling in telephone surveys is increasingly affected by the growing number of cell phones, as many pollsters do not have access to cell phone exchanges and many cell phone users, especially young people, do not have landlines, which are used in telephone polls. At this point, there is not a lot of evidence to suggest that people without landlines vote differently from those with them, but this shift concerning cell phones will continue.[14] Perhaps more important is the widespread use of caller ID and answering machines. In 2003, half of the public had an answering machine at home,[15] which means that increasing numbers of Americans can screen their calls and refuse to participate in surveys. In fact, there is a general polling fatigue among members of the public. The declining **response rate** is lessening the ability of pollsters to capture public opinion accurately. In the 1990s, the rate of response was nearly 40 percent; now it is about 25 percent.[16]

With telephone surveys in trouble, Internet polls represent the future for measuring public opinion. Through the Internet, polls can be done quickly and cheaply, but respondents may not be representative of the population. Once statisticians develop reliable ways to correct for bias, the web will become an even more powerful tool than it is now to measure the public's thinking. As more people gain access to the web, the amount of bias will decline. Such trends suggest the future of survey research lies with the Internet.

What Drives Public Opinion?

Where does public opinion come from? If it is the aggregate of citizen attitudes and beliefs, it starts with individuals. In this section, we examine the major forces that shape political thinking on a personal level, including the social and political environments in which one grows up and the generation and family into which one is born. Self-interest also affects political attitudes, as do the ideas of opinion leaders such as journalists, political observers, policy makers, and experts.

Social and Political Environment

Political attitudes are shaped by environment—the kind of place one grows up in and lives in now. Each of us is a product of our family, friends, and community. We call the process by which our attitudes are shaped **socialization**.

The way we live our lives, the kinds of foods we eat, the types of vacations we enjoy, and the house of worship we attend—all shape how we are socialized. Our political attitudes are no different. The clearest embodiment of political socialization is partisanship, and evidence shows that parents pass their partisan views along to their children. If parents are Democrats, there is a two-thirds chance that their children will identify themselves as Democrats. They might identify as **Independents**, but there is just a 10 percent chance they will be Republicans. The impact of socialization depends, of course, on whether the parents identify with the same party. If the parents are split on partisanship, the chance of the children being Independents rises considerably.[17]

It may be that political values are passed on in families by genes as well as by socialization. Recent research offers some tantalizing hints that genetics may shape political views.[18] Political scientists have been slow to embrace the possibility, but it warrants close consideration. That some people are more outgoing and willing to build social networks appears to have a basis in one's genes.[19] If so, such a tendency could explain a willingness to become involved in politics, and it may even shape political views. Studies of twins are particularly revealing. Data collected from sets of twins indicate that identical twins, who share their entire genetic code, expressed more similar political attitudes than fraternal twins, who are no more similar than any set of siblings. Such data are not conclusive, but they are suggestive. Admittedly, some political attitudes are less likely to have a genetic component, and partisanship appears to be shaped by family and friends. But ideological leanings—whether one is more or less open to change—may be shaped in part by genetics.[20] This new area of research offers fascinating possibilities for understanding the sources of public opinion.[21]

Whether through family socialization or genes, parents have the biggest impact during a child's early life, but starting in the teenage years, friends also influence attitudes and behavior, as do schools and communities.

socialization: *Impact and influence of one's social environment on the views and attitudes one carries in life, a primary source of political attitudes.*

Independents: *Individuals who do not affiliate with either of the major political parties.*

Communities that are homogeneous, in which most people share many of the same views and opinions, are likely to reinforce the attitudes of parents. Colleges, too, influence attitudes, and college attendance often offers students a chance to break out of the homogeneous settings of their early years. Students meet people from different states or other communities, people with different backgrounds and attitudes. College classes and experiences can also shape political leanings. Socialization does not end at college graduation. It continues as young people pursue careers and choose where and how they will live.

Have your political opinions ever changed? If so, what led to the change?

Generational Effects

Major events can change an entire generation's thinking about politics. The Great Depression, for example, which started in 1929 with the crash of the stock market, shaped the attitudes of millions of Americans. It was an economic calamity that even the severe economic downturn of 2008–2009 did not match. Millions lost their savings and their homes. In 1932, one of every four Americans was out of work, and incomes had declined by 50 percent. One consequence was that the public blamed the party in power, the Republicans, and switched party allegiance. The Democrats, as a result, became the majority party for the first time in generations.

generational effects: *Effects on one's personal opinions related to the era in which one lives.*

Another defining event that caused Americans to change their views, this time on national security, was the terrorist attacks of September 11, 2001. Quite suddenly, many were willing to give up some personal freedom to reduce the threat of terrorism (see Figure 6.1). Searing events, such as the Great Depression or the terrorist attacks, can have a long-term impact on public opinion, especially if the generation that experienced them most acutely reacts as a bloc.

Generational effects need not be limited to life-altering events, however. They can also be affected by the era in which is one is young and

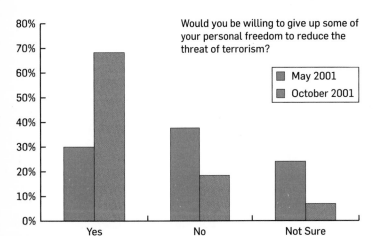

FIGURE 6.1 **Shift in Public Opinion Following the Terrorist Attacks of September 11, 2001.** The terrorist attacks of September 11, 2001, are likely to have a long-term effect on public opinion. The graph shows before-and-after responses to the question about being willing to give up personal freedom. When the question was asked again, in May 2006, 56 percent answered yes, a 17 point decline from October 2001 but still well above the levels registered before 9/11.
Source: Fox News/Opinion Dynamic Poll, May 2001, October 2001, and May 2006.

first active as a citizen. Those who were young during the time of Republican President Ronald Reagan are likely to think of politics differently than those who are young now during the time of the Democrat Barack Obama. The former will naturally think more favorably about Republicans, the latter more favorably about Democrats. Exit polls from 2008 indicated that 66 percent of all 18- to 29-year-old voters supported Obama.[22] By historical standards, this level of support is quite high. Although it remains to be seen whether being a member of what may be called the "Obama generation" will have an enduring effect on partisan identification and politics, America's Millennial generation does seem distinctive. Millennials seem to be more trusting of government than previous generations. There is also evidence to suggest that this group is less religious than previous ones.[23]

Self-Interest and Rationality

Forming political opinion is much more than just a psychological process tied to socialization, however. People also respond to the context in which they find themselves. That is, to a certain extent people are "rational" in that they act in a way that is consistent with their **self-interest**. For example, as income rises, the chance of someone being a Republican increases. Why? The Republicans have pursued tax policies that protect individual wealth, while the Democrats pursue tax policies that tax the wealthy at higher rates to pay for social programs that benefit the less wealthy. In fact, one could argue that although the transmission of partisanship reflects socialization, the reason it persists is that it is in one's self-interest.

self-interest: *Concern for one's own advantage and well-being.*

Examples of **rationality** and self-interest abound. Couples with school-age children get interested in education policy. Homeowners become more focused on issues tied to property taxes than individuals who rent. As citizens approach retirement age, they become protective of Social Security and Medicare benefits. Recently young people, too, have been concerned about these benefits, but in ways that reflect their self-interest. They wonder if the entitlement programs will be bankrupt before they are of age to receive them, and they have engaged in the debate about whether the federal government should privatize Social Security, allowing people to invest the Social Security taxes they pay while they are working directly in the stock market. Such evidence suggests the public is rational and that people act in ways consistent with their self-interest.

rationality: *Acting in a way that is consistent with one's self-interest.*

Elites

One of the big questions in the field of public opinion is what role **elites**—leaders of opinion—play in shaping citizens' thinking. A democracy is

elites: *Group of people who may lead public opinion, such as journalists, politicians, and policy makers.*

supposed to be a system in which the average person has a say in government and the people's preferences drive public policy. Yet some worry that experts, policy makers, political observers, journalists, and others in the news media have an undue influence in shaping public opinion. If elites shape public opinion, can the United States be a democratic nation? One way to approach this question of what political scientists call **elite theory** is to recognize, first, that it is not so simple a matter as elites offering an opinion and the public swallowing it. That assumption gives far too much influence to elites and far too little credit to the people. Instead, it helps to understand that elites can influence citizens if two conditions are met: first, citizens must be exposed to the message and, second, they must be open to it.[24]

This theory of who changes opinions and who does not has a number of implications. First, massive change in public opinion is not likely. Second, elites' ability to change public opinion is a product of the intensity and consistency of the message. Disagreement among elites on a new issue will decrease the potential for change. People respond only to ideas that they find appealing and that fit with their own values and opinions. As a model for how people change opinions in response to events, acting out of both self-interest and rationality, we can look at how Americans are viewed by others (see Other Places: The Rise and Fall of Anti-Americanism).

elite theory: *Idea that public opinion is shaped by discourse among elites and is a top-to-bottom process.*

Does every citizen have an equal chance to be heard?

The Shape of Public Opinion

To understand public opinion, it is essential to appreciate the ways it is shaped by partisanship and ideology. These two variables can, to a large extent, explain the opinions of citizens. Although not everyone is partisan or ideological, these forces provide useful frameworks for understanding the public's thinking on issues. With a firm understanding of partisanship and ideology in place, we can address two major questions about public opinion: How informed is the public? And is the public polarized?

Partisanship

party identification: *Attachment or allegiance to a political party; partisanship.*

perceptual lens: *Ideological framework that shapes the way partisans view the political world and process information.*

Party identification, or partisanship, is central to understanding how people think politically. Party identification represents an individual's allegiance to a political party. This psychological attachment to a party usually forms when an individual is young. This attachment, through what is called **perceptual lens**, shapes the way partisans view the political world and process information. The result, for example, is that a Republican would

otherplaces

The Rise and Fall of Anti-Americanism

Following the terrorist attacks of September 11, 2001, the world rallied to support the United States. There was an outpouring of good will and cooperation. More than forty countries joined the United States in providing military assistance to rid Afghanistan of the Taliban, hoping to root out a major source of terrorism. But this support started to erode as the United States deemphasized cooperation to pursue independent policies. The U.S. attack on Iraq in 2003 and subsequent war caused global public opinion to turn against the United States. The figure below shows a downward trend in the image of the United States held by four democracies. Israel's image of the United States remains stable, reflecting the long-standing ties.

This trend is now reversing itself. The election of Barack Obama was hailed across much of the world and has signaled a new tone of cooperation. As a result, the U.S. image abroad has begun to improve. In Europe, there has been an across-the-board upturn. Between 2008 and 2009, ratings from Britain increased from a little over 50 percent to nearly 70 percent. Ratings from Germany doubled—from about 30 percent to over 60 percent. The same is true for countries in other parts of the world, such as Indonesia and Nigeria. Ratings in India increased from 60 percent to 75 percent.

The rise and fall of anti-Americanism are not unusual. Anti-Americanism has generally increased when the United States is at war, as it did also during the Vietnam War. Each time that America has fallen out of favor, there has also been a rebound. Public opinion around the world is a product of self-interest and rationality.

- **How closely does world opinion of America coordinate with what Americans think about their country?**

- **Should American government be responsive to world opinion?**

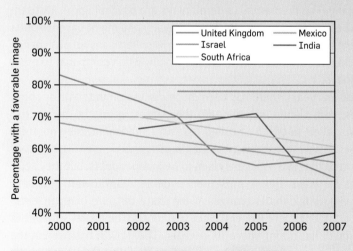

Favorable Image of the United States, 2000–2007.

Sources: Pew Research; Giacomo Chiozza, *Anti-Americanism and the American World Order* (Baltimore: Johns Hopkins University Press, 2009); Chiozza, Report to the APSA Task Force, APSA annual meeting, Toronto, Canada, September 3–6, 2009.

be slower to turn against the Iraq War, initiated by a Republican president, than a Democrat. Conversely, a Republican will be less sympathetic to Barack Obama's reform of health care than would a Democrat.[25]

By knowing party identification, political scientists can predict—with considerable accuracy—attitudes on a range of issues. Republicans, for example, are less likely than Democrats to support government spending to help the poor and elderly. Republicans are not opposed to helping such people, but they want to do so through private charities and individual initiative. More generally, Republicans are less supportive of an activist federal government, while Democrats are more open to giving government an active role in the lives of citizens.

Although partisanship shapes how an individual thinks about politics, it can subside in times of national crisis. Following 9/11, Americans put aside partisan differences. In late September, over 98 percent of Republicans and more than 80 percent (up from 25 percent) of Democrats approved of the job President Bush was doing.[26] Partisanship returned the next year, however, with the 2002 midterm elections.

Because party identification is central to understanding public opinion, pollsters have been asking about partisanship since the 1940s. The American National Elections Studies, a premier academic survey organization, has been asking the same question since 1952: *Generally speaking, do you usually think of yourself as a Republican, a Democrat, an Independent, or what?*[27] This question asks respondents how they "think" about themselves in order to "capture" political identification and the general tendency, or the perceptual lens, of one's thinking. The theoretical underpinnings are psychological. Partisanship can also be likened to loyalty, the kind of loyalty one might have to sports teams or friends that stick through ups and downs. Partisanship can change during one's life, but it tends to be stable, especially when compared to other political attitudes.

In the last few years, there has been much discussion in the press about Independents, with claims that they are the "largest group in the electorate."[28] And with the rise of the so-called Tea Party movement, their numbers are on the rise. This view that Americans are mostly Independent is, however, a myth.[29] It is true that many citizens claim to be Independents, but they actually behave as partisans. That is, most Independents "lean" toward one party or the other. Figure 6.2 charts changes in the share of "pure Independents" as opposed to "Independent leaners" since the 1950s. The "pure" variety has been pretty much flat during these six decades. The growth has been in the "leaners," and that growth has been quite substantial. But these individuals vote consistently for one party and are very much partisans despite self-professed labels. Their behavior is testimony to the strength of partisanship in the United States.

political ideology: *Set of consistent political beliefs.*

liberals: *Individuals who have faith in government to improve people's lives, believing that private efforts are insufficient. In the social sphere, liberals usually support diverse life styles and tend to oppose any government action that seeks to shape personal choices.*

Ideology

Political ideology has a complex relationship with partisanship. **Liberals** tend to be Democrats and **conservatives** tend to be Republicans, but ideology speaks to both political and social values. Conservatives view a good society as one that allows individuals to pursue their economic interests in an unfettered fashion. Liberals worry that, without some governmental regulation to curb abuse and moderate economic cycles, the rich will get very rich and the poor will get very poor. This concern leads liberals to believe that government can improve people's lives and prevent inequalities that harm society and the economy as a whole. Conservatives are much

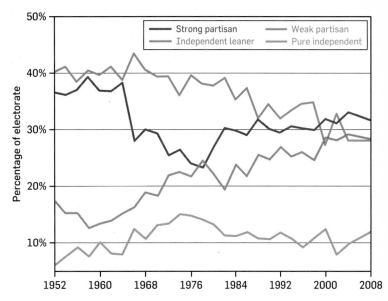

FIGURE 6.2 Independents in the Electorate. These data show that "pure Independents" constitute just a small part of the American electorate, a proportion that has remained about the same for the last fifty years. Such data are important in understanding the continuing importance of partisanship in America.
Source: John Sides, George Washington University, 2009.

more leery of government and view it as a problem in and of itself. They contend that less government interference will give the poor the opportunity to improve their lives by themselves. On social issues, the tables are turned. That is, liberals tend to believe that people should be able to make personal choices free from government interference. Conservatives, by contrast, value more traditional life styles and in fact want government, at times, to enforce such choices.

Not all citizens think of themselves as a liberal or conservative. Depending on the wording of the question, about 40 percent of Americans view themselves as ideological moderates, about 25 percent as liberals, and the remaining 35 percent as conservatives.[30] But there is also a debate among political scientists about whether citizens think ideologically at all. That is, do people have coherent views about politics? One famous effort to measure the ideological foundations, or **levels of conceptualization**, of the public's thinking found little evidence of such organized opinions. Data from the 1950s indicated that only about 12 percent of the public viewed the political parties in ideological terms, whereas over 40 percent judged the parties by the groups (such as social class or racial and ethnic groups) they were thought

conservatives: *Individuals who distrust government, believing that private efforts are more likely to improve people's lives. In the social sphere, conservatives usually support traditional life-styles and tend to believe government can play a valuable role in shaping personal choices.*

levels of conceptualization: *Measure of how ideologically coherent individuals are in their political evaluations.*

How does party
identification relate to
ideology?

to represent rather than the policies they pursued. About 25 percent evaluated the parties by "the nature of the times": Is the economy doing well? Are we embroiled in a war? The remainder—just over 20 percent—did not think about issues at all when evaluating the parties and candidates; this part of the public showed "no issue content."[31]

Over the last fifty years, there have been some changes in size of these four groups, but not major ones. Using data from 2000, about 20 percent of citizens can be thought of as being ideological thinkers, 28 percent focus on groups, another 28 percent is driven by the nature of the times, and 24 percent have no issue content at all in their political thinking.[32] From this evidence, it would be hard to argue that even a majority of the public has a coherent, ideologically driven view of politics.

Nevertheless, it is still worth looking at the public's ideological mood. Is the public, collectively, becoming more liberal or more conservative? Such changes should aid understanding of the general direction of the country. Figure 6.3 maps changes in the public's ideological thinking between 1937 and 2009.

FIGURE 6.3 **Liberal Self-Identification.** Liberal self-identification has declined since highs in the mid-1930s and early 1960s but now appears to be again on the rise.
Source: Christopher Ellis and James A. Stimson, "On Symbolic Conservatism in America," paper presented at the 2007 annual meeting of the American Political Science Association; data updated by Ellis and Stimson.

This seventy-year time period reveals some interesting trends. The liberal nature of public opinion was apparent between 1937 and 1964—an era dominated by the Democrats. In the mid-1960s, with the unpopularity of the Vietnam War and growing concerns about civil rights, crime, and excessive government involvement in the economy, conservatism grew—and grew quickly. The pattern since the 1960s has been back and forth, with liberalism on the rise of late. Even with the recent gains, however, the share of liberals in the population generally is still far less than in the time of Franklin Roosevelt, Harry Truman, and John Kennedy.

Is the public becoming more liberal or more conservative? How can you tell?

Is the Public Informed?

A democracy rests on having an engaged and well-informed electorate. Otherwise, how can the public make good choices? If the power is to rest with the people, the people need to be knowledgeable about the issues of the day and the candidates who compete for public office. But are they? When survey research began in the 1940s, it became possible to gather a systematic assessment of the public's knowledge about politics. The early evidence was not encouraging. In a detailed study of the 1940 presidential campaign, scholars from Columbia University assumed that voters were like consumers and would look for the best deal, and that the campaign would be an important source of information as they made their choices. But the data told a different tale. Instead, most voters made up their minds *prior* to the campaign, and their choices were driven by where they lived and whom they knew.[33] In a subsequent study, the Columbia researchers went so far as to argue that low turnout in elections might actually be a good thing, because the uninformed will not be choosing the nation's leaders.[34] This argument has strong elitist overtones and certainly strays far from the assumptions about government responsiveness and citizen equality on which American democracy rests. Together with previous findings about levels of conceptualization,[35] these claims suggested that the public may not be capable of meeting its democratic responsibilities. What ensued was a debate over the accuracy and interpretation of these core findings.

Political scientists went, in effect, in search of the "informed" voter, and they learned that citizens do not know many details about politics. Only 10 percent of the public knows the name of the Speaker of the House. Only about a third can name one U.S. Supreme Court justice. Only about half of Americans know which party controls Congress, and less than half know the name of their own congressional representative.[36] These facts suggest that average citizens do not possess the detailed information necessary to hold their government accountable.

Should these data be taken as evidence that the public is not able to meet its democratic responsibilities? Let us consider some findings that give reason for optimism.

First, the public, collectively, seems to make reasonable choices. For example, when the economy is doing poorly, the party in power suffers. Voters hold presidents and legislators accountable; failures are punished and successes are rewarded. Further, the public does not like it when the United States is at war and rewards candidates who pursue peace.[37]

Second, although individuals do not know all the details about candidates' views on all the issues, they do tend to know candidates' views on the issues that are **salient** to them. Hunters know candidates' views on gun control; college students know candidates' views on student loans. One study estimates that when an issue is salient to an individual, that individual knows candidates' views on that issue correctly more than 90 percent of the time.[38]

Third, the public can learn quickly if an issue is salient enough to them and receives attention in the news media. Following 9/11, the public understood the need to consider some curtailment of civil liberties to ensure security.

Fourth, public opinion is more stable than suggested by the shifting answers people give to the same question just a few months apart. The instability reflected in polls does not speak to a fickle or poorly informed public. Instead, it appears that polls themselves may be at fault.[39] That is, survey questions and the normal error associated with these questions make people's attitudes appear more unstable than they really are. Further, most issues are complex and leave many people genuinely conflicted. Being conflicted is not a sign of lack of information, but perhaps a realization that some problems are thorny and not easily answered.

Fifth and finally, personal decision making is not always based on complete information, so why should political decision making be expected to conform to rational models that scholars use? Individuals often rely on cues and instincts to make decisions, rather than on an analysis of detailed information. Scholars have termed such thinking **low information rationality**.[40] For example, in 1992, President George H. W. Bush (1989–93) asked what milk cost in grocery stores. His admission that he did not know suggested he was out of touch with ordinary Americans, who do their own shopping. His competitor, Bill Clinton, knew the price of milk and other items, such as jeans. Simple things like not knowing what groceries cost turned some voters against Bush.

It is easy to make any member of the public—even presidents!—look uninformed, and of course it would be better if the public knew more about politics. But individuals do appear to learn about the issues that matter to them. Gaining information is a gateway to influence, because individually people learn what they need to know to advance their interests, and collectively voters do hold government officials accountable.

Is the Public Polarized?

The engaged and informed citizens of a democracy cannot be expected to agree on everything. They will naturally have different views on issues. When the differences become stark, however, the danger is that

salient: *Indication of importance and relevance of an issue to an individual.*

low information rationality: *Idea that people do not need to have lots of information to make good decisions.*

polarization fuels controversy and personal attacks to the point that compromise and consensus become impossible. Congress has clearly become more polarized over the last thirty years. Figure 6.4 tries to capture the idea of polarization on a simple left–right continuum. In the 1970s, the parties adopted positions that were close to the middle; thirty years later, they are more at the extremes. In fact, Democrats and Republicans disagree

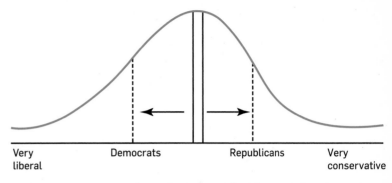

Very liberal   Democrats   Republicans   Very conservative

FIGURE 6.4 **Political Polarization in the United States.** When the parties are polarized they move toward the tail of these distributions. When parties are depolarized they adopt positions near to each other. Currently the parties are polarized, but that was not the case in the 1970s.
Source: The authors.

on more issues now than any time since the end of the Civil War.[41] What is less clear is whether the public, too, is polarized.

Some scholars have argued that the public has polarized along with parties, but there is also evidence that the public is more moderate, even though the choices the parties offer them are not.[42] For example, according to a series of surveys conducted by the Pew Center between 1987 and 2007, "the average difference between Republican and Democratic identifiers on forty political and social issues increased from 10 to 14 percent, a surprisingly small difference."[43] These data suggest that the public is more moderate than the choices that are laid before them in elections would suggest.[44]

Many worry that one effect of polarization will be more personal attacks on political figures and greater incivility in politics. Others argue, however, that increasing polarization only indicates that people care more about who wins elections and that their interest in elections has increased. In fact, the share of the public who cares about which party wins the presidential election has increased since 1988. Interest in elections, generally, also seems to be on the rise. In 1988, 44 percent of the public paid "a lot" of attention to the presidential campaign. In 2000, the proportion stood at 53 percent, a notable gain. By 2008, the percentage was a whopping 72 percent.[45] The 2008 increase surely reflects response to the candidacy of Barack Obama, but it is also true that the differences between the candidates in recent elections have been stark enough to prompt lots of interest.

Having a clear choice engages people and gives them a stake in an election outcome. If the system became **depolarized** (see Figure 6.4), the public would lack a choice. It would no longer matter if Democrats or Republicans won, because they would do the same thing once in office. For these reasons, many scholars in the 1950s called for **responsible parties** that would offer

polarization: *Condition in which differences between parties and/or the public are so stark that disagreement breaks out, fueling attacks and controversy.*

Does a polarized public prevent good policy making?

Do political parties influence public opinion, or is it the other way around?

depolarized: *Political system in which the parties adopt the same positions on issues and choice is limited, leading citizens to feel less compelled to participate in elections.*

responsible parties: *Parties that take responsibility for offering the electorate a clear and distinct range of policies and programs, thus providing a clear choice.*

the public a real choice. Citizens, under such conditions, can more effectively hold officials accountable for misdeeds and reward success.

Group Differences

Public opinion is shaped by partisanship and ideology. Social scientists find that demographics also matter—that is, the tendency for certain groups within the American population to hold similar views. These breakdowns by group are the microfoundations of public opinion. In this section, we look at the ways that socioeconomic status, religion, gender, race and ethnicity, and education tend to organize public opinion.

Socioeconomic Status

socioeconomic status:
Combined measure of occupation, education, income, wealth, and relative social standing or lifestyle.

Socioeconomic status is a combined measure of occupation, education, income, wealth, and relative social standing or lifestyle. Socioeconomic status influences where one lives, what kind of work one does, whom one knows, the kinds of schools one attends, and the kinds of opportunities one can take advantage of. These matters inevitably mold political attitudes. Working-class people favor more government programs to help the poor and provide child care, more funding for public education, and more protection for Social Security. In 2004, 70 percent of Americans earning between $15,000 and $35,000 supported spending by government on important social services. For those earning between $75,000 and $105,000, the proportion drops to about 55 percent.[46]

Part of the reason for the strong differences in opinion among different income groups is that political parties have a class bias. Republicans draw far more support from those who come from higher socioeconomic status than do Democrats. Starting in the 1980s, however, Republicans also began to draw support from working-class people who supported a conservative social agenda and a decreased role for government in the economy. These so-called **Reagan Democrats** were central to Republican success in the ensuing decades.

Reagan Democrats:
Voters traditionally affiliated with the Democratic Party based on their working-class status but who defected in the 1980s to vote for Ronald Reagan because of his conservative message on social issues, a strong national security, and limited government.

Age

Age also influences opinion on issues, because the stage of one's life affects how one thinks about issues. For instance, 70 percent of people under 30 years old favor increased spending on student loans. That drops to 42 percent for those over 55. This gap makes sense because younger people are more likely to need student loans. Younger people are much more likely to favor making marijuana legal than older people are. Those under 30 also are more supportive of gay marriage than people over 55. In general, older citizens are more socially conservative than younger citizens,[47] and there is evidence that people tend to become more conservative as they age.

Religion

Religious affiliation is another indicator of opinion. Overall, for example, Protestants are more conservative than Catholics or Jews. Only 12 percent of Jews describe themselves as conservative, compared to 36 percent of Protestants. The attitudes of Muslims have recently started to draw attention. On some issues, they have been found to be more liberal than the general population and significantly more liberal than Protestants or Catholics. For example, 70 percent of Muslims favor an activist government, whereas just 43 percent of the public as a whole subscribes to that view. On social issues, however, Muslims show a much more conservative tendency. When answering the question, *Which comes closer to your view? Homosexuality is a way of life that should be accepted by society or homosexuality is a way of life that should be discouraged by society,* 61 percent of Muslims said homosexual lifestyles should be "discouraged." Only 38 percent of all Americans gave that response.[48]

Recent studies of religion and public opinion have focused on differences within denominations, particularly with the rise of evangelical Christianity among Protestants. Starting in the 1970s, and especially after the *Roe v. Wade* (1973) Supreme Court decision made abortion legal under some conditions, evangelicals became more active in politics. They also have strong views opposing gay rights and supporting school prayer. On the issue of abortion, in 2004, only 11 percent of "evangelical" Protestants described themselves as pro-choice. Among more secular Protestants, nearly 60 percent advocated pro-choice positions. The same pattern holds for supporting same-sex marriage. Secular Protestants were six times more likely to favor same-sex marriage than evangelical Protestants.[49]

Table 6.1 explores differences among Protestants on the issue of immigration. White evangelical Protestants take a much less favorable view of immigrants than "mainline" Protestants (those belonging to older denominations such as the Presbyterian or Episcopal church) and those who describe themselves as secular, that is, without religious affiliation. Among evangelicals, 63 percent see "newcomers" as threats to "traditional American customs and values." Only 39 percent of seculars hold that opinion. A near majority of seculars (45 percent) believe immigrants "strengthen our country with their hard work and talents." Less than 30 percent of white evangelicals agree. These kinds of differences underscore the importance of looking within denominations for patterns in U.S. public opinion.

TABLE 6.1 Religious Tradition and Views on Immigrants

	All	White Evangelical Protestant	White Mainline Protestant	White Non-Hispanic Catholic	Secular
The growing number of newcomers from other countries . . .					
Threatens traditional American customs and values	48%	63%	51%	48%	39%
Strengthens American society	45%	32%	44%	47%	54%
Don't know/Refused	7%	5%	5%	5%	7%
	100%	100%	100%	100%	100%
Immigrants today . . .					
Are a burden because they take our jobs, housing, and health care	52%	64%	52%	56%	46%
Strengthen our country with their hard work and talents	41%	29%	42%	41%	45%
Don't know/Refused	7%	7%	6%	3%	9%
	100%	100%	100%	100%	100%

Source: Gregory Smith, "Attitudes toward Immigration: In the Pulpit and the Pew," Pew Research Center, April 2006.

Gender

gender gap: *Differences in the political attitudes and behavior of men and women.*

Starting in 1980, a **gender gap** emerged in U.S. politics. Prior to 1980, the differences in political attitudes among men and women were not large and did not draw much attention. However, in elections since Ronald Reagan's victory over Jimmy Carter (1977–81), women have been generally more supportive of Democrats than Republicans. Barack Obama secured 56 percent of the female vote and just 49 percent of the male vote. The differences are such that, if only women were allowed to vote, the Democrats might have won every presidential election since 1980 save for Reagan's landslide against Walter Mondale in 1984.[50]

In general, women are more liberal than men, and gender gaps are also evident on specific issues. Women were less supportive of the Iraq War, believing in larger numbers in 2004 that the war "was not worth fighting." Women favor more spending on social programs than men. In 2000, 67 percent of women favored more spending on child care, whereas 58 percent of men held this view. Men are much more likely to support the death penalty than are women (62 percent versus 38 percent). This gap is not nearly as wide when it comes to abortion. In 2009, 50 percent of women and 44 percent of men thought abortion should be legal.[51]

Race and Ethnicity

Another divide in public opinion involves race and ethnicity. The issue of slavery tore the nation apart, and one hundred years after the Civil War, Americans remained divided about issues involving race. In 1964, African Americans overwhelmingly endorsed desegregation, whereas white Americans were split on the issue. In 1974, only 25 percent of white Americans felt "government should help blacks," whereas 63 percent of African Americans believed that government should take that role.[52] Similar gaps exist in regards to support for **affirmative action**, policies that grant preferences to those who have suffered discrimination in the past (not only African Americans but women) in job hiring, school admissions, and contracting. In 2004, only 11 percent of whites favored "preferences for hiring blacks." Four times as many African Americans favored affirmative action.[53]

affirmative action:
Policies that grant racial or gender preferences in hiring, education, or contracting.

Latinos include a broad array of groups that do not necessarily share a common experience, and so opinion among them tends to be divided. The families of some Latinos in the Southwest have lived there for centuries, since before the area became a part of the United States in 1848. Others came to the United States within the last few years, from homelands throughout Central and South America. Cuban immigrants, who left their homeland following the rise of Fidel Castro and the Communists in the late 1950s, tend to be much more conservative than Puerto Ricans or Mexican Americans. According to one study, about 60 percent of Cuban Americans are Republican identifiers, whereas only about 15 percent of Mexican Americans support the GOP.[54] Latinos are divided in other ways as well. According to one group of prominent scholars:

> On many key domestic issues, significant majorities of each [Latino] group take the liberal position. On other issues, there is no consensus and, depending on the issue, Mexicans may be on the right, while Cubans and many Puerto Ricans are on the left of the nation's current political spectrum. Thus, labels such as liberal or conservative do not adequately describe the complexity of any one group's political views.[55]

Thus, both parties compete for the support of the Latino community. In 2004, Latino support for President George W. Bush helped him defeat John

Kerry. In 2008, however, Barack Obama gained two-thirds of the Latino vote, a shift partly owing to actions by Republicans in Congress to block immigration reform. As a group, Latinos favor bilingual education more than Anglos and they support policies that favor immigration more than Anglos. These differences surely reflect the fact that these issues are more salient to them.[56]

Asian American public opinion has not drawn the same level of attention as other groups. Asian Americans are, however, a growing segment of the population and constitute a sizable part of the population of some states, especially California. In general, Asians are a bit more liberal than white Americans. In 2004, for example, about 60 percent of Asian Americans supported John Kerry, whereas only 44 percent of white Americans did so. Their disapproval of the Iraq War was stronger than that of white Americans, but not nearly as strong as that of African Americans.[57] Like Latinos, Asian Americans are diverse, including people from Korea, Vietnam, Japan, and China.

Education

One of the important changes in the American population is the increasing level of education. Figure 6.5 charts the share of Americans who had at least attended a year of college over the last 60 years. The pattern is striking. In 1948, about one in seven Americans had gone to college for at least one year. By 2008, more than one in two Americans had attended college. The upward trend has been continuous since the end of World War II in 1945. There are two key reasons for this trend. The first is that more young people have access to a college education. The second is what is called "generational replacement." That is, older, less-educated citizens have passed on, and the average level of education of the American public has thus increased.

That people in the United States are more educated matters. In broad strokes, there is a long-standing belief that a democracy is best able to endure when its citizens are engaged and informed. With more education, the public

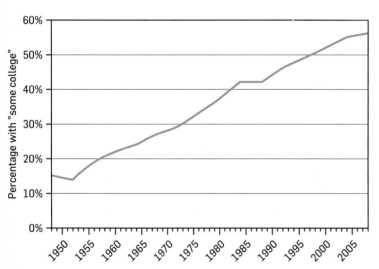

FIGURE 6.5 Percentage with "Some College" Education, 1948–2008. Since the end of World War II, education levels have steadily increased. Level of education is a factor affecting public opinion on a range of specific issues.
Source: American National Election Studies, http://www.electionstudies.org/.

should be more aware of politics and better able to find ways to ensure government responds to them. In the language of this book, a better-educated public should be in a better position to travel through the gateways of influence and find ways around the many gates in the American political system.

Think again: does being a member of a demographic group shape opinion?

Public Opinion and Public Policy: Military Action and Antiterrorism

To see how public opinion affects the policies pursued by government, we examine foreign policy, focusing on military action and antiterrorism measures. Public opinion exerts a different type of influence in each. The relationship between public opinion and domestic policy is taken for granted, but with continuing terrorist attacks around the world and a war in Afghanistan, it is important to consider the relationship between public opinion and foreign policy.

Military Action

The president, as commander in chief, has always made the decision to engage in military action. Although Congress has formally declared war only five times, U.S. troops have been sent into conflicts or potential conflicts about two hundred fifty times since the beginning of the nation.[58] For military missions that are publicized, not secret, a president usually enjoys widespread support if the mission can be clearly tied to preserving national security. In cases in which the United States is attacked on its own soil, support for a military response is even higher. This so-called **rally-around-the-flag effect** is a surge in patriotic sentiment that translates into presidential popularity.[59] For example, when President George H. W. Bush commenced the first Gulf War, his approval ratings shot up to 89 percent.[60] His son, President George W. Bush, experienced a similar spike in popularity after the aftermath of the attacks of September 11, 2001; his job approval ratings went from 52 percent to 90 percent, and they remained above 70 percent for almost an entire year.[61]

The public's influence on the president's decision to engage in military action is always limited because the amount of information available to the public is purposely restricted, both to ensure the safety of the troops involved and to preserve military advantages in conflict. The fundamental imbalance

rally-around-the-flag effect: *Surge of public support for the president in times of international crisis.*

Should public opinion influence foreign or defense policy when military secrets are withheld from the public?

Congress

President

Citizens

Military actions

Joint Chiefs
of Staff

Director
of the CIA

National
Security
Adviser

Secretary of
Defense

of information held by the government versus what the general public understands poses a major problem for the assumptions of a democracy, because the people cannot hold the government fully accountable if they are not fully informed. Nevertheless, when a president decides to send troops, he has to anticipate public reaction and hope that the public maintains its trust and confidence in his decision to take such action.

Following the rally-around-the-flag effect, public support for extended military engagements declines, as the polls reveal. Americans do not like war, and this core value drives public opinion and U.S. defense policy. The fundamental problem for the American public is that once the United States enters into a military conflict, there are few actual ways that the public can effectively change military strategy or troop levels. Only when public opinion turns against a war effort is there any real pressure on the president and Congress to take steps to end it.

For example, Figure 6.6 tracks public opinion on two major conflicts, the Vietnam War and the Iraq War. At the beginning of each war, there was considerable public support for it; only 25 percent of the public thought it was a mistake to go into the conflict. However, as time progressed and the number of American troops killed and wounded grew, public apprehension about the war also grew. From 1965 to 1968, the percentage of the public who thought the Vietnam War was a mistake more than doubled, and it became a major issue in the 1968 presidential campaign. Richard Nixon, the Republican Party presidential candidate, sensed a change in the public's attitude toward the war and pledged to end the U.S. involvement in Vietnam by promising "peace with honor." As president, Nixon did end the war, but it took him five years to do so.

In the case of the Iraq War, there is even stronger evidence that the number of casualties directly affects public support for military conflict. For example, in the 2006 House elections, voters punished Republican candidates in districts with higher casualty rates.[62] It also appears that the public's support for conflict is a product of calculations involving the likely winner, the upward or downward trend in casualties, and the possible payoff from the conflict.[63]

From 2003 to 2008, the portion of the public who thought the Iraq War was a mistake grew from 25 percent to 60 percent, and in 2008, the Democratic nominee Barack Obama promised to withdraw the majority of American troops from Iraq within two years. President Obama kept that promise, withdrawing the last of American combat troops from Iraq on August 31, 2010. But he did decide to send thirty thousand more troops to Afghanistan. The public was leery of such a move, given the problems in Iraq, but Obama nevertheless sought to secure public support.[64]

Although the power of public opinion is slow-moving, when a majority of Americans oppose a military conflict elected leaders recognize that they either must change course or find a way to rally the public to their side.

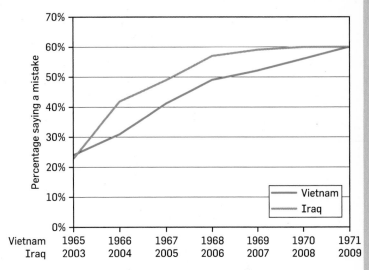

FIGURE 6.6 Percentage Who Thought Sending Troops to Vietnam and Iraq a Mistake. While only about 25 percent of Americans thought it was a mistake to send troops to Vietnam and to Iraq at the beginning of these conflicts, within three years more than 50 percent of the public thought the conflicts a mistake, and the percentages continued to grow.
Source: Gallup Poll.

Antiterrorism Measures

The terrorist attacks of September 11, 2001, prompted a huge increase in government's efforts to stop future terrorist acts against U.S. citizens at home and abroad. In general, public opinion was highly supportive of the steps that President George W. Bush claimed were necessary to fight terrorism. These steps were taken with advice from the same units that handle military policy, with the important addition of the Federal Bureau of Investigation and the Department of Justice. The Bush administration authorized the detaining of suspects, whether U.S. citizens or not, without charges or trials, and wiretapping (eavesdropping) without a warrant. With the onset of the war in Iraq, the measures employed in the name of antiterror security increased. Then, in 2004, CBS News and the *New Yorker* magazine broke the story about the Abu Ghraib facility in Iraq, where Iraqi prisoners were subject to activities that violated international norms of treatment and might be considered torture.[65] Subsequently, it was also revealed that the U.S. interrogators used waterboarding, a near-drowning technique, as a means of getting information from prisoners about potential terrorist plots. The international community

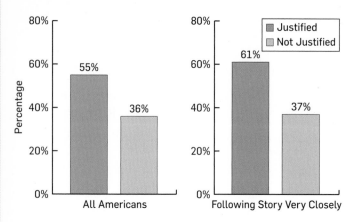

FIGURE 6.7 **Support for Harsh Interrogation Techniques.**
A majority of the public supports the use of harsh interrogation techniques for terrorism suspects. The more closely a person follows the story of the treatment of terrorism suspects, the more likely he or she is to support harsh techniques.
Source: Gallup Poll daily tracking, April 24–25, 2009.

considers waterboarding to be torture, and many Americans also objected. The issue of treatment of detainees became a major issue in the 2008 presidential campaign. After he took office, President Obama declared that the United States would no longer engage in any practice that violated international norms. The president has also been struggling with the closing of the Guantánamo Bay facility for detainees located in Cuba. Despite an early consensus in the White House to close this facility, deciding what to do with existing detainees and how best to handle others who may be engaged in terrorism have proven difficult.[66]

Americans remain conflicted in their collective opinion of the type of force necessary to preserve national security. As of 2009, a Gallup Poll reported majority support for the use of harsh interrogation techniques (see Figure 6.7) for terrorism suspects. The same poll revealed, however, that 51 percent of the respondents favored an investigation into how these techniques are used. Here is the same dilemma the public faces with military action: by their very nature, antiterrorism policies must remain secret to be effective, and the only opportunity the public has to register an opinion about government action in this area is after that action has been taken. If it can be shown that government action saved American lives by uncovering and then preventing a terrorist attack through harsh interrogation techniques, then the public will support them; otherwise, the public will want to limit them.

Public Opinion and Democracy

For a country to be considered democratic, the views of the public must affect the course of government. To do so, the public must be sufficiently well informed to be able to make good decisions and to ensure that politicians act in a way consistent with public preferences. Average Americans do not know a lot of details about politics, but the nation's many successes indicate that the public is equal to the task of self-government. In 2008, when most people thought the country was on the wrong track, they voted for change and put Barack Obama in office. By supporting Obama, the public signaled a clear break from the policies of the Bush administration.

Elections are one means by which the public expresses its will, but on a year-to-year, even day-to-day basis, public officials can stay in touch with what the public thinks through polls. Scientific polling permits researchers to measure people's thinking with considerable accuracy and gives average Americans a chance to speak out on policy and contribute to policy making. Scientific polling, introduced in the 1930s, not only created greater equality but also provided the gateways through which the public could affect the course of government. Although it is clear that public officials are generally responsive to public opinion,[67] there are legitimate questions about how responsive American government actually is. Some suggest that the connection between opinion and policy is weak. Others point out that the public has mixed feelings on many issues and does not have concrete opinions about some of the toughest questions, so can offer little guidance. Still others argue that politicians use policy to manipulate public opinion. That interaction is troubling and is not the way a democratic system in which the government is accountable to the people should work. These concerns are why it is so instructive to look at the general patterns and the nation's general successes.

It is also important to recognize that, in a democracy, politicians know the kinds of issues the public will respond to and rebel against, and so they adopt views that will not arouse the electorate's anger. They are aware, in other words, of what political scientists call **latent public opinion**,[68] and this awareness makes them responsive and accountable. The ability to anticipate public opinion is an invaluable skill, helping officials avoid quagmires and stress issues that hit a responsive chord with the public. Thus the power of public opinion in a democracy is both direct and indirect, and its effects are revealed in many ways.

FOCUS QUESTIONS

- How does public opinion influence public policy?

- In what ways are elected officials responsive to public opinion? How responsive should they be?

- Is every citizen's voice equal, or are some people more influential? Why?

- How well does polling capture public opinion? Should polls direct public policy?

- Does public opinion provide a gateway or a gate to democracy?

latent public opinion:
Underlying opinions and attitudes of the public that are not always captured in public opinion data but are recognized by public officials and influential in policy making.

GATEWAYS TO LEARNING

Top Ten to Take Away

1. Public opinion—the aggregate of citizen attitudes—is essential to the workings of a democracy. (pp. 178–182)

2. Scientific polling enables public officials to gauge public opinion with some degree of confidence, though polls can be in error. (pp. 182–186)

3. Citizens' opinions and attitudes are shaped by environment, political socialization, generational effects, and self-interest. (pp. 186–189)

4. Elites do drive public opinion, but only to the extent that citizens are exposed and open to their message. (pp. 189–190)

5. Party identification can help predict individual attitudes, and liberal or conservative leanings shape views on political and social issues. (pp. 190–193)

6. Generally, the public has been becoming less liberal, although there is a recent uptick. (pp. 193–195)

7. Although parties have grown more polarized in recent years, the electorate is more moderate than party choices allow. (pp. 196–198)

8. Political opinion is also divided by demographic groups. (pp. 198–203)

9. In recent years, efficacy and public trust in government have fallen. (p. 180)

10. In national security issues, the public is often deliberately not informed, and public officials have to work hard to maintain public trust, especially as the American public has a strong preference for peace. (pp. 203–206)

A full narrative summary of the chapter is on the book's website.

Ten to Test Yourself

1. How was public opinion gauged before scientific polling?

2. Describe how polls may be in error.

3. How does environment shape political attitudes?

4. What other factors shape political attitudes?

5. Is the public "rational"? How do you know? What are some examples?

6. What is the relationship between partisanship and ideology?

7. What do liberals generally believe? What do conservatives generally believe?

8. How well informed, or uninformed, is the American public? Does it matter?

9. What are the effects of political polarization?

10. In what way does public opinion affect military action and antiterrorism policy?

More review questions and answers and chapter quizzes are on the book's website.

Terms to Know and Use

affirmative action (p. 201)

approval rating (p. 179)

census (pp. 182, 183)

confidence interval (p. 185)

conservatives (p. 193)

depolarized (p. 197)

efficacy (p. 180)

elite theory (p. 190)

elites (p. 189)

exit polls (p. 183)

Gallup Poll (p. 182)

gender gap (p. 200)

generational effects (p. 188)

Independents (p. 187)

latent public opinion (p. 207)

levels of conceptualization (p. 193)

liberals (pp. 192, 193)

low information rationality (p. 196)

nonattitudes (p. 186)

party identification (p. 190)

perceptual lens (p. 190)

polarization (p. 197)

political ideology (pp. 192, 193)

political trust (p. 180)

polls (p. 180)

population (p. 183)

public opinion (p. 179)

push polls (p. 184)

rally-around-the-flag effect (p. 203)

random sample (p. 182)

rationality (p. 189)

Reagan Democrats (p. 198)

representative sample (p. 198)

response rate (p. 186)

responsible parties (p. 197)

salient (p. 196)

sample (pp. 182, 183)

sampling error (p. 185)

scientific polling (p. 182)

self-interest (p. 189)

socialization (p. 187)

socioeconomic status (p. 198)

straw polls (p. 182)

tracking polls (p. 183)

Use the vocabulary flash cards on the book's website.

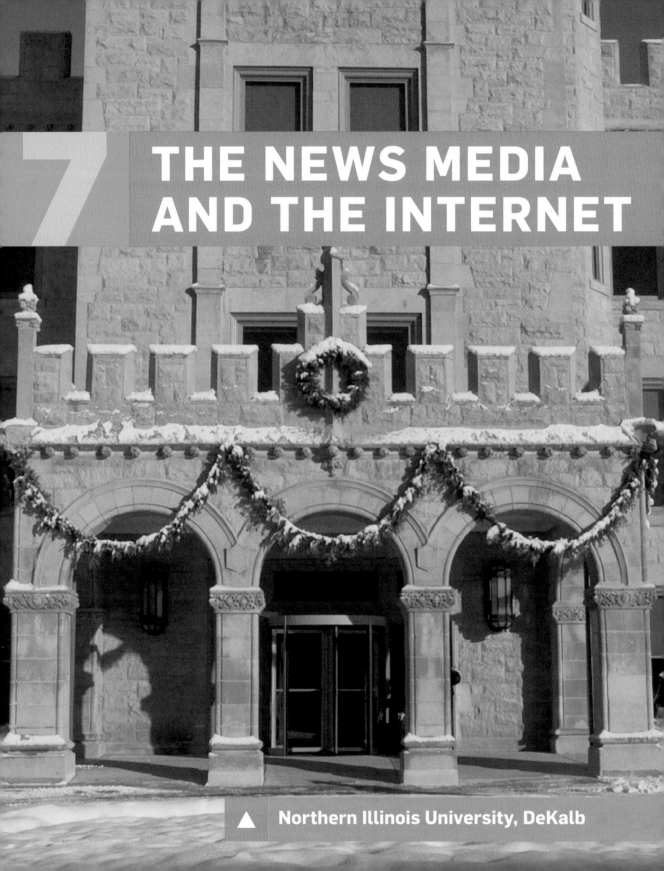

7 THE NEWS MEDIA AND THE INTERNET

Northern Illinois University, DeKalb

> *I didn't have the pedigree to be 'heard,' and the media and political gatekeepers worked to marginalize me and my new allies in the nascent but growing netroots. But it didn't matter. The floodgates were open, and technology allowed us to easily (and gleefully) crash those gates.*

In 1992, Markos ("Kos") Moulitsas Zúniga started taking classes at Northern Illinois University. He approached college a bit differently from many students, for he had just finished a three-year tour with the U.S. Army, trained as a 13P, a specialist in the Multiple Launch Rocket System. Kos did not experience combat, but he knew something of war from his childhood. Born in Chicago in 1971 to a Salvadoran mother and a Greek father, he had spent his formative years in El Salvador, where he saw firsthand the ravages of the Salvadoran civil war.

Kos was a little older than most college students, and his military training had accustomed him to a demanding schedule. It had also forged his interest in politics. With his background and interests, he sought to earn two bachelor's degrees, with majors in philosophy, journalism, and political science and a minor in German. But Kos did much more than just take a demanding set of courses. By his senior year, he was editor of Northern Illinois's student newspaper, the *Northern Star*. Following graduation in 1996, Kos went straight to law school at Boston University, but he did not want to be a

Chapter Topics

Visit http://www.cengagebrain
.com/shop/ISBN/0495906190 for
interactive tools including:

- Quizzes
- Flashcards
- Videos
- Animated PowerPoint slides,
  Podcast summaries, and more

Markos ("Kos")
Moulitsas Zúniga ▶

lawyer. Law school provided training that would further his interest in politics.

Kos had been a Republican when he joined the army. But his time in the army and college shifted his attention to liberal causes. In May 2002, he launched the Daily Kos, a blog through which he voiced his opinions, particularly his frustration with the presidency of George W. Bush. Blogging was still relatively new at the time, and Kos had no sense of what would unfold. But his blog coincided with the partisan battles that raged once the shock of the terrorist attacks of September 11, 2001, subsided. Americans' concerns about terrorism and how to combat it were reshaping political life. Kos's commentary drew a large audience, and his blog became a forum for criticism of Bush and the Iraq War, which began in 2003. He tapped into the anger surrounding the war, and his support for Howard Dean's presidential run in 2004 made him a powerful player in Democratic Party politics. Since then, prominent politicians such as Nancy Pelosi, Harry Reid, and Barack Obama have posted regularly on Daily Kos. For Kos, blogging has been a gateway to influence. In 2007, he was named one of the fifty most important people on the web by *PC World*. *Forbes* magazine listed him as the third most influential person on the web in the same year. Today, Daily Kos announces itself as "the premier online political community with 2.5 million unique visitors per month and 215,000 registered users. It is at once a news organization, community, and activist hub." As of January 2010, Daily Kos was the seventeenth most popular blog in the nation.[1]

Kos's gateway to influence involved more than just blogging. The title of a book Kos coauthored—*Crashing the Gate: Netroots, Grassroots, and the Rise of People-Powered Politics*—suggests how the Internet is transforming the way Americans learn and share news about politics. The Internet provides a new platform to distribute the news. Rather than passively learning about the news from professional journalists, citizens now take an active role in communicating news and opinion and in shaping political debate about issues that are important to them. Political information now flows from the bottom up, not just from the top down. The Internet is a gateway that makes it

FOCUS QUESTIONS

- How do the mass media help to make government accountable to the people?

- How has the rise of the Internet increased or decreased the ability of the public to hold government accountable?

- How does the bottom-up approach of twenty-first-century mass media affect citizen participation and equality? What are its other effects?

- When, and under what conditions, should government regulate the media?

- In what ways do the mass media offer gateways to American democracy? In what ways do the modern media establish new gates?

possible for more Americans to participate in the political process. But with the transformation of the news media from print to digital, there are costs as well. Not everyone has equal access to the Internet, generating a digital divide that potentially fosters inequality. In this chapter, we examine and assess the critical role that the news media play in a democracy. We analyze the functions and impact of the press, survey its history, and describe and evaluate the new forms of communication in the twenty-first century.

The News

In a democracy such as the United States, the citizens are supposed to be the ultimate source of power. The decisions made by the public shape the course of government. The public, therefore, needs information about politics to make good choices. Most people cannot directly observe political events, so they rely on the mass media for information about politics and government.

What Are the Mass Media?

The **mass media** represent the vast array of sources of information that are available to the public. These sources include newspapers, television, radio, blogs, online sources, cell phones, and social networks like Facebook. The **news media** (or the **press**) is a subset of the mass media that has traditionally provided the news of the day, gathered and reported by journalists. But, with all the new technologies of the twenty-first century, the news media are changing, because now the average citizen is able to report on politics through blogs such as Daily Kos and websites such as YouTube. These new media have recast journalism, for there is a proliferation of news outlets and no monolithic entity that shapes and defines political reporting. In this chapter, we use the term *mass media* to describe the many ways citizens learn about government and politics.

One aspect of the mass media today is speedy communication. Most young people today (the **Millennials** born between 1982 and 2003) grew up with the 24-7 news cycle, an information world that is very different from that of their parents (and their professors). This chapter takes those changes into account.

Access to information is important because an enduring and effective democracy demands a knowledgeable public.[2] And for the people to be informed, the press needs to be able to do its job free from government interference, and journalists must feel free to be critical of the government. This **watchdog** role of the press lies at the very heart of a democracy. Freedom of

mass media: *News sources, including newspapers, television, radio, and the Internet, whose purpose is to provide a large audience with information about the nation.*

news media: *Subset of the mass media that provides the news of the day, gathered and reported by journalists.*

press: *Another term for the news media or journalists, both of which provide information to the public about political events.*

Millennials: *Generation born between 1982 and 2003.*

watchdog: *Role of the press in monitoring government actions.*

the press is intertwined with the very idea of democratic government, and the First Amendment to the Constitution protects it.

The Functions of the News

The mass media help ensure government accountability and responsiveness by performing three important tasks—informing, investigating, and interpreting the news.

Informing.   Journalists, simply put, inform. In August 2008—just a month before the financial crisis that rocked the nation—about 5 percent of news stories dealt with the economy. In September, that proportion soared to nearly 30 percent.[3] Just a quick scan of any newspaper or network news website provides a great deal of information about a wide range of topics.

Investigating.   The media can also make news by researching and revealing information about events. Politicians often court the press, but they want only favorable coverage. They want journalists to advertise their accomplishments to voters. Yet journalists and politicians are usually in an adversarial relationship because journalists want to report new stories on topics of interest to the public. So reporters love to unearth a scandal—something that politicians want to avoid. Scandals are fresh and exciting, and uncovering them gives journalists real influence. The investigative function not only allows the press to fulfill its role as the watchdogs of democracy; it makes reporters' jobs exciting and important. It is also worth noting that scandals sell newspapers, and the profit motive is a central part of the process.

Why is the relationship between the press and politicians adversarial?

Interpreting.   When the media inform, they also interpret the news. Just giving one story front-page coverage and relegating another to an inside page involves interpreting what is more and less important. But the role of interpretation has taken on even greater significance in the last few decades. In 1960, for example, journalists covered presidential campaigns in a very descriptive fashion. About 90 percent of the campaign stories focused on describing what happened in the campaign that day. But in the following decades, journalists started to interpret events more frequently, assessing why something happened. By the 1990s, more than 80 percent of campaign stories were interpretive.[4]

The Law and the Free Press

The First Amendment to the Constitution states that "Congress shall make no law . . . abridging . . . freedom . . . of the press." But this protection is not unlimited. During times of war (or threat of war), national security concerns may require that the press not publish a story. The government, however, is often too eager to stop publication of controversial stories, whereas the press may be too willing to report on a controversial story that will boost sales. This conflict plays out in debates over **prior restraint**—government's ability to restrict the publication of sensitive material (see Chapter 4). When can government invoke prior restraint? At what point does prior restraint become censorship and thus undermine the ability of the press to be a watchdog?

The answers to these difficult questions have been shaped by Supreme Court decisions. In the early 1930s, for example, the state of Minnesota stopped a small newspaper from publishing controversial claims about the mayor of Minneapolis and convicted the publisher, Jay Near, under state libel laws. Near then appealed the conviction all the way to the Supreme Court. The Court ruled in *Near v. Minnesota* (1931) that only in exceptionally rare cases could the government stop the printing of a story, overturning Near's conviction and invalidating the Minnesota law that led to his conviction. The Court has also reinforced the protections of press freedom in a **libel** case, *New York Times v. Sullivan* (1964), which also set a very high standard—proof of **actual malice**—to convict in a libel suit. Justice William J. Brennan wrote, "We consider this case against the background of a profound national commitment to the principle that debate on public issues should be uninhibited, robust, and wide open, and that it may well include vehement, caustic, and sometimes unpleasantly sharp attacks on government and public officials" (see Supreme Court Cases: *New York Times v. Sullivan*).

But the landmark modern case on the freedom of the press was the *Pentagon Papers* **case** (1971). During the Vietnam War, the *New York Times* secured a copy of a top secret Department of Defense analysis detailing U.S. involvement in Vietnam and began publishing it, believing the information, some of which contradicted official statements, was essential to public understanding of government policy. Citing national security, the Nixon administration secured a court injunction forcing the *Times* to cease publication, but the newspaper appealed, and the case quickly went to the Supreme Court. While not denying the possibility that censorship can be warranted, the Court in this instance rejected the government's argument that national security took precedence over the right to publish documents embarrassing to the government. The government, said the Court, had not met the extraordinary burden of proof needed for prior restraint. In general, the courts have tended to give the edge to the press with the belief that in the long run it is better to protect press freedoms so that the press can in turn help inform the public and hold elected officials accountable.

Consistent with this general predisposition, there are very few laws that constrain the print media, such as newspapers and magazines. The electronic media, however, are more heavily regulated by government. As early as the 1920s, Congress sought to regulate radio to ensure it would serve the public interest. This was a new medium, and Congress wanted to guard against its

prior restraint: *Government restrictions on freedom of the press that prevent the material from being published.*

Near v. Minnesota **(1931):** *Supreme Court case that declared that only in exceptionally rare cases can the government prevent the printing of a news story.*

libel: *Publishing false and damaging statements about another.*

New York Times v. Sullivan **(1964):** *Supreme Court case establishing that proof of actual malice is required to convict in a libel suit.*

actual malice: *Making a statement against public officials or public figures with knowledge that the information was false or with "reckless disregard" of whether it was false or true.*

Pentagon Papers **case (New York Times Co. v. United States) (1971):** *Supreme Court case permitting publication of classified documents on the Vietnam War and thus favoring freedom of the press over the executive authority of the president.*

supremecourtcases

New York Times v. Sullivan (1964)

QUESTION: What level of negligence must be found when public officials sue newspapers for libel?

ORAL ARGUMENT: January 6–7, 1964 (listen at http://www.oyez.org/cases/)

DECISION: March 9, 1964 (read at http://www.findlaw.com/CaseCode/supreme.html)

OUTCOME: Actual malice must be found to convict for libel, thus overturning the libel conviction of the *New York Times* (9–0).

Libel is the publication of false and damaging information about someone. Prior to libel laws, people often responded to libel by challenging the libeler to a duel, as when Vice President Aaron Burr challenged *Federalist* author and former Treasury Secretary Alexander Hamilton to a duel and killed him. To prevent such acts, various states made libel a criminal act. Today, however, it is almost exclusively a question for civil suits, in which one person sues another for damages.

The *Sullivan* case derived from an advertisement placed in the March 29, 1960, *New York Times* by an ad hoc group of civil rights supporters called "The Committee to Defend Martin Luther King."* The ad condemned the "wave of terror" against nonviolent civil rights activists by unnamed "southern violators." Because some of the actions that "the violators" allegedly participated in included arresting King, the chief of the Montgomery, Alabama, police department claimed that all of the allegations were about him and that he had been libeled.

Under Alabama law, once damaging statements are found, the only defense is if the publication can prove that all the particulars are true. The ad in this case was not true in all the particulars. For example, it claimed that protesting students sang "My Country 'Tis of Thee" when they actually sang "The Star-Spangled Banner." The jury thus found against the *Times*, awarding the police chief $500,000 in damages.

The Supreme Court reversed the verdict, declaring that a law holding newspapers liable for criticisms of public officials only if they could prove that every statement in the article was true would lead to massive self-censorship by the press. Instead, the Court declared that libel against public officials required a finding of actual malice, that is, knowledge that the statement was false or reckless disregard of whether it was true or false. Under this standard, the Court found that the ad was substantially true, but even if it had not been substantially true, there was no evidence that the *Times* acted with malice.

This decision has made it much easier for newspapers to criticize public officials. The Court, though, has expanded the ruling to cover public figures as well. So when a supermarket tabloid trashes a popular actor or singer, the individual thus harmed has to prove actual malice to win a suit for libel.

- **What would happen if the media were held legally responsible for any false statement they made?**
- **Should the burden of proof for proving libel of public officials be treated equally to the burden of proof for libel of private people?**

* See http://www.archives.gov/exhibits/documented-rights/exhibit/section4/detail/heed-rising-voices.html

216

being used in a way that might undermine equality and fairness. In 1934, it created the **Federal Communications Commission** (FCC), now a powerful agency that regulates all forms of electronic media, including radio, television and cable television, cell phones, and even wireless networks. Anyone can start a newspaper, but starting a radio station requires a license from the FCC.

Federal Communications Commission: *Executive branch agency charged with regulating and overseeing radio, television, and electronic broadcasting.*

The FCC monitors media ownership as well. For a long time, the FCC worked to ensure that ownership of the news media did not concentrate in just a few hands, concerned that a monopoly would undermine the ability of the media to be fair and able to perform its watchdog function. The Telecommunications Act of 1996 eased the rules concerning multiple ownership, and the FCC has started to relax this standard. As a result, there has been a trend toward greater concentration of media ownership in the last decade. In 1995, major companies generally owned around ten television stations each; ten years later, that number stood at nearly forty. The ownership of radio has also seen a change. Clear Channel Communications owned 520 radio stations in 1999. By 2008, the number stood at 833.[5]

This recent concentration of media ownership is not unique. Without genuine competition, the press, some fear, will become lapdogs, not watchdogs. But even the changes of the last few years have not eliminated competition. It is true that newspapers are now dominated by seven major chains; Gannett alone controls more than 100 daily newspapers. But that is still just about 6 percent of all newspapers in this country.[6] With so many outlets for news in the twenty-first century, it will not happen that just one person or company will come to control it all.

What are the newspapers in your city or town? Who owns them?

The History of the Press in America

The press in America has always been dynamic. Newspapers have developed from occasional pamphlets in the early 1700s, to comprehensive daily publications that aimed for objective reporting of political news, to today's online enterprises filled with a mix of news and entertainment. Journalism emerged by the 1900s as a profession with a commitment to objectivity. In the twentieth century, radio and then television changed how Americans received the news and how they reacted to it. Throughout all this time, the press has variously supported government and elected officials and assumed an adversarial role as it has given citizens the information they need to make government accountable and responsive.

The Colonial Era, 1620 to 1750

In the early colonial period, newspapers were not widely available, and there were few printing presses. *Public Occurrences*, which began publication in Boston in 1690, had only a few pages and was more a pamphlet than a newspaper. Circulation was small, usually less than 2,000 copies.[7] Newspaper publication was more of a hobby for publishers than anything else, and the notion that the press had the right to criticize government was not widely accepted. Colonial governments in fact feared that harsh criticism would incite the public and create instability, so if publishers attacked those in power, they could be thrown into jail and have their printing presses confiscated.

In 1734, John Peter Zenger was jailed for criticizing the colonial governor of New York in his *New York Weekly Journal*. The next year, when his case came to trial, his lawyer, Andrew Hamilton of Philadelphia, decided on a bold strategy. They would admit Zenger's guilt—he had published the critical statements—then argue that the jury should find him not guilty because the statements were true. The press, in other words, had a fundamental right to criticize government, and a free press was more important than the law against **seditious libel** that had put Zenger behind bars. Much to the surprise of the governor and his supporters, the jury agreed and freed Zenger. The case is a landmark in advancing the idea of a free press.

seditious libel: *Conduct or language that incites rebellion against the authority of a state.*

The Founding Era, 1750 to 1790

As tensions between the colonies and Britain increased, interest in politics grew as well, and the press responded. The circulation of newspapers grew twice as fast as the population between 1760 and 1776.[8] That year, when Thomas Paine published *Common Sense*, a pamphlet attacking King George, it sold 150,000 copies, far more than the 2,000 copies political documents normally sold.[9] Given that there were only 2.5 million people in the colonies, that is the equivalent of 18 million copies today! The press helped spread the idea of independence because newspapers served as networks for sharing information. They reached not only subscribers but also many who could not read, for they were read aloud in taverns and town squares.

Partisanship in the press carried over to the battle for ratification of the Constitution, and newspapers provided a vital forum for debate. The Antifederalists waged a fierce campaign against the Constitution,[10] and those supporting the Constitution responded, most famously in a series of essays published in New York newspapers. These essays, by Alexander Hamilton, James Madison, and John Jay, are today known as the ***Federalist Papers*** and are still regarded as a leading source for understanding the Constitution. At the time, the essays helped to lay the groundwork for ratification of the Constitution by the state of New York—a state absolutely critical for making the

Federalist Papers: *Series of essays written by James Madison, Alexander Hamilton, and John Jay under the pseudonym of Publius, arguing for the ratification of the Constitution.*

new government a reality. It is also worth noting that the Antifederalists' criticisms led to the adoption of the Bill of Rights (see Chapter 2 and the Appendix, where *Federalist* 10 and 51 are printed).

The Partisan Era, 1790 to 1900

Following the adoption of the Constitution, most newspapers allied themselves with the Federalists or with the newly emerging Jeffersonian party. Their writers made no effort to adjudicate between the claims and ideas of competing parties. Consequently, rhetoric was often harsh. George Washington (1789–97) was attacked continually by the Jeffersonian press during his time in office.

Even worse criticism was leveled at the second president, John Adams (1797–1801), who was not as universally admired as Washington. Adams was called a liar and feebleminded, among other things.[11] His administration's **Sedition Act** (1798) made it illegal to print or publish any "false, scandalous, and malicious writing" about the federal government, either house of Congress, or the president.

Newspapers continued to have close alliances with political parties in the next decades of the nineteenth century. They not only served as an attack dog on the opposition but also provided a way for presidents and party leaders to express their opinions on the issues of the day. Some presidents, such as James K. Polk (1845–49), even started their own newspapers to get out their message.[12]

During the 1830s and 1840s, new steam presses reduced the cost of publishing newspapers. In 1833, Benjamin Day sold his *New York Sun* for a penny an issue, initiating the era of the **penny press**. At the same time, literacy throughout the nation was growing, and newspaper owners began to realize that they could make higher profits through circulation and advertising than as arms of political parties.[13] They also saw that partisanship actually drove away customers who did not share their political views. So to increase circulation, newspapers began to move toward sensationalism, printing news of crimes and scandals and stories about personalities, much as tabloids do today or as Ben Franklin did in the 1700s. In 1870, for example, only about 13 percent of all newspapers were independent of a political party. By 1900, that proportion had swelled to nearly 50 percent.[14]

The circulation of newspapers rose from about 1.4 million in 1870 to over 8 million within the next thirty years. Quest for market share led to competition over which newspaper could grab the most attention with sensational headlines and stories. Known as **yellow journalism**, this form of news reporting distorted the presentation of events and could mislead the public, all in the interest of boosting sales. Joseph Pulitzer and William Randolph Hearst, the most famous newspaper publishers at the time, used large type, provocative headlines, pictures, and color to attract readers. Hearst actually introduced comics as a way to sell more papers.

Sedition Act (1798): *Made it a crime to criticize the government, later repealed.*

What are the advantages and disadvantages of partisan control of the press?

penny press: *Newspapers sold for a penny, initiating an era in which the press began to rely on circulation and advertising for income, and not on political parties.*

yellow journalism: *Style of journalism in the late nineteenth century, characterized by sensationalism intending to capture the readers' attention and increase circulation.*

What are examples of sensationalized news stories today?

MAINE EXPLOSION CAUSED BY BOMB OR TORPEDO?

Capt. Sigsbee and Consul-General Lee Are in Doubt---The World Has Sent a Special Tug, With Submarine Divers, to Havana to Find Out---Lee Asks for an Immediate Court of Inquiry---Capt. Sigsbee's Suspicions.

CA I. SIGSBEE, IN A SUPPRESSED DESPATCH TO THE STATE DEPARTMENT, SAYS THE ACCIDENT WAS MADE POSSIBLE BY AN ENEMY.

Dr. E. C. Pendleton, Just Arrived from Havana, Says He Overheard Talk There of a Plot to Blow Up the Ship---Capt. Zalinski, the Dynamite Expert, and Other Experts Report to The World that the Wreck Was Not Accidental---Washington Officials Ready for Vigorous Action if Spanish Responsibility Can Be Shown---Divers to Be Sent Down to Make Careful Examinations.

The New York World a day after

who had been Populists and those who became Progressives — clamored for the United States to rescue the Cuban people from the Spanish malefactors.

William Randolph Hearst's *New York Journal* and Joseph Pulitzer's *New York World* competed for circulation with sensational news and screaming headlines. The frenzy they stirred up over the sinking of the USS *Maine* in Havana Harbor in February 1898 helped lead the United States into war with Spain. It is now generally believed that the explosion on the *Maine* was not caused by a Spanish mine but was accidental.

muckraking: *Journalistic practice of investigative reporting that seeks to uncover corruption and wrongdoing.*

Give other examples of investigative journalism making government responsive.

The Professional Era, 1900 to 1950

The development of mass circulation newspapers also led journalism to develop into a serious profession with an ethic of objective reporting. Pulitzer, despite his role in advancing yellow journalism, was a key figure in this transition, believing that a vibrant, independent press was essential for a democracy to endure.

The idea of a public-spirited press was increasingly realized in efforts to investigate wrongdoing in government, business, and industry. Adolph Ochs purchased the *New York Times* in 1896 with the goal of pursuing objective reporting. Such commitments led journalists, with the backing of people like Ochs and Pulitzer, to expose corruption and to encourage genuine reform. Though President Theodore Roosevelt (1901–09) labeled such efforts as **muckraking**—after a character in *Pilgrim's Progress* who rakes "muck," looking for the worst rather than the best—he came to appreciate the service these investigative journalists provided.

Muckraking gave politicians an additional reason to pursue good public policy: to avoid bad press. It is overly simplistic (and optimistic) to claim that muckraking single-handedly led to a fundamental change in how politicians behaved, but investigative journalism has helped hold public officials accountable, even as it has transformed the press into an institution that seeks to advance the public interest.

The rise of professional journalism is also tied to an ethic of objectivity. The goal of being impartial and unbiased in reporting became part of the journalist's creed, especially as taught in new schools of journalism. The American Society of Newspaper Editors adopted a set of principles that declared "news reports should be free from opinion or bias of any kind."[15] Reporters were trained to present facts, not personal opinions, and to describe, not judge.

The muckraking impulses faded by about 1916 or so, but the press's role as a watchdog did not. Now a key goal became to get **the scoop**—to write a story that presented the public with new and important information that was well researched and carefully documented. Journalists sought to cultivate politicians for access to news and stories, and this cultivation led to a different dynamic between politicians and the press. It remained adversarial, but both sides knew they needed each other. As the press and politicians formed closer relationships than they had in the past, the potential for conflicts of interest increased. To retain the relationship, politicians made certain statements **off the record**, with the understanding that journalists would not use them in a story except as **background**, information that could help set the context and provide a broader understanding for the story. As a result, journalists have a strong ethic about not revealing confidential sources.

The Television Era, 1950–2000

CBS /Landov

The rise of television in the 1950s recast the news media and the information available to the public. By the 1960s, the three major networks—ABC, CBS, and NBC—had a near monopoly of television news.

Prior to the advent of television in the 1950s, newspapers and radio had been Americans' main sources of information about their political leaders. By the 1960s, people started to rely more on television news than newspaper for their political information.[16] Television's visuals, especially, redefined the news and even political events. Politicians now aimed to look good on television, because viewers could detect nervousness and judge body language.

The Mass Media in the Twenty-First Century

The media have always been a dynamic institution, but the speed of the changes in the last few decades is truly staggering. The impact of television, for example, changed further with the rise of cable television in the 1970s, 1980s, and 1990s. It was now possible to bring news to the public any time during the day, reshaping the news environment of Americans. Recent advances in technology have opened up additional avenues of communication—nearly all at the same time. It is the pace and the depth of these changes that make the information environment of the twenty-first century different from those that preceded it.

From 1961 to 1982, Walter Cronkite was the anchor for CBS Evening News and one of the most trusted men in America. Usually calm and objective, he broke down when announcing that President John F. Kennedy, shot in Dallas on November 22, 1963, had died. His emotions on the air exemplified the feelings of all Americans.

the scoop: *Colloquial expression for journalists' goal of breaking a news story, providing original and important information to the public.*

off the record: *Information a journalist acquires from interviews that, though not intended for publication, can still be useful in setting a context for important news reports.*

background: *Information journalists gather from individuals that provides valuable context for a story.*

The Changing Media Environment

The options open to Americans for gathering information about politics have constantly expanded. Figure 7.1 displays the changing **media environment** and suggests two main lessons. First, Americans adopt new media quickly. In the early 1920s, there were only five radio stations, and few households owned radios. By 1927, there were seven hundred stations, and ownership was rapidly increasing.[17] By the end of the 1930s, almost everyone in the United States had access to a radio. Television caught on even more quickly.

Only 10 percent of Americans had TV sets in their homes in the early 1950s; by 1960, the figure was 90 percent. Today, nearly all American households have not just one television set but often two or three. Internet access also shows a steep upward trend, from few households in the mid-1990s to more than 70 percent of Americans in 2007.[18] The speed by which these new media have entered the marketplace itself increases. It took television thirteen years to reach 50 million users. In just three years on the market, more than 50 million iPods were sold. Facebook added 100 million users in just nine months![19]

Television proved its importance as a source for political information when the NBC board chair invited the 1960 presidential candidates to debate the issues on television. John F. Kennedy accepted first, saying "I believe you are performing a notable public service in giving the American people a chance to see the candidates of the two major parties face to face." More than 70 million Americans watched the Kennedy-Nixon debates, and today the presidential debates are a fixture of the fall campaign.

media environment: *Structure and design of media through which people obtain information about politics or other current events.*

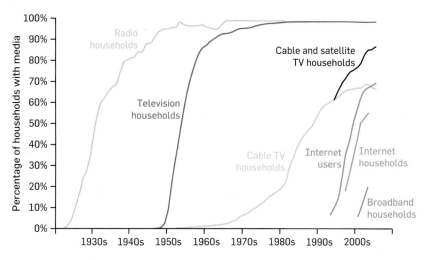

FIGURE 7.1 The Changing Media Environment.
Source: Markus Prior, *Post Broadcast Democracy* (Cambridge, U.K.: Cambridge University Press, 2007).

Second, there are more options for news than ever before. In the 1930s, newspapers and radio were the main sources. In the 1950s, television was a new option, but there were just three networks and they broadcast the news only in the evening. Now cable television, satellite TV, and the Internet make news available night and day.

The Decline of Newspapers

Traditional printed newspapers are in decline. The number of daily papers has dropped from about 1,600 in 1990 to just over 1,400 in 2007.[20] Newspaper readership is also declining. In 1977, about 70 percent of the public read newspapers; the figure is now below 50 percent. The decline of newspapers raises concerns, because newspapers tend to contain more **hard news**, more fact-based stories as opposed to interpretive narratives, than is reported on TV. In 2009, Alex Jones, one of the leading observers of the press, estimated that newspapers contained 85 percent hard news.[21] Will the decline of newspapers deprive Americans of hard news, of the facts they need to hold government accountable?

hard news: *News coverage, traditionally found in the printed press, that is more fact-based, opposed to more interpretive narratives and commentary.*

Some counter that readers are simply migrating from the printed newspapers to online versions. In January 2004, online newspapers had about 41 million visitors; just four years later, the number had jumped to 67 million.[22] While the move from the printed to online versions may offer some hope to the newspaper industry, it has not solved its financial difficulties. Fewer readers of print newspapers mean that fewer advertisers buy space, and online advertising has not been able to make up the difference.[23] It is not only commercial ad revenue that has been lost. Want ads have shrunk has well, as potential buyers and sellers turn more often to Craigslist or other specialty websites that share information without charge. With revenue plummeting, newspapers survive only by cutting staff. The *Boston Globe* once had journalists overseas reporting on international events. That is no longer true.[24] The *Los Angeles Times* has seen its newsroom decline from 1,200 reporters to 850.[25] Fewer reporters, journalists, and editors mean that newspapers have less ability to inform and investigate. If the press cannot perform its watchdog role, the people stand to lose the means by which they hold government accountable.[26]

Despite these serious concerns, Americans do want the news and continue to seek it out, so newspaper owners have an incentive to develop new ways to make a profit.[27] Moreover, today's leading newspapers, such as the *New York Times,* have been powerful for only about seventy years, whereas American democracy has survived for 230 years. Concerns about newspapers may simply indicate how much Americans depend on the press to hold government accountable. Any change in the means by which news is delivered raises fears that democracy itself may be weakened.

Photo credits (vertical): © Dennis Kleiman/Retna Ltd./Corbis; Ali Goldstein/MSNBC/NBCUPB

Bill O'Reilly and Rachel Maddow are highly visible news anchors in the media environment of the twenty-first century. Unlike Walter Cronkite, they convey the news with a clear ideological edge. Both can be informative, but they present the news in a way that is very different from news reporting in the 1960s and 1970s.

The Durability of Radio

In many ways, radio is underappreciated as a medium of communication, as current debates center on newspapers, television, and the Internet. But radio remains important, especially considering how often Americans listen to the radio in their cars. In 1998, 95 percent of the American public tuned into an AM or FM station at least once a week. That figure remains unchanged. In 2007, 94 percent had listened to the radio in the previous seven days. Radio is actually expanding its reach due to satellite radio and streaming audio on desktop and laptop computers. In fact, it may be that "radio" is becoming "audio," reflecting advances in digital technology.[28]

Political talk radio, a medium dominated largely by conservatives, is increasingly popular. In 2008, nearly 50 million Americans listened to talk radio,[29] and most of them listened to conservative programs. According to one estimate, in 2007 conservatives hosted 91 percent of programming hours, and liberals just 9 percent. Over 90 percent of stations do not even broadcast progressive (that is, liberal) talk radio.[30]

The Transformation of TV News

Newspapers are not the only news outlet facing a decline in customers. There is also a shrinking audience for the network evening news. Nearly 25 percent of Americans watched the evening news in 1980; by 2010, that figure was just 8 percent.[31] The downward trend is likely to continue because the current audience for TV news is older Americans. Young people, who represent the future audience, are not big consumers of network news. Their habits are not likely to change, painting a bleak picture for the industry in the coming years.

This decline, like that of newspapers, generates concern about how well informed the public is about politics. But these concerns are counterbalanced by the rise of cable news, increasingly available since 1980. Households are now watching two or three hours a week of cable news, a rate of viewership higher than that for network news in the 1980s. Of the cable networks, Fox has the largest audience, more than CNN and MSNBC combined. Bill O'Reilly has become exceptionally popular, though not nearly as popular as Walter Cronkite once was. Even so, his show has a substantial following.

But cable news is not like the evening news show of the 1970s, a thirty-minute broadcast around dinnertime. With cable, television news is available twenty-four hours a day. Events get live coverage, transforming the news cycle. No longer do politicians time public appearances so they can be covered on the evening news. News now comes at viewers at a rapid-fire rate, and cable networks fill out constant programming with interpretation. MSNBC's *Hardball with Chris Matthews* and *The Rachel Maddow Show,* and Fox's *The Beltway Boys* are examples. Cable news has taken the interpretive function of the news media to an entirely new level.

Of course, the web offers yet another platform for gathering news, and one that seems to be on the rise. In 2008, msnbc.com, foxnews.com, and cnn.com all registered significant gains in the number of visitors.[32] With cable TV and Internet news, the sources for news have increased. We examine the impact of these developments later in the chapter.

Infotainment

Television viewers also get political news through talk shows, such as *The Oprah Winfrey Show*, *Late Show with David Letterman,* and *Jimmy Kimmel Live*. These sources offer what is called **infotainment** or **soft news**, news with fewer hard facts of the kind newspapers generally report but with more emphasis on personal stories that engage (or shock) the public and often appeal to the emotions rather than the intellect.

Nearly 1.5 million people, especially young adults, watch *The Daily Show* hosted by Jon Stewart, which delivers the news with humor and satire, four days a week.[33] With Stewart's tough questions and hard-hitting reporting, it would be misleading to suggest that the news the show provides is "soft," but events like the murder of students and faculty at Virginia Tech drew little mention here, though it dominated more traditional outlets. The guests who appear on *The Daily Show* cover the full ideological spectrum, indicating at least some desire for balance.[34]

Blogs

A **blog** is a website that provides a forum for "bottom-up" commentary, description of events, video postings, and general conversation. Through blogs, average citizens are able to express their opinions to a wider audience, and they offer a gateway for people to influence politics. There are all kinds of blogs, with political blogs representing just a subset. But of the twenty-five most popular blogs in 2009, four were political. The Daily Kos remains popular, with nearly 600,000 visitors per month in 2009.[35] During the 2008 presidential campaign, interest in liberal blogs was very high, but their appeal has declined since the election of Barack Obama. With the Democrats now occupying the White House, conservative blogs are becoming a more popular way for people to express their unhappiness with the Obama administration.

political talk radio: *Media format dominated by conservative commentators that has become a vital gateway in disseminating political issues and events to millions.*

Which cable station do you watch? Do you think the presentation of the news is fair?

infotainment: *Sources of news geared toward a less politically attentive audience, offering less substantive and more entertaining coverage than hard news.*

soft news: *News stories focused less on facts and policies than on sensationalizing secondary issues or on less serious subjects of the entertainment world.*

Would you describe the news you seek out as hard or soft?

blog (short for weblog): *Website where people post news, commentary, pictures, video, and other pieces of information to share with other users.*

Have you ever written a blog? What inspired you?

In many ways, blogging symbolizes the modern transformation of the mass media. Blogs capture the interest of people of all ages, and some hope that blogs will provide a forum for more participation and deliberation. While there is some evidence blogs do foster participation, they do not seem to foster deliberation. Liberals read liberal blogs, and conservatives read conservative blogs: In fact, 94 percent of people read blogs that share their ideological viewpoint. These data suggest that blogs reinforce existing preferences and do not open opportunities to hear the other side.[36] Moreover, blogs are usually strong in their ideological leanings. Daily Kos is a liberal blog, as is the Huffington Post.[37] Conservative blogs include those of Matt Drudge[38] and Rush Limbaugh.[39]

Blogs also have the potential to spread false information. Because no one checks the accuracy of a posting, individuals—some call them trolls[40]—can say outrageous things merely to get attention[41] and without penalty. In contrast, the traditional press has a well-established set of norms for vetting the accuracy of information; when false statements do get through, there is a heavy penalty to journalists. Trolls, on the other hand, often gain notoriety for lying.

The importance of blogs appears to be on the rise. In early 2004, less than 20 percent of Internet users claimed to be visiting blogs. Two years later, that figure has doubled. Politicians increasingly understand the power of blogs as sources of news. Former Massachusetts Governor Mitt Romney established the Five Brothers blog as part of his 2008 presidential campaign. The intent was to have his five sons write about their dad and life on the campaign trail. The blog provided a way for the public to get a close look at Romney's children and gain an understanding of his family life. This information was valuable, because Romney's family was a real strength of his candidacy.[42] Other candidates have also used blogs as a way to communicate with followers and potential supporters.

citizen journalists: *Ordinary individuals with no formal journalistic training and independent of news organizations who play an active role in reporting the news or commenting on current events, primarily through the Internet and blogs.*

Blogs have given rise to **citizen journalists**, who clearly influenced the political debate during the 2008 presidential campaign. One example is Mayhill Fowler, who reported on Huffington Post that Barack Obama had said working-class people were "clinging" to their "guns and religion" because they were "bitter."[43] Obama made those comments at a private fundraiser, in a setting in which he did not know he was being recorded. But once the comments were posted, the Obama campaign faced a firestorm of protest. Fowler did not intend to become a media sensation, but her actions indicate how easy it is now for citizens to become part of the process of holding politicians accountable. The new media have opened more gateways for conveying news than were possible in the previous century.

Social Networking

The Internet has also enabled new social networks for sharing information. Just as personal conversations are an important source of information, social networking websites are increasingly important as ways to spread political news. The two leading websites are MySpace and Facebook.

Facebook is especially popular among college students. According to its webpage, it is "a social utility that connects people with friends and others who work, study, and live around them. People use Facebook to keep up with friends, upload an unlimited number of photos, share links and videos, and learn more about the people they meet." Mark Zuckerberg started the "utility" from his Harvard dorm room in February 2004 as a social networking service limited to the Harvard campus. Today, if Facebook were a country, it would be the world's fourth largest, sitting between the United States and Indonesia.[44]

Just as politicians began to use blogs to communicate with the public, so they have begun to use social networks. A recent study found that 32 percent of 2006 senatorial candidates and 13 percent of 2006 congressional candidates posted information on their Facebook profiles (which the company created for every candidate of that year). In total, about 1.5 million people (13 percent of the user base at the time) were connected to either a candidate or an issue group.[45]

With the exponential growth of Facebook, the website has become a vital medium of political communication, especially for young people. In December 2007, Facebook teamed up with ABC News to create a presidential campaign application entitled "U.S. Politics," allowing users to get involved in political discussions in a variety of ways, such as subscribing to the profiles of reporters on the campaign trail and giving their own reactions, or starting discussion groups based on press reports.

Facebook has become a valuable means whereby candidates reach out to a younger generation of voters, both to convey their messages and to raise money. Candidates can list biographical details, post advertisements and other Internet feeds, provide links for donations, and create discussion groups. Users are, in turn, able to become candidate supporters with access to all posted information. And aside from the candidates' profiles and solicitations on Facebook, private individuals have taken part in campaigning for the candidates on their own. It is a new way of volunteering that is less costly and may very well reach more voters.

Another development in "social networking" is the rise of Twitter. One can communicate with a large number of people through Internet-based messages (or "tweets"). Politicians, actors, sports figures, and other celebrities are using this technology to share information, and it has spread rapidly around the world. In June 2009, Iranians used Twitter to organize people to attend rallies protesting the outcome of the presidential election.[46] It is far from clear that Twitter had any real impact,[47] but its growth is phenomenal

Do you use Facebook? If so, is it a source of political news or action for you?

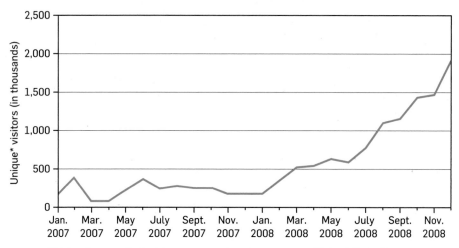

*"Unique" means that each person counts only once, so multiple visits by the same person are counted as one.

FIGURE 7.2 **Twitter Audience, 2007–2008.**
Source: Nielsen Media Research, State of the News Media, 2009.

(see Figure 7.2). In just ten months during 2008, there was a tenfold increase in Twitter use. Once again, new technologies have opened gateways for individuals to become involved in the political arena.

Cell phones have made possible yet another means of communication—text messaging. For many, especially young people, text messaging is replacing e-mails. In the United States, over 60 percent of cell phone users engage in text messaging. The percentage is even higher elsewhere: in Germany, it is 90 percent, and it is 85 percent in Britain.[48] About 10 percent of text messages contain some kind of political information.[49] Politicians and political parties have also started to use this medium to communicate with supporters. Obama, for example, announced his selection of Joe Biden as his vice presidential nominee via a text message (and e-mail) to supporters. And supporters can send messages to various political organizations as well. Text messaging is yet another gateway, and the increasing popularity of iPhones and other advanced cellular devices promises new means of communicating and sharing information in the future.

What is the future of political communication?

The News and the Millennials

The changes in the media environment do not affect all citizens equally. For example, the millennial generation consumes news differently from the way older Americans do. Americans over 40 years old read the newspaper more often, watch TV news more often, and tune into the radio with greater frequency than those under 40. By contrast, young people rely more on Internet news. Further, when younger Americans read a newspaper or listen to a radio program, they do so for a much shorter period of time than those over 40.[50] The youth seem to do more channel surfing, while older Americans are more likely to sit down and watch an entire news program. These habits may reflect differences in lifestyles between, for example, college students and adults with full-time jobs and families.[51] It may also be that older adults are more cautious about new technology, whereas younger people embrace it. When the public began to rely on TV news instead of newspapers, commentators worried that the people would be less well informed and that television would somehow cheapen the information available. Change always generates uncertainty, and with the increasingly rapid rate of technological change, worry increases as well.

Jae C. Hong, File/Associated Press

Today's media environment expects immediate news and instantaneous communication. When campaigning for president, Barack Obama relied heavily on his BlackBerry. Many thought he would have to give it up when he became president, but he loves the device and managed to keep it while ensuring that there would be no security breaches by someone trying to hack into his e-mail.

Conventional wisdom has always said that young people are less interested in politics than older Americans. But Millennials appear to be more interested in politics at this point in their lives than previous generations. This interest is not gauged by whether they watch the evening news or read newspapers, but by the ways they use new media to share information and learn about and express an interest in politics.[52] Young adults tend to reject the top-down approach for learning about politics, in which the news is filtered by professional journalists and trusted news anchors such as Cronkite. Instead, they seem much more interested in the bottom-up approach made possible by the wide-open availability of new media to citizen participation.

These changes are going to become more important over time, as more Millennials become eligible to vote and older generations pass on. In addition, technological change continues to spread, making the Internet and all its information increasingly available to more Americans. The United States is in the midst of a major transformation in the media environment, and observers are only beginning to understand the changes in how Americans transmit and consume the news.

The Impact of the News Media on the Public

The press provides information, investigation, and interpretation of the news. The news media, both old and new, make decisions about what to cover, what not to cover, and how to cover it. How does the public respond to this information? This section looks at several models ranging between two extremes: that the mass media have no effect on the public and that the mass media dominate the public's thinking.

The Propaganda Model

Few people believe the media have no influence on citizens. To hold such a view, one must either believe that the public ignores the media or that citizens learn about politics by observing the events themselves. Neither is true. We can confidently label this the *naïve model,* and dismiss it.

propaganda model:
Extreme view of the media's role in society, arguing that the press only serves the interest of the government, driving what the public thinks about important issues.

The polar opposite is what has been called the **propaganda model**. This approach is exemplified by the Nazi dictatorship in Germany in the 1930s and 1940s. The Nazi Party controlled the content of newspapers and radio. It dictated the information available to citizens, affecting the direction and shape of public opinion. Through controlled programming, the German people often heard about the greatness of Adolf Hitler and the dangers of racial impurity. By holding a monopoly on information, the government could easily marshal public support. This is a dangerous model, but also one inconsistent with how the press works in open societies. In the United States, media sources control programming, and they compete for audience share; the government does not control the flow of information. The Constitution guarantees a free press.

The Minimal Effects Model

Having seen the powerful effects of propaganda in Nazi Germany, toward the end of World War II scholars in the United States began to study public opinion and the influence of the media on it. Paul Lazarsfeld and others examined the media's influence on voting in the 1940 presidential election. The results were surprising, as the researchers discovered that people had made up their minds prior to the campaign and new information altered only a handful of people's choices.[53] Lazarsfeld's study gave rise to what has been called the

minimal effects model:
View of the media's impact as marginal, since most people seek news reports to reinforce beliefs already held rather than to develop new ones.

selective exposure:
Process whereby people secure information from sources that agree with them, thus reinforcing their beliefs.

selective perception:
Process whereby partisans interpret the same information differently.

minimal effects model. Lazarsfeld and his colleagues contended that the news media had only marginal influence on the public's thinking about politics. The public did not have much information about politics, and attitudes were shaped by long-standing forces such as partisanship or the neighborhood in which one lived.

According to this model, in a process described as **selective exposure**, people secured information from sources that agreed with them, leading to the reinforcement of beliefs, not to a change of beliefs. The minimal effects model was also based on a complementary process called **selective perception**—a concept developed in a study of the American voter published by Angus Campbell and three coauthors in 1960.[54] Selective perception describes partisans as interpreting the same information differently. In other words, partisanship involves a perceptual lens (recall Chapter 6) that shapes how outside events are viewed. So, for example, in February 2009, 70 percent of Democrats supported Obama's economic stimulus package, whereas only 24 percent of Republicans did.[55]

The Not-So-Minimal Effects Model

The minimal effects model dominated the field of political science for about forty years. Then, starting in the 1970s, scholars began to reassess it.[56] This reassessment took place at two levels. First, rather than looking at whether the news media shifted citizens' opinions about an issue, scholars examined the more subtle effects that might arise from how the press covers politics (more will be said about this later). Second, they started to gather better data that could more effectively test for the impact of the news media. This next generation of research produced the **not-so-minimal effects model**. While not overstating the power of the news media, this model acknowledges that the coverage of politics by the press matters in subtle and important ways. In particular, there are three kinds of media effects: agenda setting, priming, and framing.

not-so-minimal effects model: *View of the media's impact as substantial, occurring by agenda setting, framing, and priming.*

Have the news media changed your mind about a political issue or figure?

Agenda Setting.
By stressing certain issues, the media influence what the American public views as the most pressing concerns. This effect is called **agenda setting**. Given that on any particular day there are literally hundreds of stories that could be reported, journalists' decisions about which stories to cover (and which story to lead with and which to bury inside the paper or the end of a newscast) matter considerably. Politicians and their advisers make a huge effort to convince the media to cover some stories and ignore others. Should the news lead with a story about the casualties in the war in Afghanistan or the growing problems in the nation's public education system? As one scholar explains, a media outlet "may not be successful most of the time telling people what to think, but it is stunningly successful in telling its readers what to think about."[57] The evidence is compelling. If the media talk about crime, the public starts to care about it. If the press starts paying additional attention to the federal budget deficit, the issue becomes more salient to citizens. For these reasons, the news media's recent lack of attention to education policy is worrisome. With only about 1 percent of news coverage dedicated to the topic of education, it is not surprising that this issue rarely rises to the top of politicians' agendas.[58]

agenda setting: *Ability of the media to impact how people view issues, people, or events by controlling what stories are shown and what are not.*

What issues are the media putting on the political agenda right now?

Priming.
An extension of agenda setting is **priming**. The media can alter the criteria that citizens use when evaluating political leaders, and this priming affects the vote. In the 2008 campaign, the Republican candidate John McCain hoped the public would vote on the basis of national security, believing a majority would vote for him on that criterion. The Obama team wanted

priming: *Process whereby the media influence how the public views politicians by emphasizing criteria that make them look either good or bad.*

AP Photo/Matt York

the focus to be on the economy. By priming the public to think about gas prices or the housing crisis, the news media could give the public more reason to vote for Obama. Such effects are real. Following the terrorist attacks on September 11, 2001, for instance, the news media's coverage of terrorism was the most powerful force shaping President Bush's popularity.[59] The public gave Bush credit for dealing effectively with these tragic events. So when terrorism was the focus, Bush prospered. But if the topic shifted to the economy, for example, the public was less supportive of the president.

Media attention to a new Arizona law passed in April 2010 put immigration reform back in the political agenda. The law, which requires police officers to detain people they suspect are illegal immigrants, sparked protests all over the country, especially for its potential for racial profiling. In Phoenix on May 1 a protester suggests that the Arizona law raises constitutional issues.

framing: *Ability of the media to influence public perception of issues by constructing the issue or discussion of a subject in a certain way.*

Framing.

Framing is the ability of the media to alter the public's view on an issue by presenting it in a particular way. If the battles waged in the Middle East are framed as an issue of fighting terrorism, the public thinks about the war in a much more favorable light than if these conflicts are framed by the casualties incurred. Framing can have a very powerful effect, actually changing public opinion on an issue.

Perhaps the most famous example of framing comes from the work of Amos Tversky and Daniel Kahneman.[60] In an experiment, they told research subjects that the United States is preparing for the outbreak of an unusual disease, which is expected to kill 600 people, and asked which program should be implemented to deal with the disease:

- If program A is adopted, 200 people will be saved.
- If program B is adopted, there is a one-third probability that 600 people will be saved, and a two-thirds probability that no one will be saved.

Of those surveyed, 72 percent favored program A and 28 percent favored program B. Such a strong result suggests that the government should adopt program A.

But another group of subjects was also given a choice between two different programs. The options were described as follows:

- If program C is adopted, 400 people will die.
- If program D is adopted, there is a one-third probability that nobody will die, and a two-thirds probability that 600 people will die.

Here, 22 percent of subjects favored program C and 78 percent favored program D.

There is a 50 percentage point difference in people's willingness to support program A versus program C. Yet the programs yield the *exact same policy outcome*: 200 people live, and 400 people die. The *only* difference is that the description of program A stressed saving people, while the description of program C stressed the deaths of people. The outcomes are exactly the same. This experiment underscores the power of framing—that the public reacts to a news event or a policy depends on how it is presented.

Evaluating the News Media

The worries about the news media often center on two general concerns. One is that the media are biased and are not presenting objective information. The second, which is related, focuses on the general quality of information available to the public. The emphasis on soft news, for example, worries observers who do not think the public has enough exposure to more substantive, hard news. Without enough hard news, these observers fear, the public will not be well enough informed to hold elected officials accountable.

Whether these concerns are valid or not (and we will examine them later), it is clear that the public's faith in the press has declined (see Table 7.1). In the

TABLE 7.1 Persistent Criticisms of the Press

	Percentage of Survey Respondents							
	July 1985	Feb. 1999	Sept. 2001	Nov. 2001	July 2002	July 2003	June 2005	July 2007
News organizations . . .								
Moral	54%	40%	40%	53%	39%	45%	43%	46%
Immoral	13%	38%	34%	23%	36%	32%	35%	32%
Protect democracy	54%	45%	46%	60%	50%	52%	47%	44%
Hurt democracy	23%	38%	32%	19%	29%	28%	33%	36%
Get facts straight	55%	37%	35%	46%	35%	36%	36%	39%
Stories often inaccurate	34%	58%	37%	45%	56%	56%	56%	53%
Careful to avoid bias	36%	31%	26%	35%	26%	29%	28%	31%
Politically biased	45%	56%	59%	47%	59%	53%	60%	55%
Highly professional	72%	52%	54%	73%	49%	62%	59%	66%
Not professional	11%	32%	27%	12%	31%	24%	25%	22%

Source: Pew Research Center for the People & the Press, "Views of Press Values and Performance: 1985–2007," August 9, 2007. These survey questions were not repeated in 2008.

early 1970s, around 15 percent of the public did not have much confidence in the press; by 2004, the percentage had nearly tripled to about 45 percent. The share of the public who thinks the press gets the facts "straight" has declined over the last twenty years. In 1985, 55 percent of the public thought the press got the facts right. By 2007, that had shrunk to 39 percent. In November following the terrorist attacks of September 11, 2001, 60 percent of the public felt the press protected democracy. Now, less than half of the public holds that belief.[61]

Do you trust the news media? What source, if any, gets it right?

Is there reason to worry about the media? Are the mass media of the twenty-first century less able to fulfill their watchdog role? This section looks at media bias, the quality of information, and the implications of the Internet and media choice.

Are the Media Biased?

The press claims to be objective, and professional journalists subscribe to an ethic of neutrality. Yet given that even in selecting what stories to cover the press influences public opinion, bias may be inevitable. Nevertheless, it need not be evil or ideological. David Broder, a famous columnist for the *Washington Post*, admits to the bias but attributes it to the speed with which journalists have to act. "The process of selecting what the reader reads involves not just objective facts but subjective judgments, personal values, and, yes, prejudices," he confesses. Broder goes on to point out that "the newspaper that drops on your doorstep is a partial, hasty, incomplete, inevitably somewhat flawed and inaccurate rendering of some of the things we have heard about in the past 24 hours—distorted, despite our best efforts to eliminate bias, by the very process of compression that makes it possible for you to lift it from the doorstep and read it in about an hour."[62]

With the rise of the 24-7 news cycle, bias in selecting what to cover becomes even more evident. For example, during the 2008 presidential campaign, all three candidates—John McCain, already the Republican nominee, and Barack Obama and Hillary Clinton, still contending for Democratic nomination—were scheduled to give speeches on the evening of June 2. McCain spoke first, and all the major cable networks covered his speech. During the middle of the speech, however, Obama secured the few extra delegates that officially gave him the presidential nomination. MSNBC broke away from McCain's speech to announce this important development. Fox News did not. Fox flashed the information on the lower part of the screen, but continued to cover McCain's speech. Both networks were informing the public, but they were making different choices about what is newsworthy and what is not. Insofar as these choices seem to support a liberal or a conservative outlook, they might be described as biased.

Do you think the news media are too liberal?

A broader point is that, for many years, conservative commentators have claimed that the news media is liberal. Accuracy in Media, a conservative watchdog organization, contends that over 80 percent of mainstream journalists support the Democratic Party. Such partisan loyalties, according to critics, drive the liberal bias.[63] Yet those who own the most major media outlets, such as Rupert Murdoch—who owns the Wall Street Journal and Fox News—are conservative. Should one assume that because most news outlets are owned by conservatives the media are really conservative? It is far from clear whether the media are liberal or conservative.

Yet, complaints about a liberal press seem to resonate with the public. Gallup Poll data measuring public's belief about ideological bias in the news media indicate that about half the public believes the news media have a liberal bias. The proportion has been quite stable, ranging from 45 percent to 48 percent over the last few years. However, there has also been an increase in the share of people who think the media have a conservative bias. In 2001, only 11 percent of the public viewed the press as too conservative. By 2007, 18 percent made that claim. This trend is worth noting, but the important point is that Americans generally perceive a liberal tilt to the press's coverage of politics.[64]

Nevertheless, the debate over whether the news media are "too" liberal (or "too" conservative) actually misses the central point about the news these days. With so many sources of information, one can find news with a liberal spin and news with a conservative spin. In fact, in the second decade of the twenty-first century, much news reporting is partisan, more like the party-dominated press of the nineteenth century than the objective and neutral press of the twentieth century. Media choice and multiple outlets mean that a Democrat can easily find a Democratic-leaning source for news and a Republican can find a Republican-leaning source. It is fair to conclude that, individually, news outlets are biased, but collectively, the media provide a full range of ideological viewpoints.

If you think a media source is biased, do you ever listen to or view it? How can you evaluate it?

Quality of Information

The idea that people are getting news from Oprah rather than Jim Lehrer is disconcerting to political observers. The general worry is that people are getting less hard news and instead are relying on what we earlier called soft news[65]—feature stories that are more personal and less policy focused, more sensationalized and less objective, than the political facts of hard news. So news about crime or natural disasters can fit the soft news category when the focus is about the drama surrounding the event (such as loss of life or home) rather than a discussion about public policy that could reduce crime or perhaps provide quicker government response to disasters.[66]

Part of this underlying concern is the emphasis on image as opposed to substance. The assumption here is that visuals (television and Internet news, as opposed to print news) appeal to the emotions more than the intellect, so visual news formats are in themselves less "hard" and more superficial. It is true that visual images convey impressions that go beyond the facts, but that does not mean that such information is not valuable. All media of communication shape how information is shared and digested. Radio, for example, puts a premium on the quality of people's voices. It is also important to realize that images did not begin with the advent of TV. It may be easier to engage in "image" politics in an era of video, but politicians have always wanted to convey a favorable image and have done so within the media of their time.

In the same way, **sound bites**—very brief snippets of information—did not begin with the advent of television. Many fear the "sound bite" undermines the quality of information by stressing short catchy statements rather than more detailed substantive statements. Campaigns, however, have always made effective use of simple slogans. In 1980, for example, President Ronald Reagan (1980–88) sought election with the slogan "Are you better off than you were four years ago?"[67] reminding voters about the economic difficulties of the previous Carter administration.

The purpose of this discussion is to urge caution in making hasty judgments about the differences in the kinds of information available via the news media over the last 230 years. Soft news, which is more entertaining than hard news, may be better able to inform than hard news because people find it easier to understand and more enjoyable. It is important, therefore, not to let the definition of what counts as "news" shape judgment of the press. That news reporting is no longer filtered by Walter Cronkite but by Bill O'Reilly does not mean the news media are no longer doing their job. They are just doing it differently.

Despite all the recent changes in the mass media, evidence suggests that Americans have as much information about politics as they did before the arrival of the Internet and the 24-7 news cycle. According to a 2007 survey released by the Pew Research Center for the People and the Press, "the coaxial and digital revolutions and attendant changes in the news audience behaviors have had *little* impact on how much Americans know about national and international affairs."[68] Patterns from the 2008 presidential campaign provide further evidence. Americans were not less informed about the two candidates than in previous elections; they only secured information in new ways.[69]

Implications of the Internet

There is evidence that the arrival of the Internet has not changed the overall amount of information the public possesses, but it is important to acknowledge that the Internet is not equally available to all Americans. Only about

35 percent of those Americans making less than $20,000 a year in 2009 have access to the Internet; for those making $75,000 or more, the proportion climbs to 85 percent.[70] Older Americans also have less access to the Internet than younger Americans.

These data suggest a further inequality—that those with Internet access may be much better informed than the public generally just twenty years ago, whereas those without access may be even less informed. Variations among groups, buried in discussions of the public as a whole, are significant. These variations will likely decrease as more people secure access to the Internet. In time, the Internet will give older and less wealthy Americans a better chance to become informed about politics than they currently have.

Implications of Media Choice

Perhaps the single best word to describe today's media environment is *choice*.[71] The spread of cable television, the Internet, and satellite radio means that people have many possible sources for political information, as well as a huge array of entertainment programming that may lead them to opt out of political news altogether. In the mid-twentieth century, when the network evening news was the source for news, viewers had fewer choices and less opportunity to opt out. They might change channels at dinnertime, but they would then get similar news from a different network. The evening news was the only show on during the dinner hour. The lack of choice may have forced them to learn more about politics than their own interest indicated.[72]

The TV network news standardized the information Americans had access to. Today, with the wide array of choices now available, information is more polarized. Viewers who choose a conservative network such as Fox and listen to Rush Limbaugh in their cars will have different information from those who watch MSNBC and tune in to National Public Radio. Those who lack an interest in politics can avoid political news altogether. In other words, media choice cuts two ways: polarizing the type of information available and making it possible to receive no political information at all.

The consequences of media choice are complex and are only beginning to be understood. New technologies in the future could further fragment what Americans as a people know. Efforts to make political news more interesting may only mean a further "softening" of the news. The large point is that Americans have access to a vast amount of information, but the availability of more information does not necessarily mean that the public, as a whole, is better informed. Lurking beneath these general patterns is the real prospect that media choice will further fuel polarization, as liberals watch MSNBC and conservatives watch Fox.

What are the consequences of media choice?

The Mass Media and Public Policy: Censorship

Any effort by government to control the media or to curtail the freedom of the press faces an immediate debate and often strong protest. When the courts decide between national security concerns and press freedoms, they usually support the press. Libel suits rarely result in convictions. Yet the advent of radio and television and the recent proliferation of electronic media have brought new challenges to drawing the line between what kinds of content should be restrained and what should be allowed to flow freely. There is no government agency regulating the print media, but the Federal Communications Commission has the authority to regulate the content and ownership of radio, television, the Internet, and all electronic media. One area of special concern has been what might be considered obscene or offensive material.

Obscene Content in Broadcast Media

The landmark Supreme Court decision in *FCC v. Pacifica Foundation* (1978) established the precedent that the FCC has the legal authority to fine any media outlet that knowingly allows the expression of obscene content, under certain circumstances. The background of the case was that in 1973, a New York radio station aired George Carlin's monologue, "Filthy Words," which included seven words that could not be said on the public airwaves. The station had prefaced his monologue with a warning to listeners that it included "sensitive language which might be regarded as offensive to some." A listener filed a complaint with the FCC after hearing the broadcast with his young son in the car.

The underlying question in this case was whether the First Amendment inhibits the power of the government to restrict the public broadcast of indecent language under any circumstances. The Supreme Court ruled in a 5–4 decision that the

Should the government censor language on the air?

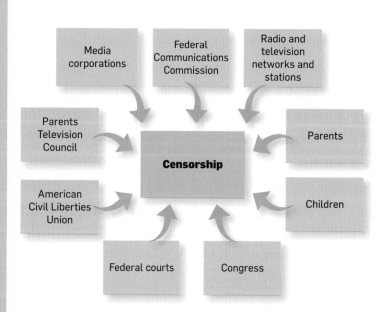

government could invoke limited civil sanctions against radio broadcast of patently offensive words dealing with sex and excretion without violating the First Amendment. The Court also said that the words did not have to be obscene to warrant sanction and that, in decisions on whether sanctions on media content are fair and justified, other factors such as audience type, time that the broadcast was aired, and how it was transmitted are relevant.[73]

In today's television, music, and video climate, the boundaries for socially acceptable visual and verbal content are constantly evolving. Two recent cases reflect the ongoing policy discussion over what are acceptable restrictions on media expression. In *FCC v. Fox Television Stations,* Fox Broadcasting Company appealed fines that the FCC imposed for its 2002 and 2003 broadcast of the Billboard Music Awards, during which participants uttered expletives. Fox claimed that on previous broadcasts, participants had used similar language and the FCC had ruled that they were "fleeting" and were not seriously harmful, so it objected to a change in FCC enforcement with no warning. In a 5–4 decision, the Supreme Court ruled that the FCC only needed to prove that its new policy was justifiable and reasonable.[74] In response to what has been viewed as a stricter crackdown on language content, broadcast outlets like network television and radio stations have taken to "bleeping" or "buzzing" over words that might be viewed as harmful by the FCC. In live broadcasts, networks typically use a five-second delay in sending their signal over the airways to make sure they have time to bleep out offensive language. Cable television outlets are not under this same type of restrictions because they broadcast to a paid subscriber base that gives audience members more control over the content that they choose to view.

Similar to the reasoning in the Fox case, the Supreme Court also ruled to support the FCC in *CBS Inc. v. FCC*, which dealt with an incident at the halftime show for the 2004 Super Bowl. During a performance by Justin Timberlake and Janet Jackson, part of Jackson's costume was ripped off and her breast was momentarily exposed. The FCC fined CBS $550,000 for allowing the viewing of indecent images, and CBS sued to appeal the fine. The Court of Appeals for the Third Circuit ruled that the fine was illegal because the FCC had changed its policy on indecent images without notifying CBS and other broadcast networks. The FCC then appealed that ruling, and in 2009, the Supreme Court sent the case back to the court of appeals for reconsideration in light of its decision in the *Fox Television* case.[75]

These three Supreme Court cases exert a significant impact on the way that government restricts expression of speech and visual images through the media. Current policy distinguishes between media outlets that are free to the public and those that audiences pay for—subscriber-based media outlets. Supporters of expanded FCC powers argue that the government has a compelling interest in keeping airways and television "clean" or at least promoting content that does not contain language or behavior deemed socially undesirable. Opponents of a strong FCC believe that media content should be restricted only when it can be shown to be seriously and deeply damaging to the social fabric of the democracy. Given the advances in the technical delivery of media content, such as print- and video-to-cell-phone converters, further controversies involving FCC restrictions are likely to occur.

Safety, Social Networking, and the Internet

The Internet is not exactly a broadcast medium, but given its wide availability to the general public, Congress has sought to restrict its content. In 1996, Congress passed the Communications Decency Act, which established broadcast-style content regulations for the Internet. The act banned the posting of "indecent" or "patently offensive" materials in a public forum on the Internet, including newsgroups, chat rooms, webpages, or online discussion lists. However, the American Civil Liberties Union (ACLU) challenged the law and in 1997, the Supreme Court ruled unanimously that the law was unconstitutional because it imposed sweeping restrictions that violated the free speech protections of the First Amendment.[76]

In 1998, Congress tried for a second time to limit the content on the Internet when it passed the Child Online Protection Act (COPA).[77] The COPA made it a crime for anyone using an Internet site, or e-mail over the Internet, to make any communication for commercial reasons considered "harmful to minors" unless the person had prohibited access by minors through requiring a credit card number to access the material. In addition, the act imposed fines of up to $50,000 a day. Again, the legislation was ultimately struck down, this time by the Court of Appeals for the Third Circuit. The court ruled that COPA, like the Communications Decency Act before it, "effectively suppresses a large amount of speech that adults have a constitutional right to receive and to address to one another" and thus is too broad. For this reason, COPA violates the First Amendment.[78] Further, in 2009, the U.S. Supreme Court refused to hear the government's appeal of this decision.

Congress subsequently responded by passing the Children's Online Privacy Protection Act (COPPA), which requires sites directed to children under the age of 13 to gain parental consent before collecting, maintaining, or using children's information. Parents can review their child's online activity under COPPA. The act also requires such sites to post a privacy policy on their home page and a link to the privacy policy on every page where personal information is collected.[79] In addition, in 2003, Congress also passed a law that is designed to prevent the exploitation of children by prohibiting pornographic websites from showing any sexually explicit material involving children on their home pages.[80]

In a related move, the government has taken action to shield consumers from receiving unsolicited e-mail. The CAN-SPAM Act (2003) requires all commercial e-mailers to provide Internet users with the opportunity to opt out of getting further messages, restricts them from sending e-mail with false header information, and sets civil penalties for misleading subject lines on commercial e-mail.[81]

Given the vastness of the Internet, and the speed at which technology evolves, it becomes fundamentally harder to keep the Internet "safe" for users of all ages as well as to preserve the security of information that is passed over the Internet. Because the Internet is an engine of commerce as well as a media outlet, it is also regulated by the Federal Trade Commission (FTC).[82] The FTC's Bureau of Consumer Protection offers detailed information to consumers about what information they should never release on the Internet, which websites are not secure, how to determine secure websites, and how to report wrongdoings. Citizens who fail to read privacy policies or are not careful about the information they release face safety concerns, and the FTC is the government agency responsible for helping to prevent Internet abuse and fraud.

Although society has a legitimate interest in censoring explicit sexual and violent images on the Internet, the Supreme Court has repeatedly ruled that using broad or vague language to create blanket restrictions jeopardizes the right to free speech guaranteed by the First Amendment. Balancing the individual right to public expression and upholding community standards of behavior, now that the Internet has created a global community, will continue to be a challenge in the twenty-first century.

The Mass Media and Democracy

The news media, as watchdogs, are a central player in democratic politics. In the twenty-first century, the mass media are far more open than they were just a few decades ago, providing additional chances to forge accountability, responsiveness, and equality. But it is only a "chance" at this point, because the media are in the midst of this transformation, and all the repercussions are not yet known.

For example, nearly all public movements and statements of political figures can now be caught on video or audiotape. Politicians, as a result, have

What should the government do about pornography on the Internet? If you think there should be a restriction of freedom of expression or access, what is the justification?

What, if anything, should the government do to make the Internet secure and safe? Under the Constitution, what could be the justification?

- How do the mass media help to make government accountable to the people?

- How has the rise of the Internet increased or decreased the ability of the public to hold government accountable?

- How does the bottom-up approach of twenty-first-century mass media affect citizen participation and equality? What are its other effects?

- When, and under what conditions, should government regulate the media?

- In what ways do the mass media offer gateways to American democracy? In what ways do the modern media establish new gates?

bubble: *State of politicians being sheltered from public scrutiny and uncontrolled situations.*

a tougher time ducking responsibility; they are more easily held accountable for their actions. At the same time, the threat of being caught on tape in an embarrassing moment may only encourage politicians to stay in the **bubble**, sheltered from public scrutiny and shielded from assertive journalists or potentially harmful situations. Politicians build staffs and organizations designed to keep them from making mistakes and from interacting with journalists and citizens. They want to appear only at staged events where they can control the message.

The more open and more "democratic" new media thus have the potential to let citizens know more about the politicians who lead them; they also give people more opportunity to express opinions, which politicians can consider as they develop and enact laws. Thus blogs and other new media may help forge responsiveness. But these gateways have potential costs, because these opinions may be from people who are on the fringe and not representative of American mainstream. Further, the "facts" offered in these settings have not been checked and are potentially erroneous.

The many changes in the news media have also led to a decline in the number of professional journalists who are covering politics. With fewer professional journalists, there is worry that the press will be less able to investigate stories that might unearth corruption or just provide a more complete account of some politicians' backgrounds.

The decline in investigative reporting could, in short, undermine accountability. But there is some reason for optimism. For example, Paul Steiger, former editor of the *Wall Street Journal*, has formed a nonprofit organization called ProPublica. This organization pursues investigations, offering the findings to newspapers and magazines. By taking advantage of funding from private sources, this organization offers a way to compensate for the decline in investigative journalism.[83] So in a sense, the rise of the Internet has lessened the need for professional journalists, but the power of the Internet has also provided a way to pool resources and undertake important investigations. It is far too early to know whether this innovation will work. But these innovative uses of the Internet demonstrate the dynamic nature of the mass media.

The worries about the media's ability to advance democratic government come mostly from those who favor a top-down approach for providing political information. For those who see the merit and appeal in a bottom-up approach, these changes will seem far less worrisome. On average, the millennial generation will not be so worried, as these young people have grown up with the transformed mass media. They see the potential that the Internet and other media have for promoting equality—for providing more chances to be part of the process. But until access to the Internet becomes universal, these changes offer more hope than reality.

Top Ten to Take Away

1. In a democracy, the people rely on the mass media for the information they need to hold government accountable and make it responsive. The press plays the role of watchdog, and the First Amendment protects the freedom of the press. (pp. 213–217)

2. The mass media perform three important tasks—informing, investigating, and interpreting the news. (p. 214)

3. When the government attempts to constrain the press, the Supreme Court generally sides with the press, believing it is better to protect press freedoms than to permit government censorship. (pp. 214–217)

4. Unlike the press, radio, television, and electronic media are heavily regulated by the Federal Communications Commission, which looks to prevent monopoly, censor obscene or offensive material, and prevent the exploitation of children. Laws and standards for the Internet continue to emerge. (pp. 215; 217)

5. The history of the press in America is dynamic, developing from occasional pamphlets to comprehensive daily publications and online enterprises with a mix of news and entertainment. The profession of journalism developed as well, with a commitment to objectivity. In the 1950s, television began to replace newspapers as the source of news. (pp. 217–221)

6. In the twenty-first century, technological advances are changing the media environment once again. The rise of cable television, satellite TV, and the Internet make news available day and night. Soft news, with personal stories and emotional content, is replacing hard news. Blogs are evidence of a new bottom-up journalism by citizens. (pp. 221–229)

7. Political scientists describe the impact of the news media on the public as agenda setting, priming, and framing. It is evident that the issues journalists decide to feature and the way they present them have the power to alter public opinion. (pp. 229–233)

8. Although the public has lost faith in the media and generally think the media are too liberal, media choice and multiple outlets ensure a full range of ideological viewpoints. The sources of information are changing, but the public has as much information about politics as ever. (pp. 233–237)

9. The decline of newspapers is a real concern, however, as fewer journalists means that newspapers have less ability to inform and investigate. If the press cannot perform its watchdog role, the public loses a means by which it holds government accountable. (pp. 223; 241–243)

10. Technology has changed the media and the way Americans receive the news since before the nation was founded. Americans quickly adopt new technologies, and they have always sought out the news. Increasing Internet access will eventually even out inequalities, giving all Americans a chance to be informed about politics. (pp. 222; 243)

Ten to Test Yourself

1. Describe the contributions of Zenger, Day, Pulitzer, and Ochs to the role of the press in American democracy.

2. What caused partisan newspapers to decline in the middle of the nineteenth century?

3. Compare and contrast freedom of the press and regulation of radio and electronic media.

4. What can the Federal Communications Commission regulate? How is the FCC regulated?

5. Describe the rise of professional journalism.

6. Describe the role of the citizen journalist.

7. What evidence is there that the press is declining?

8. What evidence is there of media bias?

9. What does "media choice" mean, and what are its effects?

10. Why is the press so important to democratic politics?

Terms to Know and Use

8 INTEREST GROUPS

University of Idaho, Moscow

> *Citizens are the engineers of their own destiny. They have to be proactive in order to achieve the goals they set for themselves and for the nation as a whole.*

At the University of Idaho, Al Baker is a mechanical engineering student and a gun rights activist. As both the Idaho state director for Students for Concealed Carry on Campus (SCCC) and the organization's Rocky Mountain regional director, he works with college students, parents, teachers, and other educators to persuade state legislators and college administrators "to grant concealed handgun license holders the same rights on college campuses that those licensees currently enjoy in most other unsecured locations." This is the group's mission statement. It is student led—Baker is also on the national board of directors and serves as the organization's vice president—and student founded. In April 2007, in response to the tragic loss of life in the shooting deaths on the Virginia Tech campus, Chris Brown, a political science major at the University of Texas, organized SCCC from his dorm room. Beginning with a website and Facebook, the organization now has more than 350 chapters on college campuses and universities and some 43,000 members. Although this group has the core principle of gun rights, it is not officially associated with the National Rifle Association or with any political party.

Baker has always lived in Idaho and enjoyed its opportunities for outdoors activities. As a sportsman and responsible firearms owner, he has been a campus leader in SCCC since

Al Baker ▶

Visit http://www.cengagebrain
.com/shop/ISBN/0495906190 for
interactive tools including:
- Quizzes
- Flashcards
- Videos
- Animated PowerPoint slides,
   Podcast summaries, and more

DianeRicePhotos.com

© www.JayBeeStock.com

its inception. He wants colleges and universities to allow members of their communities to legally carry licensed concealed weapons because, he points out, students are citizens and they have an actual need for self-defense in light of the crimes common on college campuses, including assault, robbery, and rape. On February 13, 2008, Baker testified before the Idaho state legislature in favor of a bill that would prevent localities from banning guns. He made the point that the tragedy at Virginia Tech and other campus shootings have made students afraid of being attacked on campus. Students need to be able to protect themselves, he argued. Challenged that the risk of violence from armed students in the classroom would outweigh any potential protection guns on campus might provide, Baker disagreed. Students are at the mercy of crazed gunmen, he countered. "We sit there as sitting ducks waiting and hoping some madman doesn't come and kill us." For Baker and the members of SCCC, it is better to have the opportunity to fight an attacker off with a gun than to be a victim. As an interest group, the SCCC serves as a gateway to influence that allows students to make their views about gun rights known throughout the nation.

FOCUS QUESTIONS

- How do interest groups influence economic and social policy?

- How do interest groups help or hinder government responsiveness to all citizens in an equal and fair way?

- Are interest groups themselves democratic organizations? Are their leaders accountable to their members? Explain.

- Do interest groups balance each other out across income levels, regions, and ethnic backgrounds? Explain and give examples.

- Are interest groups gates or gateways to democracy?

Currently Utah is the only state that allows concealed carry at all public colleges and universities. In other states, SCCC students offer testimony in defense of their position on campus and in the halls of state legislatures. Members sign petitions, write letters and op-ed pieces, organize e-mail drives, and plan Empty Holster protests, during which they wear empty holsters to class "as an act of silent protest," says the SCCC website, "against laws and policies that discriminate against legally armed citizens." The group also offers information packets, fliers, posters, tip sheets, and form letters that can help members get out its message, and it is considering starting a magazine. One member has initiated a lawsuit. Whether one agrees or disagrees with SCCC's perspective, its grassroots origins and current activities are examples of students engaging in collective action to generate change and using university and political resources to raise awareness and support for a cause.[1]

Small or large, student-run or established national organizations more than a century old, interest groups are a mechanism of representation in a democracy because they help translate individual opinions and interests into outcomes in the political system. Interest groups form for many reasons: to advance economic status, express an ideological viewpoint, influence public policy, or promote activism on international affairs. For a democracy, the most crucial role of interest groups is their attempt to influence public policy. In this chapter we examine the history of interest groups, why they form, what they do, and their impact on democratic processes. We also identify how and why some groups are more influential than others. Throughout the chapter we focus on interest groups as gateways to citizen participation and at the same time point out how they can erect gates when they pursue narrow policy interests.

Interest Groups and Politics

In 1831, the French political theorist Alexis de Tocqueville came to the United States to observe American social and political behavior. He later published his study as *Democracy in America,* a classic of political literature. He wrote, "The most natural right of man, after that of acting on his own, is that of combining his efforts with those of his fellows and acting together. Therefore the right of association seems to me by nature almost as inalienable as individual liberty."[2] Tocqueville noticed that Americans in particular liked to form groups and join associations as a way of participating in community and political life. To Tocqueville, the formation of groups was an important element of the success of the American democracy.

What Are Interest Groups?

Tocqueville used the term *association* to describe the groups he observed throughout his travels in America; today, we call them interest groups. **Interest groups** are groups of citizens who share a common interest, whether a political opinion, religious affiliation, ideological belief, social goal, or economic objective, and who try to influence public policy to benefit their members. Other types of groups form for purely social or community reasons, but this chapter focuses on the groups that form to exert political influence.

Most interest groups arise from conditions in public life. A **proactive group** arises when an enterprising individual sees an opening or opportunity to create the group for social, political, or economic purposes. A **reactive group** forms to protect the interests of the members in response to a perceived threat from another group, or to fight a government policy they believe will adversely affect them, or to respond to an unexpected external event. Groups whose

interest group: *Group of citizens who share a common interest—a political opinion, religious or ideological belief, social goal, or economic characteristic—and try to influence public policy to benefit themselves.*

proactive group: *Group that forms when an enterprising individual sees an opening or opportunity to create the group for social, political, or economic purposes.*

reactive group: *Group that forms in response to a perceived threat from another group, or to fight a government policy those who join believe will adversely affect them, or in response to an unexpected external event.*

members share a number of common characteristics are described as homogeneous, whereas groups whose members come from varied backgrounds are described as heterogeneous. All interest groups are based on the idea that members joining together in a group can secure a shared benefit that would not be available to them if they acted alone.

The Right to Assemble and to Petition

The First Amendment states that Congress cannot prohibit "the right of the people peaceably to assemble, and to petition the Government for a redress of grievances." This right to assemble is the **right of association**. The Framers understood that human beings naturally seek out others who are similar to them, and they believed that the opportunity to form groups was a fundamental right that government may not legitimately take away. At the same time, however, they were fearful that such groups, which Madison called **factions**, might divide the young nation. In *Federalist* 10 Madison wrote, "By faction I understand a number of citizens, whether amounting to a majority or minority of the whole, who are united and actuated by some common impulse of passion, or of interest, adverse to the rights of other citizens, or to the permanent and aggregate interests of the community." Although he recognized that such groups could not be suppressed without abolishing liberty, he also argued in *Federalist* 51 that, in a large and diverse republic, narrow interests would balance each other out and be checked by majority rule. (See *Federalist* 10 and 51 in the Appendix.) Factions are not exactly the same as political parties, which form explicitly to win elections and which we examine in Chapter 9 (Political Parties), but Madison feared they could have the same divisive or polarizing effect in a democracy. Nevertheless, the Bill of Rights contains protections for the rights of association and petition because these rights are essential for citizens to be able to hold their government accountable, ensure the responsiveness of elected officials, and participate equally in self-government.

The **right of petition** gives individuals with a claim against the government the right to ask for compensation, but it also includes the right to petition to ask for a policy change or to express opposition to a policy. It was the earliest and most basic gateway for citizens seeking to make government respond to them, and it has been used from the beginning of government under the Constitution. In the twenty-first century, the Internet has made it possible for individuals to directly "ask" Congress for a benefit via e-mail or to sign onto a virtual petition that can be presented to Congress. Interest groups also use their high membership numbers as a proxy for the direct expression of support that once came from petitioners' personal visits to lawmakers.

right of association: *Right to freely associate with others and form groups, protected by the First Amendment.*

faction: *Defined by Madison as any group that places its own interests above the aggregate interests of society.*

Do you think interest groups are divisive and polarizing? Or do they bring citizens together? Can you give examples?

right of petition: *Right to ask the government for assistance with a problem or to express opposition to a government policy, protected by the First Amendment.*

Have you ever signed a petition? What was it for?

Today, the rights of association and petition most often take the form of **lobbying**, or trying to persuade elected officials to adopt or reject a specific policy change. Lobbying is a legitimate form of petitioning, and interest groups of all sizes and purposes engage in it, from Students for Concealed Carry on Campus, to big corporations such as Microsoft or Google, to large-scale **grassroots groups** such as the Sierra Club. The term *lobbying* was coined over three hundred years ago when individuals seeking favors from the British government would pace the halls, or lobbies, of the Parliament building, waiting for a chance to speak with members. The practice was immediately adopted in the new United States.

Interest groups lobby the legislative, executive, and even judicial branches of government at the state and federal levels. For example, when groups lobby Congress or state legislatures, they typically meet with staff aides to members to make the case for their policy goals. Lobbyists may also try to influence the executive branch by meeting personally with key bureaucrats and policy makers. Lobbying of the judicial branch takes the form of lawsuits against government policies that interest groups see as fundamentally unconstitutional or that go against the original intent of law. Such lawsuits can be high profile and are initiated by groups of all political ideologies. For other cases, interest groups can also submit *amicus curiae* **briefs** that record their opinion even if they are not the primary legal participants in a case. Interest groups also lobby for and against judicial nominees, especially Supreme Court appointments. Lobbying strategies and tactics differ according to the branch of government at the state and federal levels, but no government entity is outside the scope of lobbyists' efforts.[3]

Types of Interest Groups

Because the universe of interest groups is so large and diverse, it can be helpful to categorize them by their core organizing purpose and the arena in which they seek to influence public policy. In this section, we survey three types of interest groups—economic, ideological, and foreign policy–focused—to illustrate and explain differences in interest group policy goals and strategies.

Economic Interest Groups

Economic interest groups form to advance the economic status of their members and are defined by a specific set of financial or business concerns. Economic interest groups tend to be exclusive in their membership base because their purpose is to secure tangible economic benefits for themselves; if they grow too large or too inclusive, members' benefits are necessarily diluted. However, as we will see in discussing unions, if the underlying

lobbying: *Act of trying to persuade elected officials to adopt a specific policy change, or maintain the status quo.*

grassroots movement: *Group that forms in response to an economic or political event, but does not focus on only one issue.*

amicus curiae briefs: *Briefs filed by outside parties ("friends of the court") who have an interest in the outcome of a case.*

economic interest group: *Group formed to advance the economic status of its members.*

industries represented by these groups disappear or merge with others, then the groups have to adapt in order to attract new members.

Trade and Professional Associations.

Trade associations are a subcategory of economic interest groups that focus on particular businesses or industries. Examples include the National Association of Manufacturers, Chamber of Commerce, National Retail Federation, and Semiconductor Industry Association. Trade associations form because business owners in these areas believe that collectively they will have more influence on the policy process than they would individually. **Professional associations** are similar, as they are formed by individuals who share a similar job. Examples include the American Bar Association (lawyers), the American Medical Association (doctors), and the American International Automobile Dealers Association (car dealers). These associations are frequently responsible for setting guidelines for professional conduct, from business practices to personal ethics, and for collectively representing the members in the policy process.

Corporations.

Large corporations can be included as a type of economic interest group, because they try to influence policy on their own as well as join trade associations of businesses with similar goals. Corporations such as Wal-Mart, Comcast, and Boeing have thousands of employees, and that alone encourages politicians to listen to their concerns.

Unions.

Unions are a type of economic interest group. They comprise people who share a common type of employment. Unions seek safer working conditions and better wages for their members, and they are traditionally organized as local chapters that are part of a national organization. For example, autoworkers might join the United Auto Workers (UAW), truck drivers the International Brotherhood of Teamsters, television script writers the Screen Writers Guild, health care workers the Service Employees International Union, and high school teachers the National Educational Association.

The strength of unions as economic groups rests in the fact that when workers agree to *unionize*, they agree to allow the union leaders to bargain collectively with their employers over wages and working conditions. Collective bargaining is protected by the **National Labor Relations Act**, passed by Congress in 1935. The act also provides that only one union can be selected to represent workers in a specific location, so that once a union successfully organizes a work location, those workers have to abide by that union's decisions.[4] The persuasive power of unions rests in their ability to call strikes, work stoppages that always decrease employers' profits. The mere threat of a strike is frequently enough to win benefits for workers who are represented by a union.

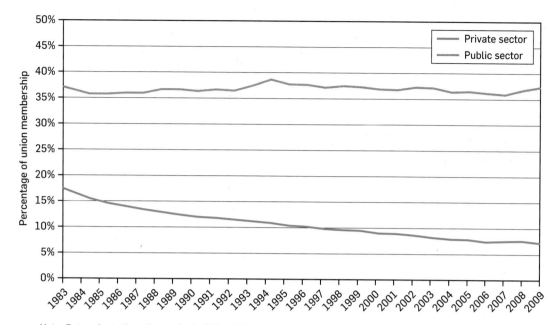

Note: Data refer to the sole or principal job of full- and part-time workers. All self-employed workers are excluded, regardless of whether or not their businesses are incorporated. Data for 1990–93 have been revised to reflect population controls from the 1990 census. Beginning in 2000 data reflect population controls from census 2000 and new industry and occupational classification systems. Beginning in 2000 private sector data refer to private sector wage and salary workers; private sector data for earlier years refer to private nonagricultural wage and salary workers.

FIGURE 8.1 **Trends in Private and Public Sector Union Membership, 1983–2009.** Private union membership has been declining over time, while public union membership has increased. *Source:* Bureau of Labor Statistics based on Current Population Survey, http://www.bls.gov.

The biggest weakness that unions face is that when the industry they represent loses jobs, union membership shrinks, and the smaller the union, the less power it can exert on both manufacturers and elected officials. The once large and powerful United Steelworkers Union has suffered a decline due to financial difficulties in the American auto industry. Overall, private sector union membership has been declining (see Figure 8.1). One effective response by unions to a declining traditional membership base is to seek to represent workers in other types of industries. For example, the UAW now represents cafeteria and janitorial staffs on campuses all over the nation. Like any other interest group, unions try to respond and adapt to changing external conditions.

Despite the recent downturn in membership in large industrial and manufacturing unions in the private sector, unions in the public sector representing teachers, health service workers, communications workers, and government employees have all made large gains over the past two decades. Table 8.1 lists the top thirty-eight unions in the country. Together, the top five unions have

TABLE 8.1 Unions in the United States with More Than 100,000 Members, 2003

Union	Number of Members
NEA—National Education Association	2,679,396
SEIU—Service Employees International Union	1,464,007
UFCW—United Food and Commercial Workers International Union	1,380,507
IBT—International Brotherhood of Teamsters	1,350,000
AFSCME—American Federation of State, County and Municipal Employees	1,350,000
LIUNA—Laborers' International Union of North America	840,180
AFT—American Federation of Teachers	770,090
IBEW—International Brotherhood of Electrical Workers	700,548
IAM—International Association of Machinists and Aerospace Workers	673,095
UAW—United Automobile, Aerospace and Agricultural Implement Workers of America	638,722
CWA—Communications Workers of America	557,136
USW—United Steelworkers of America	532,234
UBC—United Brotherhood of Carpenters and Joiners of America	531,839
IUOE—International Union of Operating Engineers	390,388
NPMHU—National Postal Mail Handlers Union	388,480
UA—United Association of Journeymen and Apprentices of the Plumbing and Pipe Fitting Industry of the United States and Canada	325,914
NALC—National Association of Letter Carriers	294,315
APWU—American Postal Workers Union	292,901
PACE—Paper, Allied-Industrial, Chemical and Energy Workers International Union	274,464
IAFF—International Association of Fire Fighters	261,551
HERE—Hotel Employees and Restaurant Employees International Union	249,151
UNITE—Union of Needletrades, Industrial and Textile Employees	209,876
AFGE—American Federation of Government Employees	200,600
AGVA—American Guild of Variety Artists	182,597
UAN—United American Nurses	152,000
OPEIU—Office and Professional Employees International Union	150,882
SMW—Sheet Metal Workers International Association	148,378
BSORIW—International Association of Bridge, Structural, Ornamental and Reinforcing Iron Workers	130,928
IUPAT—International Union of Painters and Allied Trades	115,511

TABLE 8.1 **Continued**

Union	Number of Members
BCTGM—Bakery, Confectionery, Tobacco Workers, and Grain Millers International Union	114,618
TWU—Transportation Workers Union of America	110,000
AACSE—American Association of Classified School Employees	109,188
IATSE—International Alliance of Theatrical Stage Employees, Moving Picture Technicians, Artists and Allied Crafts of the United States and Canada	104,102
AFM—American Federation of Musicians of the United States and Canada	102,000
NRLCA—National Rural Letter Carriers' Association	101,810
BAC—International Union of Bricklayers and Allied Craftworkers	101,499
TCU—Transportation Communications International Union	101,228
UMWA—United Mine Workers of America	100,570

Source: Directory of U.S. Labor Organizations (Bureau of National Affairs), 2004 ed., http://www.workinglife.org.

over 8 million members and, in total, the top thirty-eight unions, each with at least 100,000 members, have a combined membership of over 17 million workers. Today, unions represent 12.3 percent of the overall workforce in the United States.[5]

American unions are economically powerful *and* potentially politically powerful because they can mobilize their members to vote for candidates they view to be favorable on issues such as higher minimum wages, standards for overtime pay, better access to health care insurance, worker safety, and international trade agreements. In other nations, unions play important economic and political roles (see Other Places: Trade Unions in South Africa).

Ideological and Issue-Oriented Groups

Ideological interest groups form among citizens with the same beliefs about a specific issue. We describe these groups as ideological rather than economic to point out the fact that economic benefits are not the primary basis for their existence. This category of interest group can include **citizens' groups** (Common Cause or Public Citizen), **single-issue groups** (National Rifle Association or Right to Life), and grassroots movement groups (MoveOn .org or the National Organization for Women). Citizens groups are typically formed to draw attention to public issues that affect all citizens equally, such as environmental protection, transparency in government, consumer product

Give three reasons why private union membership has declined.

ideological interest groups: *Groups that form among citizens with the same beliefs about a specific issue.*

citizens' groups: *Groups that form to draw attention to purely public issues that affect all citizens equally.*

single-issue groups: *Groups that form to present one view on a highly salient issue that is intensely important to their members, such as gun control or abortion.*

⊕otherplaces

Trade Unions in South Africa

Unions play an important role in countries outside the United States. For example, in South Africa, a nation with a population of about 49 million, there are three major union federations: the Congress of South African Trade Unions (COSATU), the Federation of Unions of South Africa (FEDUSA), and the National Council of Trade Unions (NACTU). These three federations represent a total of 2.7 million workers, about 15.6 percent of the total workforce, in a varied set of industries.

Although unions have been active in South Africa for nearly sixty years, they were segregated under *apartheid*, a policy of oppression and racial segregation that governed the nation from 1948 to 1994. Under apartheid, union membership was restricted to whites, Indians, and colored (non-black). Consequently millions of black South Africans were not granted the same protections for working conditions as white workers.

As the political resistance to apartheid grew stronger in the 1980s, the international community pressured South African white leaders to eliminate racist policies and allow broader political participation. Union leaders and local organizers arranged protests and ministrikes to undermine support for the apartheid regime. In 1994, the first free elections were established, and political and economic rights were granted to black South Africans. Nelson Mandela was elected as the first black president, and his political party, the African National Congress, won control of the legislature. New laws were enacted that gave more bargaining power to unions, and the National Economic Development and Labour Council (NEDLAC) was created to negotiate labor disputes between management and workers.

This case study of unions in South Africa is designed to show how unions can be powerful economically and politically. In advocating on behalf of their members, unions implicitly make the case for full political equality and participation. These arguments are advantageous for unions because their capacity for influence only grows stronger with more members who can vote.

- **What two things did unions do to overturn apartheid in South Africa?**

- **How is political freedom connected to union power in South Africa?**

Sources: South Africa Info: Gateway to the Nation, "Trade Unions in South Africa," http://www.southafrica.info; Central Intelligence Agency, *The World Factbook: South Africa,* http://www.cia.gov. See also *Africana: The Encyclopedia of the African and African American Experience,* ed. Kwame Anthony Appiah and Henry Louis Gates Jr. (New York: Perseus Books. 1999), http://www.africanaencyclopedia.com.

safety, ethics reform, and campaign finance reform. Single-issue groups form to present *one view* on a highly salient issue that is intensely important to its members, as the right to carry a concealed weapon is to Students for Concealed Carry on Campus. In contrast, broader organizations typically emerge in response to an economic or political event but do not focus solely on one issue. For example, MoveOn.org was founded by two wealthy men who were angry that President Bill Clinton (1993–2001) was impeached despite the fact that most people opposed such proceedings. MoveOn.org advocated for more responsive government and, during the George W. Bush administration (2001–09), called for an end to the Iraq War.

Ideological groups provide a way for individual members to express their opinions on an issue with a larger, louder voice than any one person could have separately. Members of ideological groups get the benefit of knowing that others share their views and feel empowered. In this way, ideological groups can encourage political participation in a democratic society. At the same time, these groups contribute to the **polarization** of the American public. Because this type of group gets its power from the fact that it has agreement within its ranks on a highly salient issue, it discourages debate and disagreement within the group and any type of compromise outside the group.

polarization: *Condition in which differences between parties and/or the public are so stark that disagreement breaks out, fueling attacks and controversy.*

Foreign Policy Groups

Foreign policy groups form to generate support for favorable U.S. policies toward one or several foreign countries. One of the most well-known organizations of this type is the American Israel Public Affairs Committee (AIPAC). This group seeks a strongly pro-Israel American foreign policy and uses public advocacy and member mobilization to influence members of Congress to support its goals. AIPAC first formed in the early 1950s, and it claims credit for getting the first aid package to Israel, $65 million to help relocate Holocaust refugees, passed by Congress in 1951.[6] Today, AIPAC has more than 100,000 active members and is widely considered to be one of the most influential groups of its kind in Washington.

foreign policy groups: *Groups founded to create support for favorable U.S. policies toward one or several foreign countries.*

Should foreign countries or corporations be allowed to lobby the U.S. government? Why or why not?

Other foreign policy groups focus attention on human rights violations or starvation in certain areas of the world. For example, the Coalition to Save Darfur was founded in 2004 in response to intense violence and famine in Darfur, a rural part of the African nation of Somalia. It was started by a small number of human rights groups that believed U.S. and U.N. intervention were necessary. In January 2006, the group launched a grassroots personal and Internet effort to have one million postcards sent to President George W. Bush, urging the United States to join with other countries to intervene in the region. In June 2006, the group reached its goal with the millionth postcard signed by then-Senator Hillary

Michael Brown/Getty Images

Rodham Clinton (D-N.Y.), who was appointed secretary of state in 2009.[7] By the end of 2009, the situation in Darfur had stabilized and the violence had ebbed; in response, the group changed its focus from stopping the violence to supporting "a vision for peace."[8] The Coalition to Save Darfur illustrates the power of an interest group to draw attention to a situation occurring in a foreign land and to solicit a powerful response from average citizens and elected officials alike.[9]

The Coalition to Save Darfur is an interest group that mobilizes people at the grassroots to e-mail, call, or send a letter to their legislators on behalf of its effort to end violence and famine in Darfur, a rural part of the African nation of Somalia. In 2006 thousands joined a grassroots rally in New York City to express their support for sending United Nations troops to Darfur to help stop the violence there.

What Interest Groups Do

Interest groups perform a number of functions in the political process. They collect information about the implications of policy changes and convey that information to lawmakers and other policy makers. Their lobbying efforts aim to construct policies in ways that will most benefit their members. This section of the chapter examines the tactics of lobbying, from providing information, to contributing to campaigns, to orchestrating grassroots movements that increase political participation on an issue. Lobbying is one of the fundamental gateways for expressing views and securing a favorable response from government officials.

Inform

All interest groups provide information to their members, the media, government officials, and the general public. The type of interest group dictates the kind of information it disseminates. In today's information age, it is a much more difficult task to keep information confidential or limit access to it, so interest groups do more than merely report on current policy developments; they also provide members with an interpretation of how these developments will affect the group's mission and goals. For example, when President Barack

Obama's (2009–) climate control bill passed the House of Representatives on June 26, 2009, the executive director of the Sierra Club posted a letter to members on the group's website explaining the impact of the bill.[10] Even though Sierra Club members might be able to find information about how the bill's passage would affect environmental policy from other sources, it would take more time and effort to gather a complete picture. Interest groups see it as their responsibility to effectively package information to members in the most efficient and complete way possible.

Interest groups also work hard to inform government officials about the impact of specific public policies. Most of the time, lobbyists have a pro or con position on a policy proposal, and their goal is to persuade government officials to agree with their perspective. Legislators and government officials are generally knowledgeable in their areas of expertise and interest, but the vast size of the federal and state governments makes it hard to know the impact of policies on every citizen. Economic and ideological groups constantly monitor those policies that might affect their members in a positive or negative way and strive to make legislators and government officials aware of the impact of policy proposals.

Lobby

Almost every kind of group, with every kind of economic interest or political opinion, engages in one form of lobbying or another, including business firms, trade and professional organizations, citizens groups, labor unions, and even universities and colleges.[11] At the federal level, even state and county government officials maintain lobbying offices in Washington, D.C., separately and as part of larger national groups like the National Governors Association, the United States Conference of Mayors, and the National Conference of State Legislatures. Lobbyists for these government entities frequently visit with members of the state's congressional delegation to keep them informed about how federal programs are operating back home and to ask for legislation that will benefit their states. At the state level, city mayors and county executives attempt to influence their state legislators and governor by keeping them informed about how policies affect their constituents.

The Lobbyists. Groups can either use their own employees as lobbyists, or they contract with firms that specialize in lobbying. According to the Center for Responsive Politics, in 2009 there were 13,739 individuals registered as active lobbyists in Washington, D.C. That amounts to nearly twenty-six lobbyists for each member of the House and Senate.[12] The offices of many of these lobbyists are concentrated in an area of Northwest Washington known as the K Street corridor; in fact, if someone says she works on K Street, it is safe to assume that her job is to lobby.

When interest groups gather and disseminate information, are they performing a public service? Or do they do it just to advance their own causes? If so, is there anything wrong with that?

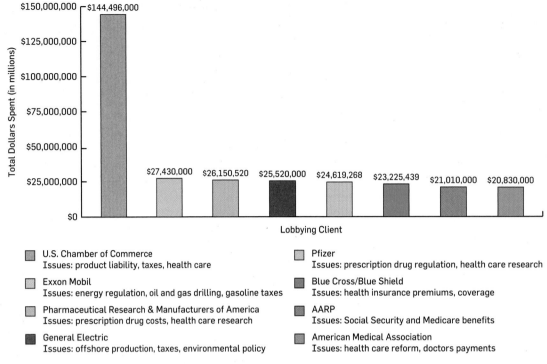

Total Dollars Spent (in millions)

$150,000,000	$144,496,000
$125,000,000	
$100,000,000	
$75,000,000	
$50,000,000	
$25,000,000	$27,430,000 $26,150,520 $25,520,000 $24,619,268 $23,225,439 $21,010,000 $20,830,000
$0	

Lobbying Client

U.S. Chamber of Commerce
Issues: product liability, taxes, health care

Exxon Mobil
Issues: energy regulation, oil and gas drilling, gasoline taxes

Pharmaceutical Research & Manufacturers of America
Issues: prescription drug costs, health care research

General Electric
Issues: offshore production, taxes, environmental policy

Pfizer
Issues: prescription drug regulation, health care research

Blue Cross/Blue Shield
Issues: health insurance premiums, coverage

AARP
Issues: Social Security and Medicare benefits

American Medical Association
Issues: health care reform, doctors payments

FIGURE 8.2 **Top Spenders on Lobbying, 2009.** Large corporations and trade associations tend to be the biggest spenders for lobbying the federal government. The amount of money they spend varies according to the subject matter of the legislation being considered by Congress and the president. *Source:* Center for Responsive Politics, "Lobbying: Top Spenders, 2009," http://www.opensecrets.org.

Although lobbyists are frequently stereotyped as representing only the narrow interests of their clients, they are typically individuals who have held public service jobs at some point in their careers. There are three common pathways to becoming a Washington lobbyist: working on Capitol Hill, working in the executive branch, or working on a political campaign. Lobbyists may start out on a political campaign for a congressional candidate, work in a congressional office, and then leave to join a corporation, lobbying firm, or a law firm with a branch that lobbies on specific legal matters. Or lobbyists may start out as practicing attorneys, then go to work in Congress or the executive branch, and subsequently join a company or lobbying firm.

Why is the public perception of lobbyists so negative?

In 2009, interest groups and lobbying firms spent nearly $2.5 billion on a wide range of expenses associated with lobbying, including salaries for in-house lobbyists, consulting fees charged by lobbying firms, overhead for office space, and travel costs of staff[13] (see Figure 8.2). In the past, the costs of lobbying also included paid trips for members of Congress and their staffs (known as junkets), as well as expensive meals. Lobbyists justified these expenses as a way of getting to know members of Congress in a smaller and more relaxed setting, which they claimed would enable them to enhance their or their client's influence in the policy process. In 2007, congressional ethics reforms prohibited paid trips and meals for members and staff.[14] Still, lobbyists can use money to maintain their influence in other ways. For example, the salaries for most lobbyists typically include an allocation for them to make strategic campaign contributions to members of Congress who preside over issues that are important to their companies or clients.[15]

During a typical day, lobbyists phone, e-mail, or meet with congressional staffers, their clients, and possibly members of the media to gather information about relevant issues for their clients or to promote their clients' policy positions. Lobbyists also attend congressional hearings, executive branch briefings, and even committee markups, where members of Congress actually write legislation, on issues of importance to their companies or clients. Interest groups, businesses, and industries do not survive by lobbying alone, but it is a natural outgrowth of their purpose, because members expect their leaders to advocate for them when it is necessary to do so.

Lobbying Strategies. Lobbying frequently involves a multipronged strategy. Groups usually try an inside lobbying strategy first, in which they deal directly with legislators and their staff in asking for a specific policy benefit or in trying to stop a policy that they oppose. These insider meetings require access to policy makers, which typically comes about as a result of longtime interactions that build mutual trust. The key aspect of the inside strategy is to keep the policy request narrowly tailored to the group's needs, because the broader the policy request, the more likely other groups will become involved in the negotiations, and then complications ensue. Either the policy request has to expand, so that each group gets a high level of benefits, or each group has to be satisfied with less, and few groups are ever satisfied with less. Nevertheless, if several groups share the same policy goals, they may form a temporary coalition, working together to improve their chances of success.

When an inside strategy does not work, groups adopt a more public or outside lobbying strategy by getting the press and their members more directly involved. A group may go straight to the press to provide details about the adverse effects of the proposal, in the hopes that journalists will then inform the general public. In this way, interest groups try to make use of the press's **watchdog** role over the government. For example, a nonprofit group called Citizens for Responsibility and Ethics in Washington consistently tries to get the press to focus on whether government officials are obeying ethics laws.[16] Early in 2009, this group was successful in launching an examination of President Obama's ethics rules for executive branch employees.

Through publicity and coordinated activities, groups also try to promote grassroots lobbying by encouraging an action among their own members and the larger public. Energizing constituents in congressional districts used to

watchdog: *Role of monitoring government actions.*

be the work of regional offices. Today interest groups can generate citizen involvement through the Internet, asking that a message be sent by e-mail, text messaging, or cell phones. In addition, marches and rallies show strength in numbers to elected officials; they also generate publicity that can attract new people to join in advocacy efforts. In these ways, groups directly give their membership a stronger voice in the policy-making process.

Engage in Campaign Activities

Interest groups also promote their views by engaging in campaign activities, though federal law regulates their participation. Groups with a tax-exempt status are prohibited from engaging in any activity on behalf of a candidate or party in an election campaign. These groups, commonly referred to as **501(c)(3) organizations** after the section of the Internal Revenue Code that governs their activities, are likely to be charities, religious organizations, public service organizations, employee benefit groups, and fraternal societies, which are exempt from paying federal tax. Although these groups cannot engage in lobbying in any significant way, they can produce voter education guides or other nonpartisan educational material that explains issues raised during a political campaign and keeps the public informed.[17]

Groups that fall outside the tax-exempt category are free to engage in lobbying and campaign activities. But to set boundaries between the group's core mission and politics, they generally create parallel organizations that make campaign contributions to legislators. These are **political action committees (PACs)**, which raise funds to support electoral candidates and are subject to campaign finance laws (see Chapter 10, Elections, Campaigns, and Voting). In one sense, PACs serve as gateways for expanding interest groups' political influence through financial involvement in campaigns.

PACs began growing in number and force after the Supreme Court's landmark decision *Buckley v. Valeo* (1976) upheld congressional limits on donations to campaigns.[18] As the costs of campaign spending increased over time, groups realized that creating or expanding an affiliated PAC could gain them more influence over elected officials through campaign contributions. Unaffiliated PACs, which are groups that make campaign contributions but do not associate with a specific interest group, also grew in size as a means of coordinating campaign contributions from individual citizens who wanted to express their campaign support as part of a larger group. All PACs make campaign contributions to candidates for office who they believe will be supportive of their policy goals (see Table 8.2). Thus PACs expand the reach of interest groups well beyond lobbying to include active engagement in the electoral arena.

501(c)(3) organizations: *Tax-exempt groups that are prohibited from lobbying or campaigning for a party or candidate.*

political action committees (PACs): *Groups formed to raise and contribute funds to support electoral candidates, subject to campaign finance laws.*

Should there be limits on how much money interest groups can contribute to campaigns? Why?

TABLE 8.2 Top Twenty PAC Contributors by Total, and Party Percentage 2009–10

PAC Name*	Total Amount	Percentage to Democrats	Percentage to Republicans
Honeywell International	$2,760,600	55%	45%
AT&T Inc.	$2,597,375	50%	50%
International Brotherhood of Electrical Workers	$2,561,123	98%	2%
National Beer Wholesalers Association	$2,244,500	56%	44%
American Association for Justice	$2,202,500	97%	3%
Operating Engineers Union	$2,109,300	89%	11%
American Bankers Association	$1,981,430	39%	61%
American Fedn of State/County/ Municipal Employees	$1,869,500	100%	0%
International Association of Fire Fighters	$1,843,500	83%	17%
National Association of Realtors	$1,818,298	58%	41%
Boeing Co.	$1,765,000	59%	41%
Teamsters Union	$1,732,910	98%	2%
American Crystal Sugar	$1,729,500	68%	32%
American Federation of Teachers	$1,682,250	100%	0%
Laborers Union	$1,670,000	96%	4%
Lockheed Martin	$1,657,950	58%	42%
Machinists/Aerospace Workers Union	$1,646,500	98%	2%
Credit Union National Association	$1,598,446	58%	42%
National Air Traffic Controllers Association	$1,594,900	83%	17%
Plumbers/Pipefitters Union	$1,554,075	96%	3%

Totals include subsidiaries and affiliated PACs, if any.

*For ease of identification, the names used in this section are those of the organization connected with the PAC, rather than the official PAC name.

Source: Center for Responsive Politics, http://www.opensecrets.org, based on data released by the Federal Election Commission on August 22, 2010.

Given the amount of money that PACs spend on campaign support, there is a concern that their money exerts a disproportionate influence over legislators, which creates an imbalance in government responsiveness toward some groups and not others. However, scholars have had difficulty establishing just exactly what PACs are getting for their money. Although campaign contributions can make it easier for groups to get access to legislators, they generally do not buy results. Interest groups tend to lobby and contribute to members of Congress who are leaning in their direction, so it is very difficult to prove the impact of a campaign contribution.[19]

More generally, campaign finance laws impose limits on what interest groups can do in terms of **issue advocacy**, the practice of running advertisements or distributing literature on a policy issue rather than a specific candidate. In general, the Supreme Court has ruled that campaign spending is a form of speech, and that like other forms of speech, Congress must show a "compelling interest" before laws can regulate it. The McCain-Feingold Bipartisan Campaign Reform Act (2002) restricted corporations and unions from using television or radio ads for "electioneering communications"—commercials that refer to a candidate by name within thirty days of a primary or sixty days of a general election. Since 2002 many groups have run ads that could be interpreted either as issue advocacy or as outright campaigning. In 2004, in *FEC v. Wisconsin Right to Life*, the Supreme Court ruled that if a campaign advertisement could be reasonably viewed as issue based, it was protected under the guarantee of free speech and could not be prohibited under the McCain-Feingold Act. Two years later, MoveOn .org ran a number of issue ads arguing that the only way to end the Iraq War was to change the leadership in Washington. Because the group did not name specific candidates, these ads were ruled not to be in violation of campaign finance laws.

The use of issue ads has now become a regular feature of interest group activity, even in nonelection years. In the summer of 2009, a wide range of interest and industry groups, such as the pharmaceutical industry, health care providers, and unions, began running ads in support of President Obama's health care reform.[20] These ads are legal: they do not advocate the election or reelection of specific candidates, and they fall outside the time limit imposed by the McCain-Feingold Act. Although they serve the purposes of interest groups, they also encourage elected officials to be more responsive to constituents' needs, because they focus attention on issues of importance to constituents. In 2010, the Supreme Court has further extended protections to issue ads (see Supreme Court Cases: *Citizens United v. Federal Election Commission*).

issue advocacy:
Sponsoring advertisements (issue ads) or distributing literature on a policy issue, rather than a specific candidate.

Are issue ads fair or unfair? Are they informative or "disinformative"?

supremecourtcases

Citizens United v. Federal Election Commission (2010)

QUESTION: Can the government restrict campaign spending by corporations and unions without violating First Amendment rights?

ORAL ARGUMENT: March 24, 2009, reargued September 9, 2009 (listen at http://www.oyez.org/cases/)

DECISION: January 21, 2010 (read at http://www.findlaw.com/CaseCode/supreme.html)

OUTCOME: No, governmental restrictions on corporate speech violate First Amendment rights (5–4).

In an attempt to equalize finances in political campaigns, Congress passed the Bipartisan Campaign Reform Act of 2002, also known as the McCain-Feingold Act after its two leading sponsors. In 1976, the Supreme Court had upheld limits on what congressional campaigns could spend, but struck down limits on what independent groups unaffiliated with the campaign could spend. In response, McCain-Feingold restricted corporations and unions from using television or radio ads for "electioneering communications"—commercials that refer to a candidate by name within thirty days of a primary or sixty days of a general election.

While corporations are often for-profit operations, such as General Motors or Microsoft, other nonprofit and political entities such as the NAACP organize as corporations under the tax code. One such political organization is Citizens United, a conservative interest group "dedicated to restoring our government to citizen control." During the 2008 Democratic primary campaign, it released a documentary called *Hillary: The Movie,* which was severely critical of Senator Clinton. Citizens United planned to show the documentary on pay-per-view television, marketing the movie with ads on broadcast television. Concerned about violating McCain-Feingold, Citizens United sued the FEC, seeking an injunction prohibiting enforcement of the act as a violation of the First Amendment rights of corporations.

In a break with past decisions, the Supreme Court declared that corporations and unions had the same First Amendment rights as U.S. citizens. Using the compelling interest test (see Chapter 4, Civil Liberties), the Court ruled that Congress cannot disfavor certain subjects or speakers. While recognizing that corporations may have more money to spend than individual citizens, the Court ruled that First Amendment protections do not depend on the speaker's "financial ability to engage in public discussion." Such limitations violate the marketplace of ideas that the First Amendment is designed to protect. The majority left open the question as to whether Congress could limit the speech rights of foreign corporations operating within the United States.

The dissenters claimed that money is not equivalent to speech and that the law was a reasonable attempt to level the playing field in campaigns. President Barack Obama attacked the decision in his State of the Union Address in February 2010.

- **Why is campaign spending a form of speech?**
- **Should corporations receive the same free speech protections as ordinary citizens?**

The Impact of Interest Groups on Democratic Processes

"I have often admired the extreme skill," wrote Tocqueville, "with which the inhabitants of the United States succeed in proposing a common object to the exertions of a great many men, and in inducing them voluntarily to pursue it."[21] Both Tocqueville and James Madison assumed that voluntary association or the forming of factions was a natural process of citizens interacting in a free society. Scholars have been interested in the same process, examining why interest groups form and what effects they have in a democratic society. In this section, we survey various perspectives on interest groups that relate to government responsiveness and citizen equality.

Natural Balance or Disproportionate Power?

Over the last fifty years, scholarly debate has centered on the process of interest group formation and its consequences. In the 1950s, David Truman agreed with Tocqueville and Madison, describing interest group formation as natural. He observed that when individuals have interests in common, they naturally gravitate toward each other and form a group. So long as those individuals share a characteristic, opinion, or interest, the group continues to exist, but if that commonality disappears, the group disappears.[22] But Mancur Olson, writing in the mid-1960s, argued that merely having something in common with other people was not enough to give a group life and keep it going as an effective organization.[23] Olson focused on the costs of organizing and maintaining a group, and noted that costs increase as a group grows in size and reach. Those who pay membership dues expect benefits in return. To Olson, the cost-benefit structure that underlies group formation contradicts Truman's claim that all groups naturally form and sustain themselves.

The debate between Truman and Olson raises the fundamental issue of whether interest groups are natural and can compete on an equal basis, or artificial because they distort public policy in favor of some citizens over others. Other scholars have addressed this question in different ways. Robert Dahl argued that in a **pluralist** society, the varied interest groups that emerge to represent their members will, in their battles over public policy, produce a consensus that serves the public's common interest.[24] And as we note in Chapter 1 (Gateways to American Democracy: Judging the Democratic Experiment), scholars such as C. Wright Mills worried that a power elite controlled power in the American democracy.[25] His concerns were echoed by Theodore Lowi, who argued that in a democracy some voices are louder than others and that government is more responsive to louder voices and will consistently

pluralist: *View of democratic society in which interest groups compete over policy goals and elected officials are mediators of group conflict.*

serve those groups at the expense of those who cannot make their voices heard. This kind of policy making is, according to Lowi, **elitist** and fundamentally antidemocratic.[26]

Traditionally, it has been the narrow focus of interest groups that has engendered a sense of illegitimacy. Interest groups form and survive by appealing to a particular segment of society (economic, ideological, or social), so they are inherently exclusive. If groups are exclusive, they act only in the best interests of their members, even if nonmembers thereby lose out. E. E. Schattschneider described this aspect of interest groups as an actual threat to democracy. He argued that if interest groups are given legitimacy because they claim to represent citizens' interests, but in fact only seek narrow benefits for their members at the expense of nonmembers, then there is an inherent unfairness to them. Moreover, citizens will be lulled into a false sense of security about living in an "interest group society" because they believe that every interest group has equal opportunity to be influential.[27]

There is a middle ground between these contrasting views. Given the approximately seven thousand registered groups in America today, it is clear that group formation is a natural outgrowth of the freedom to associate and of community life in which human beings share social, economic, and political goals. The interest group system provides multiple gateways through which individuals can see their views represented. Theoretically, because there are in fact so many different interest groups, they balance each other out in a democracy, as Madison hoped they would.

But if Olson is right, and successful cost-benefit strategies determine whether a group can survive or grow, then groups led by individuals with sufficient time and money stand a greater chance of winning a policy fight than groups without such resources. In this view, interests become **special interests**, a term with negative connotations suggesting that some groups exert a disproportionate amount of power in the arena of interest group competition. To the extent that a well-funded interest group can more easily pressure the government to produce policies that are beneficial to them, government responds unequally across all citizens. In this view, financial advantage creates an artificial imbalance of influence that acts as a gate against equality.

Take the example of MoveOn.org, which describes itself as a grassroots interest group but as we noted earlier was founded by two very wealthy Internet entrepreneurs. They formed MoveOn.org (and MoveOn PAC), which states as its mission to get individual citizens to participate more in the governing process. MoveOn.org is a nonprofit, progressive but nonpartisan organization that organizes a wide range of activities designed to inform and motivate average citizens. Its goals and mission sound very democratic, and joining the group requires little more than a click of a button on the Internet.

elitist: *View of democratic society in which only a select few interest groups shape policies in favor of a small group of wealthy or powerful citizens.*

What distinguishes a legitimate interest from an illegitimate interest?

Do interest groups balance each other out the way that Madison thought they would?

special interests: *Set of groups seeking a particular benefit for themselves in the policy process.*

For those who debate the merit of interest groups, the question is whether the public service mission of a group outweighs the fact that it is founded and run by a small, elite set of citizens.

Self-Service or Public Service

In assessing the relative power of interest groups in a democratic political system, it is essential to remember that interest groups do not pass or implement laws; they try to influence state and federal governments to enact their policy goals for them. To do so, they constantly interact with political parties, members of Congress, executive branch bureaucrats, and even the judicial system. The question of legitimacy of an interest group's activities comes when a victory for one group means a loss for another, or more broadly, a loss for the general public.

The frustrating aspect of the role that interest groups play in a democracy is that groups contesting over a single issue frequently talk over each other, not with each other; compromise is difficult to achieve. It is often left to members of Congress and the executive branch to balance their own responses to interest group requests and still maintain responsiveness to constituents and the nation at large. Over time, most interest groups experience wins and losses in the policy system; the necessary condition for a democracy is that every group has a chance to make its case.

Open or Closed Routes of Influence

Although it may be true that interests ultimately balance each other out and that changing conditions ultimately level the playing field, the fact that a tightly knit group of specialists often control policy areas raises a concern about fairness both inside and outside interest group organizations.

For example, lobbyists work to build good relationships with legislators and officials in the bureaucracy. Given their knowledge of particular policy areas, many of them move in and out of government. Are they always thinking of their groups' membership when they engage in their activities, or are they thinking about their next job? Do they constitute an insider group that is ultimately self-serving rather than serving the public?

iron triangle: *Insular and closed relationship among interest groups, members of Congress, and federal agencies.*

Scholars have long used the phrase **iron triangle** to describe the relationship among interest groups, members of Congress, and federal agencies. In essence, an iron triangle is a network forged by members in three categories that works to seal off access to public policy making. Lobbyists and interest groups want to maximize their benefits from federal programs; members of Congress want to maximize their power to shape the programs; and federal bureaucrats want to maximize their longevity as administrators of these programs.

Critics of the influence of interest groups in a democracy often describe these iron triangles as unbreakable and argue that they contribute to the inefficiency of the federal government because they sustain programs that should be eliminated or enlarge programs beyond what is necessary to meet their intended purposes. Today an iron triangle can be seen as operative in issues related to health care and prescription drugs (see Figure 8.3).

Yet the well-known interest group scholar Hugh Heclo claims that the interconnections of interest groups and the government are more benign, suggesting that the term **issue network** is better than iron triangle to describe the relationship.[28] Heclo argues that interest groups, members of Congress, and bureaucrats all share information continually, and that their interactions are actually quite open and transparent, rather than closed. Heclo wrote thirty years ago, before the advent of the 24-7 news cycle, Twitter messaging, and other telecommunications innovations, so it stands to reason that it is more difficult than ever for self-serving interconnections to go unnoticed. In addition, citizens' watchdog groups, such as Common Cause, and policy institutes, such as the Center for Responsive Politics, monitor interest group influence on government activities and policies. When these groups find evidence of wrongdoing in government, they blow a loud whistle by issuing reports and holding press conferences to inform the media and the general public.

What remains true is that lobbyists, members of Congress and their staff, and members of the executive branch do pass through what scholars describe as a **revolving door** of paid positions in each other's organizations, with knowledge and experience on a specific issue the valued commodity. The term *revolving door* has a negative connotation, suggesting that an iron triangle of influence consists of the same set of people moving from one branch of government to another, and then to the private sector. The image of a revolving door also suggests that the system does not stop to include outsiders with new perspectives; in other words, it can act as a gate against wider political participation.

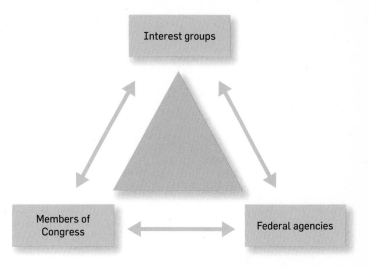

FIGURE 8.3 Iron Triangle in the Medicare Prescription Drug Improvement and Modernization Act. The iron triangle is a policy-making structure that includes congressional committees, bureaucratic agencies, and interest groups.

issue network: *View of the relationship among interest groups, members of Congress, and federal agencies as more fluid, open, and transparent than the term iron triangle.*

How does government prevent corruption among government officials?

revolving door: *Movement of members of Congress, lobbyists, and executive branch employees into paid positions in each other's organizations.*

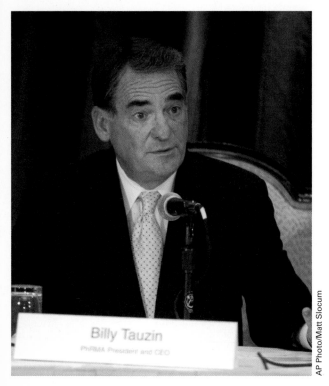

One example might be Representative Billy Tauzin (R-La.), who as chair of the Energy and Commerce Committee was instrumental in passing the Medicare Prescription Drug Improvement and Modernization Act in 2003. In 2005, Representative Tauzin left the House of Representatives to be named president of the Pharmaceutical Research and Manufacturers of America (PhRMA), a major beneficiary of that Medicare Prescription Drug bill. At the time, government watchdog groups were concerned about Representative Tauzin's behavior because he was in a position to provide disproportionate benefits to PhRMA in the Medicare bill, and PhRMA might have rewarded him for these benefits with a job when he left Congress. In 2009 Representative Tauzin led the negotiations on behalf of PhRMA with Democrats in Congress and President Barack Obama on health care reform, but the deal they worked out was subsequently abandoned. The board of PhRMA was displeased and Tauzin resigned his position in June 2010. Although it was never proven that Tauzin was "bought" by the pharmaceutical industries, the revolving door does create at least the perception that members of Congress and the bureaucracy are improperly influenced by industries seeking preferential treatment in an issue area.

It is also essential to remember, however, that not all relationships among lobbyists, members of Congress, and federal officials are tainted or suspicious. Congress and the federal bureaucracy each have an elaborate set of rules governing their behavior with respect to interest groups and lobbyists, and most members and bureaucrats follow them closely. When they do break these rules, it is easy to inform constituents.

In the iron triangle, members of Congress can serve as chair of a key committee, write legislation, and then leave to head an organization that directly benefited from it. For example, Billy Tauzin (R-La.) chaired a key committee writing legislation for the Medicare Prescription Drug Improvement and Modernization Act, then left Congress to head PhRMA, the interest group that represents drug manufacturers.

Billy Tauzin
PhRMA President and CEO

AP Photo/Matt Slocum

Characteristics of Successful Interest Groups

The measure of a successful interest group is how well it accomplishes its goals. Some groups want to stay in existence forever or for as long as they can, but other groups form temporarily for a specific purpose, such as the Students for Concealed Carry on Campus, and once they accomplish their goal, they disband. For those groups that want to establish an enduring voice in a democracy, success can be measured in four ways: leadership accountability, membership stability, financial stability, and public influence.

Identify two interest groups with "an enduring voice" in American democracy.

Leadership Accountability

As anyone who has tried to get a group of students together to perform a task, lodge a protest, or plan an event knows, coordination can be difficult. It typically takes an individual who acts as an **interest group entrepreneur** to organize citizens into a formal group that agrees on a united purpose. In return for organizing the group, these individuals typically take leadership roles in directing the group's activities. There are benefits that come from being a group leader, ranging from a salary as a paid staff member for the group, to the prestige associated with being a group leader, to extra influence over the group's goals and strategies. The well-known interest group scholar Robert Salisbury calls this tradeoff the "exchange theory of interest groups" and he argues that no one would rationally expend the energy and time to start a group if he or she could not take a prominent role in directing it.[29] Members are willing to pay their group leaders and afford them more power within the group in return for accomplishing the group's collective goals. Being an interest group leader requires the ability to keep members satisfied enough to stay in the group and, at the same time, maintain influence in the economic or political sphere on the issues that are important to those members.

interest group entrepreneurs: *Individuals who expend their own time, energy, and resources to form an interest group.*

Transparency about the group's political and financial activities in pursuit of their goals is an important democratic element of interest groups; without it, there is a risk that the leaders could act in ways that do not properly serve their members. Internally, interest groups owe it to their members to stay true to their mission. However, leaders do sometimes act in their own self-interest, by misusing group finances, for example, or they may take the group in an ideological direction that may not mirror the majority opinion in the group. Over a hundred years ago, Robert Michels coined the phrase **iron law of oligarchy** to describe this scenario, and he argued that larger interest groups were especially susceptible to unresponsive or abusive leadership. Flaws in interest group management can be a major problem for a democracy if citizens join groups with the expectation that the group will accurately represent their opinions and interests, and it does not.

iron law of oligarchy: *A theory that in any organization, the leaders eventually behave in their own self-interest, even at the expense of the rank-and-file members; the larger the organization, the greater the likelihood that the leader will behave this way.*

Members must be able to register satisfaction or dissatisfaction with the group's leadership. Yet it is difficult for the average member to hold an interest group internally accountable. Some groups elect their leaders at annual conventions, but to vote requires that members have to spend time and money to travel to attend those conventions, and few do. Other groups have ballots by mail or Internet, but again, casting a ballot for a leadership officer in a group takes time. A member can always go to the group's website to read about the group's activities, but the group's leaders write the content of that website so it is not a purely objective description. All in all, the larger the organization, the more difficult it is for members to be sure they are being represented actively and honestly.

If interest group leaders do not act in good faith on behalf of their members, the legitimacy of the policies they promote can be called into question. Legitimacy is established by accountability. Interest groups must represent their members' needs and opinions accurately to encourage government officials, in turn, to respond to citizens. Citizens have a right to expect accountability both from government officials and from interest group leaders.

Membership Stability

Whether a group is small or large, attracting and keeping members over time are essential to its survival. People join groups because they share a similar interest or political viewpoint or because they want to protect their economic livelihood. For the leaders of groups, the challenge is to find the right balance between membership size and the organization's purpose.

Selective Benefits.   One way to attract and keep members is to provide benefits exclusive to members, which Olson labels **selective benefits**.[30] These can include **material benefits**, such as direct monetary benefits from policies that the group advocates, discounts on travel or prescriptions, and even monthly magazines. **Solidarity benefits** are less tangible. They range from the simple pleasure of being surrounded by people with similar interests and perspectives to the actual networking benefits that come from interacting with people who share professional or personal concerns. **Expressive benefits** are the least tangible in that they simply consist of having a specific opinion expressed in the larger social or political sphere. When individuals join a group, they know that their viewpoint is being actively represented in the policy system, and that knowledge can be gratifying all by itself.

The Free Rider Problem.   Many of the benefits that large interest groups seek on behalf of their members—clean air by the Sierra Club, or gun rights by the National Rifle Association—are **public goods**. That is, they are available to all, whether they have contributed toward the provision of that good or not. Public goods are typically the spillover effects from public policies that affect all citizens. And if a group lobbies for public goods or collective benefits that are so widespread that members and nonmembers alike receive them, incentives to join the group disappear. Olson addressed this collective action dilemma, calling it the **free rider problem**.[31] After all, why

---

selective benefits: *Benefits offered exclusively to members of an interest group.*

material benefits: *Tangible benefits available only to members of a group, such as discounts and monthly magazines.*

solidarity benefits: *Benefits to members of a group that are intangible but come from interacting with people who share similar professional or personal interests.*

expressive benefits: *Benefits to interest group members of having a specific opinion expressed in the larger social or political sphere.*

Would you join an interest group for its material benefits? Its solidarity benefits? Its expressive benefits? What would make you decide to join?

public goods: *Goods or benefits provided by government from which everyone benefits and from which no one can be excluded.*

free rider problem: *Problem faced by interest groups when a collective benefit they provide is so widespread and diffuse that members and nonmembers alike receive it, reducing the incentive for joining the group.*

pay to join a group if one can get the benefits for free? And if the group is so large that it does not actually need one additional member, why join?

Tangible Benefits.   There is no easy answer to this question, so large interest groups take no chances with maintaining their members. The Sierra Club, for example, makes membership more attractive by providing material benefits like a knapsack or calendar. Additionally, by wearing a knapsack, a T-shirt, or a button with the name of the Sierra Club on it, members give free advertising for the group. The same is true of the National Rifle Association, which provides members with a magazine subscription, a window sticker, and small life insurance policies. Whether a group is on the left or right side of the political spectrum, as it grows larger and the public benefits it seeks become more widespread, it turns to providing tangible benefits as a necessary part of organizational maintenance.

Economic and Political Changes.   Changes in both the economy and the political environment can affect the stability of a group's membership. For economic groups, the size and number of people in a particular occupation can ebb and flow, affecting membership potential. From a political standpoint, groups can "succeed" their way out of existence; the NAACP is one such example. In the course of its 100-year history it successfully fought discrimination and secured civil rights, and today it seems less urgently needed than it was in the past. Indeed, the election of Barack Obama, the first African American president, and the selection of Eric Holder as the first African American attorney general, are mixed blessings in that they are both the culmination of everything the organization has worked for and the undermining of its reason to exist. Recently, the group has experienced leadership turmoil and a decline in membership, and it is currently reformulating its core mission to focus on multiracial human rights.[32]

Financial Stability

Together with keeping a membership base, groups must also establish financial stability. Groups of all types require money to sustain their organizations, and they collect it from various sources, including membership dues, royalties on magazines and other publications, contributions from corporations and foundations, and outside contributions from nonmembers. Membership dues are funds that individuals or businesses pay to join the group. The price of membership in a group is typically tied to the group's organizing purpose. For example, a grassroots group that seeks to attract as many members as possible to support its cause, such as the National Rifle Association, keeps it dues relatively modest, ranging from $25 to $150. A smaller professional organization, such as the American Political Science Association (APSA), scales its membership fees according to salary and academic position; full professors, for example, contribute more money than assistant professors, who are usually paid less.

Second, groups find ways to make money by creating not-for-profit businesses within the organization. For example, the AARP is a classic example of a large interest group that wears two hats: a politically powerful lobby on policies that affect senior citizens, and a multimillion-dollar business that provides health insurance, life insurance, and discounts on movies, travel, and prescriptions to members, who have to be at least 50 years old to join. A basic AARP membership only costs $12.50 a year, and membership provides the opportunity to purchase the other services at discounted rates. In turn, the AARP can receive payments from businesses that it contracts with to provide services to its members.[33] The AARP is among the most successful large-scale interest groups in American history; in 2008, it claimed a membership of 40 million and it took in over $249 million in membership dues.[34] Its size alone gives it power and influence. Indeed, it ranks seventh out of all groups in the amount of money it spent on lobbying in 2009 (see Figure 8.2).

Imagine an AAYP—American Association for Young People. What would it lobby for? What benefits would it offer?

The financial challenge for many groups is to keep their operating costs in line with their expected income. For the very largest interest groups, such as the AARP, a single year's operating budget can be over $1 billion.[35] For most other groups, the operating budget ranges from thousands to millions of dollars per year.[36] Groups can get into financial difficulty from financial mismanagement by group leaders, or, in some cases, they may simply outlive their usefulness and members cease paying dues. When groups get into financial difficulty, they may be forced to scale back their activities and close local chapter offices.

Influence in the Public Sphere

The extent to which an interest group appears to influence public debate on an issue of concern to its members is another characteristic of success. There are several indicators of influence: being quoted in the press when a bill in the group's policy area is considered in Congress, being asked to testify before House and Senate committees during hearings on such a bill, drawing a comment from a member of Congress about a policy paper or "issue brief" that the group has written, or being quoted during final debate on the bill on the chamber floor. Another public sign of influence is when the president or members of his cabinet meet with representatives of the group and either the press or the group informs the public about it.

Interest Groups and Public Policy: Immigration

Among the most contentious issues in the public policy sphere is the question of immigration reform. Immigration has fueled U.S. population growth since the nation's founding, and the United States now comprises citizens with ancestries from many different foreign lands. In 2008, there were 37,264,000 foreign-born people in the United States—12 percent of the total population. The largest percentage of foreign-born people are from Latin America (mostly Mexico), followed by people from Asia and then Europe.[37] Immigration laws serve simultaneously as gates to entry into the United States and gateways to eventual citizenship.

The Legal Immigration Process

The legal immigration process is jointly administered by the U.S. Department of State and the U.S. Citizenship and Immigration Services (USCIS). Immigrants seeking to come to the United States apply for visas, which are granted by the Department of State; once they arrive in the United States, their journey toward citizenship is overseen by the U.S. Citizenship and Immigration Services (USCIS).[38] To come to the United States with the intention of staying on a permanent basis, individuals can apply for a general immigration visa, a family relations visa, or an employment visa. The Immigration and Nationality Act of 1990 sets an annual limit of between 416,000 and 675,000 on these types of visas.[39] In addition, 50,000 visas are set aside for people born in countries that have recently had the lowest numbers of immigrants to the United States.[40]

To become a naturalized citizen, an immigrant must first apply to be a legal permanent resident of the United States, a step known as getting a **green card**, which is the permanent resident card issued to those who are eligible. The green card is no longer green but the name has remained. To get a green card, an individual must secure a sponsor who will attest that the individual has some means of financial support. The individual must also take a medical exam and secure proof of employment if he or she intends to hold a job in the United States. This last criterion can present a significant barrier to permanent residency, because the federal government requires that an individual seeking permanent residence have talents or skills for a particular job that a current U.S. citizen could not provide. To become a fully naturalized U.S. citizen, a green card holder must reside in

green card: *Permanent resident card issued to those immigrants who are eligible.*

the United States continuously for at least five years; be able to read, write, and speak English; pass a citizenship test on the history and government of the United States (see Chapter 5, Civil Rights); and pledge support for the United States.[41]

Because the number of immigration visas is limited, there is significant competition among interest groups representing people of various ethnic origins who seek to come to the United States. There is also competition between "old" and "new" immigrant groups. For example, the Ancient Order of Hibernians represents Irish Americans, who began large-scale immigration to the United States in the 1840s. In contrast, the South Asian Americans Leading Together (SAALT) represents a relatively newer immigrant group including Indians, Pakistanis, and Sri Lankans who came to the United States after 1965. In any battle over legal immigration policy, each group tries to construct grassroots lobbying campaigns that might give it an edge in influence. For example, in 2009, SAALT held a national summit that brought together students, professionals, and politicians to address issues of importance to South Asians living in the United States and abroad.[42] The purpose of the summit was to draw attention to immigration, civil rights, and housing issues that affect the South Asian community.

In contrast, groups such as NumbersUSA seek to limit legal immigration to the United States. NumbersUSA, founded in 1996 by Roy Beck, argues that the United States does not have the natural resources to sustain increased domestic population growth and increased immigration. The organization makes it easy for individuals who want to make their voices heard on the issue of immigration to e-mail or fax a letter to a state or federal official directly through its website. All people have to do to join the group is register their name and address; there is no membership fee. The group relies on voluntary donations and foundation money to maintain its activities.[43]

The Illegal Immigration Debate

In Chapter 5, we described the reasons for historical restrictions on immigration from certain countries. Today, the drive to reform immigration laws stems from the number of individuals who enter the country illegally. The last major piece of legislation to deal specifically with illegal immigration was the 1986 Immigration Reform and Control Act, which granted amnesty, or forgiveness, to almost 2.8 million individuals who had entered the country illegally and wished to stay as legal residents.[44] Since then, amnesty has been extended to specific groups of illegal residents from Latin America and Haiti, and amnesty is still available to anyone who was eligible under the 1986 law

In the immigration debate, would you side with NumbersUSA or with interest groups representing immigrants?

but has not yet filed for legal residence.

Nevertheless, in the past two decades, up to 12 million more people have entered the United States illegally. In 2007, President George W. Bush and the Democratic Congress tried to produce a new immigration reform bill that would give illegal immigrants who are already in the United States an opportunity to become citizens but would, at the same time, discourage future illegal immigration. They failed to reach agreement, and the issue was featured prominently in the 2008 presidential election campaign. In 2010, President Obama signaled his intention to work with Congress to revisit immigration reform.

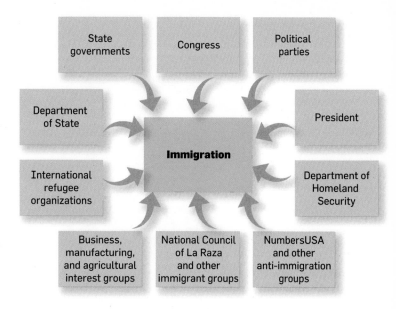

One position toward immigration reform holds that individuals who broke the law to enter the United States must not be allowed to stay and must be forced to return to their country of origin and apply for legal immigration status. Another position toward immigration reform argues that individuals who arrived illegally but have since established productive lives should be legally incorporated into society and have the opportunity to be full and active citizens.

Interest groups align along both sides of the debate. Proponents of amnesty argue that bringing illegal residents into legal society would make it possible for them to earn fair wages, participate in politics, and pay taxes on their earnings. Without amnesty, proponents argue, families would be torn apart as parents forced to leave the United States might leave children behind who were born in the United States and therefore are citizens. One of the most vocal proponents has been the National Council of La Raza, founded in 1968 and today the largest Hispanic civil rights and advocacy organization in the nation. It is made up of local chapters as well as 300 affiliated community-based organizations, and the group claims to speak for millions of Hispanic residents in the United States. During the immigration reform debate, the group has relied on local chapters to organize marches and rallies across the country to express support for immigration reform legislation.[45]

Through the use of mass media and advanced technology, groups can organize protest marches on a much larger scale than ever before. On March 21, 2010, Reform America staged a huge march on the National Mall in Washington, D.C., calling for immigration reform that includes a secure border strategy, expansion of the number of legal immigration visas, and amnesty for illegal immigrants currently in the United States.

Douglas Graham/Roll Call/Getty Images

What is your position on immigration reform?

Opponents of immigration reform argue that the previous amnesty program has only encouraged more people to enter the United States illegally and that a new bill would do the same. They also contend that illegal immigrants take away jobs from the legal resident population, because illegal immigrants are willing to work for lower wages and their employers may not pay Social Security tax on their earnings. During the most recent debate, NumbersUSA launched a campaign to stop immigration reform that generated close to one million faxed messages to members of Congress, though it had just 447,000 members at the time.[46]

There are strong sentiments on both sides of this debate. One could side with the National Council of La Raza and point out that this country was literally built by waves of immigrants from foreign lands, so to close the door on immigration is to reject one of the founding principles of the American democracy. Or one could side with NumbersUSA's policy positions holding that the laws of the land must be respected and that the modern United States cannot economically support a large influx of new immigrants every year. No matter which position one takes, actions by each group illustrate how grassroots movements enable individuals to get their opinions heard in the policy process. Ultimately it will be a major challenge to policy makers to construct a holistic immigration policy that is both fair and practical.

Refugees and Political Asylum

The Department of State grants special immigration status to individuals whose lives are at great risk in their homelands, in two categories: refugee status and political asylum. Refugee status is granted when the U.S. government determines that individuals are at risk because of their race, religion, political views, or social, ethnic, or tribal group; refugees apply to enter the United States from their homeland, or another foreign nation.[47] Political asylum status is a narrower category and is granted to individuals who are already in the United States and would face persecution if they returned to their homeland. Moreover, once individuals are granted political asylum, they are subsequently treated as someone with refugee status. In 2009 the United States resettled 74,654 refugees across forty-nine states and the District of Columbia.[48]

Interest groups, religious organizations, and charity groups play an important role in making the case that individuals deserve refugee status because of the conditions of their homelands, and they subsequently assist refugees when they arrive in the United States. For example, the U.S. Committee for Refugees and Immigrants (USCRI) has worked for nearly 100 years to help refugees navigate a new life in the United States.[49] These private organizations coordinate with the Office of Refugee Resettlement, located in the Department of Health and Human Services, to implement programs in local communities that assist with language, job training, health care, and other resettlement issues. Government efforts to grapple with legal and illegal patterns of immigration, as well as to deal with the millions of refugees caught up in foreign conflicts, have created an environment in which groups have worked harder than ever to elicit the political participation of their members on a grassroots level.

Interest Groups and Democracy

Interest groups are a powerful instrument of democracy because they crystallize the opinions and interests of average citizens and present those views to elected officials during the policy-making process. It was precisely this power to influence policy that Madison feared so much, and why he hoped that in a large republic competition among interest groups would prevent any single one of them from gaining too much influence. Interest groups contribute to a democracy by holding the government accountable for its actions, pressuring elected officials to be responsive to their constituents, and serving as a vehicle to equalize the influence of different groups of citizens in the policy process.

- How do interest groups influence economic and social policy?

- How do interest groups help or hinder government responsiveness to all citizens in an equal and fair way?

- Are interest groups themselves democratic organizations? Are their leaders accountable to their members? Explain.

- Do interest groups balance each other out across income levels, regions, and ethnic backgrounds? Explain and give examples.

- Are interest groups gates or gateways to democracy?

A group can channel the power of separate individuals into one collective voice that is more likely to be heard throughout the policy system. Moreover, the very existence of an interest group can keep citizens informed about the direct impact of policy on their lives, and with that information, constituents can better hold their elected officials accountable for those policies.

Interest groups engage in several methods to influence economic and social policy, including direct lobbying, media campaigns, legal challenges, and grassroots informational movements. For example, when Congress considered the bill to overhaul health care insurance, groups such as the American Medical Association, the Health Insurance Association of America, and the U.S. Chamber of Commerce all conveyed their group's opinions to members of Congress on regulation of doctors' fees, insurance coverage, and small business insurance premiums (see Chapter 11, Congress, for more details on health care reform).

In today's democracy, elected officials, bureaucrats, and even the judiciary often end up acting as intermediaries of interest group conflict. In Congress, political parties adopt positions that are favored or opposed by specific interest groups, and thus create alliances between parties and interest groups. Although there are more interest groups today than ever before, political parties serve as a counterweight to the influence of interest groups. As partisanship has grown stronger in the House, Senate, and even the White House, members who are asked to choose between an interest group and a political party will choose the party. However, given the fact that political parties tend to align very closely with supportive interest groups, members do not have to make that choice very often. To the extent that interest groups can influence politicians to address only narrow or exclusive interests, to the detriment of what is best for all citizens, they can be viewed as a negative aspect of the U.S. democracy.

Yet interest groups also represent a positive aspect of democracy when they serve to express wide-ranging viewpoints, and they continue to be an effective way of giving voice to citizens' needs and concerns. Interest groups continually win and lose within the American policy-making system, and they reinvent their lobbying strategies in response to changing political and economic conditions. However, sole reliance on interest groups as a means of citizen participation is dangerous, because some groups have more resources—time, money, and membership—than others and consequently win more often than others. In this way, interest groups can be both gateways and gates to citizen equality and the securing of policy benefits. Ultimately, citizens must hold both their interest group leaders and their elected officials accountable for public policy outcomes.

Top Ten to Take Away

1. Interest groups are groups of citizens sharing a common interest, whether it is a political opinion, religious affiliation, ideological belief, social goal, or economic objective, who try to influence public policy to benefit their members. (pp. 249–250)

2. The constitutional basis for interest groups lies in the First Amendment, which guarantees both the right to assemble and the right to petition the government for redress of grievances. (pp. 250–251)

3. Individuals and interest groups have lobbied legislators from the nation's earliest days. The number of groups has vastly increased in the course of the nation's development, and today groups also lobby executive branch officials and attempt to influence judicial appointments and the courts through lawsuits and briefs. (pp. 250–251)

4. Interest groups can be categorized into three types— economic, ideological, and foreign policy. Each has different policy goals and strategies. (pp. 251–258)

5. Generally, interest groups gather and disseminate information with regard to their issue area, lobby using a variety of strategies, and contribute to political campaigns and advertising to the extent that federal law allows. (pp. 258–266)

6. Scholars who study why interest groups form and their effects in a democratic society debate whether the wealthy have disproportionate power to use interest groups to their advantage, and so to the disadvantage of others. Scholars also debate whether interest groups balance each other out. (pp. 266–268)

7. Lobbyists, federal regulators, and members of Congress form networks that some describe as "iron," and closed to citizen influence, and some describe as transparent and open to citizen influence. (pp. 268–270)

8. One aspect of an issue network that can tend to make them self-serving, or appear to be self-serving, is that members of Congress and federal agency employees sometimes leave their jobs to become lobbyists in the issue area of their specialty. (pp. 269–270)

9. The success of interest groups can be measured in four ways: leadership accountability, membership stability, financial stability, and public influence. (pp. 270–275)

10. In today's democracy, elected officials, bureaucrats, and even the judiciary often end up acting as intermediaries of interest group conflict. (pp. 279–281)

A full narrative summary is on the book's website.

Ten to Test Yourself

1. What is an interest group?

2. What is an interest group entrepreneur?

3. What is the role of interest groups in American government and society?

4. Compare and contrast interest groups, factions, political parties, special interests, and movements.

5. Identify the three types of interest groups in terms of their core organizational purpose.

6. What do lobbyists do?

7. What campaign activities can interest groups engage in? What are the limits?

8. What is the free rider problem and how do interest groups solve it?

9. Compare and contrast iron triangles and issue networks.

10. Describe interest group pressures on immigration policy.

More review questions and answers and chapter quizzes are on the book's website.

Terms to Know and Use

amicus curiae briefs (p. 251)

citizens' groups (p. 255)

economic interest
group (p. 251)

elitist (p. 267)

expressive benefits (p. 272)

faction (p. 250)

501(c)(3) organizations (p. 262)

foreign policy groups (p. 257)

free rider problem (p. 272)

grassroots movement (p. 251)

green card (p. 275)

ideological interest groups
(p. 255)

interest group (p. 249)

interest group entrepreneurs
(p. 271)

iron law of oligarchy
(p. 271)

iron triangle (p. 268)

issue advocacy (p. 264)

issue network (p. 269)

lobbying (p. 251)

material benefits (p. 272)

National Labor Relations
Act (p. 252)

pluralist (p. 266)

polarization (p. 257)

political action committees
(PACs) (p. 262)

proactive group (p. 249)

professional associations
(p. 252)

public goods (p. 272)

reactive group (p. 249)

revolving door (p. 269)

right of association (p. 250)

right of petition (p. 250)

selective benefits (p. 272)

single-issue groups (p. 255)

solidarity benefits (p. 272)

special interests (p. 267)

trade associations (p. 252)

unions (p. 252)

watchdog (p. 261)

Use the vocabulary flash cards on the book's website.

9 POLITICAL PARTIES

> *Self-government is not an easy thing to do. It requires a lot from citizens. . . . I believe it is my obligation, not a choice, to be informed about my local, state, and national government.*

Josh McKoon, elected to the Georgia Senate in 2010, credits his experience at Furman University in Greenville, South Carolina, for launching "his lifetime commitment to conservative politics." As a political science and communications major, he volunteered on Republican Bob Dole's 1996 presidential campaign and worked for both a state representative running for Congress and a U.S. congressman running for the Senate. His wealth of campaign experience was one reason he was elected president of the College Republicans chapter at Furman. McKoon maintains that his time at Furman was what allowed him to really become plugged into the Republican network. "I learned very early," he said in a phone interview, "that it is 90 percent about who you know, and making those contacts with the right individuals."

In 1999, McKoon met George W. Bush, the governor of Texas who was running for president. By making contacts with Bush's campaign team, McKoon landed a job as a director of field operations on Bush's primary campaign in South Carolina. As a field director, he coordinated campaign activities with Bush supporters at Clemson and

Chapter Topics

CourseMate

Visit http://www.cengagebrain.com/shop/ISBN/0495906190 for interactive tools including:

- Quizzes
- Flashcards
- Videos
- Animated PowerPoint slides, Podcast summaries, and more

Josh McKoon ▶

Furman universities and built volunteer networks that facilitated Bush's get-out-the-vote efforts. When Bush won the primary, McKoon organized the victory rally on Furman's campus.

After completing law school, McKoon headed back to Columbus, the Georgia city where he was born, and reconnected with the Muscogee County Republican Party. Using his networking and leadership skills, he started a Young Republicans chapter, and by 2007 he had risen to party chair.

Because the goal of any party chair is to get more party members elected to public office, McKoon sought to get more Republicans involved in state and local government using a three-pronged approach. First, he worked to expand grassroots campaign operations throughout Muscogee County to give Republican challengers the capacity to wage better campaigns. To that end, he created an executive director position to lead Republican committee outreach efforts. Second, he tried to recruit more viable Republican candidates with the talent and qualifications to challenge incumbent Democrats in the Georgia statehouse. Third, he used his fundraising skills to fill the party coffers to support local races. As it turned out, McKoon became one of those Republican candidates himself, running to represent the 29th district in the state senate. And his fundraising skills came in handy; as early as April 2010, he had already raised nearly $200,000 for his state senate campaign.

McKoon calls the Republican Party his "gateway." "In Columbus as a high school student and as an attorney," he says, "in Tuscaloosa as a law student, and in Greenville as a college student, the Republican Party offered me an access point to candidates, campaigns, and political experiences." At age 31, he built on these experiences and put them to the test by taking a successful leap into electoral politics.[1]

Political parties offer every citizen in America the opportunity to participate in politics and even to run for elected office. In this chapter, we look at the role of political parties in the American constitutional system by examining what they do, how they formed and evolved over time, and what role they play in shaping electoral choices for candidates and voters alike.

FOCUS QUESTIONS

- How do political parties shape the choices voters face in local, state, and federal elections?

- In what ways do political parties allow voters to hold their elected officials accountable for the policies they produce?

- How do political parties respond to changes in public opinion on key issues?

- Do political parties enable all citizens to participate equally in self-government, or do they help give more power to some people and less to others? Explain.

- Are political parties a gate or a gateway to democracy?

The Role of Political Parties in American Democracy

A democratic government must be responsive to its citizens; for government to be equally responsive, all citizens must have an equal opportunity to influence it. But mobilizing the more than 308 million citizens in the United States to take an active role in monitoring their government is a truly momentous challenge. In the United States, political parties fill an essential need by shaping the choices that voters face in elections, which serve as the key mechanism by which voters hold their government accountable. With so many public offices to fill, voters need some sort of road map to compare candidates and make the choice that will serve their best interests. The potential danger in relying on parties to shape these choices is that parties become interested only in winning office, not serving the interests of the people. It takes action and vigilance on the part of voters to ensure that parties do not go in this direction.

In this section, we look at the role parties play in the American democratic system, specifically at the way they organize the electorate, the elections that can put their candidates in office, and those elected once in office.

What are Political Parties?

A **political party** is a group of individuals who join together to choose candidates for elected office—whether by informal group voting or a formal nominating process—and these candidates agree to abide by the **party platform**, a document that lays out the party's core beliefs and policy proposals. Parties operate through national, state, and county committees; members include party activists, citizen volunteers, and elected officials. The party's main purpose is to win elections in order to control governmental power and implement their policies.

At the national level, the party issues its platform during presidential election years. In their 2008 platforms, for example, the Republican Party and the Democratic Party stated their positions on national security, health care, environment, and taxes. These platforms not only define the positions of the presidential and vice presidential candidates but also serve as a general guide to the policy positions of all the candidates running under the party label. From time to time, individual candidates may disagree with elements of the party's platform, but in general, candidates who choose to run under a party label are defined by it. Using party labels as a shortcut for the party platform, voters can hold the elected officials accountable for their policy successes, and blame them for policy failures.

political party: *Broad coalitions of individuals who organize to win elections in order to enact a commonly supported set of public policies.*

party platform: *Document that lays out a party's core beliefs and policy proposals for each presidential election.*

party in the electorate:
Percentage of voters who are likely to choose a party's candidates in an election.

party in government:
Members of government who share the same party affiliation and work together to accomplish the party's electoral and policy goals.

party as an organization:
Internal structure of a political party at the city, county, state, and federal levels.

With which political party's ideas do you identify? What ideas do you agree with from the opposing party?

party identification:
Attachment or allegiance to a political party; partisanship.

Citizens tend to vote for one party over the other in somewhat predictable patterns. Classic political scientists, such as V.O. Key, use the term **party in the electorate** to describe the general patterns of voters' party identification and their behavior on election day. A main goal of any political party is to maximize party affiliation among voters so that it translates into a solid majority of the party in the electorate, which can in turn translate to a solid majority of the **party in government**. To accomplish this goal, the **party as an organization** is created, with internal structures that guide how the party functions.[2] The modern American political party is multilevel, with committees at the federal, state, and local level.

What Political Parties Do

In this section, we move from the theoretical ideas about political parties to what they actually do in the American political system.

Parties in the Electorate.   Parties offer several layers of opportunity for political participation. Most simply, a person can claim to be a member of a party simply by stating that he or she identifies with it: for example, "I am a Republican." That statement is an acknowledgment of **party identification**—an attachment or allegiance to a political party. Voters identify with parties for several reasons. The simplest is the belief that the policies put forth by one party will serve their interests better than policies proposed by other parties in the political arena. Another reason to join a party stems from family or social environments, in which being a member of a party is similar to other personal characteristics. As Chapter 6 (Public Opinion) explains, many young people simply adopt the party identification of their parents. Although parties always ask for contributions, there are no membership fees. For this reason, parties provide the broadest and most open gateway to participation in American politics.

A more formal step of party identification is stating party affiliation when registering to vote. **Voter registration** rules vary by state, but they typically require a citizen to show proof of identity and address to an official government office. In some places, voters can register by mail, or when they get their driver's license, but in others, they must fill out the forms in person at a local board of elections.

At the next level of participation, voters can become active in the party at the town, county, state, and federal level. Parties encourage people to volunteer on campaigns at every level—making phone calls to prospective voters, passing out bumper stickers, or maintaining e-mail contact through the campaign website. Of course, political parties expect their members to vote on election day, and to bring their friends, coworkers, and family members to the polls with them. Parties also rely on supporters to build up the organization and candidates by making financial contributions.

voter registration:
Enrollment required prior to voting to establish eligibility.

Have you formally affiliated with a political party? What would be the advantages and the disadvantages of doing so?

Political parties also serve as a gateway to elected office. Josh McKoon, for example, got his start in politics through volunteer work with a local party on a campaign and then he ran for the Georgia state senate. Many candidates who seek public office start out by affiliating with a party in college and rise through the ranks of party organizations, as McKoon did. Parties also actively recruit individuals in their county, district, or state to run for elected office. Candidate recruitment involves party leaders at all levels trying to identify people who will make good candidates for elected office, either because they are well known in the community, have personal wealth, or have a professional record that speaks to current issues and would appeal to voters.

Parties in Government.
Parties also serve to organize members of Congress and state legislatures into cohesive groups, known as **party caucuses**, that consistently vote, year after year, for the policies that the parties promise in their platforms. The party in government consists of elected officials who share the same party affiliation and work together to accomplish the party's electoral and policy goals. Elected officials often hold positions in party organizations as well. For example, Tim Kaine, Democratic governor of Virginia from 2006 to 2010, served as chair of the national Democratic Party during his last two years in office. Even the president, whose primary responsibility is to govern, is also expected to serve as leader of his political party by setting the agenda according to party policy goals. The president is also increasingly expected to engage in political support for party candidates, from campaign appearances to party fundraisers.

party caucus: *Group of party members in a legislature.*

Party Organization.
The modern political party structure is multilevel, with units at the federal, state, and local levels. **National committees** are at the top of the party organization, and their members are chosen by each state party organization (see Figure 9.1). A new president can select the national committee chair from his party; for other parties, the national committee itself elects the party chair. National committees are responsible for running their party's presidential nominating convention every four years, while state and local party structures are obviously more active, given the greater frequency of electoral activities at those levels. Key to that effort is overseeing the states' primary delegate selection process and officially recognizing a state's delegation at the convention.

national committee: *Top level of national political parties; coordinates national presidential campaigns.*

The main job of the national committee is to do everything possible to elect the party's presidential nominee every four years, and that requires strengthening all party organizations, from the national down to the local levels. The national committees run training workshops on party-centered activities like candidate recruitment and fundraising. The national committee has to raise money; for example, in the 2008 presidential campaign, the Democratic National Committee raised $260 million and the Republican

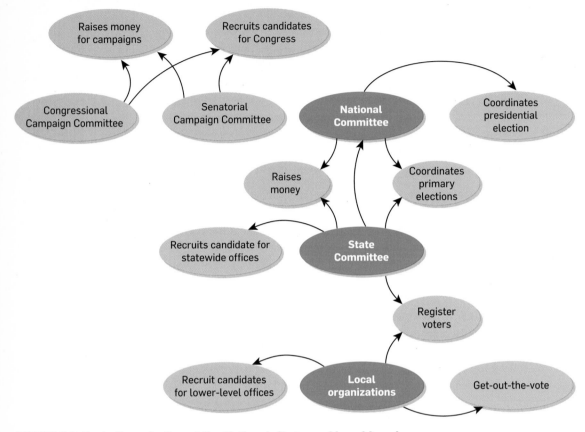

FIGURE 9.1 **Party Organization at the National, State, and Local Levels.**

National Committee raised $428 million.[3] The national party can spend its money on coordinated expenditures, which are funds spent in cooperation with the presidential campaign, and it can make independent expenditures, which are funds spent separately on general efforts to increase voter turnout for the party's nominee.

Each major political party has committees dedicated to raising money for **incumbent** House and Senate members. For the Democrats it is the Democratic Congressional Campaign Committee and the Democratic Senatorial Campaign Committee, and for the Republicans, the National Republican Congressional Committee and the National Republican Senatorial Committee. These congressional party committees are also responsible for recruiting qualified challengers to run for seats held by the opposing party and helping to fund their campaigns. These four congressional party organizations raised a combined $529.7 million in the 2005–06 electoral cycle and $551 million in the 2007–08 electoral cycle.[4]

incumbent: *Occupant of elected office.*

state central committee: *Top level of state political parties; helps recruit and raise money for statewide candidates and drafts state party policies.*

State political parties are the next level of party organization, and they are regulated by state law, so their responsibilities can vary by state. Typically a political party has a **state central committee** that tries to elect candidates for statewide office and also works with local organizations to recruit new voters and raise money. Each state party organization has its own website, which displays the structure of the state party organization and provides information about how to become involved with the party.

Local party organizations exist at the county, town, and precinct or ward levels. The Muscogee County Republican Party, which Josh McKoon chaired, is an example of a local party organization. The essential functions of local party organizations are to recruit candidates for lower-level elected offices, register voters, and most important, ensure that voters get to the polls on election day.[5]

The Party Nomination Process

One of the most important functions of parties is to nominate candidates for office and then elect them, a process accomplished in two stages. First, parties hold **primary elections**, and in some cases **runoff elections**, in which voters determine who should be the party's choice to run in the next stage, the **general election**.

Primaries.

Primary elections are a very important way that each voter can have an equal voice in nominating his or her party's candidates for elected office. Although most states rely heavily on the primary, some states authorize both the primary and a nominating convention of state party members to approve the party's set of nominees.[6]

As noted, state laws regarding elections vary, and there are several types of primaries. A **closed primary** is one in which voters must affiliate with a party before casting a vote (either by registering prior to the election or on primary election day). A **semiclosed primary** is one in which party-affiliated voters cast votes in their party's primary, and nonaffiliated (Independent) voters can choose which party's primary to vote in. An **open primary** is one in which voters do not have to affiliate with a party before voting. Instead, in an open primary, voters are given **ballots** with each party's list of candidates; they can choose which ballot to use but are restricted to voting for only one party's set of nominees.

Primary elections are a fact of political life, but insofar as they create competition within a political party and encourage candidates to reveal negative aspects of each other's professional or personal lives, they can weaken the party's eventual nominee when he or she faces opponents in the general election. Because party organizations always want the candidate who is most likely to win the election to be nominated under the party banner, they try to

local party organization: *First level of political parties; recruits candidates for lower-level elected office, registers voters and ensures they get to the polls on election day.*

primary election: *Elections in which voters select the candidates who will run on the party label in the general election; also called direct primary.*

runoff election: *Election held after an initial primary in which voters select from the top two primary candidates, guaranteeing a candidate's nomination by majority vote.*

general election: *Election in which voters choose their elected officials.*

closed primary: *Primary election in which the voter must affiliate with a party before casting a vote.*

semiclosed primary: *Primary election in which party-affiliated voters cast votes and nonaffiliated voters can choose which party's primary to vote in.*

open primary: *Primary election in which voters do not have to affiliate with a party before voting.*

ballot: *List of candidates who are running for elected office, used by voters to make their choices.*

Have you voted in a primary election? What kind of primary was it? Did you have to identify your party affiliation?

exert control over the primary election process in several ways. First, state laws govern party ballot access—literally, who can actually get on the primary election ballot. The relationship between elite state party members and state legislators is very close, so the party controls the gate by determining how open or restrictive ballot access is for candidates seeking to run for office on the party label. Second, although party organizations remain technically neutral during the primary election season, they can steer donors toward their preferred candidates, and away from candidates who do not agree with their goals. As a consequence, individuals who are perceived as weak, or not loyal to the party, may run into major roadblocks set up by the party organization.

The Presidential Nomination.

The process by which each party nominates its presidential candidate has evolved from one that was concentrated in the hands of a small group of elites to the modern process that allows millions of voters to participate directly in choosing the party's presidential nominee.

In a presidential primary, voters cast a vote for a particular candidate, but what they are really doing is choosing **delegates** who will support that nominee at the party's national nominating convention. In a **presidential party caucus**, which serves the same nominating purpose, the process is less formal and more personal in that party members meet together in town halls, schools, and even private homes to choose a nominee. Each state is awarded a number of delegates to the convention by the national party organization based largely on the number of Electoral College votes the state has but also on the size of party support in that state. The candidate who wins a majority of the delegates from the primary and caucus elections is selected at the national convention as the party's nominee for president.

The Democratic Party and Republican Party allocate their delegates within the primaries and caucuses differently. The Democratic Party has had a more tumultuous nominating process due in large part to some key rule changes in the 1970s and 1980s. In the 1960s, members of underrepresented groups, such as women and African Americans, began calling for a change in the presidential nominating procedures for the Democratic Party. Specifically, they objected to the use of the unit rule, or **winner-take-all system**, which meant that whoever won the majority of primary or state nominating convention votes would win the entire state's delegates. Activists believed that the unit rule allowed white conservative men to dominate the nominating process. In response to this grassroots movement, the Democrats formed the **McGovern-Fraser Commission**, which recommended changes in the way that delegates were chosen and awarded to candidates during the primary season. In 1972, the Democratic Party instituted requirements that states' delegations accurately reflect the distribution of preferences for presidential

delegate: *Individual selected by party voters in a primary or caucus election who is committed to supporting a particular presidential nominee at the party's national nominating convention.*

presidential party caucus: *Meeting of party members in town halls, schools, and even private homes to choose a presidential party nominee.*

winner-take-all system: *Electoral system in which whoever wins the most votes in an election wins the election.*

McGovern-Fraser Commission: *Democratic Party commission whose reforms of the party's presidential nominating system increased access by underrepresented groups.*

candidates in the state. For the 1976 election, the Democrats formally instituted **proportional representation**, that is, the number of delegates that a candidate receives is based on the percentage of the vote received in the primary or caucus, either at the state level or in each congressional district. In most states, delegates are committed to a candidate before the primary election takes place.

To further address the activists' concern that the nominating process was dominated by white men, the 1972 reforms instituted requirements that a certain percentage of each state's delegates would be women, African Americans, and other underrepresented groups, based on their proportion in each state's population. If states did not comply with this requirement, the national party reserved the right not to "seat" or count their delegates in the final nominating vote held at the party's national convention. Although the party stated its goal to increase delegates from underrepresented groups, it did not really increase African American convention participation until the presidential election of 1984, when Jesse Jackson, an African American, ran for the Democratic nomination. Although he was defeated for the nomination by former vice-president Walter Mondale, he was successful enough to be able to insist that more people of color be delegates to the convention. The cumulative effect of all these reforms was to create a gateway for members of underrepresented groups to exert influence in determining the Democratic Party presidential nominee.

In 1981, the Democratic Party made several other changes, including requiring that each state's delegation be composed of an equal number of men and women, and creating a category of delegates known as **superdelegates**. Superdelegates are not chosen through the primary voting process but rather are invited to the convention based on the fact that they are active members of the party who will be instrumental in turning out party voters in the general election. Most superdelegates are elected officials in the party, such as governors and members of Congress from each state, as well as state party committee chairs and key activists in interest groups that are loyal to the Democrats. They are uncommitted and free to choose whomever they wish to support at the convention.

In the 2008 Democratic nomination contest between Senator Barack Obama (D-Ill.) and Senator Hillary Clinton (D-N.Y.), superdelegates played the most important role since their creation. By the end of the regular primary season, Obama led in the primary and caucus delegate count but not by enough votes to win the nomination outright. The nomination would be determined by the 823 superdelegates. Only about half had committed to one or the other candidate early in the process. As it became clear that Obama had more support among party members generally, many of the remaining superdelegates swung their support to him. In the end, Obama won 463 superdelegates, for a final delegate count of 2229.5; Hillary Clinton won 257 superdelegates, for a total of

proportional representation: *Electoral system that assigns multiple seats to a geographic district according to the proportion of votes a political party receives in an election.*

What difference does proportional representation make for the Democratic Party?

superdelegates: *Democratic Party delegates who have a vote at the national nominating convention on the basis of party status or position in government and are free to support the presidential nominee of their choice.*

Senator Hillary Clinton (D-N.Y.) closely competed with Barack Obama for the presidential nomination in 2008 and was the most successful female candidate for president in Democratic Party history. Her ability to make such progress was in part due to the 1970s Democratic reforms in the nomination process.

Compare and contrast the nominating system for the Democratic and Republican Parties.

In the primary system, some states have a greater impact on candidates' chances than others. Is that fair to party voters? Does frontloading have a negative impact on American democracy?

Chip Somodevilla/Getty Images

1896.5 delegates.[7] The 2008 contest for the Democratic nomination was one of the closest ever. Very often, close nominating contests encourage the nominee to choose one of his opponents as a running mate, or if he wins the election, as a member of his cabinet. In this case, Obama chose Senator Joe Biden (D-Del.), who had briefly run for the 2008 nomination, as his running mate, and he later appointed Hillary Clinton to be secretary of state.

Unlike the Democratic Party, the Republican Party has rarely faced an internal demand for more diverse representation, so it has not significantly changed its nominating system. However, in August of 2010, the Republican National Committee approved a plan that would award some delegates on a proportional basis. In the past, with a winner-take-all nomination system, the Republican Party tended to resolve its nomination process more quickly than the Democrats.[8] The shorter nomination process typically gave Republicans an advantage in the general election because their nominee could develop his strategy for the general election far sooner than the Democratic nominee. Although the Democratic candidate ultimately won the presidential election in 2008, the Democrats have begun discussions on how to simplify and shorten their nomination process.

The timing of primaries has become an integral part of the presidential nomination strategy. Larry Bartels's work demonstrates that states that hold primaries early in the process exert disproportional influence by giving one or another candidate an early stamp of approval and momentum.[9] Candidates who win in the early primaries can solicit more campaign money and garner more endorsements from key constituent groups than those who lose. It also literally pays off economically to be a state with an early presidential primary because candidates, their staff, and members of the media spend a disproportionate amount of time in the state prior to the primary, generating income for local businesses. Traditionally, the two earliest presidential contests have been the New Hampshire primary and the Iowa caucus; in 2008, both were held in January. Even though these are two relatively small states, the fact that they are the first two presidential contests for each major party makes them disproportionately influential in generating publicity and momentum for the winners.[10] In fact, for the 2008 elections, other states moved their primary dates up closer to Iowa and New Hampshire to elevate their own importance in the nomination contest. Ultimately, such **front-loading**, holding many primaries simultaneously early in the year, creates an imbalance of influence across states in determining the party's nominee; a candidate who manages to do well in early primary states diminishes the chances for other candidates and reduces the influence of the voters in later primary states.

AP Photo/Paul Sancya

Senator Barack Obama (D-Ill.) made history as the first African American presidential nominee of any party, and the first African-American president. Joe Biden (D-Del.) was an early candidate for the 2008 nomination but quickly dropped out, and was later chosen by Obama as his vice presidential running mate.

The Dynamics of Early Party Development

Political parties in 2011 seem very well organized, as if they have existed as long as the nation itself. But parties were not intended to be part of the original fabric of the political system. They emerged from the disagreements among the Framers who were able to compromise just enough to adopt the Constitution but not enough to suppress different perspectives on the role of government. Today, rather than the narrow organizations that the Framers feared, there are two large parties that each include a broad swath of the electorate and must make internal compromises to stay unified. In this section, we trace the background to these developments.

Political Factions: Federalist versus Antifederalist

James Madison and Alexander Hamilton, writing in the *Federalist Papers* 10 and 51 (see the Appendix), predicted the rise of **factions**, groups of individuals who share a common political goal and ally with each other on a temporary basis to accomplish that goal. They recognized that factions

front-loading: *Holding many primaries simultaneously early in the year.*

faction: *Defined by Madison as any group that places its own interests above the aggregate interests of society.*

Given the Framers' views on factions and political parties, do you think the development of parties has been good or bad for American democracy?

Federalists: *Initially, those who supported the Constitution during the ratification period; later, the name of the political party established by supporters of Alexander Hamilton.*

Antifederalists: *Those who opposed the new proposed Constitution during the ratification period.*

Try to relate the two parties today to the viewpoints of the Federalists and the Antifederalists. Which party comes closest to which viewpoint?

Democratic-Republicans: *Political party formed by Thomas Jefferson to oppose the strong central government policies of the Federalists.*

would be a natural outgrowth of different interests among citizens and that there was little government could do to stop them without denying citizens important civil liberties. Although factions were not considered the same thing as actual political parties, of the kind that had emerged in Britain, the Framers also feared that both factions and parties might encourage divisions in the young democracy that could threaten its very existence.

Yet factions emerged even before the Constitution was adopted. In the debate over ratification (see Chapter 2, The Constitution), those who argued for the Constitution called themselves **Federalists**. They believed that a stable federal government that could collect tax revenue, fund and regulate a national army, regulate foreign and domestic trade, and stabilize currency would make the American democratic experiment a success. Opponents of a strong national government, however, viewed the future of the United States in terms of loosely affiliated but sovereign states that governed themselves, managing their own tax policies and internal security. These were the **Antifederalists**. In their view, the United States had just fought a war to overturn a strong monarch and they did not want to put themselves under the rule of an oppressive new centralized government that would govern from the top down.

Ultimately, the Federalist viewpoint triumphed, and the Constitution was ratified. But the debate did not end there. The nation's first president, George Washington (1789–97) formed a government that included both proponents of a strong national government, led by Alexander Hamilton and John Adams (1797–1801), and of strong state governments, led by Thomas Jefferson (1801–09). Washington worried that opposing views could lead to organized political parties that would cause conflict in the new nation.[11] Tensions between the factions accelerated after John Adams's election as president, especially following passage of the Alien and Sedition Acts in 1798. The Sedition Act severely restricted freedom of the press and freedom of speech critical of the government (see Chapter 4, Civil Liberties). Jefferson opposed this law and, in 1800, mounted a campaign against Adams for the presidency, arguing that the Federalists were too heavy-handed in their approach to governing.

Thomas Jefferson, Andrew Jackson, and the Emergence of the Democratic Party

Jefferson won the election of 1800, and it marked the beginning of established partisan politics. The new president used his victory to transform his fledgling political party into a viable long-term organization known as the **Democratic-Republicans** (most candidates shortened the name to

Republican).[12] The Democratic-Republicans occupied the White House for the next twenty-eight years with the terms of Jefferson, James Madison (1809–17), James Monroe (1817–25), and John Quincy Adams (1825–29). Meanwhile, the Federalists diminished in number and faded away as a force in politics.

Despite their electoral success and lack of opposition, the Democratic-Republicans themselves grew divided. The conflict was led by Andrew Jackson (1829–37), an ambitious politician who wanted to take the party to a new level of inclusiveness and use that wider reach to become president. Jackson, from Tennessee, had served in both the House and the Senate, but he made his national reputation as the hero of the Battle of New Orleans in 1815, at the end of the War of 1812. After his military service ended, Jackson returned to Congress and made an attempt to win the presidential nomination of the Democratic-Republicans in 1824.[13] At that time, presidential nominations were decided by party caucuses in Congress, and Jackson was challenging John Quincy Adams, the son of President John Adams. Although the congressional party caucus nominated William H. Crawford of Georgia, less than one-third of the members of the party showed up to cast their vote, reflecting a lack of consensus around a majority candidate. Consequently, there was no clear choice among the Democratic-Republicans in the election of 1824, and no one won a majority in the Electoral College. The outcome then had to be determined by the House of Representatives, which selected Adams (for an explanation of this process, see Chapter 10, Elections, Campaigns, and Voting).

By 1828, the nomination process had been taken over by party members in state legislatures who voted on their preferred nominee either in the legislature or at state party conventions. By locating the nomination process in the states, instead of in Congress, parties were enlarging the sphere of people involved in making the decision about who could run for president. As we note in Chapter 11 (Congress), Jackson wanted states to open up the voting process to as many people as possible by eliminating barriers to voting such as property ownership requirements. In 1828, using a grassroots state-level strategy to attract both the support of state legislators and the voters themselves, Jackson worked closely with Martin Van Buren, a powerful New York politician, to again challenge Adams for the nomination of the Democratic-Republicans; this time, he won the nomination and the presidential election.

By 1832, the end of Jackson's first term in office, politics had changed in fundamental ways because of the nation's rapid geographic and population growth.[14] The Jackson-led Democrats emerged as a large grassroots majority political party, and President Jackson used all the powers of the presidency to strengthen his political party around the country. In the meantime, the anti-Jackson wing of the old Democratic-Republicans had taken the name of the National Republicans. In the presidential election of 1832, the National Republicans nominated Henry Clay, a U.S. senator from Kentucky, to run against Jackson, but Jackson was victorious.

Although Henry Clay lost that election to Jackson, he returned to the Senate and started laying the groundwork for a new political party that would oppose Jackson's policies. He encouraged members of the National Republicans to join forces with others who opposed Jackson and to form the **Whig Party**, which objected to what they viewed to be Jackson's abuse of presidential power for partisan gains. As Clay put it, "The Whigs of the present day are opposing Executive encroachments, and a most alarming extension of Executive power and prerogative."[15] From 1832 to 1856, these two parties, the Democrats and the Whigs, dominated American politics and presidential elections. However, the issue of slavery soon emerged to shake up the party balance once again.

The Antislavery Movement and the Formation of the Republican Party

The Democratic Party's general strategy for opening up a larger gateway for citizen participation in politics inadvertently encouraged alternate groups and political parties to emerge on the political scene. In 1833, William Lloyd Garrison, a white journalist, formed the American Anti-Slavery Society to press for the abolition of slavery. Several years later, Frederick Douglass, an African American, began organizing free blacks in the North for the same purpose. Over time, groups that opposed slavery combined under the umbrella of the **abolitionist movement**. Although the movement was not a political party per se, it grew large and vocal enough to pressure the Democrats and Whigs to take a formal position on slavery, especially the extension of slavery into western territories.

Further complicating party politics were smaller, **third parties** that arose in the North, some explicitly antislavery. Third parties are minor political parties that present a third alternative to the two dominant political parties in the American political system. Typically, third parties focus on a single issue, as in the case of the Liberty Party, which focused on slavery, but as frequently happens in American politics, this smaller party was absorbed into a larger coalition of groups, led by the Free Soilers, which opposed the expansion of slavery in the territories. Then, these groups were also joined by some antislavery northern Democrats, and the modern Republican Party was born. In the words of one activist, Alvan E. Bovay, "We went into the little meeting held in a schoolhouse Whigs, Free Soilers, and Democrats. We came out of it Republicans."[16] Six years later, the Republican Party had

Whig Party: *Political party formed to oppose the Jackson Democrats.*

abolitionist movement: *Grassroots movement to abolish slavery.*

third parties: *Minor political parties that present a third alternative to the two dominant political parties in the American political system.*

consolidated its support and elected Abraham Lincoln (1861–65) to the presidency.

Shortly, seven southern states seceded from the Union, and on April 12, 1861, with the Confederate firing on the federal government's fort in Charleston Harbor, the Civil War began. Four more southern states seceded, leaving the Republicans in complete control of Congress. On January 1, 1863, in issuing the Emancipation Proclamation (see Chapter 5, Civil Rights), Lincoln publicly affirmed that ending slavery was a fundamental aim of the war. After the war ended in 1865, the Confederacy dissolved, but southerners held great resentment toward northerners and the Republican Party, on account of both the South's physical and economic losses and the continued occupation of the South by northern troops. Since then, the Democrats and the Republicans have been the nation's two major political parties.

Party Loyalty and Patronage

Andrew Jackson set an example for how to build a political party organization using government resources. Just as Jackson worked to expand the electorate, he sought to expand the size of the federal government in order to increase the number of federally funded jobs his party could control. The Jacksonian era provided many opportunities to bring the federal government into the state and local arena by the building of forts, post roads (for mail delivery), customhouses, and lighthouses. Whoever controlled the jobs associated with these programs could also demand political allegiance from those who filled them. By the late nineteenth century, a system emerged whereby the politician became the "patron" of the businessmen and workers who were on the payrolls of the federal or state governments. Jobs built party loyalty, and those hired often had to declare their political allegiance to the politician who arranged for the job, and promise to vote for him. Such a system is commonly referred to as a **patronage system**.

As the government expanded, so did the party organization. At each level—federal, state, and local—there were parallel party committees. Parties became the organizations they are today, with a national committee, state committees, and local chapters at the county, ward, town, or precinct levels. At each level, leaders who had power within the party acted as **party bosses**, controlling the distribution of public funds by rewarding supporters and withholding them from opponents. The key element in this system was the loyalty of supporters, who on election day voted for the boss's preferred set of candidates. Voter support in this kind of system was so reliable and predictable that it became known as **machine politics**; it ran like a well-oiled machine.

patronage system: *Political system in which government programs and benefits are awarded based on political loyalty to a party or politician.*

Do you see the patronage system still at work today in American politics?

party boss: *Party organization leader who controlled the distribution of public funds by rewarding party supporters and punishing party opponents.*

machine politics: *Party organization dominated by a "boss" who controlled the distribution of public jobs and commanded groups of voters to support his preferred candidates.*

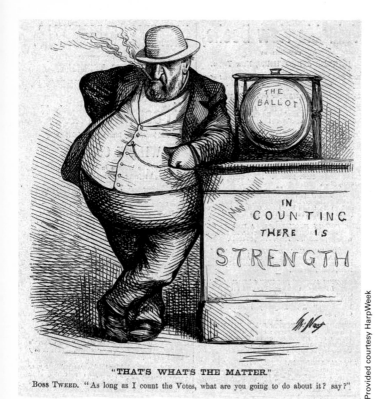

"THAT'S WHAT'S THE MATTER."

Boss Tweed. "As long as I count the Votes, what are you going to do about it? say?"

Provided courtesy HarpWeek

William Marcy "Boss" Tweed was the head of a Democratic Party machine in New York City in the 1850s and 1860s. He was notorious for using political office to hand out favors and benefits to loyal party members and to accumulate personal wealth. The editorial cartoons of Thomas Nast helped expose the graft and corruption of the "Tweed Ring."

Progressives: *Coalitions of Democrats and Republicans who believed that government had been captured by corrupt elites who were using government resources to enrich themselves rather than serve citizens.*

Reform and the Erosion of Party Control

A critical factor in the success of machine politics was party control of voting. In contrast to today's system—in which states manage all aspects of elections, including ballot design and ballot counting—local parties in the late nineteenth century printed up their own ballots, called party strip ballots, which listed only their candidates, and gave them to voters on their way into the polling places. In many places, party officials counted the votes as well, further manipulating the voting process to their advantage.

However, three developments in the late nineteenth and early twentieth centuries eroded party organizations' control over government jobs and elections: the creation of a merit-based system of government employment, the introduction of ballot reforms, and a change in the way nominees for elected office were selected. All three reforms were led by **Progressives**, coalitions of Democrats and Republicans who believed that government had been captured by corrupt elites who were using government resources to enrich themselves rather than serve citizens.

Since Jackson's day, bosses in the old patronage system had taken for granted the right to distribute government jobs to their supporters. But in 1883, the Pendleton Act reformed the **civil service** by requiring that government jobs be filled based on merit, not political connections (see Chapter 13 on the Bureaucracy for more on the civil service). It was the first of several laws that slowly transformed the federal bureaucracy from a corrupt insider organization to a neutral, policy-based organization.[17]

Voting procedures were also reformed between 1888 and 1911 as states adopted the so-called **Australian ballot** system, which originated in Australia in 1858, to replace the party strip ballots[18] (see Figure 9.2). When parties printed the ballots and gave them to voters, who then put them in the ballot

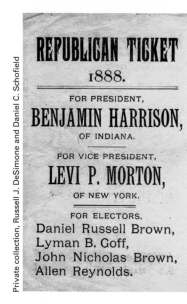

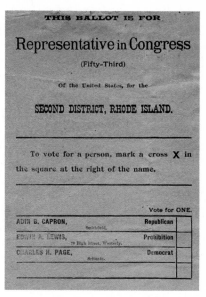

FIGURE 9.2 Ballot Reform. On the left are examples of party strip ballots used in Rhode Island in 1888. These types of ballots were printed by political parties and handed to voters on election day. They gave voters no opportunity to split their vote among different parties. On the right is an example of the so-called Australian ballot. Like this ballot used in Rhode Island in 1892, Australian ballots were printed by state governments rather than political parties. They listed all candidates for elected office, not just candidates from a single party, and therefore gave voters a choice to split their vote among different parties. *Source:* Russell J. DeSimone and Daniel C. Schofield, "Rhode Island Election Tickets: A Survey," Technical Services Department Faculty Publications (Kingston, R.I.: University of Rhode Island, 2007), http://digitalcommons.uri.edu/lib_ts_pubs/17/.

box, there was no privacy and party officials monitored citizens' votes. This Australian ballot system introduced the secret ballot, because each ballot listed all the candidates, from all parties, running for office, and voters marked their choices in private. In addition, poll watchers and ballot counters were expected to perform their tasks without favoring any specific party and without intimidating voters. This reform greatly reduced party boss control over election outcomes.[19]

Lastly, Progressives launched grassroots campaigns for direct primaries, run by the state, as a means of nominating party candidates. These primaries replaced the practice of nominating candidates in local and state party conventions, which were typically dominated by party bosses. Direct primaries opened up the party nomination system to voters generally, and they are the nominating process used today. The effect of direct primaries was to greatly reduce the control that party bosses and machines had over the choices offered in elections. As party bases

civil service: *System of employment in the federal bureaucracy under which employees are chosen and promoted based on merit.*

Australian ballot: *Voting system in which state governments run elections and provide voters the option of choosing candidates from multiple parties; also called the secret ballot.*

broadened, leaders turned their attention to finding ways to keep coalitions of voters together.

The Effects of a Two-Party System

Following the Civil War, party divisions ran largely along geographic lines, with Republicans dominant in the Northeast and West, and Democrats dominant in the South and increasingly in the nation's largest cities. Today, the Democratic and Republican parties have reversed their geographic strongholds somewhat, but the two-party system remains intact. In this section we examine the effects of a two-party system not only on citizens' choices but also on the ways that government can respond. We also examine the reasons why the United States, even before the Civil War, never had more than two major parties, and we explore the role of the third parties that have occasionally arisen to challenge two-party dominance.

Limited Political Choice

Surely there are more than two views on how to solve important policy problems. It might seem logical, therefore, that a large democracy like the United States should have as many political parties as there are diverse viewpoints. But the United States has only two major parties, standing in stark contrast to each other, and scholars have debated whether this two-party system adequately reflects the range of views among citizens.

In 1957, the scholar Anthony Downs argued that voters whose views fall between the two parties were actually represented in a two-party system. His **median voter theorem** proposed that if voters select candidates on the basis of ideology and everyone participates equally, then in a two-party race, the party closer to the middle will win. As candidates from each party seek to attract a majority of votes, and because most voters fall in the middle of the ideological spectrum, both parties move toward a compromise, or middle position. In this way **moderates** do have political influence in a two-party system.[20]

Nevertheless, the impact of ideologically extreme campaign activists and interest groups that align with a party can pressure parties and candidates to move away from the center.[21] In today's highly partisan atmosphere, it seems as though the political center has almost entirely disappeared. Each party appears to be so dominated by its more extreme wing that there is little opportunity within each party to make moderate views known or for politicians to

median voter theorem: *Theory that if voters select candidates on the basis of ideology and everyone participates equally, then in a two-party race, the party closer to the middle will win.*

moderate: *Ideological viewpoint that falls between liberal and conservative, can be associated with Democrats or Republicans, and does not hold consistently strong ideas about whether government should be involved in people's lives.*

compromise. The current two-party system increasingly appears to contradict Downs' expectations about convergence to the middle. In regions where one party is very dominant, elected officials may not be responsive to voters from the other party.

Despite its limitations, the two-party system is built into the American electoral system, as the political scientist Maurice Duverger explains. The American electoral system is a **single-member plurality system**, in which one legislative seat (on a city council, in a state assembly, in the House of Representatives) represents citizens who live in a geographically defined district.[22] To win that seat, a candidate usually needs only a **plurality** of votes, not a pure **majority**, that is, more votes than any other candidate but not necessarily 50 percent plus 1. Because there is only one seat to be won in a district, voters have become accustomed to choosing between candidates from the two major parties.

Other electoral systems work differently. Many democracies assign the number of seats a party wins according to proportional representation, based on the percentage of votes it receives in a particular election (see Other Places: Proportional Representation Electoral Systems).

In the United States the single-member plurality system encourages a two-party system, and the two-party system in turn encourages political debates that ask Americans to take a "for" or "against" position on an issue. There is little effort during an election to arrive at a middle ground, although there is often debate within a party as to what its position will be. In fact, the two-party system works to transfer the battleground from between parties to within parties. Each party—rather than government itself—is a coalition.

The Role of Third Parties

In one sense, a two-party system stands as a gate that blocks the emergence of alternative viewpoints and reduces the choices available to voters in terms of perspectives on how to govern. On the other hand, when the two parties together do not offer policy proposals that a significant number of voters want to see enacted, third parties form. These third parties can mount challenges so significant that the major parties are compelled to act, often by incorporating the third party's policy proposal into their platforms.

Several contenders representing significant third parties have entered presidential elections, but no third party has been able to build a sustained organization over time. Two of these candidates, Strom Thurmond (Dixiecrats) and George Wallace (American Independent Party), ran on

Do you think the major political parties do or do not reflect the views of citizens? What can be done about that?

single-member plurality system: *Electoral system that assigns one seat in a legislative body to represent citizens who live in a defined area (a district) based on which candidate wins the most votes.*

plurality vote: *Vote in which the winner needs to win more votes than any other candidate.*

majority vote: *Vote in which the winner needs to win 50 percent + 1 of the votes cast.*

Proportional Representation Electoral Systems

In contrast to the United States' single-member plurality system, many nations in Europe and in Central and Latin America have proportional representation electoral systems. This system assigns multiple seats to a geographic district according to the proportion of votes a political party receives in an election. In this system, there are rewards for forming more than two parties because parties that receive even a small percent of the vote, for example 10 percent, are likely to be awarded seats in the legislature. In turn, these legislatures typically have coalition majorities, where members from different parties agree on policies and form a working majority in the legislature. In this way, proportional representation grants multiple parties the power to make policy and deliver benefits to voters.

There are tradeoffs in terms of participation, responsiveness, and accountability in each type of electoral system. Single-member plurality electoral systems tend to produce fewer political parties, which in turn reduces the number of opinions that can be actively represented in a political system. Two-party systems also encourage strict partisanship among officeholders and discourage bipartisanship. On the other hand, this stark contrast allows voters to more easily hold their elected officials accountable.

Proportional representation systems produce multiple parties and greater diversity of representation. However, this system tends to produce coalition government because no party can gain a straight majority. Coalitions

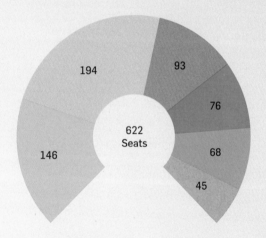

622 Seats

93
76
68
45
146
194

- Sozialdemokratische Partei Deutschlands (Socialist Party of Germany)
- Christlich Demokratische Union (Christian Democratic Union)
- Freie Demokratische Partei (Free Democratic Party)
- Die Linke (The Left)
- Die Grünen (The Green)
- Christlich-Soziale Union (Christian Social Union)

Seats Allocated by Party in the German Bundestag, 2009. The German Bundestag, which is equivalent to the U.S. House of Representatives, awards a percentage of seats to each party depending on its vote share in the election (each citizen votes for a district representative and for a party). Following an election in 2008, the Christian Democrats and their Bavarian ally, the Christian Social Union, formed a coalition government with the Free Democrats. *Source:* The Federal Returning Officer, www.bundeswahlleiter.de.

encourage compromise among parties, but it is also true that the parties that make up the coalition can withdraw at any time, which makes the ruling government potentially unstable.* Moreover, voters cannot easily identify which party in the coalition should be rewarded or blamed for government policies, so accountability is more difficult than in single-member plurality systems.

- **How does a proportional representation electoral system translate votes into legislative power in the government?**

- **Why are governments established under proportional representation systems inherently unstable?**

* Ko Maeda and Misa Nishikawa, "Duration of Party Control in Parliamentary and Presidential Governments," *Comparative Political Studies* 39 (2006): 352–74.

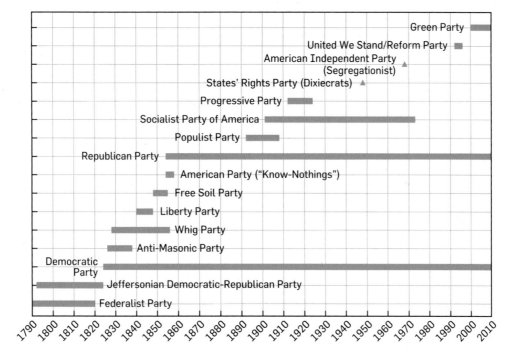

FIGURE 9.3 **Major American Political Parties, 1789–2010.**

segregationist party platforms and were a splinter group of the Democratic Party. John Anderson (National Unity Party) and Ross Perot (United We Stand) each ran on platforms that favored moderate social policy and strict fiscal discipline. (For a list of significant parties in American politics, see Figure 9.3.)

Third parties thus present an alternative to the two dominant political parties. Today the Green Party is one example. However, being an alternative can also mean being a spoiler for major party candidates and can, as a consequence, alienate potential voters. Some Democratic Party activists argued that if Ralph Nader had not run for president on the Green Party ticket in 2000, and received 97,488 votes in the state of Florida,[23] Al Gore would have been elected president instead of George W. Bush.

What are the benefits and the risks of voting for a third-party candidate?

Obstacles to Third Parties and Independents

Because third-party candidates can act as spoilers, the two major parties do everything they can to discourage them. The Democrats and Republicans have controlled state legislatures and Congress for so long that they have successfully structured electoral laws to favor a two-party system over a multiple-party system. For example, if a candidate is a third-party candidate, or an **Independent**, not affiliated with any political party, state laws typically require thousands of signatures to get that candidate on the ballot, and the names and addresses of the signers have to be exactly right or the signature will not count. To prevent candidates who are not from the major parties from getting on the ballot, state and local political parties frequently challenge the signatures on ballot petitions in court to try to get them invalidated. Moreover, without the backing of a major party in terms of get-out-the-vote efforts, campaign contributions, and media coverage, most third-party or Independent candidates do not stand much chance of being elected. Consequently, voters who consider themselves Independents do not have the opportunity to vote for candidates who might be closest to them in terms of policy preferences.

Independent: *Voter or candidate who is not affiliated with a political party.*

Parties also directly influence the policy agendas of state legislatures and the U.S. Congress. The party that wins the majority of seats in the legislature becomes the majority party, and consequently controls the legislative process. Once the legislative session begins, members are asked to express their opinion in subcommittee, committee, and on the floor, by voting with or against their party's proposed legislation, and it is rare that an alternative to the major party proposal is considered.

Should laws that discourage third parties be changed? What would be the effects in terms of government responsiveness?

Challenges to Party Power from Interest Groups

What are the advantages and disadvantages of being an Independent?

In addition to challenges from third parties, the two major parties also face challenges from established interest groups and from broader social groups formed at the grassroots of American politics (see Chapter 8, Interest Groups). These groups draw attention to each party's failings in specific issue areas and mobilize members around specific issues. They are important in a democracy because they can force political parties to be more responsive to the policy concerns of voters generally, even if they are not party members. Interest groups and grassroots movements can also force parties to be accountable to their own members on issues that the membership feels should be included in the party's platforms. When they are large enough, these groups have the potential to move the party platform in new directions and, in turn, to change federal laws.[24]

Over the past two decades, interest and social movement groups have become more tightly aligned with specific political parties, and that alignment has undermined their capacity to serve as independent checks or competitors with political parties. For example, unions such as the American Federation of Labor and Congress of Industrial Organizations (AFL-CIO), or environmental groups, such as the Sierra Club, are generally supportive of the Democratic Party, whereas business groups, such as the Chamber of Commerce and the National Rifle Association, are supportive of the Republican Party. For interest groups, the risk in continuously supporting one party is that the party will take their support for granted. In fact, parties are most responsive to interest groups when they threaten to withdraw their support or start their own party organization.

Identify the differences in gatekeeper approaches between interest groups and political parties.

Party Alignment and Ideology

Throughout U.S. history, there have been long stretches of time during which the party affiliations of voters remained stable, but there have also been key elections in which parties lost or gained significant blocs of voters. Scholars have tried to identify the factors that explain why voters make large, permanent shifts from one party to another. Such shifts of **party alignment**—voters identifying with a party in repeated elections—can occur when there is an external shock to the nation, such as an economic depression or a foreign military attack. Shifts in party allegiance can also occur when public attitudes change considerably and one party appears to respond more quickly to those changes than another.

party alignment: *Voter identification with a political party in repeated elections.*

The Parties after the Civil War

From 1896 to 1932, the basic geographic pattern of party alignment stayed the same, but the combination of the stock market crash of October 24, 1929, a global depression that followed, and a drop in worldwide agricultural prices brought political trouble to the Republican Party. By 1932, voters in every part of the country were ready for a change, not only in political leadership but also in the entire approach to government itself.

The New Deal and the Role of Ideology in Party Politics

political ideology: *Set of consistent political views.*

During the election of 1932, voters were exposed to a new **political ideology**, or set of consistent political views, about the way that the federal government could work. Today voters might describe themselves as "liberal" or "conservative," but voters before 1932 typically just identified themselves with a political party. In that election year, Franklin Delano Roosevelt (1933–45), governor of New York State, ran for president on a platform designed to reverse the effects of the Great Depression. The idea that the federal government would help individuals to help themselves was transformative in American politics. The Democratic Party platform resonated with voters, and Roosevelt was elected president.

New Deal: *Franklin D. Roosevelt's program for ending the Great Depression through government intervention in the economy and a set of safety-net programs for workers.*

After he took office, Roosevelt championed a vast array of new government programs, commonly referred to as the **New Deal**. These programs were designed to help individuals who were jobless, homeless, or otherwise in financial need; essentially the New Deal was a promise by the federal government to provide a safety net for workers who fell on hard times. Following his electoral victory in 1932, Roosevelt built a coalition of white southerners, working-class ethnic northerners, liberal advocates for socialist policies, and northern African Americans who had previously been Republicans. For African Americans, this was a radical shift, because after the Civil War they had followed the party of Abraham Lincoln and shunned the Democrats, whom they associated with racism and slavery. This electoral coalition was large but fragile, and to maintain it, Roosevelt engaged in a great deal of political balancing and a wide distribution of government benefits.

liberal: *Ideological viewpoint that has faith in government to improve people's lives, believing that private efforts are insufficient. In the social sphere, liberals usually support diverse lifestyles and tend to oppose any government action that seeks to shape personal choices.*

In supporting the New Deal, voters came to accept the ideological viewpoint that government involvement in the economic aspects of individuals' lives was legitimate and, on balance, a good thing. As we noted in Chapter 1 (Gateways to American Democracy: Judging the Democratic Experiment), this perspective on government serves as the foundation for the modern definition of a **liberal**. Today the liberal viewpoint builds on the New Deal perspective by favoring government redistribution of income through higher taxes on the wealthy to provide social benefits, such as health care, unemployment insurance, and welfare payments to the poor. Those who opposed the New Deal are the forefathers of the modern **conservative**, who believes in lower taxes and less government involvement in economic life.

conservative: *Ideological viewpoint that distrusts government, believing that private efforts are more likely to improve people's lives. In the social sphere, conservatives usually support traditional lifestyles and tend to believe government can play a valuable role in shaping personal choices.*

In response to Roosevelt's big government approach, the Republicans seized what they saw as the main weakness of the New Deal, which was the high cost of all these newly created programs. To pay for them, the federal and state governments would have to raise taxes on businesses and workers alike. The Republicans recognized that they had an opportunity to reshape their party platform to exploit the Democrats' weakness.

In the aftermath of 1932, the two parties transformed; in fact, it was almost as if they had switched places. The Democrats changed from a party that believed in state's rights, low taxes, and little government intervention in individuals' lives to a party that created a large social safety net that relied on the federal government to ensure personal economic stability. The Republicans changed from a party that believed in a strong central federal government and in intervention in the economy when necessary to a party of a strictly limited federal government and fiscal responsibility. Alongside these opposing economic viewpoints, modern liberals and conservatives also differ on social issues, including abortion, gun control, affirmative action, prayer in school, and same-sex marriage.

Voters responded to these partisan and ideological changes by changing their own party allegiances over time, essentially producing a **realignment** of the electorate. In the broadest sense, Democrats today support expanding the size of government to accomplish specific policy goals, even if it means raising taxes, as well as supporting liberal social values. In contrast, Republicans support limiting the size of government by keeping taxation and regulation of the economy to a minimum as well as preserving conservative social values. A majority of voters today, however, indicate a reluctance to identify themselves conclusively with either party. Such a situation suggests an alternative to realignment, known as **dealignment**—voters express no particular allegiance to either political party, frequently splitting their votes—termed **split-ticket voting**—between the two major parties. This situation may mean that the parties are too extreme in their beliefs for most voters or are "polarized." As an example, a voter would vote for a Republican for president and then select a Democratic Senator or House member on the same ballot. Such a scenario presents particular problems for a party attempting to implement its platform of ideas and could suggest that the power of interest groups, with more specific or singular ideas, dominates the political spectrum and officeholders, as well as voters, overall.

The Modern Partisan Landscape

The results of the 2008 elections may be a sign that the party landscape is shifting[25] (see Figure 9.4). Clearly the election of an African American president is a significant turning point in race relations; Barack Obama received 43 percent of the white vote in 2008, 2 percentage points higher than white candidate John Kerry received in 2004. Obama won five states that had been considered solid Republican states in previous presidential elections: Florida,

realignment: *Long-term shift in voter allegiance from one party to another.*

dealignment: *A reluctance by voters to identify themselves with either party, often accompanied by increased split-ticket voting.*

split-ticket voting: *Practice of voting for candidates from different parties for different elected offices in a single election.*

Is the political ideology of the modern era dealigned? If so, what are the consequences to the political system of dealignment?

Which perspective comes closest to your own views—liberal or conservative?

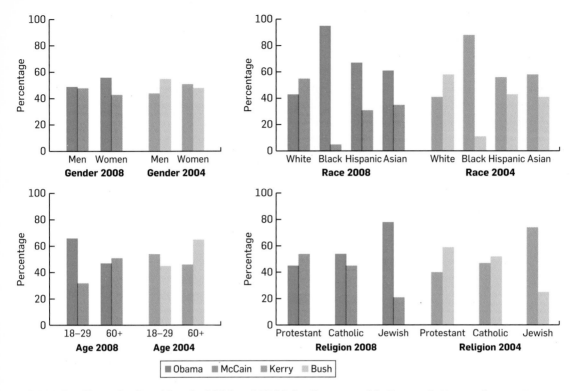

FIGURE 9.4 Votes for President in 2004 and 2008, by Demographic Group. Patterns of support among voters can change from one election to the next depending on who the party chooses as its nominee.
Source: New York Times, elections.nytimes.com.

responsible parties:
Parties that offer the electorate a clear and distinct range of policies and programs, thus providing voters a means for holding the party in government accountable for policy outcomes.

Indiana, North Carolina, Ohio, and Virginia. In addition, Democrats won an additional twenty-two seats in the House of Representatives and nine seats in the Senate from states that had also been considered traditional Republican strongholds.

However, when voters give one party control of the White House and Congress, they have high expectations for a strong governing track record. In one way, that is what political scientists mean by **responsible parties**; if the parties offer voters clear choices, voters can hold the party in charge responsible for policy outcomes. When President Obama and the Democrats took charge of government in 2009, they faced some of the greatest economic challenges since the Great Depression, ongoing wars in Iraq and Afghanistan, and the task of trying to make health insurance available to all Americans. The 2010 congressional midterm elections were the first opportunity that voters had to register their satisfaction or dissatisfaction with the president and his party. The Democratic losses and Republican gains showed the responsible party system in action because voters held the incumbent majority party accountable for its performance on the economy, health care, and the ongoing wars.

What are the advantages and disadvantages of responsible parties?

There is a trade-off between responsible party government and bipartisan cooperation; where there is one, there is almost never the other. Although the divisions between Democrats and Republicans are clearer than ever, this same divide is causing the greatest level of disagreement between the parties in Congress since the Civil War.[26] In the past two decades, parties have taken on starker opposing positions and have ramped up the rhetoric to the point that it has become difficult for members of opposing parties to communicate at all. Elected officials from each party draw such sharp distinctions between themselves and their partisan opponents that voters sometimes wonder if partisanship is taking precedence over policy making. In addition, the current level of partisanship has reduced the incentive for the parties to cooperate to solve problems. As a result, government is less responsive to overall public needs.

Do you think partisanship is taking precedence over policy making? What can be done about that?

Political Parties and Public Policy: The Environment

Political parties lay out their platforms during the campaign season, and elections serve as a key link between parties and policy outcomes. The extent to which candidates honor their party's platform can differ depending on external conditions and opportunities available to them. Not every element of a party platform can be enacted into law, but lawmakers, from the president to state legislators, recognize that they must try to address the issues raised in their campaign platforms to retain the trust of voters.

Party Platforms on Environmental Policy

In the 2008 presidential election, the platforms of both parties addressed environmental protection and energy conservation. The Democratic Party platform centered on creating "green" jobs and renewable energy sources and on reducing greenhouse emissions.[27] As the Democratic Party nominee, Barack Obama made this approach to environmental problems a key part of his presidential campaign. The Republican Party platform focused on promoting clean and reliable sources of energy in America, funding an energy trust fund, and increasing emphasis on energy conservation and efficiency.

The Republican Party nominee John McCain promoted this approach in his presidential campaign, with a special emphasis on tax incentives for energy innovators.[28]

As is typically the case, the political party that wins control of the White House tries to implement its policy platform. One of President Obama's first environmental initiatives was to ask Congress to pass a bill to reduce carbon emissions. H.R. 2454, originally known as the "cap and trade bill," establishes a system whereby the government establishes a maximum amount of carbon emissions for the entire country, with a goal of reducing these emissions 17 percent by 2020. Within the maximum, each company that produces carbon gases is granted a permit for a set amount of emissions. Companies can buy, sell, and trade permits with each other if they expect their emissions to exceed or fall below expectations. Over time, the government will reduce the maximum to reduce pollution.[29] The policy, if enacted into law, would implement the Democratic Party's agenda for reducing emissions, creating new energy resources, and making the United States more energy independent in the future.[30]

H.R. 2454 passed the House of Representatives in a close vote (219–212) on June 26, 2009. Many House Republicans opposed the bill because they argued it would increase energy costs for companies, which would result in higher costs for consumers as well as potential job losses as companies cut back on hiring.[31] This line of opposition is consistent with the Republican Party platform of trying to use tax credits, which lower taxes, to decrease energy use rather than adopting tax increases or requiring the purchase of government permits. Republicans also argued that any real decrease in carbon emissions would take too long to accomplish, at too great a cost.[32]

Competing Constituent and Interest Group Pressures

party-line vote: *Voting in Congress according to party position, so that a majority of one party votes against a majority of the other party.*

The vote on the climate change bill in the House of Representatives was not a straight **party-line vote**; members of both parties crossed the political aisle to vote against their party's official position. Specifically, eight Republican members of Congress, predominantly from the East and West coasts, voted for the bill, saying that their local constituents supported it. Even more surprising was the fact that forty-four Democratic members of Congress—from the Southeast, Northern Tier, and western states—voted against the bill.[33] These Democrats, who were going against their majority party leadership and their president, cited concerns over job displacement, increased taxation, and disproportionate costs imposed on oil-, gas-, and coal-producing states. The voting patterns on the bill suggest that these members weighed the local interests of their regions and constituents more heavily than national party platforms.[34]

In the Senate, a bipartisan trio consisting of Senators John Kerry (D-Mass.), Joseph Lieberman (I-Conn.), and Lindsay Graham (R-S.C.) worked together to produce a version of the bill that could pass the Senate. One of the first things they did was

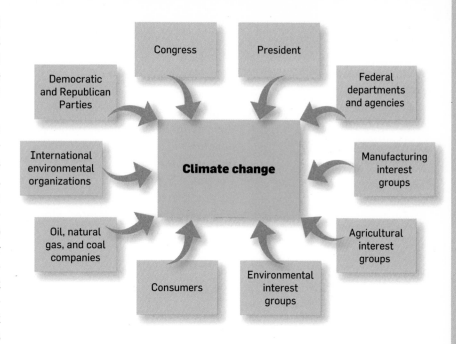

to remove the "cap and trade" label and use the less controversial name of "climate change" to describe the bill. They were set to introduce the bill to the full Senate in April 2010, but their efforts were interrupted when immigration replaced climate change as a priority for the Obama administration and Senator Graham withdrew his support for their bill. Because the Senate relies so heavily on bipartisan cooperation to consider legislation (see Chapter 11, Congress), the bill could not proceed successfully without his support. However, the stakes for both major political parties remain high when it comes to environmental policy because voters will hold them responsible for their promises. The case of the climate change bill illustrates how party platforms and the policy-making process can intersect to produce conflicting incentives for elected officials.

Do political parties help voters hold government responsible? Why or why not?

Political Parties and Democracy

Political parties, which emerged in the nation's first decade, now play a major role in American democracy. The Democrats and Republicans together claim the allegiance of about 80 percent of voters. Political parties determine the choices voters have at the polls by crafting the laws that allow candidates to be on the ballot and overseeing the primaries that allow voters to choose candidates. Parties also recruit candidates for elected office, raise funds for

- How do political parties shape the choices voters face in local, state, and federal elections?

- In what ways do political parties allow voters to hold their elected officials accountable for the policies they produce?

- How do political parties respond to changes in public opinion on key issues?

- Do political parties enable all citizens to participate equally in self-government, or do they help give more power to some people and less to others? Explain.

- Are political parties a gate or a gateway to democracy?

campaigns, register voters, and organize get-out-the-vote drives. In sum, parties shape the selection of candidates who seek, run, and win elected office.

Do political parties make it easier for voters to hold elected officials accountable? Party platforms tell voters what candidates intend to do if elected, and voters can compare their actions against their campaign pledges. If pledges and policies match up, voters typically reelect the official; if they do not, voters can vote for his or her opponent in the next election. One advantage of clear dividing lines between the parties is that it makes the job of monitoring the government easier for the average voter. However, such clear divisions also bring the disadvantages associated with conflict and stalemate between the parties that make bipartisan policy making difficult.

Parties do a mixed job of promoting equal political participation among all citizens. On the one hand, they are a gateway to participation because membership in a political party is free and citizens can work a little or a lot on behalf of the party. Primaries and caucuses give every party member a say in determining who will represent the party in elected office, and they force candidates who seek the party's endorsement to shape their campaign platforms according to party voters' preferences. Because voters are free to join and leave political parties as frequently as they wish, parties are always seeking to represent their members' viewpoints.

On the other hand, parties can discourage political participation by putting obstacles in the way of third-party formation. The U.S. party system is structured around two major parties, and even though third parties have arisen at various times, they are quickly subsumed or defeated by one of the two major parties. The two-party system reduces major policy issues to two-sided questions, when in fact the complexity of these issues warrants multiple perspectives. The problem for democracy is that there is no formal venue for presenting these multiple perspectives, either in elections or in the governing institutions.

The larger question is whether the twenty-first-century U.S. party system fulfills the role of enabling widespread participation in the governing process. In terms of responding to changes in public opinion, political parties fall short of meeting their responsibilities as agents of democratic government. They are large, entrenched organizations, with multiple layers—federal, state, and local—that can differ in their viewpoints on specific issues. The breadth of the national parties makes it difficult to reach internal consensus on issues at every level of government.

The combination of intraparty divisions with interparty polarization and conflict has produced a party-dominated democracy that is not consistently responsive to voters' interests and opinions. However, in a democracy, power rests on winning elections, and for that, parties will always depend on voters like you, who hold the power to change parties by staying loyal or switching allegiance.

GATEWAYS TO LEARNING

Top Ten to Take Away

1. Political parties are the broadest and most open gateway to participation in American politics. (pp. 287–288)

2. They have one primary purpose—to win elections in order to control government power and implement their policies. (p. 287)

3. Parties organize the electorate by giving them choices of policies and candidates, and they also organize Congress and state legislatures into cohesive groups that consistently vote for the policies that their parties promise in their platforms. (pp. 288–291)

4. Parties nominate candidates for office in primary elections, which are open to all voters, although in some states voters must affiliate with a party before voting. (pp. 291–295)

5. The basic division between the Federalists and the Antifederalists over the ratification of the Constitution survived into the Washington administration to become factions; by the time of Jefferson's election in 1800, the factions had become political parties. (pp. 295–296)

6. Between 1800 and the Civil War, various parties rose and fell, but since the end of the war the two major parties—the Democratic Party and the Republican Party—have dominated the American political system. (pp. 296–302)

7. The effects of the two-party system are to limit voter choices to "for" and "against" and to discourage third parties, although the issues third parties arise to address are frequently adopted by one of the major political parties. (pp. 302–307)

8. Voter realignments occur when the parties readjust the focus of their policies, typically as a result of a major event such as depression or military conflict. (pp. 307–311)

9. Since the 1930s, with Franklin D. Roosevelt's New Deal, liberals have generally aligned with the Democratic Party and conservatives with the Republican Party. (pp. 308–309)

10. The modern political landscape is marked by a partisan divide, as the parties have taken on starker opposing positions and have ramped up the rhetoric to the point that voters sometimes wonder if partisanship is taking precedence over policy making. (pp. 309–311)

A full narrative summary is on the book's website.

Ten to Test Yourself

1. What is a faction? What is a political party? How are they different?

2. When, and how, did the first nationally organized political party emerge?

3. How is the presidential nomination system organized?

4. How do the rules and practices for nominating presidents and members of Congress influence who runs and who can win?

5. What was the Australian ballot and how did it transform the American political party system?

6. What is the difference between party identification and political ideology?

7. What are the roles of third parties and interest groups in the American political party system?

8. How did the New Deal change the party balance among voters between Republicans and Democrats?

9. How do the Democratic and Republican Party each differ from what they were a century ago in terms of voter base, geography, and party policy?

10. How do the Democrats and Republicans differ on environmental policy?

More review questions and answers and chapter quizzes are on the book's website.

Terms **to Know and Use**

abolitionist movement (p. 298)
Antifederalists (p. 296)
Australian ballot (pp. 300, 301)
ballot (p. 291)
civil service (pp. 300, 301)
closed primary (p. 291)
conservative (p. 308)
dealignment (p. 309)
delegate (p. 292)
Democratic-Republicans (p. 296)
faction (p. 295)
Federalists (p. 296)
front-loading (p. 295)
general election (p. 291)
incumbent (p. 290)
Independent (p. 306)
liberal (p. 308)
local party organization (p. 291)
machine politics (p. 299)
majority vote (p. 303)

McGovern-Fraser
  Commission (p. 292)
median voter theorem (p. 302)
moderate (p. 302)
national committee (p. 289)
New Deal (p. 308)
open primary (p. 291)
party alignment (p. 307)
party as an organization (p. 288)
party boss (p. 299)
party caucus (p. 289)
party identification (p. 288)
party in government (p. 288)
party in the electorate (p. 288)
party-line vote (p. 312)
party platform (p. 287)
patronage system (p. 299)
plurality vote (p. 303)
political ideology (p. 308)
political party (p. 287)

presidential party caucus (p. 292)
primary election (p. 291)
Progressives (p. 300)
proportional representation (p. 293)
realignment (p. 309)
responsible parties (p. 310)
runoff election (p. 291)
semiclosed primary (p. 291)
single-member plurality
  system (p. 303)
split-ticket voting (p. 309)
state central committee
  (pp. 290, 291)
superdelegates (p. 293)
third parties (p. 298)
voter registration (p. 288)
Whig Party (p. 308)
winner-take-all system (p. 292)

Use the vocabulary flash cards on the book's website.

10 ELECTIONS, CAMPAIGNS, AND VOTING

▲ **Bradley University, Peoria, Illinois**

> *As far as this generation, I think we're a very involved and engaged demographic. I think you saw that in the last election.*

Aaron Schock, Republican member of the House from Illinois, was voted the "hottest Congressional Freshman" in a 2009 reader's poll. There is no question that Schock is good-looking, single, and just 30, but he is also a near-perfect example of what dedication and hard work can accomplish in the American political system. In just two years, he graduated from Bradley University, in Peoria, Illinois, with a bachelor's degree in finance. But he was already a successful business-man. As a child, he had grown strawberries on his father's farm, which he harvested and sold. After graduation from college, he and a partner started a small business that employed three people.

The next year, Schock entered politics. Running as a write-in candidate for the Peoria School Board, he knocked on enough doors to introduce himself and win with 60 percent of the vote. Four years later, his fellow board members unanimously elected him president. He was 23 years old. But by this time he was already a member of the Illinois House of Representatives, having run, and won, a difficult campaign in a traditionally Democratic district. In the Illinois House he was appointed to five committees, including one on school appropriations and one on financial services. In 2007, he shared with Barack Obama (then a U.S. senator) an award for "outstanding legislative and constituency service"

Aaron Schock

CourseMate

Visit http://www.cengagebrain.com/shop/ISBN/0495906190 for interactive tools including:

- Quizzes
- Flashcards
- Videos and more

Courtesy of Bradley University

AP Photo/Seth Perlman

- In what ways do elections encourage accountability and responsiveness in government?

- How does citizen equality work, or not work, in elections and campaigns? Are elections and campaigns fair?

- How well do campaigns work to inform the public so as to allow voters to hold candidates accountable?

- Why is voting such an important gateway for any democracy?

- Is more participation always good?

- How does citizen participation in the political system affect the prospects for accountability and equality?

- Do young citizens participate enough to make the system responsive to their preferences? What about other groups?

- How do other forms of participation, besides voting, serve as gateways to democracy? Are they more or less effective than voting?

- Do laws that regulate the financing of campaigns impede or advance equality and accountability in elections?

- In what ways are elections, campaigns, and voting gateways to American democracy? What are the gates?

from the Illinois Committee for Honest Government. The next year Schock entered national politics, campaigning and winning election to the U.S. House of Representatives from the 18th Congressional District in Illinois. This young Republican was the youngest member of the 111st Congress and the first person born in the 1980s to serve in Congress.[1]

Elections and campaigns, as the experience of Aaron Schock demonstrates, offer a gateway into the American political system. They provide many opportunities for participation, not only running for office but also volunteering and working at the polls. During campaigns, candidates offer competing visions of the role of government and promise to enact specific policies. The people decide to support the candidate and the campaign program, or not, when they go to the polls. Elections provide the most common (and easiest) gateway for the people to express their opinions and to hold elected officials accountable. Together, elections and campaigns offer the public a chance to shape the course of government. In this chapter, we examine how elections, campaigns, and voting work, asking whether, and how, these institutions promote government responsiveness and equality for citizens.

The Constitutional Requirements for Elections

Given the importance of elections to the democratic process, it is surprising that the Constitution says so little about them (see Figure 10.1). The Constitution is nearly silent on the rules about voting in elections, leaving such choices to the states. As Article I, Section 4 of the Constitution states, "The Times, Places and Manner of holding Elections for Senators and Representatives, shall be prescribed in each State by the Legislature thereof." The Constitution does spell out in some detail the workings of

FIGURE 10.1 **Amendments That Pertain to the Right to Vote.**

Color Code :
Participation   Equality

Fifteenth (1870): Prohibits states from denying the right to vote on account of race

Seventeenth (1913): Gives the people (instead of state legislatures) the right to choose U.S. senators

Nineteenth (1920): Guarantees women the right to vote

Twenty-Third (1961): Grants residents of the District of Columbia votes in the Electoral College

Twenty-Fourth (1964): Prohibits poll taxes

Twenty-Sixth (1971): Guarantees 18-year-olds the right to vote

the **Electoral College**, which chooses the president. But even for the College, states were given latitude about how to choose electors. The consequence of this delegation of authority is to create a system of voting that is very complicated, because state rules vary considerably. These differing rules also lead to inequalities among the states. It is, for example, easier in some states to vote than others. What requirements the Constitution does lay out for elections indicate that the Framers wanted to set up barriers against a direct democracy. Only the House of Representatives was to be elected directly by the people. In elections for the president and for the Senate, the public's role was indirect and complex. Today, senators are elected directly by the people. Presidential elections also give citizens more say in the process, but these contests continue to be shaped by constitutional requirements that serve as a gate between the people and the presidency. In this section, we explain the constitutional requirements for American elections as background for understanding the ways in which presidential and congressional campaigns are run.

Electoral College: *The 538 presidential electors, elected to represent the votes of their respective states, who meet every four years to cast the electoral votes for president and vice president of the United States.*

Why did the Framers set up gates against popular participation in elections?

Presidential Elections

The constitutional rules governing the selection of the president reflect three fundamental themes that guided the Framers' thinking. First, the states were given broad discretion on key matters regarding presidential elections to ensure their importance and to counterbalance the power of the national government. Second, the Framers designed the presidency with George Washington in mind and really did not spell out in great detail all aspects of the presidency, including elections. Over time, the details were filled in. Third, the presidency was envisioned as an office that would be above party politics, doing what was right for the nation as opposed to supporting one faction over another. But that assumption went awry early on, as parties formed almost from the start.

The Electoral College.

The means by which the president of the United States is elected was born of compromise between the interests of the states and the interests of the people, yielding a system that even today is indirect and confusing. The formal selection of the president is in the hands of **electors**, who collectively constitute the Electoral College.

Why did the Framers give so much authority over elections to the states?

electors: *The individuals who actually serve in the Electoral College, casting votes for president.*

The selection of electors was originally the responsibility of state legislatures, whose members were, for the most part, elected by the people. This arrangement gave the public an *indirect* say in the choice. Today, the people of each state, not the members of state legislatures, choose the electors, in an arrangement that has given citizens a new gateway for influence (see Figure 10.2).

The electors, however, remain the formal decision makers for choosing the president. The actual electors are selected in a variety of ways in the fifty states. In broad strokes, each party lines up electors for its candidate prior to the election. Each state receives a number of electoral votes equal to the number of senators and members of the House of Representatives. The minimum number is three, because every state has at least one House member and two senators. California has the most electoral votes with fifty-five. All the electoral votes in a state are allocated to the candidate who finishes first in the voting. This **winner-take-all system** means that if a candidate wins California by just a single vote, that candidate gets all fifty-five of the state's electoral votes. There are two exceptions: Nebraska and Maine allocate votes by congressional district and so can split their electoral votes.

winner-take-all system: *Electoral system in which whoever wins the most votes in an election wins the election.*

Is the winner-take-all system fair?

To win the presidency, a candidate needs to win a majority (270) of the 538 electoral votes (538 is the total of 435 representatives plus 100 senators plus 3 votes from the District of Columbia, which can vote for president but does not have a dedicated voting representative in Congress). If no one wins a majority of electoral votes, the election is thrown into the House of Representatives. At that point, each state gets a single vote, and the candidate who wins a majority of the states becomes the next president. The last time that happened was 1824.

Problems with the Electoral College and Reform.

The Electoral College has never worked as the Framers envisioned—an institution that would allow for a group of independent decision makers to get together in the many states and deliberate over who would make the best president. Other difficulties with this gate to direct democracy include:

popular vote: *Tally of total votes from individual citizens, as opposed to the electoral vote.*

What inequalities do state control of elections introduce?

- A source of problems in the system was that states were free to set their own rules for selecting electors, and as a consequence, state's rules for selecting electors and the timetable for selection vary widely.
- The biggest problem with the Electoral College occurs when winning the nation's **popular vote** does not automatically translate into a win

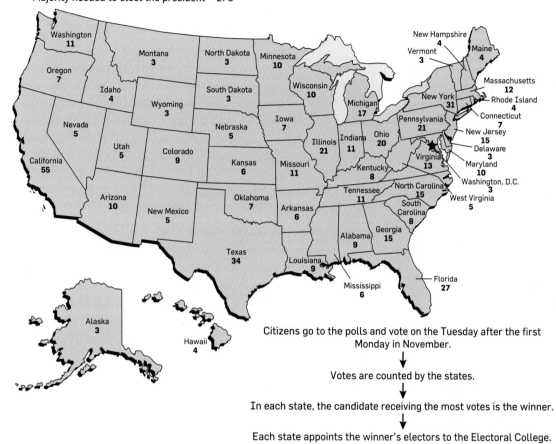

Electoral votes per state = number of senators (2) + number of representatives
Total number of electoral votes = 538
Majority needed to elect the president = 270

Citizens go to the polls and vote on the Tuesday after the first Monday in November.

↓

Votes are counted by the states.

↓

In each state, the candidate receiving the most votes is the winner.

↓

Each state appoints the winner's electors to the Electoral College.

↓

The electors meet in their respective state capitals and vote for the winner on the Monday after the second Wednesday in December.

↓

Congress meets in joint session to count the electoral votes and announce the next president.

Each state's number of electors for the 2004 and 2008 elections, allocated on the basis of the 2000 census.

Note: In every state but two the winner of the popular vote takes all of the electoral votes. Maine and Nebraska allocate votes by congressional district and so can split their electoral votes.

FIGURE 10.2 How the Electoral College Works.

in the Electoral College, meaning that the individual who received *fewer* votes could become the president. Such outcomes raise questions about equality; because of the Electoral College, votes in some states matter more than votes in others. In fact, the votes citizens cast in Alaska have more than twice the influence of those cast in California.[2] In addition, if a democracy rests on the idea of majority rule—that is, the candidate with the most support in the public wins the election—then four (or five) presidential elections (about 10 percent) have been undemocratic.

Some may wonder why the country does not just change the rules to select the president through the popular vote. This method would appear more democratic, because all votes would be treated equally. But the current system has some advantages. For example, the Electoral College does encourage candidates to secure support in all corners of the country, not just areas with dense populations. Eliminating the Electoral College would decrease the role of the states, dampening the significance of state interests. There are also practical problems. Doing away with the Electoral College would require a constitutional amendment, and it is not clear that the three-quarters of the states needed to ratify an amendment would support such a reform.

The Controversy Surrounding the 2000 Presidential Election.

Because elections are a centerpiece of democracy, it is important that they be viewed as fair. For these reasons, the events surrounding the 2000 presidential election tested the credibility of the American electoral process. The margin between Vice President Al Gore (1993–2001) and George W. Bush (2001–09) was razor thin. In the popular vote, Gore received about 600,000 more votes than Bush—just a .5 percentage point difference (48.4 percent to 47.9 percent). The Electoral College did not, however, produce a winner on election night. The state of Florida was too close to call and, without that state's electoral votes, neither Bush nor Gore had a majority in the Electoral College. Bush led Florida by 537 votes out of 5.8 million votes cast—a .0001 percent difference. Demands for a recount ensued, and the Florida recount revealed how difficult it is to produce an accurate vote count. A series of court cases resulted in a Supreme Court decision that determined the outcome of the election (see Supreme Court Cases: *Bush v. Gore*).

Many votes had not been counted in Florida, and some had been counted for the wrong candidate. Citizens across the country lost faith in American elections. Nearly one in five had doubts about whether his or her vote had been counted.[3] Only 32 percent thought there was "a fair and accurate vote count in Florida."[4] In January 2001, just a few days before George W. Bush was to be sworn in as president, only 51 percent of the public felt he had won the presidency "legitimately."[5] More than 60 percent wanted to do away with the Electoral College.[6]

Fortunately, the public's confidence has been restored. By 2008, only one in twenty Americans had doubts about whether his or her vote had not been counted.[7] Few people had any doubt that Senator Obama had beaten Senator McCain.[8] The 2000 election raised distrust in the short run, but with little lasting damage to the nation's electoral institutions.

Was the outcome of the 2000 presidential election fair? Does it matter if it was or wasn't fair?

supremecourtcases

Bush v. Gore (2000)

QUESTION: Does Florida's subjective recount mechanism violate equal protection of the law? If so, should there be a recount using more objective standards?

ORAL ARGUMENT: December 11, 2000 (listen at http://www.oyez.org/cases)

DECISION: December 12, 2000 (read at http://www.findlaw.com/casecode/supreme.html)

OUTCOME: Yes, Florida's recount procedures violate the equal protection clause (7–2); there is insufficient time to conduct a recount (5–4).

The presidential election of 2000 came down to Florida's electoral votes. Whoever won the state—Republican Governor George W. Bush of Texas or Democratic Vice President Al Gore—would win the election. The early counts were excruciatingly close, with the networks first calling the election for Gore, then declaring it undecided, then declaring Bush the winner, and then putting it back in the undecided column.

Due to the closeness of the race, an automatic machine recount took place. Bush led Gore by 537 votes out of nearly 6 million cast. Because elections, even for federal office, are administered under state law, Gore went to state court in Florida, asking for a hand recount in four counties that would require election officials in those counties to determine, from each ballot, the intent of the voter. In punch card ballots, the machine will not read a ballot unless the chad—to be punched out by the voter—is completely removed. But a hand count might be able to determine the voter's intent from a "hanging" or "dimpled" or "pregnant" chad—indented but not sufficiently punched out so as to break off or even break the corners.

The Florida Supreme Court ruled for Gore by a 4–3 vote on December 8. Bush then filed suit in federal court, claiming that the standard of the intent of the voter that Florida used, which could mean different standards by different officials, was so arbitrary as to violate the equal protection clause. The Bush legal team asked for an injunction, an order blocking further recounts. Both the U.S. District Court and the U.S. Court of Appeals rejected Bush's request. Bush then appealed to the Supreme Court.

The Supreme Court agreed to hear the case, and on December 9, it decided, by a 5–4 vote, to halt the recount prior to the Court's decision. The Court heard oral arguments on December 11, and announced its decision at 10:00 p.m. on December 12.

The Supreme Court ruled by a 7–2 vote that the absence of specific standards for gauging the intent of the voter was so arbitrary as to violate the equal protection clause. The Court also declared by a 5–4 vote that Florida's legislature intended all recounts to be completed by December 12, thus making a recount impossible.

The dissenters declared that the machinery of running elections is a state question that should not involve the federal courts; that the Court's prior interpretation of the equal protection clause has allowed differential treatment as long as there is no intent to discriminate against certain groups; and that the Court's December 12 deadline was never stated in Florida law.

Vice President Gore conceded the election the next day.

- **Why was the Supreme Court so rushed in its decision?**
- **In what way did Florida's recount plan violate equality?**

Congressional Elections

The constitutional guidelines for congressional elections again reflect the compromise between the interests of states and the interests of the people. The Senate was intended by the Framers to bring state interests to bear on the legislative process, while the House was intended to represent the people.

Senate Elections.   As with the choice of electors, the Constitution originally gave the choice of senators to state legislatures. The adoption of the Seventeenth Amendment in 1913 changed this; however, there are barriers against overwhelming change in the composition of the Senate because Senate elections are staggered; only one-third of senators are up for election at a time. This arrangement ensures the Senate is insulated from large shifts in public sentiment.

House Elections and Redistricting.   In contrast to the Senate, the entire House of Representatives is up for election every two years. Also in contrast to the Senate, House members have always been elected directly by the people. The Constitution requires that representatives be apportioned, within each state, according to population, which is counted every ten years in a **census**. Every ten years, new district lines are drawn following a census. Depending on patterns of population growth or decline, states win or lose congressional seats with each new census.

State legislatures are responsible for drawing the district lines, in a process known as **redistricting**. While the official aim of redistricting is to try to keep districts equal in terms of population, the majority party in the state legislature tries to construct each district in such a way that makes it easier for its candidates to win congressional seats. An imposed limitation on this redistricting process is that the boundaries of the district must be contiguous (uninterrupted).

Redistricting has also been used as a tool to achieve greater minority representation in the House of Representatives. Following passage of the Voting Rights Act in 1965, some states sought to dilute the effect of minority voters by drawing district lines so as to split their voting strength. In 1982, amendments to the Voting Rights Act forbade this practice, and in response, state legislatures created majority-minority districts, in which African Americans or Hispanics would constitute a majority of the voters in the district, thereby increasing the

How do differences in term lengths and constituencies affect how senators and House members behave?

census: *Constitutionally mandated count of the population every ten years.*

redistricting: *Process whereby state legislatures redraw the boundaries of congressional districts in the state to make them equal in population size.*

Do majority-minority districts help advance equality or introduce inequalities?

possibility of their electing African American or Hispanic candidates. In the past decade, however, the federal courts have ruled that state legislatures have overemphasized the racial composition of these districts to the point where districts made no geographic sense. As a result, current guidelines on redistricting call for the consideration of race in drawing district lines, but not to the extreme that it has been employed in the past.[9]

Any change to the size and shape of a district can have political implications, because shifts in its partisan makeup alter which party might be able to capture the seat. For these reasons, there are major battles over the composition of districts. The politicization of drawing districts is called **gerrymandering**. Chapter 11 provides more details about this process and explains how different compositions of districts can alter the kind of gateway these congressional elections offer.

© Bettmann/CORBIS

THE GERRY-MANDER.

The term *gerrymander* comes from this salamander-shaped district in Massachusetts, which Governor Elbridge Gerry approved following the census of 1800. Political rivals denounced the blatant seeking of political advantage that had produced such an oddly shaped congressional district, and the made-up taunt stuck, passing into common usage in politics.

Other Elections

The only type of election mentioned in the Constitution in which the people could directly participate was for members of the U.S. House of Representatives. Today, however, U.S. citizens elect the president (through electors), members of Congress, governors, state legislators, and a range of local officials, which can include positions at the city, town, or village level. In some states, voters can cast ballots on specific policies through **initiatives** and **referenda**.[10] Further, thirty-nine of the fifty states have some sort of election involved in either the selection or retention of judges.[11] No developed country has as many elections as the United States.[12]

The Presidential Campaign and Issues

Presidential campaigns capture the interest of nearly all Americans. Every move a presidential candidate makes is watched and assessed. The course of the modern presidential campaign is long and difficult. From the decision to run to the final victory and concession speeches, the road to the White House is shaped by constitutional requirements, interparty struggles, and strategies for attracting votes that highlight the many gates and gateways along the road.

gerrymandering: *Redistricting that blatantly benefits one political party over the other or concentrates (or dilutes) the voting impact of racial and ethnic groups.*

initiative: *Process by which citizens place proposed laws on the ballot for public approval.*

referendum: *Process by which public approval is required before states can pass laws.*

The Decision to Run and the Invisible Primary

invisible primary: *Period just before the primaries begin, during which candidates attempt to capture party support and media coverage.*

Once a candidate decides to run for president, he or she enters what has been called the **invisible primary**. No votes are cast, but candidates are jockeying for position so they can be ready to do well in the initial primaries and caucuses. They must line up party support, financial backing, and credibility with journalists in the news media. Candidates who can get attention from the news media can raise more money and secure more endorsements from party leaders. It is a game that relies heavily on momentum.

Incumbent presidents usually win their party's nomination for a second term. If that part of the contest is a struggle, it is a sign that the incumbent is in trouble and he usually goes on to lose the general election. But when the seat is open (when an incumbent is in his second term or decides not to run again), a big battle unfolds. These struggles tend to be multicandidate affairs, often with seven or eight serious candidates seeking the nomination. Over the last thirty years, this phase of the campaign has tended to favor **party insiders**, candidates who have deep ties to major party leaders and are not challenging the existing party leadership. Of these nomination contests in which there was no incumbent, the party insider won all but one time. The sole exception over the last three decades was Barack Obama's 2008 defeat of Hillary Clinton. Because Clinton had nearly all the insider support, it was widely assumed she would win the nomination. Obama had substantial support, but few thought he had a chance against the power of the Clintons.[13]

party insiders: *Candidates with deep ties to party leaders and views that comport well with the political viewpoints of the party leadership.*

The Caucuses and Primaries

What gates are imposed by the primary system?

To win a party's nomination, candidates must secure a majority of delegates to the national party conventions. These delegates are allocated to each of the fifty states (plus the District of Columbia, Guam, and Puerto Rico) by the two parties, and then the states decide how to choose the delegates. The national party sets guidelines that the states must follow. If they fail to do so, the party can refuse to accept their delegates to the national convention.

primary election: *Elections held in which citizens directly vote for candidates who will run on the party label in the general election; also called direct primary.*

About 70 percent of the states use some form of **primary election**, an election in which citizens go to the polling booths and vote for their favorite party candidates. The other 30 percent use **caucuses**, which are something like a town meeting. The Iowa caucus, the nation's first and most famous caucus, requires that people attend a meeting of about two hours in which they indicate their preferences and then try to convince those who are undecided to join their candidate's group. Because caucuses demand more time from voters, participation is usually low.

caucus: *Meeting of party members in town halls, schools, and even private homes to choose a vote for a presidential party nominee.*

Caucuses and primaries take place over six months, from January through June of the election year. Some states hold these events earlier than others, and the first states to hold primaries and caucuses wield tremendous influence because in most election years the early primaries quickly build momentum for a front-runner and yield a likely nominee. Iowa and the first state to hold a primary, New Hampshire, get a great deal of attention from candidates and the media. In a process called **front-loading**, other states have been moving their dates earlier to avoid the possibility of holding a primary after the winner has already been determined. A stark exception to the usual pattern was the Democratic primary season in 2008, in which Clinton and Obama battled to the very last primary in one of the closest contests in recent memory.

front-loading:
Holding many primaries simultaneously early in the year.

The National Convention

Following the primary season, each party meets in a national convention. Prior to the 1960s, conventions were often exciting, because it was far from clear who would be the nominee. In 1924, for example, it took the Democrats 124 ballots to decide on their nominee. But by the 1960s, conventions began to be televised, so parties wanted to ensure they were orderly. To avoid projecting an image that would lose votes in the upcoming election, party leaders instituted rule changes designed to increase the odds that the likely nominee would be known well in advance of the convention. Convention planners could, then, stage the event to emphasize party unity, rather than discord, to impress television viewers.

Issues

Citizen participation in American politics peaks during presidential campaigns. Supporters and those who are undecided have the chance to attend rallies, hear speeches, read blogs, and watch the never-ending advertisements on television. Because these campaigns are important gateways for public participation, we look in particular at concerns regarding fundraising and campaign strategies that make public engagement possible but may also introduce some inequalities.

Fundraising and Money.   Of course, no one could run for president without funding, and spending by presidential candidates has risen sharply in recent years, despite legislation to control it. In 1971, Congress tried to put candidates on an equal financial footing and make them less beholden to special interests through the Federal Election Campaign Act (FECA). Under the rules of this act, candidates seeking their party's nomination are given public funds for the campaign in the form of **matching funds**: a dollar amount equal to the amount the candidates raise from private contributors with a limit per individual contributor and an overall cap. In 2008, the limit per contributor was $2,400 in the primary and $2,400 in the general campaign; the cap was $42 million for the primary and $84 million for the general election. Some

matching funds:
Public funding given to a presidential candidate equaling the dollar amount the candidate raises from private contributors.

bundling: *Organizing and influencing others to donate to a political campaign so as to raise more money than the $2,400 contribution FEC rules permit per individual.*

political action committees (PACs): *Groups formed to raise and contribute funds to support electoral candidates and that are subject to campaign finance laws.*

What are the pros and cons of laws that regulate campaign finance?

Should FEC rules work to encourage third parties? Why or why not?

Are campaigns too expensive?

swing voters: *Voters who are neither reliably Republican nor reliably Democratic and who are pursued by each party during elections, as they can determine which candidate wins.*

swing states: *States that are not clearly pro-Republican or pro-Democrat and therefore are of vital interest to presidential candidates, as they can determine election outcomes.*

contributors try to amplify their impact though the practice of **bundling**—amassing individual contributions. **Political action committees (PACs)**, groups formed with the express purpose of donating money to candidates who agree with the PAC's policy agenda, can also give money to candidates—in some cases $5,000 per candidate.[14]

The rules for the public financing of presidential nomination campaigns are complicated and are designed to ensure candidates are serious contenders before receiving them. The Federal Election Commission (FEC) monitors campaign finance compliance. First, candidates must raise at least $5,000 in twenty states, made up of donations that are less than $250 each. Most candidates can meet this standard, but staying eligible for funds is much harder. A candidate who does not get at least 10 percent of the vote in two consecutive primaries loses eligibility, and to reestablish it, he or she must get 20 percent of the vote in a subsequent primary. These standards are hard to meet when four or five other serious candidates are also seeking votes. They also discourage third-party candidates from running.

Increasingly, candidates have decided to forego matching funds in their quest for the nomination. One reason is to be able to spend money in states important to the contest without regard to FEC limits. But primarily, they believe they can raise (and spend) more money if they do not accept federal matching funds. In 2000, George W. Bush believed he could raise much more than the $40 million existing limit and, foregoing matching funds, raised $70 million *prior* to the first primary.[15]

During the 2008 presidential campaign, McCain did use public funds, receiving about $80 million from the government, but Obama opted out of general election funding, the first candidate to do so since the system began in 1976. By so doing, he had access to far more money than McCain. Over the course of the yearlong campaign, he spent $730 million, breaking all previous fundraising records. McCain spent $333 million dollars during that same period, a huge amount by historical standards, but it was dwarfed by Obama's spending (see Figure 10.3 for total spending). Obama's record fundraising will change how presidential campaigns are funded. As we approach the 2012 presidential election, the financing system is entering a new era. Serious candidates for the nomination and eventual nominees will almost surely not use federal funds, raising and spending their own money instead. The key constraint will be the approximate $2,500 limit an individual can contribute to a campaign in 2012.[16] Given the amounts Obama raised in 2008, the total amount spent on the next presidential campaign can be expected to approach $2 billion (see Chapter 8, p. 265, for a discussion of the *Citizens United case*).

Swing States.   Even though partisanship is extremely high, **swing voters** still exist—those who do not fall into either the Republican or Democratic camp—and so do **swing states**, those that might vote either

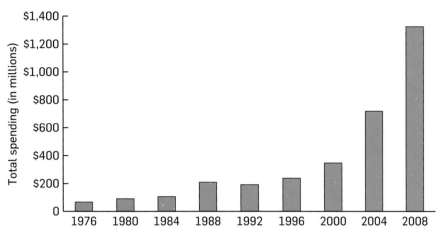

FIGURE 10.3 Total Spending by Presidential Candidates, 1976–2008.
Source: Opensecrets.org

Democratic or Republican in a particular election. Parties avidly pursue swing voters during a presidential election, as they can swing an election one way or the other. Though the number of swing voters varies from year to year, it is usually about 20 percent of the electorate.

More important for a campaign strategy, however, are the swing states, which can mean the difference between victory and defeat. Because of the Electoral College's winner-take-all system, presidential candidates invest time and effort only in states that they can win. Both McCain and Obama campaigned hard in Pennsylvania—a **battleground state** that each thought he had a chance to win. Citizens in these states got lots of attention. Nearly 90 percent of campaign visits were to battleground states. TV viewers were deluged with campaign ads, and party-based get-out-the-vote organizations were active in even the smallest of towns. Citizens in these states were well informed and increasingly interested in the campaign. But the strategy of pursuing votes in swing states yields an important inequality, for citizens in non–swing states do not get such attention, and their interest in the campaign lags, especially among the poor. According to one estimate, "the seven battleground states targeted by both major parties contained only 18% of the nation's population" in 2004, "with another 24% residing in states that were classified as leaning, but not quite safe."[17] Much the same was true for 2008, considering that nearly 25 percent of all visits by McCain and Obama were to Ohio and Pennsylvania.[18]

Microtargeting.   Today, the technique of **microtargeting** (also called *narrowcasting*) has become a boon to political parties and electoral campaigns. By identifying and tracking potential supporters, campaign strategists

Do you live in a swing or battleground state? What is the impact on you?

battleground state: *State in which the outcome of the presidential election is uncertain and in which both candidates invest much time and money to win, especially if vital for a victory in the Electoral College.*

microtargeting: *Gathering detailed information on cross-sections of the electorate to track potential supporters and tailor political messages for them; also called* narrowcasting.

What is your "microtargeting" profile? Can these categories predict how you will vote?

What should shape a presidential campaign—issues or character?

valence issues: *Noncontroversial or widely supported campaign issues that are unlikely to differentiate among candidates.*

position issues: *Political issues that offer specific choices in policy and often differentiate candidates' views and plans of action.*

wedge issue: *Divisive issue focused on a particular group of the electorate that candidates use to gain more support by taking votes away from their opponents.*

Identify three wedge issues that are important to you. Do they determine your vote?

negativity: *Campaign strategy of telling voters why they should not vote for the opponent and highlighting information that raises doubts about the opponent.*

What is your response to negative ads?

can design specific political messages tailored for each of the "voting profiles" found from the data. As a campaign strategy, microtargeting has begun to replace traditional polling techniques and precinct-by-precinct get-out-the-vote drives. By combining information from polling surveys with political participation and consumer information obtained, political parties and campaigns can establish a profile of the many different types of voters and the issues they support.

Campaign Issues. Campaigns are very much shaped by issues. Many observers think that the personality of the candidates dictates the race, but that view is not consistent with the evidence. Between 1960 and 2000, for example, 56 percent of the content of advertising in presidential campaigns involved policy, with 26 percent concerning the personal traits of the candidates, and the remaining 18 percent about general values such as freedom, hard work, and patriotism.[19] In 2008, the economy dominated the discussion between McCain and Obama. According to one estimate, over 50 percent of the appeals made by these two contenders dealt with the economy alone.[20]

For greater understanding of how issues influence campaigns, political scientists have drawn a distinction between **valence issues** and **position issues**.[21] A valence issue is a vague claim to a goal, such as a "strong economy," "improved education," or "greater national security." Valence issues provide limited insight into what policies a candidate might pursue once in office. A position issue is different. Here candidates adopt views that allow voters to understand specific plans for government.

Because campaigns are competitive struggles for votes, candidates look for ways to secure extra votes while maintaining existing support. This dynamic is especially true for candidates who trail, because they need to find some way to break up the existing support for the candidate in the lead. One strategy is to use a **wedge issue** that has the potential to break up the opposition's coalition.[22] Wedges usually involve controversial policy concerns, such as abortion or gay marriage, which divide people rather than build consensus.

Negativity. Candidates are very good at telling voters why they should vote for them, but they are also good at telling the public why they should not vote for their opponents. These reasons often involve issues. A candidate might, for example, remind voters that his or her opponent raised taxes. But other times, a campaign releases an array of information about a candidate that raises doubts and concerns about fitness for office. Because the public does need to know both the good and the bad, **negativity** plays an important, and usually underappreciated, role in campaigns.

One of the most famous negative ads was the "Daisy spot," aired only once by President Lyndon Johnson (1963–69) in his 1964 campaign against the Republican nominee, Barry Goldwater. The implication was that Senator

Goldwater, if president, would start a nuclear war. Goldwater had called for the tactical use of nuclear weapons and made some loose statements about attacking the Soviet Union with nuclear weapons. This issue was among the most important facing the nation—much like terrorism is now. The public needed to know Goldwater's views, and this negative ad helped generate that debate.

In recent years, the amount of negativity has been on the rise. In the 2008 campaign, about two-thirds of all statements were negative. Many worry about this trend, viewing attacks on the opposition as weakening the fabric of democracy. In fact, nearly 80 percent of the public dislikes negative ads.[23] But negative ads do serve a purpose. To ensure accountability, candidates do need to be able to critique the other side.

Polls and Prediction Models.

Given Obama's victory in 2008, it is easy to overestimate his skill and McCain's lack of skill. The winners always look brilliant and the losers misguided. But such judgments are not very useful. To look beyond a single case, political scientists have developed **prediction models** that yield specific estimates of the vote share in presidential elections. The goal is to provide a general understanding of who wins and why.

The best prediction models use some combination of the following key structural factors:

1. *The economy.* What is the condition of the economy? A strong economy leads voters to support the incumbent party. A struggling economy gives an edge to the challenger.
2. *Presidential popularity.* How popular is the sitting president? An unpopular president will hurt the chances for his party's candidate.
3. *The incumbent party's time in office.* How long has the incumbent party controlled the presidency? The American public has showed a consistent preference to support change. A party that has been in power for a long time usually has made enough mistakes to lead citizens to vote for the other side.

Considering these three factors, it becomes clear that McCain faced a tough road. The economy was struggling. With the stock market and banking sector in turmoil, President Bush's popularity was the lowest of any president

LBJ Library Photo by the Democratic National Committee

The "Daisy spot" is perhaps the most famous negative ad in American history. Yet it was only aired once by President Lyndon Johnson in the 1964 campaign and in fact never explicitly mentioned his opponent, Senator Barry Goldwater (R-Ariz.). But Goldwater had made statements about possible use of nuclear weapons, and they made this ad so memorable.

prediction models:
Formulas that take into account an array of factors, such as a candidate's popularity or the state of the national economy, to project a winner.

since such measurements began in the 1930s. And finally, the Republicans had controlled the White House for eight years.

Congressional Campaigns and Issues

Nearly all congressional campaigns start with a primary election at which the party's official candidate is selected. The general election then follows.

The Decision to Run and the Primaries

Those who choose to run for Congress are usually visible residents of their district or state. Often they already hold a local or state-level elected office. They might, like Aaron Schock, be a school board member, city council member, or state legislator. Contenders with strong local roots can organize core supporters who volunteer time, and often money, to advance their candidacy. The contests that occur in between the four-year presidential election cycles are called **midterm elections**.

midterm elections:
Congressional elections held between the presidential elections.

The Fall Campaign

What is the personal background of your representative? Of your senators?

Following the primaries, the two winning candidates often revise their campaign message to attract more moderate voters. Anthony Downs explained this shift in message with the theory of the median voter, which argues that candidates in their quest for votes should adopt moderate positions on issues. If one candidate fails to do so, the other candidate can move to the center, winning a majority of votes and the election.[24] To win the general election, candidates usually need votes from party members as well as Independents and members of the opposing party. It is for these reasons that elections are often battles over the so-called middle.

Issues

Congressional elections do not draw as much attention as presidential elections, but they involve many of the same issues. Money and fundraising are concerns, and again the FEC sets limits. Voters almost always reelect House and Senate members, so whether congressional elections actually serve to hold Congress accountable is a question for American democracy. Voters know less about these candidates than about those in presidential elections, suggesting perhaps there is not much accountability. Nevertheless, the composition of Congress changes in response to conditions in the country. If times are good, the party in power is rewarded. In general, the pattern of

Republican and Democratic gains and losses indicates that voters hold members of Congress accountable and that Congress is, therefore, a responsive institution.

Fundraising and Money.   A key element in launching and running a congressional campaign is fundraising. Every campaign needs an office, staff members, computers, posters and pamphlets, a website, and money for television and radio ads. Senate campaigns generally cost more than House campaigns.

Federal campaign finance laws set the same limits on congressional elections as on presidential elections: an individual can contribute up to $2,400 to a candidate for the primary election in 2010, and the same amount for the general election. Individuals can contribute to candidates in different races, up to a total of $45,600 for primaries and the same amount for general election campaigns. Candidates also raise money from PACs, which are limited to donating $5,000 for a primary election, and $5,000 for a general election, to a single candidate.[25]

The amount of money required to wage a competitive contest for a seat in Congress is formidable, and it gives an advantage to those who are personally wealthy and able to make good use of personal or business connections. In 2006, on average, a challenger had to raise at least $1.5 million to win a seat in the House of Representatives, and an incumbent had to raise at least $1.2 million to keep his or her seat. For Senate races, on average a challenger had to raise $8.2 million and an incumbent $9 million.[26]

The Role of Political Parties.   Of the other sources of financial support available to candidates, the most important is the political party. Parties are forbidden by campaign finance laws from actively coordinating a specific individual's congressional or senatorial campaign, but local parties can engage in general activities, such as voter registration drives, partisan rallies, and get-out-the-vote efforts on election day that help party-endorsed candidates at every level.

The role of national political parties in congressional elections is more complex. They can pay for campaign training for candidates and their staffs, hold general party fundraisers, and buy campaign advertisements that attack the opposing candidate so long as they do not mention their party's candidate. They can also share lists of campaign donors and party members who are likely to volunteer their time to candidates' individual campaigns.

Both the Democratic and Republican parties have congressional campaign organizations designed to recruit and support candidates for the House and Senate. These party committees are arms of the congressional party leadership, and they can choose to be more or less supportive of incumbents seeking reelection, depending on how loyal the incumbents have been to the

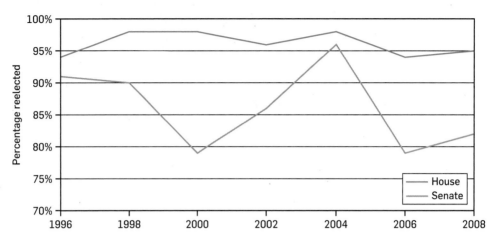

FIGURE 10.4 Reelection Rates of Incumbents in Congress, 1996–2008.
Source: Open Secrets / Bruce Oppenheimer.

party. In 2006, these national party committees spent more than $230 million overall, with about $150 million devoted to House races, and $80 million to Senate races.[27]

Incumbency Advantage.   Incumbents almost always win.[28] In House races, they are reelected about 95 percent of the time, and in Senate races, at least 80 percent of the time (see Figure 10.4). In the last two decades, more than 70 percent of House incumbents received 60 percent or more of the vote. And since the 1960s, the number of competitive races has been in decline, a trend called **vanishing marginals**. The idea here is that fewer and fewer congressional elections are competitive. Such districts are often referred to as **safe seats**. These high rates of incumbent reelection may indicate that incumbents are doing a good job, especially with constituent services that build support with voters (see also Chapter 11, Congress). Or they might raise concerns about whether elections really foster accountability. Concerns about the lack of accountability are extensive enough that some observers call for **term limits**, which would force members to retire after serving a maximum number of terms.

More turnover actually occurs in the House than the data in Figure 10.4 suggest. Members often engage in **strategic retirement**, deciding against running for reelection when the outcome is likely to be unfavorable. Incumbents also win reelection at high rates because they are known commodities to their constituents. Name recognition for House and Senate incumbents is over 80 percent. Being an incumbent can be a disadvantage, however, if one's party falls out of favor with voters. This was the case in 1994, 2006, and 2010, when a large number of incumbents of the party in power lost seats in the House and the Senate. In 1994 and 2006 Congress changed hands, becoming Republican in 1994 and Democratic in 2006. In 2010, voters handed the Republicans major victories that allowed them to take control of the House and significantly

vanishing marginals: *Trend marking the decline of competitive congressional elections.*

safe seat: *Seat in Congress considered to be reliably held by one party or the other.*

term limits: *Rule restricting the number of terms an elected official can be in a given office.*

Why do incumbents usually win reelection?

strategic retirement: *Decision to retire from Congress based on the unlikelihood of winning the next election.*

Are term limits for Congress a good idea? What are the pros and the cons?

reduce the Democratic majority in the Senate. Usually such a strong tide would have swept both chambers, but the Democrats held fifty-nine seats prior to the election, enough of a cushion for them to sustain losses but maintain control.

Relative Lack of Interest. Voting rates in congressional elections, particularly in midterm elections, are always lower than in presidential elections. Presidential elections are "high-stimulus" elections, whereas congressional elections are "low-stimulus." The attention and excitement of a presidential election means that voters are bombarded with information about the contest. Congressional elections generate far less attention. A major consequence of these differences is that voters in congressional elections often do not know much about the candidates.

As a result, voting is driven largely by two major forces: partisanship and incumbency. Voters follow **party identification** and vote for their party's candidates. And, as we have seen, voters also tend to vote for incumbents. There is also the effect of **presidential coattails**—that is, a popular president running for reelection brings additional party candidates into office. Voters going to the polls in "high-stimulus" elections to vote for president cast ballots for other members of the party for lower-level offices. While scholars debate this effect, it is clear that the partisan makeup of Congress reflects the popularity of the president or presidential candidate.[29] The normal occurrence is that the president's party loses seats in midterm elections. Only three times in the last twenty-one midterm elections (1930–2010) has the president's party gained seats. The average seat loss for the president's party in midterm elections is about twenty-five. Nevertheless, the extent of these losses, or whether they can even be turned into gains, depends on the approval rating of the president. In 2010 the pendulum swung back and the Republicans captured more than 60 seats, giving them control of the House.

party identification: *Attachment or allegiance to a political party; partisanship.*

presidential coattails: *Effect of a popular presidential or presidential candidate has on congressional elections, boosting votes for members of his party.*

What is the basis for your vote in the 2010 congressional elections?

The Practice and Theory of Voting

Americans enjoy near universal opportunities to vote. Even so, no one should assume such opportunities have always existed or that they are permanent. Despite the widespread belief in the importance of elections for democratic institutions, some Americans have argued that voting rights should not be universal. Voting, in short, is a gateway to power, and so there are always battles over who gets access to the ballot. In this section, we examine the arguments.

Competing Views of Participation

Debates about voting, and the removal of obstacles to voting, often centered on whether potential voters would be qualified to cast ballots. Others worried that too much participation yields too many demands on government, making government less able to respond to these demands.

We label these ideas the **Hamiltonian model of participation**. Alexander Hamilton represents a perspective that sees risks in greater participation and, thus, favors a larger role for **elites**. In this model, not only would the quality of the decision be diluted by more participation, but government would be less able to advance the national interest of the country because it would be responding to uninformed voters. The Hamiltonian model stands in stark contrast to the **Jeffersonian model**, which holds that more participation yields a more involved and engaged public and that, in turn, produces better outcomes.[30] In other words, democracy thrives with more democracy. Thomas Jefferson had more faith than Hamilton in the people's ability and worried that excessive reliance on elites would make government less responsive to its citizens.

Figure 10.5 offers a summary of these competing views. Proponents of the Hamiltonian model do seek accountability, but they place much more faith in the ability of elites than in the general public to make the right decisions. The people, they contend, are often uninformed and cannot make the best choices. In contrast, proponents of the Jeffersonian model want to see more participation, believing that the people can be trusted and that getting more people involved will push government to be more responsive to the people's interests. They contend that if certain groups of people are disenfranchised, government will be less responsive. It may be that people are not well informed about politics, but if they have a chance to be involved, they will become better informed. An informed citizenry that actively participates in politics will ensure that government is both accountable and responsive.

Obviously the Jeffersonian model holds equality as an important political value, whereas the Hamiltonian model places more emphasis on efficient and effective outcomes. The reality of which groups evidence greater voting participation leads to a more thorough understanding of the electoral gateway.

Hamiltonian model of participation: *View of participation that suggests that too much participation is a bad thing and that many people are not well-enough informed to cast votes.*

elites: *Well-educated and often wealthy people who lead public opinion, such as journalists, politicians, and policy makers.*

Jeffersonian model of participation: *View of participation that suggests more is better. That is, as people get involved more they learn more about politics and want to get even more involved.*

Do you lean toward the Hamiltonian or the Jeffersonian model of participation?

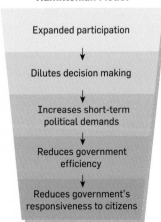

FIGURE 10.5 Hamiltonian and Jeffersonian Models of Participation.

Who Votes?

Voting is an important gateway to influence, but not everyone has the inclination or the desire to do so. Yet failure to vote has real implications for the political process, for it affects which representatives govern and make laws, and these have real policy consequences that affect everyone in the United States. Low turnout raises questions about government's responsiveness, and unequal turnout by various demographic groups suggests that government's response is unequal, too. Low turnout among young people, for example, as opposed to older Americans, means that elected officials may give more attention to issues affecting senior voters, such as Social Security, than to issues affecting younger voters, such as the costs of education (see Figure 10.6). In this section, we examine turnout rates generally, and then look at turnout rates by various demographic groups.

Turnout

Even with widespread opportunity to cast ballots and shape the course of government, Americans often choose not to vote. In 1996, less than half of the eligible electorate (about 48 percent) took the time to vote. By 2008, the rate of participation improved to over 57 percent. But presidential elections are high-stimulus events. In midterm congressional elections, which are low-stimulus elections, turnout is usually less than 40 percent. For primary elections during presidential nominations, turnout is even lower. In the all-important New Hampshire presidential primary, turnout is often less than 40 percent, and that represents the high end in the primaries and caucuses that decide party nominees. If we consider local school board elections, we find an even smaller electorate. Often, less than 10 percent of eligible citizens votes in these contests. A general assessment of turnout in the United States is offered later in the chapter. Here, we turn to the demographics of turnout.

FIGURE 10.6 Gap in Voter Turnout by Age in Presidential Elections, 1972–2008. Young voters (ages 18–29) have turned out in greater numbers in the last two presidential elections, but their rate of turnout is less than that for people over 30, decreasing the likelihood that government will be responsive to young people's interests. *Source:* Nonprofit Voter Engagement Network, America Goes to the Polls, "Voting Gaps in the 2008 Election," October 2009.

The Demographics of Turnout

Given the important power that voting brings in a democracy, a central question becomes: Who votes? Do various demographic groups vote in equal proportions? If not, what are the consequences for government responsiveness? The following sections answer these questions with statistics. The data suggest that those who are most likely to vote tend to be better educated, better paid, and older. There are some modest race and gender differences. But when scholars control for differences in education and income, differences on race pretty much disappear.[31] The key lesson here is that the driving force of participation is developing the kinds of skills and habits as a young person that prepare one for active citizenship.

Why do better educated, better paid, and older people vote at higher rates than less educated, less well paid, younger voters? What is the effect on government?

Race and Ethnicity.   Whites have a slightly higher rate of participation than blacks. In 2004, 60 percent of blacks and 67 percent of whites voted. But by 2008, the gap disappeared: 66 percent of whites reported voting, whereas 65 percent of African Americans did so.

Other minority groups participate less frequently. About 47 percent of Asian Americans vote.[32] Native Americans appear to have the lowest rate of turnout, although precise estimates have been difficult to gather.[33] Latinos vote less frequently than whites or blacks, at about 50 percent. But it is clear that Latino voting rates are increasing and will become a more significant force in U.S. elections. In 1988, Latinos constituted less than 4 percent of voters. Twenty years later, the proportion had more than doubled to nearly 8 percent.[34]

In general, turnout rates among ethnic minorities tend to be below the average for the entire country. Part of the reason for this gap is that these groups often tend to be less well off, and lower income generally means lower turnout. In other cases, many of the individuals are not eligible to vote because they are not citizens. This is especially true for Asians and Latinos.

Sex.   Women turn out at a slightly higher rate than men, by perhaps 3–5 percentage points. In 2008, 68 percent of women reported voting and 62 percent of men claimed to have cast ballots.[35] The **gender gap** is important in American politics. But the gap focuses mostly on different political preferences, such as the greater tendency of women to identify themselves as Democrats than men. The gap in turnout is far less consequential.

gender gap: *Differences in the political attitudes and behavior of men and women.*

Age.   Age affects rates of participation. Turnout peaks once voters are about 45 years old and continues at that rate until advanced age sets in (about 80 years or older). Even when differences in education and income are controlled for, participation remains higher for older Americans. In 2004, around 70 percent of citizens over 65 years old claim to have voted. The proportion is just 47 percent for those under 24 years of age.

Income. The higher one's income, the more likely one is to vote. More income generally means that the person has more at stake and thus more reason to vote. Political knowledge is strongly correlated with the propensity to vote. Further, individuals with higher incomes are more likely to be able to arrange to vote than those with low-paying jobs, who may be less able to take time off from work to vote.

Data from the Census Bureau strongly document this pattern. In 2004, over 80 percent of those with total family incomes of more than $100,000 report that they went to the polls. For the income range that represents the median annual family income in America, which is $40,000 to $50,000, turnout is 69 percent. For the least well off (those earning less than $20,000), the proportion who claim to have voted is 48 percent. As we show later (Figure 10.8), this pattern is consistent.

Education. Although race and ethnicity, sex, age, and income have some effects on the propensity of people to vote, years of formal education seem to be the most important influence on the tendency of someone to vote. Social science research has documented this connection between education and voting.[36] When the youngest voting-eligible citizens (18- to 24-year-olds) have a college degree, they are 14 percentage points more likely to vote than older citizens (65 and above) who do not have a high school education.[37] Table 10.1 indicates propensity to vote by education from 1988 to 2008. The gap between those with the least education and those with the most is 50 percentage points in 2008, a huge difference. Nearly three-fourths of college-educated people vote, whereas less than one-quarter of those with just a grade school education vote.

The relationship between education and voting may not be as simple as these data suggest, however. New evidence indicates that going to college

TABLE 10.1 **Rates of Turnout (percent) in Presidential Elections by Education, 1988–2008**

	1988	1992	1996	2000	2004	2008
Education						
8 years or less	37	35	30	27	24	23
Less than high school	41	41	34	34	34	27
High school	55	58	49	49	50	50
Less than college	65	69	61	60	66	65
College or more	78	81	73	72	74	73

Source: Stanley, Harold W., and Richard G. Niemi, *Vital Statistics on American Politics 2009–2010* (Washington, D.C.: CQ Press, 2010).

socialization: *Process of learning the customs, attitudes, and values of one's social group, community, or culture.*

does not matter as much as childhood **socialization**, which imbues the values of citizenship and similarly affects the decision to attend college. It is not, therefore, spending four years in college that makes college graduates more likely to vote. Rather, it is having been raised in an environment that stresses the importance of education that shapes willingness to vote.[38]

This gap in turnout between higher-educated people and those with little education has increased over the last forty or so years. This increase can be explained by increased access to education. Individuals who lack a high school education are at a much bigger disadvantage than in the past. These patterns suggest that inequalities may result as government responds more effectively to those who vote than those who do not.

Why Vote?

With the right to vote guaranteed and widely available, why do some people choose not to vote, and some groups prove more likely to vote than others? Perhaps we can start to answer that question by reversing it, that is, by looking at why people do vote. Political scientists have developed three approaches to explain why eligible voters choose to cast ballots. One model draws from the field of economics, a second draws from psychology, and a third focuses on the rules and context of the election. In this section we present these explanations, as well as some new ideas about the relationship between socialization and voting.

An Economic Model of Voting

self-interest: *Concern for one's own advantage and well-being.*

Did you vote in the in the 2010 midterm election? Why or why not?

The economic model of voting starts with the assumption that all choices involve a calculation about **self-interest** that balances costs and benefits. According to the economic model, citizens consider the costs and benefits of voting, and if the benefits exceed the costs, they turn out. So, according to this model, if voting becomes less costly to all citizens, there should be a rise in participation. If it becomes more costly, fewer people will turn out. Voters, under this model, act in a rational, self-interested fashion.

public good: *Goods or benefits provided by government from which everyone benefits and no one can be excluded.*

The benefits of voting are less clear. If benefits are defined in a narrow, self-interested fashion, there are no tangible benefits to be had from voting. A voter may favor a candidate (or party) because of a specific policy, such as a promise of a tax cut that would provide a big financial benefit. But a tax cut is a **public good** that is shared by all in society, regardless of whether one votes or not. Moreover, and perhaps most important, the chance that one vote will alter the outcome of the election is very small—so small in fact that there is a greater chance of being killed in an accident on the way to the polls than of changing the outcome of the election. Thus, given that there are some financial costs to voting, why should a self-interested person participate?

In short, the conclusion of the economic model was that voting was not in one's self-interest and in fact is irrational. If the decision to vote is driven by a self-interested assessment of costs and benefits, people should not take the time to vote. That is a troubling conclusion for the workings of democratic government. Obviously, if citizens do not bother to vote, then government cannot be responsive and public officials will not be held accountable. Yet many people do cast ballots, so the economic model of voting has clear weaknesses. Political scientists, instead, tend to think of voting as more of a psychological process than as a narrow economic or self-interested process.

What can, or should, government do to lower the "cost" of voting?

A Psychological Model of Voting

The psychological model views voting as a product of citizens' attitudes about the political system. These attitudes are often a product of socialization and early political experiences. Those who are raised in households in which voting is important are likely to think that participation matters. Those who have a strong sense of trust in government or believe that their vote matters are more likely to participate.

Another psychological component tied to the act of voting is **partisanship**. Those citizens who align themselves with the Democratic or the Republican parties are more likely to vote. Being a partisan implies an engagement in politics, and partisans see a great stake in the outcome of elections. Partisanship increases the prospects that an individual will vote.

partisanship: *Attachment or allegiance to a political party; party identification.*

Both civic duty and partisanship are attitudes formed in childhood. The relationship between socialization and voting holds even after education and other important variables that drive participation are taken into account. Socialization continues to have a long and powerful reach.

It is also clear that citizens who express greater trust in government are more willing to participate. In addition, people who think they have a voice in government are more likely to vote. Political scientists call this attitude **efficacy**—the belief that one's involvement influences the course of government.

efficacy: *Extent to which people believe their actions can have an impact on public affairs and the actions of government.*

An Institutional Model of Voting

A third explanation of voting looks at political context. In the **institutional model**, voting is understood to be shaped by the rules of the system, by political party behavior, by the ways candidates run their campaigns, and by the context of the election.[39] This model does not ignore individuals' personal resources or psychological attitudes; it simply points out that the political environment is a factor that shapes participation.

institutional model: *Model of voting that focuses on the context of the election, including whether it is close and whether the rules encourage or discourage participation.*

The competitiveness of an election also influences motivation. Elections that look to be close draw voters' interest and attention, especially if they think their votes might influence the outcome. A close race is exciting and people like to be part of it. But elections often are not competitive, lessening the incentive citizens have for making the time to cast their ballots.

Because voting takes time, efforts by parties, interest groups, or civic organizations to bring people to the polls can make a difference. "Get-out-the-vote" drives seem to pay big dividends, especially at the local level. For example, direct personal contact, such as going door to door, may increase the rate of voting by 7–10 percentage points in local elections.[40] Parties, too, can increase turnout by mobilizing their base to participate.[41] Efforts to help people vote can obviously alter citizens' decisions to vote.

Have you participated in, or been contacted by, a get-out-the-vote program? What was the effect on you?

Assessing Turnout

As this chapter has established, most Americans do not vote in most elections. Even in presidential elections, for which turnout is highest, only slightly more than half of eligible voters actually go to the polls. In this section we assess turnout in the United States. Is it too low for responsive, and responsible, government? Even more important, does turnout increase the prospects of governmental action that ensures equality? These two questions are addressed here.

Is Turnout Low?

There is a widespread belief among political scientists, political observers, and journalists that turnout in American elections is "low." Certainly, when less than 40 percent of the American public took the time to vote in the 2006 congressional elections, the concern about low turnout expressed in these books seems justified. Even with all the attention and interest surrounding the 2008 presidential elections, turnout of the voting age population was about 57 percent.[42] Such percentages strike many as disappointing. But further investigation of turnout can offer a different way to assess what some consider to be a problem.

What does it mean for democracy when only 40 percent of Americans vote in midterm elections?

The United States Compared to Other Democracies.
Compared to other democracies, turnout in the United States is near the very bottom. The average rate of turnout in U.S. presidential elections between 1945 and 2008 was 56 percent. In Australia, turnout is 95 percent; in Malta it is 98 percent. The only country that is significantly lower than the United States is Afghanistan, where turnout is 48 percent. A survey of twenty-five nations reveals that a typical rate of participation is about 71 percent— 15 percentage points more than in the United States.[43] These numbers compel an assessment of why U.S. turnout is so low.

One reason has to do with rules for voting. Australia has **compulsory voting**. That is, citizens are required by law to vote. Those who do not vote receive a $20 fine, and the fine increases to $50 if the nonvoter does not answer the Australian Election Commission's inquiry as to why he or she did not vote. New Zealand requires all citizens to register to vote. In most of the countries of western Europe, the government is responsible for registering citizens to vote. In the United States, by contrast, both voting and registering are voluntary, and only about 70 percent of the public is registered to vote. That means that nearly one-third of potentially eligible voters cannot cast a vote at the polls on election day even if they want to do so.

Another reason has to do with the convenience of voting. Most European countries lessen the costs of voting by allowing voting to take place on Sunday. In the United States, voting takes place on Tuesday, a workday for most people. Federal law stipulates that the first Tuesday after the first Monday in November is the day on which voting for president and members of Congress will take place, and most states have also selected Tuesdays as the day for voting in primaries and in state and local elections. Holding voting on a workday increases the costs of voting, because people are often at work and may have difficulty finding the time to vote. With more costs to voting, turnout is lower in the United States than in many European democracies. This discussion highlights the importance of considering the context of each election, which is the theoretical focus of the institutional model of voting.

According to one estimate, turnout in the United States would be 27 percentage points higher (or more than 80 percent) if the nation had laws and rules that foster voting.[44] At the least, this figure suggests that comparisons of turnout in various democracies require a careful accounting of the rules and institutions that shape the willingness of citizens to go to the polls.

Trends in Turnout.
A second way turnout in American elections looks problematic is to examine the trend over the last fifty years. One of the lines in Figure 10.7 (on p. 347) represents the percentage of turnout in presidential elections measured against the **voting age population (VAP)**, or the number of voters eligible to vote. In the United States, all citizens over 18 years old constitute the VAP. The graph shows that there has been an overall decline in voting since 1960, despite a recent upswing. This pattern is much the same for midterm elections. In 1962, turnout for congressional elections was 48 percent. It fell to a low of 38 percent in 1986, with a slight rebound to about 40 percent in 2006.

This downward trend becomes more worrisome in light of rising levels of education since 1960, as education is one of the strongest predictors of turnout. Even though education levels have increased over the last fifty years (see Table 10.1), the rate of participation in elections has not increased.

compulsory voting: *Practice that requires citizens to vote in elections or face punitive measures such as community service, fines, or imprisonment.*

Should the United States adopt compulsory voting?

Should the United States vote on Saturday or Sunday instead of a weekday?

voting age population (VAP): *Used to calculate the rate of participation by dividing the number of voters by the number of people in the country who are over 18 (and hence able to vote).*

generational replace-
ment: *Cycle whereby
younger generations replace
older generations in the
electorate.*

These data have led political scientists to study why fewer Americans seem to be voting.[45] Their explanations have varied. One explanation lies in the difference between those who enter the electorate and those who leave. The concept of **generational replacement** describes a trend in which older voters who pass away and leave the electorate are replaced by less reliable young voters.[46] It is very difficult, however, to sort out generational differences from changes in self-interest. That is, do older voters turn out to vote because of the generation they were part of, or because they are just older and have more experience in dealing with politics, or because they want to protect their interests or expand the benefits that directly affect them, such as Medicare and low payments for prescription drugs?

A second explanation has been the decline of party organizations.[47] Local parties have been less able to turn out the vote on election day than they were in the late nineteenth and early twentieth century, and therefore the voting rate has declined. Some scholars have estimated that half of the decline in turnout can be attributed to the drop in mobilization efforts.[48] This explanation has appeal, but parties in many ways are stronger today than they were in the past. The Republican Party was successful in turning out the vote in 2004, especially in key states like Ohio,[49] and citizens are voting more along party lines than any time since scientific surveys began in the 1950s. So a decline in party strength (perceived or real) is not an adequate explanation for low turnout.

A third explanation for declining turnout is the increasingly harsh tone of political campaigns. Some argue that negative campaigns have fueled voter apathy. It is clear that negative advertising on TV often fosters voters' disgust with politics. About 80 percent of the public say they do not like these campaign tactics.[50] Initial studies suggested that negative campaigns could decrease turnout by about 5 percentage points.[51] Moreover, there is clear evidence that negativity in campaigns has been on the rise since the 1960s so there was an apparent correlation between the two trends.[52] Scholars and pundits rushed to endorse this hypothesis. But subsequent studies have called this hypothesis into question.[53] A harsh campaign is likely to be competitive, and competitive campaigns draw interest and therefore increase turnout. Further, negative attacks can activate partisanship, which also increases turnout. It is often the case that people choose a party affiliation in part because they do not like members of the opposite party. An attack ad by the Republicans can remind their supporters why they oppose the Democrats, giving them more reason to participate. A recent comprehensive study of all research on this topic shows quite clearly that negativity is not responsible for a decline in turnout.[54]

What effect do negative ads have on you?

The Voting Eligible Population Measure. Two political scientists, Samuel Popkin and Michael McDonald, offer a fourth explanation by

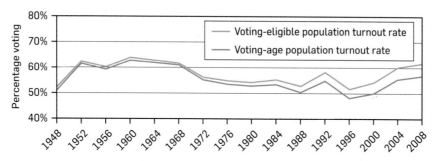

FIGURE 10.7 Presidential Turnout Rates, 1948–2008. The VAP measure is the traditional approach to assessing turnout, dividing the number of voters by the "voting age population." The VEP seeks to correct for overcounting in the voting age population by removing illegal immigrants and those in jail who are not in fact eligible to vote. Until 1972, this correction made only a modest difference. But with the surge of immigration and growth in the number of convicted felons since that time, the VEP measure is more accurate. Turnout in the 2004 and 2008 elections is actually comparable to turnout in the 1950s and 1960s. *Source:* http://elections.gmu.edu/voter_turnout.htm.

arguing that turnout has not declined over the last thirty years: the VAP measure has been in error because it does not take into account increases in the numbers of convicted felons and immigrants who are ineligible to vote. The number of immigrants is estimated to be about 13 million (or about 4 percent of the population).[55] Over the last twenty years there has also been nearly a three-fold increase in the number of people in prison (from 585,000 to 1.6 million), reflecting tougher sentencing in American courts of law.[56]

Popkin and McDonald correct for these trends by introducing a new measure called the **voting eligible population (VEP)**. The second line in Figure 10.7 presents the VEP estimates for turnout. It indicates that in the 2008 presidential election turnout was actually about 62 percent. By this measure, turnout has *not* declined over the last thirty years. In fact, measured against turnout in the presidential election of 1948, which was 52 percent, turnout is now a full 10 percentage points higher. These revised estimates put a new spin on what has been perceived as a problem with U.S. elections, suggesting that Americans are not less willing to vote than in the past, or than citizens in other democracies.

voting eligible population (VEP): *Used to calculate the rate of participation by dividing the number of voters by the number of people in the country who are eligible rather than just able to vote.*

Do Turnout Rates Promote Inequality?

Voting is a hallmark of democratic politics and is certainly a cherished American value. Yet the fact that those who are better educated or better off participate at a greater rate is a potential source for concern. Further, the income gap between the rich and the poor is increasing.[57] With the rich becoming richer,

Do Americans have equality in voting? Explain.

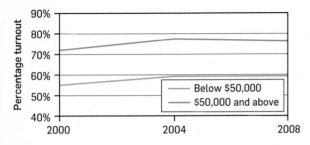

FIGURE 10.8 **Voter Turnout by Income, 2000–2008.** *Source:* Nonprofit Voter Engagement Network, America Goes to the Polls, "Voting Gaps in the 2008 Election," October 2009.

they are even better able to contribute money to parties and candidates.[58] Such donations only further advance their potential influence.

The data in Figure 10.8 indicate that individuals making over $50,000 a year are much more likely to vote than those making less than $50,000 a year. The pattern is consistent. In 2008, for instance, 76 percent of people with incomes above $50,000 participated in the 2008 elections. For those making less than $50,000, the proportion declined to 59 percent.[59] The 2000 and 2004 elections tell the same story.

Participation Beyond Voting

Voting is by far the most common form of participation. But in a democracy, citizens have the opportunity to express their views in other ways. In fact, voting is a very constrained form of participation. Voters select from among a limited set of candidates, and the ballot permits them to support only one of them. There is no way to tell from a single vote whether that citizen agrees or disagrees with the candidate on the key issues of the day. But the American political system gives individuals the opportunity to express their preferences and the intensity of those preferences in other ways. Although far smaller numbers of Americans join political campaigns or protest movements, both are important gateways for the expression of political views.

Aside from voting, how have you participated in politics and civic life?

Involvement in Political Campaigns

Campaigns give citizens a chance to talk about politics, volunteer, promote an issue they care about, and make financial donations to candidates and causes. At the same time, the weeks prior to an election provide candidates and various interest groups a chance to connect with the public. The campaign is an important gateway that allows for the public to influence politics and for politicians to influence the public.

As a result, political scientists try to understand the motivations for people's involvement in campaigns and the nature of their involvement. Do Americans try to influence other citizens to vote a certain way? Table 10.2 reports the percentage of Americans who say they do. Over the last few decades, about 40 percent of Americans have reported that they talk about presidential politics with their fellow citizens.[60] In 2008, 45 percent of Americans said they tried to influence others' votes, a greater than 50 percent jump from 1996. In another poll, nearly two-thirds of Americans claimed to be

TABLE 10.2 Nonvoting Measures of Political Participation (percent), 1980–2008

	Tried to Influence Others' Votes	Attended a Political Meeting	Worked for a Party or Candidate	Wore a Button or Displayed a Bumper Sticker	Gave Money to a Campaign
1980	36	8	4	7	8
1984	32	8	4	9	8
1988	29	7	3	9	9
1992	37	8	3	11	7
1996	28	5	2	10	8
2000	34	5	3	10	9
2004	48	7	3	21	13
2008	45	9	4	18	14

Source: American National Election Study, 1948–2008.

"more excited and interested in voting" in the 2008 campaign than in recent contests.[61]

By contrast, the proportion of people who work in a campaign has been small and very stable over the last three decades (see Table 10.2), hovering around 3 percent. Nearly 10 percent of citizens attended a political meeting during the course of the 2008 campaign. Willingness to give money to a campaign was a bit higher, reaching 14 percent in 2008. More citizens also claimed to display a bumper sticker or wear a button than engaging in other campaign activities except trying to influence others' votes.

Have you ever contributed time or money to a political campaign? Why or why not?

This body of evidence about political participation suggests some important conclusions. First, if "active" citizens are defined as individuals who vote and engage in at least one of the activities reported in Table 10.2, nearly 40 percent meet the standard over this twenty-eight-year period. More than 15 percent of the public voted and engaged in two of these activities. Second, recent presidential elections have shown a real jump in these kinds of political activities. More people were willing to give money, wear campaign buttons, and try to influence others' votes. Such increases underscore the importance of the contest to many voters and indicate the American public's willingness to engage in politics when elections matter to them.

Some might wonder whether 15 percent is an impressive number. A comparison to other countries can put it in perspective. In 2004, 44 percent of Americans tried to persuade others how to cast their ballots. In Brazil, the proportion was 37 percent; in France, it was 29 percent; and in Sweden, it was just 13 percent.[62] The same pattern holds for attending a meeting or displaying a bumper sticker. Americans are far more engaged in campaigns than citizens in other democracies.

Protest Politics

Political protests are an important means for expressing opinion and bringing about change. The **Boston Tea Party** is perhaps the first and most famous American protest, as the protesters dumped tea into Boston Harbor rather than support the British government-backed monopoly. More recently, protests over the 2009 stimulus package and 2010 health care reform have sought to recall the spirit of the "Boston Tea Party" by calling their gatherings "tea parties."[63] Upset with the massive amount of spending enacted by Congress in the last few years, these protesters were calling for a return of small government.

Throughout American history, abolitionists seeking an end to slavery, women seeking to vote, working people seeking the right to strike and organize unions, civil rights activists calling for an end to segregation and discrimination, antiwar activists seeking to end the war in Vietnam and the war in Iraq, and many others have called attention to their causes though marches, street demonstrations, petitions, and advertising campaigns.

How is the Boston Tea Party like, and not like, the Tea Party protesters?

In general, very few Americans actually participate in protests. In March 2003, only 3 percent of the public claimed to have joined any of the "recent antiwar protests."[64] Overall, only about 5 percent of Americans claim to have participated in a "protest, march, or demonstration" over the last five years. Australians report a three times greater willingness to engage in such activities. In Spain and France, about 25 percent of the citizenry claim to have undertaken such an act.[65] High rates of protest activities in other

Does the fact that few Americans protest mean they are satisfied with government? What does it mean?

Library of Congress

The American colonists hated the British tax on tea, but the famous Boston Tea Party, December 16, 1773, was also a protest against the monopoly over the tea trade that the British had given the struggling East India Company. This 1846 lithograph has become a classic image of the event.

HALEY/SIPA/AP Images

In 2009–10, critics of taxes, big government generally, and government spending in the Stimulus Bill and the health care reform act came together to label their protests "tea parties."

democracies can be attributed to strong labor parties—some of them socialist and Communist—that make protests common and symbolic.

E-Participation

In the past decade, many Americans have engaged in politics through e-mail and the Internet. It is easier and cheaper to send an e-mail to a member of Congress than to write a letter, and Americans do so with increasing frequency. In 1998, members of Congress received over 23 million e-mails; two years later, that number had doubled to 48 million.[66] Recent figures are not available, but that number has surely exploded over the last decade, underscoring the ease and convenience of e-mail, and transforming the way voters communicate with their politicians.

Participation in blogs and other e-communications will continue to rise. As of May 2008, nearly 75 percent of the public made at least occasional use of e-mail or the Internet.[67] Of those who have access to e-information, as much as 20 percent claim to participate in blogs, online discussions, or e-mail lists for political issues of interest.[68] These data suggest that, overall, about 14 percent of the public may be participating in politics through blogs.

The Internet has also transformed fundraising and campaign involvement. Candidates have made use of the Internet and have developed websites and various outreach programs. The Internet is a means to gather small contributions cheaply, as Barack Obama's 2008 campaign for president exemplifies.[69] Obama broke all records for fundraising during the primary, raising $32 million in January 2008, $28 million via the Internet.[70] In fact, David Plouffe, Obama's campaign manager, argued in 2009 that the ability to raise money through the Internet had been a key ingredient to Obama's winning the election. Formerly, it cost more to secure a $25 donation than it was worth, but now campaigns solicit contributions as small as $5. Ron Paul, who ran for the Republican nomination for president in 2008, raised $4 million on the Internet in a single day.[71]

Voting Laws and Regulations

The rules surrounding voting alter participation rates. State governments continue to manage most voting laws and procedures, though the federal government steps in to prevent discrimination at the polls. Both state and federal governments are committed to increasing participation by making voting as easy as possible. At the same time, both work to prevent voter fraud. Thus, policy making regarding voting is undertaken at both the federal and state levels, and it has the effect of both expanding and potentially contracting turnout. This section reviews recent policies that have altered how voting works in the United States.

The National Voter Registration Act and Voter Identification

In 1993, Congress sought to streamline voter registration procedures so that more Americans would exercise their right to vote, at least in federal elections. The National Voter Registration Act, commonly known as the "Motor Voter" law, requires states to allow citizens to register to vote at the same time they apply for or renew their driver's license. This law also requires that states inform citizens if they are removed from the approved voter roll and limits removal to a change of address, conviction for a felony, and, of course, death. The 1993 law imposes criminal penalties on anyone who tries to coerce or intimidate voters on their way to the polling place or tries to prevent registered voters from casting their ballots.[72]

Should government take steps to increase voting? Why?

To avoid voter fraud, many states have now instituted voter identification requirements on election day. Seven states (Florida, Georgia, Indiana, Louisiana, Hawaii, Michigan, and South Dakota) require photo identification at the polls on election day. Two states (Kansas and Pennsylvania) require photo ID of first-time voters only. Eighteen other states require personal identification but not necessarily a photo ID, and the remaining twenty-three states do not require identification on election day.

The implementation of voter identification requirements on election day has been controversial, and opponents sued in federal court to strike down Indiana's photo identification law. The fundamental issue in this case was whether state laws that were intended to prevent voter fraud had the result of preventing citizens who were legally entitled to vote from doing so because of a lack of proper identification. Indiana argued that the requirement of a photo ID was not unduly burdensome because the state provided voter identification cards if citizens had no other photo ID. But the opponents argued that the process of getting such a card was too complicated and the overall effect of the law would be to disenfranchise thousands of citizens. In 2008, the Supreme Court upheld the Indiana law by a 6–3 vote. Justice John Paul Stevens wrote on behalf of the majority, "The state interests identified as justifications for [the law] are both neutral and sufficiently strong to require us to reject" the lawsuit. However, Justice David Souter wrote in dissent that "Indiana has made no such justification [for the statute] and as to some aspects of its law, it hardly even tried." Further, Souter said this law "threatens to impose nontrivial burdens on the voting right of tens of thousands of the state's citizens."[73]

Is it a good idea or a bad one to require voters to show a photo ID before voting?

With the Hamiltonian and Jeffersonian views of voting in mind, it is important to decide what standards should be imposed for citizens to vote. Clearly, the federal government has taken steps to make the voting process easier and more convenient. But ultimately, states and localities administer and oversee elections, and states have responded inconsistently to these federal efforts. Some states appear to have made it easier to vote, but others, such as Indiana, have made it ostensibly harder to vote by requiring photo identification at the polling place. It would seem that, in a democracy, all citizens should have an equal opportunity to cast their votes because voting is the fundamental mechanism by which we hold government accountable. As states introduce more laws regarding identification, disparities in the opportunity to vote may be growing.

New Forms of Voting

At the same time, states are also experimenting with laws that make voting easier. Some have instituted "early voting," allowing voters to cast ballots prior to the Tuesday on which a general election is held. This flexibility helps working people, who might find it hard to find time to vote on a Tuesday. It also allows for more than a single day for voting, so that schedule conflicts (such as a dental appointment or a sick child) do not interfere. Other states, such as Oregon, have started to make use of a **vote-by-mail system**. Voters get ballots in the mail two weeks prior to the election, providing them a chance to research the candidates and cast their ballots. They can make their choices at home and avoid the often long lines at the polling booth. This innovation lowers the cost of voting, and it has increased participation. In 2004, 87 percent of registered voters in Oregon voted—the highest rate in the nation.[74]

In the future, other forms of voting may be used, including the Internet and cell phones. A study conducted in 2008 by Credo Mobile and the Student PIRGS sent text messages to 3,600 young mobile phone users chosen at random from a pool of 5,400 people who had registered to vote for the presidential primary. They found that just reminding voters through text messages to go to the polls on election day increased voter turnout by 4.6 percent. The study suggests that cell phone technology could increase voter turnout, so if citizens could actually vote via their cell phones or the Internet, voting rates might also rise, especially among the elderly and the handicapped who find it physically challenging to get to a polling place. Issues of security must be resolved, however, before these technologies can be widely employed.

vote-by-mail system:
Method of voting in an election whereby ballots are distributed to voters by post, completed, and returned by post.

What are the risks, and benefits, of early voting? Of voting by mail?

Elections, Campaigns, and Public Policy: Campaign Finance and Promises

Campaigns and elections are the key instruments of American democracy because they allow voters to judge their elected officials and replace them if they disapprove of their job performance. As such, the playing field of elections

Should elections be read as signals about the direction of public policy?

has to be fair, and the rules have to be enforced equally across all candidates, parties, and interest groups. The federal government has sought to enact rules with these goals in mind. Moreover, elections are intrinsically connected to public policy outcomes because politicians take them as indicators of which policies voters want the government to pursue. In this section we detail how the rules of campaigns are enforced and how closely policy follows from the promises that elected officials make to voters on the campaign trail.

Campaign Finance Laws

The 1971 Federal Election Campaign Act (FECA) transformed how campaigns are conducted and monitored, as it requires candidates, political parties, and PACs to disclose their campaign financial records. In 1974, Congress amended the law to set strict limits on how much money could be contributed by individuals, parties, and PACs to campaigns and, more important, created the Federal Election Commission as an independent agency to closely monitor campaign finance.[75] Senator James Buckley (R-N.Y.) challenged these rules on contributions on the grounds they interfered with freedom of speech (see also Chapter 4). The Supreme Court's decision in *Buckley v. Valeo* (1976) declared that limits on contributions and enforcement of those limitations were constitutional but that limits on how much money candidates spent were not constitutional.[76] In 2002, the Bipartisan Campaign Reform Act (BCRA) raised the legal contribution allowances for campaigns; prohibited political parties from accepting and spending unlimited amounts of money directly on campaigns; restricted the ability of interest groups to run campaign ads without fully identifying themselves; and prohibited them from running these ads within thirty days of a primary, and sixty days of the general election.[77] The 2010 ruling of the Supreme Court in *Citizens United v. Federal Election Commission* (see Supreme Court Cases in Chapter 8) undoes many of these restrictions, now allowing unions and businesses to spend money on campaigns.

The FEC takes its job seriously. If an individual citizen makes a complaint against a candidate, group, or political party for violating campaign finance law, the FEC will investigate that complaint. In 2006, in response to complaints about campaign-related behavior in the 2004 presidential election, the FEC

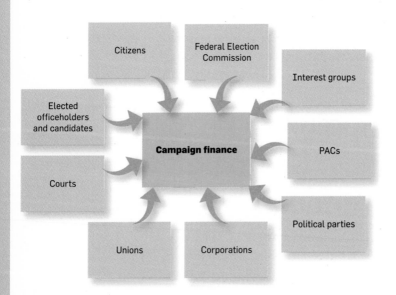

assigned stark penalties to three prominent advocacy groups—MoveOn.
org Voter Fund ($150,000), League of Conservation Voters ($180,000), and
the Swift Boat Veterans and POWs for Truth ($299,500)—for violations of
campaign finance laws. Note that the FEC's enforcement decisions are even-
handed, not favoring or targeting groups representing one ideology or the
other. The FEC has been responsive to citizen concerns and continues to serve
as a tool whereby citizens can help ensure a fair playing field in elections.

Campaign Promises and Electoral Mandates

Elections are supposed to send signals to politicians about what policies should
be pursued, and winning candidates like to claim that their election constituted
a **mandate**, a clear signal from the public about the policies government should
pursue. The bigger a candidate's win, the stronger the belief in a mandate. But
how can an election result, even a lopsided one, be viewed as evidence of a
mandate? The key link between a campaign and a policy outcome is the extent
to which candidates are specific in their campaign promises. Vague promises do
not translate well into actual public policy because they fail to provide a blueprint for Congress and the public. Moreover, claiming a mandate presupposes
that the candidates' policies were sufficiently distinct or that voters' decisions
can be read as a real choice between two different plans for federal policies.

mandate: *Political power the president claims after a decisive electoral victory.*

Do you take campaign promises seriously?

If it is not possible to truly connect campaign promises to voters' decisions,
why do successful candidates claim mandates? Mandates serve a political purpose for the winners of campaigns in American politics in that they help persuade Congress, the media, and interest groups that the president has majority
public support for his program. Even without the specifics, when voters choose a
president by a large percentage over the opposition candidate, they are sending
a strong message that they have trust and confidence in him to run the country.
So long as the president does not stray too far from his campaign promises, he
can use the idea of a mandate to successfully accomplish his goals.

Party Platforms and Campaign Promises

Campaign promises are not made solely by presidential candidates. They are
also made by the party in the form of the **party platform**, which lays out
its vision for government. These party platforms are adopted at the national
conventions. Overall, one study has concluded that about 66 percent of campaign promises have been enacted, only about 10 percent were ignored, and
the remaining 20 percent or so were blocked in Congress.[78] A study comparing
campaign appeals in House elections to subsequent introduction and cospon-
sorship of legislation finds that House members also keep their promises.[79]

party platform: *Document that lays out a party's core beliefs and policy proposals for each presidential election.*

Has President Obama kept his promises? The data in Figure 10.9 suggest
that he has done a pretty good job of doing what he said he would do during
the campaign. He made 415 promises during the campaign and, fifteen months
into his term (March 2010), had broken only sixteen of them. A great many are

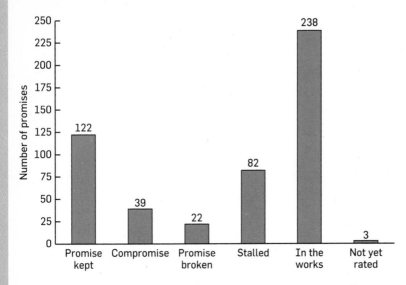

PolitiFact compiled more than five hundred promises that Barack Obama made during the campaign and has tracked their progress, rating those that are completed as "promise kept," "compromise," or "promise broken," and the others as "not yet rated," "in the works," or "stalled."

FIGURE 10.9 Obama's Campaign Promises Kept and Broken, as of October 1, 2010. Despite the common perception that politicians do not keep their campaign promises, these data suggest that President Barack Obama has at least tried to keep his. This pattern applies for politicians in general, including recent presidents George W. Bush and Bill Clinton. *Source:* PolitiFact, "The Obameter: Tracking Obama's Campaign Promises," *St. Petersburg Times*, PolitiFact.com.

still "in the works" and not yet tackled.[80]

Elections serve an important public policy purpose because they allow voters to declare their approval or disapproval of government actions. Politicians recognize that they have to offer voters some blueprint for their future actions in office, and that is the purpose of campaign promises. Campaigns themselves are the selling of contrasting political products, and voters choose the one they think they will like the best. The policies that are produced after every election are the products that are sold to the public by candidates and political parties during each election cycle. But just as citizens require truth in advertising about consumer goods, citizens also require that politicians live up to their promises. In the end, it is up to each citizen to judge the public policies that are enacted after every election to ensure that the electoral connection between campaigns and policy is strong.

Elections, Campaigns, Voting, and Democracy

American elections and the campaigns that precede them are the means by which citizens participate in selecting those who will govern them. It is inevitable that they are at the center of concerns about American democracy. Many worry that campaigns are too long, candidates spend too much money, and the voters are not very well informed. These concerns often focus on the fairness of the process and of the outcome. In the long term, the process has worked reasonably well. In the short term, it is those who lose who see the process as unfair.

The general lesson here is that elections, campaigns, and voting, although imperfect, provide a real chance to ensure government responsiveness. It is through this competitive struggle that American democracy works. Many worry that the public does not know many of the details of candidates and their platforms, and that is clearly true. But the American public should not be underestimated. The fact that the public collectively seems to act in reasonably coherent ways is testimony to political scientist V. O. Key's classic observation that "voters are not fools."[81]

There is one danger to a democracy from a distortion in turnout—the rich do participate more than the poor, and this gap seems to be growing. With nonvoters being poorer and less educated, their failure to participate may help explain why government is not as responsive to their needs. Or put another way, the government may be overly responsive to the needs of the well off. This disparity in responsiveness threatens the underpinnings of a democratic and egalitarian society. If the political system responds only to one segment of the population repeatedly, and ignores other segments systematically, then general support for democracy, based on principles of fairness, could drop significantly.

With the Internet's growing influence, there may be other dangers to democracy. Wealthier citizens have more access to the information and resources on the Internet and therefore become even more informed and better able to make government responsive to their needs. The rich have always had advantages, but they may be growing. At the same time, however, the Internet might be used to extend participation. This technology can be used to expand the number of contributors from just the very wealthy to those people who have only a few dollars to contribute or who might want to show up to a local meeting to learn about an issue of relevance to them.

Let us now return to Figure 10.5 on p. 338, which offered two models of participation. The Hamiltonian model argued that more participation is not always a good thing, and the government works best with limited involvement from the public. The Jeffersonian model contended that greater participation improves both the quality of the input and the lives of citizens. Within our book's gateway approach, the participatory model of voting has more appeal than the elite model. Democracy becomes more responsive, more accountable, and more equal if more people participate. The cycle is reinforcing. Citizens themselves need to do all they can to encourage participation, in their self-interest and their civic interest. Democracy rests on the active and healthy participation of its citizenry. In other words, the more gateways there are, the better America's civic life is.

FOCUS QUESTIONS

- In what ways do elections encourage accountability and responsiveness in government?

- How does citizen equality work, or not work, in elections and campaigns? Are elections and campaigns fair?

- How well do campaigns work to inform the public so as to allow voters to hold candidates accountable?

- Why is voting such an important gateway for any democracy?

- Is more participation always good?

- How does citizen participation in the political system affect the prospects for accountability and equality?

- Do young citizens participate enough to make the system responsive to their preferences? What about other groups?

- How do other forms of participation, besides voting, serve as gateways to democracy? Are they more or less effective than voting?

- Do laws that regulate the financing of campaigns impede or advance equality and accountability in elections?

- In what ways are elections, campaigns, and voting gateways to American democracy? What are the gates?

Top Ten to Take Away

1. The constitutional requirements for elections set up gates against a direct democracy by allowing only the House of Representatives to be elected by the people. The choice of senators was the responsibility of state legislatures, as was the selection of electors who would elect the president. Today senators are elected directly by the people, and presidential elections give the people more influence, but the structure of the Electoral College enhances the influence of small states over states with large populations and affects the strategy of presidential campaigns. (pp. 320–327)

2. Presidential campaigns are demanding on the candidates and are shaped by constitutional requirements, interparty struggles, and strategies for attracting votes. (pp. 327–334)

3. Congressional elections take place every two years, when terms end for one-third of senators and all members of the House. Congressional incumbents almost always win. Congressional campaigns do not draw as much attention as presidential elections. (pp. 334–337)

4. Participation is essential to the functioning of democracy, and voting is the most common means by which people get involved. (pp. 337–339).

5. Because voting shapes the outcome of elections and the conduct of government, there have always been debates over who gets access to the ballot. The Hamiltonian model of participation sees risks in the extension of the franchise to groups that may be uninformed and favors a larger role for elites. The Jeffersonian model of participation maintains that greater participation produces better outcomes and encourages citizens to get more involved in self-government. (p. 338)

6. Unequal turnout by various demographic groups suggests that government's response is unequal.

A full narrative summary is on the book's website.

Most troubling for democracy is the tendency for those with higher incomes to vote at higher rates than the poor. Older people and those with more education also tend to vote at higher rates than younger people and those with less education. (pp. 339–342)

7. Political scientists explain why people vote (and choose not to vote) by building theoretical models. The economic model examines the costs and benefits of voting. The psychological model examines attitudes, including the idea of civic duty and the influence of partisanship. The institutional model examines the rules and regulations surrounding voting, including political party behavior, campaign strategy, and the context of the election. Socialization is a new consideration. (pp. 342–344)

8. Turnout in the United States is lower than in many other democracies, but it can be explained by the institutional model. (pp. 344–348) Americans participate in the political system in other ways, including being involved in a political campaign, participating in protests that call attention to causes, and, with the rise of the Internet and other new technologies, engaging in political debates, fundraising, and political campaigns on the web. (pp. 348–351) Voter registration helps prevent fraud in elections but it also poses a gate to participation that lowers turnout. (pp. 351–353)

9. The federal government regulates the financing of campaigns to help equalize opportunities to run for federal office. (pp. 353–356)

10. The presidency and the composition of Congress change in response to economic conditions and foreign relations, and the pattern of party gains and losses indicates that voters use elections to hold officials accountable and that the presidency and Congress are responsive institutions. (pp. 356–357)

Ten to Test Yourself

1. What is the difference between a primary election and the general election?

2. What are some election and campaign inequalities? What are the roles of issues and advertising in campaigns?

3. What are the primary factors in determining who wins a presidential campaign?

4. Why do incumbents in congressional races almost always win?

5. What are the differences between the Hamiltonian and Jeffersonian models of participation?

6. What are the demographic characteristics of a typical voter? A typical nonvoter?

7. How does turnout in the United States compare to turnout in other nations? What is the trend in turnout in U.S. presidential elections?

8. How do political scientists explain voters' decisions to vote and not to vote?

9. What is the role of money in campaigns, and how is it regulated? What rules of American elections serve as gates against voting? What rules are gateways to voting?

10. What other ways do Americans participate in politics and civic life, aside from voting? How are the Internet and other new technologies affecting participation?

More review questions and answers and chapter quizzes are on the book's website.

Terms to Know and Use

battleground state (p. 331)
Boston Tea Party (p. 350)
bundling (p. 330)
caucus (p. 328)
census (p. 326)
Compulsory Voting (p. 345)
efficacy (p. 343)
Electoral College (p. 321)
electors (p. 322)
elites (p. 338)
front-loading (p. 329)
gender gap (p. 340)
generational replacement (p. 346)
gerrymandering (p. 327)
Hamiltonian model of participation (p. 338)
initiatives (p. 327)
institutional model (p. 343)
invisible primary (p. 328)

Jeffersonian model of participation (p. 338)
mandate (p. 355)
matching funds (p. 329)
microtargeting (p. 331)
midterm elections (p. 334)
negativity (p. 332)
partisanship (p. 343)
party identification (p. 337)
party insiders (p. 328)
party platform (p. 355)
political action committees (PACs) (p. 330)
popular vote (p. 322)
position issues (p. 332)
prediction models (p. 333)
presidential coattails (p. 337)
primary election (p. 328)
public good (p. 342)

redistricting (p. 326)
referendum (p. 327)
safe seat (p. 336)
self-interest (p. 342)
socialization (p. 342)
strategic retirement (p. 336)
swing states (p. 330)
swing voters (p. 330)
term limits (p. 336)
valence issues (p. 332)
vanishing marginals (p. 336)
vote-by-mail system (p. 353)
voting age population (VAP) (p. 345)
voting eligible population (VEP) (p. 347)
wedge issue (p. 332)
winner-take-all system (p. 322)

Use the vocabulary flash cards on the book's website.

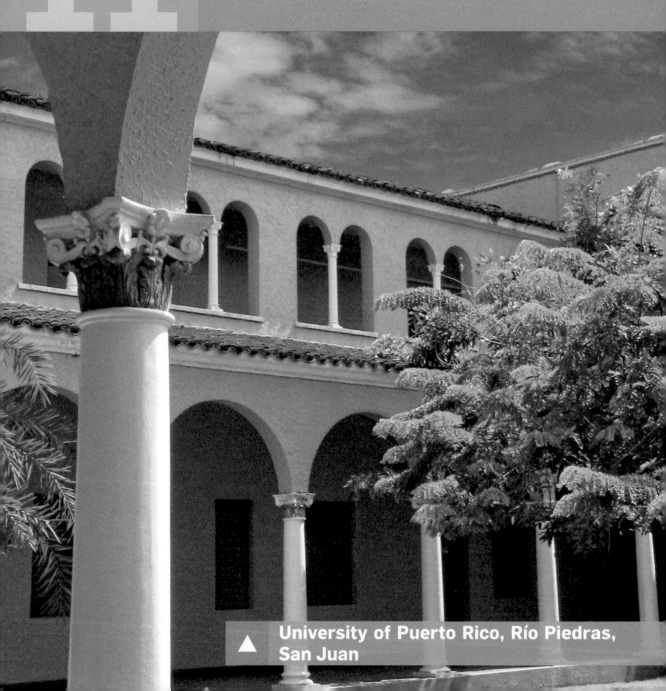

11 CONGRESS

▲ **University of Puerto Rico, Río Piedras, San Juan**

> *The future of our nation is held in the hands of our youth, and we must do all we can to prepare them for the competitive, international job market they will enter.*

As a young girl, Nydia Velázquez had to convince her family to let her start school early. By age 16, she was already a student at the University of Puerto Rico. Her major—political science—was no surprise to her family, though, for her father, a sugarcane cutter, had long been a political activist. He founded a political party in Yabucoa, where the family lived, and dinner conversations, Nydia remembered, were full of talk about workers' rights. She credits him with passing on to her a strong social conscience. "I always wanted to be like my father," she told the *New York Times*.

After graduating with honors in 1974, Velázquez pursued a master's degree in political science at New York University and went on to serve as a legislative aide to African American Congressman Ed Towns of New York. She also worked as the director of the Department of Puerto Rican Community Affairs for the governor of Puerto Rico and, like her father, was a community activist on behalf of Latinos, organizing massive voter registration drives in the New York City area.

But the key element to Velázquez's story is how she won a seat in the U.S. House of Representatives in 1992. Running in a newly created congressional district that was designed to include a majority of Latino voters, she faced challenges from other Latino candidates and from a white former congressman seeking to reclaim his seat. During her

CourseMate

Visit **http://www.cengagebrain .com/shop/ISBN/0495906190** for interactive tools including:
- **Quizzes**
- **Flashcards**
- **Videos**
- **Animated PowerPoint slides, Podcast summaries, and more**

Nydia Velázquez ▶

campaign, she and her volunteers went door to door in the district's poorest neighborhoods to register voters and ask for their support. On election day, she emerged victorious with the help of thousands of Latino voters, and she has never forgotten them. "Her biggest commitment," reports an observer, "is to her district and her 'pueblo'—the Latino community she says has historically been shut off from access to power and information." With her election, Nydia Velázquez did not win just a seat in Congress; she gave the Latino residents of her district a voice in national policy making that they never had before.[1]

FOCUS QUESTIONS

- How are members of Congress held accountable, both individually and for the collective output of Congress as a whole?

- In what ways is Congress responsive as a decision-making body? How does Congress address the pressing needs of the American people?

- What opportunities are there for the average person to influence the policy process in Congress? Is Congress accessible to citizens equally?

- How do the institutional structures in the House of Representatives and in the Senate each work as a gate blocking the enactment of legislation? Are there any gateways in these chambers that can help overcome these obstacles? Why did the Framers set up the legislative branch this way?

- Is Congress a gate or a gateway to democracy?

In the House, Congresswoman Velázquez has been a strong advocate on behalf of Latinos, especially Latino women, as well as the Chinese and African American residents in her district. She has focused on immigration issues and on strengthening ties with Latin America. She has spoken out against "English-only" laws because, she argues, Latinos need both Spanish and English in their early years of education to overcome language barriers and become full citizens. In 2007, Congresswoman Velázquez became chair of the House Committee on Small Business, and in 2009 she became chair of the Congressional Hispanic Caucus. She believes that economic empowerment for the working poor is her district's chief challenge, and her position in Congress gives her the opportunity to bring home federal dollars, in the form of projects and grants, to provide economic and political opportunity for her constituents.

In this chapter, we explain how members of Congress navigate the gates and gateways embedded in the legislative branch to best serve the interests of their constituents. The fact that members of Congress must repeatedly return home to ask the voters to reelect them helps to keep them responsive to their constituents, who hold them accountable for the policies they enact into law. But the process of congressional representation—that is, of putting good ideas into practice as law—is difficult and complex. There are structural gates embedded in a separation of powers system of government and in a democratic legislative process that encourages competition among groups with conflicting interests. Navigating this terrain is not easy, but Nydia Velázquez's efforts on behalf of her district show how an individual member of Congress can be an advocate as well as a legislator.

Congress as the Legislative Branch

In Chapter 2 (The Constitution), we discussed the ideas of representation that shaped the Framers' thinking. They believed that a democratic government had to be responsive and accountable to the people. In such a government, leaders would not inherit power; rather, they would be elected by the people at regular intervals, and these elections would be the primary way that voters would hold government officials accountable for their actions. The Framers of the Constitution designed Congress to be the legislative branch of the federal government, and they gave it broad powers to enact laws. At the same time, the Framers wanted the process of lawmaking to be complex and deliberative, so that members of Congress would not succumb to rash or impulsive actions that might harm constituents or violate fundamental constitutional rights. Over time, Congress as the legislative branch has increased the scope and range of its powers, but the added responsibilities have added a layer of complexity that makes it harder than ever before to achieve legislative change.

Representation and Bicameralism

In Chapter 1 (Gateways to American Democracy), we asked whether the people's representatives in the legislature should act as **trustees** who exercise independent judgment about what they believe is best for the people, or act as **delegates** who do exactly as the people wish. In Chapter 6 (Public Opinion), we examined the polls and other means by which legislators try to determine what the people wish. We also learned that citizens do not have informed views on every issue. Thus, members of Congress have to act as both trustees and delegates.

Essential to understanding how Congress facilitates **representation** in the American democracy is to recognize that it is **bicameral**: that is, it is divided into two separate chambers, the House of Representatives and the Senate. This structure reflects the Framers' fear that the power of the legislative branch might grow to the point where it could not be controlled by the other two branches. Because the legislative branch is closest to the people—its members represent specific population groups, by region, and can be removed by election—the Framers believed that Congress would have a democratic legitimacy that neither the executive nor the judicial branches would possess.

trustee: *Idea of representation that says elected officials should do what they think best, even if the public disagrees.*

delegate: *Idea of representation that says elected officials should do what the public wants and not exercise independent judgment.*

Who are your representatives and senators? Do you want them to be trustees or delegates?

representation: *Idea that government officeholders are elected by the people to act on their behalf.*

bicameral: *A legislature having two chambers.*

The Framers created the House of Representatives and the Senate as separate chambers of Congress, but both are located in the U.S. Capitol. In this view from the mall, the Senate chamber is on the left, and the House chamber is on the right. There are six office buildings for members of Congress and their staff members, three on each side of the Capitol.

istockphoto

The solution, according to James Madison, was to divide the legislature into two parts that would check each other. The House of Representatives would be a large body that reflected population size within states and was directly elected frequently (every two years), and the Senate would be an elite chamber, with two senators for every state regardless of population size, elected by state legislatures every two years. In that way, both the popular opinions of average voters, and the elite opinion of the well educated and the wealthy would each be represented in Congress. This arrangement also guaranteed that large states could not overwhelm smaller states in determining the content of laws. The specific differences between the two parts of Congress are discussed in the next section.

Constitutional Differences between the House and Senate

To accomplish Madison's goal, the Constitution establishes four key differences between the two chambers of Congress: qualifications for office, mode of election, terms of office, and constituencies (see Table 11.1).

Qualifications for Office. The qualifications for the House are that an individual must be at least 25 years old, reside in the state that he or she represents, and have been a U.S. citizen for seven years prior to running for office. The qualifications for the Senate are that an individual must be at least 30 years old, reside in the state he or she represents, and have been a U.S. citizen for nine years prior to running for office. Senators were expected to be older and to have lived in the United States for a longer period of time than House members because the Framers believed those characteristics would make the Senate the more stable partner in the legislative process.

TABLE 11.1 Comparison of House and Senate Service

	House	Senate
Qualifications	25 years old	30 years old
Citizenship	7 years	9 years
Term of office	2 years	6 years
Geographic constituency	District	State
Redistricting	Every 10 years	Never
Mode of election until 1914	Direct	Indirect through state legislatures
Mode of election after 1914	Direct	Direct

Although the members of the First Congress (1789–91) were all white men, there is no provision in the Constitution that dictates a specific race, gender, income level, or religion as a prerequisite to being elected to serve in Congress. Twenty-first century Congresses are much more diverse, with female, African American, Hispanic, Pacific Islander, and American Indian members in the House (see Figure 11.1). The average House and Senate member is older than 55. House members tend to serve an average of five terms (ten years) and Senators an average of two terms (twelve years).[2] The House includes members from the Protestant, Catholic, Jewish, Greek Orthodox, Mormon, Buddhist, Quaker, and—for the first time—Muslim faiths. The religious background of senators is slightly less varied, but also includes members from the Protestant, Roman Catholic, Mormon, and Jewish faiths.[3]

House members have more varied prior experience than their Senate colleagues. A majority of House members served in their state legislature before coming to Congress. Just as House members use state legislatures as stepping-stones, senators use the House of Representatives to launch their bids for the Senate. Forty-nine senators served in the House of Representatives before coming to the Senate.

Mode of Election. House members are elected directly by citizens. Senators are elected directly as well, but that is a more recent development. From 1789 to 1914, the mode of election for the Senate was indirect: citizens voted for members of their state legislatures, who then selected the U.S. senators. The mode of election for the House and Senate was different on purpose. The House was supposed to be more immediately responsive to the opinions of the people, but the Framers designed the Senate to insulate senators from the direct voice of the people, in other words, to make them *less* directly responsive to the people. The mode of election for the Senate was

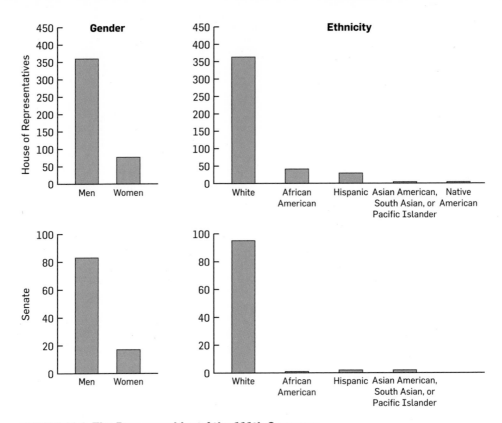

FIGURE 11.1 The Demographics of the 111th Congress.

changed from indirect to direct in 1913, with the ratification of the Seventeenth Amendment. The change to direct elections opened up a much more direct gateway of influence for constituents over their U.S. senators.

Terms of Office.   A term of office is the length of time that an elected official serves before facing the voters again in an election. The term of office for House members is two years, and the term of office for U.S. senators is six years. The difference in term of office leads to key differences in how each chamber operates. House members have a shorter amount of time to demonstrate their effectiveness before they face reelection, so the House of Representatives as a whole is usually in a greater hurry to pass legislation than the Senate. Senators know they have six years before they have to face their voters, so they have a bit more flexibility in working out disagreements among their constituents and balancing constituents' interests against the interests of the nation as a whole. Because senators know they have a longer time in which to establish a good reputation among their home state voters, the Senate takes more time to deliberate over legislation.

In any given election year, the entire membership of the House of Representatives must face the voters, but only one-third of senators stand for reelection. To guarantee that the entire Senate would never stand for reelection all at once, the Constitution divided the first Senate into three classes of senators, which would be elected at different six-year intervals.[4] To this day, the maximum number of senators who stand for regularly scheduled reelection in the same year is thirty-four (out of a possible 100), thereby ensuring that a majority of the Senate is never up for reelection at the same time as the entire House of Representatives.[5] This electoral condition reinforces the stability of the Senate's membership; it also limits the electoral incentives for House and Senate members to cooperate with one another to pass legislation.

Constituencies.   A **constituency** is the set of people that officially elects the House or Senate member; in the United States, constituency is defined geographically. For the House of Representatives, each member represents a congressional district that has established geographic boundaries within each state. For the Senate, each U.S. senator represents an entire state, and two U.S. senators are elected from each state. The Framers wanted to have two senators for each state to make sure there was always at least one senator actively representing a state in the Senate.[6]

In 1789, the average size of a congressional district was about 30,000 people, and the average size of a state was about 300,000 people; today, a congressional district has about 640,000 people, and the nation's largest state, California, has approximately 37 million residents.[7] Because the Framers knew that the country would grow, they required a count, or **census**, of the population every ten years. Following the census, the number of congressional districts in each state would be adjusted to reflect population changes. The House started with 65 members, and eventually grew to 435 members by 1911, an increase of 670 percent.[8] That year, Congress passed a law that limited the size of the House to 435, concerned that if the House grew any larger it would not be possible to conduct legislative business.[9] Today, because there is an absolute limit on the total number of House members, population growth or decline has a direct bearing on a state's representation, increasing or decreasing a state's number of representatives and thus its relative influence in the House.

Geographic boundaries on constituencies have a direct impact on congressional representation. A member of the House is responsive to the needs of the residents of a district, but a U.S. senator is responsive to the needs of the residents of an entire state. As a result, members of the House and Senate from the same state can react differently to the same issue. For example, in 1999, Congresswoman Velázquez supported President Bill Clinton's

constituency: *Defined group of citizens officially designated to elect a legislative representative.*

census: *Constitutionally mandated count of the population every ten years.*

(1993–2001) proposal to grant clemency to members of the FALN, a Puerto Rican opposition group who were convicted and serving prison sentences for a series of violent protests, including a bombing in the U.S. Capitol. In contrast, the senior Democratic senator from New York, Daniel Patrick Moynihan, opposed the measure because he believed it was inconsistent with a tough stand on terrorism. Congresswoman Velázquez felt a duty to her own heritage, as well as that of many of the residents of her district, to support clemency for the FALN members, but Moynihan, who was elected by the entire state of New York, did not feel the same obligation to respond to the opinions of the residents of Congresswoman Velázquez's district on this issue. In this case, the House and Senate were checking and balancing each other, as the Framers' had envisioned.

Redistricting.

redistricting: *Process whereby state legislatures redraw the boundaries of congressional districts in the state to make them equal in population size.*

Only the House of Representatives is subject to **redistricting**, which is the redrawing of the boundaries of congressional districts in a state to make them approximately equal in population size. Because the size of the House is limited to 435, the overall number of congressional seats per state must be adjusted following a census if there have been population changes. Based on the state's allocation of congressional districts, the state legislature redraws the districts, and the only real limitation on redistricting is that the boundaries of the district must be contiguous (uninterrupted). During redistricting, the majority party in the state legislature tries to influence the process to construct each district in such a way that a majority of voters favor its party, thereby making it easier for its candidates to win in a process known as **gerrymandering**.

gerrymandering: *Redistricting that blatantly benefits one political party over the other or concentrates (or dilutes) the voting impact of racial or ethnic groups.*

Sometimes the majority party will combine two existing districts that have House members from the other party, forcing them to run against each other.

How do majority-minority districts provide a gateway for better representation of minority interests?

Redistricting has also been used as a tool to achieve greater minority representation in the House of Representatives. Many states initially redrew congressional districts to group minority voters in such a way as to deny them the voting strength to elect a minority member of Congress. In 1982, Congress amended the Voting Rights Act of 1965 to prevent this kind of manipulation. In response, some state legislatures created so-called majority-minority districts in which African Americans or Latinos would constitute a majority of the voters in the district and would have enough votes to elect an African American or Latino candidate.[10] The New York district from which Congresswoman Velázquez was first elected was one of them. Since then, the federal courts have ruled that state legislatures overemphasized the racial composition of these districts to the point where districts made no geographic sense. Current guidelines on redistricting call for the

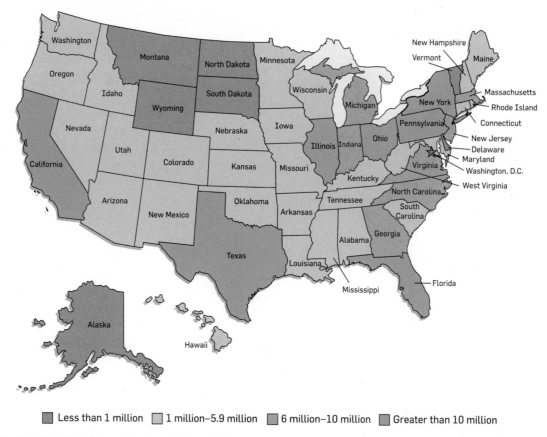

| Less than 1 million | 1 million–5.9 million | 6 million–10 million | Greater than 10 million |

FIGURE 11.2 States by Population, 2009. The U.S. Senate has two senators for every state, regardless of state population size. This arrangement makes states equal in Senate votes: Wyoming has the same number of votes as California. But it also means that the 1 million citizens of Wyoming have the same voice in the Senate as the 37 million citizens of California. Equal representation in the Senate did not seem so imbalanced when states had more similar population sizes, but today, with such huge differences among states, some observers think representation in the Senate is inherently unfair. *Source:* U.S. Census Bureau.

consideration of race in drawing district lines, but not to the extreme that it has been employed in the past.[11]

Because representation in the Senate is not related to population size, but to state boundaries, some scholars have argued that the Senate is less responsive than the House. It is true that there are vast differences in population size among the states[12] (see Figure 11.2). As we will explore later in this chapter, the rules of the Senate amplify this imbalance of influence by granting each senator equal power to block legislation. As a result, a senator who represents a state like Wyoming, with fewer than 1 million

With each state having the same number of senators, what are the consequences for citizen equality across small and large states?

people, can block a policy that might benefit a state like California, with 37 million people.

The Powers of Congress

As Chapter 2 describes, the Framers granted Congress powers that were necessary to construct a coherent and forceful federal government. The Framers also worried that the legislative branch would grow too powerful. So they limited the powers of Congress to a list in Article I, Section 8 of the Constitution, together with a few stated responsibilities in other sections. The following discussion highlights the most important powers of Congress. It also examines the ways that Congress has used its constitutional powers to expand its role in the policy-making system, and ways that Congress, as the legislative branch, is balanced and checked by the executive and judicial branches.

How have the powers of Congress increased? Why?

Taxation and Appropriation

Congress has the power "to lay and Collect Taxes." In a division of this important power, the Constitution states that all bills for raising revenue should originate in the House of Representatives, but the Senate "may propose or concur with Amendments as on other Bills." Initially, the Framers thought tax revenue would come primarily from levies placed on imported goods. However, as the industrial economy grew, so did the need for government services and programs that cost money. With the Sixteenth Amendment, passed in 1913, Congress gained the power "to lay and collect taxes on incomes," whatever the source. This amendment overturned prohibitions on certain types of income taxes.

Paralleling the power to tax, Congress also has the power to spend—"to pay the Debts and to provide for the common Defence and general Welfare." The **general welfare clause** has proven to be a major means by which Congress's power has expanded. Congress **appropriates** (or allocates) federal monies on programs it **authorizes** (or creates) through its lawmaking power. Although all laws, including appropriations, must be signed by the president, Congress's "power of the purse" has been instrumental in its expansion of power.[13] The Constitution also gives Congress the authority to borrow money, to coin money, and to regulate its value, and it requires a regular accounting of revenue and expenditures of public money.

general welfare clause (Article I, Section 8): *Gives Congress the power to tax to provide for the general welfare.*

appropriate: *Allocate a set amount of federal dollars for a specific program or agency.*

authorize: *Grant the power to create a federal program or agency and spend federal funds to support that program or agency.*

War Powers

The Constitution gives Congress authority to "provide for the common Defense." In reality, the war powers are shared with the president. For example, Congress has the sole power to declare war, but this power is typically only used after the president has requested a declaration of war. In many cases, the president may ask Congress for specific authorization to take military action, even though it is not a full declaration of war; under its power of taxation and appropriation, Congress has the authority to fund or refuse to fund those military operations. Generally, Congress also has the power "to raise and support Armies," "to provide and maintain a Navy," "to provide for calling forth the Militia," and to make rules and regulations regarding the armed forces and their organizations. Relations between Congress and the president over war powers have sometimes been harmonious, but in recent decades they have become contentious. The struggle between the president and Congress over the war powers is examined in detail in Chapter 12 (The Presidency).

Regulation of Commerce

The Constitution gave Congress an important power that it did not have under the Articles of Confederation: the power "to regulate Commerce with foreign Nations, and among the several States, and with the Indian Tribes." Using the power in this **commerce clause**, Congress established a national set of laws regulating commerce that are applicable to all states equally.[14] In time, this authority to regulate interstate commerce has allowed Congress to expand its power to the point that almost no economic activity is beyond its reach. In the name of regulating interstate commerce, Congress has passed laws that permit the federal government to break up monopolies, protect labor unions, set a minimum wage, and outlaw racial discrimination by businesses and commercial enterprises.

> **commerce clause (Article I, Section 8):** *Gives Congress the power to regulate commerce with foreign nations, with Indian tribes, and among the various states.*

Appointments and Treaties

In recognition of the Senate's perceived wisdom and stability, the Framers gave the Senate, and not the House, the power of **advice and consent**. In the appointment of high-level executive branch appointees, such as cabinet secretaries and ambassadors, this power allows the Senate to evaluate the qualifications of a presidential nominee and, by majority vote, to approve or reject the nominee. Similarly, the appointment of all federal judges, from district courts to the Supreme Court, is subject to the approval of the Senate (see Chapter 14, The Judiciary, for more details on this process). Additionally, the Senate acts as a check on the president's power to make treaties with foreign nations, because treaties must be approved by a two-thirds vote or they fail to take effect (see Chapter 12 for more on treaty negotiation and ratification). The advice and consent role of the Senate acts as a gateway for citizen influence over presidential appointments and treaties because senators are more

> **advice and consent:** *Power of the Senate to approve or disapprove presidential appointments, such as cabinet secretaries, ambassadors, and judges, as well as international treaties.*

The Senate exercises its advice and consent powers when it holds hearings on presidential nominees and then votes to approve or disapprove them. In summer 2009, senators questioned President Barack Obama's Supreme Court nominee, Sonia Sotomayor, an appeals court judge from New York. The hearings generated considerable interest, as Sotomayor, if confirmed, would be the third woman and first Hispanic justice ever to serve on the Court. She was confirmed on August 6, 2009, by a vote of 68 to 31.

impeachment: *Process whereby the House brings charges against the president (or other federal officials) that will, upon conviction by the Senate, remove him from office.*

enumerated powers: *Powers of Congress listed in Article I, Section 8 of the Constitution.*

likely to block such appointments when they believe they are unpopular with their constituents.

Impeachment and Removal from Office

Congress's ultimate check on the executive and judicial branches is its power to remove officials and judges from office by **impeachment**. The president, vice president, and high officials are subject to impeachment for "Treason, Bribery, or other high Crimes and Misdemeanors." This power is rarely used. In Chapter 12, we examine the two times in which presidents have been impeached but not removed from office.

The process takes place in two steps. First, a majority of the House of Representatives votes to bring formal charges against the president, which is impeachment. Then the Senate conducts the trial, with the chief justice presiding. The Senate votes to convict or acquit. If two-thirds of the senators present vote to convict, the federal official or judge is removed from office.

Lawmaking

Congress, as the legislative branch, is responsible for lawmaking. Unlike the **enumerated powers** listed at the beginning of Section 8 and explained above, the final paragraph of Section 8 gives Congress the broad authority "to make all Laws which shall be necessary and proper for carrying into Execution the fore-going Powers." In combination with the general welfare clause and the commerce clause, this **necessary and proper clause** allows Congress a great deal of leeway to carry out its responsibilities, under the assumption that additional powers are **implied** in these clauses rather than explicit. Over time, Congress has made full use of this flexibility to expand its authority over a wide range of areas, such as regulating interstate railroads, establishing civil rights protections, funding school lunch programs, limiting greenhouse gases, and providing student loans. Essentially, if an argument can be made that a service or program is important for the nation, Congress has used its powers to create it.

Authorization of Courts

In Article I, the Constitution also gave Congress the power to "constitute Tribunals inferior to the Supreme Court." Article III, the section on the judiciary, reiterates congressional control by saying that Congress may "ordain and establish" courts at levels lower than the Supreme Court. In 1789, Congress used this power to pass the **Judiciary Act**, which established federal district courts and circuit courts of appeal. Today, there are ninety-four district courts and twelve regional appellate circuits, plus a Court of Appeals for the Federal Circuit.[15]

The federal judicial branch asserted more authority over the other two branches in the Supreme Court case of *Marbury v. Madison* (1803) (see Chapter 2, The Constitution). This case established **judicial review**, which is the federal judiciary's power to declare laws passed by Congress as unconstitutional. That decision gave the courts the power to interpret the Constitution and see how congressional laws (and even executive branch actions) conform to its explicit language and its intent (see Chapter 14, The Judiciary, for further explanation of this decision).

In recent years, the Senate has tried to reassert its influence over the federal courts through the nomination process.[16] As we discuss later in the chapter, individual senators can try to stall or block presidential nominees for federal judgeships with whom they disagree on key constitutional questions.

Oversight

Once a law is signed, the executive branch, headed by the president, is supposed to carry out the law according to Congress's wishes. But the executive branch is a bureaucracy with many departments and agencies that have authority to implement laws. The sheer size and complexity of the federal bureaucracy make it difficult for Congress to determine whether laws are being administered according to their intent (see Chapter 13, The Bureaucracy, for more details). Over time, Congress has asserted its **oversight** authority to monitor the ways in which the executive branch implements law. This authority stems from Congress's responsibility to provide for the general welfare of the nation, and its power to appropriate money. Congress constantly exercises this power, but less so under **unified government**, when the same party controls Congress and the White House, than under **divided government**, when the party that controls Congress is not the party of the president. Under unified government, members of Congress assume that because they share the same partisan affiliation as the president, his administration is more likely to implement laws according to congressional intent.

In contrast, legislatures in countries that have a parliamentary system typically choose their executive from among the members of the majority party so that the executive and legislative branches always share the same policy goals. Consequently, legislative oversight is not a fundamental element of those political systems (see Other Places: The Parliamentary System of Great Britain).

necessary and proper clause (Article I, Section 8): *Gives Congress the power to pass all laws necessary and proper to the powers enumerated in Section 8.*

implied powers: *Powers not explicitly granted to Congress but added through the necessary and proper clause.*

Judiciary Act (1789): *Created the lower federal judiciary, district courts, and circuit courts of appeal.*

Marbury v. Madison **(1803):** *Established the Supreme Court's power of judicial review.*

judicial review: *Authority of courts to declare laws passed by Congress and acts of the executive branch to be unconstitutional.*

oversight: *Power of Congress to monitor how the executive branch implements laws.*

unified government: *Situation when the same party controls the executive and legislative branches.*

divided government: *Situation when one party controls the executive and the other party controls the legislature.*

The Parliamentary System of Great Britain

All democracies have a legislature and an executive, but their relationship to each other produces differences in the way that people are represented. The United States has separated legislative and executive branches. In Great Britain, however, the executive and the legislative branches are intertwined. Great Britain is a limited monarchy democracy, with a queen as the head of state and a parliament for its legislature. The British Parliament is bicameral; the House of Commons has 646 members and elections are held in single-member districts, as they are in the United States; whichever party wins the most seats wins control of the chamber. The House of Lords has 730 members; some inherit their seats and others are appointed by the queen. The approval of both branches of the legislature is necessary to pass legislation.

In the British system, the prime minister, who is the chief executive of the government, is an elected member of the House of Commons chosen by the majority party and officially recognized by the queen. He appoints ministers and advisers to his cabinet without the formal approval of the legislature. Because the prime minister comes from the majority party in the legislature, the executive and the legislature typically agree on the legislation that needs to be passed to accomplish the party's goals.

THE HOUSE OF COMMONS

1. Speaker
2. Pages
3. Government Members
4. Opposition Members
5. Prime Minister
6. Leader of the Official Opposition
7. Leader of Second Largest Party in Opposition
8. Clerk and Table Officers
9. Mace
10. Hansard Reporters
11. Sergeant-at-Arms
12. The Bar
13. Interpreters
14. Press Gallery
15. Public Gallery
16. Official Gallery
17. Leader of the Opposition's Gallery
18. Members' Gallery
19. Members' Gallery
20. Members' Gallery
21. Speaker's Gallery
22. Senate Gallery
23. T.V. Cameras

The British have a parliamentary system, where the legislative and executive branches are combined. The prime minister, who is the chief executive, is an elected member of Parliament chosen by members of the majority party and officially recognized by the queen. In the House of Commons, members of the two major parties sit on opposite sides, as in the U.S. Congress, but they are identified as "government" and "opposition."

The prime minister is the party leader in Great Britain and is thus responsive to the party's voting base. There are no regularly scheduled parliamentary elections, but they must be held at least once every five years, and they last less than three weeks. The prime minister calls for elections either when the majority party is very popular, so that it can retain power, or when it is so unpopular that the public calls for a change. In 2010, Prime Minister Gordon Brown, a member of the Labour Party, was losing popularity, and in the May 6 election the Conservatives, led by David Cameron, won more seats than the Labour Party but fell short of a working majority. As a result, the Conservatives joined with members of a third party, the Liberal Democrats, to form a working majority party in Parliament. The end result of the elections was a complete change of majority party control.

- **How does the British parliamentary system differ from the separation of powers system in the United States?**
- **Is there a difference in citizen control in elections that are regularly scheduled versus elections that are scheduled by the majority party in power? Explain.**

Source: http://www.parliament.uk.

Members of Congress engage in oversight activities in several ways. They hold **hearings** with cabinet officials and bureaucrats to analyze how well programs are working, and they frequently invite members of the public to describe how federal programs operate in their communities. Members of Congress constantly write letters to executive branch agency heads to inquire about specific programs, and they keep careful track of the responses they receive. In cases of special investigations or suspected wrongdoing by members of the executive branch, Congress can even legally require members of the administration to testify. In some instances, Congress convenes special committees to investigate actions involving members of the president's staff or even the president himself. In these ways, members of Congress provide a gateway for the people to constantly monitor and hold the federal government accountable for how it implements the law.

hearings: *Congressional committee meetings to gather information or hear testimony on a bill, issue, or appointment.*

The Organization of Congress

The House and the Senate have evolved into very different institutions by virtue of their differences in size, rules, structure, and responsibilities. The Constitution establishes few guidelines for how the House and Senate should operate, so it was left to the members to determine how to choose their leaders and how much power to give them. Some aspects of leadership are shared by the House and Senate, but there are important differences in the amount of power each grants to its leaders. Notably, the power of political parties to shape policy is vastly different in each chamber.

The Role of Political Parties

In today's political world, political parties seem natural and intrinsic to the organization of Congress. Party affiliation and party loyalty have become the defining features of how policy is made in the House of Representatives. The reason parties could become so powerful inside the House chamber was because they were important outside Washington, back home in local districts. Being identified with a political party became an essential stepping-stone to political office. Political parties controlled the nomination process for Congress, and anyone who wanted to run on a party ticket had to pledge support for the party's policies. Consequently, each individual member had a strong incentive to align with a political party, both at home in the district and in Washington (see Chapter 9, Political Parties, for more on party affiliations).

Are political parties in the House too powerful? Are they a gate or gateway to passing legislation?

With the rise in party strength at the district level, House members were increasingly judged on the performance of their party in office, and elections became centered on gaining majority control of the chamber. If the majority party could pass policies that it favored, and prevent those who disagreed with them (the minority party) from gaining any power, majority party members could return to their districts and claim credit for being effective legislators.

Although the Senate also became more party-oriented at the end of the nineteenth century, its members never changed the rules of the chamber to give the majority party complete dominance. Because the number of senators remained small, it was, and is, still possible to conduct legislative business in a personal manner, and each senator exerts individual influence over policy outcomes. Senators also have the chance to make an individual impression on voters over a longer time (six years) and from a more visible vantage point, as they represent an entire state rather than just one district. Voters still consider a senator's party affiliation in their voting decision, but it is not as important a factor as it is in House elections. Consequently, senators have had fewer incentives to hand over their individual powers to a single party leader to accomplish party goals.

The Senate has remained small enough that each individual senator can wield relatively equal amounts of power. As a result, members of the minority party in the Senate have far more power in the policy-making process than do their counterparts in the House.[17] In essence, getting any legislation passed in the Senate requires compromise and cooperation among all senators—majority and minority party members—in one way or another.

What evidence of compromise and cooperation do you see in the Senate today?

The House of Representatives

As is the case with any large organization, success requires leadership, so members of the House meet in a **party caucus** ("to caucus" literally means "to gather") as members of separate political parties. Each party's caucus chooses the party leadership: for the majority party, the top official is the Speaker of the House, and for the minority party, it is the minority leader.

The Speaker of the House.
The **Speaker of the House** is the only formal leadership position written into the Constitution. Article I, Section 2, states that "the House of Representatives shall chuse their Speaker and other Officers," but there the official description ends. The Speaker is elected by a majority of House members every two years, on the first day of the first session of a Congress. The position of Speaker includes the power to appoint all committee chairmen, approve all members' committee assignments, refer bills to committee, bring bills to the House floor that reflect the majority party's ideas, and refuse to allow the minority party the ability to delay legislation.[18] Throughout the twentieth century, leadership style of Speakers varied according to how much power the rank-and-file party members wanted to give to their leader. The Speaker's most important responsibility is to maintain power in the House for the majority party, and that means getting the members of the majority party reelected. To do so, the Speaker supports a set of policies that he or she believes are popular with voters, and then tries to get those policies enacted into law.

House Party Leaders.
The **House majority leader**, as second in command, works with the Speaker to decide which issues the party will consider. He or she also coordinates with committee leaders on holding hearings and reporting bills to the House floor for a vote. The House majority leader must strike a compromise among many competing forces, including committee chairs and external interest groups. He or she is also expected to raise a significant amount of campaign contributions for party members, and that role produces more pressure to appease as many interest groups as possible. The majority leader also has nine majority **whips** to help "whip up" support for the party's preferred policies and keep lines of communication open between the party leadership and the rank-and-file membership. The majority party leaders work hard to track members' intended votes—in a process called the whip count—because they want to bring to the floor only those bills that will pass; any defeat on the floor could weaken voter confidence in the majority party.[19]

The minority party in the House is the party that has the largest number of House members who are not in the majority party. The highest-ranking member of the minority party is the **House minority leader**, and his or her

---

party caucus: *Group of party members in a legislature.*

Speaker of the House: *Constitutional and political leader of the House.*

Why is the House Speaker so powerful? Why is the person who holds this position third in line in presidential succession, after the vice president?

House majority leader: *Leader of the majority party in the House.*

whips: *Legislators designated to count votes within the majority or the minority party.*

House minority leader: *Leader of the minority party in the House.*

main responsibility is crafting the minority party's position on an issue and serving as the public spokesperson for the party. If the minority party is the same as the president's party, the House minority leader is also expected to garner support for the president's policies among minority party members. The House minority leader also works with minority whips, who are responsible for keeping all the minority members in line with the party's public positions.

The challenge for the minority party in the House of Representatives is that it has very little institutional power; the majority party uses its numerical advantage to control committee and floor actions. Because of its institutional disadvantages, the modern minority party in the House of Representatives rarely has the power to stop majority party proposals from passing. Minority party members can vote no, but their real power lies in making speeches, issuing press releases, and stirring up grassroots opposition to majority party proposals.

Does the institutional structure of the House promote party dominance? Responsible lawmaking? What can be done about the structure of Congress?

The Senate

The Senate has always been a smaller chamber than the House because it is based on the number of states in the union and does not adjust according to population growth. Since 1959, when Hawaii and Alaska joined the union, the Senate has had one hundred members and the magic number to secure majority control in the Senate has been fifty-one senators. However, the Senate majority leader has fewer formal powers to advance the party's agenda compared to the Speaker of the House. Because the Senate never grew to be as large and unwieldy as the House, the individual members have rarely seen the benefit of giving up power to party leaders to make the Senate run efficiently or enact the party's agenda.

President Pro Tempore.   Article 1, Section 3 of the Constitution states that the vice president shall be the president of the Senate, but that in his absence, the Senate may appoint a **president *pro tempore*** (temporary president) to preside over the Senate. For most of the Senate's history, the vice president presided over the Senate, and his main functions were to recognize individual senators who wished to speak and rule on which procedural motions were in order on the Senate floor. The vice president can also break a tie vote in the Senate. This power can give the president's party control of the outcome on the floor. But in the 1950s, the vice president became more active in executive branch business and less active in the Senate. Subsequently, the Senate began appointing the oldest serving member from the majority party as the president pro tempore to serve as the temporary presiding officer. The president pro tempore is closely advised by the **Senate parliamentarian**, who is responsible for administering the rules of the Senate.

president *pro tempore*: *Constitutional leader of the Senate.*

Senate parliamentarian: *Official in charge of interpreting the rules of the Senate.*

Senate Party Leaders. The majority party elects the **Senate majority leader**, but unlike the Speaker of the House, this position is not written into the Constitution. The job of the Senate majority leader is to make sure the Senate functions well enough to pass legislation. To accomplish that goal, the Senate majority leader tries to craft that legislation as closely to the preferred policies of his party as possible, necessitating a great deal of compromise. As the scholar Ralph Huitt describes it, the power of the Senate majority leader is predominantly the "power of persuasion."[20]

Still, the Senate majority leader does have several formal powers. For instance, he is the official scheduler of Senate business and is always recognized first to speak on the Senate floor. Every senator has the right to speak on the Senate floor, but senators must speak one at a time. Being recognized first, before any other senator, gives the majority leader the power to control the floor and prevent any other senator from speaking. But because the Senate majority leader relies on the senators' voluntary cooperation to conduct the business of the Senate, there are limits on how tough he or she can be on Senate colleagues. If a Senate majority leader tries to bully senators, they might retaliate by constantly using their individual floor powers to delay or block key legislation.

The **Senate minority leader** is the leader of the minority party in the Senate and is expected to represent the minority party senators in negotiations with the majority leader on which bills are brought to the Senate floor and under what circumstances. Similar to the House counterpart, the Senate minority leader's job is to organize minority party senators into a coherent group that can present viable alternatives to the majority party's proposals.

The extended leadership structure of the Senate looks similar to the House except that it is smaller (see Figure 11.3). It consists of an assistant majority leader, majority and minority whips, and conference chairs, all of whom are responsible for uniting the senators in their respective parties and crafting legislative proposals that can garner enough support to pass the Senate.

The Committee System

Almost all legislation that passes the House or Senate goes through a committee. The House and Senate are organized into separate committees to deal with the different issues that fall under the purview of the federal government. Whichever party has the majority in the entire House or Senate also has the majority of seats on each committee, and the **committee chair** is chosen from the majority party, with the approval of the party caucus. Typically, a House member or senator gives the party leadership a "wish list" of committee assignments, and the leadership then assigns committee seats according to seniority and the availability of seats on specific committees.

Senate majority leader: *Leader of the majority party in the Senate.*

Does the institutional structure of the Senate promote party dominance? Responsible lawmaking? Individual careers? What can be done about the structure of Congress?

Senate minority leader: *Leader of the minority party in the Senate.*

committee chair: *Majority party member of a House or Senate committee who has been chosen to lead the committee and determine which issues the committee considers.*

FIGURE 11.3 **The Structure of Party Leadership in the 112th Congress.** Each chamber of Congress has its own separate party leadership structure designed to help party leaders keep rank-and-file members united and accomplish the party's policy goals. This figure illustrates the Democratic and Republican Party organizations in the House and Senate.

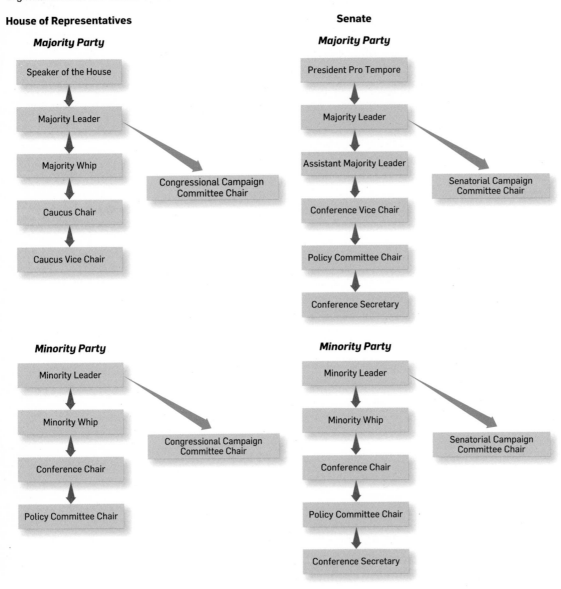

House of Representatives

Majority Party

- Speaker of the House
- Majority Leader
- Majority Whip
- Caucus Chair
- Caucus Vice Chair

Congressional Campaign Committee Chair

Minority Party

- Minority Leader
- Minority Whip
- Conference Chair
- Policy Committee Chair

Congressional Campaign Committee Chair

Senate

Majority Party

- President Pro Tempore
- Majority Leader
- Assistant Majority Leader
- Conference Vice Chair
- Policy Committee Chair
- Conference Secretary

Senatorial Campaign Committee Chair

Minority Party

- Minority Leader
- Minority Whip
- Conference Chair
- Policy Committee Chair
- Conference Secretary

Senatorial Campaign Committee Chair

standing committee:
Permanent committee in the House or Senate.

The House and Senate each have several types of committees. A **standing committee** is a permanent committee with the power to write legislation and report it to the full chamber. **Select committees**, **joint committees**, and **special committees** are usually focused on a more narrow set of issues, such as aging or tax policy, but none has the same legislative clout and authority of a standing committee. In the House, there are twenty standing committees, and the average House committee has forty-three members. In the Senate, there are sixteen standing committees, and the average Senate committee has twenty members.[21] The committee system is the central hub of legislative activity in Congress. Committees hold hearings to consider members' bills, to conduct oversight of the executive branch, or to draw attention to a pressing issue. Committees also write the legislation that is eventually considered on the House and Senate floors. Table 11.2 lists the standing committees in each chamber.

During committee hearings, committee members literally "hear" testimony on the content and impact of a bill from other members of Congress, executive branch officials, interest groups, businesses, state and local government officials, and citizens' groups. For the public, hearings are a direct gateway for influence on members of Congress because important information is conveyed in a public setting. Committee hearings serve five basic functions for members of Congress: (1) to draw attention to a current problem or issue that needs public attention, (2) to inform the committee members about the consequences of passing a specific bill, (3) to convey constituents' questions and concerns on an issue, (4) to exert oversight of the executive branch to determine whether congressional intent is being honored, and (5) to provide an arena where individual members make speeches to attract media attention that is often used later in a campaign as evidence that the member is doing his or her job. Committee chairs decide which bills receive hearings and which go on to **markup**, a meeting in which committee members write the version of the bill that they send to the entire chamber for a vote. In both the hearing and markup process, the committee chair gives preference to the views of the majority party members of the committee.

Committee chairs have powerful roles. They are typically the majority party member who has the most seniority (longest time) on the committee. However, the Speaker or the Senate majority leader reserves the right to suggest a less senior member be chair if either believes it will better serve the party's interests. The minority party leader on a committee is called the **ranking member** and is the member of the committee from the minority party with the greatest seniority.

Until 1994, there was no limit on the number of terms that committee chairs could serve. However, in 1995, the Republican majorities in the House and the Senate adopted six-year term limits on chairs. Limiting the tenure of committee chairs makes it harder for them to amass long-term individual power, so the Speaker retains more control over the committees' legislative agendas. In 2007, when the Democrats took the majority in the House and

select committee: *Committee in the House or Senate that has very limited powers over a specific issue.*

joint committee: *Committee that includes members of both the House and Senate.*

special committee: *Committee formed to address a specific issue area or controversy, typically for a defined period of time.*

markup: *Process where bills are literally "marked up," or written by the members of the committee.*

Identify the functions of hearings. How do they serve as gateways?

ranking member: *Leader of the minority party members of the committee.*

TABLE 11.2 Standing Committees in Congress

House of Representatives (20 committees)	U.S. Senate (16 committees)
Agriculture	Agriculture, Nutrition, and Forestry
Appropriations	Appropriations
Armed Services	Armed Services
Financial Services	Banking, Housing, and Urban Affairs
Budget	Budget
Education and Labor	Health, Education, Labor, and Pensions
Energy and Commerce	Commerce, Science, and Transportation
	Energy and Natural Resources
	Environment and Public Works
Foreign Affairs	Foreign Relations
Homeland Security	Homeland Security and Governmental Affairs
Oversight and Government Reform	
House Administration	Rules and Administration Committee
Judiciary	Judiciary
Natural Resources	
Transportation and Infrastructure	
Rules	
Science and Technology	
Small Business	Small Business and Entrepreneurship
Standards of Official Conduct	
Veterans' Affairs	Veterans' Affairs
Ways and Means	Finance

Source: U.S. House of Representatives and Senate Website, www.house.gov and www.senate.gov. See the committee membership lists.

Senate, House Democrats retained term limits but Senate Democrats did not; in January 2009, House Democrats eliminated term limits on committee chairs.[22]

In general, when a bill is referred to a committee, it is assigned to a subcommittee, a smaller group of committee members who focus on a specific subset of the committee's issues. Subcommittees can consider legislation, but only the full committee can report a bill to the chamber floor for consideration. In 1973, the House expanded the number of subcommittees and subcommittee chairs, largely as a result of the efforts of young congressmen who wanted to enact policies that older committee chairs opposed. By creating more subcommittees, the House created smaller centers of power in which individual members could exert influence over the content of legislation.[23] The Senate did not make similar changes; each senator already had individual power and did not see the need to make changes in the committee structure.

Advocacy Caucuses

In addition to committees in the House and Senate, there are also **advocacy caucuses**, groups whose members have a common interest and work together to promote it. Members might have similar industries located in their districts and states, such as coal mining; or they share a background, such as the Congressional Black Caucus or the Hispanic Caucus; or they hold similar opinions on issues, such as abortion or land conservation. Members join a caucus because it gives them an opportunity to work closely with colleagues to represent specific interests and to draw attention to issues that are of concern to them and to their constituents. Most caucuses are bipartisan, that is, they allow both Democrats and Republicans to join as members. These caucuses are important to the interactions of Congress because they bring members together from different parties and regions that might not otherwise have the possibility to interact.[24]

Advocacy caucuses have no formal legislative power, but they can be influential on a bill, especially in the House, because they represent a bloc of members who could vote together in support or opposition. As an alternative to joining a caucus, senators can simply join together in a temporary coalition and call a press conference to draw attention to the group, industry, or issue that unites them. Senators can also join a congressional caucus even though it is lodged in the House. When he was a senator from Illinois (2005–8), Barack Obama joined the Congressional Black Caucus.

advocacy caucus: *Group of members of Congress from both parties who share a common background, economic interest, or opinion on an issue that reflects their constituents' interests.*

How do advocacy caucuses counteract the role of parties in Congress? How can they be a gateway for citizen influence?

The Lawmaking Process

In this section, we examine the lawmaking process. The process by which a policy proposal becomes a bill and then a law is long and winding, and the Framers made it so deliberately, to ensure that laws were reasonable and well thought out. In fact, the gates against passage are almost too successful. In the 110th Congress (2007–8), for example, members introduced 7,271 public bills in the House of Representatives, and 3,676 public bills in the Senate. Of the total 10,947 public bills, Congress enacted only 334 bills—or 3 percent—into law.[25] It requires compromise and cooperation for a bill to become a law. For an overview of the process, see Figure 11.4.

FIGURE 11.4 **How a Bill Becomes a Law.**

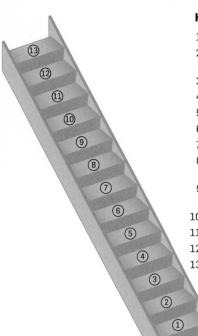

House of Representatives

1. Bill is introduced by a House member on the House floor.
2. Bill is referred by the Speaker of the House to a committee and subcommittee.
3. Subcommittee holds hearings on the bill.
4. Subcommittee holds a markup session on the bill.
5. Subcommittee reports the bill to the full committee.
6. Full committee may hold hearings on the bill.
7. Full committee marks up the bill.
8. Committee votes to recommend the bill to the full House, and the bill is sent to the House Rules Committee (the gatekeeper).
9. Rules Committee writes the rule on the bill, which determines what amendments, if any, can be offered when the bill is considered on the House floor.
10. Members of the House vote to adopt or reject the rule.
11. If the House accepts the rule, the bill is debated, and amendments may be offered.
12. House votes to pass or defeat the bill.
13. House bill is reconciled with Senate version to produce one bill, which is sent by Congress to the president for his approval or rejection.

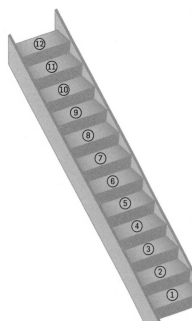

Senate

1. Bill is introduced by a senator on the Senate floor.
2. Bill is referred to a committee by the Senate parliamentarian.
3. Committee may refer the bill to a subcommittee.
4. Subcommittee may hold hearings on the bill; depending on the committee, the subcommittee may or may not mark up the bill.
5. Full committee may hold hearings on the bill.
6. Full committee holds a mark up and recommends the bill to the Senate.
7. Bill is placed on the Senate legislative calendar.
8. Majority leader brings up the bill on the Senate floor.
9. Majority leader tries to craft a unanimous consent agreement outlining which amendments will be offered and how long debate will continue; if unanimous consent is not achieved, there is unlimited debate on the bill.
10. Senators may offer amendments to the bill and debate the bill.
11. Senate votes to pass or defeat the bill.
12. Senate bill is reconciled with House version to produce one bill, which is sent by Congress to the president for his approval or rejection.

The Procedural Rules of the House and Senate

Just as the role of political parties and leaders differs in the House and Senate, so do the internal rules of these chambers. Over time, House and Senate members have adopted different procedures for considering legislation, and they can make compromise between the two chambers more difficult.

The House Committee on Rules.

To proceed from committee to the House floor, most bills must pass through the **House Rules Committee**. Because the House is so large, bills cannot proceed to the floor from committee unprotected; otherwise the number of **amendments** that could be offered by 435 members of the House would overwhelm lawmaking.

The Rules Committee maintains control before the bill goes to the floor by issuing a **rule** dictating how many amendments may be considered. A closed rule means no amendments may be offered at all; a modified closed rule allows a few amendments; and an open rule, as its name suggests, allows any number of amendments. The most typical rule is a modified closed rule, which allows the minority party to offer at least one alternative to the bill supported by the majority party. The rule is voted on by all members of the House, and if it is approved, debate on the bill begins. If the rule is defeated, the bill is returned to the House Rules Committee or the originating committee for further consideration.

As we explained earlier, the majority party has learned over time how to use the Rules Committee to maintain policy advantages over the minority party. The majority party uses its numerical advantage on the Rules Committee (9–4) to structure floor debate to limit the minority party's opportunity to amend or change a bill. The Speaker appoints all the majority party members to the Rules Committee, and they are expected to use their powers to advance the party's preferred version of a bill.

Agenda-Setting Tools in the Senate.

The Senate does not have a gatekeeper committee like the Committee on Rules in the House; all senators have the power to try to amend legislation on the floor. The tool that they use is Rule XIX of the Standing Rules of the Senate, which grants senators the right to speak on the Senate floor. Over time, senators have used this right to make speeches, offer amendments to bills, object to consideration of a bill on the floor, or engage in a **filibuster**, an extended debate whose purpose is to delay or even prevent a bill's passage.[26] All senators, in the majority and the minority parties, can use the filibuster. Throughout Senate history, a wide range of bills, from civil rights legislation to product liability legislation, have been delayed or defeated by filibusters.[27]

The only way to stop a filibuster is by invoking **cloture**, a motion to end debate that requires a supermajority of sixty votes to pass. Once cloture has

Do the procedural rules of the House and Senate serve as gates or gateways to legislation? Why would there be gates that prevent Congress from fulfilling its fundamental responsibility to pass laws?

House Rules Committee: *Gatekeeping committee that sets the guidelines for debating, changing, and voting on a bill on the floor.*

amendment: *In Congress, a proposed change to a bill.*

rule: *Guidelines issued by the House Rules Committee that determines how many amendments may be considered for each bill.*

filibuster: *Delay tactic of extended speech designed to delay or block passage of a bill in the Senate.*

Is the filibuster a legitimate means of protecting minority rights?

cloture: *Vote that can stop a filibuster and bring debate on a bill to an end.*

been invoked on a bill, no more than thirty additional hours of debate are permitted. All amendments must be germane to the bill's issues, and a time for a final vote is set.

In addition, Senate rules no longer require those seeking to block a bill to speak continuously on the floor. Senators who oppose a bill can merely state their intention to filibuster and that will be sufficient to block it from consideration on the floor. Senators also use the threat of a filibuster to block the president's judicial nominations at all levels, a practice that has come under increasing scrutiny. To counteract the filibuster in recent years, the Senate has resorted to a two-track system, in which a bill that is being filibustered can be set aside to allow the Senate to proceed to other bills. But even with this two-track system, the filibuster has imposed substantial costs on the Senate, both in terms of the legislation that has failed to pass and legislation that could not be brought to the floor.

Some scholars have argued that the filibuster has been used too frequently as a way of blocking action on important public policies and is not a legitimate democratic instrument of power.[28] Others argue that filibustering is a responsive and effective means of representation in Congress; if there is intense opposition to a bill in a senator's state, or from a minority of voters nationwide, the senator may consider it a responsibility to block the bill's passage.[29]

Without a gatekeeper like the House Committee on Rules and with the constant threat of a filibuster, there are few restrictions on a bill when it comes to the Senate floor. When the Senate majority leader wishes to bring a bill up for consideration, he or she must ask unanimous consent of every senator. Consequently, the Senate typically operates under **unanimous consent agreements** to establish guidelines for debating a bill. Senators strike a deal as to how a bill will be debated on the Senate floor, how and when amendments will be offered, how much time will be allocated to debate and vote on amendments, and a time and date for the final vote on the complete bill. Senators have accepted this form of limitation on their rights to amend or block a bill because it requires their consent and enables the Senate to move forward and pass key legislation.

Nevertheless, a senator can object to a unanimous consent request to bring a bill to the Senate floor, in a practice known as a **hold**. A hold is a less drastic measure than a filibuster, but it still can be used by any senator to delay a bill for twenty-four hours. If a senator wants to block the bill for longer than that, he must request a hold every twenty-four hours. Typically senators hold up a bill to extract concessions from Senate leaders, or from the administration, on the legislation being considered. They also use the hold to draw increased attention to a bill, or to delay a presidential nominee that they oppose, in the hopes that public opposition to it will develop.

unanimous consent agreement: *Agreement among all 100 senators for how a bill will be debated, changed, and voted on in the Senate.*

hold: *Power available to a senator to keep a bill from coming to the Senate floor for twenty-four hours without having to filibuster it.*

Twenty-four hours may not seem like a long time, but in an age of 24-7 media and the Internet, public impressions can form quickly. In March 2010, Senator Jim Bunning (R-Ky.) used his power to object to unanimous consent to delay a bill that would have extended benefits to unemployed workers. Although he explained that he was doing so to avoid increased deficit spending, the bill was perceived by members of both parties to be vital, and Senate leaders managed to bring sufficient public pressure to bear on him that he dropped his objection.

Legislative Proposals

The lawmaking process starts with an idea. Ideas for legislation can come from a number of sources, including constituents, interest groups, local or national newspaper stories, state or local governments, staff members, and finally, the members' own personal interests.[30] When an idea is agreed upon, the House or Senate member's staff consults with the Office of Legislative Counsel, which turns the general outlines of a bill into the technical language that will alter the U.S. Code, the set of federal laws that governs the United States. After approving the final legal language of a bill, the member introduces the bill into the respective chamber (House or Senate), an action known as **bill sponsorship**. Once a bill is introduced, other members can sign on to be cosponsors (sponsorship of legislation is discussed in more detail later in this chapter). In reality, many freestanding bills that are introduced separately are later incorporated into larger **omnibus bills** that are passed by Congress. Omnibus legislation can be an attractive tool for Congress, especially in periods of divided government. These big bills allow Congress to pass numerous provisions that might not pass if each were presented separately.[31]

Committee Action

After a member introduces a bill, it is referred to the committee(s) or subcommittee(s) that have jurisdiction over its subject matter. The first step on the route to getting a bill enacted into law is to secure a hearing on a bill in subcommittee or full committee. In general, a committee tends to act first on bills that are sponsored by the chair of the committee, then the subcommittee chairs, and lastly, regular members of the committee. If the sponsor is not on the committee to which the bill is assigned, it is much harder to get action on the bill, but this arrangement also makes sense because committee members are more likely to have expertise on the issues covered by the committee than are others, so their bills are taken more seriously by their fellow committee members.[32] In rare cases, however, as a result of intense interest group lobbying or media pressure, a committee might hold a hearing on a bill

Are filibusters unnecessary gates to the legislative process? What about holds?

bill sponsorship: *Act of introducing a bill on the House or Senate floor.*

omnibus bill: *One very large bill that encompasses many separate bills.*

How can you as a citizen influence legislation in Congress?

How do omnibus bills make accountability more difficult?

sponsored by a non–committee member, but the committee typically drafts its own bill to address the same issue.

After a bill has been the subject of hearings, the committee may move to the markup phase, where committee members write the version of the bill that will be reported to the full House or Senate. At this point, the stakes intensify as to what the bill will ultimately look like, so the stakeholders in the policy process try to exert influence. Stakeholders know that the language of the full committee bill is likely to stay intact because the process of amending a bill on the chamber floor is difficult, especially in the House. Once the full committee approves a bill, then the bill and an accompanying committee report are sent to the full House or Senate for consideration by all the members.

Floor Action and the Vote

When a bill is sent to the full House or Senate, it is commonly known as "going to the floor" because all the members of the chamber gather together to debate and vote on the bill. Debate takes different forms in each chamber. In the House, it is heavily structured, and most members are allowed no more than five minutes to speak on a measure, leaving almost no time for actual deliberation among members. But in the Senate, as we noted earlier, there are few limits on the time allowed to members to speak on an issue on the floor. If the Senate is operating under a unanimous consent agreement or cloture, then time is limited; otherwise, senators can make speeches and even engage in active debate on an issue for much longer than their House counterparts. Unfortunately for the current political system, real debate on issues rarely occurs on the floor; instead, House members and senators use their opportunity to speak to make partisan speeches on a bill or to direct their remarks to their constituents back home.

roll call vote: *Vote that a House or Senate member casts on a bill or amendment when his or her name is called.*

During a **roll call vote**, the clerks of the House or Senate call the names of each member, who registers his or her vote electronically. Members cast votes up or down on legislation (to pass or reject), to table (set aside) legislation, or to approve a motion to recommit (send it back to committee with instructions to rewrite it). In addition to individually recorded votes, general voice votes can be taken when a consensus exists and there is no perceived need to record each member's vote. A roll call vote is the most fundamental way that a member of Congress represents his or her constituents and therefore is a key gateway for citizen influence in the legislative process.

Scholars have long characterized roll call voting by partisan dimension and by ideological or spatial dimension,[33] because in the past both the Democratic and Republican parties contained both liberals and conservatives.

Currently, the vast majority of Democratic members are liberal, and the vast majority of Republican members are conservative. Consequently, scholars now can examine roll call voting through both the partisan and ideological lens simultaneously. They confirm that most votes in the House and Senate are **party-line votes**, in which a majority of one party votes yes on a bill and a majority of the other party votes no. In the 110th Congress, for example, 89 percent of House votes and 84 percent of Senate votes were party-line votes.[34] In today's Congress, leaders frame the content of bills and the choices for roll call votes along the lines of party platforms and ideology. Essentially, they are engaging in **message politics**, designing legislation to push members into casting votes that may later be used in campaigns against them.[35] This framework reflects a responsible parties system (see Chapters 6 and 9), in which voters can clearly distinguish between Democratic and Republican legislative policy goals. Although the increased emphasis on partisanship makes it easier for citizens to more clearly hold Congress accountable, it decreases the likelihood of bipartisan cooperation and makes it more difficult to pass legislation that addresses pressing needs of citizens on an equal basis.

party-line votes: *Voting in Congress according to party position, so that a majority of one party votes against a majority of the other party.*

message politics: *Strategy of framing choices on legislation so as to push members into casting votes that could later be used against them in campaigns.*

Conference Committee

For a bill to become law, the House and Senate have to pass an identically worded version of it to send to the president for his signature. The last stage in the congressional legislative process is when the House and Senate meet in **conference committee** to resolve any differences that exist in the versions that passed each chamber. The Speaker of the House and the Senate majority leader typically appoint the chairs and ranking members from the committees that originated the bills, and other members who have been active on the bill. If the bill is very important to the party leaders, they also have the power to appoint themselves to the committee, though this does not happen very often. If the conferees are successful, then the conference committee issues a conference report that must be voted on by the entire House and Senate. Because the conference report represents the end of the negotiation process between the two chambers, members cannot offer amendments to change the contents of it. However, if a majority of members of the House or Senate are displeased with the final results of the conference, they can defeat the report outright or vote to instruct the conference committee to revise the agreement.

conference committee: *Temporary committee created after a bill passes the House and the Senate to resolve any differences in the provisions of the bills so a single bill can be sent to the president.*

In the past two decades, however, Congress has also used alternative ways of constructing a compromise between versions of House and Senate bills. When a bill involves the work of several committees, party leaders have sometimes chosen not to form an official conference committee but instead take on the responsibility for producing a final bill themselves. In choosing this path, they concentrate power over the final bill in the hands of fewer members of Congress than the traditional conference committee system does.[36] Although this alternative provides a more streamlined way of legislating between the House and Senate, it also acts as a gate against input from committee members who wish to represent their constituents' views on the final version of the bill.

The Budget Process and Reconciliation

Although the federal government tries to spend about as much money as it takes in from revenues, it does not typically succeed. Instead, the federal government usually runs a budget **deficit**, which requires it to borrow money to meet all of its obligations (see Table 11.3 and Figure 11.5). Although the process is complex, essentially this means that the federal government pays interest on outstanding loans, and the loans and interest that accumulate over time constitute the **national debt**.

The modern Congress operates under a budget process created in the Congressional Budget and Impoundment Control Act of 1974, which was enacted to give Congress more power over the federal budget.[37] It was passed at a time of relatively low deficit amounts, but many new government programs were being implemented and government financial obligations were steadily rising. The act created the House and Senate Budget Committees and the Congressional Budget Office so that Congress could construct its own budget blueprint, as an alternative to the president's annual budget (the

federal deficit: *Difference between the amount of money the federal government spends in outlays and the amount of money it receives from revenues.*

national debt: *Sum of loans and interest that the federal government has accrued over time to pay for the federal deficit.*

TABLE 11.3 **Federal Deficits and the National Debt 1970–2009**

Year	Revenues	Outlays	Total Deficit	National Debt
1970	192.8	195.6	−2.8	283.2
1975	279.1	332.3	−53.2	394.7
1980	517.1	590.9	−73.8	711.9
1985	734.0	946.3	−212.3	1,507.3
1990	1,032.0	1,253.0	−221.0	2,411.6
1995	1,351.8	1,515.8	−164.0	3,604.4
2000	2,025.2	1,789.0	236.2	3,409.8
2005	2,153.6	2,472.0	−318.3	4,592.2
2009	2,104.6	3,518.2	−1,413.6	7,544.0

Source: Congressional Budget Office, January 24, 2010, www.cbo.gov.

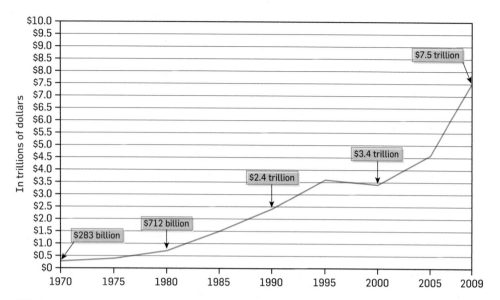

FIGURE 11.5 The National Debt, 1970–2009. Since 1970, the federal government has operated under a budget deficit for most years, except between 1998 and 2000, when it ran a surplus. The United States government borrows money, with interest, to fill the gap between what it takes in and what it spends, and the total outstanding loan balance is the national debt. *Source:* For historical tables on the U.S. federal budget, see Congressional Budget Office, "The Budget and Economic Outlook Fiscal Years 2010 to 2020," Worksheet F-1 entitled "Revenues, Outlays, Surpluses, Deficits, and Debt Held by the Public 1979 to 2009."

federal government's fiscal year begins on October 1 and ends on September 30). The key aspect of the budget process (see Figure 11.6) is that the congressional budget, known as the **concurrent budget resolution**, is supposed to be approved by both chambers by April 15, but because it does not have the force of law, it is not sent to the president for his signature. Rather it serves as general instructions to congressional committees about how much money can be allocated for federal programs in any given fiscal year. The authorizing committees take this blueprint into account when they reauthorize existing programs or create new ones, and the appropriations committees in the House and Senate use it to allocate funds in twelve separate bills; they typically begin their work in May in the hopes of enacting all appropriations bills by September 30. If Congress and the president fail to agree on any one of the twelve appropriations bills, a **continuing resolution** is enacted that funds the government temporarily while disagreements about spending can be worked out.

The 1974 Budget Act also created a parallel budget bill, known as **reconciliation**, which does require the president's signature. Reconciliation was specifically designed as umbrella legislation to bring all bills that contain

concurrent budget resolution : *Congressional blueprint outlining general amounts of funds that can be spent on federal programs.*

continuing resolution: *Measure passed to fund federal programs when the appropriations process has not been completed by the end of the fiscal year on September 30.*

Does the congressional budget process help or hurt deficit reduction efforts?

reconciliation: *A measure used to bring all bills that contain changes in the tax code or entitlement programs in line with the congressional budget.*

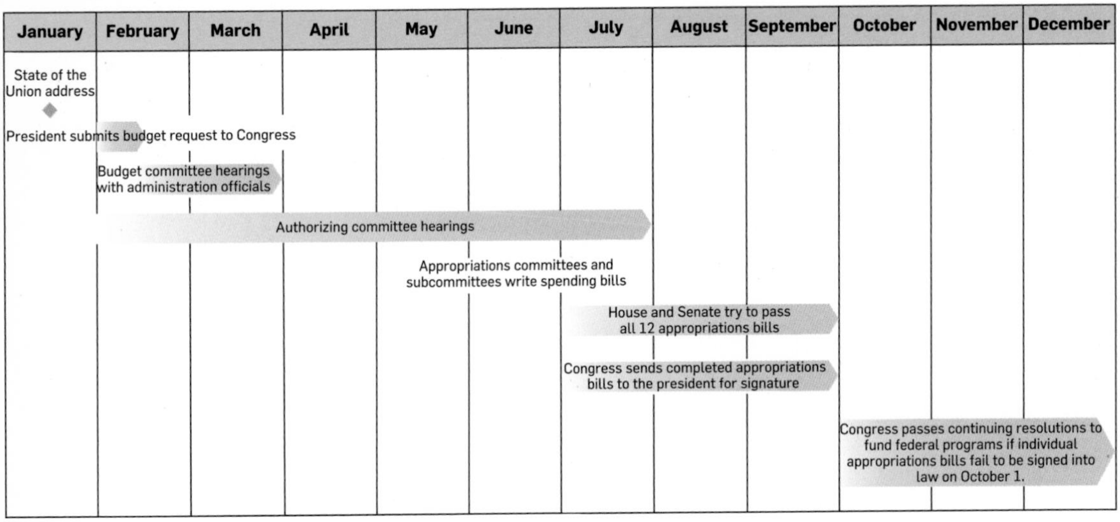

January	February	March	April	May	June	July	August	September	October	November	December

State of the Union address
◆

President submits budget request to Congress ▶

Budget committee hearings with administration officials ▶

Authorizing committee hearings ▶

Appropriations committees and subcommittees write spending bills

House and Senate try to pass all 12 appropriations bills ▶

Congress sends completed appropriations bills to the president for signature ▶

Congress passes continuing resolutions to fund federal programs if individual appropriations bills fail to be signed into law on October 1. ▶

FIGURE 11.6 The Federal Budget Timeline. Congress produces its own blueprint for the federal budget to serve as an alternative to the president's budget and guide the appropriations process. If necessary, Congress also produces a reconciliation bill to make changes to tax and entitlement programs.
Source: Author, based on the Budget and Impoundment Control Act of 1974, Title III, Section 300 (Washington D.C.: Government Printing Office, 1987), 72.

entitlement programs:
Federal programs, such as Social Security, Medicare, or Medicaid, that pay out benefits to individuals based on a specified set of eligibility criteria.

changes in the tax code or entitlement programs in line with the congressional budget. **Entitlement programs**, such as Social Security, Medicare, or Medicaid, are considered mandatory because they are federal programs that pay out benefits to individuals based on a specified set of eligibility criteria. When Congress wishes to make a change to these types of programs, it must pass a reconciliation bill. This type of bill has special procedural protections in the Senate, where it cannot be filibustered and can be debated for no more than twenty hours. A bill that cannot be filibustered was a tempting target for those who wanted to add non-budget-related provisions. Consequently, in 1985 the budget process was modified to include the Byrd rule, which required that reconciliation be used only to reduce the federal deficit, which at the time was $212.3 billion.[38] In subsequent years, the Byrd rule has been interpreted to mean that all provisions of reconciliation must be directly related to the budget.[39]

Despite the Byrd rule, Congress has found ways to use the reconciliation process to pass controversial legislation. Most recently, the Democratic majority in Congress used it to pass comprehensive health care reform, which we discuss below. Both Democrats and Republicans have used the reconciliation process to go beyond changes in the tax code, or to balance the budget, on issues ranging from welfare reform to children's health insurance.[40]

Presidential Signature or Veto, and the Veto Override

The last step in the legislative process is sending a bill to the president for his approval or disapproval. A president can actively disapprove, or **veto** a bill. If Congress will be going out of session within ten days, the president can wait for Congress to go out of session and simply not sign a bill, a practice known as a **pocket veto**. In cases where the president refuses to sign the bill but Congress remains in session, the bill becomes law (see Chapter 12 for more discussion on the presidential use of the veto power).

The veto is a powerful balancing tool for the president against the overreach of Congress; but at the same time, the Framers gave Congress the **override**, the power to overturn a presidential veto with a two-thirds vote in each chamber. When the president vetoes a bill, it is returned to the chamber from which it originated; if two-thirds of that chamber vote to override the veto, then it is sent to the other chamber. A two-thirds vote, rather than just a majority vote, is required for an override because the Framers wanted to enable the president to be able to block a bill passed by Congress if he does not believe it is in the best interest of the nation as a whole. From a legislating point of view, presidents use the veto either to prevent a bill from becoming law or to pressure Congress into making changes to a bill that are closer in line with his policies.[41] In the 110th (2007–08) Congress, President George W. Bush (2001–09) vetoed nine bills, and Congress overrode four of them.[42]

veto: *Authority of the president to block legislation passed by Congress.*

pocket veto: *Automatic veto that occurs when Congress goes out of session within ten days of submitting a bill to the president and the president has not signed it.*

override: *Congress' power to overturn a presidential veto with a two-thirds vote in each chamber.*

Why did the Framers give Congress the final say in whether a bill should become a law?

The Members of Congress at Work

The cardinal rule of succeeding in the House or Senate is simple: Never forget where you came from. Representative Nydia Velázquez has shown how a member tries to balance all the competing demands of legislator with the core responsibility to serve constituents. The following sections describe in depth just exactly what the job of a House or Senate member entails.

Offices and Staff

For all newly elected members in the House and Senate, the first steps are to set up an office and hire staff members. Most members bring some of their campaign workers with them to Washington to work on their staffs and try to hire people from their districts or states. New members of Congress also seek out individuals with prior Capitol Hill experience to help orient them to their new surroundings and provide specific issue expertise.

Generally, a member of Congress's Washington office has a chief of staff who oversees the entire office, a scheduler who makes the member's appointments, a press secretary who handles all interactions with the media, and a legislative director who oversees the member's legislative work. In addition, legislative assistants handle specific issues, and legislative correspondents are responsible for answering constituent mail.

House and Senate members aim to be responsive to constituents, and that means providing prompt and extensive **constituent services**. To do so, they establish district offices—in the congressional district, or for senators, in the state—which are run by district directors. These offices help constituents navigate federal agencies if they have difficulty, for example, getting a Social Security check or a passport, and advise constituents on how to win federal contracts. Specific requests for help are assigned to caseworkers. These local offices serve as a direct and important link between voters and members of Congress that affects both accountability and responsiveness.[43]

constituent services:
Individualized services performed by a member of Congress for a constituent, such as help with a passport, Social Security problem, or any other issue that requires federal government involvement.

Legislative Responsibilities

A successful legislator typically fulfills four responsibilities: securing desired committee assignments and performing committee work, sponsoring and cosponsoring bills, casting votes, and obtaining federal funds for the district or state.

Committee Work.   Just before the start of each new Congress, members are asked which committees they would like to join, and party leaders try to accommodate their wishes, although freshman members rarely get their most favored committees immediately. Freshman members make their choice of committee assignments based on the needs of their district or state, their professional background, and their personal experience. However, new senators have to accommodate their committee assignment wish list to the reality of the senior senator's existing committee assignments. All members of the House and Senate try to put themselves in the best possible institutional position to address issues that matter to their constituents.

Committee work consists of attending hearings and participating in markups as well as initiating ideas for legislation that could be considered by the committee. Committee members also meet with interest groups, businesses, and citizens groups that are specifically concerned about bills to be considered in that committee. The extent to which members participate actively in committee business varies according to the local concerns of their constituents, their personal interests, and whether the committee might provide an opportunity for political advancement.[44]

Committees themselves provide different gateways for members to serve their constituents and advance their careers. For example, the Appropriations and Environment and Public Works Committees distribute federal funds for a wide range of programs and projects, enabling members of these committees to have a lot of influence over how these funds are spent. Serving on other committees, such as the Armed Services Committee, can provide members with credentials in the area of defense policy, which can be useful if they represent areas with high military employment or envision themselves running for president one day.

Bill Sponsorship. Members can sponsor a bill by themselves, or they can ask colleagues to cosponsor bills with them; the greater the number of cosponsors, the greater the show of support for the bill. Members sponsor and cosponsor for three important reasons. First, bill sponsorship is an effective tool for giving voters in a district or state a voice in the federal policy-making system. Second, it is a means of staking out specific territory that members can claim as their area of expertise and can be a means of fulfilling campaign promises.[45] Third, it draws attention from the media, relevant interest groups, and the press, and thereby can help House and Senate members build their reputations as legislators.

A bill that accomplishes all three goals is H.R. 44, the Stabilizing Affordable Housing for the Future Act, which Congresswoman Velázquez sponsored and introduced on January 4, 2007. This bill asked Congress to increase the amount of affordable, federally sponsored housing available to citizens with low incomes; it would have directly benefitted Velázquez's constituents because it tried to equalize the opportunity for finding affordable housing. The bill fell directly under the jurisdiction of the Committee on Small Business that she chaired. Although it did not pass, it drew media attention to the national problem of a shortage in affordable housing.

Roll Call Votes. Each representative or senator is expected to cast a roll call vote on the bills and amendments that reach the floor of the House and Senate. In the House alone, members cast 1,876 roll call votes during the 110th Congress.[46] Given this large number of roll call votes, voters have difficulty identifying votes that affect them directly. Because most members of Congress vote the party line, party identification can provide a helpful shortcut to voters in holding their members accountable for their roll call votes. If members do not vote the party line, they risk losing the support of party voters in their district or state. However, most members will not vote for a measure that goes against their constituents' opinion or interests. For this reason, majority party leaders try to construct bills that will benefit the constituents of the members of their party.

Federal Funds. Most members of Congress try to secure federal funds for their districts and states. The effort to carve out some piece of the

funding formula: *Formula written into law by Congress that determines how funds will be distributed in a federal program.*

earmark: *Amount of federal dollars devoted specifically to a local project in a congressional district or state.*

Federal funds for local projects are often denounced as "pork." How does "pork" figure in your decision to vote for or against an incumbent?

federal financial pie is typically referred to as "bringing home the bacon" or pork barrel spending, and can work through **funding formulas** for federal programs or **earmarks**, which are narrowly defined, federally funded projects.[47] Federal funds can be used to rebuild a highway, build a fairground, fund a local orchestra, construct a research center on the effects of pig odor, and even support a water taxi service in Connecticut.[48] Over the past decade, spending on earmarks has increased tenfold; in fiscal year 2009, Congress devoted $19.1 billion to fund 10,160 earmarks.[49] Although Democrats promised to cut spending on earmarks when they assumed control of Congress in 2007, spending on these programs has not declined.

While the purposes of these earmarks always sound useful, they can range in price from $100,000 to $200 million and prove to be wasteful. One of the most infamous earmarks in recent years was the so-called "bridge to nowhere" in Alaska. The bridge was championed by former Senator Ted Stevens (R-Alaska), chair of the Senate Appropriations Committee. When a combination of conservative members of Congress and public watchdog groups raised media awareness about the enormous cost of this bridge, which would have served only a few thousand people at most, the House and Senate were embarrassed into canceling approval for the bridge. The funding itself was not canceled; instead, Congress directed the state of Alaska to spend the money on other, more necessary transportation projects.[50]

Despite the conflict over the earmark and federal funding process generally, one could argue that obtaining federal dollars for the district is a form of responsiveness to the local needs of voters. After all, voters are taxpayers, and members of Congress are simply seeking to bring some of that tax money back home in a directed fashion. On the other hand, many of these projects are not really necessary to most voters, and they create waste and inefficiency that can make the federal government less effective.

Communication with Constituents

Congressional representation depends on good communication between constituents and their representatives and senators. It is important to remember that members of Congress have two distinct places of work: Washington, D.C., and their home district or state.

In Washington, members take advantage of technological innovations, such as e-mail and the Internet, to stay in touch with their constituents. Before e-mail and the Internet, members used the **franking privilege**, which is free mail service, to respond to constituent letters and to send quarterly newsletters as updates on their activities. Much of that hard-mail correspondence has disappeared, and today members of Congress use their own congressional websites, Facebook, and Twitter to transmit information about their activities to constituents.

franking privilege: *Special free mail that a House or Senate member can use to send letters to constituents.*

Is the franking privilege necessary today? Should it be eliminated? How might this privilege be abused?

To help members stay in touch with their constituents, the federal government pays for House and Senate members to return home to their districts or states approximately thirty-three times a year. These trips home are crucial for building bonds with voters, and members make sure they use this opportunity to meet with individuals, speak to local interest groups, attend local parades and business openings, and be seen on local television.

Cultivating direct links with constituents and making a good impression on them is what the political scientist Richard Fenno calls **home style**, or the way members portray themselves to constituents.[51] Members can choose to emphasize their local work for constituents, or they can emphasize their influence on the national policy scene; some try to do both. Members can be very good at giving charismatic speeches, or they can be quiet, unassuming worker bees; successful members adapt their home style to the expectations and customs of constituents.

home style: *Way that incumbents portray themselves to constituents.*

The Next Election

As political scientist David Mayhew explains, members of Congress look to the next election.[52] Elections are the means by which constituents express approval, or disapproval, of the job members of Congress are doing, and elections are the fundamental tool that voters use to hold their members accountable for individual legislative work and the collective performance of their party in office.

The fact is that most **incumbents** in the House and Senate win reelection; in 2008, 94 percent of all House incumbents won reelection, and 84 percent of all Senate incumbents won reelection.[53] Most of this textbook's discussion of congressional elections is contained in Chapter 10 (Elections, Campaigns, and Voting), but in this section, we focus on the interaction of incumbency advantage and reelection. Congressional campaigns are typically divided into two categories: those with an incumbent seeking reelection and those with open seats, where no incumbent is seeking reelection. In elections in which an incumbent is running, the contest becomes an evaluation of the job he or she has done in office compared to what the **challenger** promises to do if elected. Incumbents have major advantages because they have already won at least one election in the district, they are likely to have moderate name recognition, and they have the power of their congressional office to provide services to constituents.

incumbent: *Occupant of elected office.*

challenger: *Candidate who runs against an incumbent.*

In 2010, did you vote for the incumbent or challenger in your district? What was the basis for your decision?

In fact, members' concern for their local districts or states can be one of the biggest gates standing in the way of a productive Congress, and frequently it is the party that works to overcome division among its members. Parties provide a collective set of policy goals that will benefit or appeal to party members at the local level. For a member of Congress, however, tying electoral fortunes to the political party can be risky if the majority party falls out of favor with the voters who can hold it accountable for policy outcomes. In 1994 and 2006 large numbers of incumbents from each major party lost their seats in the House and Senate, and party control of the chambers changed hands as a result; in 2010 the Democrats lost more than sixty seats and majority control of the House but retained a slim majority in the Senate. Although elections with such significant changes are infrequent, they are powerful reminders to incumbents that they must constantly balance the needs of their constituents against the ideas of their party, and stay responsive at all times or risk losing their bid for reelection.

Congress and Public Policy: Health Care

A central challenge to the institution of Congress in carrying out its fundamental responsibility of lawmaking is to balance the separate individual interests of its members against the collective need of the nation. The party leaders and committee chairs in each chamber try to write legislation that will attract the support of enough rank-and-file members to pass. At the same time, Congress considers opinions from organized interest groups, and of course, the president, whose approval is necessary to enact laws. The health care reform efforts in the 111th Congress reflect the challenges of congressional policy making precisely because the proposal was national in scope but faced opposition from members' constituencies all over the country.

The American Health Care System

The health care reform process has a very long history in American politics, dating back to the New Deal, and it always attracts intense support and opposition from various sectors of the policy-making arena. Essentially, the United States has a mixture of private and public health care insurance systems. Most Americans receive health insurance through their employment or purchase it independently from private insurance companies. People over the age of 65 are covered by Medicare, a federally funded health insurance program, and very low income people are covered by Medicaid, a jointly funded health insurance program offered by the federal, state, and local governments.[54] However, in 2008, approximately 45 million Americans did not have access to any health insurance coverage because they were self-employed and could not afford to purchase it, unemployed but not poor or old enough for a government program, or deemed ineligible by private insurance companies because they had health conditions that make them high risk and expensive to cover[55] (see Figure 11.7).

During the past twenty years there have been attempts to reform health care; the two central issues have been the availability of health insurance coverage and the cost of health care programs. President Bill Clinton tried to reform health care in 1993–94 but did not succeed. President Obama

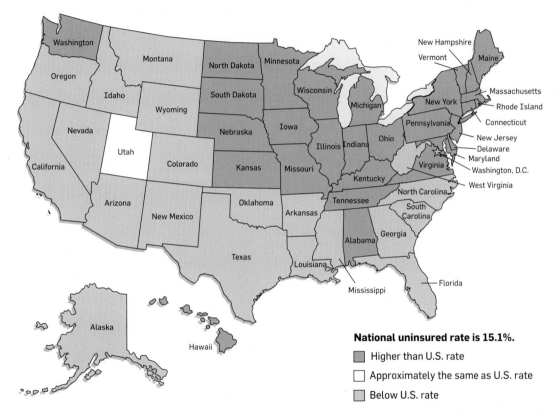

National uninsured rate is 15.1%.

- Higher than U.S. rate
- Approximately the same as U.S. rate
- Below U.S. rate

FIGURE 11.7 Percent of Individuals without Health Insurance by State. Inequalities in access to health care, and especially the problem of 45 million uninsured Americans, made health care reform an issue in the 2008 presidential campaign. Even so, it took until 2010 for health care reform to become law, and implementation of the law will occur over several years. Health care reform illustrates the complexities of the policy process, from internal congressional rules and procedures, to external involvement by the president and interest groups.
Source: Joanna Turner, Michael Boudreaux, and Victoria Lynch, "A Preliminary Evaluation of Health Insurance Coverage in the 2008 American Community Survey," Health Insurance Coverage Working Paper: 2008 American Community Survey, U.S. Census Bureau, issued September 22, 2008, http://www.census.gov.

promised to address health care reform during his 2008 presidential campaign and followed through by asking Congress to write legislation in the summer of 2009. Although Congress did not meet that deadline, the House and Senate each passed versions of health care reform by the end of December 2009 and ultimately passed a compromise version, the Patient Protection and Affordable Care Act in 2010. The process by which health care policy moved from proposal to bill to law was long and winding, as lawmaking always is, but it was especially complicated because of the nature of America's health care system, party politics and partisanship, and the heightened political rhetoric that surrounded the effort.

Where do you stand on health care reform?

Committee Action

The complication for Congress in beginning the task of addressing health care reform was committee jurisdiction. Normally, a bill might be referred to one or two committees at most, but multiple committees claimed jurisdiction over the vast number of programs that constitute the American health care system: the publicly funded Medicare, Medicaid, and related public health service programs, as well as a large private sector component that includes insurance companies and medical professionals. Because of the vast scope of the health care system, there are many different viewpoints on how to reform it and many organizations have a major stake in the outcome of reform efforts.

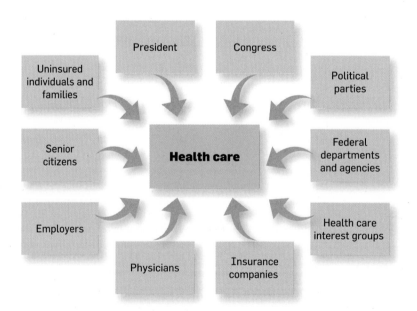

In the House, Representative John Dingell (D-Mich.) introduced the America's Affordable Health Choices Act of 2009 (H.R. 3200), on July 14, 2009. Importantly, the chairs of three committees with primary jurisdiction for health care—Energy and Commerce, Ways and Means, and Education and Labor—were cosponsors of the bill, and the House leadership simultaneously referred the bill to their committees. These three committees produced separate bills that dealt with their sections of health care policy. Henry Waxman (D-Calif.), chair of Energy and Commerce, who had a long history of legislative involvement in health care policy, led the coordination effort. Despite the efforts of House leadership, this bill did not pass the House. On October 29, 2009, Representative Dingell introduced the Affordable Health Care for America Act (H.R. 3962), a merged version of bills proposed by the committee chairs and the House Democratic Party leadership. On November 7, 2009, the House passed this bill with a vote of 220–215 and sent its version of the bill to the Senate. Key to the House bill was the inclusion of a "public option," which would authorize the creation of a federal health insurance program to create competition with private health insurance providers.[56] This sequence demonstrates the complexity of policy reform: reforming a policy requires the cooperation and approval of many players, and even when a bill passes one chamber of Congress, it still must pass the other.

In the Senate, the Health, Education, Labor, and Pensions Committee (HELP) and the Finance Committee have primary jurisdiction. Each committee worked on drafting a separate version of health care reform, and the HELP committee reported its bill, the Affordable Health Choices Act of 2009 (S. 1679), to the full Senate on September 17, 2009. However, the Senate Finance Committee could not come to any agreement on its version of health care reform, and because it has jurisdiction over key components of the health care system, no single bill could be brought to the Senate floor without it. On October 20, 2009, Senator Max Baucus (D-Mont.) introduced America's Healthy Future Act of 2009 (S. 1796), which was amended and approved by the Senate Finance Committee.[57] Although finding consensus in the Senate Finance Committee was a great leap forward for health care reform, Senate leaders still had to reconcile this bill with the HELP committee's bill in order for health care reform legislation to pass the Senate. On Christmas Eve, 2009, the Senate stayed in session for a roll call vote on a compromise version of health care reform entitled America's Healthy Future Act of 2009. The bill passed with a vote of 60 to 39; voting was strictly by party lines.[58] Senate leaders believed passage to be great progress, but the bill differed greatly from that passed by the House, notably because it did not contain the public option. For legislation to be enacted, each chamber has to agree on the same version of the bill and send it to the president for his consideration.

Party Politics

Blue Dog Democrats:
Democratic House members from conservative-leaning districts and who care deeply about fiscal discipline.

The strongest opposition to the bill in the Democratic caucus in the House came from **Blue Dog Democrats**, fifty-two Democratic members who come from conservative-leaning districts and who care deeply about fiscal discipline.[59] They were concerned that the health care bill was too costly and would contribute to an unacceptable level of deficit spending. At the same time, however, the Blue Dogs also expressed concern that if Congress made cuts in federal services to pay for the bill, they would fall disproportionately in rural areas, which constitute a large base of constituents for Blue Dog Democrats. The debate over health care reform within the Democratic caucus in the House reflects the constant tension between party goals and local concerns involved in congressional policy making.

For their part, the Republicans in the House also opposed the bill's provisions on the grounds that it was too costly and that it would introduce government interference into individual choice on health care decisions. Because the minority party in the House is outnumbered in committee and on the House floor and minority party members have few procedural tools to obstruct the majority, they do not have the power to stop the bill.

In contrast, the Senate Republicans, despite being the minority party, have the power to filibuster any health care bill on the Senate floor, and the Democrats needed sixty votes to invoke cloture to shut down a filibuster. Democrats technically had a coalition of sixty senators, including two independent senators, Joseph Lieberman (I-Conn.) and Bernie Sanders (I-Vt.), for all of 2009. However, in January 2010, Scott Brown, a Republican, was elected to fill the Massachusetts Senate seat held by the late Senator Edward Kennedy, a Democrat, so the Democrats lost their sixtieth vote.

Without the necessary sixty votes to invoke cloture, the Democrats feared they could not pass any new or revised version of health care reform. So Democratic leaders in the House and Senate, working with President Obama, decided that the House would have to approve the version of the bill that had already passed in the Senate so that the Senate would not technically have to vote on it again. Democratic House members who supported a more liberal version of the bill were not happy about this compromise, especially about the loss of the public option, so they insisted that in addition to approving the Senate bill, a second bill would have to be passed to include changes that would expand the group of people who would be covered by the bill. Senate Democrats turned to the reconciliation procedure to make these changes in order to avoid a new filibuster by the bill's opponents in the Senate.

As noted earlier, reconciliation bills cannot be filibustered and only require a majority (fifty-one votes) to pass. Ultimately the House passed the Senate version of health care, the Patient Protection and Affordable Care Act, on March 21, 2010, by a vote of 219-212, and President Obama signed it on March 23, 2010. The second bill, the Health Care and Education Reconciliation Act of 2010, was

Sarah L. Voisin/The Washington Post/Getty Images

passed by the Senate on March 25, 2010, by a vote of 56-43, passed by the House on March 25, 2010, by a vote of 220-207, and was signed by President Obama on March 30, 2010. The education part of this bill was included because federal student loan programs have budgetary implications and using the reconciliation process was necessary to revamp the program.

The health care reform act establishes a number of new programs, the most notable of which extends health insurance coverage to approximately 32 million uninsured citizens and legal immigrants through an expansion of Medicaid and the provision of federal subsidies to workers to purchase private health insurance.[60] The act also provides for increased regulation of private insurance company practices; mandates that young adults under the age of 26 be able to stay on a parent's insurance policy; and bans the denial of health insurance based on a preexisting condition. The bill also increases payment levels to doctors who participate in the Medicaid program and helps senior citizens by closing an existing loophole in Medicare coverage for prescription drugs.

The process of health care reform in the House and Senate starkly illustrates the differences between the two chambers, especially the procedures by which they each consider a bill. The House of Representatives uses majority rules and does not give members the opportunity to individually block or delay legislation, so compromise occurs within the majority party more than it does between the majority and minority parties. But in the Senate, the power for the minority party to filibuster makes compromise essential to successful legislating; without it the majority party must resort to invoking cloture and other procedural maneuvers to pass a bill.

Policy discussion occurs in a number of different places in Congress, including in members' offices, in committee rooms, on the House and Senate floors, and among staff members. Such discussion plays an important internal and external role in shaping legislation. Here senators are shown considering health care legislation in committee, with their aides sitting behind them to provide additional information if they need it.

As this brief account of health care policy and reform demonstrates, the internal structure of Congress, the intensity of partisan politics, and the role of citizens and the president each present gates and gateways for legislative policy making.

In 2010 the media and public debated this question: is government broken? Do you think Congress is broken? Defend your answer.

Congress and Democracy

The composition of Congress has changed considerably over the nation's 230 years. This lawmaking body has tripled in size, and now includes men and women from a wide range of ethnic, racial, and religious backgrounds. Certainly from the standpoint of equality of opportunity to serve in Congress, the increased diversity is a very positive step.

Is Congress a *responsive* decision-making body? Individual members clearly work hard to address the concerns of their constituents, both at home in the district or state and in their Washington offices. But Congress as a whole is not always capable of addressing the immediate needs of the nation in a timely fashion. The bicameral nature of the institution, with each chamber's separate rules of operation, makes the legislative process time-consuming and complex. In the House, the majority party almost always succeeds in passing legislation that reflects the party's policy goals. In the Senate, the minority has much greater power to block the majority through the threat of a filibuster, so minority party views are typically incorporated into legislation. These differences offer advantages and disadvantages; if Congress acts too hastily, it can pass harmful legislation, but if it acts too slowly, it can fail to meet its fundamental responsibilities to address issues that citizens care about.

Are individual members of Congress *accountable* for the collective output of the Congress as a whole? Not always. The fundamental difficulty with the representative structure of Congress is that each member is elected separately, so that voters may reelect their own congressperson or senator but still be unhappy with the Congress as a whole. Only in the rarest of election years do voters actually hold all the members of the Congress accountable for their collective performance. This lack of collective accountability can be a significant obstacle or gate to Congress's productivity and responsiveness to important policy needs.

Is Congress *equal* in its treatment of each citizen relative to all others? Are the citizens of small states more powerful in the Senate than those who live in large states, because each state has

FOCUS QUESTIONS

- How are members of Congress held accountable, both individually and for the collective output of Congress as a whole?

- In what ways is Congress responsive as a decision-making body? How does Congress address the pressing needs of the American people?

- What opportunities are there for the average person to influence the policy process in Congress? Is Congress accessible to citizens equally?

- How do the institutional structures in the House of Representatives and in the Senate each work as a gate blocking the enactment of legislation? Are there any gateways in these chambers that can help overcome these obstacles? Why did the Framers set up the legislative branch this way?

- Is Congress a gate or a gateway to democracy?

the same number of senators, regardless of population size? Are the laws that Congress passes fair and balanced, or do they benefit one group more consistently than any other? There is no simple answer to these questions. It is not clear that Congress sets out to give some people greater advantages than others, but the process of balancing all the different individual and regional interests in national policy making produces winners and losers. The fundamental challenge to Congress is to make sure that there are no permanent winners or losers. The challenge to all citizens is to monitor their members of Congress to be sure they are performing their legislative responsibilities.

GATEWAYS TO LEARNING

Top Ten to Take Away

1. The Framers designed Congress as a bicameral legislature so that the House of Representatives and the Senate, with different qualifications for office, modes of election, terms of office, and constituencies, would check and balance each other. (pp. 363–364)

2. Although the enumerated powers of Congress are limited, it has built upon its implied powers to become the powerful legislative branch that it is today. (pp. 370–375)

3. Differences in size, rules, structure, and responsibility influenced the evolution of the House and Senate into very different institutions. (pp. 364–370)

4. Political parties play a stronger role in the organization and operation of the House than the Senate. (pp. 376–378)

5. In the Senate, each member has relatively equal power, and passing legislation requires compromise and cooperation. (pp. 378–379)

6. The procedures through which a bill becomes a law are different in the House and Senate, but each chamber engages in committee work, hearings, floor debate, and voting. Following passage by each chamber individually, a formal conference committee or an informal group of party leaders

resolves differences between the two bills to produce a single bill that is presented to the president for his signature. (pp. 379–383)

7. If a president vetoes a bill, Congress can override the veto with a two-thirds majority in each house. (p. 393)

8. The process of lawmaking is not smooth or efficient, and there are structural gates against a bill's passage. Only a very small percentage of bills introduced are enacted into law. Lawmaking requires that competing interests be balanced through cooperation, compromise, and deal-making. (pp. 383–393)

9. In recent years, intense partisanship, including party-line voting and message politics, has decreased the likelihood of bipartisan cooperation and made it even more difficult for Congress to pass legislation. (pp. 388–389)

10. Members of Congress try to balance the competing demands of legislation and constituent services and they are always anticipating the next election. A successful legislator seeks to be responsive to constituents by engaging in committee work, sponsoring and voting on bills, and securing federal funds for his or her district or state. (pp. 393–398)

A full narrative summary is on the book's website.

Ten to Test Yourself

1. Compare and contrast the constitutional differences between the House and Senate.

2. How do these differences explain the different paths of development for the House and the Senate?

3. What are two key differences in the ways bills are considered in the House and Senate?

4. What is a committee markup?

5. Compare and contrast the power of political parties to shape policy in the House and in the Senate.

6. Who is more powerful—the Speaker of the House or the Senate majority leader?

7. Describe the rules and procedures in the House and Senate that make passage of legislation difficult.

8. Identify and describe three ways that a member of Congress builds a bond with constituents.

9. Why do representatives and senators vote with their party leaders on legislation?

10. Describe the various factors that complicated consideration of health care reform in 2009–10.

More review questions and answers and chapter quizzes are on the book's website.

Terms to Know and Use

advice and consent (p. 371)

advocacy caucus (p. 383)

amendment (p. 385)

appropriate (p. 370)

authorize (p. 370)

bicameral (p. 363)

bill sponsorship (p. 387)

Blue Dog Democrats (p. 402)

census (p. 367)

challenger (p. 397)

cloture (p. 385)

commerce clause (p. 371)

committee chair (p. 379)

concurrent budget
  resolution (p. 391)

continuing resolution (p. 391)

conference committee (p. 389)

constituency (p. 367)

constituent services (p. 394)

delegate (p. 363)

divided government (p. 373)

earmark (p. 396)

entitlement programs (p. 392)

enumerated powers (p. 372)

federal deficit (p. 390)

filibuster (p. 385)

franking privilege (p. 396)

funding formula (p. 396)

general welfare clause (p. 370)

gerrymandering (p. 368)

hearings (p. 375)

hold (p. 386)

home style (p. 397)

House majority leader (p. 377)

House minority leader (p. 377)

House Rules Committee (p. 385)

impeachment (p. 372)

implied powers (pp. 372, 373)

incumbent (p. 397)

joint committee (pp. 380, 381)

judicial review (p. 373)

Judiciary Act (p. 373)

Marbury v. Madison (p. 373)

markup (p. 381)

message politics (p. 389)

national debt (p. 390)

necessary and proper clause
  (pp. 372, 373)

omnibus bill (p. 387)

override (p. 393)

oversight (p. 373)

party caucus (p. 377)

party-line votes (p. 389)

pocket veto (p. 393)

president *pro tempore* (p. 378)

ranking member (p. 381)

reconciliation (p. 391)

redistricting (p. 368)

representation (p. 363)

roll call vote (p. 388)

rule (p. 385)

select committee (pp. 380, 381)

Senate majority leader (p. 379)

Senate minority leader (p. 379)

Senate parliamentarian (p. 378)

Speaker of the House (p. 377)

special committee (pp. 380, 381)

standing committee (p. 380)

trustee (p. 363)

unanimous consent
  agreement (p. 386)

unified government (p. 373)

veto (p. 393)

whips (p. 377)

Use the vocabulary flash cards on the book's website.

Smith College, Northampton,
Massachusetts

> *I can't stress how important it is to simply get involved. Get into the fight. Do everything you can to get hands-on experience.*

As a government and economics major at Smith College, Stephanie Cutter enjoyed politics, but it was her adviser's encouragement that turned interest into involvement. Her work on the 1988 presidential campaign of Michael Dukakis opened a whole new world and, it turned out, a career. After college, she took a job as a receptionist in the Washington office of New York's Governor Mario Cuomo, but she shortly returned to presidential campaign work, serving as staff on the campaigns of Bill Clinton, John Kerry, and Barack Obama. Campaign work led, in turn, to White House work. For Clinton, Cutter was communications director. For Obama, she has served as chief spokesperson for his transition team, head of communications at the Department of the Treasury, and coordinator of press strategy for Obama's first Supreme Court nomination. In May 2010, she became an assistant to the president for special projects and was given the task of coordinating public outreach on the implementation of health care reform. Over the past years, in between White House assignments, Cutter got a law degree and worked for Senator Ted Kennedy, First Lady Michelle Obama, and the Democratic National Committee.

Stephanie Cutter's career exemplifies the gateways that open when one gets involved in politics. It also reveals the political networks that

Chapter Topics

CourseMate

Visit http://www.cengagebrain.com/shop/ISBN/0495906190 for interactive tools including:

- Quizzes
- Flashcards
- Videos
- Animated PowerPoint slides, Podcast summaries, and more

Stephanie Cutter ▶

Stephen Crowley/The New York Times/Redux

© Jim Gip/Pivot Media, Inc.

- In what ways is the president held accountable, both individually and for the collective economic, military, and social condition of the federal government?

- How responsive is the presidency as a democratic office? How can the president address the vital public policy concerns of the American people?

- What opportunities are there for the average citizen to influence the decisions of the president?

- What powers does the president have to ensure equality across all citizens?

- Is the modern presidency a gate or a gateway to democracy?

talented and hard-working volunteers establish on presidential campaigns and how they use them to secure influential positions in the executive branch. Cutter's specialty is communications. She describes handling the press for political leaders as "a game of ping-pong," planning press briefings and pushing back on stories. Her skills at this game offer insight into the management of the modern presidency and into the importance of presidential agendas and citizen response.[1]

In this chapter, we examine how the president governs and how responsive he can be to the people. We look at his constitutional powers and the way he uses the executive power to achieve his policy goals. We also look at the limits on presidential power. As presidential scholar Charles Jones has argued, successful presidents work within a separation of powers system and alongside the legislative and judicial branches.[2] The most successful presidents are also strong leaders with clear policy vision and excellent communication and negotiation skills. In the twenty-first century, the American president has to implement existing law but, equally important, he must lead the effort to turn his policy goals into law and achieve his vision for the nation.

Presidential Qualifications

The American presidency was invented at the Constitutional Convention in 1787. The Framers had no definitive models to help them determine what sort of person should serve as a democratically elected head of state, because nations were still ruled by monarchs whose power to rule was hereditary. But the Framers had George Washington, the hero of the Revolutionary War, in mind for the office, and he helped shape the idea of what a president should be. Still, they left the qualifications as open as possible, and men with diverse experiences have served as president.

What is the prior experience of the current president?

Constitutional Eligibility and Presidential Succession

natural-born citizen: *Citizen in a nation from birth, usually by being born there.*

Article II, Section 1 of the Constitution states that the president must be a **natural-born citizen** (or a citizen at the time the Constitution was adopted), at least 35 years old, and a resident of the United States for at least fourteen years. The original Constitution did not specify eligibility for the vice presidency, as the person who came in second in the vote for president would be vice president. But in 1800, Thomas Jefferson and Aaron Burr ended up in a tie in the Electoral College when in fact supporters wanted to elect them as a team, with Jefferson as president and Burr as vice president. The Twelfth Amendment, ratified in 1804, changed the process so that candidates are elected for president and vice president separately. The amendment also directs that vice presidents must meet the same eligibility requirements as presidents and that electors cannot vote for both a president and a vice president from the elector's home state.

The Constitution also states that when the president is removed from office, by death, resignation, or inability to perform the duties of the office, the vice president becomes president. It stipulates that if neither the president nor the vice president is able to complete the elected term, Congress should designate a successor by law. In 1947, Congress changed presidential succession, putting the order of succession as vice president, **Speaker of the House**, **president pro tempore**, followed by the **cabinet secretaries**, starting with the secretary of state and again following in order of date of the **cabinet department's** creation.

But there was no actual constitutional provision for replacement of the vice president. Eventually, the Twenty-Fifth Amendment, ratified in 1967, required the president to nominate a replacement vice president, who must be approved by a majority vote of the House and the Senate. The first vice president to assume office in this manner was Gerald R. Ford (1974–77), nominated by President Richard M. Nixon (1969–74) in 1973, following the resignation of Vice President Spiro T. Agnew. The amendment also allows for a temporary transfer of power from the president to the vice president in cases of incapacity. This clause is invoked typically only if the president has to have surgery that would require sedation.

Another constitutional amendment, the Twenty-Second (1951), limits the president to two elected terms. For a century and a half, presidents followed the precedent established by George Washington (1789–97) when he stepped down after two terms. But in 1940, President Franklin D. Roosevelt (1933–45) chose to run for a third term and won; he also won election to a fourth term in 1944. Though the dangers of World War II were a factor in his staying in office, many Americans, especially Republicans, worried that a long-standing president could expand executive branch power too much, so they sought a way to limit presidential terms of service. In 1946, Republicans captured a majority in the House and Senate, and on the very first day the new Congress met, they proposed a constitutional amendment limiting the president to two full terms in office.[3] For a list of constitutional amendments that pertain to the presidency, see Figure 12.1.

Speaker of the House: *Constitutional and political leader of the House.*

president pro tempore: *Constitutional leader of the Senate.*

cabinet secretaries: *Heads of cabinet departments and chief advisers to the president on the issues under their jurisdiction.*

cabinet departments: *Executive branch organizations responsible for carrying out federal policy in a specific set of issue areas.*

FIGURE 12.1 **Constitutional Amendments That Pertain to the Presidency.**

Color Code :

Structure

Twelfth (1804): Requires that electors cast separate votes for president and vice president and specifies requirements for vice presidential candidates

Twentieth (1933): Declares that presidential term begins on January 20 (instead of March 4)

Twenty-Second (1951): Limits presidents to two terms

Twenty-Fifth (1967): Specifies replacement of the vice president and establishes the position of acting president during a president's disability.

term limits: *Limits on the number of elected terms an elected official may serve.*

lame duck: *Term-limited official in his or her last term of office.*

How do term limits make the president less responsive to public opinion?

Term limits enforce turnover and open opportunity for new leadership, but they also act as a gate that prevents voters from reelecting a popular president whom they want to stay in office. Because a president in his second term cannot seek reelection, he is commonly referred to as a **lame duck**. Lawmakers know that the president's time in office is limited, so they are less likely to cooperate or compromise with him. On the other hand, a president who wants to chart a policy course that is unpopular may be more likely to do so when he does not have to face the voters. Lame duck status therefore has the advantage of giving the president more political freedom, but the disadvantage of making him less directly responsive to public opinion.

Background and Experience

In keeping with the democratic spirit of the founding of the United States, the Framers did not specify qualifications for the presidency beyond age and citizenship, and in the ensuing 230 years, men of varying backgrounds have served in the office. Presidents have come from all walks of life and all regions. There is no one gateway profession that leads to the presidency. Harry Truman (1945–53), born in Missouri, was a farmer and owner of a men's clothing store. Ronald Reagan (1981–89), born in Illinois, was a radio sports announcer. Barack Obama (2009–), born in Hawaii, was a community organizer and constitutional law professor.[4] Until the Catholic John Kennedy (1961–63) was elected in 1960, all presidents were from a Protestant background. Until Obama, an African American, was elected in 2008, all presidents were white. All presidents have been male, but the 2008 election saw a serious run by Hillary Clinton for the Democratic nomination, and the Republican nominee John McCain selected Sarah Palin as his vice presidential candidate.

Unlike members of Congress, presidents represent all the people of the United States. How can a president represent all the people?

The clearest path to the White House is through the office of the vice president, but most presidents have some combination of service in the military, in state legislatures or as governor, in the U.S. House of Representatives or Senate, or in prior presidential administrations. There are advantages and disadvantages to specific types of experience prior to becoming president. Lyndon Johnson (1963–69) was very successful in passing his domestic policy agenda in large part due to his experience as a House member, U.S. senator, and Senate majority leader. His prior experience taught him crucial negotiating skills with members of Congress, and he used his skills to their fullest extent. In contrast, Jimmy Carter (1977–81) was generally considered to have failed in getting his domestic policy agenda enacted because of his lack of experience in Washington. He came to the White House from the governor's mansion in Georgia, and he was used to exercising executive power with little challenge from the legislature. When he faced a Congress that did not embrace his agenda, he lacked the negotiating skills to be successful. Of course there is no single set of qualifications or experiences that will guarantee success as a president. When voters cast their ballots for president, they take a leap of faith that the person who wins will be trustworthy, accountable, responsive to their needs, and implement the laws equally for every citizen. For a full list of the men who have been president of the United States and a map showing where they lived when they were elected president, see Figure 12.2.

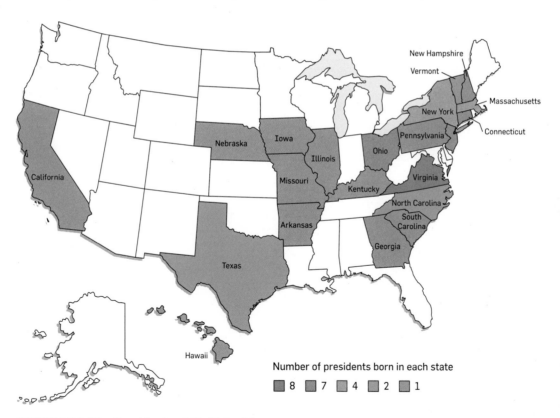

Number of presidents born in each state

■ 8　■ 7　■ 4　■ 2　■ 1

FIGURE 12.2 The Presidents of the United States.

Table of Presidents for Figure 12.2

	President	Term Dates and Number of Terms	Party	Prior Experience
1	George Washington	1789–97 (2)	General	
2	John Adams	1797–1801 (1)	Federalist	Vice president
3	Thomas Jefferson	1801–1809 (2)	Democratic-Republican	Vice president, secretary of state
4	James Madison	1809–17 (2)	Democratic-Republican	Secretary of state, state legislator
5	James Monroe	1817–25 (2)	Democratic-Republican	Minister to France, U.S. Senate
6	John Quincy Adams	1825–29 (1)	Democratic-Republican	Secretary of state, U.S. Senate
7	Andrew Jackson	1829–37 (2)	Democrat	U.S. House, U.S. Senate, general
8	Martin Van Buren	1837–41 (1)	Democrat	Vice president, U.S. Senate
9	William Henry Harrison	1841 (died in office)	Whig	General, governor
10	John Tyler	1841–45 (1)	Whig	Vice president, governor, U.S. Senate, U.S. House
11	James K. Polk	1845–49 (1)	Democrat	Governor, U.S. House
12	Zachary Taylor	1849–50 (died in office)	Whig	General
13	Millard Fillmore	1850–53 (died in office)	Whig	U.S. House, Vice president
14	Franklin Pierce	1853–57 (1)	Democrat	State legislator, U.S. Senate, U.S. House
15	James Buchanan	1857–61 (1)	Democrat	U.S. House, U.S. Senate, secretary of state
16	Abraham Lincoln	1861–65 (2; died in office)	Republican	State legislator
17	Andrew Johnson	1865–69 (1)	Democrat; National Union	U.S. House, U.S. Senate, vice president
18	Ulysses S. Grant	1869–77 (2)	Republican	General
19	Rutherford B. Hayes	1877–81 (1)	Republican	Governor, U.S. House, general
20	James A. Garfield	1881 (died in office)	Republican	U.S. House, general, state legislator
21	Chester A. Arthur	1881–85 (1)	Republican	Vice president, collector of the Port of New York

(Continued)

Table of Presidents for Figure 12.2 (Continued)

	President	Term Dates and Number of Terms	Party	Prior Experience
22	Grover Cleveland	1885–89 (1)	Democrat	Governor, mayor
23	Benjamin Harrison	1889–93 (1)	Republican	U.S. Senate
24	Grover Cleveland	1893–97 (1)	Democrat	President, governor, mayor
25	William McKinley	1897–1901 (2; died in office)	Republican	Governor, U.S. House
26	Theodore Roosevelt	1901–1909 (2)	Republican	Governor, lieutenant colonel
27	William Howard Taft	1909–13 (1)	Republican	Secretary of war, federal judge
28	Woodrow Wilson	1913–21 (2)	Democrat	Governor, university president
29	Warren G. Harding	1921–23 (died in office)	Republican	State legislator, lieutenant-governor, U.S. Senate
30	Calvin Coolidge	1923–29 (2)	Republican	Vice president, governor
31	Herbert Hoover	1929–33 (1)	Republican	Secretary of commerce
32	Franklin Delano Roosevelt	1933–45 (4; died in office)	Democrat	Governor, assistant secretary of the Navy, state legislator
33	Harry S. Truman	1945–53 (2)	Democrat	Vice president, U.S. Senate
34	Dwight D. Eisenhower	1953–61 (2)	Republican	General
35	John F. Kennedy	1961–63 (died in office)	Democrat	U.S. Senate, U.S. House
36	Lyndon Baines Johnson	1963–69 (2)	Democrat	Vice president. U.S. Senate, U.S. House
37	Richard M. Nixon	1969–74 (2; resigned)	Republican	Vice president, U.S. Senate, U.S. House
38	Gerald R. Ford	1974–77 (1)	Republican	Vice president, U.S. House
39	Jimmy Carter	1977–81 (1)	Democrat	Governor
40	Ronald Reagan	1981–89 (2)	Republican	Governor, actor
41	George H. W. Bush	1989–93 (1)	Republican	Vice president, CIA director, U.S. House
42	William J. Clinton	1993–2001 (2)	Democrat	Governor, state attorney general
43	George W. Bush	2001–2008 (2)	Republican	Governor
44	Barack Obama	2009–	Democrat	U.S. Senate, state senator

The Expansion of the Presidency

President George Washington had the enormous responsibility of setting the standard for how a president should govern in a democracy, and he was very careful not to infuse the office with airs of royalty or privilege. The Framers anticipated the executive branch would be led by one person, whose primary responsibility would be the defense of the United States. As commander of the Continental Army during the Revolutionary War, Washington had military experience, but he was also a cautious and thoughtful statesman who wanted to establish a precedent for how the chief executive should operate.

In the course of the nineteenth century, from the presidency of Thomas Jefferson (1801–09) to Andrew Jackson (1829–37) to Abraham Lincoln (1861–65) and finally to William McKinley (1897–1901), the nation grew in size, population, and economic power. The job of the chief executive grew accordingly, but though increasingly demanding and complex, it remained essentially focused on internal security. In the twentieth century, however, the United States became a leading international military and economic power. Its role in World War II and the subsequent **Cold War** against the Soviet Union expanded the authority of the presidency. The historian and presidential adviser Arthur Schlesinger Jr. used the term **imperial presidency** to describe the power of the president to speak for the nation on the world stage and to set the policy agenda at home. Schlesinger's view suggests that as long as the United States is engaged in military conflicts all over the world to promote and protect its interests, the president will be considered the most important figure in American politics.[5]

Cold War (1948–89):
Economic competition and political conflict between Communist and democratic nations.

imperial presidency:
Power of the president to speak for the nation on the world stage and to set the policy agenda at home.

What defines an imperial presidency?

Presidential Power: Constitutional Grants and Limits

As we saw in Chapter 11 (Congress) the Framers enumerated Congress's powers, both to assert powers that were missing under the Articles of Confederation, such as the power to collect taxes and to regulate commerce, and to constrain the branch they anticipated would be the most powerful. The Framers expected that the executive branch would be smaller and less powerful and did not believe it was necessary to enumerate the executive powers as they did with the legislative powers (see Table 12.1). Instead, in the very first sentence of Article II, they "vested" the president with a general grant of "executive power" and then, later in the article, stated certain additional powers and responsibilities of the executive. It is this general grant of executive

TABLE 12.1 A Comparison of Legislative and Executive Authority under the Constitution

While the Constitution grants specific legislative authority to Congress, it provides a general grant of authority to the president that does not require specific enumerated grants of power. Nor is there an executive equivalent of Article I, Section 9, which specifically limits congressional authority.

Category	Legislative	Executive
Authority	"All legislative Powers *herein granted* shall be vested in a Congress of the United States . . . ."	"The executive Power shall be vested in a President of the United States of America."
Specific Powers	Article I, Section 8, including: • lay and collect taxes • provide for the common defense • regulate interstate and foreign commerce • authorize courts • set uniform rules for naturalization and bankruptcy • establish post offices • make all laws that are "necessary and proper" for carrying out the listed powers	Article II, Section 2, including: • commander in chief of armed forces • grant pardons • make treaties • receive foreign ministers • appoint ambassadors, judges, cabinet-level officials • ensure that the laws are faithfully executed Article I, Section 7: • veto legislation
Limits on Power	Explicit limits on powers: Article I, Section 9, including: • no bills of attainder • no ex post facto laws • no titles of nobility Bill of Rights: • substantive limits of the First through Eighth Amendments Ninth Amendment: • enumeration of rights does not grant general authority Tenth Amendment: • people and states retain reserved powers not granted to Congress	Mostly through checks and balances: • veto override • Senate confirmation on appointments • removal by impeachment

power that has allowed the presidency to become the powerful office it is today. In this section, we look at the constitutional sources of the president's powers, the ways in which presidents have sought to expand their constitutional powers, and the ways in which the other branches, especially Congress, act to check and balance the president.

Commander in Chief

The president is the commander in chief of the armed forces of the United States, which includes the Army, Navy, Air Force, Marines, Coast Guard, and the National Guard. An elected commander in chief, rather than an appointed military officer, is a distinctly important element of American democracy. The president directs all war efforts and military conflicts. Congress, however, has the power to officially declare war and to authorize funding for the war effort. Because the war powers, divided between the president and Congress, are so contentious, we examine them later in the chapter.

Why is it important that the commander in chief of the U.S. military is a civilian?

Power to Pardon

clemency: *General power of president to grant mercy for a federal criminal offense.*

pardon: *Full forgiveness for a crime.*

commutation: *Decision to shorten a federal prison sentence.*

The president has the power to grant **clemency**, or mercy, for crimes against the United States, except in the case of impeachment from federal office. Clemency is a broad term that includes a **pardon**, which is forgiving an offense altogether, and a **commutation**, which is shortening a federal prison sentence; in general, a pardon is considered a more sweeping act of clemency than commuting a sentence.

Should the president have the power to pardon? What impact does this power have on citizen equality?

Treaties and Recognition of Foreign Nations

The president or his designated representative has the power to negotiate and sign treaties with foreign nations, but he must do so with the "Advice and Consent of the Senate," as specified by the Constitution; for a treaty to be valid, two-thirds "of the Senators present" must approve. Historically, there have been notable treaties that the Senate has refused to approve, ranging from the Treaty of Versailles ending World War I, signed by President Woodrow Wilson (1913–21), to the Kyoto Protocol on climate change, signed by Vice President Al Gore who was representing President Bill Clinton (1993–2001). These examples illustrate how the requirement that the Senate approve treaties serves as a gateway for public input into presidential actions, and how it can be a gate that blocks a president's attempt to reach agreements with foreign nations. Today, with the expansion of globalization, the president's representatives negotiate treaties over a wide range of areas, such as military alliances, human rights accords, environmental regulations, and trade policy.

The president's authority in foreign affairs also includes the power to "receive Ambassadors and other public Ministers," which allows the president to recognize the legitimacy of foreign regimes. Such decisions are frequently based on the internal political system of the nation. For example, revolutionaries overthrew Russia's czarist regime in 1917, but the new Soviet Union, a Communist nation, was not recognized by the United States until 1933, through the action of President Franklin Roosevelt. In contrast, in 2008, when Kosovo, a young democracy, declared its independence from Serbia, President George W. Bush (2001–09) immediately recognized it as an independent nation.[6]

Appointments and Judicial Nominations

The president has the power to appoint all federal officers, including cabinet secretaries, heads of independent agencies, and ambassadors. The presidential appointment process has two steps: nomination and subsequent approval by a majority of the Senate. These individuals are typically referred to as **political appointees**, and they are expected to carry out the president's political and policy agenda (in contrast to **civil servants**, who are hired through a merit-based system and are politically neutral; see Chapter 13, The Bureaucracy). During Senate recesses, the president can make appointments that will expire at the end of the Senate's next session, unless the appointee is subsequently confirmed. Presidents have sometimes used recess appointments to bypass the Senate. In 2005, George W. Bush appointed John Bolton as United Nations ambassador in a recess appointment, but at the end of 2006, Bolton resigned when it was clear he would not win Senate approval. The president also nominates judges in the federal judicial system, from district court level to the Supreme Court, who again must receive majority approval in the Senate. In recent years, this process has become more ideological and contentious; rather than only considering qualifications for the job, presidents and members of the Senate also consider a nominee's ideological views on key issues such as abortion (see Chapter 14, The Judiciary, for more information on the nomination process). As with the treaty process, the Senate's advice and consent role in appointments and nominations is a gateway for citizen influence.

The president has the power to fire federal officers, but not to remove judges, who can be removed only by impeachment. Even though they have the formal power to do so, presidents rarely remove cabinet members because that would entail an admission of error in making the appointment in the first place. However, there have been cases in which cabinet secretaries have disagreed with presidents about policies, or worse, committed acts of corruption and were subsequently fired or asked to resign.

political appointees: *Individuals appointed to federal jobs by the president with the explicit task of carrying out his political and partisan agenda.*

civil servants: *Federal employees hired through a merit-based system to implement federal programs and who are expected to be neutral in their political affiliation.*

Consider the Senate's power to check the president in treaty making and appointments. What are the costs and benefits of this power sharing in terms of government efficiency and responsiveness?

The Veto and the Veto Override

veto: *Authority of the president to block legislation passed by Congress.*

The president has an important role in the enactment of legislation. He has the power to **veto** bills passed by Congress before they become law, by refusing to sign them and sending them back to the chamber in which they originated, with his objections. Or if Congress will be going out of session within ten days, he can simply not sign the bill, a practice known as a **pocket veto**. In cases where the president refuses to sign the bill but Congress remains in session, the bill is enacted into law.

pocket veto: *Automatic veto that occurs when Congress goes out of session within ten days of submitting a bill to the president and the president has not signed it.*

To counter the power of the veto, the Framers gave Congress the veto **override**, the power to overturn a presidential veto with a two-thirds vote in each chamber. Because the two-thirds threshold is higher than the majority vote needed to pass a bill in the first place, it is difficult for Congress to overcome presidential opposition to a bill. The high threshold reinforces the power of the president in blocking congressional action and so serves as a gateway for presidential influence in the legislative process. One could also see the veto as a gate that legislation must pass through to become law, which can be unlocked only with a congressional supermajority.

override: *Congress' power to overturn a presidential veto with a two-thirds vote in each chamber.*

The veto is the most direct way that the president checks the power of Congress. Presidents use the veto power either to prevent a bill from becoming law or to pressure Congress into making changes to a bill to bring it closer into line with his policies and his view of the national interest (see Table 12.2). For most of the twentieth century, Congress sent the president a large number of single-issue or narrowly drawn bills each year. In recent decades, however, Congress has learned to get around the threat of a presidential veto by passing only a few **omnibus bills**, which include provisions affecting a wider number of issue areas. These omnibus bills are costly to veto because they affect a wide range of voters, and thus give Congress an advantage in negotiating with the president.[7] Presidents naturally tend to veto more bills when Congress is controlled by the opposite party, a condition known as **divided government**.

How does the veto power give the president influence in the legislative process?

omnibus bills: *Lengthy pieces of legislation that include provisions affecting a wide range of programs.*

divided government: *Situation when one party controls the executive and the other party controls the legislature.*

Other Powers

The president works within this framework of formal powers and constraints to lead the nation, and in doing so, becomes the chief agenda setter for domestic and foreign policy. In a later section of this chapter, we discuss agenda setting in more detail; here it is important to note that, over time, smaller tasks assigned to the president in the Constitution have evolved into powerful tools for influencing legislation. One tool is the **State of the Union address**, which is authorized in Article II, Section 3: the president "shall from time to time give to the Congress Information of the State of the Union, and recommend to their Consideration such Measures as he shall judge necessary

State of the Union address: *Speech given by the president to Congress every January on the condition of the country.*

TABLE 12.2 Presidential Vetoes, 1789–2010

President	Congresses	Regular Vetoes	Pocket Vetoes	Total Vetoes	Vetoes Overridden
George Washington	1st–4th	2	...	2	...
John Adams	5th–6th	...	...	...	...
Thomas Jefferson	7th–10th	...	...	...	...
James Madison	11th–14th	5	2	7	...
James Monroe	15th–18th	1	...	1	...
John Quincy Adams	19th–20th	...	...	...	...
Andrew Jackson	21st–24th	5	7	12	...
Martin Van Buren	25th–26th	...	1	1	...
William Henry Harrison	27th	...	...	...	...
John Tyler	27th–28th	6	4	10	1
James K. Polk	29th–30th	2	1	3	...
Zachary Taylor	31st	...	...	...	...
Millard Fillmore	31st–32nd	...	...	...	...
Franklin Pierce	33rd–34th	9	...	9	5
James Buchanan	35th–36th	4	3	7	...
Abraham Lincoln	37th–39th	2	5	7	...
Andrew Johnson	39th–40th	21	8	29	15
Ulysses S. Grant	41st–44th	45	48	93	4
Rutherford B. Hayes	45th–46th	12	1	13	1
James A. Garfield	47th	...	...	...	...
Chester A. Arthur	47th–48th	4	8	12	1
Grover Cleveland	49th–50th	304	110	414	2
Benjamin Harrison	51st–52nd	19	25	44	1
Grover Cleveland	53rd–54th	42	128	170	5
William McKinley	55th–57th	6	36	42	...
Theodore Roosevelt	57th–60th	42	40	82	1
William H. Taft	61st–62nd	30	9	39	1

(Continued)

TABLE 12.2 (Continued)

President	Congresses	Regular Vetoes	Pocket Vetoes	Total Vetoes	Vetoes Overridden
Woodrow Wilson	63rd–66th	33	11	44	6
Warren G. Harding	67th	5	1	6	0
Calvin Coolidge	68th–70th	20	30	50	4
Herbert C. Hoover	71st–72nd	21	16	37	3
Franklin D. Roosevelt	73rd–79th	372	263	635	9
Harry S. Truman	79th–82nd	180	70	250	12
Dwight D. Eisenhower	83rd–86th	73	108	181	2
John F. Kennedy	87th–88th	12	9	21	. . .
Lyndon B. Johnson	88th–90th	16	14	30	. . .
Richard M. Nixon	91st–93rd	26	17	43	7
Gerald R. Ford	93rd–94th	48	18	66	12
James Earl Carter	95th–96th	13	18	31	2
Ronald Reagan	97th–100th	39	39	78	9
George Bush*	101st–102nd	29	15*	44	1
William J. Clinton	103rd–106th	36	1	37	2
George W. Bush	107th–110th	9	0	9	2
Barack Obama	111th	0	1	0	0
Total		**1,493**	**1,067**	**2,559**	**108**

* President Bush attempted to pocket veto two bills during intrasession recess periods. Congress considered the two bills enacted into law because of the president's failure to return the legislation. The bills are not counted as pocket vetoes in this table.

Source: Congressional Research Service.

and expedient." Nothing in this passage requires the president to inform Congress on a yearly basis or to do so in person. Indeed, President Woodrow Wilson (1913-21) was the first president to deliver the State of the Union address in person; up until then, it had been delivered to Congress in writing.[8] Over the last century, presidents have turned this obligation into an opportunity to outline a broad policy agenda for the nation. That same passage also says that the president "may, on extraordinary Occasions, convene both Houses, or either of them." Thus the president can call Congress into a special session to consider legislation or to hear him deliver an important speech.[9]

Congress's Ultimate Check on the Executive: Impeachment

Congress's ultimate check on the president is its power to remove him from office. Article II, Section 4 of the Constitution stipulates that the president, vice president, and all civil officers (including cabinet secretaries and federal judges) are subject to removal for "Treason, Bribery, or other high Crimes and Misdemeanors." Should these officers be removed from office, they then may be subject to normal criminal charges and proceedings, where applicable.

The process of removal begins with **impeachment** in the House of Representatives. Typically, the House Judiciary Committee investigates charges and makes a recommendation to the full House whether to impeach or not. If the House votes to impeach a federal officer, the Senate then holds a trial, with the chief justice of the Supreme Court presiding. If two-thirds of the senators vote to convict, the official is removed from office.

At the highest level of federal office, two presidents—Andrew Johnson and Bill Clinton—have been impeached, but neither was convicted. When the Senate failed to convict them, they remained in office. There have been impeachment resolutions introduced by individual members of the House of Representatives against other presidents, but they were not acted on. The case of Richard Nixon shows, however, that just the threat of impeachment can be enough to remove a president from office. Knowing he was about to be impeached, Nixon resigned instead. In addition to charges of wrongdoing, partisan disagreements can influence some members of Congress in their votes to move forward with impeachment proceedings.

As the following discussion will show, impeachment is a rarely used but powerful instrument for Congress to hold the president accountable for his actions. In a democratic nation guided by the rule of law, all citizens are equally obligated to obey the laws of the land, including the president.

Richard M. Nixon. President Nixon was embroiled in a serious scandal known as Watergate, after the name of a complex in Washington where the Democratic National Committee had its headquarters. It was there that the scandal began on June 17, 1972, with a break-in. In August, the *Washington Post* reported that one of the five men caught in the act and arrested had, in his bank account, $25,000 in funds originally given to the Nixon 1972 reelection campaign.[10] Nixon denied any connection and was reelected in the fall, but all the while, he and his aides were working to cover up the fact that

Have you watched a State of the Union address? What do you think its purpose was? What did you learn from it?

impeachment: *Process whereby the House brings charges against the president (or other federal officials) that will, upon conviction by the Senate, remove him from office.*

Think about the impeachments (and near-impeachment) described here. What was the basis for impeachment in each case?

his reelection committee had ordered the break-in to install listening devices on Democratic Party phones. Two *Washington Post* reporters, Bob Woodward and Carl Bernstein, continued to investigate the story, and as connections between Nixon and the break-in were revealed, several of his aides were convicted of conspiracy, burglary, and wiretapping, and others resigned.

In the months that followed, when a Nixon staffer revealed that the president had tape-recorded all his White House conversations, both the Senate Watergate Committee and the House Judiciary Committee formally issued **subpoenas** demanding that Nixon turn over the recordings. The turning point in the what became known as the **Watergate scandal** came on Saturday, October 20, 1973, when President Nixon fired Archibald Cox and abolished the office of special prosecutor entirely and, in response, his own attorney general and deputy attorney general resigned as well. What had been a struggle for information became a question of obstruction of justice by the president.

President Nixon turned over a limited number of tapes; but there was an 18½-minute gap in one tape, and Congress wanted to know what was discussed during that time period and why it was erased. The administration claimed that the tape was erased by mistake. During the next months, Nixon released only partial transcripts and said that others were protected by **executive privilege**—the president's right to engage in communications with his advisers that he does not have to reveal. The justification for this privilege is that the president must make difficult choices and, without the guarantee of privilege, he may not receive or deliver the fullest information in the course of his deliberations.

The Supreme Court created an exception to this privilege in *United States v. Nixon*, when on July 24, 1974, it unanimously ruled that executive privilege is not absolute and must give way when the government needs the information for a trial. The tapes showed that Nixon and his aides had conspired to cover up the Watergate break-in. Three days later, the House Judiciary Committee approved three articles of impeachment against Nixon.[11] With the full House of Representatives ready to vote articles of impeachment against him, President Nixon resigned on August 8, 1974.

William Jefferson Clinton. The most recent case of impeachment involved President Bill Clinton.[12] This case began in 1979 when President Clinton and his wife Hillary formed a real estate company called Whitewater with some business associates. After he was elected in 1992, foes of President Clinton pushed for an investigation into the Whitewater dealings, and in January 1994, public pressure led the attorney general to authorize an independent counsel investigation into these dealings. The first independent counsel was Robert Fiske, but he was perceived to be less than vigorous in pursuit of the investigation, and in August 1994, he was replaced by Kenneth Starr.[13]

subpoenas: *Orders issued by a legal authority demanding that an individual appear to testify at, or turn over documents relevant to, a legal proceeding.*

Watergate scandal (1972–74): *Scandal uncovered by* Washington Post *reporters that led to the resignation of President Richard M. Nixon.*

executive privilege: *President's right to engage in confidential communications with his advisers.*

Should the president have executive privilege?

Should the president be subjected to civil lawsuits while he is in office? State the reasons for your answer.

Meanwhile, in an unrelated event, a woman named Paula Jones who had met with Bill Clinton, then governor of Arkansas, in an Arkansas hotel room in 1991, had filed a sexual harassment suit against Clinton. President Clinton's lawyers moved to prevent the lawsuit from proceeding while he was still in office.[14] That case, *Jones v. Clinton*, made its way to the Supreme Court, which on May 27, 1997, ruled that a sitting president has no immunity from a civil suit arising from acts occurring before he took office and that Jones's lawsuit could proceed, and it did. In the course of their work, Jones's lawyers uncovered information alleging that Clinton had engaged in a sexual affair with a White House intern named Monica Lewinsky, and they were prepared to question both women. Independent counsel Kenneth Starr found out about Lewinsky and her possible testimony in the Jones case, and he won permission to question the president about the affair. In essence, he was trying to secure evidence about whether President Clinton had committed **perjury** (lied under oath) about his relationship with Lewinsky during his deposition in the Jones trial.

perjury: *Lying under sworn oath.*

articles of impeachment: *List of charges against the president in an impeachment proceeding.*

abuse of power: *Charge against officeholders for taking advantage of the powers of their office for personal gain.*

In the impeachment process, what evidence do you see of checks and balances?

Starr concluded that there was sufficient evidence that Clinton had committed perjury. On September 9, 1998, Starr released his report to members of the House of Representatives; on October 8, the House approved an impeachment inquiry. On December 19, the House debated four

AP Photo/U.S. Senate

articles of impeachment against President Clinton for two counts of perjury, one count of obstruction of justice, and one count of **abuse of power**. The House voted to impeach Clinton on two of the four counts against him: perjury and obstruction of justice.[15] On January 7, 1999, the Senate began the formal phase of the trial, and it lasted until February 8. In the Senate, voting on the two counts fell far short of the two-thirds (67) vote necessary to convict President Clinton of the charges against him. He was acquitted and served out the remainder of his second term. Ironically, the original Whitewater investigation, which had led to the impeachment proceedings, failed to unearth solid evidence that President Clinton or his wife Hillary committed any crime.

Based on charges that President Clinton lied under oath during the Whitewater special investigation, the House of Representatives impeached him on December 19, 1998. In a trial that began the following month, the Senate failed to convict him.

What should be done about the growth of executive power? Is it a problem for checks and balances among the separate branches?

Impeachment is not a power to be used lightly, but it does serve as a gateway for the public, through their elected officials in Congress, to hold the president, cabinet officials, and federal judges accountable for abuses of power.

The Growth of Executive Influence

presidential directive:
Official instructions from the president regarding federal policy.

With all these formal constitutional restrictions on the president, one has to wonder how the modern presidency has become so powerful. The answer lies with the general grant of "executive power" that we discussed earlier in the chapter. In addition to this power being vested in the president at the beginning of Article II, the president is also required to "take Care that the Laws be faithfully executed," which he promises to do when he takes the oath of office. Presidents have found ways to unlock the enormous powers inherent in the general grant of power and in the "take care" clause to expand their role and authority by means not explicitly granted in the Constitution, and they draw

Wally McNamee/CORBIS

The power of the presidency is symbolized by the unique presidential seal. Photographs of the president working in the Oval Office capture the enormous power vested in a single elected official.

on these powers to help them get their preferred policies enacted into law. The president's veto power, and Congress's power to override the veto and to impeach the president, counteract each other and help ensure that each branch remains responsive to its governing responsibilities. However, Congress has no formal means to balance and check the president's growing executive power, though at times the judicial branch has been able to do so.

Presidential Directives and Signing Statements

executive order:
Presidential directive that usually involves implementing a specific law.

Presidents use the executive power to issue **presidential directives** that give specific instructions on a federal policy that do not require congressional approval. The presidential scholar William Howell argues that recent presidents have used this "unilateral" power much more frequently than previous presidents, especially under conditions of divided government or interbranch policy conflict.[16] Presidential directives might take the form of executive orders, proclamations, or military orders. These directives are the primary way that presidents shape policy implementation, and the instrument they use to act quickly in case of national emergencies.[17]

The most well-known type of directive is the **executive order**, which can be used for a wide range of purposes. Typically, executive orders instruct federal employees to take a specific action or implement a policy in a particular way. The scholar Kenneth Mayer argues that executive orders are an important source of "independent authority" that is used solely at the discretion of the president.[18]

Even though presidents since Washington have issued executive orders, they were not officially numbered until 1862 and not published in the *Federal Register* until 1935.[19] In 1957, President Dwight D. Eisenhower (1953–61) used a combination of executive orders, **proclamations**, and **military orders** to enforce school integration in Little Rock, Arkansas. Following Supreme Court rulings (*Brown v. Board of Education* 1954, 1955) that struck down the practice of segregation in public schools, the governor of Arkansas, Orval Faubus, called up the Arkansas National Guard to block nine African Americans from attending Central High School in Little Rock. President Eisenhower responded by issuing a proclamation calling on the governor to cease and desist, but when the governor ignored the proclamation, Eisenhower issued Executive Order 10730 to send the 101st Airborne Division to Little Rock to ensure that the students would be allowed into the school. He also used his authority as commander in chief to take command of the Arkansas National Guard and order it to assist in the school's integration. Eisenhower intervened because he believed it was his obligation as president to enforce the laws of the land as set forth by the rulings of the Supreme Court.[20]

Federal Register: *Official published record of all executive branch rules, regulations, and orders.*

proclamation: *Presidential directive usually issued to declare a change in federal policy.*

military orders: *Presidential directive that gives instructions to a branch of the armed forces.*

© Bettmann/CORBIS

In September 1957, in a move that demonstrated federal power over state power and the authority of the commander in chief, President Dwight D. Eisenhower sent the 101st Airborne Division to Little Rock, Arkansas, to protect nine African American students attempting to attend previously all-white Central High School. He also nationalized the Arkansas National Guard for the same purpose.

Still, a presidential directive is not completely immune from scrutiny or accountability. In 1952, during the Korean War, the United Steelworkers union threatened to stop work at steel mills. In response, President Harry Truman used his executive powers to order the seizure of steel mills and put them under the control of the United States government. Although the steel workers were willing to put off the strike and work in government-owned mills, the steel mill owners sued to challenge the legality of the seizure. In *Youngstown Sheet and Tube Co. v. Sawyer*, better known as the *Steel Seizure* case, the Supreme Court ruled against the president, claiming he had no statutory authority from Congress to seize the mills, nor did his commander in chief status allow him to seize domestic property when the United States was at war in a foreign land (see Supreme Court Cases: *Youngstown Sheet and Tube Co. v. Sawyer*.)

presidential directive on national security:
Presidential directive that deals with government action in the area of foreign policy and is not publicly released.

In foreign and military affairs, presidents can issue **presidential directives on national security**, which have a similar purpose to executive orders but are not published in the *Federal Register*. These directives can announce specific sanctions against individuals who are considered enemies of the United States or make larger statements about U.S. policy toward a foreign country. President George W. Bush used this power frequently in what he described as a war on terror and in the conduct of the wars in Afghanistan and Iraq. For example, he issued an order in 2001 to create **military tribunals** that would try suspected enemy combatants and terrorists, rather than allowing them to be tried in a regular military court. He also created a special subcategory called Homeland Security Presidential Directives, which are not as widely publicized as other directives and deal only with homeland security policy.

military tribunal:
Specially created court that determines the innocence or guilt of enemy combatants.

signing statements:
Written remarks issued by the president when signing a bill into law that often reflect his interpretation of how the law should be implemented.

When a president signs a bill into law, he can issue **signing statements**, written remarks that reflect his interpretation of the law, although they are not required or authorized by the Constitution. Signing statements can be classified as nonconstitutional and constitutional (see Table 12.3 on p. 430). Nonconstitutional statements are typically symbolic, celebrating the passage of the law or providing technical instructions for implementing a bill. Constitutional statements are more serious in that the president uses them to indicate a disagreement with Congress on specific provisions in the bill. In constitutional signing statements, the president may go so far as to say he refuses to implement specific provisions of a bill. This kind of statement is a challenge to Congress's constitutional authority to legislate.[21] Even when the presidency and the Congress are controlled by the same party, signing statements can be used to shift the implementation of policy toward presidential preferences. President Obama recognized the controversy over signing statements, and he issued a memorandum early in his administration stating that he would use signing statements "to address constitutional concerns only

What limits can Congress, the courts, and/or the American people place on the president?

supremecourtcases

Youngstown Sheet and Tube Co. v. Sawyer (1952) (*Steel Seizure Case*)

QUESTION: Can the president seize steel mills to prevent a strike during wartime?

ORAL ARGUMENT: May 12, 1952

DECISION: June 2, 1952 (read at http://www.findlaw.com/casecode/supreme.html)

OUTCOME: No, overturning the seizure (6–3)

Following North Korea's invasion of South Korea in June 1950, President Harry Truman sought and received a United Nations (UN) resolution permitting intervention on behalf of South Korea. In 1952, with the Korean War still raging, the United Steelworkers announced plans for an April 1952 strike. President Truman feared that the strike would severely harm America's war effort. One alternative for putting off the strike was to seek a temporary court order prohibiting a strike when national security is at stake, a provision allowed under the Taft-Hartley Labor Act. Uncomfortable with what was perceived to be anti-labor policy, Truman instead ordered Secretary of Commerce Charles Sawyer to seize the steel mills and run them under the flag of the United States. Because the steelworkers preferred working at the steel mills under the flag of the United States to the Taft-Hartley alternatives, they agreed to come back to work following the seizure.

The steel mill owners then brought suit challenging the seizure. Truman claimed the authority to do this under his powers to make sure that the laws were faithfully executed and his powers as commander in chief of the armed forces. The Court's decision rejected the president's authority to seize the steel mills, noting that Congress had not passed a law allowing the seizure, thus there were no laws involving the seizure to be faithfully executed. The Court also ruled that the president's authority to rule as commander in chief did not extend to domestic seizures during foreign wars. Without congressional authorization, the president could not seize the steel mills.

The *Steel Seizure* case still stands as the leading decision on presidential authority. The Supreme Court relied heavily on the *Steel Seizure* case in deciding that President George W. Bush did not have the authority to hold enemy combatants from the war in Afghanistan at the U.S. naval base at Guantanamo Bay, Cuba, without a hearing, as Congress had not authorized actions.*

- **Why did the Court block President Truman's seizure of the steel mills?**

- **Did the decision place the president above Congress, below Congress, or equal to Congress in terms of making policy?**

* *Hamdan v. Rumsfeld*, 548 U.S. 557 (2006).

TABLE 12.3 Presidential Signing Statements, 1969–2008

President	Nonconstitutional	Constitutional	Total
Nixon	111 (94.9%)	6 (5.1%)	117
Ford	123 (89.8%)	14 (10.2%)	137
Carter	198 (86.8%)	30 (13.2%)	228
Reagan	165 (66.3%)	84 (33.7%)	249
Bush	106 (46.5%)	122 (53.5%)	228
Clinton	294 (77.4%)	86 (22.6%)	380
Bush	32 (19.9%)	129 (80.1%)	161
Obama			
Total	**1,029 (68.6%)**	**471 (31.4%)**	**1,500**

Source: Michael J. Berry, "Controversially Executing the Law: George W. Bush and the Constitutional Signing Statement," *Congress and the Presidency* 36 (2009): 244–71, see p. 252.

when it is appropriate to do so as a means of discharging my constitutional responsibilities."[22] In issuing this memorandum, President Obama was trying to alleviate concerns about abusing executive power but at the same time preserve the presidential power to interpret legislation that is inherent in signing statements.

Presidential directives and signing statements create tension between the president and Congress, and between the president and the judiciary, because they are an expansion of presidential power and have at times even been deemed illegal.[23] Many presidents, from Lincoln to Franklin Roosevelt to George W. Bush, have taken temporary actions that have violated constitutional rights in the name of national security, from suspending *habeas corpus* to interning Japanese Americans to eavesdropping on U.S. citizens (see Chapter 4, Civil Liberties, and Chapter 5, Civil Rights, for expanded discussions of these actions). Judging the merit of such actions is a difficult task because citizens have to decide whether the president is indeed acting in good faith on behalf of the country or merely seeking to expand his own power and agenda.

Power to Persuade

bully pulpit: *Nickname for the power of the president to use the attention associated with the office to persuade the media, Congress, and the public to support his policy positions.*

Presidents understand that communicating well with the public is essential to building support for their policies. President Theodore Roosevelt (1901–09) described the office of the president as a **bully pulpit**, where presidents could use the attention associated with the office to make a public argument in favor of or against a policy.[24] The key to using the bully pulpit effectively is to explain a policy in simple and accessible terms, to get the public's attention, and to frame an issue in the public's mind in a way that is favorable to the president's policy position. Presidential scholar George Edwards makes a persuasive case that using the bully pulpit can only accomplish the president's goals if he already has a receptive audience. In today's highly partisan and divided political climate, there is no guarantee that the president's detractors will listen to his message.[25]

A president's relationship with the members of the news media is a crucial factor in successful communication, and it has evolved dramatically over time. Samuel Kernell, a presidential media scholar, argues that over the last seventy years, presidents have increased the extent to which they control their interactions with the press. Press conferences are one important way of sustaining a relationship with the media and presidents have tried to use them to their advantage. Press conferences are somewhat risky because unlike speeches, presidents do not control the content of the questions that are asked, and they can sometimes make unrehearsed statements that have political consequences. For this reason, Barack Obama has also used new technologies to bypass the media and speak directly to the people by creating a blog on the White House website, posting videos of his speeches, and sending mass e-mails to citizens who make inquiries on specific proposals.[26]

The political scientist Richard Neustadt has argued that the real power of the presidency can be measured in how successfully a president persuades members of Congress and other policy makers to support his policies. Several factors affect a president's power to persuade, notably his professional reputation and his **approval ratings**.[27] When a president comes to the Oval Office with executive experience, or a strong reputation as a productive legislator, he is likely to have a reservoir of respect with members of Congress, the public, and the media. That reservoir can become depleted, however, if the president makes missteps and is not successful with his legislative agenda.

Lawmakers are more likely to pass a president's policy proposal when his approval rating is high, and they are less cooperative when the president is unpopular. Members of Congress pay attention to presidential approval ratings because national polls are a barometer of public opinion. Public approval

© Bettmann/CORBIS

President Theodore Roosevelt was a larger-than-life figure who challenged corporate monopolies, sought to strengthen U.S. international power, and increased federal efforts at land conservation. He was known for using the office of the president as a bully pulpit to persuade the public to support his policies.

Does the bully pulpit serve as a communication gateway between the president and citizens?

approval rating: *Job performance evaluation for the president, Congress, or other public official or institution that is generated by public opinion polls and typically reported as a percentage.*

can be essential to presidential policy success, which is why the president tries to maintain public support throughout his years in the White House (see Chapter 6, Public Opinion, for more on presidential approval ratings and presidential effectiveness).[28]

Agenda Setting

As the chief executive officer of the entire federal government, the president has an obligation and an opportunity to work with Congress to set the foreign and domestic policy agenda for the nation, from determining how to configure military strength, to overseeing economic growth, to ensuring the health and safety of individual citizens. The president has formal and informal advantages over Congress in directing the federal agenda toward his policy preferences, starting with the fact that he is the sole occupant of his elected office, as compared with 535 members of the House and Senate. Consequently, the president has the power to focus the nation's attention on his ideas and policy proposals.

head of state: *Title given to the president as national leader.*

In dealing with foreign powers, the president is **head of state** and commander in chief. As head of state, the president oversees a vast organization of employees in the State Department and the office of the U.S. Trade Representative who lay the groundwork for negotiations with foreign leaders on issues ranging from nuclear weapons control to trade policy. Upon their recommendation, the president proposes new treaties or revisions to existing agreements as needed. Ultimately the president is the public face, and authority, behind U.S. foreign policy decisions. He must establish working relationships with foreign leaders and demonstrate an understanding of how other nation's political systems operate, especially the extent to which the executive power is placed in one person, or shared, as it is in parliamentary systems.

Because the president is presumed to serve the best interest of the entire nation, the American public frequently gives its support, at least initially, for most of his foreign policies. The main congressional counterweights to the president's powers in this area are the power of the Senate to ratify treaties and the power of Congress to appropriate money for federal programs, including foreign aid and diplomatic programs. However, these congressional powers come in the form of *responses* to the president's proposals. Congress can have some influence on the president's foreign policy agenda through hearings and press statements, but if the president is able to persuade the public to support his positions, he is typically able to forge his own path on foreign policy.

Identify two of the president's agenda setting tools.

federal budget: *Budget of all federal programs, typically released by the president in early February.*

In the area of domestic policy, the president uses the State of the Union address, the **federal budget**, the power to make executive appointments, the bully pulpit, the executive power to implement laws, and the veto power as his agenda-setting tools. The president issues his federal budget in early February, shortly after he delivers the State of the Union address. It is a blueprint that indicates his spending priorities for all areas of the federal government. Congress does not have to abide by this budget; frequently, Congress simply ignores it and constructs its own federal budget (see Chapter 11 for discussion of the budget). However, all measures raising taxes and spending federal money can be vetoed by the president, and, as we have seen, the veto or even the threat of a veto gives the president a means of exerting pressure on Congress to follow his budget priorities. He can also be even more proactive by issuing presidential directives that direct the bureaucracy to implement laws as he sees fit. The president always commands media attention, through major speeches, press conferences, interviews, and coverage of his travels, and therefore he has a constantly open forum to try to persuade voters to support his proposals.[29]

The President in Wartime

As executive branch powers have grown, presidents have increasingly come into conflict with the other two branches of government, especially in times of national crisis and war. As Chapter 4 (Civil Liberties) and Chapter 7 (The News Media and the Internet) have demonstrated, the judicial branch frequently protects the right of the free press to exercise its watchdog role, even in reports related to national security. In this section, we examine the power struggle between the president and Congress over war powers, which the Constitution divides between the two branches, and the power struggle between the president and the judiciary, which focuses largely on the scope of presidential powers and civil liberties.

What powers should the president have during wartime?

Power Struggles between the President and Congress

The Constitution gives Congress the power to declare war, but it has been the practice for presidents to formally ask Congress for a declaration of war first. Once Congress declares war, the president as commander in chief has the authority to direct the conflict. However, through its constitutional powers in Article I to "to raise and support Armies" and "to provide and maintain a Navy," Congress still retains the power to cut off the flow of money for the war effort. Generally, the president and Congress have worked together in times of military conflict, but in the late 1960s, opposition to the Vietnam War brought about significant divisions between the executive and legislative branches over war powers.

Vietnam and the War Powers Act.

Vietnam had been a divided nation since 1954, with Communist forces controlling North Vietnam and anti-Communists controlling South Vietnam, and a civil war had erupted between them. President Eisenhower, and then Presidents Kennedy and Johnson, believed it was important to contain Communism and to keep the North Vietnamese Communists from taking over South Vietnam, but at first the U.S. troop buildup was slow. In 1964, however, President Lyndon Johnson presented evidence to Congress that the North Vietnamese were attacking U.S. ships on patrol duty in international waters off the shores of North Vietnam in the Gulf of Tonkin. Johnson asked Congress for the authority to fight back, and Congress responded with the Tonkin Gulf Resolution, stating, "The Congress approves and supports the determination of the President, as Commander in Chief, to take all necessary measures to repel any armed attack against the forces of the United States and to prevent further aggression."[30]

By 1968, the United States had more than 500,000 troops in Vietnam, and the conflict was commonly referred to as the Vietnam War although there was never any formal declaration of war by Congress. The conflict had become highly unpopular, and Johnson was forced to give up his bid for reelection. That year, Richard Nixon was elected president and promised to end the Vietnam War; instead, he broadened the conflict to neighboring countries Cambodia and Laos.

By 1971, Congress had repealed the Tonkin Gulf Resolution, and, following the Paris Peace Accords, signed in January 1973, U.S. troops were withdrawn from Vietnam. In October 1973, Congress passed a more formal proposal to limit presidential authority to engage in military conflict. This **War Powers Act** states that the president cannot send troops into military conflict for more than ninety days without seeking a formal declaration of war from Congress. Nixon, under increasing pressure from the Watergate scandal, vetoed the act, but Congress overrode the veto.

The War Powers Act was ostensibly supposed to be a gate that would stand in the way of a president's decision to launch a war without first gauging congressional support. Although the act tried to clarify presidential authority and limits, the scholar Louis Fisher argues that it is flawed because the ninety-day limit does not begin until the president has officially reported the troop engagement to Congress; consequently, a president could send troops into a conflict and simply not report it to Congress, thereby avoiding a trigger of the War Powers Act.[31] Moreover, the act did not really give Congress the power to end a military conflict except by denying all funding for it, as it ultimately did with Vietnam. However, if there is considerable public support for an ongoing military engagement, the president can make the case that it is too dangerous to cut off all funding, and Congress would be reluctant to cut off all funding if troops are still in the field and could be harmed. The

War Powers Act (1973): *Provides that the president cannot send troops into military conflict for more than 90 days without seeking a formal declaration of war from Congress.*

irony of the War Powers Act is that it actually gives presidents an incentive to seek a declaration of war, or authorization to use military force, after which time Congress loses much of its control over the operation of the conflict.[32] In other words, once the Congress gives the president permission to go to war, it is next to impossible for Congress to end it.[33]

What were the problems with congressional attempts to limit presidential power in the War Powers Act?

The Iraq War. The most recent intense struggle between the president and Congress over a military conflict has been the Iraq War (2003–2010). By 2002, it had become increasingly difficult for UN inspectors to accurately assess Iraq's capabilities for producing weapons of mass destruction. Although there had been no concrete evidence of such weapons, President George W. Bush argued that a preemptive strike against Iraq was necessary to preserve the security of the United States. In accordance with the War Powers Act, President Bush asked Congress for a resolution authorizing military action against Iraq. On October 10, 2002, the House of Representatives approved a joint resolution that gave the president the authority to use all military force to "defend the national security of the United States" and to ensure that Saddam Hussein, the Iraqi leader, complied with a UN resolution allowing inspectors into Iraq to search for weapons of mass destruction.[34] The Senate approved the resolution the next day, October 11, 2002, by a vote of 77 to 23.

The Iraq War was launched on March 19, 2003. The initial phase of the war went very quickly. Saddam Hussein was captured in December 2003, and was eventually tried and hanged for war crimes. Nevertheless, instability in Iraq continued. By 2006, with the violence in Iraq at a high, the Democrats in Congress—many of whom had initially supported the war—now withdrew their support and called for the return of all U.S. troops and an end to the war. During the midterm congressional elections that year, Democrats made ending the war a campaign issue, and they won majority control of the House and the Senate. However, they were unable to make significant progress in bringing U.S. involvement in the Iraq War to an end. On the contrary, in January 2007 President Bush increased the number of troops in Iraq in an effort known as the "surge," which was designed to try to reduce the violence there.

In January 2009, when President Obama was inaugurated, the three dominant groups in Iraq—the Sunnis, the Shiites, and the Kurds—operated under a parliamentary system of government. In March 2010, the Iraqis held their second round of national elections. Although a great deal of instability remains, the Iraqis are making progress toward a legitimate democracy. President Obama announced that he would keep his campaign promise to initiate the return of the majority of U.S. troops within sixteen months. He worked with the secretary of defense and the Iraqi army to safely withdraw U.S. troops, and on August 31, 2010, he announced the end of the nation's formal combat involvement in Iraq.

THE PRESIDENT IN WARTIME   **435**

The Afghanistan War.
At a time when the Iraq War seemed to be coming to a close, the ongoing war in Afghanistan flared up considerably. This conflict began in 2001, after the September 11 terrorist attacks were traced back to al Qaeda operatives harbored by the Afghan Taliban regime. President George W. Bush addressed Congress on September 20, 2001, indicating that the Taliban would be held responsible for the attacks, and in early October, the United States with its allies launched a military action on Afghanistan designed to find those responsible for the 9/11 attacks and bring down the Taliban regime. Although the Taliban regime was subsequently toppled, and a new leader, Hamid Karzai, was elected and reelected, the Taliban has remained active in Afghanistan. In 2009, President Obama, as commander in chief, responded to resurgent Taliban-sponsored attacks on U.S. troops and civilian Afghanis by increasing the number of troops there by 30,000; by September 2010, there were 98,000 American troops there.[35]

After President Obama outlined his Afghanistan strategy, public opinion was narrowly supportive of the effort (51 percent to 40 percent, with 9 percent undecided).[36] With such limited support, it might become difficult to maintain U.S. involvement there, and, as President Bush learned in Iraq, an unpopular war can erode the president's popularity and effectiveness, as we discussed in Chapter 6, Public Opinion.

Power Struggles between the President and the Judiciary

Power struggles between the president and the judiciary in wartime generally focus on civil liberties. But the leading case on presidential authority in wartime is the *Steel Seizure* case, which ruled that the Constitution grants "all legislative powers" to Congress. Because Congress had enacted no law authorizing such a seizure and indeed, had explicitly rejected giving the president such power, the president could not have done so under any constitutional authority. Nor did the president's role as commander in chief of the armed forces authorize the action, because the steel mills were not part of the theater of war. Supreme Court Justice Robert H. Jackson's concurring opinion agreed with the result but set out a separate rationale, which is now widely cited as precedent. Jackson argued that the president's authority is at its peak when he acts consistent with the express or implied will of Congress, is in a middle territory when he acts in the absence of a congressional grant or denial of power, but is at its lowest when he acts, as he did in seizing the mills, contrary to the express or implied will of Congress.[37]

The most recent clashes between the president and the judiciary over wartime powers arose during President George W. Bush's declared "war on

How much responsibility should Presidents Bush and Obama assume for the Iraq and Afghanistan Wars, respectively? Does Congress have any shared responsibility in those conflicts?

terror." Following 9/11, President Bush greatly expanded the powers of the executive branch of government. Specifically, he created separate military tribunals to try captured terrorists, he claimed exemption from the **Geneva Convention** rules on the treatment and detainment of prisoners, and he authorized the National Security Agency to monitor conversations of suspected terrorists with residents of the United States without requiring a warrant. President Bush's justification was that as commander in chief, he had the foremost responsibility to protect American citizens and that actions taken for that purpose should be not be subject to the approval of Congress or the courts.

A combination of congressional action and Supreme Court decisions, following the guidelines of the *Steel Seizure* case, constrained most of these presidential actions. In 2004, the Supreme Court's *Hamdi v. United States* decision rejected Bush administration attempts to deny *habeas corpus* protections to an enemy combatant who was a U.S. citizen because federal law prohibits such denial to U.S. citizens.[38] But that same day, the Court also rejected the administration's authority to deny *habeas corpus* to an enemy combatant who was not a U.S. citizen.[39] The Bush administration then established special military tribunals to review the detention of enemy combatants at Guantanamo, but the Court rejected the authority of the tribunals because Congress had not authorized them.[40] The Court also rejected congressional and presidential efforts to limit the Court's jurisdiction to hear such appeals, claiming that those limits did not apply to cases that had been filed before Congress passed the law. But even when Congress and the president did authorize such tribunals, the Supreme Court declared that neither Congress nor the president have the authority to suspend *habeas corpus*, which the Constitution only allows during "Cases of Rebellion or Invasion."[41] Thus, in cases involving terrorism, the Court has put up gates in the way of Congress and the president in their efforts to restrict civil liberties in the name of national security. Two days after President Obama was inaugurated, he issued three executive orders requiring a complete evaluation of all policies related to interrogation, detention, and military tribunals for military prisoners, and he ordered an immediate stop to practices that constituted torture under international law.[42]

At the same time, he declared his intent to close the detention center at Guantanamo Bay but not in a way that would put U.S. citizens at risk from terrorism threats. Because of security concerns about sending prisoners back to their home countries, that process has taken longer than expected. In May 2009, President Obama decided that the United States would continue the use of military tribunals to prosecute terrorism suspects so long as they were guaranteed fundamental constitutional rights in the process.

Geneva Conventions: *Set of treaties that define lawful military combat and protect the rights of prisoners of war.*

What limits should the judiciary impose on presidential actions in wartime? Give examples.

How are acts of terrorism different from, or the same as, acts of war? How should the president, Congress, and the judiciary respond to terrorist attacks?

The Organization of the Modern White House

How a president organizes the Executive Office and the cabinet reveals a great deal about his management style as well as his policy preferences. The president relies on his White House advisers for policy recommendations. The modern president has the challenge of encouraging cooperation between political appointees and members of the civil service and making sure that employees in each category are held accountable for their decisions.

The Executive Office of the President

Executive Office of the President: *Organization that houses all staff who work directly for the president.*

White House Office: *President's personal staff organization.*

Office of Management and Budget (OMB): *President's budget office.*

National Security Council (NSC): *President's personal set of advisers on international security.*

Council of Economic Advisers (CEA): *President's personal set of advisers on the economy.*

How have presidents chosen to manage all the responsibilities of the Executive Office?

chief of staff: *Person who coordinates and oversees interactions among the president, his personal staff, and his cabinet secretaries.*

The president runs a large organization known as the **Executive Office of the President**, a loosely knit overseer of several key organizations that report directly to him. These include the **White House Office**, **Office of Management and Budget (OMB)**, the **National Security Council (NSC)**, and the **Council of Economic Advisers (CEA)**. Each office has influence over budgetary, military, and economic policies. The growth of the Executive Office in the past seventy-five years is stunning. President Franklin Delano Roosevelt had only sixty employees; President George W. Bush had more than 5,000 people working directly or indirectly for him, and the Obama administration is expected to equal that number.[43]

Staff organizations can have a real impact on the success of a presidential administration. In general, a tightly organized White House staff organization yields a productive presidency, and the **chief of staff** is central to that effort in several ways. He serves as a gatekeeper by controlling the flow of staff and paperwork and focuses the president's attention on key issues. The chief of staff also monitors the coherence of presidential policies across cabinet departments and can serve as a referee for disagreements among members of the president's senior staff. Lastly, he can be important in forming bridges between the president and Congress; President Obama acknowledged that this was a major reason why he chose Rahm Emanuel, a former congressman from Illinois, as his first chief of staff (Emanuel resigned October 1, 2010 to run for mayor of Chicago; Peter Rouse was appointed Interim Chief of Staff). Another important element in presidential productivity is staff continuity, and new presidents often bring former executive branch personnel into their administration.

The Office of the Vice President

Traditionally, the office of the vice president has not had many important responsibilities. It was not until the twentieth century that vice presidents were chosen by presidential candidates to enhance their electoral prospects, and even then, once they were elected, they were given little more than ceremonial tasks. However, with the increasing complexity and international significance of the presidential role, the role of the vice president has increased in responsibility. Each vice president tries to carve out a role that he is most comfortable with and that the president finds acceptable. Ultimately, the people hold the president accountable for the actions and policies of his administration; even if a vice president exerts influence, it is the president who bears the responsibilities for the outcomes.

What constitutional responsibilities does the vice president have? What authority should he have?

Presidential Greatness

President Obama is the forty-fourth president of the United States, and the men who came before him served with varying degrees of success as leaders in both foreign and domestic policy. Presidential leadership is judged by whether a president is able to get his preferred policies passed by Congress and enacted into law and by how well he oversees the bureaucracy to make the government run effectively and efficiently (for more on the bureaucracy, see Chapter 13).

Name two presidents you think should be called "great."

The American people like to rank their presidents, and scholars also assess presidential greatness, looking at the clarity of a president's vision for policy, his communication and negotiation skills, and the effectiveness of his use of presidential powers, especially the general grant of executive power (see Figure 12.3). Good presidents do not have to excel in every one of these categories, but they have to compensate for a weakness in one area with greater strength in another. Stephen Skowronek's work argues that presidents have opportunities to continue the policies of their predecessors or forge new paths, and that the decisions they make in this regard affect their presidential greatness factor. He also points out that a president's success is often determined by external events, such as a terrorist attack or a global economic downturn.[44] The scholar Aaron Wildavsky suggests that there are actually "two presidencies": a foreign policy presidency and a domestic policy presidency.[45] On foreign policy, the president often must work quickly, and in private, as negotiations must be conducted discretely. In contrast, domestic politics rarely require immediate action and usually entail open debate, with many citizens and interest groups vested in the outcome.[46]

The following discussion focuses on three presidents: Franklin Roosevelt, from a New York wealthy elite family; Lyndon Johnson, from a very poor Texas family; and Ronald Reagan, from a middle-class family in Illinois. Each exerted a major impact on domestic and foreign policies during the twentieth century.[47] These three presidents are frequently singled out for their impact on public policy. Each had strengths and weaknesses, and each knew how to maximize their greatest asset, from intellect, to negotiating skills, to public communications, to try and accomplish their goals.

FIGURE 12.3 Historians Presidential Leadership Survey. This list shows the top twenty presidents (out of thirty-eight) in the survey and also shows where the modern presidents rank.

President's Name	2009 Final Score	Overall Ranking	
		2009	2000
Abraham Lincoln	902	1	1
George Washington	854	2	3
Franklin D. Roosevelt	837	3	2
Theodore Roosevelt	781	4	4
Harry S. Truman	708	5	5
John F. Kennedy	701	6	8
Thomas Jefferson	698	7	7
Dwight D. Eisenhower	689	8	9
Woodrow Wilson	683	9	6
Ronald Reagan	671	10	11
Lyndon B. Johnson	641	11	10
James K. Polk	606	12	12
Andrew Jackson	606	13	13
James Monroe	605	14	14
Bill Clinton	605	15	21
William McKinley	599	16	15
John Adams	545	17	16
George H. W. Bush	542	18	20
John Quincy Adams	542	19	19
James Madison	535	20	18
Gerald Ford*	509	22	23
Jimmy Carter*	474	25	22
Richard M. Nixon*	450	27	25
George W. Bush*	362	36	NA

*Modern presidents not ranked in the top twenty

Source: C-SPAN Historians Presidential Leadership Survey, www.c-span.org.

Franklin Delano Roosevelt (1933–45): The New Deal and World War II

When Franklin Delano Roosevelt (known as "FDR") took office in 1933, the nation was experiencing the Great Depression. Unemployment had reached 25 percent, and Americans were suffering, many homeless and hungry. To combat the effects of the depression, FDR had a clear policy vision, which he called the **New Deal**. In the first three years of his presidency he succeeded in getting Congress to pass legislation that radically altered the size and shape of the federal government. His immediate need was to find a way to get cash into the hands of individual citizens, but he opposed handouts. Instead, he created various job programs, including the Conservation Corps, the Works Progress Administration, and the Tennessee Valley Authority, all of which both employed and trained workers.

The White House Historical Association (White House Collection)

Franklin D. Roosevelt

New Deal: *Franklin D. Roosevelt's program for ending the Great Depression through government intervention in the economy and a set of safety-net programs for workers.*

FDR also expanded the government's role in regulating the economy. The creation of the Securities and Exchange Commission and other laws relating to banking and finance helped restore confidence in banks and the stock market. The National Labor Relations Act established the federal oversight of working conditions, labor standards, and labor disputes. This legislation brought the government and the business and labor sectors closer together. The Social Security program, a pension program to which workers contributed through a payroll tax that was also paid by employers, further entwined business with government.

Just as his distant cousin Teddy Roosevelt did, Franklin Roosevelt used the bully pulpit and advanced the use of communication technology in the office of the president. He invented the **fireside chat**, a radio address to voters explaining the reasoning behind his governing decisions. Because fewer than half of all Americans owned radios at this time, FDR also turned the chats into newsreels that were shown in movie theaters. Ever since, presidents have found direct communications with voters to be an effective governing device.[48] President Roosevelt was also open and available to the Washington press corps, and his very first press conference in 1933 was a success. As a media-savvy president, FDR created the formal position of White House press secretary.[49]

Identify one of Franklin D. Roosevelt's successes and one of his failures.

fireside chat: *Radio addresses by President Franklin D. Roosevelt that were the first regular communications from the president to a large portion of the American public.*

Roosevelt took a personal role in negotiating legislative deals with the members of the House and Senate, which were controlled by the Democrats. He allowed his staff to lay out the conditions for a compromise, but Roosevelt would finish the negotiations himself.[50] During his first five years in office, Roosevelt had great success in getting legislation through Congress. But in 1937, he overstepped his powers by proposing to expand the size of the Supreme Court. The Court had struck down several of Roosevelt's favored policies, often by closely divided votes, and his so-called **Court-packing plan** would have allowed him to appoint additional justices and so secure a majority favorable to him. However, Congress rejected Roosevelt's attempt to upset the checks and balances, and after that, his relationship with Congress began to falter.

On December 7, 1941, Japan attacked the United States at Pearl Harbor in Hawai'i, drawing the United States into World War II. From that point on, foreign affairs dominated Roosevelt's presidency, but the New Deal legislation of the previous decade laid the groundwork for the modern structure of domestic programs in the United States.

Court-packing plan: *President Franklin Roosevelt's proposal to add new justices to the Supreme Court so that the Court would uphold his policies.*

Great Society: *Lyndon B. Johnson's program for expanding the federal social welfare programs in health care, education, and housing, and ending poverty.*

Lyndon Baines Johnson

The White House Historical Association (White House Collection)

Lyndon Baines Johnson (1963–69): The Great Society and Vietnam

President Lyndon Johnson ("LBJ") focused his mission on improving race relations and ending poverty, because he believed they stood in the way of social, political, and economic progress. Most of his programs, which he called the **Great Society**, built on the infrastructure of FDR's New Deal, but they went much further in connecting the individual to the federal government. In the area of race relations, Johnson believed it was the obligation of the federal government to guarantee civil rights to all Americans. He convinced Congress to pass the Civil Rights Act of 1964, the Voting Rights Act of 1965, and the Fair Housing Act of 1968, which together combined to form a powerful set of laws that protected the rights of African Americans and have been subsequently used to protect the rights of other minority groups as well (see Chapter 5).

LBJ believed that it was possible for people to work very hard but still remain poor and that the poor were severely disadvantaged in terms of education, access to jobs, and affordable housing. He transformed the social contract between the individual and the federal government into one that included pure need, rather than merit based on work. He created two major federal health insurance programs: Medicaid, a health insurance program for the poor, and Medicare, a health insurance for the elderly. He was also responsible for creating the Food Stamp Program, the School Lunch Program, Head Start, Jobs Corps, and the Elementary and Secondary Education Act.

Johnson was not a skilled communicator or comfortable speech giver, and he did not come across well on television, which by this time had succeeded radio as the dominant form of political communication. LBJ compensated for his lack of communication skills by relying more heavily on his very strong negotiation skills. From his prior experience as a member of Congress and Senate majority leader, Johnson understood how to convince members of Congress when it was in their interest to pass legislation. Johnson made sure that his programs would benefit all poor people, white and black, rural and urban. By creating sweeping eligibility criteria, Johnson almost guaranteed that every congressional district in the country would receive some benefit from these programs. For example, both Medicaid and Medicare legislation included subsidies to rural hospitals and to big inner-city hospitals for services and capital expenditures such as improving facilities and building new ones. School lunch programs benefited schoolchildren as well as farmers, who sold the federal government their meat, milk, cheese, and grains at a guaranteed price, so they always had a market.

Johnson also used his presidential powers to distribute and award federal contracts and federal funds to key members of Congress and key state officials in return for their support of his programs. He understood that if a member of Congress needed to explain his vote in support of a liberal bill, he could do so more easily if he could point to some other federal benefit he had secured, such as a bridge, navy or army base, or new hospital wing. Legislators and lobbyists who opposed Johnson were invited to the Oval Office at the White House, where he lectured and intimidated them.

Although Johnson's personal relationship with the press and the public started out reasonably well, as the U.S. involvement in the Vietnam War escalated the press began to distrust Johnson, and many journalists believed he was not being candid about the war with them or the American people. By the end of his presidency, Johnson's relationship with the press was downright hostile on both sides, and the press gave the president much negative publicity. In fact, negative reporting on the progress of the Vietnam War and its unfavorable impact on Johnson's approval ratings are widely believed to be the reasons Johnson decided not to seek reelection in 1968.

> Identify one of Lyndon Baines Johnson's successes and one of his failures.

Ronald Reagan (1981–89): The Reagan Revolution and the End of the Cold War

President Ronald Reagan had a vision of the relationship between the federal government that was different from the views of Roosevelt and Johnson. Reagan believed that the combined effect of the New Deal with the Great Society had sapped individual initiative and responsibility. When he took office, he mounted an aggressive campaign to scale back federal programs that provided benefits to individuals.

Ronald Reagan

federal budget deficit: *Difference between the amount of money the federal government spends in outlays and the amount of money it receives from revenues.*

Identify one of Ronald Reagan's successes and one of his failures.

Tax cuts were the first thing on Reagan's agenda for two reasons. First, he reasoned that if taxes went down, the economy would flourish. Second, he knew that if tax revenue went down, and spending increased, **federal budget deficits** would be created. These deficits would, in turn, give him justification for proposing cuts in entitlement programs, such as Social Security, Medicaid, and Aid to Families with Dependent Children (today called Temporary Aid to Needy Families). These entitlement programs put a strain on the federal budget, especially as the number of people living in poverty grew and the elderly lived longer. Reagan managed to make cuts in the programs for the poor and elderly by restricting eligibility requirements for benefits, but he did not succeed in dismantling them.

At the same time Reagan was implementing his domestic policy vision, he was also implementing his foreign policy vision. He took a firm stand against the Soviet Union, which he perceived as a direct threat to the United States and as a major promoter of Communism throughout the world. The defense buildup he ordered set off a military spending race that strained the Soviets' state-controlled economy to the breaking point. By the end of Reagan's second term, it was clear that the Soviet Union was on the way toward collapse and could no longer control its satellite nations in Eastern Europe. Reagan's foreign policy was arguably an important factor in the end of Communism and the Cold War.

Ronald Reagan is referred to as the "Great Communicator" because he came across very well on television, and as a former actor, he was able to give engaging, persuasive, and even comforting speeches. In January 1986, when

The White House Historical Association (White House Collection)

the space shuttle *Challenger* blew up shortly after takeoff as literally millions of Americans watched in horror, Reagan's words eased the national pain: "The crew of the space shuttle *Challenger* honored us by the manner in which they lived their lives. We will never forget them, nor the last time we saw them, this morning, as they prepared for their journey and waved goodbye and 'slipped the surly bonds of earth' to 'touch the face of God.'"[51] In any analysis of presidential success, the power of speech cannot be underestimated because it is the most basic way that the president tries to connect with the people.

President Reagan delegated much of the actual negotiating over policy to his staff members. He also enhanced the power of the director of the Office of Management and Budget to negotiate with Congress on budgetary matters. He and his staff knew how to position themselves in a favorable way on most issues, but on issues on which they were at a public disadvantage, Reagan knew when to compromise. During his last two years in office, 1987–88, he had considerable success working with a Democratic-controlled Congress to pass trade legislation, welfare reform, and the first comprehensive AIDS funding and treatment bill. Although Reagan enjoyed relatively consistent popularity and was perceived as highly responsive to his base of supporters, his record came under greater scrutiny after he left office because his policies resulted in higher federal budget deficits and lower spending on programs for the disadvantaged.

The example of Reagan, in the context of Roosevelt and Johnson, shows how the office of the presidency can shape domestic and foreign policy for future generations. Reagan ran for president thirty-five years after Roosevelt died, and eleven years after Johnson left office, on a campaign platform of scaling back the New Deal and the Great Society. In turn, Reagan left a conservative political legacy about the limited role of the federal government that remains a powerful rallying cry for Republicans today.

Describe the legacy of Franklin D. Roosevelt, of Lyndon Baines Johnson, and of Ronald Reagan. How did each of these men change the office of the president?

The President and Public Policy: Tax Policy and Government Spending

Presidents can set the policy agenda not only for their terms in office but for generations that follow. How successful they are is greatly determined by their ability to combine the agenda-setting tools available to them with their natural leadership skills. All presidents confront a vast policy landscape, but their performance with regard to the economy is a primary point on which they are judged. In fact, presidents are generally held accountable for the economy, despite the fact that they cannot actually control it. As chief executive, the president oversees a large economic infrastructure in areas related to taxation and government spending. In the section that follows we describe his direct and indirect roles in implementing economic policy.

Tax Policy

Beginning with Theodore Roosevelt and accelerating under Franklin Roosevelt, presidents have led federal intervention in the economy: regulating business practices, ensuring workplace safety, overseeing banking and finance, and constructing a safety net of unemployment and disability benefits, among many other programs. When the economy is weak, there is pressure on the president to take extraordinary steps to address it. This is what Franklin Roosevelt did during the Great Depression, and what Barack Obama did in 2009 in response to a deep recession. A **recession** is typically defined as a downturn in economic activity, with declines in employment levels, income, retail spending, and industrial production. The recession of 2008–10 was largely attributed to inflated housing prices, irresponsible lending by banks, and excessive borrowing by consumers, all of which led to widespread foreclosures and the collapse of major sectors of the financial and construction industries. The U.S. economy has long been driven by consumer spending, so as people lose jobs, consumer spending declines, forcing business and industry to cut back production and lay off their workers.

Government can use **fiscal policy** to intervene in the economy, that is, by manipulating the money supply through taxing and spending. Increasing spending or decreasing taxes increases the money supply. Decreasing spending or increasing taxes decreases the money supply. In times of severe economic crises, the president may support a policy of increasing the money supply to ward off a recession. Alternatively, an

recession: *Downturn in economic activity, with declines in employment levels, income, retail spending, and industrial production.*

fiscal policy: *Means of controlling the money supply through taxing and spending.*

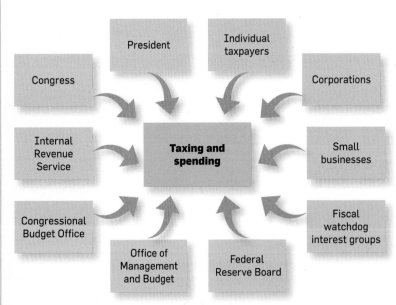

increase in prices can lead to workers demanding raises, and higher wages and lead to even larger increases in prices, setting off **inflation**. In this case, the president may support a decrease in the money supply to ward off or reduce the extent of inflation.

The Constitution grants Congress the explicit power to raise (or lower) federal taxes, but the executive branch has always been responsible for collecting taxes. The **Internal Revenue Service**, a unit in the Department of the Treasury, monitors the payment of federal taxes. Americans pay a wide range of federal taxes to support federal programs, including the income tax as well as taxes supporting Medicare, Social Security, disability benefits, and unemployment compensation. There are also corporate taxes and customs fees. The federal government also collects taxes on goods and services, such as gasoline, cigarettes, and cell phones.

As chief executive of the federal government, the president must make decisions about fiscal policy in terms of taxes and federal spending. Republican presidents have typically wanted to lower all taxes, a policy that provides less revenue to the federal government and subsequently decreases federal spending. Democratic presidents have typically wanted to cut taxes for individuals with lower incomes and to raise taxes on wealthier citizens to support federal programs. In 2009, President Obama responded to the severe economic crisis by asking Congress to pass a nearly $800 billion stimulus bill—a combination of spending increases favored by Democrats and tax credits (which amount to tax cuts) to increase the money supply.

The problem that modern presidents face is the complexity of the tax code itself, with thousands of pages of rules and regulations, and that complexity means that hundreds of groups and businesses lobby Congress for provisions that will help them. Some economists argue that business decisions and job growth are tied too strongly to tax incentives rather than to the marketplace. In 1986, Congress passed and President Reagan signed the Tax Reform Act, which tried to simplify the tax code and make it work for citizens at all income levels. However, those changes did not last, because the Reagan administration produced large federal budget deficits and the next two presidents, George H. W. Bush and Bill Clinton, each raised taxes to balance the budget. President George W. Bush cut taxes in the early years of his administration, but by the end of his administration, the federal budget deficit and the **national debt** had each increased dramatically (see Chapter 11 for further explanation). President Obama's federal stimulus package added to that deficit and his administration now bears the responsibility of bringing the federal budget back into balance.

The constant revisiting of the tax code and the changing levels of spending in the federal budget create an unpredictable economic environment for the country. With tax policy so complicated and vast, it becomes increasingly

inflation: *Condition in which money supply and higher wages leads to large increases in prices.*

Should the government intervene in the economy to ward off recession and prevent inflation?

Internal Revenue Service: *Executive branch agency that collects federal taxes.*

national debt: *Sum of loans and interest that the federal government has accrued over time to pay for the federal deficit.*

difficult for the president to be equally responsive to all citizens and, in turn, for citizens to hold the president accountable for the spending of their tax dollars. Even more frustrating for the president is the fact that he might propose a tax plan but Congress has the power to accept it, alter it, or reject it. In this way, Congress checks presidential influence in the management of the federal budget.

Monetary Policy

monetary policy:
Means of controlling the money supply through control of interest rates and availability of credit, managed by a central bank, the Federal Reserve.

The president is limited in his power to directly influence the nation's economic condition because **monetary policy** is in reality under the control of the **Federal Reserve Board**, an independent agency (see Chapter 13). Monetary policy, enacted by a nation's central bank, increases or decreases the money supply by changing the reserve requirements—the amount of cash reserves that banks must keep on hand (see Table 12.4). Congress created the Federal Reserve in 1913 as a system of twelve regional banks that all belong to one national banking system, in an effort to stabilize American currency and control the flow of money in the economy.

Federal Reserve Board:
Independent regulatory commission that affects the money supply by setting the reserve requirements of member banks, establishing a discount rate for loans to member banks, and buying or selling government securities.

The Federal Reserve System is led by a seven-member board of governors. Each member is nominated by the president and confirmed by the Senate. Members serve fourteen-year terms and the president selects the board chair, who serves a four-year term. The chair of the Federal Reserve is typically

TABLE 12.4 Comparison of Tax and Monetary Policy

Actions by the Congress and the president affect fiscal policy, while actions by the Federal Reserve Board affect monetary policy.

Type of Policy	Policy Maker	Action	Direct Effect	Effect on Money Supply
Fiscal	Congress/president	Increase spending or cut taxes	Consumers have more money to spend.	increases
	Congress/president	Decrease spending or increase taxes	Consumers have less money to spend.	decreases
Monetary	Federal Reserve Board	Increase reserve requirement	Banks have less money to loan.	decreases
	Federal Reserve Board	Decrease reserve requirement	Banks have more money to loan.	increases
	Federal Reserve Board	Increase the discount rate	Loans are more expensive.	decreases
	Federal Reserve Board	Decrease the discount rate	Loans are less expensive.	increases

a public figure who testifies before Congress frequently and also goes before banking and investment firms to explain federal monetary policy. The current chair of the Federal Reserve is Ben Bernanke, who was nominated by George W. Bush. In 2009, President Obama nominated Bernanke to a second term, making it clear that Bernanke's views and policies were in line with his own.

The Federal Reserve Board can increase or decrease the money supply using monetary policy. When the Federal Reserve increases reserve requirements, banks have less money to lend, and the money supply decreases. When the Federal Reserve decreases reserve requirements, banks have more money to lend, and thus the money supply increases. The Federal Reserve Board also controls the money supply through the discount rate, or the interest rate that the Federal Reserve charges other banks on loans. When the Federal Reserve lowers the discount rates, member banks can loan money out at lower rates, increasing the amount of money borrowed and thus the money supply. When the Federal Reserve increases the discount rate, member banks have to charge higher interest on loans, lowering the amount of money borrowed and thus reducing the money supply. During the recession of 2008–10, the Federal Reserve dropped the discount rate to nearly zero percent in an effort to increase borrowing.

Although the president can name people to the Federal Reserve, he cannot fire them if they push monetary policy in a direction different from the one he wants. His only real power over the Federal Reserve comes with the nomination process, especially in choosing the chair. Despite the fact that the president has very limited control over the actions of the Federal Reserve, he is ultimately held accountable for whether those actions improve or worsen economic conditions.

The Presidency and Democracy

From George Washington to Barack Obama, the presidency has evolved from an institution with strictly limited responsibilities to the large and powerful institution it is today. Certainly the Framers would be surprised by the growth of the presidency, and they might wonder whether the executive branch is too focused on serving the president individually, and not focused enough on the needs of the citizens more generally.

Is the president held accountable for the performance and policies of the federal government? Probably much more than he deserves. The president operates in a separation of powers system, and laws must be passed with the cooperation of Congress, so the president cannot be rewarded or blamed entirely for the federal government's policies.[52] Voters can render

- In what ways is the president held accountable, both individually and for the collective economic, military, and social condition of the federal government?

- How responsive is the presidency as a democratic office? How can the president address the vital public policy concerns of the American people?

- What opportunities are there for the average person to influence the decisions of the president?

- What powers does the president have to ensure equality across all citizens?

- Is the modern presidency a gate or a gateway to democracy?

their direct verdict on the president's job performance when they choose whether to reelect him, provided he runs for a second term. Voters also indirectly register their opinions in congressional midterm elections, which focus on members of the House and Senate but are also interpreted as judgments on the president's record. Because there is no possibility of a third term in office, presidents in their second term are typically freer from public accountability. In cases of very serious wrongdoing, Congress has the power to impeach and convict the president, but the threshold for impeachment is extremely high and it happens very rarely. No president has ever been impeached, convicted, and removed from office.

Overall, it is actually quite difficult for the average citizen to hold the president personally accountable for his actions. Surrounded by so many staff members, presidents do not give ordinary citizens much chance to influence him, nor does he often make himself available to be responsive to citizen needs. Given the vast size of the nation and security concerns for the president's safety, it is not easy for citizens to convey their opinions directly to the president. In the course of the nation's history presidents have grown less accessible to the average voter. However, technological innovations as simple as fast airplane travel, and more recently, e-mail, texting, blogging, and social networking websites, provide many more modes of communication between voters and the president or the president's staff. Although the president will not meet most of the people he represents, each town meeting he holds and public speech he gives is an opportunity for an exchange of views. The job of presidential staff is to keep him as well informed on public opinion as possible.

Despite the limited opportunities for accountability, presidents do tend to be responsive to public opinion over the course of their time in office, although less so in their second term. However, each president strives for success and wants to leave behind a legacy that is respected and honored. In the modern age of politics, presidents are considered their party's leader, and they want their records to reflect well on other elected officials from their party. And all presidents see it as their responsibility to do what they believe to be best for the country, even in the face of opposition from the media, the public, and Congress. At times, this opposition can result in a less effective president than some might want, but the operation of checks and balances on presidential power accords with the Framers' vision of presidential leadership.

In terms of equality under the law, there is no question that the president's professional and moral obligation is to enforce all laws equally, with no bias or prejudice against any one type or group of citizen. Presidents cannot enact laws individually, however, and if Congress refuses to cooperate, presidents are forced to use their executive powers to do what they believe to be right. Ultimately, as the single occupant of the most powerful office in America, the president is first in line to uphold the principle of equality. The president is also equal to every other citizen in that he is subject to the law.

Overall, the modern presidency acts as both a gate and a gateway to democracy at the same time. It is a gate in that the president oversees a very large federal government that can be complex and difficult to change in response to public needs. It is a gateway in the fact that any natural-born citizen can run for the most powerful office in the land, and although wealth, education, and connections are extremely helpful in winning, they are not prerequisites for victory. The men who have been elected president have come from a wide range of income, educational, and professional backgrounds. After the 2008 presidential election, when both racial and gender barriers were broken, one can argue that the path to the White House is more open than ever before.

Top Ten to Take Away

1. The American presidency was an innovation in governance. The Framers thought the executive branch would be led by one person whose primary responsibility would be the defense of the United States. As the nation grew, the presidency grew accordingly. Today the president speaks for the nation on the world stage and sets the policy agenda at home. (pp. 410–412)

2. Presidents have come from a wide range of income, educational, and professional backgrounds. All have been male, although women were serious contenders during the 2008 presidential election cycle. (pp. 412–416)

3. Among the president's constitutional powers are those associated with being commander in chief. The president also has the power to pardon, to negotiate and sign treaties and recognize foreign nations, to veto bills passed by Congress, and to appoint federal officers, cabinet secretaries, agency heads, ambassadors, and federal judges. (pp. 416–423)

4. Congress's ultimate check on the executive is the power to impeach and remove from office. Two presidents have been impeached but not convicted and so not removed from office. One president resigned under threat of impeachment. (pp. 423–426)

5. The Constitution vests the president with a general grant of executive power and requires that he "take Care that the Laws be faithfully executed." These responsibilities have been used by presidents to vastly increase presidential power. (p. 426)

6. The president uses his executive power to issue presidential directives. He also uses the office to persuade the people and Congress and to set the agenda for domestic and foreign policy. (pp. 426–433)

7. As presidential power has grown, the president has come into increasing conflict with the other two branches of government, particularly during wartime. Congress has tried to clarify and limit the president's war powers. The struggle with the judiciary during wartime is largely over civil liberties. (pp. 433–438)

8. The modern Executive Office of the President includes organizations that have great influence over budgetary, military, and economic policies, although presidents are held accountable for the economy in a way that exceeds their ability to control it. The office of the vice president has grown in recent years and increased in influence. (pp. 438–439)

9. Presidential leadership is generally judged on how successful a president is in getting his preferred policies passed into law by Congress and in getting the bureaucracy, which he oversees, to be effective and efficient. Americans also judge their presidents on their communication and negotiation skills. (pp. 439–441)

10. Presidents have the power to shape domestic and foreign policy not only during their administrations but for future generations. Franklin Roosevelt, Lyndon Johnson, and Ronald Reagan are examples of powerful presidents. (pp. 441–445)

A full narrative summary of the chapter appears on the book's website.

Ten to Test Yourself

1. How did the Executive Office of the President change from Roosevelt to Obama?

2. Does a president's prior experience shape his leadership style? If so, how?

3. What is the president's most powerful bargaining chip with Congress?

4. How does the power of impeachment restrict presidential abuse of power?

5. What was the relationship between the Vietnam War and the War Powers Act?

6. Give one example of an executive order that changed U.S. history, and explain why.

7. What are the roles of the chief of staff and vice president in helping to carry out the president's agenda?

8. How do presidents use the bully pulpit to accomplish their policy goals?

9. Compare Franklin Delano Roosevelt's and Ronald Reagan's visions of the federal government's responsibilities toward individual citizens.

10. What role does the president play in the economy?

More review questions and answers and chapter quizzes are on the book's website.

Terms **to Know and Use**

abuse of power (p. 425)
approval rating (p. 431)
articles of impeachment (p. 425)
bully pulpit (p. 430)
cabinet departments (p. 411)
cabinet secretaries (p. 411)
chief of staff (p. 438)
civil servants (p. 419)
clemency (p. 418)
Cold War (p. 416)
commutation (p. 418)
Council of Economic Advisers (CEA) (p. 438)
Court-packing plan (p. 442)
divided government (p. 420)
Executive Office of the President (p. 438)
executive order (pp. 426, 427)
executive privilege (p. 424)
federal budget (p. 432)
federal budget deficit (p. 444)
Federal Register (p. 427)

Federal Reserve Board (p. 448)
fireside chat (p. 441)
fiscal policy (p. 446)
Geneva Conventions (p. 437)
Great Society (p. 442)
head of state (p. 432)
impeachment (p. 423)
imperial presidency (p. 416)
inflation (p. 447)
Internal Revenue Service (p. 447)
lame duck (p. 412)
military orders (p. 427)
military tribunals (p. 428)
monetary policy (p. 448)
National Security Council (NSC) (p. 438)
natural-born citizen (p. 410)
national debt (p. 447)
New Deal (p. 441)
Office of Management and Budget (OMB) (p. 438)
omnibus bills (p. 420)

override (p. 420)
pardon (p. 418)
perjury (p. 425)
pocket veto (p. 420)
political appointees (p. 419)
president pro tempore (p. 411)
presidential directive (p. 426)
presidential directive on national security (p. 428)
proclamation (p. 427)
recession (p. 446)
signing statements (p. 428)
Speaker of the House (p. 411)
State of the Union address (p. 420)
subpoenas (p. 424)
term limits (p. 412)
veto (p. 420)
War Powers Act (p. 434)
Watergate scandal (p. 424)
White House Office (p. 438)

Use the vocabulary flash cards on the book's website.

13 THE BUREAUCRACY

▲ College of the Redwoods,
Eureka, California

> *Get involved. You have no idea what you can accomplish until you become unstoppable. . . . If I had a nickel for every time someone said we would fail I would never have to work again.*

When Kate Hanni was a student at the College of the Redwoods, she was a theater arts major who dreamed of being a rock star—"to be in front of a gazillion people with their lighters on," as she put it. Today she is a different kind of rock star, founder and head of the Coalition for an Airline Passengers' Bill of Rights (see FlyersRights .org), which claimed a major victory in December 2009 when the Department of Transportation ruled that airlines must allow passengers stuck on stranded planes to get off.

Hanni had not planned to be a political activist. For years, she was a successful real estate broker in Napa County, California, who enjoyed family and friends and still sang on occasion with her rock band, The Toasted Heads. But on December 29, 2006, her life took a new direction. With 134 other passengers, she and her family were stranded for nine hours and sixteen minutes in a jet parked at the Austin, Texas, airport. There was little food or water; the lavatories reeked. "People got so angry they were talking about busting through the emergency exits," Hanni recalled. "I was fuming. It was imprisonment."

When Hanni got home, she drafted an online petition demanding legal rights for airline passengers. The following month, when an ice storm at New York's Kennedy International Airport stranded thousands of passengers

CourseMate

Visit http://www.cengagebrain
.com/shop/ISBN/0495906190 for
interactive tools including:
- **Quizzes**
- **Flashcards**
- **Videos**
- **Animated PowerPoint slides,**
  Podcast summaries, and more

Kate Hanni ▶

in planes for up to eleven hours, her cause took off. She gave up her real estate business, and she and her husband took out a line of credit on their house to build a website. Soon her petition had 18,000 signatures, and those in her e-mail network wrote to Congress and the Federal Aviation Administration and posted videos of the stranded flight experience on YouTube. Hanni got media attention, promoting passengers' rights in radio and TV interviews. Her coalition gained support from airline labor unions, air traffic controller unions, and consumer groups. She talked her congressman, Mike Thompson (D-Calif.), into introducing legislation. In September 2007, Hanni staged a "strand-in" near the Capitol in Washington, with a tent outfitted to resemble the interior of an airplane and invitations to members of Congress to see what it felt like to be trapped. As the movement's theme song, she got The Toasted Heads to rewrite the Animals' 1965 hit, "We've Gotta Get Out of This Place."

As the movement grew, the airlines fought back, claiming that conditions were not as bad as Hanni reported. The Air Transport Association argued that deplaning would only cause delays and cancellations and might compromise passenger safety. A version of Congressman Thompson's bill passed the House, but a similar one introduced by Barbara Boxer (D-Calif.) did not pass the Senate. New York and California passed airline passenger laws, but a federal court of appeals struck down New York's law on the grounds that only the federal government has the authority to regulate airline service.

In the end, that's exactly what happened. On December 21, 2009, Transportation Secretary Ray LaHood announced new airline regulations. After two hours on the tarmac, airlines must give passengers food and water. After three hours, they must let them off or face stiff fines—$27,500 per passenger. In an e-mail to supporters, an elated Hanni called the regulations "an early Christmas present," but reminded them that "we're not done yet!" Citing fees for checked bags and chronically delayed or canceled flights, she will continue to push for passenger rights legislation. Already, she has jumped into the debate over body scanners.[1]

The story of Kate Hanni is remarkable because she, as an ordinary citizen, demanded that the federal government

FOCUS QUESTIONS

- How does the federal bureaucracy play a role in responding to the individual needs of ordinary citizens?

- How does the structure of the federal bureaucracy shape the way policies are implemented?

- What powers does the bureaucracy have to ensure that federal policies are administered equally across all citizens?

- How can the average citizen influence the decisions of the bureaucracy?

- Is the bureaucracy a gate or a gateway to democracy? Explain.

live up to its responsibility of ensuring the safe travel of passengers. She took matters into her own hands and used the gateways of citizen influence on policy making to draw attention to the issue. Her activism got the Federal Aviation Administration, a subdivision of the Department of Transportation, to respond. In this chapter we will examine the cabinet-level departments, agencies, and other organizations that constitute the executive branch. We look at their structure, characteristics, rationale, procedures, accountability, and responsiveness to citizens' concerns. A fundamental question for students of American government is whether the sprawling nature of the bureaucracy makes it possible to serve the people effectively.

The American Bureaucracy

Just mention the word *bureaucracy* and most people roll their eyes and utter phrases like "red tape" or "slow as molasses." Of all the components of American government, the bureaucracy is most likely to be perceived as annoying and daunting, as a gate against getting things done. And of all the components of American government, the bureaucracy is also the most likely to have a direct impact on citizens' lives. Most Americans have never met a president or a member of Congress or a federal judge, but every American has interacted with an employee of the government. The U.S. Postal Service employees who deliver the mail may be very friendly, but anyone who has waited in line to mail a package might find the rules and regulations of the postal service frustrating.

What federal employees have you come in contact with in the past? What was the most recent experience like?

Bureaucracies generally are not afforded much respect because they seem so complicated and impenetrable, and bureaucrats are often portrayed as faceless automatons who merely enforce the rules. Yet enforcing the rules is the bureaucracy's job; as an extension of the presidency, bureaucratic implementation is the means by which the president executes the law. And rules must be enforced equally across all citizens. In the most obvious example, a first-class stamp costs the same in every state and will get the letter to any place in the nation, just across town or from Houston to Honolulu.

Chris Slane/CartoonStock

Despite the well-known problems associated with bureaucracies, organization is essential to modern government. In the late nineteenth century the German sociologist Max Weber described bureaucracies as highly rational organizations that enabled large numbers of people to get difficult jobs done efficiently.[2] If the federal bureaucracy does not seem efficient today, that may be because of the enormous responsibilities it bears, not only to implement complex policy and law established by the president and Congress but to do so in a way that is orderly, predictable, fair, equal for all citizens, and transparent. The formal aspects of bureaucratic structure promote accountability, while the informal operations—bureaucratic culture—determine how well the organization carries out its own mission and how well it interacts with other organizations. We will discuss these elements in detail to draw a practical road map not only to understanding the federal government but to actually making it work better for ordinary citizens.

What Is the Bureaucracy?

bureaucracy: *Executive branch departments, agencies, boards, and commissions that carry out the responsibilities of the federal government.*

regulations: *Guidelines issued by federal agencies for administering federal programs and implementing federal law.*

What is your impression of the federal bureaucracy? Which branch of government do you think works best? Which works least well?

The **bureaucracy** is the large collection of executive branch departments, agencies, boards, commissions, and other government organizations that carry out the responsibilities of the federal government. These responsibilities are established by laws passed by Congress and signed by the president, but for execution they often entail expertise, so the legislature relies on specialists—the bureaucrats—to write the **regulations** that implement the law.

Today, the total number of federal employees, including the armed services, is almost 5 million people.[3] The jobs of federal employees vary widely. A national park ranger is a federal employee, as is a border patrol officer, a dam inspector with the Army Corps of Engineers, an accountant with the Securities and Exchange Commission, and a lawyer with the Department of Justice. For every federal job classified as "professional," there are also staff jobs, including clerks, office managers, janitors, mechanics, and delivery personnel, who keep the bureaucracy running. Skills and specialties in almost any type of work can be a gateway to employment in the federal government, which we discuss in more detail later in the chapter.

cabinet: *Set of executive departments responsible for carrying out federal policy in specific issue areas.*

One simple way to understand the basic structure of the bureaucracy is to imagine a piece of furniture called a cabinet that stores different types of items in different drawers. It is no accident that the term *bureaucracy* has "bureau" at its base, an old-fashioned term for a cabinet. Today, a president builds his **cabinet**, which is his set of key advisers who are responsible for the areas under their jurisdiction. For example, President Barack Obama appointed Janet Napolitano as secretary of the Department of Homeland Security based on her experience with border control as governor of Arizona, and Senator

Ken Salazar (D-Colo.) as the secretary of the Interior based on his experience with land management policy in Colorado. Most cabinet members are **cabinet secretaries** and head executive departments, but presidents may select additional advisers for cabinet-rank status. In the Obama administration, these include the vice president, the chief of staff, the heads of the Environmental Protection

Official White House Photo by Chuck Kennedy

On April 20, 2009, President Obama posed in the East Room of the White House with Vice President Joe Biden and members of his cabinet.

Agency and of the Office of Management and Budget, the U.S. trade representative, the U.S. ambassador to the United Nations, and the chair of the Council of Economic Advisers.[4]

Constitutional Foundations

The word *bureaucracy* does not appear in the U.S. Constitution, but the foundations of the federal bureaucracy can be traced to a few key sentences in Article II that relate to the powers of the president.

Appointments. Article II, Section 2 gives the president the power to "nominate, and by and with the Advice and Consent of the Senate, . . . appoint . . . all other Officers of the United States, whose Appointments are not herein otherwise provided for, and which shall be established by Law." This section goes on to state that Congress can "by Law vest the Appointment of such inferior Officers, as they think proper, in the President alone, in the Courts of Law, or in the Heads of Departments." Thus the discussion of the president's appointment power implies the existence of executive departments.

Opinions on Federal Policies. Article II, Section 2 references the executive branch more directly when it authorizes the president to "require the Opinion, in writing, of the principal Officer in each of the executive Departments, upon any Subject relating to the Duties of their respective Offices." The Framers envisioned that the president would manage a staff

cabinet secretary: *Head of a cabinet department and chief adviser to the president on the issues under the department's jurisdiction.*

Why did the Framers provide so little direction in the Constitution for the bureaucracy?

of federal officers who would oversee executive departments managing the operations of government, although it is doubtful that they expected the president's staff to be as large as it is today.

Execution of the Laws.   Article II, Section 3 gives the president broad powers to "take Care that the Laws be faithfully executed." At the same time that the Framers wanted to make sure that the president would follow the intention of Congress, they also gave him wide discretion in how he carried out the laws. This broad executive power is the foundation for the growth of the federal bureaucracy as well as for the growth of the presidency, as we saw in Chapter 12 (The Presidency).

The Structure of the Bureaucracy

For more than two centuries, the federal bureaucracy has been changing, growing, and developing into the modern-day interlinked set of organizations that implement federal policy. Some organizations are vast, such as the executive departments, but some are small advisory boards and commissions. Coordinating the authority and operations of these different types of organizations is a significant challenge for the executive branch as it carries out its constitutional duties. The structure of the U.S. bureaucracy is not unique, nor are the challenges it faces.

What made the bureaucracy grow? Is it too big?

Executive Departments.   Today there are fifteen executive, or cabinet-level, departments in the federal bureaucracy. A cabinet department is an executive branch organization led by a cabinet secretary appointed by the president. Cabinet departments are responsible for implementing laws and policies in specific areas, and the job of the secretary is to oversee implementation, provide advice to the president about the issues under the department's control, and develop an annual budget for the department. Congress has the authority to create a cabinet department, but once it is created, it is under the control and supervision of the president as head of the executive branch. Table 13.1 lists each department, the year it was created, its website, and its number of employees.

Each cabinet department consists of subdivisions arranged in a hierarchical form to divide up its tasks and theoretically maximize efficiency and responsiveness. Each department has many subdivisions, or layers, each assigned a specific federal policy to implement. HHS is one of the largest cabinet departments. It oversees 300 programs, with 65,100 employees and a budget of $868.2 billion.[5] This massive and complex organization is necessary to respond to the needs of all the individuals affected by the programs that HHS manages.

For example, HHS is responsible for administering the Supplemental Children's Health Insurance Program (SCHIP), which provides funding to

TABLE 13.1 **Cabinet Departments of the Federal Government, 2010**

Department	Year	Website	Employees (thousands)
State	1789	www.state.gov	35.0
War (later named Defense)	1789	www.dod.gov	720.2
Treasury	1789	www.treasury.gov	113.5
Interior	1849	www.interior.gov	70.6
Agriculture	1862	www.usda.gov	101.0
Justice	1870	www.justice.gov	119.3
Commerce	1903	www.commerce.gov	141.5
Labor	1913	www.labor.gov	17.9
Housing and Urban Development	1965	www.hud.gov	9.7
Transportation	1966	www.transportation.gov	57.9
Energy	1977	www.energy.gov	16.6
Education	1979	www.education.gov	4.3
Health and Human Services	1980	www.hhs.gov	65.1
Veterans Affairs	1989	www.va.gov	284.3
Homeland Security	2003	www.dhs.gov	177.0

Sources: www.whitehouse.gov; United States Office of Management and Budget; *Analytical Perspectives, Budget of the U.S. Government, Fiscal Year 2011* (Washington D.C.: Government Printing Office, 2010): 107. Accessed online at www.whitehouse .gov/omb/budget/fy2011/assets/spec.pdf.

state governments to provide health insurance coverage for children living in working families that are not able to afford private health insurance but are also not poor enough to receive benefits through the **Medicaid** program. The Medicaid program was created in 1965 as a government-provided health insurance program for individuals in poverty, and it falls under the jurisdiction of the Centers for Medicaid and Medicare Services (www.cms.hhs.gov), a division of HHS. But Medicaid is strictly limited to specific income levels, and millions of children are not eligible for health care insurance under this program. To care for the health of these children, Congress created SCHIP in 1997, but it expired in 2007, and President George W. Bush (2001–09) could not agree with the Democratic-controlled

Medicaid: *Government health insurance program for the poor.*

Congress on a reauthorization plan. Consequently, states were limited in the coverage they could offer to children in 2007–08. Without continued permission and federal funds to offer medical services to eligible children, the states had no choice but to pull back. But on February 3, 2009, Congress passed the State Children's Health Insurance Program Reauthorization, and President Obama signed the legislation the next day, extending this program to 11 million children.[6] SCHIP and health care reform are two examples of federal policy that are implemented by a cabinet department, in conjunction with state governments.

Other Types of Federal Organizations.

In addition to cabinet-level departments, there are numerous independent organizations that constitute the federal government, including agencies, commissions, administrations, boards, corporations, and endowments (see Table 13.2). These organizations vary by structure, mission, and degree of independence from the president. For example, the **Office of Management and Budget (OMB)** has final authority over the entire federal budget, and each agency and department must submit its proposed budget to OMB for approval before it is included in the president's official proposed budget. The director of OMB is part of the president's cabinet, although OMB is not a cabinet department. Additionally, all regulations must go through OMB before they take effect.

The **Environmental Protection Agency (EPA)** is an **independent agency**, a type of federal organization established by Congress with authority to regulate an aspect of the economy or a sector of the federal government. Independent agencies do not operate within a cabinet department. Congress designs these agencies to operate with their own authority, depriving the president of the customary authority to remove officers of these agencies without cause. The EPA has a unique role in the federal government, with responsibility for preserving the quality of air, water, and land. It can issue regulations and create policy, as it did on greenhouse gas emissions in January 2010, which are subject to OMB approval, just like regulations from any cabinet department. We discuss the regulatory process, and environmental policy making more specifically, in further detail later in this chapter.

A **federal commission** is an agency typically run by a small number of officials, known as commissioners, who are appointed by the president and have responsibility for overseeing a sector of the economic or political arena. One example is the **Securities and Exchange Commission (SEC)**, which has the responsibility for monitoring all business practices involving the stock market. The SEC has five commissioners who serve staggered five-year terms and manage 3,800 employees.[7] The SEC oversees the work of accountants, stockbrokers, hedge fund managers, financial advisers, and small business

Office of Management and Budget (OMB): *Federal agency that oversees the federal budget and all federal regulations.*

Environmental Protection Agency (EPA): *Federal agency responsible for monitoring pollution levels in air, water, and land.*

independent agency: *Federal organization that has independent authority and does not operate within a cabinet department.*

federal commission: *Federal organization that has a defined number of appointed overseers known as commissioners for a particular issue area.*

Securities and Exchange Commission (SEC): *Federal organization responsible for monitoring business practices involving the stock market.*

TABLE 13.2 Selected Independent Agencies, 2010

Department	Year	Website	Employees (thousands)
Environmental Protection Agency (EPA)	1970	www.epa.gov	17.4
Equal Employment Opportunity Commission (EEOC)	1965	www.eeoc.gov	2.5
Federal Deposit Insurance Corporation (FDIC)	1933	www.fdic.gov	7.6
General Services Administration (GSA)	1949	www.gsa.gov	13.0
International Broadcasting Bureau (IBB)	1999	www.bbg.gov	2.1
National Aeronautics and Space Administration (NASA)	1958	www.nasa.gov	18.6
National Archives and Records Administration (NARA)	1934	www.archives.gov	3.2
National Labor Relations Board (NLRB)	1935	www.nlrb.gov	1.7
National Science Foundation (NSF)	1950	www.nsf.gov	1.4
Nuclear Regulatory Commission (NRC)	1974	www.nrc.gov	4.0
Office of Personnel Management	1978	www.opm.gov	4.9
Peace Corps	1961	www.peacecorps.gov	1.3
Railroad Retirement Board	1935	www.rrb.gov	1.0
Securities and Exchange Commission (SEC)	1935	www.sec.gov	3.8
Small Business Administration (SBA)	1953	www.sba.gov	3.5
Social Security Administration (SSA)	1935	www.socialsecurity.gov	67.6
Tennessee Valley Authority	1933	www.tva.gov	13.0
U.S. Agency for International Development	1961	www.usaid.gov	2.8

Source: www.whitehouse.gov; United States Office of Management and Budget; *Analytical Perspectives, Budget of the U.S. Government, Fiscal Year 2011* (Washington D.C.: Government Printing Office, 2010): 107. Accessed online at www.whitehouse.gov/omb/budget/fy2011/assets/spec.pdf.

owners. It has legal authority to demand information from these professionals, impose fines for bypassing investment rules, and even bring formal charges for serious violations of the law.

federal administration:
Federal organization responsible for running or administering a federal program.

federal board: *Federal organization with a narrow scope of authority over a specific area of jurisdiction.*

A **federal administration** is responsible for running a federal program or overseeing specific areas of federal responsibility. The Federal Aviation Administration (FAA), as we saw at the beginning of this chapter, is located within the Department of Transportation and is responsible for overseeing the entire airline industry and setting the requirements and guidelines for safe travel. It has approximately 48,000 employees, including air traffic controllers and safety inspectors.[8] Its stated mission is "to provide the safest, most efficient aerospace system in the world."[9] This is a huge responsibility, and the internal complexity of the FAA makes it difficult for air travelers, such as Kate Hanni, to find the right office to contact about a problem. Her efforts to get the FAA to respond to travelers' needs are therefore all the more inspiring.

AP Photo/Steven Day

The National Transportation Safety Board is an example of a federal board that has the specific responsibility of investigating all transportation-related accidents. The board assesses the causes of an accident, such as the bird strike incident that forced US Airways Flight 1549 to land in the Hudson River on January 15, 2009. Not all accidents have such fortunate outcomes, and the NTSB makes recommendations for preventing similar accidents in the future.

A **federal board** typically has a more narrow scope of authority but can possess the power to require changes in operating procedures and suggest fines. It usually consists of individuals appointed for a specific term and who ideally have expertise in the area of the board's jurisdiction. For example, the **National Transportation Safety Board (NTSB)** has the responsibility of investigating transportation-related accidents such as the "Miracle on the Hudson" airplane landing in January 2009, when a US Airways jetliner lost power because geese flew into its engines. There were no fatalities in that water landing, and only a few injuries. Whenever an accident involves any form of transportation, one of the five board members is appointed to oversee an investigation. Ultimately the NTSB issues a report on the accident in an effort to make sure it does not happen again. The NTSB can issue recommendations for safe transportation practices, but it does not have the power to issue federal regulations.

A **federal corporation** is a type of federal organization similar to a private business in that it provides a service or commodity for a price to the public, but it also receives federal funding. For example, the **National Railroad Passenger Corporation**, better known as Amtrak, is essentially a for-profit railroad, but it receives federal funding and is subject to federal restrictions and controls.

A **national endowment** is also a type of federal organization that uses funds specifically allocated to promote a public good or service. The **National Endowment for the Arts**, for example, was created to support scholarship and art that would be available to the general public, but this endowment does not have any formal responsibility to monitor private- and public-sector activities in a specific set of issue areas. However, because endowments are funded by the federal government, they are expected to serve as a gateway for the expression of a wide range of viewpoints and perspectives in the work that they support.

Core Components of the Bureaucracy

All these bureaucratic organizations share four core components that determine how government implements policy and, more immediately, how government responds to the individual needs of its citizens. These components are mission, a hierarchical decision-making process, expertise, and a bureaucratic culture.

Mission

Each federal agency has a stated **mission** that defines its role and responsibilities within the federal bureaucracy. For example, the Department of Health and Human Services' mission is stated on its website:

> The Department of Health and Human Services (HHS) is the United States government's principal agency for protecting the health of all Americans and providing essential human services, especially for those who are least able to help themselves.[10]

A mission statement is important as the public face of the department, and it is the measure by which members of Congress and the general public can hold the department accountable for the success or failure of its efforts.

Hierarchical Decision-Making Process

To carry out its mission, every federal organization has a hierarchical decision-making process that structures how policy is implemented. The hierarchy of authority in bureaucracies means that an employee's decision on the implementation of policy is reviewed at each higher level in the organization. For example, HHS contains the following levels of authority, in ascending order: bureau chief, assistant secretary, deputy secretary, secretary. Each of these officials puts his or her expert input into policy implementation and then

National Transportation Safety Board (NTSB): *Federal organization responsible for investigating transportation-related accidents and recommending safety standards.*

federal corporation: *Federal organization that is similar to a private business in that it provides a service or commodity for a price to the public but also receives federal funding.*

National Railroad Passenger Corporation (Amtrak): *Railroad that receives federal funding.*

Why would the government fund a for-profit railroad?

national endowment: *Federal organization that distributes funds to promoting a public good or service.*

National Endowment for the Arts: *Federal organization that funds scholarships and art made available to the general public.*

mission: *Federal organization's defined role and set of responsibilities.*

sends the decision to the next level for approval. Not every department uses these levels of authority in the same way, but each leads up to the secretary, who is responsible for all the policy decisions that come out of a department, and ultimately to the president.

The hierarchical decision-making process has advantages and disadvantages. It ensures that the unit responds consistently and predictably. The process also requires careful consideration of a policy before it is implemented. These two structural characteristics, taken together, are designed to ensure that policies are administered equally across citizens. However, this same hierarchical structure can present an obstacle to speedy decision making. Despite efforts to streamline this process, the step-by-step review of decision making inevitably slows down the implementation of federal laws.

Expertise

expertise: *Specialized knowledge and experience in an issue area.*

Fundamental to the core of the federal bureaucracy is the presumption that the people who hold bureaucratic positions have **expertise** in the issue areas they oversee and implement. Such expertise can come from a number of sources. Individuals can enter the bureaucracy at the lowest possible levels and stay in their jobs long enough to acquire knowledge about federal programs. Or they may have worked in a particular area, such as nuclear energy, and then bring their preexisting knowledge to the bureaucracy as a mid-level employee. Other bureaucrats acquire knowledge about federal policy in an area by studying it in academia or policy think tanks and are then asked to join the government. Lastly, Congress, with members who have chaired or served a long time on relevant congressional committees, is a major source of cabinet secretary appointments.

Bureaucratic Culture

bureaucratic culture: *Set of beliefs and behaviors that governs how a federal agency operates.*

The fourth core component of a bureaucracy is **bureaucratic culture**. As the political scientist James Q. Wilson has explained, "Every organization has a culture, that is, a persistent, patterned way of thinking about the central tasks of and human relationships within an organization. Culture is to an organization what personality is to an individual. Like human culture it is passed on from one generation to the next."[11] Fundamental to bureaucratic culture is the constant drive to self-perpetuate; employees in a bureaucratic organization want to preserve their jobs and their influence in the policy-making system. For this reason, bureaucratic culture can act as a gate that prevents efficiency and responsiveness in government because it can create situations in which employees in different organizations duplicate tasks, counterbalance each others' efforts, and ultimately fail to accomplish their agency's or department's mission.

What are the causes of bureaucratic failure?

At its worst, bureaucratic failure can result in a terrible loss of life, as in the case of the terrorist attacks of September 11, 2001. Many politicians, members of the media, and even the general public blame the federal agencies that oversee intelligence gathering—the Federal Bureau of Investigation (FBI), the Central Intelligence Agency (CIA), and the National Security Agency (NSA)—for failing to uncover and prevent the attacks. Each agency detected warning signs of such an attack, but the agencies did not work together. The bureaucratic culture of each agency was insular and distrustful, and lack of coordination among them resulted in an intelligence failure.[12]

To remedy the lack of coordination among the nation's national security and disaster relief agencies, Congress created the cabinet-level Department of Homeland Security in 2003. The hope was that a single large federal organization, presumably with one culture and one overarching mission, would be more effective. The new department consolidated several key units that had been operating independently, including the Coast Guard, U.S. Citizenship and Immigration Services, Customs Service, Secret Service, and the Federal Emergency Management Agency, and also created new intelligence offices that would try to serve as a bridge between the FBI and the CIA. However, it was not functioning well enough to coordinate the government's response to Hurricane Katrina in 2005, where once again, warnings of possible catastrophe—from the National Weather Service and the Army Corps of Engineers that the levees might break and flood New Orleans—went unheeded. As in the case of the 9/11 attacks, key federal emergency agencies failed to coordinate with one another. In the case of Hurricane Katrina, the Federal Emergency Management Agency in particular was blamed for the loss of life and property that occurred during and after the hurricane, attributed in large part to the inexperience of the director and his top aides in dealing with disasters.[13] A common lack of communication and expert direction exposed the inherent dangers of a flawed bureaucratic culture.

This lack of communication and cooperation remains a particular concern for national security, for the FBI, CIA, and NSA remain independent agencies, outside the authority of the Department of Homeland Security. In addition, the FBI, CIA, and NSA may continue to resist change, not wanting to give up authority that overlaps with the authority of other agencies. The dangers of a lack of cooperation among these agencies were on display again in late December 2009, when an alleged al Qaeda operative managed to smuggle explosives aboard an international flight bound for Detroit. Fortunately, he failed in his bombing attempt, but it was later revealed that both the CIA and State Department had ample warning of this terrorist plot yet did not communicate with each other about it. Change in any long-standing organization is difficult to achieve and generally happens only when the people at the top of the chain of command tear down the barriers to cooperation across agencies.

Bureaucratic culture can be shaped by the type of person drawn to work in a government bureaucracy. Bureaucrats are often depicted as narrow-minded and resistant to innovation. But, as Wilson points out, many different types of people seek jobs in the bureaucracy.[14] A person who works in a long-standing government division may seek job security and stability, but someone who joins a newly formed department or agency might seek opportunities for creativity. Moreover, policies evolve over time in response to changing external conditions. For example, twenty years ago the Department of Energy might have focused on more efficient ways of drilling for oil and subsequently hired geologists; today, with the emphasis on reducing national dependence on fossil fuels, the Department of Energy seeks to hire individuals with expertise in new energy technologies. There is no one personality type in the bureaucracy. The bureaucracy is so complex and diverse that individuals with a wide range of skills and interests choose to work within it. Finally, bureaucrats also know that when an agency becomes viewed as incompetent, it risks budget and personnel cuts, being rolled into a larger agency, or being dissolved altogether.

What are the advantages of a government job? What are the disadvantages?

The Historical Evolution of the Bureaucracy

The federal bureaucracy is as old as the nation itself, but it has evolved in ways that the Framers would barely recognize. Although they understood that the population would increase and the country's borders would expand, they could never have imagined that the federal government would have so many responsibilities and be so integral to citizens' daily lives. Over time, in tandem with economic, social, and technological developments, Congress passed laws creating new executive departments and other bureaucratic organizations. Next we trace the growth of the federal bureaucracy and the development of professional staff positions to implement federal policy.

The Expansion of Executive Branch Departments

The first departments created by Congress in 1789 were State, War, and Treasury. The attorney general also sat on the president's cabinet, though he did not yet head a department. In addition, the Post Office, first created in 1775 by the Continental Congress to serve the vital function of establishing communication routes among the colonies, became a permanent government organization in 1794.[15] Through these organizations, Congress intended to fulfill the constitutional responsibilities set forth in Article I, Section 8—to regulate commerce among the states and with foreign nations, to provide for defense, to collect taxes and borrow money, and to establish post offices and post roads.

In 1849, Congress created the Department of the Interior, consolidating under its direction several organizations that regulated the sale and development of federal lands and the management of Indian affairs. The Department of Agriculture came into existence in 1889 in response to the importance of the agricultural sector in the nation's economy and to the hardships caused by crop and price fluctuations. To address these hardships, Congress created crop subsidies that remain in place today. In 1870, the Office of the Attorney General, first set up in 1793, was transformed into the Department of Justice, which employed lawyers to handle the legal business of the nation and managed all prosecutions and suits in which the United States had an interest.

As with the departments of the Interior and Agriculture, the next two departments, Commerce and Labor, represented economic concerns. Congress addressed them by creating a single department in 1903, but within a decade the issues of child safety and workers' standards became so important that Congress divided the department, giving Labor its own cabinet status. This sequence was paralleled later in the twentieth century by the creation of the Department of Health, Education, and Welfare in 1953 and its subsequent division into two departments: the Department of Education, created in 1979 to coordinate programs dealing with elementary, secondary, and postsecondary education, and the Department of Health and Human Services in 1980 to oversee health care and welfare programs, such as Medicare and Medicaid. In 1947 and 1949 the War Department was transformed into the Department of Defense, coordinating the army, navy, and air force. In 1965, Congress created the Department of Housing and Urban Development to oversee federal programs designed to build more affordable housing for people with low incomes and to help restore inner cities that were losing residents. The Department of Transportation was created in 1966, following a decade of interstate highway building authorized by the Highway Act of 1956. Increases in trucking also put pressure on the federal government to maintain highways and regulate business and labor practices in trucking and the air travel industry. As a direct response to the energy crisis of the early 1970s, the Department of Energy was created in 1977 to promote fuel conservation as well as the development of alternatives to fossil fuels, including nuclear, ethanol, and solar power.

In 1989 the Department of Veterans Affairs was created with the support of President George H. W. Bush (1989–93). It elevated the Veterans Administration, which oversaw a separate, federally funded health care system for veterans, to a cabinet-level department and was intended to give visibility and support to veterans' critical needs. Finally, as we noted earlier, Congress created the Department of Homeland Security in 2003 in a direct response to

The expansion of executive departments reflects the growth of the nation. What do you think will be the next executive department created? Which executive department has authority over your future career?

the widely perceived intelligence failures associated with the terrorist attacks of September 11, 2001.

The Growth of Regulatory Agencies and Other Organizations

In addition to the formal cabinet departments, the executive branch also contains numerous regulatory agencies and other organizations that are responsible for administering the details of laws in specific areas, as well as for overseeing the practices of businesses and individuals involved in all facets of economic and political life. These agencies serve as a gateway for the federal government to respond to citizens in targeted ways and on a localized level, and they are especially important in ensuring safety and economic fairness for citizens in daily life. Among the concerns these agencies address are highway and air travel, food inspection and product labeling, and the practices of banks and the stock market.

Interstate Commerce Commission: *First regulatory agency, created in 1887, specifically to monitor and prevent unfair business practices by interstate railroads.*

The first regulatory agency, the **Interstate Commerce Commission**, was created in 1887 specifically to monitor the business practices of large railroad companies and their owners to make sure that consumers were given fair and equal access to rail services. More than a hundred years later, this agency still exists, but is now known as the Surface Transportation Board and has a portfolio that includes railroads, trucking companies, bus companies, and moving companies.[16]

Food and Drug Administration (FDA): *Federal organization that monitors food safety and handling as well as pharmaceutical drug development.*

Perhaps a more familiar type of regulatory agency is the **Food and Drug Administration (FDA)**, which monitors food safety and handling practices as well as pharmaceutical drug development and approval procedures. The motto of the FDA summarizes its mission: "Protecting and Promoting *Your* Health." The agency fulfills its mission by issuing guidelines and standards for companies to follow. Yet the well-publicized cases of E. coli contamination in ground beef in 2007, 2008, and 2009, and lettuce in 2010, which resulted in illness and even death, illustrate just how difficult it is for the FDA to monitor food safety. Americans consume billions of pounds of ground beef each year, most of it processed by private companies that are subject to FDA inspection but are expected to do most of the food quality and safety monitoring themselves.[17]

Is protecting you from food poisoning the government's job? Why or why not?

As the nation's economy has grown, so has the number of industries, products, and services that may warrant government regulation, and this growth in turn expands the workload for existing agencies and can require the creation of new ones. For example, the Federal Trade Commission was established to protect consumers from unfair financial and marketplace practices and the Consumer Product Safety Commission to ensure that basic goods purchased by consumers are safe.[18] Yet in 2010 President Obama and

Congress proposed establishing a new regulatory agency—the Consumer Financial Protection Agency—that would help consumers to navigate mortgages and other housing loans, as well as real estate investments.[19] In making this proposal, the president was responding to the financial crisis and severe recession that began in 2008, and in doing so, displayed how the federal government tries to adapt to the invention of new products, services, and economic practices.

There are limits to the effectiveness of regulatory agencies. They have authority to monitor practices, issue fines, and even shut down businesses, but for the vast majority of private businesses, the government must rely on voluntary cooperation on following agency guidelines. The distinct separation between the government and private businesses that is the hallmark of the American economy can also stand as a gate against effective government regulation and oversight. On the other hand, regulatory agencies are gateways through which citizens can ask government to protect them from fraudulent and unsafe products sold in the marketplace.

From Patronage to the Civil Service

For the nation's first forty years, jobs in the executive branch were filled by wealthy elites who had personal, political, and social connections to members of Congress and the president.[20] But President Andrew Jackson (1829–37) used the executive powers of the president to appoint people to federal positions who came from wider social and economic backgrounds. He also demanded political loyalty from federal employees; to get a job in the Jackson administration, one had to be an active political supporter of Jackson and of the Democratic Party. This arrangement, in which the politician appoints employees who pledge loyalty to him, is generally referred to as the **patronage** system. Jackson's political enemies called it the **spoils system**, charging Jackson with awarding jobs to political friends in the manner of the saying "To the victor belong the spoils."

For most of the nineteenth century, Congress and the president shared the patronage power, as the president allowed members of Congress to recommend individuals for government posts. With each election, if a different party assumed office, there was a large turnover in staff. As the nation grew larger and the economy more complex, more expertise and stability were needed in the federal bureaucracy. The assassination of President James A. Garfield in 1881 by an individual who had sought, but not received, a federal job, caused a public outcry against patronage in government employment. Although the assassin had had no direct contact with President Garfield, he evidently held the president responsible for his failure to secure a federal job. In response, Congress passed the **Pendleton Act**. It was the first of several

patronage: *Political system in which government programs and benefits are awarded based on political loyalty to a party or politician.*

spoils system: *Term used by Jackson's critics to describe his brand of the patronage system.*

Pendleton Act (1883): *Established a merit- and performance-based system for federal employment.*

Civil Service
Commission: *Created
by the Pendleton Act to
administer entrance exams
for the federal civil service
and set standards for
promotion based on merit.*

civil service: *System of
employment in the federal
bureaucracy under which
employees are chosen and
promoted based on merit.*

political appointees:
*Federal employees appointed
by the president with the
explicit task of carrying out his
political and partisan agenda.*

career civil servants:
*Federal employees hired
through a merit-based
system to implement federal
programs and who are
expected to be neutral in
their political affiliations.*

Compare the patronage
system to the merit-based
civil service system.
Which is more efficient?

reforms that slowly changed the federal bureaucracy from a corrupt and partisan insider organization to a neutral, policy-based organization.[21]

The Pendleton Act created the **Civil Service Commission** to administer entrance exams for the federal civil service and set job requirements and promotion standards based on merit and performance, not political affiliation. At first the civil service covered only a small fraction of federal jobs; the rest were controlled primarily by powerful members of Congress who used their influence to direct federal jobs to loyal supporters. But over time, successive presidents asserted more control over the federal bureaucracy, issuing executive orders to classify a greater percentage of jobs as merit-based and as part of the **civil service**. By 1897, 50 percent of federal jobs were covered by the civil service, and by 1951, 88 percent of federal jobs were civil service jobs.[22] The remaining federal employees are **political appointees** appointed by the president to carry out his political and partisan agenda within the federal policy-making system.

Career Civil Service

Career civil servants are nonpolitical personnel who must pass an exam to secure their jobs and compete on an equal playing field with anyone else who has the same credentials. For the number of executive branch employees, and other members of the federal workforce, see Figure 13.1.[23] The vast majority of executive branch employees are located in the metropolitan Washington, D.C., area.[24] In general, federal civil service employees fall into three categories: blue-collar, white-collar, and senior executive positions. Blue-collar jobs consist of "craft, repair, operator, and laborer jobs," and employees in this category are under the Federal Wage System, which sets pay levels associated with specific jobs.[25] White-collar workers fill a wide range of professional positions ranging from clerks and administrative assistants to engineers, informational technology specialists, and lawyers. These types of jobs are governed by the General Schedule (GS), which has fifteen grades or levels of pay assigned according to level of responsibility and

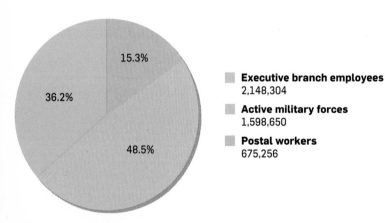

Executive branch employees
2,148,304

Active military forces
1,598,650

Postal workers
675,256

FIGURE 13.1 Distribution of Federal Government Workforce.
Federal employment is divided into several categories: executive branch, active forces, and the U.S. Postal Service.
Source: Office of Management and Budget, "The Budget for Fiscal Year 2011," http://www.omb.gov; and United States Postal Service, "Postal Facts 2010," http://www.usps.com.

work experience. In 2010, for example, the entry-level pay was $17,803 for GS 1 and $99,628 for a GS 15.[26] Executive-level management employees are governed by the Senior Executive Service guidelines, which generally follow the GS pay scale. All federal employees are subject to performance evaluations and may receive gradual raises, promotions up the career ladder, and incentive and merit bonuses for outstanding job performance. Civil servants remain in their positions from one administration to the next, and they cannot be asked to resign for partisan reasons.

Political Appointees

Political appointees, unlike civil servants, get their jobs because they are members of the same party that controls the executive branch, they have connections to politically powerful people, or they have served in a prior presidential administration. Political appointees can occupy a wide range of positions, from cabinet secretary to commissioner to administrator. Although it is uncommon, political appointees can also come from the opposition party, especially when they have a particular expertise in a policy area or a president wants continuity in department leadership early in his administration. This was the case with Secretary of Defense Robert Gates, who served in the George W. Bush administration and was asked to stay on by President Obama. No matter their personal views, political appointees are expected to carry out the president's policy agenda.[27] Top-level political appointees require Senate confirmation, and that number has risen from 73 under Franklin Roosevelt to 526 for President Obama.[28]

How much authority should the president have over executive branch employees?

In 1978, President Jimmy Carter (1977–81) created the **Senior Executive Service (SES)**, experienced personnel who can be assigned by the president to senior management positions throughout the federal bureaucracy. For SES positions, the president generally chooses career civil service employees who have shown expertise in their jobs, but he also has the authority to bring individuals in from the private sector. The SES provides a layer of administration over federal programs that is directed by the president, infusing the federal bureaucracy with political perspectives that can clash with the goal of objective implementation of federal policy. Since 1980, the total number of political appointees has averaged about 3,000.[29] Although that may not seem like a high number compared to the total federal workforce, the category of political appointee has been used successfully by many presidents to expand their direct influence within the bureaucracy.

Senior Executive Service (SES): *Senior management personnel in the federal government appointed by the president.*

Private-Sector Contract Workers

In addition to civil service employees and political appointees, the federal government hires thousands of individuals and companies from the private sector to administer programs and carry out tasks associated with specific policies. These companies can range from nonprofit community organizations, to midsize security firms, to large health care conglomerates. These organizations are not under the direct control of the federal bureaucracy, but they carry out crucial tasks for it. During the Clinton administration, Vice President Al Gore took on the job of revamping the bureaucracy. His Reinventing Government plan sought to reduce the complexity and size of the federal bureaucracy through efforts to "contract out" the provision of key services and administration of federal programs. Other presidents had made similar efforts, but President Clinton was the first Democrat since the 1930s to suggest that some of the services provided by the federal government could be more efficiently done by the private sector. In addition, incentive programs were put in place to reward federal civil servants for efficiency, in the same way that employees in the private sector receive bonuses.

Should government services be contracted out to the private sector? Why or why not?

President George W. Bush continued this trend of contracting out the performance of government tasks to private companies. For example, during the Iraq War, the federal government contracted with major construction companies to work with the Army Corps of Engineers to rebuild war-torn areas of Iraq. It also contracted with private security firms to provide additional security for U.S. diplomatic and civilian personnel. At home, much of the actual administering and provision of benefits under the Medicare and Medicaid programs are carried out by large private health maintenance organizations.

There are costs and benefits to privatization of federal services. One concern is that the federal government does not have close oversight over the quality, experience, or job performance of the employees who work in these private companies. Although company employees have an incentive to do their jobs well, fraud, waste, and abuse can go undetected for years because of a lack of direct federal oversight. Sometimes the federal government ends up paying more for the provision of these services through private contractors than if federal employees administered the program directly. Occasionally private employees commit crimes in foreign nations while they are under contract with the federal government, which can only punish them after the fact.

The benefit to using private firms is that they do not technically count as additional federal employees, so when they are used instead of hiring permanent federal employees, the overall size of the federal workforce appears smaller. In some cases, it is more efficient to use a private firm that has expertise in an area and can provide a specific service at a lower cost than permanent employees, achieving the same outcome.

Bureaucrats and Politics

The creation of the civil service was intended to protect federal employees from partisan politics, but by 1939 it had become clear that political influence was still rampant throughout the bureaucracy, not only at the federal level but at state and local levels, too. In response, Congress passed the **Hatch Act**, which prohibited government employees from working on political campaigns, using their positions to solicit campaign donations, or promoting candidates for elected office. This mandated separation of politics from the bureaucracy was designed to eliminate the last vestiges of patronage. It took pressure off bureaucrats, who could simply tell campaigning politicians that they were prohibited from engaging in certain political activities. In 1993, the **Hatch Act Reform Amendments** significantly loosened restrictions on political activities by government employees as long as they occurred while they were off duty. Now political appointees are explicitly allowed to engage in political activities on behalf of the president so long as the costs for these activities are not paid for with tax dollars. However, bans on political activities are retained for employees in law enforcement and intelligence agencies as well as the Federal Election Commission, which monitors federal campaign activities.[30]

By 1977, when President Jimmy Carter took office, the civil service was demoralized by the increasing numbers of political appointees and the general public perception that the merit-based branch of the federal government was not working well. Civil servants remain in the government even when presidential administrations change parties, so they outlast almost every political appointee. These two factors—neutrality and longevity—frequently bring about conflict between political appointees who want to accomplish the president's partisan policy agenda and civil servants who take a programmatic approach, aiming instead to do what is necessary to make the program work efficiently. To encourage cooperation between political appointees and civil servants, and to make sure that each was held accountable for decision making, President Carter proposed the **Civil Service Reform Act** of 1978. This act created the Office of Personnel Management (OPM) to oversee both categories of federal employees. The OPM, under the direct control of the Executive Office of the President, can expand the number of political appointees and reduce the number of career civil servants. With more politically appointed personnel in the bureaucracy, presidents assert greater control over how federal policy is formulated and implemented. To preserve the essential political neutrality of the career civil service, the act also created the Merit Systems Protection Board, which ensures that the protections afforded to career civil servants through the merit system remain in place.

Nevertheless, bureaucrats do face conflicting pressures when Congress is controlled by one political party and the executive branch is controlled by the other political party, a condition known as **divided government**. Under divided government, federal bureaucrats are frequently caught in the middle because they are pressured by Congress to implement policy one way and by political appointees in their agency to implement policy in a different way. Objectively, policy is supposed to be implemented in a manner that will

Hatch Act (1939): *Limits the political activities of federal, state, and local government employees.*

Hatch Act Reform Amendments (1993): *Permits political activity by government employees as long as the activities are not conducted during business hours.*

Should there be a gate blocking government employees from engaging in certain kinds of political activities? Are these prohibitions more important than compromising citizen equality?

Civil Service Reform Act (1978): *Replaced the Civil Service Commission with the Office of Personnel Management, which oversees both civil servants and political appointees.*

divided government: *Situation when one party controls the executive and the other party controls the legislature.*

produce the most efficient and responsive results, but trying to please two powerful "bosses" can result in inefficient and ineffective policy. Fortunately, the career nature of the civil service, with its built-in protections against political pressure, helps to mitigate the negative consequences of divided government. Moreover, because career civil servants frequently outlast presidents and some members of Congress, they have a longer-term perspective on the impact of their decisions.

At the same time, bureaucrats do tend to form long-term working relationships with members of Congress and even with interest group lobbyists in the policy areas in which they specialize. In Chapter 8 (Interest Groups), we explored the concepts of **iron triangle** (see Figure 8.3) and **issue networks**, both of which are used to describe these relationships. Bureaucrats want to maximize their longevity as administrators of federal programs, so they try to be as responsive as possible to the other members of the network, and each member constantly shares information with the others.[31] Critics of these iron triangles and issue networks argue that they contribute to the inefficiency of the federal government because they sustain programs that may be duplicative or outdated, and they may encourage corruption within the government. However, given the 24-7 news cycle and the amount of government information available on the Internet, these relationships are now more transparent than ever before, as the public, media, and watchdog groups are able to monitor them. Nevertheless, they are another indication that despite the protections of a merit-based civil service, politics will always influence, to some degree, the bureaucrats who implement federal policy.

iron triangle: *Insular and closed relationship among interest groups, members of Congress, and federal agencies.*

issue networks: *View of the relationship among interest groups, members of Congress, and federal agencies as more fluid, open, and transparent than the term* iron triangle.

Why was the civil service designed so that employees remain in place despite turnover in the presidency and in Congress?

The Bureaucracy and Public Policy: The Regulatory Process and Financial Oversight

For a law to be implemented, there must be rules to instruct policy makers, government officials, and businesses in the private sector about how to follow the law. The bureaucracy makes the rules, and the bureaucratic role in federal policy making begins the day a law is enacted. In this section, we examine the regulatory process, from issuing regulations to congressional oversight and judicial interpretation, and we focus our examination on environmental policy because of its widespread reach into citizens' daily lives. In the last part of this section we look at what happens when the regulatory process fails to prevent fraud and abuse in private financial markets.

The Regulatory Process and the Role of the Executive Branch

The formal responsibility for policy implementation falls to the bureaucracy in what is commonly called the **regulatory process**. In Chapter 1, we provided a broad overview of this process, from policy proposals, to implementation, to evaluation and updating of existing programs. We identified key stakeholders in the policy process, including the president, Congress, political parties, interest groups, and of course the voters. Here, we get more specific by tracking how an idea that is enacted into law is put into practice.

The current framework for the regulatory process has its foundation in the **Administrative Procedures Act (APA)** that Congress passed in 1946 to provide a consistent blueprint for all federal agencies in the issuing of regulations. In 1947, the Attorney General's Manual on the Administrative Procedures Act was issued to explain APA guidelines.[32] Although it has been modified over the years, the APA is still the predominant blueprint for the federal regulatory process.

The federal government typically issues regulations when a law is first enacted and when a new circumstance or policy need arises that requires updates to the way the law is implemented. One such circumstance might be a change in the political control of the White House. Frequently, an incoming president of a different party from his predecessor issues new regulations to reverse the previous administration's policies. This reversal can be accomplished in an expedited form through a **presidential memorandum**. For example, President Obama used a presidential memorandum to reverse an EPA decision, issued in 2008, that denied California the right to set stricter motor vehicle emission standards than those set forth by the EPA. Obama's memorandum requested that the EPA reconsider its denial in light of the fact that administrations previous to George W. Bush had granted California such authority.[33] Subsequently the EPA granted California its request to set stricter motor vehicle emission standards.

More commonly, a new president instructs federal agencies and OMB to revise existing regulations to better reflect his policy preferences. The president can also influence policy earlier in the process by issuing **signing statements** when he signs a congressional bill into law that reflect his interpretation of what the law should accomplish (see Chapter 12, The Presidency, for a longer discussion of signing statements).

regulatory process: *System of rules that govern how a law is implemented; also called the* rule-making process.

Administrative Procedures Act (1946): *Provides a consistent blueprint for all federal organizations to issue regulations.*

Why is the regulatory process so complicated?

presidential memorandum: *Presidential directive that can reverse an existing regulation.*

signing statements: *Written remarks issued by the president when signing a bill into law that often reflect his interpretation of how the law should be implemented.*

Issuing Regulations.

The primary means by which the bureaucracy implements the law is by issuing regulations. To see how this works, we will examine environmental policy.

Clean Air Act (1963, with amendments): *Allows government to monitor and limit the levels of air pollution.*

In 1963, Congress passed the **Clean Air Act** to reduce pollution, in response to growing public concerns and calls for stricter government controls.[34] The first step in implementing the law was to identify the agency that has jurisdiction over air pollution. In this case, administration of the Clean Air Act was ultimately assigned to the Environmental Protection Agency, which was created in 1970 in part to administer this act.

preliminary regulations: *Draft instructions for implementing a law.*

The next step is for the policy experts at the EPA to write **preliminary regulations**, the draft instructions for following or implementing a law. The political appointees at the EPA then review these preliminary regulations to see if they are in line with the president's policy views. Although the bureaucracy is theoretically supposed to be insulated from direct political pressure, the reality is that the president's policies are considered during this process.

Federal Register: *Official published record of all executive branch rules, regulations, and orders.*

Once there is some agreement on the content of the preliminary regulations, they are submitted to the Office of Information and Regulatory Affairs (OIRA) within OMB for approval to be printed in the *Federal Register*, the official published record of all executive branch rules, regulations, and orders. As noted previously, OMB must review all regulations before they take effect. The OMB, created by President Richard Nixon in 1970 from the old Bureau of the Budget, is now an important gatekeeper in the implementation of federal policy. Its power was expanded by President Ronald Reagan (1981–89), who issued executive orders to specify the types of considerations that agencies should take into account in issuing regulations, including cost-benefit analysis and risk assessment. President Bill Clinton also expanded the control of the president over the regulatory process by issuing an executive order that required all agencies to submit proposed regulations to the OIRA for approval.[35] By increasing OMB's role in the regulatory process, each of these presidents has further consolidated presidential power over the bureaucratic policy-making process (see Chapter 11, Congress, for more on the congressional and executive budget processes).

When the preliminary regulations appear in the *Federal Register*, there is a defined period of time for public comment (typically outlined in the originating legislation) ranging from thirty to ninety days. During this period, ordinary citizens, interest groups, and relevant industries and businesses can submit their opinions to the agency about the regulations. In addition, the agency or its local affiliate can hold public hearings in locations across the country to solicit opinions on the regulations.

Based on all the responses it receives, the responsible agency—in this case, the EPA—revises the preliminary draft regulations and issues

FIGURE 13.2 The Regulatory Process.

Implementation

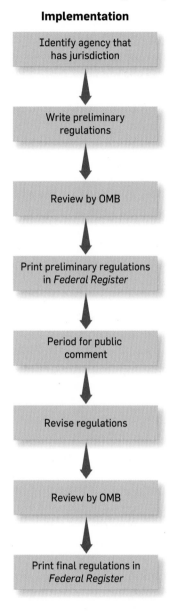

final regulations. These are once again sent to OMB and then are published in the *Federal Register* thirty days in advance of taking formal effect. Once the final regulations are issued, the program is officially ready to be implemented (see Figure 13.2).

Revising Regulations.

An example of the challenge of implementing environmental regulations concerns the Clean Air Interstate Rule (CAIR). In 2005, the EPA issued the CAIR regulation in response to the 1990 Clean Air Act Amendments that set significant targets for reducing pollution around coal-fired power plants, which contribute to acid rain. The intent of the regulation was to improve the air quality in the downwind states that are affected by the emissions.[36] A summary of the final regulation was printed in the *Federal Register*:

On March 10, 2005, EPA issued the Clean Air Interstate Rule (CAIR), requiring reductions in emissions of sulfur dioxide (SO_2) and nitrogen oxides (NO_x) in 28 eastern States and the District of Columbia. When fully implemented, CAIR will reduce SO_2 emissions in these states by over 70 percent and NO_x emissions by over 60 percent from 2003 levels. The CAIR imposes specified emissions reduction requirements on each affected State, and establishes an EPA-administered cap and trade program for EGUs [electric generating units] in which States may participate as a means to meet these requirements.[37]

The regulation was issued in final form, but it was not immediately implemented. What happened next exemplifies not only how a gateway for one interest can set up a gate against another interest but also how the courts can become directly involved in the policy implementation process.

Lawsuits and the Role of the Judicial Branch

In response to CAIR, Duke Energy, a major utility company that used coal-fired utility plants, sued to prevent the regulation from taking effect. The case reached the Court of Appeals for the District of Columbia, which struck down CAIR in July 2008, saying that the EPA exceeded its authority and was going beyond the intent of the Clean Air Act of 1990, on which the regulation was based.[38]

In response, members of Congress, environmental activists, and the George W. Bush administration united to get this judicial ruling reversed so that the regulation could be implemented. Environmental groups quickly asked Congress and the EPA to rewrite or replace the regulation. Even electric companies were in favor of the regulation. William Bumpers, an attorney representing Entergy Corp., was quoted by MSNBC as saying that few electric companies flatly opposed the regulation but most generally favored it because it included cap and trade provisions. Such provisions allow companies that exceed emissions caps to buy credits from companies that do not. "The power-generating industry had already invested billions and billions of dollars in anticipation of the trading market," Bumpers said. "They're not happy with this development."[39]

On December 23, 2008, the same federal appeals court reversed itself and reinstated the regulation in response to further arguments made by the EPA, industries, and environmental interest groups. The court said it was persuaded by arguments by the EPA and others, including environmental advocates, that "allowing CAIR to remain in effect until it is replaced by a rule consistent with our opinion would at least temporarily preserve the environmental values covered by CAIR."[40] In other words, the appeals court ruling affirmed that the bureaucracy issued a regulation that followed the intent of Congress and should therefore be upheld.

The CAIR case offers insights into the context of policy making in a separation of powers system. First, the CAIR ruling and subsequent reversal illustrates how and why the policy implementation is complex and time consuming; it is this complexity and balancing of interests that can make the bureaucracy seem slow and impenetrable. Second, this case highlights the potential for judicial interference in the regulatory process. The courts can serve as effective monitors of executive implementation of congressional legislation because they are a gateway for participation by which groups adversely affected by a federal regulation can argue their case. Typically, the courts intervene when there is a dispute between Congress and the executive on the interpretation of a law, and not when the two branches agree. Eventually the court reversed its own ruling, indicating that when Congress and the president strongly agree on how a law should be implemented, the judiciary generally limits its role in the regulatory process.

President Obama and Congress may face similar legal challenges to EPA final regulations on limiting emissions to reduce pollution that were issued on January 5, 2010.[41] This time the challenges not only come from affected industries but from state governments themselves, which either have their own standards in place or fear imposing strict standards on industry and thwarting economic growth.[42] In this case, judicial involvement may not be necessary because opponents of the rule argue that the timeline for reaching the goals set forth in the regulations should be extended, an aspect of regulatory enforcement that is at the EPA's discretion. In other words, the Obama administration could reach an agreement with industries and states that they will ultimately reach the standards set forth in the regulations, but they may take longer to do it.

Oversight, Funding, and the Role of the Legislative Branch

Congress also contributes to the regulatory process through its oversight of bureaucratic agencies and through its so-called power of the purse.

Congressional Oversight.   Congressional oversight is a powerful legislative check on the executive. It can occur in two phases: before a bill is passed into law, and as the law is being implemented.

oversight: *Power of Congress to monitor how the executive branch implements laws.*

As a bill is debated and voted on in both houses of Congress, the legislative process allows members of Congress to make their views known as to how they and their constituents would like to see a law implemented. The official record is comprised of their remarks during hearings and bill markups, and a separate committee report is issued when the bill is reported to the House and Senate floors. Once the final version of the bill is agreed upon in conference committee, then the conference committee issues an explanation of the provisions of the bill.

markup: *Process whereby bills are literally "marked up," or written by the members of the congressional committee.*

In the second phase of congressional oversight, congressional committees with jurisdiction in a set of issue areas can request that agency and cabinet officials testify before them to explain the way they implement programs under their jurisdiction.[43] This phase can get complicated because the House and Senate each have oversight committees, namely the House Committee on Oversight and Government Reform and the Senate Committee on Homeland Security and Governmental Affairs, but any congressional committee with jurisdiction over an issue area can request information from a federal agency. In addition, at the individual level, members of Congress can write to agencies and request information about a program or offer their opinion as to how it should be run. Consequently, when the time comes to write new regulations for a federal program, the relevant agency is typically well aware of the opinions of the key members of Congress who oversee their agency.

conference committee: *Temporary committee created after a bill passes the House and the Senate to resolve any differences in the provisions of the bills, so a single bill can be sent to the president.*

Agency Funding.

Another way Congress tries to assert its influence over the federal bureaucracy and policy making is through their powers to **authorize** and **appropriate**. When Congress authorizes, it grants the power to create a federal program or agency and spend federal funds to support that program or agency, as it did when it created the SCHIP program discussed earlier in the chapter. When Congress appropriates, it allocates a set amount of federal dollars for a specific program or agency. When the president believes a need exists that is not being met by existing federal agencies, he may seek to create a new one, like the Consumer Financial Services Protection Agency discussed earlier in the chapter. However, creating a new agency requires approval and funding by Congress, which then has a great deal of influence over the agency's mission and policy goals. Thereafter, because Congress sets funding levels for all federal programs on a yearly basis, it has the opportunity to evaluate federal agencies. If members of Congress are unhappy with the way that a federal agency or a specific federal program has been run, its funding levels may be reduced. Agency heads are fully aware of this congressional power, and it is a key reason that they take congressional opinion into account when they implement federal programs. Congressional influence of this type serves as a gateway for the public—who elect members of Congress—to hold the bureaucracy accountable for its actions.

Financial Oversight and Failure to Act

The bureaucracy has grown because Congress has continually responded to changes in the U.S. economy and society that have required government action. But what happens if Congress fails to respond adequately to developments in a policy area? The absence of regulation of an industry or policy area is itself a type of policy; the government is essentially allowing activity in this area to go without oversight, and there can be severe consequences. The deep recession of 2008–10 revealed how Congress failed to properly regulate banks and financial markets.

The primary organization responsible for controlling the flow of money is the **Federal Reserve**, which is discussed at length in Chapter 12 (The Presidency).[44] From 1998 to 2007, through a combination of deregulation in the banking and investment industries, the Federal Reserve's decisions to lower interest rates, and Congress's priority of making loans available to low-income families to purchase homes, a situation arose in which large numbers of individuals could no longer meet their mortgage payments. Compounding the problem was that the banks that made these "subprime" loans to riskier individuals began packaging large groups of these loans and selling them as investment opportunities. In other words, instead of holding onto the loan

---

authorize: *Congress's power to create a federal program or agency and set levels of federal funds to support that program or agency.*

appropriate: *Congress's power to allocate a set amount of federal dollars for a specific program or agency.*

Identify two ways that Congress oversees the federal bureaucracy.

Federal Reserve: *National banking system created in 1913 to control the flow of money in the economy.*

---

and receiving the interest, banks sold groups of loans to investors who hoped to receive the interest on the loans as a return on their investment.

This type of investment was a new invention in the financial industry, and Congress, which had not recognized its importance, failed to take active steps to regulate it. Unfortunately, when so many people defaulted on their mortgages, the return on investment disappeared; as defaults grew in number, so did foreclosures on properties whose worth declined rapidly. As a result, major banking institutions lost billions of dollars and pulled back on their willingness to make loans for housing, businesses, and consumer purchases, including automobile loans.

What caused the recession that began in 2008? Who or what was to blame?

In late fall 2008, President Bush and Congress responded by enacting the Troubled Asset Relief Program (TARP), commonly referred to as the banking bailout bill. The TARP program authorized $700 billion to subsidize banks by purchasing the packaged loans that had lost their value because of consumer defaults. The condition that the government imposed on this "rescue" was that banks had to resume lending to businesses and individuals. When President Obama took office in January 2009, more than $300 billion of TARP money had been distributed to banks, but lending had not loosened up and members of Congress and voters began to wonder how their taxpayer money had been spent. When the public learned that several of the companies receiving bailout money had distributed multimillion-dollar bonuses to their employees and continued to plan lavish retreats and purchase corporate jets, anger over the irresponsibility of Wall Street intensified.

Public pressure built quickly on Congress and the president to hold these banks accountable, and Congress reacted by holding oversight hearings in both the House and Senate Banking Committees. On February 11, 2009, the House Banking Committee asked the chief executive officers of eight of the nation's largest banks that received TARP money to come together and explain how they had used the funds to increase lending and dispose of bad assets. It is exactly these types of forums that Congress uses to exercise its oversight function, and it was all the more important to do so at this time because the government was on the brink of distributing more funds to these very same banks.

The factors that led up to such a dramatic intervention in the nation's economy raise serious questions about the effectiveness of congressional oversight of the bureaucracy. Ultimately, Congress and the president will be held accountable for the long-term success of the TARP program; as of 2010, most of the major banks that had participated in the program had repaid part or all of these loans but they had not opened up lending to the level it was at before the crisis began.[45] In this case, congressional failure to act imposed hardships on millions of homeowners, banks, and on the executive branch itself.

Accountability and Responsiveness in the Bureaucracy

Typically the power of the vote in regularly scheduled elections is used to monitor elected officials, but the bureaucracy does not offer any means for the average voter to register his or her opinion about the collective job performance of federal employees. Because the federal bureaucracy varies by type of agency, size of agency, and type of employee, it is difficult for citizens to evaluate job performance and hold bureaucrats collectively accountable for their actions. At the individual level, the job performance of civil servants is reviewed by supervisors at regular intervals, and political appointees can be removed by the president if he is unhappy with their work. But democracy requires that citizens be able to hold their entire government accountable for the policies it implements, and there is no readily available mechanism for the public to hold civil servants accountable for their job performance. There are, however, certain standards and procedures that Congress has put in place to hold the bureaucracy accountable and encourage responsiveness.

Is it easy or hard for citizens to hold the bureaucracy accountable for its actions? Why?

Efficiency and Transparency

One of the biggest challenges a bureaucratic organization faces is carrying out its mission efficiently while maintaining transparency to the American public. A chronic complaint about the bureaucracy is that it is slow. Yet the reason issuing rules and regulations takes so long is that the process solicits input from all sectors, including members of Congress, businesses and industries that are being regulated, and average citizens with a stake in the issue. The government can justify the slowness of the decision-making process on the grounds that it considers many points of view in implementing policy. Unfortunately, inclusiveness comes at the expense of efficiency.

Moreover, the issues at stake for bureaucrats can literally be matters of life and death if they are dealing with food and drug safety, transportation safety, working conditions, or antiterrorism measures. Citizens expect the federal government to act in their best interests, but the very nature of these types of issues requires caution, and caution can lead to delay. On the other hand, if the government fails to make its practices transparent and does not consider all the implications of its decisions, citizens may lose trust in government.

These concerns were part of the rationale behind a series of bills designed to open up the workings of the federal bureaucracy to the general public. In

Why is transparency important in a democracy?

1966, the **Freedom of Information Act** established a procedure by which ordinary citizens can request documents and reports from the federal government directly by paying a nominal fee, so long as the documents are not classified. Labeling a document or report "classified" automatically restricts access to it to federal employees who hold security clearances. In times of military conflict, such as the Vietnam and Iraq wars, presidents typically restrict access to public documents relating to war efforts. In response to

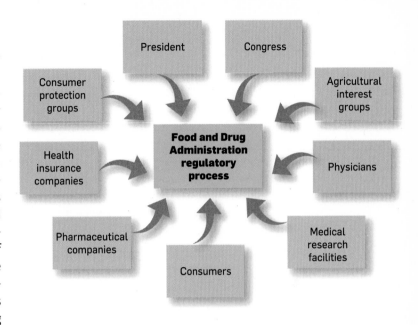

the mistrust of the federal government that grew out of the Vietnam War and the Watergate scandal, in 1976 Congress enacted the **Government in the Sunshine Act**. The Sunshine Act tried to increase transparency by requiring that government agencies hold open forums to allow the public to comment on their decisions, regulations, and performance. This process illustrates the trade-off between efficiency and transparency.[46]

To highlight the tension between efficiency and transparency, let us look at the Food and Drug Administration. One of the agency's most important responsibilities is monitoring pharmaceutical development from the initial testing of drugs to final approval for widespread use. Even before a drug is submitted to the FDA for approval, pharmaceutical companies have conducted three phases of clinical trials—experiments and applications on human subjects that measure the efficacy and safety of the drug. If the drug shows promise, the company submits a New Drug Application to the FDA. If agency employees agree that the clinical trial results are reliable, the FDA forms a review panel whose members have different types of expertise about the potential effects of the drug. Members of the panel consider all the results of the trials and offer opinions as to whether the drug can be approved for sale. Ultimately, the FDA makes the final decision.

This process illustrates the trade-off between efficiency and transparency.[47] When a new drug is effective against disease, the public wants access to that drug as soon as possible. However, every new drug has unforeseen side effects, some of which may not be visible in the short term, so the more information the FDA has, the more likely the drugs it approves for the market

Freedom of Information Act (1966): *Established procedures by which citizens can request documents from the federal government about its operations.*

Government in the Sunshine Act (1976): *Requires government agencies to hold open forums to allow the public to comment on their decisions.*

will be safe. Forming review committees with members from outside the agency is one way of collecting a wide range of information about the possible impacts of the drug. Yet this process is time-consuming; the more participants, the more slowly it moves. Like many federal agencies, then, the FDA must weigh the cost of efficient decision making against the cost of approving a drug before it has been thoroughly tested.

The issue of transparency is especially highlighted when the federal government enacts large spending bills, like the TARP plan or the American Recovery and Reinvestment Act, usually called the Stimulus Bill, that was signed into law in February 2009. The nearly $800 billion act authorized a combination of spending and tax cuts, including funds for infrastructure, education, extension of unemployment benefits, and tax breaks for homeowners and businesses. The challenge confronting the federal bureaucracy in implementing this bill was getting the funds to recipients as quickly as possible while at the same time enforcing federal program rules and being clear about where the money was going.[48] Critics of this bill pointed to the huge amount of money involved and questioned the practical effect stimulus funds could have on the economy because of the length of time it would take to distribute the funds according to standard federal practices. President Obama responded by saying that he would consider revamping standard bureaucratic practices to streamline the process of distributing these funds. However, such streamlining could reduce accountability and transparency. President Obama, aware of the importance of transparency to voters, created a website (www.recovery.gov) that pinpointed how and where the funds were distributed, down to the street block level.

Whistleblowing

Most federal employees are careful, dedicated, and hardworking. However, like all organizations run by human beings, there can be inefficiency, error, abuse of power, and, at worst, corruption. Each federal agency has an **Office of Inspector General (IG)**, which monitors the activities of all the agency's employees. But unless a wrongdoing is identified and brought to the IG's attention, it frequently goes unpunished.

To encourage more candid disclosure of wrongdoing in federal agencies, Congress passed the Whistleblower Protection Act in 1989 to protect government employees, known as **whistleblowers**, who report mismanagement, corruption, or illegal activity within their agencies.[49] Prior to the passage of this act, whistleblowers had no real protection against reprisals from their colleagues, especially at higher levels of authority. The act established grievance and appeal procedures for employees who believe they have

What is more important— transparency or efficiency?

Office of Inspector General (IG): *Office within federal organizations that monitors the activities of all the employees in the organization to ensure they are doing their jobs properly.*

whistleblowers: *Employees who report mismanagement, corruption, or illegal activity within their agencies.*

Are private contractors working for the government likely to be whistleblowers? Why or why not?

been retaliated against for reporting wrongdoing in their agencies. However, it is important to note that employees in law enforcement and national security are not currently covered by this act. Members of Congress have introduced legislation to expand coverage to such employees, as well as employees of private companies that do business with the federal government. As of yet, this legislation has not become law.

Mario Tama/Getty Images

Bureaucratic Failure

Whether whistleblowers come from inside or outside the federal government, it is up to the federal government to respond to them in an effective fashion. Unfortunately, there are serious cases in which a government agency has failed to respond. What happens when an entire agency fails to accomplish its mission, as in the case of the Securities and Exchange Commission (SEC) failing to recognize the illegal and fraudulent activities of investor and financial manager Bernard Madoff?

One of the realities of federal management and oversight is that unless a federal agency or congressional committee is aware of a problem, neither can address it. The Madoff scandal is an example of bureaucratic and congressional oversight after the fact. In December 2008, Madoff confessed to fraudulent investment practices over the span of thirty years, with an estimated cost of $50 billion to individual investors (many of whom are retirees who lost their life savings), financial management firms, and charitable foundations. His activities fell under the jurisdiction of the SEC, which was accused of failing to do its job properly.

In fact, the SEC had been warned about Madoff repeatedly over a ten-year period by Harry Markopolos, an investment fund manager. Markopolos contacted a Boston regional officer with the SEC about Madoff's scheme in 2000, after he tried to replicate Madoff's stated earnings and could not find any sound way to do so. Over the next six years Markopolos actively tried to get the SEC to act, but not until 2006 did it start an inquiry into Madoff's dealings. Even then, following interviews of Madoff and some of his business associates, SEC lawyers found no wrongdoing and dropped the case.[50] Two years later, when Madoff confessed, his financial pyramid came quickly crashing down around him.

In June 2009, 71-year old financial investment manager Bernard Madoff was sentenced to 150 years in prison for fraud. His financial scam was estimated to have cost investors close to $50 billion.

Mark Wilson/Getty Images

When the House Banking Committee questioned SEC commissioners about why they had literally acted as a gate against investigating Madoff based on Markopolos's charges and, more important, why they found no wrongdoing, they had very little response. As a general explanation, they said that the SEC was understaffed and ill-equipped to investigate such a massive fraud.

How could such major financial dealings go unnoticed, even with information provided over time by a very determined private citizen pointing to something amiss with Madoff's accounting? The SEC's failure to monitor and prevent such frauds, and the lack of congressional intervention until it was too late, illustrate the limits of the federal bureaucracy as well as of congressional oversight.

A private citizen turned whistleblower, Harry Markopolos tried to inform the SEC that Bernard Madoff was a fraud and that his financial dealings were unsound, but the agency did not act on his warnings.

What can be done about lack of responsiveness by the bureaucracy?

The dual responsibilities of accountability and responsiveness in the federal bureaucracy require that it do its job well enough to protect its citizens from physical and financial harm. Unfortunately, the American people are so familiar with the failures of the federal bureaucracy that its successes are overlooked. The fact that close to 300 million people live in relative peace and security, experience safe and reasonable working conditions, trust that the medications they take are well tested, travel on trains, buses, and planes without incident, drink clean water, and even receive their mail every day is a testament to the ways in which the federal bureaucracy meets its obligations. It is up to the voters to hold their elected officials—in Congress as well as the White House—accountable for the performance of the federal bureaucracy.

The Bureaucracy and Democracy

What started as a federal government with three cabinet departments has grown to one with fifteen cabinet departments and many powerful independent agencies. The federal bureaucracy employs nearly 4.5 million people, including those in the armed services. Their jobs affect the lives of every citizen, from the quality of the grains in breakfast cereal you eat in the morning, to the safety of the highways you drive during the day, to the purity of the water you drink.

In some important ways, the federal bureaucracy has become far more responsive to the needs of average individuals in the course of the nation's history, especially in the areas of social benefits, health care for the elderly, environmental protection, and civil rights enforcement. The federal bureaucracy has tried to be more transparent in its operations by placing comprehensive information on the Internet for the entire public to access at any time. However, as the response to Hurricane Katrina in 2005 shows, there have been notable and serious failures in the government's response to disaster, especially in areas with higher concentrations of poor and rural residents.

The structure of the bureaucracy includes many gates against speedy implementation of federal policy. The fact that there are so many layers of authority even within one agency, much less an entire cabinet department, adds considerable delay to the process of policy implementation. Multiple agencies can have jurisdiction over the same federal program or share responsibility to respond to natural disasters such as hurricanes. Such overlap can lead to miscommunication and to competition over authority and power. The hierarchy and procedural barriers that come with a large federal bureaucracy can stand in the way of efficient government.

At the same time, the rules and guidelines governing decision making in the bureaucracy are designed to ensure equal implementation of the law, which is a crucial element of a democracy. Americans expect that federal laws will be applied in a consistent and equal manner, with openness and vigilant congressional and public oversight. Understanding how laws are implemented, especially the gateways through which federal regulations are issued and enforced, gives citizens the power to hold the government accountable.

FOCUS QUESTIONS

- How does the federal bureaucracy play a role in responding to the individual needs of ordinary citizens?

- How does the structure of the federal bureaucracy shape the way policies are implemented?

- What powers does the bureaucracy have to ensure that federal policies are administered equally across all citizens?

- How can the average citizen influence the decisions of the bureaucracy?

- Is the bureaucracy a gate or a gateway to democracy? Explain.

GATEWAYS TO LEARNING

Top Ten to Take Away

1. The bureaucracy is the collection of executive branch departments, regulatory agencies, and other organizations that carry out the responsibilities of the federal government. Today nearly 4.5 million people, including those in the armed services, work for the federal government. (pp. 457–459)

2. Each bureaucratic organization has a clear mission, a hierarchical decision-making process, an area of expertise, and a bureaucratic culture. Aside from cabinet departments, there are various types of organizations within the bureaucracy, some designed to be more or less independent of the president. (pp. 465–468)

3. The constitutional foundations for the bureaucracy include the president's power to nominate and appoint officers of executive departments, from whom he may request advice. The bureaucracy is also based in the president's broad grant of executive power. (pp. 459–465)

4. Since 1789, the bureaucracy has grown from three to fifteen executive departments as government's responsibilities have grown, primarily in the area of the economy. The first regulatory agency was established in 1887 to regulate railroad practices. (pp. 468–470)

5. Federal employment has developed from a corps of wealthy elites who had political connections

to members of the Congress and the president into a merit- and performance-based civil service designed to be protected from political influence. (pp. 470–474)

6. The president appoints cabinet secretaries and other high-level political appointees who are expected to carry out the president's agenda. (pp. 474–476)

7. Following a consistent regulatory process, agencies draft regulations, which are open to comment by citizens, members of Congress, interest groups, and relevant businesses and industries before they are made final. (pp. 476–480)

8. Lawsuits can involve the judicial branch in the interpretation of public policy. Congress exercises influence over policy through its oversight responsibilities and power to authorize and allocate funds. (pp. 480–484)

9. The bureaucracy is subject to criticism for acting slowly, but in a democracy the need for efficiency is counterbalanced by the need for transparency. Reform efforts have improved transparency by providing protections for whistleblowers. (pp. 484–487)

10. It is up to the voters to hold their elected officials accountable for the performance of the federal bureaucracy. (pp. 487–488)

A full narrative summary of the chapter is on the book's website.

Ten to Test Yourself

1. What is the role of a cabinet department in the bureaucracy?

2. What explains the growth in the number of cabinet departments over time?

3. What is the difference between a federal commission and a federal corporation?

4. What are the four core components of a bureaucracy?

5. What is the relationship between bureaucratic culture and bureaucratic reputation?

6. What is the difference between a civil servant and a political appointee?

7. What do the Pendleton Act and the Civil Service Reform Act have in common?

8. Describe the steps involved in the federal regulatory process.

9. What are the two phases of congressional oversight of the bureaucracy?

10. Who are the stakeholders in food and drug oversight?

More review questions and answers and chapter quizzes are on the book's website.

Terms **to Know and Use**

Administrative Procedures Act (APA) (p. 477)
appropriate (p. 482)
authorize (p. 482)
bureaucracy (p. 458)
bureaucratic culture (p. 466)
cabinet (p. 458)
cabinet secretary (p. 459)
career civil servants (p. 472)
civil service (p. 472)
Civil Service Commission (p. 472)
Civil Service Reform Act (p. 475)
Clean Air Act (p. 478)
conference committee (p. 481)
divided government (p. 475)
Environmental Protection Agency (EPA) (p. 462)
expertise (p. 466)
federal administration (p. 464)
federal board (p. 464)
federal commission (p. 462)
federal corporation (pp. 464, 465)
Federal Register (p. 478)
Federal Reserve (p. 482)

final regulations (p. 479)
Food and Drug Administration (FDA) (p. 470)
Freedom of Information Act (p. 485)
Government in the Sunshine Act (p. 485)
Hatch Act (p. 475)
Hatch Act Reform Amendments (p. 475)
independent agency (p. 462)
Interstate Commerce Commission (p. 470)
iron triangle (p. 476)
issue networks (p. 476)
markup (p. 481)
Medicaid (p. 461)
mission (p. 465)
national endowment (p. 465)
National Endowment for the Arts (p. 465)
National Railroad Passenger Corporation (Amtrak) (pp. 464, 465)

National Transportation Safety Board (NTSB) (pp. 464, 465)
Office of Inspector General (IG) (p. 486)
Office of Management and Budget (OMB) (p. 462)
oversight (p. 481)
patronage (p. 471)
Pendleton Act (p. 471)
political appointees (p. 472)
preliminary regulations (p. 478)
presidential memorandum (p. 477)
regulations (p. 458)
regulatory process (p. 477)
Securities and Exchange Commission (SEC) (p. 462)
Senior Executive Service (SES) (p. 473)
signing statements (p. 477)
spoils system (p. 471)
whistleblowers (p. 486)

Use the vocabulary flash cards on the book's website.

▲ University of Michigan—Dearborn

> *In 1997, I read an article . . . about a possible lawsuit against the University of Michigan. . . . I knew I wanted to be involved. . . . I thought I'd be stuffing envelopes . . . even at that moment I never thought I'd become a plaintiff in a historic lawsuit.*

"The envelope was way too thin," thought **Jennifer Gratz, a high school senior, class of 1995, at Southgate Anderson High School, in Southgate, Michigan.** Despite graduating in the top 5 percent of her class, having a 3.8 (out of 4.0) GPA, and receiving 25 out of 36 (83rd percentile) on her ACT, she received a wait-list letter and then, ultimately, a rejection letter from her first choice for college, the University of Michigan.

Elsewhere in Michigan, Barbara Grutter, a mother of two in her mid-forties who decided to attend law school, did not get admitted to her first and only choice for law school. Despite a 3.8 undergraduate GPA and a score of 161 out of 180 (86th percentile) on her LSAT, she, too, was wait-listed and ultimately denied admission to the law school at the University of Michigan.

Gratz and Grutter then took a step that most rejected students do not take: they chose to sue the school that rejected them. Both challenged the university's affirmative action policies, policies that gave underrepresented minority students preferential advantages in admissions compared to whites with similar GPAs and standardized test scores. The preference at the undergraduate college, for example, was equivalent to a full point on a 4-point GPA scale. That is, a student

Jennifer Gratz ▶

CourseMate

Visit http://www.cengagebrain .com/shop/ISBN/0495906190 for interactive tools including:
- Quizzes
- Flashcards
- Videos
- Animated PowerPoint slides, Podcast summaries, and more

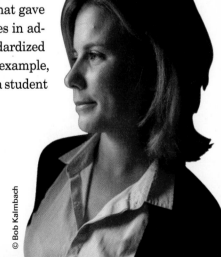

from an underrepresented minority group with a 2.8 GPA would have the same chance of admissions as a middle-class white student with a 3.8 GPA. Gratz and Grutter claimed that these policies denied them "equal protection of the law" as guaranteed by the Fourteenth Amendment. Instead of an equal opportunity to gain admission to the university of their choice, they were, as individuals, disadvantaged. Supporters of affirmative action, on the other hand, claim that affirmative action policies enhance equality generally by increasing the chances that the university student body as a whole better represents the population as a whole. The consequence is a greater equality of outcomes.[1]

In this chapter, we track the *Gratz* and *Grutter* cases all the way to the Supreme Court. Lawsuits such as these provide a gateway for a single person to have an enormous impact on the political system of the United States. The Supreme Court ultimately delivered a set of decisions that upheld the affirmative action plan as practiced by the law school, but found constitutional violation in the plan as practiced by the undergraduate college. As these cases help show, the judicial system of the United States, because of its authority to rule on the constitutionality of federal and state laws and policies, has an extraordinary amount of power in the American political system. The Supreme Court, as the highest court in the land, decides not only whether affirmative action may be allowed, but also other issues such as whether abortion can be prohibited or death penalties inflicted. The justices on the Court make important decisions that affect the lives of individuals and the policies of the nation at large despite the fact that they are not elected by the people and cannot be removed from office if the people disagree with the decisions that they make. Thus we examine, too, the controversial role and power of the judiciary in a democracy.

FOCUS QUESTIONS

- Why is the apparently simple requirement of providing "equal protection of the laws" in fact more difficult than it seems?

- In what ways do the federal courts lack traditional means of accountability?

- How are courts, nevertheless, responsive?

- Do citizens have equal access to the justice system? Does the justice system treat them equally?

- Is the judiciary a gate or a gateway to democracy?

The Role and Powers of the Judiciary

The job of courts is to resolve legal disputes. The American legal system is based largely on the English system, which is the system that the colonists knew best. The legal system under the Constitution kept many of the same practices, but added some innovations.

English Legal Traditions

Resolution of legal disputes follows an **adversary process**. Under an adversarial system, each party, usually represented by an attorney, presents its version of events, with virtually all attempts to slant information short of lying under oath deemed acceptable. According to a noted Supreme Court scholar, "The underlying assumption is that two persons arguing, as partisanly as possible, will produce the fairest decision."[2]

While in some cases a judge decides which side in such legal battles is correct, a group of ordinary citizens more usually determines the outcome. The right to **trial by jury** dates back in England to the Magna Carta (1215), where it replaced trial by ordeal, the practice of subjecting people to drowning or burning to see if they were innocent. Trial by jury is crucial to liberty, for it inserts a gate of citizen judgment between the accused and the government that protects the accused from arbitrary detention and unjust punishment.

Trials involve questions of fact (for example, did the University of Michigan set different standards for white and minority students?) and questions of law (for example, do such differing standards violate the Fourteenth Amendment?). Trial court decisions about questions of fact are presumed to be valid because it is the trial judge or jury that directly hears the evidence in the case. But because trial courts sometimes make mistakes about questions of law, the American legal system followed the British practice by allowing **appeals** from trial court rulings of law. Appeals are heard by appeals courts and by the Supreme Court.

Trials resolve two distinct types of disputes. In **criminal cases**, the government prosecutes an individual for breaking the law. Criminal cases are based almost exclusively on prohibitions on behavior written into statutes (laws) passed by federal, state, or local legislatures. In **civil suits**, a plaintiff, such as Jennifer Gratz, sues a defendant, such as the University of Michigan, to enforce a right or to win monetary damages. The U.S. Constitution guarantees jury trials in all criminal cases and in all civil suits over twenty dollars. Today, Congress limits access to the federal courts in monetary civil suits to claims of seventy-five thousand dollars or more. Suits for lesser amounts must go to state courts.

Criminal law is based on statutory authority, but statutory authority cannot cover all of the possible civil disputes between individuals. Many disputes are simply actions that no legislative authority could have ever imagined. As such, when there are gaps in statutory law, courts rely on judge-made law known as **common law**. Common law requires that judges accept and rely on previous decisions (if each judge makes his own decisions on each case, there can be no common law). Thus, British royal judges developed the practice of reaching decisions based on **precedents**, or the previous decisions of other royal judges. Deciding cases based on precedent means that similar cases are decided similarly.

adversary process: *Confrontational legal process under which each party presents its version of events.*

Is this assumption correct? That is, do courts produce the fairest decision possible? Can you give examples?

trial by jury: *Method of placing the determination of issues of fact in a trial into the hands of fellow citizens.*

appeals: *Legal proceeding whereby the decision of a lower court on questions of law can be challenged and reviewed by a higher court.*

criminal cases: *Government prosecutions of an individual for breaking the law.*

civil suits: *Lawsuits by a person, organization, or government against another person, organization, or government.*

common law: *Judge-made law in England and the United States that results from gaps in statutory law.*

precedent: *Practice of reaching decisions based on the previous decisions of other judges.*

standing: *Requirement that a party bringing a lawsuit has suffered a harm that the law arguably protects.*

Judiciary Act (1789): *Created the lower federal judiciary, district courts, and circuit courts of appeals.*

district (trial) courts: *Federal trial courts, at the bottom of the federal judicial hierarchy.*

courts of appeals: *Intermediate federal courts in the United States, above the district courts but below the Supreme Court.*

jurisdiction: *Lawful authority of a court to hear a case.*

original jurisdiction: *Authority to hear a case directly from a petitioning party as in a trial.*

appellate jurisdiction: *Authority of a court to hear cases on appeals from lower courts.*

judicial independence: *Ability of judges to reach decisions without fear of political retribution.*

equity: *Doctrines of fairness followed in countries that follow the English common law.*

statutory interpretation: *Cases in which the courts have to determine what Congress meant by a statute.*

Constitutional Grants

Article III of the Constitution establishes the judicial branch of government. It briefly refers to a Supreme Court of the United States and grants Congress the authority to create lower courts at its discretion. The Constitution grants the federal courts the authority to hear "cases or controversies," which the Supreme Court has interpreted to require that people who initiate lawsuits have **standing**, that is, have suffered a harm that the law arguably protects.

Because the Constitution says so little about the judicial branch, one of the early acts of the First Congress, the **Judiciary Act** of 1789, established thirteen **district (trial) courts** and three circuit courts, with both trial and appellate authority, serving at an intermediate level between the district courts and the Supreme Court. Today, there are 678 district court judges serving in ninety-four separate district courts and 179 **court of appeals** judges serving in thirteen intermediate appellate circuits.[3]

The lawful authority of a court to hear a case is its **jurisdiction**. In general, jurisdiction for any federal court requires either that the case involve federal law (including the Constitution and treaties), that the parties include the United States, ambassadors, or other public ministers, states that sue other states, or that the parties are residents of different states. These latter suits are called diversity suits, and parties also must satisfy the threshold amount of seventy-five thousand dollars. As for the Supreme Court, the Constitution further divides its jurisdiction into **original jurisdiction**, that is, authority to hear a case directly from a petitioning party (as in a trial), and **appellate jurisdiction**, authority to hear cases on appeals from lower courts. Specifically, the Supreme Court has original jurisdiction in "all cases affecting ambassadors, other public ministers and consuls, and those in which a state shall be party" (Article III, Section 4). The Constitution then declares that "in all other cases" properly before the Court, it would have appellate jurisdiction subject to such exceptions and regulations that Congress shall make.

The Constitution grants the president the authority to nominate judges, but these nominations are subject to the advice and consent of the Senate. Judges confirmed by the Senate serve during "good behavior," which short of impeachment essentially means a life term. The House has impeached only one Supreme Court justice, Samuel Chase (1805), in an attempt by the Democratic-Republicans to remove an ardent Federalist from the bench. The Senate rejected every charge against Chase, establishing a custom crucial to **judicial independence**: that judges would not be removed due to partisan disagreements with their decisions.

The Constitution grants the federal courts the authority to hear cases of law and **equity**. These cases can involve (1) the common law, when there are gaps in legislative authority; (2) **statutory interpretation**, where the courts have to determine what Congress meant by a statute (for example, is discrimination on the grounds of pregnancy included in the prohibition on sex discrimination in the Civil Rights Act of 1964?), and (3) **constitutional interpretation**, where the courts must decide whether a law or practice violates a provision of the Constitution, such as the Fourteenth Amendment's guarantee of **equal protection of the laws**.

Constitutional interpretation brings forth the greatest power of the federal judiciary, **judicial review**. This power is not explicitly in the Constitution, but is a power that Alexander Hamilton, the author of *Federalist* 78, expected would belong to the courts.[4] Judicial review is the power of courts to declare actions of Congress, the president, or state officials unconstitutional, and therefore void. The Supreme Court used this extraordinary power to strike down segregated schools in *Brown v. Board of Education* (1954), and the antiabortion laws of forty-seven states in *Roe v. Wade* (1973), as well as to rule on the Michigan **affirmative action** cases in 2003. The Supreme Court granted itself the power of judicial review in the case of *Marbury v. Madison* (1803).

Marbury v. Madison

The *Marbury* case arose out of the election of 1800, which resulted in the defeat of President John Adams (1797–1801) by Thomas Jefferson (1801–09). It also resulted in the defeat in Congress of Adams's Federalist Party by Jefferson's Democratic-Republicans (see Chapter 9). In the closing days of the Adams administration, the defeated Federalists, seeking to maintain some bit of power, passed the Judiciary Act of 1801. This act created many new judgeships that presumably would be filled by Federalists nominated by outgoing President Adams and confirmed by the outgoing Federalist Senate.

One of the judges nominated by Adams and confirmed by the Senate was William Marbury. In the hectic final hours of the Adams administration, Secretary of State John Marshall, who had also recently been confirmed as chief justice on the Supreme Court, failed to deliver Marbury's judicial commission, thus preventing Marbury from assuming his position. After Jefferson's presidential term began, Marbury requested that Jefferson's secretary of state, James Madison, deliver the commission, but Madison refused. Marbury then took his case directly to the Supreme Court, seeking a writ of *mandamus*, that is, an order compelling Madison to deliver the commission. Marbury believed that the Judiciary Act of 1789 gave the Supreme Court original jurisdiction to hear cases involving writs of *mandamus*.

The decision of the Supreme Court, written by Chief Justice John Marshall—the same John Marshall who as secretary of state failed to deliver the commission in the first place—unanimously decreed that Marbury had a legal right to his commission, but the Supreme Court could not order Madison

constitutional interpretation: *Decisions by a court defining the meaning of a constitutional provision, often to determine whether a law or practice violates a provision of the Constitution.*

equal protection of the laws: *Guarantee in the Fourteenth Amendment that no state shall deny any person equal treatment.*

judicial review: *Authority of courts to declare laws passed by Congress and acts of the executive branch to be unconstitutional.*

affirmative action: *Policies that grant racial or gender preferences in hiring, education, or contracting.*

Marbury v. Madison (1803): *Supreme Court case that established the Supreme Court's power of judicial review.*

to provide it because the Court did not have jurisdiction to hear the case. The Court did not have jurisdiction, Marshall wrote, because the section of the Judiciary Act of 1789 that expanded the Court's original jurisdiction to cover writs of *mandamus* was unconstitutional. The decision was brilliant. In declaring that the Court did not have jurisdiction to hear the case, Marshall established that the Court has the power to decide whether a law passed by Congress is valid under the Constitution or not.

In declaring the authority to declare acts of Congress to be unconstitutional, the Court noted that if Congress passes a law that violates a provision of the Constitution, either that law is valid or the constitutional provision is valid, but not both. So, argued the Court, if the Constitution specifically limits the Supreme Court's original jurisdiction to certain types of cases, but Congress passes legislation to expand it beyond those cases, either the legislation expanding jurisdiction is valid or the constitutional limit on jurisdiction is valid. Which is it? And who gets to decide?

Although it is obvious to us today that the Constitution is supreme over regular legislation, that relationship was not so clear in 1803. In *Marbury v. Madison,* Chief Justice Marshall clarified that the Constitution must be supreme and that regular laws cannot overrule constitutional requirements. Which branch gets to decide whether a law violates the Constitution? Marshall answered simply: "It is emphatically the province of the judicial department to say what the law is."[5] In short, Marshall was interpreting the Constitution to say that the Court has the power to interpret the meaning of the rules laid down by the Constitution's Framers and to hold those rules supreme over legislative acts passed by Congress. More than 200 years later, this decision stands as the foundation of judicial power in the United States (see Chapter 2, The Constitution, where *Marbury* is explained further in Supreme Court Cases). Since that time, approximately 120 nations have adopted this constitutional arrangement, but in 1803 it was an innovative departure even from the British system of justice (see Other Places: Judicial Review).

Historical Trends in Supreme Court Rulings

In *Federalist* 78, Alexander Hamilton described the judiciary as "the least dangerous branch" because it has no power over the sword or the purse. But due to the power of judicial review, the Supreme Court has actually played a major role in dividing authority between the nation and state, between Congress and the president, and between government, whether state or local, and the people. Throughout the Court's history, its interpretations have expanded,

otherplaces

Judicial Review

The notion of judicial review arguably began in England in 1610 when Lord Coke declared in *Dr. Bonham's Case* that "when an act of parliament is against common right and reason, or repugnant, or impossible to be performed, the common law will control it, and adjudge such act to be void." The case, though, involved an unlawful imprisonment, not an unconstitutional law, so Lord Coke was only speaking hypothetically.

Judicial review did not catch on in Great Britain for two reasons. First, unlike the United States, where Congress's powers are limited, Parliament is supreme. Second, Great Britain does not have a written constitution, thus depriving courts a basis to declare that a law is unconstitutional.

The United States thus became the first modern nation to establish judicial review, but until recently few countries followed this

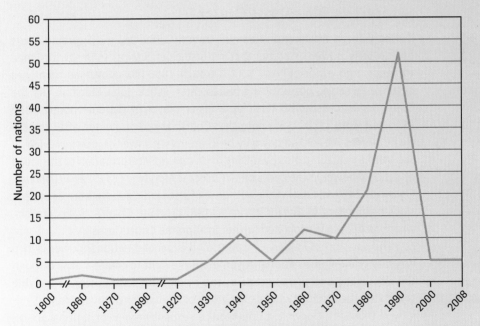

Number of Nations Adopting Judicial Review, 1800–2008
Source: Tom Ginsberg, *Judicial Review in New Democracies: Constitutional Courts in Asian Cases* (Cambridge, U.K.: Cambridge University Press, 2003); Robert Maddex, *Constitutions of the World* (Washington, D.C.: Congressional Quarterly, 1995); CIA World Factbook; various national supreme court websites; *Dr. Bonham's Case,* 8 Co. Rep. 114 (Court of Common Pleas [1610]).

practice. With greater attention to human rights around the world, most countries have moved in recent years toward some form of judicial review.

Great Britain still does not have a system of judicial review but has shown some movement in that direction. The British Human Rights Act, which went into effect in 2000, allows British courts the authority to declare that laws are not compatible with the European Convention on Human Rights, a European treaty that protects certain rights and liberties. Such a declaration does not void the law, but can be used to embarrass Parliament into changing the law.

Great Britain also has power-sharing agreements with Scotland and Northern Ireland. If Parliament passes laws that violate these agreements, British courts may be unwilling to enforce them.

then contracted, and once again expanded national powers. After a long and slow start, it has also moved, fairly consistently, toward greater protections of equality.

Expansion of National Power under the Marshall Court

Marshall Court (1801–35): *Named after Chief Justice John Marshall, the Court that greatly expanded national power.*

In *Marbury*, the Court established its power over laws made by Congress. Why, then, did the Marshall Court also expand Congress's power?

necessary and proper clause (Article I, Section 8): *Gives Congress the power to pass all laws necessary and proper to the powers enumerated in Section 8.*

commerce clause (Article I, Section 8): *Gives Congress the power to regulate commerce with foreign nations, with Indian tribes, and among the various states.*

During George Washington's administration (1789–96) the Supreme Court had so little power or status that its first chief justice, John Jay, resigned to become governor of New York. Through 1836, six confirmed nominees declined to serve. Not until the fourth chief justice, John Marshall, did the Court begin to establish itself as a major player in national politics. The **Marshall Court** (1801–35; note that Courts are often named after the sitting Chief Justice) did so not only by affirming its power of judicial review in the *Marbury* case, but also by setting forth a broad interpretation to the scope of national power in the cases of *McCulloch v. Maryland* (1819) and *Gibbons v. Ogden* (1824)[6] and limiting the authority of state judiciaries in a series of decisions culminating in *Cohens v. Virginia* (1821).[7] (See Chapter 3, Federalism, where *McCulloch* is explained further in Supreme Court Cases.)

The decision in *McCulloch v. Maryland* expanded national power in two ways: by granting the national government the right to create a bank through the **necessary and proper clause**, and by limiting state power by denying the states the authority to tax activities of the national government. Similarly, in *Gibbons v. Ogden*, the Court took an expansive view of national power, declaring that the **commerce clause**, which granted the national government the authority to regulate commerce "among the several states," would be broadly defined to include not just the shipping of goods across state lines but also the economic activities within a state that concern other states. As in *McCulloch*, what the Constitution grants as a legitimate object of national authority (here, interstate commerce) could not be regulated by a state.

This supremacy of federal law over state law is explicitly stated in the Constitution's **supremacy clause**. But the fact that federal law is supreme over state law does not necessarily answer who gets the final say over what federal law means: the national courts or the state courts. In decisions made necessary by state court refusals to abide by its initial decisions, the Supreme Court declared that federal courts have the final say over what federal law means, establishing the federal judiciary as supreme over state judiciaries on questions of national law. These cases, culminating in *Cohens v. Virginia,* are not as famous as *Marbury* or *McCulloch,* but they have been essential in preventing the sort of divisions that would arise if state judges had final say on what federal tax laws or any other federal laws meant in their home states.

By establishing judicial review, expanding national power, and ensuring the uniformity of federal law, the Marshall Court set the United States on the path to a strong and unified nation.

supremacy clause (Article VI): *Makes federal law supreme over state laws.*

Limits on National Power, 1830s to 1930s

Beginning in the 1830s, the Supreme Court began limiting national power over slavery and later, civil rights, and over governmental efforts to regulate the economy.

Although the Constitution permitted slavery, the justices did not address the issue until the case of *Dred Scott v. Sandford* (1857).[8] As noted in Chapter 5 (Civil Rights), the Supreme Court declared that no black person could be an American citizen and that Congress did not have the authority to regulate slavery in the territories. It took a civil war to undo the damage the Court had done to the nation.

Following the Civil War, Congress passed and the states ratified the Fourteenth Amendment, which overturned the *Scott* case by making "all persons born in the United States citizens of the United States." The amendment further prevented states from denying any person due process of law or the equal protection of the laws and from abridging the privileges or immunities of citizens of the United States. The amendment granted Congress the means to enforce the amendment's commands by appropriate legislation, thus adding to Congress's enumerated powers. The Supreme Court, however, interpreted these clauses narrowly, thus limiting national power.

The Supreme Court limited national authority in the economy, too. Following the Civil War, as the shift in the American economy from agriculture to industry accelerated, powerful business and industrial interests sought to limit attempts by Congress and the states to regulate economic activity and labor. The Supreme Court generally backed business and industrial interests by setting up barriers to regulation. Instead, it promoted *laissez faire,* the belief that the government should not intervene in the economy, through two constitutional doctrines. First, when Congress attempted to regulate the economy, the Court narrowly read the commerce clause, declaring that economic regulation was to be left to the states.

On what basis did the Court say, in *Dred Scott v. Sandford,* that Congress did not have the authority to regulate slavery in the territories?

Why did the Court, in this era, reduce or limit federal power?

But when states tried to regulate the economy, the Court prohibited them from doing so under its reading of the Fourteenth Amendment's due process clause.

For example, Congress attempted to control business monopolies by passing the Sherman Antitrust Act of 1890, which made "every contract, combination . . . or conspiracy in restraint of trade or commerce among the several states, or with foreign nations . . . illegal." Responding to this law, the Justice Department sought to break up the Sugar Trust, a company that had acquired control of 98 percent of the nation's sugar refining. In 1895, in what is known as the *Sugar Trust Case*,[9] the Court conceded that the Sugar Trust was an illegal monopoly but stated that Congress had no power to suppress monopolies. These were a matter for state regulation. Manufacturing, according to the Court, precedes commerce and thus cannot be regulated by the federal government. In this way the Court established that it would determine what constituted interstate commerce.

right to contract: *Court-created right not explicitly in the Constitution that prohibited restrictions on labor contracts, such as minimum wages or maximum hours.*

If a right is not explicitly stated in the Constitution, should it be protected?

But when the states attempted to regulate economic activity by setting maximum hours and minimum wages, the Court ruled such laws invalid because they violated the Fourteenth Amendment clause that prohibits states from depriving individuals of "life, liberty, or property without due process of law." Such limits on the conditions of labor deprived individuals of liberty, said the Court, specifically of a judicially created **right to contract**, a right not explicitly in the Constitution. According to the Court, individuals must have the right to contract their labor for more than the allowable number of hours or less than the minimum allowable wage, free of interference from state regulations.[10]

Strengthened National Power, 1930s to the Present

Following the onset of the Great Depression in 1929, citizens called on the states and the national government to try to regulate the economy and to assist workers, but the Supreme Court held firm in creating a constitutional gate that declared much economic legislation passed in the early years of the Franklin Roosevelt administration (1933–45) unconstitutional (the New Deal). Then, under pressure from Congress and Roosevelt, the Court eventually opened a gateway by allowing the federal and state governments greater leeway in regulating the economy. During this same period, the Court began restricting state government limits on civil rights and liberties, while strengthening national power to protect civil rights.

Increased Protections for Civil Liberties and Civil Rights. With the government's authority over the economy established, cases before the Court dealt increasingly with questions of civil rights and civil liberties, topics discussed more fully in Chapters 4 and 5. As noted in Chapter 4, paving the way for closer scrutiny of these rights were Court decisions incorporating various provisions of the Bill of Rights, making them binding on the states. This **incorporation doctrine** began slowly, with First Amendment rights among the few incorporated before the 1950s. This doctrine expanded during the liberal **Warren Court** (1953–69), which made most of the criminal procedure guarantees of the Bill of Rights binding on the states.

Outside of incorporation, the Warren Court greatly expanded the interpretation of liberties involving the First Amendment, equal protection, criminal procedure, and the right to privacy. In First Amendment cases, the Court protected the speech rights of those advocating violence against religious and racial minorities,[11] the press rights of newspapers against libel suits by public figures,[12] and the right to publish allegedly obscene materials as long as they had even the slightest amount of redeeming social value.[13] It also limited school prayer and Bible readings.[14]

Regarding equal protection, beyond the momentous *Brown v. Board of Education* decision striking at segregation,[15] the Court launched a **reapportionment** revolution, striking down arrangements in which some congressional or state legislative districts had ten or twenty times the population of other districts. Setting forth a "one person, one vote" requirement, the Court demanded equality in the number of citizens represented in each legislative district.[16]

The Warren Court also created a **right to privacy** that is not explicitly in the Constitution, striking down a Connecticut statute that prohibited any person—including married couples—from using birth control, and any person—including doctors—from counseling people or patients on such use.[17] The Burger Court (1969–86) later expanded this privacy right to cover a woman's decision to terminate her pregnancy in the 1973 decision *Roe v. Wade*.[18]

Regarding criminal justice, the Warren Court demanded that evidence obtained by police in violation of the Fourth Amendment's protection against unreasonable searches or seizures should be excluded at trial (the exclusionary rule) and that subjects in custody not be interrogated without being informed of their right to remain silent and have an attorney (the so-called *Miranda* warnings, after the plaintiff in the case).[19]

Conservatives decried liberal Warren Court decisions on civil rights, school prayer, and criminal procedure, and this opposition led to unsuccessful grassroots attempts to impeach Earl Warren. In 1968, Republican presidential candidate Richard Nixon attacked the Supreme Court for "hamstringing the peace forces in our society and strengthening the criminal forces."[20] Nixon (1969–74) won the election and was able to appoint four new justices to the Court, including Chief Justice Warren Burger. But with greater social acceptance of racial integration, and police acceptance of the *Miranda* warnings,

incorporation doctrine: *Process by which the Supreme Court made some provisions of the Bill of Rights binding on the states.*

Warren Court (1953–69): *Liberal Supreme Court that made landmark decisions on equal protection, criminal procedure, and the right to privacy.*

reapportionment: *Redistricting to achieve equal numbers in legislative districts.*

right to privacy: *Constitutional right inferred by the Court that has been used to protect unlisted rights such as sexual privacy, reproductive rights, plus the right to end life-sustaining medical treatment.*

Is there a right to privacy? Where should the line be drawn against government intrusion in private life?

neither the more conservative Burger Court nor the Rehnquist Court (1986–2005) undid what the liberal Warren Court had done.

Indeed, while school desegregation originally meant allowing children to go to their neighborhood school regardless of race, such desegregation did little in areas where whites and blacks lived in separate areas. In these areas, neighborhood schools would still be segregated. To remedy this situation, the Burger Court allowed children to be bused away from their neighborhood schools to increase integration. The Burger Court also established abortion rights, limited the death penalty, protected women's rights under the equal protection clause of the Fourteenth Amendment, and in a precursor to the *Gratz* and *Grutter* lawsuits, first allowed affirmative action at colleges and universities.[21] On the other hand, the Burger Court chose not to extend equal protection rights to the unequal funding of school districts, and, in the criminal justice area, limited the reach of the exclusionary rule and the *Miranda* warnings.[22]

Although conservative, the Rehnquist Court, over Chief Justice William Rehnquist's dissent, first extended privacy rights to homosexual conduct.[23] On the other hand, the Rehnquist Court limited, however slightly, the scope of abortion rights and cut back, again only slightly, the scope of congressional authority under the commerce clause and sovereign immunity (see Chapter 3, Federalism). It also issued split decisions in the *Gratz* and *Grutter* cases.[24] And perhaps most important, as noted in Chapter 10 (Elections, Campaigns, and Voting), it ended the dispute over the 2000 presidential election with its decision in *Bush v. Gore.*[25]

The Appointment Process for Federal Judges and Justices

Among the important consequences of the George W. Bush presidency (2001–09) was his nomination of two Supreme Court justices who share his conservative ideology, John Roberts and Samuel Alito. Given the importance that a John Marshall or an Earl Warren can have on the nation, Supreme Court nominations may in fact be among the most important decisions a president makes.[26] Article III of the Constitution, however, says no more about appointments of judges and justices other than that the president shall nominate federal judges "with the Advice and Consent of the Senate." As procedures have evolved, the president and Senate accommodate each other on district court appointments, but there is some Senate resistance at the appeals court level. At the Supreme Court level, presidential nominees face intense scrutiny by the Senate, which often reflects concerns by citizens and interest groups.

Describe the lasting impact of Supreme Court appointments.

The District Courts

When a vacancy occurs in a district court, the president selects a nominee, but with awareness of how the senators from the state in which the court is located might react. Ahead of time, presidential staff consult with this state's senators if they are members of the president's party, because if one of them is opposed, he or she can invoke the norm of **senatorial courtesy** and receive the support of other members of the Senate in blocking that nominee. When the state's senators are from different parties, the senator from the president's party sometimes offers the other senator a percentage of the appointments, hoping the favor will be returned if the other party wins the presidency. Thus Democrat Sonia Sotomayor received her district court nomination during the presidency of Republican George H. W. Bush (1989–93), due to an appointment-sharing deal between Republican Senator Alfonse D'Amato and Democratic Senator Daniel Patrick Moynihan. Like the president, senators use a variety of criteria in naming district court judges, including ideology, qualifications, and the rewarding of party loyalty.[27]

Patrick Duggan, the district court judge in the *Gratz* case, and Bernard Friedman, the judge in the *Grutter* case, had fairly similar backgrounds. Both parlayed campaign work for the Republican Party into state court judgeships, and both received federal court nominations from President Ronald Reagan (1981–89).

Confirmation of district court judges is generally routine, with nearly 90 percent of nominees since the Carter administration (1977–81) approved.[28] Following the president's nomination, the **Senate Judiciary Committee** conducts hearings on nominees. At the hearings, the American Bar Association (ABA), an organized interest group representing the nation's attorneys, evaluates the merits of nominees. District court nominees may also be requested to testify. If the Judiciary Committee approves the nomination, it moves to the Senate floor for a vote. Unless the vote is blocked by a filibuster, a majority is all that is needed for approval.[29]

senatorial courtesy: *Informal norm allowing a senator of the president's party to block judicial appointments from that state.*

Senate Judiciary Committee: *Standing Senate committee charged with reviewing judicial affairs, including federal court nominations.*

The Courts of Appeals

The formal process of appointment of court of appeals judges is the same as that of district court judges, but the greater authority of court of appeals judges means that the Senate and outside interest groups pay much closer attention to the president's nominees. First, note that whereas court of appeals judges formally represent multiple states, seats are informally considered to belong to particular states. Thus, senatorial courtesy still applies. This norm is enhanced by the practice of the chair of the Judiciary Committee to send "blue slips," so-called because of the paper color, to home state senators of the president's party, asking whether they approve of the choice. Without a positive response, the Judiciary Committee generally will not even hold a hearing on the nominee, and with no hearing, there is no vote. Indeed, even with a positive response to the blue slip, the Judiciary chair may choose not to hold a hearing, particularly if the chair is of the opposite party of the president.

For example, Senate Democrats twice blocked the nomination of future Chief Justice John Roberts, a conservative Republican, to the U.S. Court of Appeals. President George H. W. Bush first nominated Roberts to the court of appeals in 1991, but the Democrats never gave Roberts a hearing, thus killing the nomination. Ten years later, President George W. Bush renominated Roberts to the court of appeals, and again, the Democrats in charge of the Judiciary Committee did not provide Roberts a hearing. Only after a third nomination in 2003, at which point Republicans controlled the Senate (and thus the Judiciary Committee), did Roberts receive a hearing and a vote. Of course, Republicans withheld hearings from many of President Bill Clinton's (1993–2001) nominees when they controlled the Senate during his administration, including Elena Kagan, who never received a vote after Clinton nominated her in 1999 to the D.C. Court of Appeals. Overall, the Senate has failed to confirm more than 20 percent of court of appeals nominees since Jimmy Carter's administration, with the overwhelming majority being blocked at the Judiciary Committee.[28] With a short-lived filibuster-proof majority in the Senate, President Barack Obama (2009–) had little trouble appointing lower court judges in 2009, but he has been historically slow in making such nominations.[31] In 2010, Senate Republicans began extensive use of **holds**, a process by which a single senator can block the **unanimous consent agreements** by which the Senate operates, to prevent votes on many of President Obama's nominees.[32]

hold: *Power available to a senator to keep a bill or presidential nomination from coming to the Senate floor.*

unanimous consent agreement: *Agreement among all 100 senators for how a bill or presidential nomination will be debated.*

The Supreme Court

Given the Supreme Court's authority, the appointment of a Supreme Court justice is a high-stakes affair, with extensive media coverage, interest group mobilization, public opinion polls, and even the occasional scandal. Often, presidents choose nominees in part because of perceived electoral advantages. Presidential candidate Ronald Reagan promised to nominate the first woman to the Court and did so with his 1981 appointment of Sandra Day O'Connor. Fear that George W. Bush would get credit for nominating the first Latino to the Supreme Court was one of the factors that led Democratic interest groups to oppose Miguel Estrada's court of appeals nomination.[33] Keeping him off the court of appeals denied him the judicial experience that would be important for a Supreme Court nomination. President Obama then received credit for nominating the first Hispanic to the Supreme Court with Sonia Sotomayor's appointment in 2009.

Though electoral advantage certainly influences presidential decisions, presidents also try to choose nominees who are close to them ideologically, hoping to shape the direction of the Court, not just in the present, but also for years to come. But considerations of ideology are not new. George Washington (1789–97) named eleven consecutive Federalists to the first Supreme Court, and Franklin Roosevelt appointed only supporters of his New Deal programs, most of whom were Democrats.

In recent times, nominees for the Supreme Court always receive hearings from the Senate Judiciary Committee. These hearings include testimony by the ABA on the qualifications of the nominee, comments by organized interests for and against the nominee, and testimony by the nominee. Other interest groups mobilize for and against nominees, too. When in 1987 Ronald Reagan nominated Robert Bork, who was outspoken in opposing the constitutional right to privacy, Planned Parenthood released an ad stating "State controlled pregnancy? It's not as far-fetched as it sounds. Carrying Bork's position to its logical end, states could ban or require any method of birth control, impose family quotas for population purposes, make abortion a crime, or sterilize anyone they choose."[34]

Figure 14.1 presents the number of interest groups supporting or opposing nominees at Judiciary Committee hearings since 1969. There has been a substantial growth in interest group involvement in Supreme Court

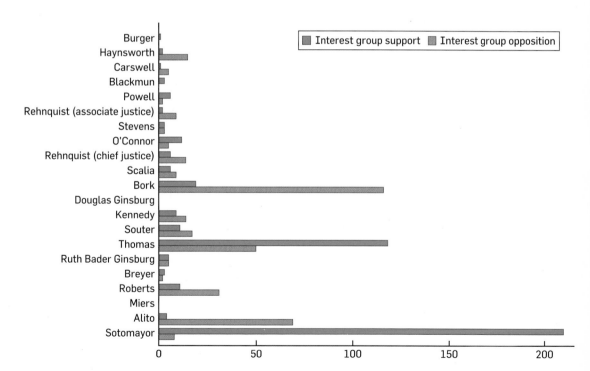

FIGURE 14.1 Number of Interest Groups Supporting and Opposing Supreme Court Nominees, Senate Judiciary Committee Hearings, 1970–2009.
Source: Derived from GPO Access, "Senate Committee on the Judiciary: Supreme Court Nomination Hearings," http://www.gpoaccess.gov/congress/senate/judiciary/scourt.html.

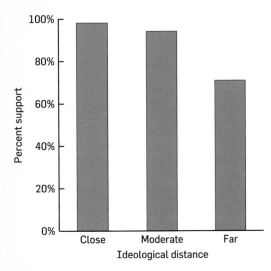

FIGURE 14.2 Ideological Distance and Voting for Supreme Court Nominees, 1937–2006. U.S. senators overwhelmingly (98.2 percent) vote for Supreme Court nominees who are ideologically close to them—liberal senators for liberal nominees and conservative senators for conservative nominees. When senators are moderately close to nominees (moderates and liberals, or moderates and conservatives), the approval rate drops to 94 percent. But when senators are ideologically distant from nominees (liberals and conservatives), senators vote for the nominee only 70.9 percent of the time. *Source:* Updated by authors from Lee Epstein and Jeffrey A. Segal, *Advice and Consent: The Politics of Judicial Appointments* (New York: Oxford University Press, 2005).

nominations, largely due to the crucial role that the Court plays in so-called values issues such as abortion, the death penalty, and affirmative action. Lobbying by interest groups can substantially influence senators' votes for and against nominations.[35]

While the Judiciary Committee can kill a nomination by refusing to report it to the Senate floor, the committee has reported every recent Supreme Court nominee, even when the recommendation is negative, as it was in 1987 for Robert Bork (9 to 5 against) and in 1991 for Clarence Thomas (voting 13 to 1 to forward without recommendation).

Bork's hearings changed the nature of testimony by nominees. An outspoken conservative, Bork answered questions about his legal beliefs directly, openly discussing his opposition to the right to privacy. The result: a 58 to 42 vote against the nominee. Since the Bork rejection, nominees have dodged questions about their beliefs. Recently, they have simply stated that it would be improper to answer any questions about any issue that might conceivably come before the Court.

Once on the floor, senators debate the pros and cons of the nominee until the vote is set. Floor votes can be postponed indefinitely through a filibuster, a tactic used on occasion for court of appeals nominees, but Abe Fortas's chief justice nomination (1968) is the only Supreme Court nomination to be defeated by a filibuster.

Overall, the votes by senators largely depend on two crucial factors about the nominees: their perceived ideology and their perceived qualifications.[36] Figure 14.2 shows the relationship for ideology. Senators are much more likely to vote for nominees who are ideologically close to them, as either liberals or conservatives. Constituent preferences matter, as six of the nine Republicans who voted for Sotomayor represented states that had voted for Obama in 2008. In contrast, only three of the thirty-one Republicans who opposed her represented states that had voted for Republican John McCain in the 2008 presidential election.

The nominees' perceived qualifications are no less important. Figure 14.3 shows the likelihood of voting for a nominee given high, medium, and low levels of perceived qualifications. Until recently, highly qualified nominees typically received overwhelming support, even if they were very conservative

Does diversity on the Court matter? Should the Supreme Court be age diverse?

Should public opinion affect judicial appointments?

(such as Antonin Scalia, 1986, who passed unanimously) or very liberal (such as Ruth Bader Ginsburg, 1993, who received only three no votes). But the increased partisanship since the 1970s means that John Roberts (2005), Samuel Alito (2006), and Sonia Sotomayor (2009), all highly qualified, received 22, 42, and 31 no votes, respectively. In each case, all the opposition came from the opposing party of the nominating president.

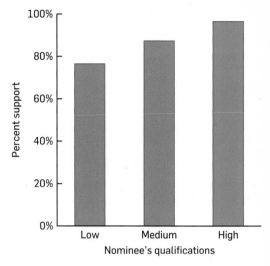

State and Lower Federal Courts

While the Supreme Court is the highest court in the United States, it hears only a small percentage of cases filed in federal court. Litigants might insist that they "will take their case all the way to the Supreme Court," but the overwhelming majority of federal cases get resolved at the district courts, which conduct civil and criminal trials. Cases appealed from the district courts go to one of the U.S. Courts of Appeals, which usually decide cases in three-judge panels. From those panels, losing litigants can appeal cases to the entire circuit for an *en banc* ("by the full court") hearing, or they can appeal directly to the U.S. Supreme Court (see Figure 14.4).

FIGURE 14.3 Qualifications and Voting for Supreme Court Nominees, 1937–2006. U.S. senators are much more likely to support Supreme Court nominees perceived to be high in qualifications (96.6 percent favorable) than nominees perceived to be low in qualifications (76.5 percent favorable).
Source: Updated by authors from Lee Epstein and Jeffrey A. Segal, *Advice and Consent: The Politics of Judicial Appointments* (New York: Oxford University Press, 2005).

State Courts in the Federal Judicial System

Each state has its own judicial system, and unless a case involves federal law or the type of parties that create federal jurisdiction, cases get resolved in state courts, each of which has its own hierarchy of trial and appellate courts. Cases that begin in one of the fifty separate state court systems that nevertheless involve federal issues can be appealed to the federal court system in one of two ways. First, criminal defendants who have exhausted their state appeals, that is, have gone through their last appeal at the state level, can file a **writ of *habeas corpus*** with a U.S. District Court, which then allows the court to determine whether one or more of the defendant's federal legal rights have been violated. Second, any parties who have exhausted their state appeals can file a request for review, known as a **writ of *certiorari***, directly with the Supreme Court. Additional explanation of this process occurs later in this chapter.

writ of *habeas corpus*: *Right of individuals who have been arrested and jailed to go before a judge, who determines if their detention is legal.*

writ of *certiorari*: *Request to the Supreme Court that it review a lower court case.*

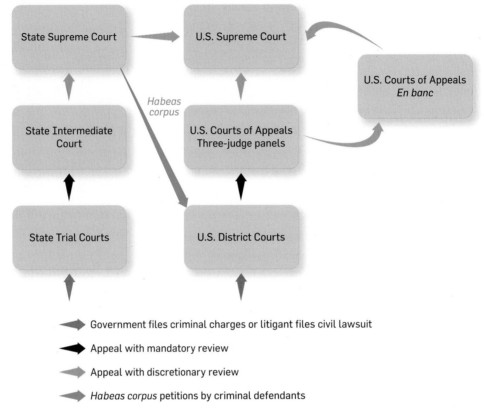

FIGURE 14.4 **Judicial Organization in the United States.**
Source: Adapted from Lee Epstein, Jeffrey A. Segal, Harold J. Spaeth, and Thomas G. Walker, *The Supreme Court Compendium*, 4th ed. (Washington, D.C.: CQ Press, 2007), Figure 7-3.

The District Courts

class action: *Lawsuit filed by one person on behalf of that person plus all similarly situated people.*

discovery: *Process in a lawsuit prior to trial in which each side receives relevant information held by the other side.*

Should Gratz and Grutter have sought monetary damages?

The Judiciary Act of 1789 established thirteen district courts for the thirteen states. Today, there are ninety-four districts. Many states have more than one district, but no district covers more than one state. Those districts that cover only part of a state receive geographical names, as in the Northern District of Illinois. Altogether there are 678 district judgeships.

Trials at the district courts are either criminal or civil. Plaintiffs (the parties bringing the suit) in civil suits often request monetary damages to compensate for harms done to them, such as by a broken contract or a defective product. When rights are alleged to have been violated, they may ask that the practice be stopped. Litigants filed over 267,000 civil suits with the district courts in 2008, and the government commenced nearly 71,000 criminal prosecutions.[37]

When Gratz and Grutter sued the University of Michigan over its admissions policies, their first stops were the U.S. District Courts. They had standing to sue, as their rejection by the university was a real injury, and because they claimed their rights to equal protection under the Fourteenth Amendment had been violated, their cases raised a constitutional issue and entered the federal court system. Gratz and Grutter sought not only their own admission to the University of Michigan, but also an end to the university's use of race in admissions decisions. The district courts allowed both suits to move forward as **class action** lawsuits, meaning that Gratz and Grutter were suing not only on behalf of themselves but also on behalf of all people denied admission at Michigan on account of their race.

Civil Procedure. The overwhelming majority of lawsuits filed in federal court settle out of court with a negotiated agreement between the plaintiff and the defendant. In 2005, plaintiffs filed suit in federal court in over 250,000 cases, but the district courts commenced only 5,000 civil trials. Of these, slightly more than half, including the Grutter and Gratz cases, were bench (nonjury) trials.

Once a case is assigned to a judge, the next step in a civil suit is **discovery**. Discovery grants each side access to information relevant to its suit held by the other side. Crucial to the *Gratz* and *Grutter* suits were University of Michigan documents showing differential admission rates for whites and minorities who had similar grades and standardized test scores. During discovery, the attorneys for each side can also question witnesses for the other side in a process known as **deposition**. Following discovery, litigants file briefs with the court, laying out their arguments.

Outside interests can file *amicus curiae* **briefs** ("friends of the court" briefs), stating their concerns in a case.[38] The most influential *amicus* briefs are those filed in the name of the United States, as represented by the Office of the **Solicitor General** in the Justice Department.[39] In the *Gratz* and *Grutter* cases, the Clinton administration filed briefs in favor of the University of Michigan, which argued that affirmative action was necessary to obtain a diverse student body. General Motors also filed a brief in favor of the university's affirmative

AP Photo/Susan Walsh

Barbara Grutter was in her 40s when she applied to law school. The mother of two children, she also ran a consulting business.

deposition: *Process in a lawsuit prior to trial in which each side gets to interview witnesses from the other side.*

amicus curiae briefs: *Briefs filed by outside parties ("friends of the court") who have an interest in the outcome of a case.*

Solicitor General: *Official in the Justice Department who represents the president in federal court.*

How important is a
diverse student body?
How important is a
diverse work force? What
is your experience?

action program, stating that it needed a diverse pool of highly qualified attorneys, managers, and the like. Eventually, twenty Fortune 500 companies, including Microsoft, signed briefs supporting the university.[40]

Civil trials begin with opening statements by the plaintiff and respondent. The plaintiff then calls its witnesses, who can be cross-examined by the respondent's attorney. Once the plaintiff rests her case, the respondent calls his or her witnesses, who can be cross-examined by the plaintiff's attorney.

Trial courts make determinations as to fact and as to law, whereas appellate courts generally make determinations only as to law, applying the facts as determined by the trial court. That would normally mean it would be up to the district court to determine factually whether race played a role in admissions at Michigan and how much of a role it played. Then it would decide as a matter of law whether that role was allowable or not. The parties in the *Gratz* and *Grutter* cases made the decision a bit easier for the judges, for the University of Michigan readily admitted—indeed, strongly defended—its use of race in admissions. Therefore, the question for the trial judge was not a question of fact, but a question of law: Does the equal protection clause of the Fourteenth Amendment prohibit the use of race as a factor in university admissions?

Should race be a factor in
university admissions?

While trial judges or juries have nearly complete discretion in deciding questions of fact, they are constrained by the courts above them as to questions of law. In affirmative action, the key precedent was a 1978 Supreme Court decision *Regents of the University of California v. Bakke*.[41] In *Bakke*, a divided Court ruled that the University of California's quota system of reserving a certain number of seats for minorities was unconstitutional, but that a system in which race was a "plus" in admissions could be justified due to the benefits that a diverse student body provides all of the students (see Chapter 5).

In December 2000, Judge Duggan ruled in the *Gratz* case that the point system used by the university—in which each applicant could receive up to 150 points including 20 for being from an underrepresented minority group—was a valid and necessary means of obtaining a diverse student body. On the other hand, Judge Friedman ruled in March 2001 that the law school's use of race in admissions violated the Constitution, finding that it was an "enormously important factor" in admissions, and not the mere "plus" approved by the Supreme Court in *Bakke*. The University of Michigan appealed Friedman's decision to the Sixth Circuit Court of Appeals, while the Center for Individual Rights backed Gratz's appeal to the same circuit.

Criminal Procedure. Beyond civil cases like the Michigan affirmative action suits, trial courts also conduct criminal trials. Criminal prosecutions begin with an alleged violation of federal criminal law. In the U.S. federal system, states have primary authority over law enforcement, but the federal government frequently prosecutes drug, weapons, and immigration cases, plus other crimes that involve interstate commerce or the instrumentalities of the federal government, such as the post office and government buildings.

The clearance rate for state and federal crimes, that is, the percent of reported crimes in which someone is arrested, charged, and turned over for prosecution, is highest for violent crimes (over 45 percent in 2002) but much lower for property crimes such as burglary (16.5 percent).[42] Under the Constitution, accused criminals in federal courts have a right to indictment by a **grand jury**, a specially empanelled jury consisting of between sixteen and twenty-three citizens who determine whether the government has sufficient evidence to charge the suspect with a crime. In the rare occasions in which a grand jury chooses not to indict, the suspect is freed.

Following indictment, the accused is arraigned, or informed of the charges against him or her, and asked to enter an initial plea of guilty or not guilty. About 90 percent of federal criminal cases are resolved through a **plea bargain**, in which the accused pleads guilty, usually in exchange for a reduced charge or a lesser sentence.[43]

In the small number of cases that proceed to trial, the accused has the right to a trial by jury, but defendants are free to request a bench trial, in which the judge decides guilt or innocence. Juries in federal felony cases consist of twelve individuals who must reach a verdict unanimously. (Neither twelve people nor unanimity is required in state courts.) The accused can appeal a guilty verdict, but the double jeopardy clause of the Constitution prohibits the government from appealing a verdict of not guilty. If the accused is found guilty, the judge determines the sentence, based on guidelines that depend on the nature of the offense, the number of prior convictions, and other factors as recommended by the U.S. Sentencing Commission. In death penalty cases, the decision on the punishment is left to the jury. That is, following a guilty verdict, the jury hears new testimony by the prosecutor and defense attorney as to whether death is the appropriate punishment.

grand jury: *Special jury charged with determining whether people should be put on trial.*

plea bargain: *Agreement by a criminal defendant to plead guilty in return for a reduced sentence.*

Do plea bargains make efficiency more important than justice?

The Courts of Appeals

Sitting hierarchically above the ninety-four district courts are the U.S. Courts of Appeals. They are divided geographically into eleven numbered circuits plus a circuit for the District of Columbia and a "federal circuit" that hears appeals from specialized lower courts that deal with patents and customs (see Figure 14.5). Each of the numbered courts of appeals has jurisdiction over several states. For example, the Sixth Circuit Court of Appeals, which sits in Cincinnati, hears appeals from district courts in Kentucky, Michigan, Ohio, and Tennessee.

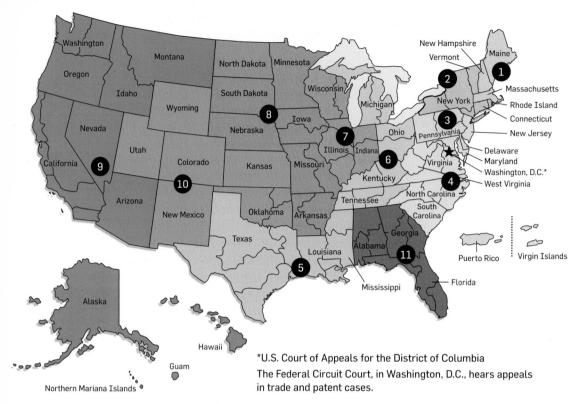

FIGURE 14.5 U.S. Courts of Appeals and U.S. District Courts.
Source: United States Courts, Court Locator, www.uscourts.gov/.

*U.S. Court of Appeals for the District of Columbia
The Federal Circuit Court, in Washington, D.C., hears appeals in trade and patent cases.

The number of judgeships in each circuit ranges from just six in the First Circuit, which covers the New England states, to twenty-nine in the Ninth Circuit, which covers California and eight other western states. Regardless of the number of judgeships, the courts usually hear appeals from the district courts in three-judge panels.

The courts have mandatory jurisdiction over cases appealed to it. That is, if a losing party from the district court appeals to the appropriate court of appeals, the court must hear the case. Because the circuit courts are in the middle of the federal judicial hierarchy, cases can be both appealed to the court of appeals and appealed from the court of appeals (see Figure 14.4). This can happen in two ways. First, losing litigants at the court of appeals who believe that the three-judge panel that heard their case did not represent the judgment of the circuit as a whole can request *en banc* review. Alternatively, losing litigants can request review by the Supreme Court. In both cases, further review is at the discretion of whichever court is being appealed to.

Given the importance of the *Grutter* and *Gratz* cases, they made it through the U.S. Court of Appeals in anything but a normal manner. Rather than a hearing with a three-judge panel, possibly followed by *en banc* and/or Supreme Court review, the Center for Individual Rights, which represented Gratz and Grutter, requested and was granted immediate *en banc* review. On May 14, 2002, the Sixth Circuit ruled in favor of the university in the law school case by a 5–4 vote. The **majority opinion** argued that the law school's approach resembled the "plus" system approved by the Supreme Court in the *Bakke* case. All three Republicans on the circuit sided with Grutter; five of the six Democrats sided with the university, consistent both with generally greater support among Democrats than Republicans for **equality of outcome** over **equality of opportunity**, and with evidence that such attitudes often influence judicial decisions. Not surprisingly, Barbara Grutter appealed the decision to the Supreme Court.

On October 1, 2002, ten months after oral arguments, the court of appeals still had not issued its ruling in the undergraduate case. In an unusual step, Gratz's attorneys asked the Supreme Court to bypass the court of appeals and rule directly on their appeal. On December 1, the Supreme Court accepted review in both cases.

The Supreme Court

The Supreme Court's procedure in handling cases consists of deciding whether or not to grant review, and if review is granted, receiving briefs, hearing oral arguments, deciding who wins, and writing the majority opinion. If desired, justices who do not agree with the majority opinion can write concurring and dissenting opinions. The majority opinion, however, stands as the precedent for lower court judges to apply in similar cases dealing with the same issue.

Granting Review

Each year, about 8,000 losing litigants ask the Supreme Court to review their cases. Most of these cases have lost one decision in the U.S. Courts of Appeals or one of the fifty state supreme courts. The vast majority of appeals to the Supreme Court come in the form of a petition for a writ of *certiorari* (often shortened to "cert"). The Court's decision to grant cert is purely discretionary, but the Supreme Court's rules suggest that a grant of cert will be more likely when a lower court resolves issues of law differently from the way other lower courts have or issues a decision that conflicts with decisions of the U.S. Supreme Court. The Supreme Court is also more likely to grant review when the government of the United States, represented by the Solicitor General's office, requests it, either as a petitioning party or as an *amicus*

majority opinion: *Opinion of a court laying out the official position of the court in the case.*

equality of outcome: *Expectation that equality is achieved if results are comparable for all citizens regardless of race, gender, or national background, or that such groups are proportionally represented in measures of success in life.*

equality of opportunity: *Expectation that citizens may not be discriminated against on account of race, gender, or national background, and that every citizen should have an equal chance to succeed in life.*

In 1929, Chief Justice William Howard Taft—the only chief justice who was also a president—convinced Congress to move the Supreme Court out of the U.S. Capitol to "a building of dignity and importance suitable for its use as the permanent home of the Supreme Court of the United States." The new building, across the street from the Capitol, was completed in 1935.

© Bill Ross/CORBIS

curiae. The filing of *amicus* briefs by other parties can also be important to the Court, as it signals the Court that the case involves important questions of public policy.[44]

The large number of petitions for cert prevents the justices from fully reviewing each one. Instead, they rely on their clerks, usually recent law school graduates, to write summaries. Most of the justices' chambers have joined the "cert pool," which splits the cert petitions among the justices in the pool.

The large number of petitions also prevents the justices from fully discussing each one. Rather, the chief justice passes around a "discuss list," a set of cases he thinks worthy of discussion. Any other justice can add any other case to the list if he or she wishes. Cases not on the discuss list are automatically denied cert, leaving the lower court's decision as final. The justices then meet in conference to consider each of the cases on the discuss list. The Court grants cert through a **rule of four**. That is, although five votes constitute a majority, the Court will agree to hear a case if any four justices vote to grant. Overall, the Court grants only about 1 percent of cert petitions, leaving the lower court decision as final in the remaining 99 percent of the cases.

The justices' votes on *certiorari* remain secret unless a justice leaves his or her papers to the public, as they sometimes do after they retire. To date,

rule of four: *Supreme Court rule that grants review to a case if as few as four of the justices support review.*

the justices' votes in the *Gratz* and *Grutter* cases are unavailable, but the importance of the issue plus a split between the Sixth Circuit Court upholding affirmative action and an earlier Fifth Circuit decision striking it down at the University of Texas[45] made a grant of *certiorari* highly likely. On December 2, 2002, the Court granted review to both cases.

Oral Arguments

Following a grant of cert, the justices receive written briefs from the litigants explaining why their position should win. Other parties may file *amicus curiae* briefs urging the Court to affirm or reverse the lower court decision. Thus, while the Clinton administration sided with the university at the district court level in the *Gratz* and *Grutter* cases, the George W. Bush administration switched sides and asked the Supreme Court to strike down the law school and undergraduate admissions programs. On the other hand, seventy-four organizations filed *amicus* briefs supporting the university, the most ever in a Supreme Court case.

Parties normally receive thirty minutes each for oral argument, although the justices frequently interrupt with questions. The quality of these arguments, not surprisingly, can certainly influence which party wins.[46] The Supreme Court heard oral arguments in the *Gratz* and *Grutter* cases on April 1, 2003, hearing the *Grutter* case first. Grutter's attorney, Kirk Kolbo from the Center for Individual Rights, spoke first, arguing that the Constitution prohibits distinctions based on race. Justice O'Connor immediately interrupted, asking the attorney about Court precedents holding that race could be used if the government had a compelling interest in doing so. Kolbo responded that the school could legally achieve a diverse student body without using racial preferences by using factors that are not explicitly racial, such as economic status. The U.S. Solicitor General, Theodore Olson, spoke next, opposing Michigan's use of affirmative action but, under President Bush's directive, not calling for a complete ban on the use of race. Olson chose not to answer questions about the military's use of affirmative action, stating that he had not examined their policies. Michigan's attorney, Maureen Mahoney, a former law clerk for Chief Justice Rehnquist, tried to distinguish between the university's attempt to obtain a diverse student body and the type of quota system declared unconstitutional in the *Bakke* case.

Kolbo represented Gratz as well as Grutter, arguing in Gratz's case that the use of race as a factor must be extraordinary and rare, and that diversity does not meet that extraordinary standard. Michigan's attorney in the undergraduate case defended the need for a "critical mass" of minority students, so that those students would not feel like tokens.

Should the federal government be allowed to try to influence a court decision?

Oral arguments in the *Gratz* and *Grutter* cases, as well as hundreds of other cases, are available at the U.S. Supreme Court Media website, www .oyez.org.

The Decision

Within a few days of oral argument, the justices meet in conference to vote on the merits of the case, that is, to decide which side wins and to assign a justice to write the Opinion of the Court in the case. If the chief justice is in the majority, he assigns who writes the opinion. If the chief is not in the majority, the assignment is made by the senior justice who is in the majority.

The opinion is the heart of the Court's legal and policy-making power. It explains the Court's justification for its decision and sets guidelines for other courts to follow in subsequent cases. But to have this authority, it must become a majority opinion by gaining the assent of a majority of the justices.

Assigning the writing of the Opinion of the Court to a justice does not mean that a majority opinion will result. If a justice writes an opinion siding with one side, and other justices agree with the result (that is, who wins) but not with the reasoning, they can concur in the judgment. That means that they are not joining the Opinion of the Court. Such justices will typically write a **concurring opinion** that explains their reasoning, or join the concurring opinion of another justice. Justices who disagree with the result reached by the majority (again, who wins) can write a **dissenting opinion** explaining why they believe the Court's decision was in error. If, due to a combination of concurring and dissenting justices, fewer than five justices join the opinion of the court, that opinion becomes a **plurality judgment** rather than a majority opinion. Plurality judgments have lesser value as precedent than majority opinions.

The conference on the affirmative action cases revealed a split in the justices' preferences: 5–4 in favor of the law school program but 6–3 against the undergraduate program. As Figure 14.6 shows, four conservative justices thought that both the undergraduate and the law school affirmative programs violated the Fourteenth Amendment and were unconstitutional, whereas the three most liberal justices thought that both programs were acceptable because of the university's compelling interest in creating a diverse student body and the narrow tailoring of the affirmative action program to meet that interest. Justices Sandra Day O'Connor and Stephen Breyer were the swing justices. They agreed that diversity constituted a compelling interest but did not believe that the undergraduate program, which automatically gave a set number of points to minority applicants, was narrowly tailored to meet that interest. They thus voted with the more conservative justices to strike the

concurring opinion:
Opinion by a judge that agrees with the court majority's result (that is, which party wins) but sets out a separate rationale.

dissenting opinion:
Opinions written by judges who disagree with the result reached by the majority as to who should win a case.

plurality judgment:
Opinion of the court that results when a majority of the justices cannot agree on the rationale for a decision.

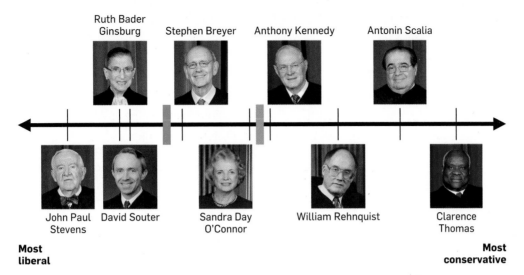

Ruth Bader Ginsburg   Stephen Breyer   Anthony Kennedy   Antonin Scalia

John Paul Stevens   David Souter   Sandra Day O'Connor   William Rehnquist   Clarence Thomas

Most liberal   **Most conservative**

FIGURE 14.6 **Ideology and Votes of Supreme Court Justices in the *Gratz* and *Grutter* Cases.** The justices are aligned from most liberal to most conservative. The six justices to the right of the blue line voted with Gratz to strike the undergraduate affirmative action program at the University of Michigan. The five justices to the left of the brown line voted with the University of Michigan in upholding the law school's affirmative action program. *Source for justices' ideology:* Martin-Quinn Scores, http://mqscores.wustl.edu/. *Photos:* Ginsburg, Breyer, Kennedy, Scalia, Stevens, and Thomas by Steve Petteway, Collection of the Supreme Court of the United States; Souter by Joseph Bailey, National Geographic Society, Courtesy of the Collection of the Supreme Court of the United States; O'Connor by Dane Pennland, Smithsonian Institution, Collection of the Supreme Court of the United States; Rehnquist by Dane Pennland, Smithsonian Institution, Collection of the Supreme Court of the United States.

undergraduate program. But O'Connor and Breyer voted with the liberals to uphold the law school program, which overall gave strong preferences to underrepresented minorities but was more careful in considering the importance of race in each individual's application.

Should Gratz have won her case? Should Grutter?

Because Chief Justice Rehnquist dissented in the law school case, Justice Stevens, the senior justice in the majority, assigned the opinion. Given Justice O'Connor's role as the swing justice in the case, he assigned the opinion to her. O'Connor declared that while racial categorizations could be used only if the state had a compelling interest in doing so, the need for diversity was such an interest. Chief Justice Rehnquist was in the majority in the undergraduate case, and he assigned the majority opinion to himself. His opinion accepted the notion that diversity was a compelling interest—he did not have the votes to declare otherwise—but wrote that the automatic granting of 20 points toward admission to every minority student did not meet the precedent required in *Bakke* of considering each particular applicant as an individual.

Though Gratz won her case, she had by this point graduated from a different Michigan campus, the University of Michigan—Dearborn. The University of Michigan then changed its admissions procedures to be more like the law school's: race would still be used as an admissions factor but there would be no automatic point total added just because of an applicant's race.

Impact

The fact that the Supreme Court issues a decision does not necessarily mean that governmental officials charged with implementing it will comply. The courts, after all, have no power of enforcement. The Court's school desegregation decision in *Brown*, for example, met with massive resistance from supporters of segregation: elected officials urged disobedience, local boards of education ignored the decision, and lower courts complied with the decision half-heartedly at best. And the fact that a decision might be complied with does not necessarily mean that it will have the impact that the Court intended. The advances in school desegregation over time have not meant that educational equality has been achieved in the United States.

Additionally, many types of court decisions can be overturned by Congress, state legislatures, or other legislative mechanisms such as state-level referenda. When a court's decision is based on the meaning of a statute (for example, is carbon dioxide considered a pollutant under the Clean Air Act?), Congress can simply overturn the court's decision if it disagrees with the Supreme Court's conclusion.

In the constitutional realm, if the Court declares that a practice is *not* unconstitutional, as in the affirmative action case, that practice can still be prohibited through the legislature or, if the state allows, through a referendum. So when the Supreme Court rules that affirmative action is not prohibited by the Constitution, that does not mean that the university is required to implement an affirmative action program or that the state is required to allow such a program. Following the Supreme Court decision in her case, Jennifer Gratz used the gateway provided by Michigan's **initiative** procedure, organizing a Michigan statewide proposal that banned the use of race, gender, or ethnicity for higher education. The initiative passed decisively in November 2006, by a 58 percent to 42 percent margin. Thus despite the Supreme Court's decision in the affirmative action cases, affirmative action in admissions is illegal at all public colleges in Michigan, including the University of Michigan.

Alternatively, when the Supreme Court declares that the Constitution prohibits an activity, legislatures find that prohibition difficult to overturn. For example, when the Court declared that Congress did not have the authority to set the voting age at 18 for state elections, the only recourse was for Congress and the states to pass a constitutional amendment overturning that decision. Congress occasionally overturns the Supreme Court's statutory decisions; however, only five of the Court's constitutional decisions have ever

How are court decisions enforced? Would government work better if the courts had the power of enforcement?

initiative: *Process by which citizens place proposed laws on the ballot for public approval.*

Did the Michigan ballot initiative undermine justice or help ensure it?

TABLE 14.1 Constitutional Amendments Overturning Supreme Court Decisions

Decision	Amendment
Chisolm v. Georgia (1793) allowed citizens to sue other states in federal court.	Eleventh (1795) establishes sovereign immunity for states.
Dred Scott v. Sandford (1857) denied citizenship to African Americans.	Fourteenth (1868) makes all people born in the United States citizens of the United States.
Minor v. Happersett (1874) denied voting rights to women.	Nineteenth (1920) guarantees women the right to vote.
Pollock v. Farmers' Loan and Trust (1895) limited Congress's authority to tax income.	Sixteenth (1913) grants Congress the authority to tax income from whatever source derived.
Oregon v. Mitchell (1970) prompted Congress to set the voting age at 18 for all elections. The case struck the law as applied to state elections.	Twenty-Sixth (1971) sets the voting age of 18 for all elections.

been overturned via amendment (see Table 14.1). Most Supreme Court decisions, however, and virtually all of its constitutional decisions, are not overturned by Congress or via amendment.

The Judiciary and Public Policy: Activism and Restraint

An overly simple view of American politics holds that the legislative branch makes the law, the judicial branch interprets the law, and the executive branch enforces the law. But the president can issue executive orders, and executive branch agencies can issue regulations that often are indistinguishable from legislation. The legislative branch holds hearings on executive branch agencies that often focus on how those agencies enforce the law. What about courts? Their job is to interpret the law, but in doing so, they often appear to go beyond mere interpretation and instead get actively involved in policy making. Supporters and critics of the *Roe* abortion decision often agree that the decision, which established different degrees of abortion rights depending on the trimester of the pregnancy (see Chapter 4), reads more like the making of policy than the interpretation of law.

Consider also affirmative action. We have noted throughout this book that representative democracy requires the government to treat people equally. Does the government do so when, to make up for past discrimination and current inequalities that exist in society, it provides preferences to some groups over others? The Supreme Court's answer was a tentative yes. But how did the Court come to that decision? We will consider two broad approaches to understanding judicial policy making: a *legal* approach, which suggests that courts rely on legally relevant factors, and an *extralegal* approach, which suggests that courts rely on legally irrelevant factors. We look at affirmative action policy in particular and then examine the consequences for a democracy of the reliance on extralegal factors by an unelected judiciary.

The Legal Approach

According to the legal approach, justices base their decisions on legally relevant materials, such as prior court precedents, the **plain meaning** of the text of the law under consideration, and the **intent of the Framers** of the law.

As we explained earlier in the chapter, precedent means a reliance on the prior decisions of the Court. Thus in the *Grutter* case the Court accepted the arguments from the *Bakke* case that the government had a compelling interest in achieving a diverse student body but concluded that systems that establish racial quotas go too far. Lower courts are bound by Supreme Court precedents, but the Supreme Court does not necessarily consider itself strictly bound to its own precedents. Otherwise there would be no growth in the law, and, for example, the United States might still have the separate-but-equal school systems that were declared unconstitutional in *Brown v. Board of Education*.

Beyond precedent, legal-based approaches consider the plain meaning of the law being interpreted. Justice Antonin Scalia is the Court's foremost proponent of this approach. If there is no right to privacy written in the Constitution, he claims, then the Supreme Court should not be creating privacy rights. According to Scalia, if such rights are to be protected, they should be granted by democratically elected legislatures, not life-appointed judges. Similarly, Justice Clarence Thomas often argues for decision making based on the intent of the Framers. This approach places the meaning of the Framers ahead of the literal meaning of the words that they wrote. Thus, while dissenting in a case that upheld federal prohibitions on medicinal marijuana under Congress's authority to regulate interstate commerce, Thomas ignored

In the *Gratz* and *Grutter* cases, was government responsive? Did the decisions help ensure equality?

What should judges and justices base their decisions on?

plain meaning:
Interpretation of laws or constitutional provisions based on the literal meaning of what the law says.

intent of the Framers:
Interpretation of a law or constitutional provision based on what the Framers of the law intended.

more than seventy years of precedent that had expanded the scope of the commerce clause. He argued that local activities such as the medical use of homegrown marijuana were not what the Framers meant by commerce.[47] This may well be true, but in many circumstances it is difficult to know what the Framers meant, or what they would have thought if they could have envisioned modern American society.

The Extralegal Approach

Legal approaches often fail to provide a good indicator of what the Supreme Court will do. While some precedents, notably the 1978 *Bakke* decision, supported affirmative action, more recent cases prior to *Grutter* had pushed in the opposite direction. The text of the Fourteenth Amendment guarantees equality, but there is no evidence that the Framers of the amendment intended it to prohibit policies that tried to help disadvantaged groups.

Alternatively, we can consider extralegal approaches to Supreme Court decision making. Extralegal factors are those that go beyond the legal factors that courts are supposed to consider. The most important extralegal considerations include the justices' own preferences and strategic considerations based on the preferences of others.

The Justices' Preferences. Recall from the affirmative action cases that the four most conservative justices voted to strike down both the undergraduate and the law school plans, the three most liberal justices voted to uphold both, and two justices in the middle voted to uphold the law school program but to strike down the undergraduate program. (For the ideology of the justices currently on the Court, see Figure 14.7).

This sort of relationship between the justices' ideology and their votes is fairly common. But because Supreme Court scholars cannot obtain information from the justices themselves about their ideology, they use indirect measures. As Figure 14.8 (see page 525) shows, whether scholars use the justices' party identification, the ideology of their appointing president, or public perceptions of the nominees' ideology prior to confirmation, there exists a very strong relationship between the justices' ideology and their votes once on the Court.[48]

What role should ideology play in judicial decisions? What role does it play?

Strategic Considerations. Justices cannot, however, behave solely on the basis of their own ideological preferences. Justice Rehnquist, while writing the *Gratz* opinion, may have preferred to declare that virtually all affirmative action plans are unconstitutional, but if he had done so he might have lost the support of Justices O'Connor, Breyer, and Kennedy. So he compromised and accepted diversity as a rationale but nevertheless was able

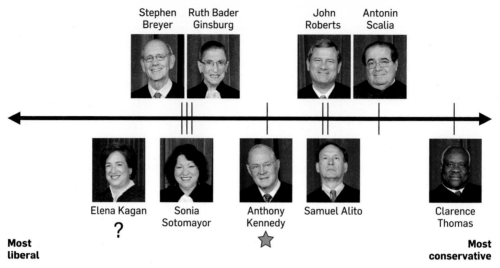

Stephen Breyer Ruth Bader Ginsburg   John Roberts Antonin Scalia

Elena Kagan Sonia Sotomayor   Anthony Kennedy   Samuel Alito   Clarence Thomas

?

Most liberal

Most conservative

★ = Median (swing) justice
? = Ideology on the Court not yet determined

FIGURE 14.7 Ideology of the Supreme Court Justices. Although liberalism and conservatism mean different things at different times, liberalism on the Supreme Court is usually associated with support for women and minorities in civil rights cases, support for governmental authority in economic cases, support for defendants and convicts in criminal cases, and support for individuals claiming an abridgement of rights in First Amendment and privacy cases. Conservatism is associated with the opposite values. The figure shows the ideology of the Court in June 2010, after the resignation of Justice John Paul Stevens and before the voting record of replacement Elena Kagan was available. Assuming that Kagan votes more liberally than Kennedy, Kennedy will remain the swing justice. In other words, when he votes liberally, the four more liberal colleagues probably will also vote liberally, and when he votes conservatively, the four more conservative colleagues probably will vote conservatively as well. *Source:* Judicial liberalism: Lee Epstein, Jeffrey A. Segal, Harold J. Spaeth, and Thomas G. Walker, The Supreme Court Compendium, 4th ed. (Washington, D.C.: CQ Press, 2007), Table 6-4. The justices' ideology: http://mqscores.wustl.edu/. *Photos:* Steve Petteway, Collection of the Supreme Court of the United States.

to strike down the undergraduate program. Negotiations over the content of the majority opinion are a routine part of Supreme Court decision making.[49]

Affirmative Action

The phrase *affirmative action* first made its way into federal policy through Executive Order 10925, signed by President John Kennedy (1961–63) in 1961. The order required federal contractors to "take affirmative action to ensure that applicants are employed, and that employees are treated during employment, without regard to their race, creed, color, or national origin."[50] In 1964 the Civil Rights Act, while generally prohibiting discrimination on account of race or sex, specifically allowed preferential treatment for Native

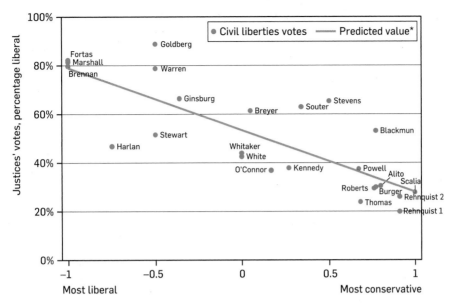

*Predicted value is the percent of time the justice is predicted to vote liberally given his or her ideology.

Note: Rehnquist 1 indicates his term as an associate justice; Rehnquist 2 indicates his term as chief justice.

FIGURE 14.8 Justices' Votes by Justices' Ideology, 1953-2009 Terms. The graph shows that, as justices line up from left (most liberal) to right (most conservative), the percentage of the time they vote liberally drops substantially. Generally speaking, the most liberal justices, those furthest to the left on the graph (Fortas, Marshall, and Brennan), vote in the liberal direction (toward the top of the graph), whereas the most conservative justices (Rehnquist and Scalia) vote conservatively most of the time. *Source:* Justices' ideology: http://ws.cc.stonybrook.edu/polsci/jsegal/qualtable .pdf. Justices' votes: Lee Epstein, Jeffrey A. Segal, Harold J. Spaeth, and Thomas G. Walker, *The Supreme Court Compendium*, 4th ed. (Washington, D.C.: CQ Press, 2007).

Americans living on or near reservations. Today federal funding acts for education, defense, and transportation routinely grant contracting preferences for minority- and female-owned business. The Department of Education interprets the nondiscrimination provisions of the Civil Rights Act to encourage voluntary affirmative action plans that help achieve a diverse student population.[51]

As the *Gratz* and *Grutter* cases show, the courts have a large role in this democratic process, balancing the equality of opportunity against affirmative action policies aimed at providing greater equality of outcome. Given the play of extralegal factors in such decisions, are judges, in fact, policy makers?[52] Certainly, when the Supreme Court decides for the nation that affirmative action programs are allowed as long as they provide individualized assessments of students' records, they are making policy. The fact that this is not

Which is more important—equality of opportunity or equality of outcome?

Congress

President

Litigants

State courts

Affirmative action

Interest groups

Federal courts

Senate Judiciary Committee

Voters

merely "interpretation" of the law is supported by the fact that the justices' policy preferences overwhelmingly explain their votes on the Court.

But we might reach a different conclusion when we deal with lower courts. Consider a district court judge faced with a suit by a white student to gain admission to a university that has an affirmative action program similar to the Michigan law school program. The judge applies the precedent from *Grutter* and rejects the student's challenge. Although that judge has made a decision that is crucial to the student, both the scope of the decision (which applies only to that student) and the low level of discretion involved in reaching it (the judge felt bound by the Supreme Court precedent in *Grutter*) make this sort of behavior distinct from what can be considered to be policy making.

Activism and Restraint

Is the judicial branch, as Hamilton said, "the least dangerous branch"? Defend your answer.

judicial activists: *Judges who go beyond what the law requires and seek to impose their own policy preferences on society through their judicial decisions.*

judicial restraint: *Respecting the decisions of other branches, or, through the concept of precedent, the decisions of earlier judges.*

Because judges are unelected and serve for life, they are not accountable to the people in the same way as presidents and members of Congress. Nevertheless, they have an extraordinary power—the power of judicial review. Judicial review allows an unelected branch of government to overturn the laws and actions of the elected branches of government—Congress and the president. This authority by the judicial branch is questionable in a democracy, where the people are supposed to have the final say. The Supreme Court first held an act of Congress unconstitutional in 1803, and then did not hold another one unconstitutional until 1857. Since that time, however, the Court has struck down 165 congressional laws, slightly more than one per year, with seven laws struck down in 1935 alone, during the height of the Court's battle with the New Deal. Since 1986, the Court has struck down nearly three times as many state and municipal laws (97) as federal laws (36).[53]

Given the undemocratic nature of judicial review, politicians frequently decry **judicial activists**, judges who go beyond what the law requires and seek to impose their own policy preferences on society through their judicial decisions. These critics insist that judges should act with **judicial restraint**,

AP Photo/Rick Bowmer

When oral arguments in the *Gratz* and *Grutter* cases were being heard before the Court on April 3, 2010, the National Association for the Advancement of Colored People (NAACP) and other interest groups rallied in support of affirmative action. While Supreme Court justices are not directly responsive to public opinion, the same factors that influence the public (war, crime, the economy) also influence the justices, leading to a general congruence between public opinion and the justices' decisions.

that is, judges should respect the decisions of other branches, or, through the concept of precedent, the decisions of earlier judges.

Contemporary research suggests that justices respect the decisions of legislatures and earlier judges when those decisions are consistent with the justices' ideology. Thus, for example, liberal justices such as Ginsburg or Stevens overwhelmingly vote to uphold liberal precedents[54] or federal laws favored by liberals.[55] But when conservative precedents are under consideration, or laws favored by conservatives, liberal justices are more than willing to strike them down. Similarly, conservative justices such as Scalia or Thomas overwhelmingly vote to uphold conservative precedents or the constitutionality of federal laws favored by conservatives. But when precedents are liberal in direction, or when liberals favor the laws under review, conservative justices are more than willing to strike them down. The vast majority of justices, however, are restrained toward laws and precedents that they agree with ideologically, but are quite willing to overturn laws and precedents that they

Is judicial review a problem for democracy?

How do elections affect judicial decisions? Should they?

are distant from ideologically. Elections have consequences, and one of the consequences of presidential elections is that the president gets to choose which judges will make judicial policy in the United States.

The Judiciary and Democracy

The judicial system of the United States promotes the equal right of participation by allowing a single individual who has been harmed by a law to challenge its constitutionality. Those who have financial resources or who can find support from organized interests may fare better than those who have to act on their own. The action may not be successful. Nevertheless, the judiciary provides a separate gateway to the political system, one that is different in kind from the gateway to the legislative or executive branch.

Representative democracy requires that government be accountable and responsive to the public. Yet the judicial branch is not accountable in any meaningful way: even if the public is dissatisfied with judges' decisions, judges cannot be removed from office. Yet this does not mean that the Court is not responsive to the public or to the public's representatives. This responsiveness can happen through four different gateways.

The first gateway is through the electoral process.[56] During the 1960s, the Warren Court made a series of decisions on contentious issues such as criminal procedure and religious freedom that were significantly more liberal than many Americans might have preferred. Richard Nixon campaigned for president in 1968 with promises to appoint justices who were significantly more pro-police and significantly less pro-defendant. Nixon won the election and, in the course of his first term, appointed four justices, all of whom were considerably more conservative on criminal procedure than the rest of the Court. The result: a conservative shift in Supreme Court decisions in criminal cases that mirrored public preferences.

Second, in cases where the Court is unresponsive to congressional preferences, Congress can threaten the Court's institutional authority. During the Civil War, Congress took away the Court's appellate jurisdiction over *habeas corpus* appeals. During Franklin Roosevelt's presidency, Roosevelt threatened to dilute the Court by adding six new members. In both cases, the Court backed down and responded favorably to congressional (and thus, presumably, public) preferences.

The third gateway is through current events, which can move public opinion and judges' behavior in the same direction. Immediately following the terrorist attacks of September 11, 2001,

FOCUS QUESTIONS

- Why is the apparently simple requirement of providing "equal protection of the laws" in fact more difficult than it seems?

- In what ways do the federal courts lack traditional means of accountability?

- How are courts, nevertheless, responsive?

- Do citizens have equal access to the justice system? Does the justice system treat them equally?

- Is the judiciary a gate or a gateway to democracy?

Americans were increasingly willing to allow the government to examine personal mail, Internet activity, and the like (see Chapter 6, Public Opinion), and judges moved in the same direction. And as society became more progressive on women's rights or other issues, judges, who are members of that society, became more progressive on those issues, too.

Fourth, judges might believe that they have an obligation to rule consistently with public opinion, even if they are not subject to electoral sanctions. It is probably no accident that the Supreme Court's split decision in the Michigan affirmative action cases reflected America's ambivalence about whether equality meant treating everybody exactly the same, or whether, to promote equality of outcomes, underrepresented groups should be given advantages in admissions. Justice O'Connor, who split the difference over what can be done in the name of equal protection in the *Gratz* and *Grutter* cases, has spoken often about the need of the Supreme Court not to vary too far from public preferences.

But this argument cuts both ways. As Justice Robert Jackson declared in a case striking down mandatory flag salutes, "The very purpose of a Bill of Rights was to withdraw certain subjects from the vicissitudes of political controversy, to place them beyond the reach of majorities and officials and to establish them as legal principles to be applied by the courts. One's right to life, liberty, and property, to free speech, a free press, freedom of worship and assembly, and other fundamental rights may not be submitted to vote; they depend on the outcome of no elections."[57] If justices are responsive, it is not because the Constitution's framework encourages it; it is because they choose to be.

GATEWAYS TO LEARNING

Top Ten to Take Away

1. The American legal system is based on the English system in following an adversary process, guaranteeing a right to trial by jury, and depending on common law in the absence of statutory authority. (pp. 494–496)

2. The Constitution established the Supreme Court. Congress has created federal district courts and courts of appeal. The Supreme Court has both original jurisdiction and appellate jurisdiction. (pp. 496–497)

3. Through the power of judicial review, established in *Marbury v. Madison,* the Supreme Court has the authority to declare laws and executive actions unconstitutional, and thus void. In this decision, and others, the Marshall court set the United States on the path to a strong and unified nation. (pp. 497–498)

4. Through the Court's history, its interpretations have expanded, then contracted, and once again expanded national powers, especially with regard to economic regulation. After a long and slow start it has also moved, fairly consistently, toward greater protections of equality. (pp. 498–504)

5. The president appoints federal judges with the advice and consent of the Senate. The higher the court, the more likely the Senate is to scrutinize nominees and refuse consent, on the basis of a nominee's ideology or qualifications or both. (pp. 504–506)

6. The Supreme Court, which once contained only white, male Protestants, has increasingly diversified with respect to religion, race, and gender. This more equal access to the Supreme Court may also make the Court more responsive to an increasingly diverse nation. (pp. 506–509)

7. District courts conduct civil and criminal trials, while courts of appeal hear appeals from the district courts. Cases from the courts of appeal can be appealed to the Supreme Court. (pp. 509–515)

8. Supreme Court decisions are made by a majority, though the justices sometimes write concurring opinions that agree with the majority but give a different rationale. The minority who disagree may write dissents. (pp. 515–521)

9. Judicial policy making can be explained by both legal and extralegal approaches, with legal approaches having more sway at lower levels and extralegal approaches at higher levels, where judicial activism can be problematic for a democracy. (pp. 521–528)

10. Although the Supreme Court is not directly accountable to the public, it is to some degree responsive to public opinion. (pp. 528–529)

A full narrative summary of the chapter is on the book's website.

Ten to Test Yourself

1. Why does common law require a system of precedent?

2. What is the federal courts' jurisdiction?

3. What is judicial review?

4. Describe the broad trends and eras in Supreme Court rulings over the nation's history.

5. Describe the current federal judicial system.

6. Why was the Supreme Court's ruling in *Cohens v. Virginia* crucial to national unity?

7. What are the most important determinants of a senator's vote for or against a Supreme Court nominee?

8. In what way is judicial review problematic for a representative government?

9. How has the Supreme Court acted in response to attacks on it by Congress or the president?

10. What guidance has the Court provided on affirmative action?

More review questions and answers are on the book's website.

Terms **to Know and Use**

THE DECLARATION OF
INDEPENDENCE

In Congress, July 4, 1776

The Unanimous Declaration of the Thirteen United States of America

When, in the course of human events, it becomes necessary for one people to dissolve the political bands which have connected them with another, and to assume, among the powers of the earth, the separate and equal station to which the laws of nature and of nature's God entitle them, a decent respect to the opinions of mankind requires that they should declare the causes which impel them to the separation.

We hold these truths to be self-evident: That all men are created equal; that they are endowed by their Creator with certain unalienable rights; that among these are life, liberty, and the pursuit of happiness; that, to secure these rights, governments are instituted among men, deriving their just powers from the consent of the governed; that whenever any form of government becomes destructive of these ends, it is the right of the people to alter or to abolish it, and to institute new government, laying its foundation on such principles, and organizing its powers in such form, as to them shall seem most likely to effect their safety and happiness. Prudence, indeed, will dictate that governments long established should not be changed for light and transient causes; and accordingly all experience hath shown that mankind are more disposed to suffer, while evils are sufferable, than to right themselves by abolishing the forms to which they are accustomed. But when a long train of abuses and usurpations, pursuing invariably the same object, evinces a design to reduce them under absolute despotism, it is their right, it is their duty, to throw off such government, and to provide new guards for their future security. Such has been the patient sufferance of these colonies; and such is now the necessity which constrains them to alter their former systems of government. The history of the present King of Great Britain is a history of repeated injuries and usurpations, all having in direct object the establishment of an absolute tyranny over these states. To prove this, let facts be submitted to a candid world.

He has refused to assent to laws, the most wholesome and necessary for the public good.

He has forbidden his governors to pass laws of immediate and pressing importance, unless suspended in their operation till his assent should be obtained; and, when so suspended, he has utterly neglected to attend to them.

He has refused to pass other laws for the accommodation of large districts of people, unless those people would relinquish the right of representation in the legislature, a right inestimable to them, and formidable to tyrants only.

He has called together legislative bodies at places unusual, uncomfortable, and distant from the depository of their public records, for the sole purpose of fatiguing them into compliance with his measures.

He has dissolved representative houses repeatedly, for opposing, with manly firmness, his invasions on the rights of the people.

He has refused for a long time, after such dissolutions, to cause others to be elected; whereby the legislative powers, incapable of annihilation, have returned to the people at large for their exercise; the state remaining, in the mean time, exposed to all dangers of invasions from without and convulsions within.

He has endeavored to prevent the population of these states; for that purpose obstructing the laws for naturalization of foreigners; refusing to pass others to encourage their migration hither, and raising the conditions of new appropriations of lands.

He has obstructed the administration of justice, by refusing his assent to laws for establishing judiciary powers.

He has made judges dependent on his will alone, for the tenure of their offices, and the amount and payment of their salaries.

He has erected a multitude of new offices, and sent hither swarms of officers to harass our people and eat out their substance.

He has kept among us, in times of peace, standing armies, without the consent of our legislatures.

He has affected to render the military independent of, and superior to, the civil power.

He has combined with others to subject us to a jurisdiction foreign to our constitution, and unacknowledged by our laws, giving his assent to their acts of pretended legislation:

For quartering large bodies of armed troops among us:

For protecting them, by a mock trial, from punishment for any murders which they should commit on the inhabitants of these states;

For cutting off our trade with all parts of the world;

For imposing taxes on us without our consent;

For depriving us, in many cases, of the benefits of trial by jury;

For transporting us beyond seas, to be tried for pretended offenses;

For abolishing the free system of English laws in a neighboring province, establishing therein an arbitrary government, and enlarging its boundaries, so as to render it at once an example and fit instrument for introducing the same absolute rule into these colonies;

For taking away our charters, abolishing our more valuable laws, and altering fundamentally the forms of our governments;

For suspending our own legislatures, and declaring themselves invested with power to legislate for us in all cases whatsoever.

He has abdicated government here, by declaring us out of his protection and waging war against us.

He has plundered our seas, ravaged our coasts, burned our towns, and destroyed the lives of our people.

He is at this time transporting large armies of foreign mercenaries to complete the works of death, desolation, and tyranny already begun with circumstances of cruelty and perfidy scarcely paralleled in the most barbarous ages, and totally unworthy the head of a civilized nation.

He has constrained our fellow-citizens, taken captive on the high seas, to bear arms against their country, to become the executioners of their friends and brethren, or to fall themselves by their hands.

He has excited domestic insurrections among us, and has endeavored to bring on the inhabitants of our frontiers the merciless Indian savages, whose known rule of warfare is an undistinguished destruction of all ages, sexes, and conditions.

In every stage of these oppressions we have petitioned for redress in the most humble terms; our repeated petitions have been answered only by repeated injury. A prince, whose character is thus marked by every act which may define a tyrant, is unfit to be the ruler of a free people.

Nor have we been wanting in our attentions to our British brethren. We have warned them, from time to time, of attempts by their legislature to extend an unwarrantable jurisdiction over us. We have reminded them of the circumstances of our emigration and settlement here. We have appealed to their native justice and magnanimity; and we have conjured them, by the ties of our common kindred, to disavow these usurpations, which would inevitably interrupt our connections and correspondence. They, too, have been deaf to the voice of justice and of consanguinity. We must, therefore, acquiesce in the necessity which denounces our separation, and hold them, as we hold the rest of mankind, enemies in war, in peace friends.

We, therefore, the representatives of the United States of America, in General Congress assembled, appealing to the Supreme Judge of the world for the rectitude of our intentions, do, in the name and by the authority of the good people of these colonies, solemnly publish and declare, that these United Colonies are, and of right ought to be, FREE AND INDEPENDENT STATES; that they are absolved from all allegiance to the British crown, and that all political connection between them and the state of Great Britain is, and ought to be, totally dissolved; and that, as free and independent states, they have full power to levy war, conclude peace, contract alliances, establish commerce, and do all other acts and things which independent states may of right do. And for the support of this declaration, with a firm reliance on the protection of Divine Providence, we mutually pledge to each other our lives, our fortunes, and our sacred honor.

John Hancock, *President and delegate from Massachusetts*

Georgia
Button Gwinnett
Lyman Hall
George Walton
North Carolina
William Hooper
Joseph Hewes
John Penn
South Carolina
Edward Rutledge
Thomas Heyward Jr.
Thomas Lynch Jr.
Arthur Middleton
Maryland
Samuel Chase
William Paca
Thomas Stone
Charles Carroll of Carrollton
Virginia
George Wythe
Richard Henry Lee
Thomas Jefferson
Benjamin Harrison
Thomas Nelson Jr.
Francis Lightfoot Lee
Carter Braxton
Pennsylvania
Robert Morris
Benjamin Rush
Benjamin Franklin
John Morton
George Clymer
James Smith
George Taylor

James Wilson
George Ross
Delaware
Caesar Rodney
George Read
Thomas McKean
New York
William Floyd
Philip Livingston
Francis Lewis
Lewis Morris
New Jersey
Richard Stockton
John Witherspoon
Francis Hopkinson
John Hart
Abraham Clark
New Hampshire
Josiah Bartlett
William Whipple
Matthew Thornton
Massachusetts
Samuel Adams
John Adams
Robert Treat Paine
Elbridge Gerry
Rhode Island
Stephen Hopkins
William Ellery
Connecticut
Roger Sherman
Samuel Huntington
William Williams
Oliver Wolcott

THE CONSTITUTION
OF THE UNITED STATES

We the People of the United States, in Order to form a more perfect Union, establish Justice, insure domestic Tranquility, provide for the common defence, promote the general Welfare, and secure the Blessings of Liberty to ourselves and our Posterity, do ordain and establish this Constitution for the United States of America.

Article I.

Section 1.   All legislative Powers herein granted shall be vested in a Congress of the United States, which shall consist of a Senate and House of Representatives.

Section 2.   The House of Representatives shall be composed of Members chosen every second Year by the People of the several States, and the Electors in each State shall have the Qualifications requisite for Electors of the most numerous Branch of the State Legislature.

No Person shall be a Representative who shall not have attained to the age of twenty five Years, and been seven Years a Citizen of the United States, and who shall not, when elected, be an Inhabitant of that State in which he shall be chosen.

Changed by the Fourteenth Amendment, Section 2.

Representatives and direct Taxes shall be apportioned among the several States which may be included within this Union, according to their respective Numbers, which shall be determined by adding to the whole Number of free Persons, including those bound to Service for a Term of Years, and excluding Indians not taxed, three fifths of all other Persons. The actual Enumeration shall be made within three Years after the first Meeting of the Congress of the United States, and within every subsequent Term of ten Years, in such Manner as they shall by Law direct. The Number of Representatives shall not exceed one for every thirty Thousand, but each State shall have at Least one Representative; and until such enumeration shall be made, the State of New Hampshire shall be entitled to chuse three, Massachusetts eight, Rhode-Island and Providence Plantations one, Connecticut five, New-York six, New Jersey four, Pennsylvania eight, Delaware one, Maryland six, Virginia ten, North Carolina five, South Carolina five, and Georgia three.

When vacancies happen in the Representation from any State, the Executive Authority thereof shall issue Writs of Election to fill such Vacancies.

The House of Representatives shall chuse their Speaker and other Officers; and shall have the sole Power of Impeachment.

Section 3.   The Senate of the United States shall be composed of two Senators from each State, chosen by the Legislature thereof, for six Years; and each Senator shall have one Vote.

Changed by the Seventeenth Amendment.

Immediately after they shall be assembled in Consequence of the first Election, they shall be divided as equally as may be into three Classes. The Seats of the Senators of the first class shall be vacated at the Expiration of the second Year, of the second Class at the Expiration of the fourth Year, and of the third Class at the Expiration of the sixth Year, so that one third may be chosen every second Year; and if Vacancies happen by Resignation, or otherwise, during the Recess of the Legislature of any State, the Executive thereof may make temporary Appointments until the next Meeting of the Legislature, which shall then fill such Vacancies.

Changed by the Seventeenth Amendment.

No Person shall be a Senator who shall not have attained to the Age of thirty Years, and been nine Years a Citizen of the United States, and who shall not, when elected, be an Inhabitant of that State for which he shall be chosen.

The Vice President of the United States shall be President of the Senate, but shall have no Vote, unless they be equally divided.

The Senate shall chuse their other Officers, and also a President pro tempore, in the Absence of the Vice President, or when he shall exercise the Office of President of the United States.

The Senate shall have the sole Power to try all Impeachments. When sitting for that Purpose, they shall be on Oath or Affirmation. When the President of the United States is tried the Chief Justice shall preside: And no Person shall be convicted without the Concurrence of two thirds of the Members present.

Judgment in Cases of Impeachment shall not exceed further than to removal from Office, and disqualification to hold and enjoy any Office of honor, Trust or Profit under the United States: but the Party convicted shall nevertheless be liable and subject to Indictment, Trial, Judgment and Punishment, according to Law.

Section 4.   The Times, Places and Manner of holding Elections for Senators and Representatives, shall be prescribed in each State by the Legislature thereof; but the Congress may at any time by Law make or alter such Regulations, except as to the Places of chusing Senators.

The Congress shall assemble at least once in every Year, and such Meeting shall be on the first Monday in December, unless they shall by Law appoint a different Day.

Changed by the Twentieth Amendment, Section 2.

Section 5.   Each House shall be the Judge of the Elections, Returns and Qualifications of its own Members, and a Majority of each shall constitute a Quorum to do Business; but a smaller number may adjourn from day to day, and may be authorized to compel the Attendance of absent Members, in such Manner, and under such Penalties as each House may provide.

Each House may determine the Rules of its Proceedings, punish its Members for disorderly Behaviour, and, with the Concurrence of two thirds, expel a Member.

Each House shall keep a Journal of its Proceedings, and from time to time publish the same, excepting such Parts as may in their Judgment require Secrecy; and the Yeas and Nays of the Members of either House on any question shall, at the Desire of one fifth of those Present, be entered on the Journal.

Neither House, during the Session of Congress, shall, without the Consent of the other, adjourn for more than three days, nor to any other Place than that in which the two Houses shall be sitting.

Amplified by the Twenty-Seventh Amendment.

Section 6. The Senators and Representatives shall receive a Compensation for their Services, to be ascertained by Law, and paid out of the Treasury of the United States. They shall in all Cases, except Treason, Felony and Breach of the Peace, be privileged from Arrest during their Attendance at the Session of their respective Houses, and in going to and returning from the same; and for any Speech or Debate in either House, they shall not be questioned in any other Place.

No Senator or Representative shall, during the Time for which he was elected, be appointed to any civil Office under the Authority of the United States, which shall have been created, or the Emoluments whereof shall have been encreased during such time; and no Person holding any Office under the United States, shall be a Member of either House during his Continuance in Office.

Section 7. All Bills for raising Revenue shall originate in the House of Representatives; but the Senate may propose or concur with Amendments as on other Bills.

Every Bill which shall have passed the House of Representatives and the Senate, shall, before it become a Law, be presented to the President of the United States; If he approve he shall assign it, but if not he shall return it, with his Objections to that House in which it shall have originated, who shall enter the Objections at large on their Journal, and proceed to reconsider it. If after such Reconsideration two thirds of that House shall agree to pass the Bill, it shall be sent, together with the Objections, to the other House, by which it shall likewise be reconsidered, and if approved by two thirds of that House, it shall become a Law. But in all such Cases the Votes of both Houses shall be determined by yeas and Nays, and the Names of the Persons voting for and against the Bill shall be entered on the Journal of each House respectively. If any Bill shall not be returned by the President within ten Days (Sundays excepted) after it shall have been presented to him, the Same shall be a Law, in like Manner, as if he had signed it, unless the Congress by their Adjournment prevent its Return, in which Case it shall not be a Law.

Every Order, Resolution, or Vote to which the Concurrence of the Senate and House of Representatives may be necessary (except on a question of Adjournment) shall be presented to the President of the United States; and before the Same shall take Effect, shall be approved by him, or being disapproved by him, shall be repassed by two thirds of the Senate and House of Representatives, according to the Rules and Limitations prescribed in the Case of a Bill.

Section 8. The Congress shall have Power To lay and Collect Taxes, Duties, Imposts and Excises, to pay the Debts and provide for the common Defence and general Welfare of the United States; but all Duties, Imposts and Excises shall be uniform throughout the United States.

To borrow Money on the credit of the United States;

To regulate Commerce with foreign Nations, and among the several States, and with the Indian Tribes;

To establish an uniform Rule of Naturalization, and uniform Laws on the subject of Bankruptcies throughout the United States;

To coin Money, regulate the Value thereof, and of foreign Coin, and fix the Standard of Weights and Measures;

To provide for the Punishment of counterfeiting the Securities and current Coin of the United States;

To establish Post Offices and post Roads;

To promote the Progress of Science and useful Arts, by securing for limited Times to Authors and Inventors the exclusive Right to their respective Writings and Discoveries;

To constitute Tribunals inferior to the Supreme Court;

To define and punish Piracies and Felonies committed on the high Seas, and Offences against the Law of Nations;

To declare War, grant Letters of Marque and Reprisal, and make Rules concerning Captures on Land and Water;

To raise and support Armies, but no Appropriation of Money to that Use shall be for a longer Term than two Years;

To provide and maintain a Navy;

To make Rules for the Government and Regulation of the land and naval Forces;

To provide for calling forth the Militia to execute the Laws of the Union, suppress Insurrections and repel Invasions;

To provide for organizing, arming, and disciplining, the Militia, and for governing such Part of them as may be employed in the Service of the United

General welfare clause gives Congress the power to tax to provide for the general welfare.

Commerce clause gives Congress the power to regulate commerce with foreign nations, with Indian tribes, and among the various states.

States, reserving to the States respectively, the Appointment of the Officers, and the Authority of training the Militia according to the discipline prescribed by Congress;

To exercise exclusive Legislation in all Cases whatsoever, over such District (not exceeding ten Miles square) as may, by Cession of Particular States, and the Acceptance of Congress, become the Seat of the Government of the United States, and to exercise like Authority over all Places purchased by the Consent of the Legislature of the State in which the Same shall be, for the Erection of Forts, Magazines, Arsenals, dock-Yards and other needful Buildings;—And

Necessary and proper clause gives Congress the power to pass all laws necessary and proper to the powers enumerated in Section 8.

To make all Laws which shall be necessary and proper for carrying into Execution the foregoing Powers, and all other Powers vested by this Constitution in the Government of the United States, or in any Department or Officer thereof.

Section 9. The Migration or Importation of such Persons as any of the States now existing shall think proper to admit, shall not be prohibited by the Congress prior to the Year one thousand eight hundred and eight, but a Tax or duty may be imposed on such Importation, not exceeding ten dollars for each Person.

The Privilege of the Writ of Habeas Corpus shall not be suspended, unless when in Cases of Rebellion or Invasion the public Safety may require it.

No bill of Attainder or ex post facto Law shall be passed.

Changed by the Sixteenth Amendment.

No Capitation, or other direct, Tax shall be laid, unless in Proportion to the Census or Enumeration herein before directed to be taken.

No Tax or Duty shall be laid on Articles exported from any State.

No Preference shall be given by any Regulation of Commerce or Revenue to the Ports of one State over those of another; nor shall Vessels bound to, or from, one State, be obliged to enter, clear or pay Duties in another.

No Money shall be drawn from the Treasury, but in Consequence of Appropriations made by Law; and a regular Statement and Account of the Receipts and Expenditures of all public Money shall be published from time to time.

No Title of Nobility shall be granted by the United States: And no Person holding any Office of Profit or Trust under them, shall, without the Consent of the Congress, accept of any present, Emolument, Office, or Title, of any kind whatever, from any King, Prince, or foreign State.

Section 10. No State shall enter into any Treaty, Alliance, or Confederation; grant Letters of Marque and Reprisal; coin Money; emit Bills of Credit; make any Thing but gold and silver Coin a Tender in Payment of Debts; pass any Bill of Attainder, ex post facto Law, or Law impairing the Obligation of Contracts, or grant any Title of Nobility.

No State shall, without the Consent of the Congress, lay any Imposts or Duties on Imports or Exports, except what may be absolutely necessary for executing its inspection Laws; and the net Produce of all Duties and Imposts, laid by any State on Imports or Exports, shall be for the Use of the Treasury of the United States; and all such Laws shall be subject to the Revision and Control of the Congress.

No State shall, without the Consent of Congress, lay any Duty of Tonnage, keep Troops, or Ships of War in time of Peace, enter into any Agreement or Compact with another State, or with a foreign Power, or engage in War, unless actually invaded, or in such imminent Danger as will not admit of delay.

Article II.

Section 1.   The executive Power shall be vested in a President of the United States of America. He shall hold his Office during the term of four Years, and, together with the Vice President, chosen for the same Term, be elected, as follows

Each State shall appoint, in such Manner as the Legislature thereof may direct, a Number of Electors, equal to the whole Number of Senators and Representatives to which the State may be entitled in the Congress: but no Senator or Representative, or Person holding an Office of Trust or Profit under the United States, shall be appointed an Elector.

The Electors shall meet in their respective States, and vote by Ballot for two Persons, of whom one at least shall not be an Inhabitant of the same State with them-selves. And they shall make a List of all the Persons voted for, and of the Number of Votes for each; which List they shall sign and certify, and transmit sealed to the Seat of the Government of the United States, directed to the President of the Senate. The President of the Senate shall, in the Presence of the Senate and House of Representatives, open all the Certificates, and the Votes shall then be counted. The Person having the greatest Number of Votes shall be the President, if such Number be a Majority of the whole Number of Electors appointed; and if there be more than one who have such Majority, and have an equal Number of Votes, then the House of Representatives shall immediately chuse by Ballot one of them for President; and if no Person have a Majority, then from the five highest on the List the said House shall in like Manner chuse the President. But in chusing the President, the Votes shall be taken by States, the Representation from each State having one Vote; a quorum for this Purpose shall consist of a Member or Members from two thirds of the States, and a Majority of all the States shall be necessary to a Choice. In every Case, after the Choice of the President, the Person having the greatest Number of Votes of the Electors shall be the Vice President. But if there should remain two or

Vesting clause gives the president the executive power.

Changed by the Twelfth Amendment.

more who have equal Votes, the Senate shall chuse from them by Ballot the Vice President.

The Congress may determine the Time of chusing the Electors, and the Day on which they shall give their Votes, which Day shall be the same throughout the United States.

No Person except a natural born Citizen, or a Citizen of the United States, at the time of the Adoption of this Constitution, shall be eligible to the Office of President; neither shall any person be eligible to that Office who shall not have attained to the Age of thirty five Years, and been fourteen Years a Resident within the United States.

Changed by the Twenty-Fifth Amendment.

In Case of the Removal of the President from Office, or of his Death, Resignation, or Inability to discharge the Powers and Duties of the said Office, the Same shall devolve on the Vice President, and the Congress may by Law provide for the Case of Removal, Death, Resignation or Inability, both of the President and Vice President, declaring what Officer shall then act as President, and such Officer shall act accordingly, until the Disability be removed, or a President shall be elected.

The President shall, at stated Times, receive for his Services, a Compensation, which shall neither be increased nor diminished during the Period for which he shall have been elected, and he shall not receive within that Period any other Emolument from the United States, or any of them.

Before he enter on the Execution of his Office, he shall take the following Oath or Affirmation:—"I do solemnly swear (or affirm) that I will faithfully execute the Office of President of the United States, and will to the best of my Ability, preserve, protect and defend the Constitution of the United States."

Section 2.   The President shall be Commander in Chief of the Army and Navy of the United States, and of the Militia of the several States, when called into the actual Service of the United States; he may require the Opinion, in writing, of the principal Officer in each of the executive Departments, upon any Subject relating to the Duties of their respective Offices, and he shall have Power to grant Reprieves and Pardons for Offences against the United States, except in Cases of Impeachment.

He shall have Power, by and with the Advice and Consent of the Senate, to make Treaties, provided two thirds of the Senators present concur; and he shall nominate, and by and with the Advice and Consent of the Senate, shall appoint Ambassadors, other public Ministers and Consuls, Judges of the supreme Court, and all other Officers of the United States, whose Appointments are not herein otherwise provided for, and which shall be established by Law: but the Congress may by Law vest the Appointment of such inferior Officers, as they think proper, in the President alone, in the Courts of Law, or in the Heads of Departments.

The President shall have Power to fill up all Vacancies that may happen during the Recess of the Senate, by granting Commissions which shall expire at the End of their next Session.

Section 3.   He shall from time to time give to the Congress Information of the State of the Union, and recommend to their Consideration such Measures as he shall judge necessary and expedient; he may, on extraordinary Occasions, convene both Houses, or either of them, and in Case of Disagreement between them, with Respect to the Time of Adjournment, he may adjourn them to such Time as he shall think proper; he shall receive Ambassadors and other public Ministers; he shall take Care that the Laws be faithfully executed, and shall Commission all the Officers of the United States.

> **Take care clause** requires the president to make sure that the laws are "faithfully executed."

Section 4.   The President, Vice President and all civil Officers of the United States, shall be removed from Office on Impeachment for, and Conviction of, Treason, Bribery, or other high Crimes and Misdemeanors.

Article III.

Section 1.   The judicial Power of the United States, shall be vested in one supreme Court, and in such inferior Courts as the Congress may from time to time ordain and establish. The Judges, both of the supreme and inferior Courts, shall hold their Offices during good Behaviour, and shall, at stated Times, receive for their Services, a Compensation, which shall not be diminished during their Continuance in Office.

Section 2.   The judicial Power shall extend to all Cases, in Law and Equity, arising under this Constitution, the Laws of the United States, and Treaties made, or which shall be made, under their Authority;—to all Cases affecting Ambassadors, other public Ministers and Consuls;—to all Cases of admiralty and maritime Jurisdiction;—to Controversies to which the United States shall be a Party;—to Controversies between two or more States;—between a State and Citizens of another State;—between Citizens of different States;— between Citizens of the same State claiming Lands under Grants of different States, and between a State, or the Citizens thereof, and foreign States, Citizens or Subjects.

> Changed by the Eleventh Amendment.

In all Cases affecting Ambassadors, other public Ministers and Consuls, and those in which a State shall be Party, the supreme Court shall have original Jurisdiction. In all the other Cases before mentioned, the supreme Court shall have appellate Jurisdiction, both as to Law and Fact, with such Exceptions, and under such Regulations as the Congress shall make.

The Trial of all Crimes, except in Cases of Impeachment, shall be by Jury; and such Trial shall be held in the State where the said Crimes shall have been committed; but when not committed within any State, the Trial shall be at such Place or Places as the Congress may by Law have directed.

Section 3.   Treason against the United States, shall consist only in levying War against them, or in adhering to their Enemies, giving them Aid and Comfort. No Person shall be convicted of Treason unless on the Testimony of two Witnesses to the same overt Act, or on Confession in open Court.

The Congress shall have Power to declare the Punishment of Treason, but no Attainder of Treason shall work Corruption of Blood, or Forfeiture except during the Life of the Person attainted.

Article IV.

Full faith and credit clause requires states to accept civil proceedings from other states.

Section 1.   Full Faith and Credit shall be given in each State to the public Acts, Records, and judicial Proceedings of every other State. And the Congress may by general Laws prescribe the Manner in which such Acts, Records and Proceedings shall be proved, and the Effect thereof.

Privileges and immunities clause requires states to treat nonresidents equally to residents.

Section 2.   The Citizens of each State shall be entitled to all Privileges and Immunities of Citizens in the several States.

A person charged in any State with Treason, Felony, or other Crime, who shall flee from Justice, and be found in another State, shall on Demand of the executive Authority of the State from which he fled, be delivered up, to be removed to the State having Jurisdiction of the Crime.

Fugitive slave clause required states to return runaway slaves; negated by the Thirteenth Amendment.

No Person held to Service or Labour in one State, under the Laws thereof, escaping into another, shall, in Consequence of any Law or Regulation therein, be discharged from such Service or Labour, but shall be delivered up on Claim of the Party to whom such Service or Labour may be due.

Section 3.   New States may be admitted by the Congress into this Union; but no new State shall be formed or erected within the Jurisdiction of any other State; nor any State be formed by the Junction of two or more States, or Parts of States, without the Consent of the Legislatures of the States concerned as well as of the Congress.

The Congress shall have Power to dispose of and make all needful Rules and Regulations respecting the Territory or other Property belonging to the United States; and nothing in this Constitution shall be so construed as to Prejudice any Claims of the United States, or of any particular State.

Guarantee clause provides a federal government guarantee that the states will have a republican form of government.

Section 4.   The United States shall guarantee to every State in this Union a Republican Form of Government, and shall protect each of them against Invasion; and on Application of the Legislature, or of the Executive (when the Legislature cannot be convened) against domestic Violence.

Article V.

The Congress, whenever two thirds of both Houses shall deem it necessary, shall propose Amendments to this Constitution, or, on the Application of the Legislatures of two thirds of the several States, shall call a Convention for proposing Amendments, which, in either Case, shall be valid to all Intents and Purposes, as Part of this Constitution, when ratified by the Legislatures of three fourths of the several States, or by Conventions in three fourths thereof, as the one or the other Mode of Ratification may be proposed by the Congress; Provided that no Amendment which may be made prior to the Year One thousand eight hundred and eight shall in any Manner after the first and fourth Clauses in the Ninth Section of the first Article; and that no State, without its Consent, shall be deprived of its equal Suffrage in the Senate.

Article VI.

All Debts contracted and Engagements entered into, before the Adoption of this Constitution, shall be as valid against the United States under this Constitution, as under the Confederation.

This Constitution, and the Laws of the United States which shall be made in Pursuance thereof; and all Treaties made, or which shall be made, under the Authority of the United States, shall be the Supreme Law of the Land; and the Judges in every State shall be bound thereby, any Thing in the Constitution or Laws of any State to the Contrary notwithstanding.

Supremacy clause makes federal law supreme over state laws.

The Senators and Representatives before mentioned, and the Members of the several State Legislatures, and all executive and judicial Officers, both of the United States and of the several States, shall be bound by Oath or Affirmation, to support this Constitution; but no religious Test shall ever be required as a Qualification to any Office or public Trust under the United States.

Article VII.

The Ratification of the Conventions of nine States, shall be sufficient for the Establishment of this Constitution between the States so ratifying the Same.

Done in Convention by the Unanimous Consent of the States present the Seventeenth Day of September in the Year of our Lord one thousand seven hundred and Eighty seven and of the Independence of the United States of America the Twelfth In witness whereof We have hereunto subscribed our Names,

George Washington, *President and deputy from Virginia*

Delaware
George Read
Gunning Bedford Jr.
John Dickinson
Richard Bassett
Jacob Broom

Maryland
James McHenry
Daniel of St. Thomas Jennifer
Daniel Carroll

Virginia
John Blair
James Madison Jr.

North Carolina
William Blount
Richard Dobbs Spaight
Hugh Williamson

South Carolina
John Rutledge
Charles Cotesworth Pinckney
Charles Pinckney
Pierce Butler

Georgia
William Few
Abraham Baldwin

New Hampshire
John Langdon
Nicholas Gilman

Massachusetts
Nathaniel Gorham
Rufus King

Connecticut
William Samuel Johnson
Roger Sherman

New York
Alexander Hamilton

New Jersey
William Livingston
David Brearley
William Paterson
Jonathan Dayton

Pennsylvania
Benjamin Franklin
Thomas Mifflin
Robert Morris
George Clymer
Thomas FitzSimons
Jared Ingersoll
James Wilson
Gouverneur Morris

[The first ten amendments, known as the Bill of Rights, were ratified in 1791.]

First Amendment

Establishment clause prohibits governmental establishment of religion.

Free exercise clause protects the free exercise of religion.

Congress shall make no law respecting an establishment of religion, or prohibiting the free exercise thereof; or abridging the freedom of speech, or of the press; or the right of the people peaceably to assemble, and to petition the Government for a redress of grievances.

Second Amendment

A well regulated Militia, being necessary to the security of a free State, the right of the people to keep and bear Arms, shall not be infringed.

Third Amendment

No Soldier shall, in time of peace be quartered in any house, without the consent of the Owner, nor in time of war, but in a manner prescribed by law.

Fourth Amendment

The right of the people to be secure in their persons, houses, papers, and effects, against unreasonable searches and seizures, shall not be violated, and no Warrants shall issue, but upon probable cause, supported by Oath or affirmation, and particularly describing the place to be searched, and the persons or things to be seized.

Fifth Amendment

No person shall be held to answer for a capital, or otherwise infamous crime, unless on a presentment or indictment of a Grand Jury, except in cases arising in the land or naval forces, or in the Militia, when in actual service in time of War or public danger; nor shall any person be subject for the same offence to be twice put in jeopardy of life or limb; nor shall be compelled in any criminal case to be a witness against himself, nor be deprived of life, liberty, or property, without due process of law, nor shall private property be taken for public use, without just compensation.

Double jeopardy clause prevents the government from retrying someone for a crime after an initial acquittal.

Self-incrimination clause protects people from having to testify against themselves at trial.

Due process clause prevents the federal government from denying any person due process of law.

Takings clause requires just compensation when the government seizes private property for a public purpose.

Sixth Amendment

In all criminal prosecutions, the accused shall enjoy the right to a speedy and public trial, by an impartial jury of the State and district wherein the crime shall have been committed, which district shall have been previously ascertained by law, and to be informed of the nature and cause of the accusation; to be confronted with the witnesses against him; to have compulsory process for obtaining witnesses in his favor, and to have Assistance of Counsel for his defence.

Seventh Amendment

In Suits at common law, where the value in controversy shall exceed twenty dollars, the right of trial by jury shall be preserved, and no fact tried by a jury, shall be otherwise reexamined in any Court of the United States, than according to the rules of the common law.

Eighth Amendment

Excessive bail shall not be required, nor excessive fines imposed, nor cruel and unusual punishments inflicted.

Cruel and unusual punishment clause prohibits cruel and unusual punishments.

Ninth Amendment

The enumeration in the Constitution, of certain rights, shall not be construed to deny or disparage others retained by the people.

Tenth Amendment

The powers not delegated to the United States by the Constitution, nor prohibited by it to the States, are reserved to the States respectively, or to the people.

Reserve powers clause reserves to the states or to the people those powers not delegated to United States.

Eleventh Amendment (1798)

The Judicial power of the United States shall not be construed to extend to any suit in law or equity, commenced or prosecuted against one of the United States by Citizens of another State, or by Citizens or Subjects of any Foreign State.

Twelfth Amendment (1804)

The Electors shall meet in their respective states and vote by ballot for President and Vice President, one of whom, at least, shall not be an inhabitant of the same state with themselves; they shall name in their ballots the person voted for as President, and in distinct ballots the person voted for as Vice President, and they shall make distinct lists of all persons voted for as President, and of all persons voted for as Vice President, and of the number of votes for each, which lists they shall sign and certify, and transmit sealed to the seat of the government of the United States, directed to the President of the Senate;—The President of the Senate shall, in the presence of the Senate and House of Representatives, open all the certificates and the votes shall then be counted;—The person having the greatest number of votes for President, shall be the President, if such number be a majority of the whole number of Electors appointed; and if no person have such majority, then from the persons having the highest numbers not exceeding three on the list of those voted for as President, the House of Representatives shall choose immediately, by ballot, the President. But in choosing the President, the votes shall be taken by states, the representation from each state having one vote; a quorum for this purpose shall consist of a member or members from two-thirds of the states, and a majority of all the states shall be necessary to a choice. And if the House of Representatives shall not choose a President whenever the right of choice shall devolve upon them, before the fourth day of March next following, then the Vice President shall act as President, as in the case of the death or other constitutional disability of the President.— The person having the greatest number of votes as Vice President, shall be the Vice President, if such number be a majority of the whole number of Electors appointed, and if no person have a majority, then from the two highest numbers on the list, the Senate shall choose the Vice President; a quorum for the purpose shall consist of two-thirds of the whole number of Senators, and a majority of the whole number shall be necessary to a choice. But no person constitutionally ineligible to the office of President shall be eligible to that of Vice President of the United States.

Changed by the Twentieth Amendment, Section 3.

Thirteenth Amendment (1865)

Section 1. Neither slavery nor involuntary servitude, except as a punishment for crime whereof the party shall have been duly convicted, shall exist within the United States, or any place subject to their jurisdiction.

Section 2.   Congress shall have power to enforce this article by appropriate legislation.

Fourteenth Amendment (1868)

Section 1.   All persons born or naturalized in the United States and subject to the jurisdiction thereof, are citizens of the United States and of the State wherein they reside. No State shall make or enforce any law which shall abridge the privileges or immunities of citizens of the United States; nor shall any State deprive any person of life, liberty, or property, without due process of law; nor deny to any person within its jurisdiction the equal protection of the laws.

Section 2.   Representatives shall be apportioned among the several States according to their respective numbers, counting the whole number of persons in each State, excluding Indians not taxed. But when the right to vote at any election for the choice of electors for President and Vice President of the United States, Representatives in Congress, the Executive and Judicial officers of a State, or the members of the Legislature thereof, is denied to any of the male inhabitants of such State, being twenty-one years of age, and citizens of the United States, or in any way abridged, except for participation in rebellion, or other crime, the basis of representation therein shall be reduced in the proportion which the number of such male citizens shall bear to the whole number of male citizens twenty-one years of age in such State.

Section 3.   No person shall be a Senator or Representative in Congress, or elector of President and Vice President, or hold any office, civil or military, under the United States, or under any State, who, having previously taken an oath, as a member of Congress, or as an officer of the United States, or as a member of any State legislature, or as an executive or judicial officer of any State, to support the Constitution of the United States, shall have engaged in insurrection or rebellion against the same, or given aid or comfort to the enemies thereof. But Congress may by a vote of two-thirds of each House, remove such disability.

Section 4.   The validity of the public debt of the United States, authorized by law, including debts incurred for payment of pensions and bounties for services in suppressing insurrection or rebellion, shall not be questioned. But neither the United States nor any State shall assume or pay any debt or obligation incurred in aid of insurrection or rebellion against the United States, or any claim for the loss or emancipation of any slave; but all such debts, obligations and claims shall be held illegal and void.

Section 5.   The Congress shall have power to enforce, by appropriate legislation, the provisions of this article.

Citizenship clause makes all persons born in the United States citizens of the United States and of the state in which they reside.

Privileges or immunities clause prohibits states from abridging certain fundamental rights.

Due process clause prevents state governments from denying any person due process of law.

Equal protection clause prevents states from denying any person the equal protection of the laws.

Changed by the Nineteenth and Twenty-Sixth Amendments.

Fifteenth Amendment (1870)

Section 1.   The right of citizens of the United States to vote shall not be denied or abridged by the United States or by any State on account of race, color, or previous condition of servitude.

Section 2.   The Congress shall have power to enforce this article by appropriate legislation.

Sixteenth Amendment (1913)

The Congress shall have power to lay and collect taxes on incomes, from whatever source derived, without apportionment among the several States, and without regard to any census or enumeration.

Seventeenth Amendment (1913)

The Senate of the United States shall be composed of two Senators from each State, elected by the people thereof, for six years; and each Senator shall have one vote. The electors in each State shall have the qualifications requisite for electors of the most numerous branch of the State legislatures.

When vacancies happen in the representation of any State in the Senate, the executive authority of such State shall issue writs of election to fill such vacancies: *Provided,* That the legislature of any State may empower the executive thereof to make temporary appointments until the people fill the vacancies by election as the legislature may direct.

This amendment shall not be so construed as to affect the election or term of any Senator chosen before it becomes valid as part of the Constitution.

Eighteenth Amendment (1919)

Repealed by the Twenty-First Amendment.

Section 1.   After one year from the ratification of this article the manufacture, sale, or transportation of intoxicating liquors within, the importation thereof into, or the exportation thereof from the United States and all territory subject to the jurisdiction thereof for beverage purposes is hereby prohibited.

Section 2.   The Congress and the several States shall have concurrent power to enforce this article by appropriate legislation.

Section 3.   This article shall be inoperative unless it shall have been ratified as an amendment to the Constitution by the legislatures of the several States, as provided in the Constitution, within seven years from the date of the submission hereof to the States by the Congress.

Nineteenth Amendment (1920)

The right of citizens of the United States to vote shall not be denied or abridged by the United States or by any State on account of sex.

Congress shall have power to enforce this article by appropriate legislation.

Twentieth Amendment (1933)

Section 1. The terms of the President and Vice President shall end at noon on the 20th day of January, and the terms of Senators and Representatives at noon on the 3rd day of January, of the years in which such terms would have ended if this article had not been ratified; and the terms of their successors shall then begin.

Section 2. The Congress shall assemble at least once in every year, and such meeting shall begin at noon on the 3d day of January, unless they shall by law appoint a different day.

Section 3. If, at the time fixed for the beginning of the term of the President, the President elect shall have died, the Vice President elect shall become President. If a President shall not have been chosen before the time fixed for the beginning of his term, or if the President elect shall have failed to qualify, then the Vice President elect shall act as President until a President shall have qualified; and the Congress may by law provide for the case wherein neither a President elect nor a Vice President elect shall have qualified, declaring who shall then act as President, or the manner in which one who is to act shall be selected, and such person shall act accordingly until a President or Vice President shall have qualified.

Section 4. The Congress may by law provide for the case of the death of any of the persons from whom the House of Representatives may choose a President whenever the right of choice shall have devolved upon them, and for the case of the death of any of the persons from whom the Senate may choose a Vice President whenever the right of choice shall have devolved upon them.

Section 5. Sections 1 and 2 shall take effect on the 15th day of October following the ratification of this article.

Section 6. This article shall be inoperative unless it shall have been ratified as an amendment to the Constitution by the legislatures of three-fourths of the several States within seven years from the date of its submission.

Twenty-First Amendment (1933)

Section 1. The eighteenth article of amendment to the Constitution of the United States is hereby repealed.

Section 2. The transportation or importation into any State, Territory, or possession of the United States for delivery or use therein of intoxicating liquors, in violation of the laws thereof, is hereby prohibited.

Section 3. This article shall be inoperative unless it shall have been ratified as an amendment to the Constitution by conventions in the several States, as provided in the Constitution, within seven years from the date of the submission hereof to the States by the Congress.

Twenty-Second Amendment (1951)

Section 1. No person shall be elected to the office of the President more than twice, and no person who has held the office of President, or acted as President, for more than two years of a term to which some other person was elected President shall be elected to the office of the President more than once. But this Article shall not apply to any person holding the office of President when this Article was proposed by the Congress, and shall not prevent any person who may be holding the office of President, or acting as President, during the term within which this Article becomes operative from holding the office of President or acting as President during the remainder of such term.

Section 2. This Article shall be inoperative unless it shall have been ratified as an amendment to the Constitution by the legislatures of three-fourths of the several States within seven years from the date of its submission to the States by the Congress.

Twenty-Third Amendment (1961)

Section 1. The District constituting the seat of Government of the United States shall appoint in such manner as the Congress may direct:

A number of electors of President and Vice President equal to the whole number of Senators and Representatives in Congress to which the District would be entitled if it were a State, but in no event more than the least populous State; they shall be in addition to those appointed by the States, but they shall be considered, for the purposes of the election of President and Vice President, to be electors appointed by a State; and they shall meet in the District and perform such duties as provided by the twelfth article of amendment.

Section 2. The Congress shall have power to enforce this article by appropriate legislation.

Twenth-Fourth Amendment (1964)

Section 1. The right of citizens of the United States to vote in any primary or other election for President or Vice President, for electors for President or Vice President, or for Senator or Representative in Congress, shall not be denied or abridged by the United States or any State by reason of failure to pay any poll tax or other tax.

Section 2. Congress shall have power to enforce this article by appropriate legislation.

Twenty-Fifth Amendment (1967)

Section 1. In case of the removal of the President from office or of his death or resignation, the Vice President shall become President.

Section 2.   Whenever there is a vacancy in the office of the Vice President, the President shall nominate a Vice President who shall take office upon confirmation by a majority vote of both Houses of Congress.

Section 3.   Whenever the President transmits to the President pro tempore of the Senate and the Speaker of the House of Representatives his written declaration that he is unable to discharge the powers and duties of his office, and until he transmits to them a written declaration to the contrary, such powers and duties shall be discharged by the Vice President as Acting President.

Section 4.   Whenever the Vice President and a majority of either the principal officers of the executive departments or of such other body as Congress may by law provide, transmit to the President pro tempore of the Senate and the Speaker of the House of Representatives their written declaration that the President is unable to discharge the powers and duties of his office, the Vice President shall immediately assume the powers and duties of the office as Acting President.

Thereafter, when the President transmits to the President pro tempore of the Senate and the Speaker of the House of Representatives his written declaration that no inability exists, he shall resume the powers and duties of his office unless the Vice President and a majority of either the principal officers of the executive department[s] or of such other body as Congress may by law provide, transmit within four days to the President pro tempore of the Senate and the Speaker of the House of Representatives their written declaration that the President is unable to discharge the powers and duties of his office. Thereupon Congress shall decide the issue, assembling within forty-eight hours for that purpose if not in session. If the Congress, within twenty-one days after receipt of the latter written declaration, or, if Congress is not in session, within twenty-one days after Congress is required to assemble, determines by two-thirds vote of both Houses that the President is unable to discharge the powers and duties of his office, the Vice President shall continue to discharge the same as Acting President; otherwise, the President shall resume the powers and duties of his office.

Twenty-Sixth Amendment (1971)

Section 1.   The right of citizens of the United States, who are eighteen years of age or older, to vote shall not be denied or abridged by the United States or by any State on account of age.

Section 2.   The Congress shall have power to enforce this article by appropriate legislation.

Twenty-Seventh Amendment (1992)

No law varying the compensation for the services of the Senators and Representatives shall take effect, until an election of Representatives shall have intervened.

10

James Madison

November 22, 1787

To the People of the State of New York

Among the numerous advantages promised by a well constructed Union, none deserves to be more accurately developed than its tendency to break and control the violence of faction. The friend of popular governments, never finds himself so much alarmed for their character and fate, as when he contemplates their propensity to this dangerous vice. He will not fail therefore to set a due value on any plan which, without violating the principles to which he is attached, provides a proper cure for it. The instability, injustice and confusion introduced into the public councils, have in truth been the mortal diseases under which popular governments have every where perished; as they continue to be the favorite and fruitful topics from which the adversaries to liberty derive their most specious declamations. The valuable improvements made by the American Constitutions on the popular models, both ancient and modern, cannot certainly be too much admired; but it would be an unwarrantable partiality, to contend that they have as effectually obviated the danger on this side as was wished and expected. Complaints are every where heard from our most considerate and virtuous citizens, equally the friends of public and private faith, and of public and personal liberty; that our governments are too unstable; that the public good is disregarded in the conflicts of rival parties; and that measures are too often decided, not according to the rules of justice, and the rights of the minor party; but by the superior force of an interested and over-bearing majority. However anxiously we may wish that these complaints had no foundation, the evidence of known facts will not permit us to deny that they are in some degree true. It will be found indeed, on a candid review of our situation, that some of the distresses under which we labor, have been erroneously charged on the operation of our governments; but it will be found, at the same time, that other causes will not alone account for many of our heaviest misfortunes; and particularly, for that prevailing and increasing distrust of public engagements, and alarm for private rights, which are echoed from one end of the continent to the other. These must be chiefly, if not wholly, effects of the unsteadiness and injustice, with which a factious spirit has tainted our public administrations.

By a faction I understand a number of citizens, whether amounting to a majority or minority of the whole, who are united and actuated by some common impulse of passion, or of interest, adverse to the rights of other citizens, or to the permanent and aggregate interests of the community.

There are two methods of curing the mischiefs of faction: the one, by removing its causes; the other, by controlling its effects.

There are again two methods of removing the causes of faction: the one by destroying the liberty which is essential to its existence; the other, by giving to every citizen the same opinions, the same passions, and the same interests.

It could never be more truly said than of the first remedy, that it is worse than the disease. Liberty is to faction, what air is to fire, an aliment without which it instantly expires. But it could not be a less folly to abolish liberty, which is essential to political life, because it nourishes faction, than it would be to wish the annihilation of air, which is essential to animal life, because it imparts to fire its destructive agency.

The second expedient is as impracticable, as the first would be unwise. As long as the reason of man continues fallible, and he is at liberty to exercise it, different opinions will be formed. As long as the connection subsists between his reason and his self-love, his opinions and his passions will have a reciprocal influence on each other; and the former will be objects to which the latter will attach themselves. The diversity in the faculties of men from which the rights of property originate, is not less an insuperable obstacle to a uniformity of interests. The protection of these faculties is the first object of Government. From the protection of different and unequal faculties of acquiring property, the possession of different degrees and kinds of property immediately results: and from the influence of these on the sentiments and views of the respective proprietors, ensues a division of the society into different interests and parties.

The latent causes of faction are thus sown in the nature of man; and we see them every where brought into different degrees of activity, according to the different circumstances of civil society. A zeal for different opinions concerning religion, concerning Government and many other points, as well of speculation as of practice; an attachment to different leaders ambitiously contending for pre-eminence and power; or to persons of other descriptions whose fortunes have been interesting to the human passions, have in turn divided mankind into parties, inflamed them with mutual animosity, and rendered them much more disposed to vex and oppress each other, than to co-operate for their common good. So strong is this propensity of mankind to fall into mutual animosities, that where no substantial occasion presents itself, the most frivolous and fanciful distinctions have been sufficient to kindle their unfriendly passions, and excite their most violent conflicts. But the most common and durable source of factions, has been the various and unequal distribution of property. Those who hold, and those who are without property, have ever formed distinct interests in society. Those who are creditors, and those who are debtors, fall under a like discrimination. A landed interest, a manufacturing interest, a mercantile interest, a monied interest, with many lesser interests, grow up of necessity in civilized nations, and divide them into different classes, actuated by different sentiments and views. The regulation of these various and interfering interests forms the principal task of modern Legislation, and involves the spirit of party and faction in the necessary and ordinary operations of Government.

No man is allowed to be a judge in his own cause; because his interest would certainly bias his judgment, and, not improbably, corrupt his integrity. With equal, nay with greater reason, a body of men, are unfit to be both judges and parties, at the same time; yet, what are many of the most important acts of legislation, but so many judicial determinations, not indeed concerning the rights of single persons, but concerning the rights of large bodies of citizens; and what are the different classes of legislators, but advocates and parties to the causes which they determine? Is a law proposed concerning private debts? It is a question to which the creditors are parties on one side, and the debtors on the other. Justice ought to hold the balance between them. Yet the parties are and must be themselves the judges; and the most numerous party, or, in other words, the most powerful faction must be expected to prevail. Shall domestic manufactures be encouraged, and in what degree, by restrictions on foreign manufactures? are questions which would be differently decided by the landed and the manufacturing classes; and probably by neither, with a sole regard to justice and the public good. The apportionment of taxes on the various descriptions of property, is an act which seems to require the most exact impartiality; yet, there is perhaps no legislative act in which greater opportunity and temptation are given to a predominant party, to trample on the rules of justice. Every shilling with which they over-burden the inferior number, is a shilling saved to their own pockets.

It is in vain to say, that enlightened statesmen will be able to adjust these clashing interests, and render them all subservient to the public good. Enlightened statesmen will not always be at the helm: Nor, in many cases, can such an adjustment be made at all, without taking into view indirect and remote considerations, which will rarely prevail over the immediate interest which one party may find in disregarding the rights of another, or the good of the whole.

The inference to which we are brought, is, that the *causes* of faction cannot be removed; and that relief is only to be sought in the means of controlling its *effects*.

If a faction consists of less than a majority, relief is supplied by the republican principle, which enables the majority to defeat its sinister views by regular vote: It may clog the administration, it may convulse the society; but it will be unable to execute and mask its violence under the forms of the Constitution. When a majority is included in a faction, the form of popular government on the other hand enables it to sacrifice to its ruling passion or interest, both the public good and the rights of other citizens. To secure the public good, and private rights, against the danger of such a faction, and at the same time to preserve the spirit and the form of popular government, is then the great object to which our enquiries are directed: Let me add that it is the great desideratum, by which alone this form of government can be rescued from the opprobrium under which it has so long labored, and be recommended to the esteem and adoption of mankind.

By what means is this object attainable? Evidently by one of two only. Either the existence of the same passion or interest in a majority at the same time, must be prevented; or the majority, having such co-existent passion or interest, must be rendered, by their number and local situation, unable to concert and carry into effect schemes of oppression. If the impulse and the opportunity be suffered to coincide, we well know that neither moral nor religious motives can be relied on as an adequate control. They are not found to be such on the injustice and violence of individuals, and lose their efficacy in proportion to the number combined together; that is, in proportion as their efficacy becomes needful.

From this view of the subject, it may be concluded, that a pure Democracy, by which I mean, a Society, consisting of a small number of citizens, who assemble and administer the Government in person, can admit of no cure for the mischiefs of faction. A common passion or interest will, in almost every case, be felt by a majority of the whole; a communication and concert results from the form of Government itself; and there is nothing to check the inducements to sacrifice the weaker party, or an obnoxious individual. Hence it is, that such Democracies have ever been spectacles of turbulence and contention; have ever been found incompatible with personal security, or the rights of property; and have in general been as short in their lives, as they have been violent in their deaths. Theoretic politicians, who have patronized this species of Government, have erroneously supposed, that by reducing mankind to a perfect equality in their political rights, they would, at the same time, be perfectly equalized and assimilated in their possessions, their opinions, and their passions.

A republic, by which I mean a government in which the scheme of representation takes place, opens a different prospect, and promises the cure for which we are seeking. Let us examine the points in which it varies from pure democracy, and we shall comprehend both the nature of the cure and the efficacy which it must derive from the union.

The two great points of difference, between a democracy and a republic, are, first, the delegation of the government, in the latter, to a small number of citizens, elected by the rest; secondly, the greater number of citizens, and greater sphere of country, over which the latter may be extended.

The effect of the first difference is, on the one hand, to refine and enlarge the public views, by passing them through the medium of a chosen body of citizens, whose wisdom may best discern the true interest of their country, and whose patriotism and love of justice, will be least likely to sacrifice it to temporary or partial considerations. Under such a regulation, it may well happen, that the public voice, pronounced by the representatives of the people, will be more consonant to the public good, than if pronounced by the people themselves, convened for the purpose. On the other hand the effect may be inverted. Men of factious tempers, of local prejudices, or of sinister designs, may by intrigue, by corruption, or by other means, first obtain the suffrages, and then betray the interest of the people. The question resulting is, whether small or extensive republics are most favorable to the election of proper guardians of the public weal, and it is clearly decided in favor of the latter by two obvious considerations.

In the first place, it is to be remarked that, however small the republic may be, the representatives must be raised to a certain number, in order to guard against the cabals of a few; and that however large it may be, they must be limited to a certain number, in order to guard against the confusion of a multitude. Hence, the number of representatives in the two cases not being in proportion to that of the constituents, and being proportionally greatest in the small republic, it follows, that if the proportion of fit characters be not less in the large than in the small republic, the former will present a greater option, and consequently a greater probability of a fit choice.

In the next place, as each Representative will be chosen by a greater number of citizens in the large than in the small Republic, it will be more difficult for unworthy candidates to practise with success the vicious arts, by which elections are too often carried; and the suffrages of the people being more free, will be more likely to center on men who possess the most attractive merit, and the most diffusive and established characters.

It must be confessed, that in this, as in most other cases, there is a mean, on both sides of which inconveniences will be found to lie. By enlarging too much the number of electors, you render the representatives too little acquainted with all their local circumstances and lesser interests; as by reducing it too much, you render him unduly attached to these, and too little fit to comprehend and pursue great and national objects. The Federal Constitution forms a happy combination in this respect; the great and aggregate interests being referred to the national, the local and particular, to the state legislatures.

The other point of difference is, the greater number of citizens and extent of territory which may be brought within the compass of Republican, than of Democratic Government; and it is this circumstance principally which renders factious combinations less to be dreaded in the former, than in the latter. The smaller the society, the fewer probably will be the distinct parties and interests composing it; the fewer the distinct parties and interests, the more frequently will a majority be found of the same party; and the smaller the number of individuals composing a majority, and the smaller the compass within which they are placed, the more easily will they concert and execute their plans of oppression. Extend the sphere, and you take in a greater variety of parties and interests; you make it less probable that a majority of the whole will have a common motive to invade the rights of other citizens; or if such a common motive exists, it will be more difficult for all who feel it to discover their own strength, and to act in unison with each other. Besides other impediments, it may be remarked, that where there is a consciousness of unjust or dishonorable purposes, communication is always checked by distrust, in proportion to the number whose concurrence is necessary.

Hence it clearly appears, that the same advantage, which a Republic has over a Democracy, in controlling the effects of factions, is enjoyed by a large over a small Republic—is enjoyed by the Union over the States composing it. Does this advantage consist in the substitution of Representatives, whose enlightened views and virtuous sentiments render them superior to local prejudices, and to schemes of injustice? It will not be denied, that the Representation of the Union will be most likely to possess these requisite endowments. Does it consist in the greater security afforded by a greater variety of parties, against the event of any one party being able to outnumber and oppress the rest? In an equal degree does the increased variety of parties, comprised within the Union, increase this security? Does it, in fine, consist in the greater obstacles opposed to the concert and accomplishment of the secret wishes of an unjust and interested majority? Here, again, the extent of the Union gives it the most palpable advantage.

The influence of factious leaders may kindle a flame within their particular States, but will be unable to spread a general conflagration through the other States: a religious sect, may degenerate into a political faction in a part of the Confederacy but the variety of sects dispersed over the entire face of it, must secure the national Councils against any danger from that source: a rage for paper money, for an abolition of debts, for an equal division of property, or for any other improper or wicked project, will be less apt to pervade the whole body of the Union, than a particular member of it; in the same proportion as such a malady is more likely to taint a particular county or district, than an entire State.

In the extent and proper structure of the Union, therefore, we behold a Republican remedy for the diseases most incident to Republican Government. And according to the degree of pleasure and pride, we feel in being Republicans, ought to be our zeal in cherishing the spirit, and supporting the character of Federalists.

PUBLIUS

51

James Madison

February 6, 1788

To the People of the State of New York

To what expedient then shall we finally resort for maintaining in practice the necessary partition of power among the several departments, as laid down in the constitution? The only answer that can be given is, that as all these exterior provisions are found to be inadequate, the defect must be supplied, by so contriving the interior structure of the government, as that its several constituent parts may, by their mutual relations, be the means of keeping each other in their proper places. Without presuming to undertake a full development of this important idea, I will hazard a few general observations, which may perhaps place it in a clearer light, and enable us to form a more correct judgment of the principles and structure of the government planned by the convention.

In order to lay a due foundation for that separate and distinct exercise of the different powers of government, which to a certain extent, is admitted on all hands to be essential to the preservation of liberty, it is evident that each department should have a will of its own; and consequently should be so constituted, that the members of each should have as little agency as possible in the appointment of the members of the others. Were this principle rigorously adhered to, it would require that all the appointments for the supreme executive, legislative, and judiciary magistracies, should be drawn from the same fountain of authority, the people, through channels, having no communication whatever with one another. Perhaps such a plan of constructing the several departments would be less difficult in practice than it may in contemplation appear. Some difficulties however, and some additional expense, would attend the execution of it. Some deviations therefore from the principle must be admitted. In the constitution of the judiciary department in particular, it might be inexpedient to insist rigorously on the principle; first, because peculiar qualifications being essential in the members, the primary consideration ought to be to select that mode of choice, which best secures these qualifications; secondly, because the permanent tenure by which the appointments are held in that department, must soon destroy all sense of dependence on the authority conferring them.

It is equally evident that the members of each department should be as little dependent as possible on those of the others, for the emoluments annexed to their offices. Were the executive magistrate, or the judges, not independent of the legislature in this particular, their independence in every other would be merely nominal.

But the great security against a gradual concentration of the several powers in the same department, consists in giving to those who administer each department, the necessary constitutional means, and personal motives, to resist encroachments of the others. The provision for defense must in this, as in all other cases, be made commensurate to the danger of attack. Ambition must be made to counteract ambition. The interest of the man must be connected with the constitutional rights of the place. It may be a reflection on human nature, that such devices should be necessary to control the abuses of government. But what is government itself but the greatest of all reflections on human nature? If men were angels, no government would be necessary. If angels were to govern men, neither external nor internal controls on government would be necessary. In framing a government which is to be administered by men over men, the great difficulty lies in this: You must first enable the government to control the governed; and in the next place, oblige it to control itself. A dependence on the people is no doubt the primary control on the government; but experience has taught mankind the necessity of auxiliary precautions.

This policy of supplying by opposite and rival interests, the defect of better motives, might be traced through the whole system of human affairs, private as well as public. We see it particularly displayed in all the subordinate distributions of power; where the constant aim is to divide and arrange the several offices in such a manner as that each may be a check on the other; that the private interest of every individual, may be a sentinel over the public rights. These inventions of prudence cannot be less requisite in the distribution of the supreme powers of the state.

But it is not possible to give each department an equal power of self defense. In republican government the legislative authority, necessarily, predominates. The remedy for this inconveniency is, to divide the legislature into different branches; and to render them by different modes of election, and different principles of action, as little connected with each other, as the nature of their common functions, and their common dependence on the society, will admit. It may even be necessary to guard against dangerous encroachments by still further precautions. As the weight of the legislative authority requires that it should be thus divided, the weakness of the executive may require, on the other hand, that it should be fortified. An absolute negative, on the legislature, appears at first view to be the natural defense with which the executive magistrate should be armed. But perhaps it would be neither altogether safe, nor alone sufficient. On ordinary occasions, it might not be exerted with the requisite firmness; and on extraordinary occasions, it might be perfidiously abused. May not this defect of an absolute negative be supplied, by some qualified connection between this weaker department, and the weaker branch of the stronger department, by which the latter may be led to support the constitutional rights of the former, without being too much detached from the rights of its own department?

If the principles on which these observations are founded be just, as I persuade myself they are, and they be applied as a criterion, to the several state constitutions, and to the federal constitution, it will be found, that if the latter does not perfectly correspond with them, the former are infinitely less able to bear such a test.

There are moreover two considerations particularly applicable to the federal system of America, which place that system in a very interesting point of view.

First. In a single republic, all the power surrendered by the people, is submitted to the administration of a single government; and usurpations are guarded against by a division of the government into distinct and separate departments. In the compound republic of America, the power surrendered by the people, is first divided between two distinct governments, and then the portion allotted to each, subdivided among distinct and separate departments. Hence a double security arises to the rights of the people. The different governments will control each other; at the same time that each will be controlled by itself.

Second. It is of great importance in a republic, not only to guard the society against the oppression of its rulers; but to guard one part of the society against the injustice of the other part. Different interests necessarily exist in different classes of citizens. If a majority be united by a common interest, the rights of the minority will be insecure. There are but two methods of providing against this evil: The one by creating a will in the community independent of the majority, that is, of the society itself, the other by comprehending in the society so many separate descriptions of citizens, as will render an unjust combination of a majority of the whole, very improbable, if not impracticable. The first method prevails in all governments possessing an hereditary or self appointed authority. This at best is but a precarious security; because a power independent of the society may as well espouse the unjust views of the major, as the rightful interests, of the minor party, and may possibly be turned against both parties. The second method will be exemplified in the federal republic of the United States. While all authority in it will be derived from and dependent on the society, the society itself will be broken into so many parts, interests and classes of citizens, that the rights of individuals or of the minority, will be in little danger from interested combinations of the majority. In a free government, the security for civil rights must be the same as for religious rights. It consists in the one case in the multiplicity of interests, and in the other, in the multiplicity of sects. The degree of security in both cases will depend on the number of interests and sects; and this may be presumed to depend on the extent of country and number of people comprehended under the same government. This view of the subject must particularly recommend a proper federal system to all the sincere and considerate friends of republican government: Since it shows that in exact proportion as the territory of the union may be formed into more circumscribed confederacies or states, oppressive combinations of a majority will be facilitated, the best security under the republican form, for the rights of every class of citizens, will be diminished; and consequently, the stability and independence of some member of the government, the only other security, must be proportionally increased. Justice is the end of government. It is the end of civil society. It ever has been, and ever will be pursued, until it be obtained, or until liberty be lost in the pursuit. In a society under the forms of which the stronger faction can readily unite and oppress the weaker, anarchy may as truly be said to reign, as in a state of nature where the weaker individual is not secured against the violence of the stronger: And as in the latter state even the stronger individuals are prompted by the uncertainty of their condition, to submit to a government which may protect the weak as well as themselves: So in the former state, will the more powerful factions or parties be gradually induced by a like motive, to wish for a government which will protect all parties, the weaker as well as the more powerful. It can be little doubted, that if the state of Rhode Island was separated from the confederacy, and left to itself, the insecurity of rights under the popular form of government within such narrow limits, would be displayed by such reiterated oppressions of factious majorities, that some power altogether independent of the people would soon be called for by the voice of the very factions whose misrule had proved the necessity of it. In the extended republic of the United States, and among the great variety of interests, parties and sects which it embraces, a coalition of a majority of the whole society could seldom take place on any other principles than those of justice and the general good; and there being thus less danger to a minor from the will of the major party, there must be less pretext also, to provide for the security of the former, by introducing into the government a will not dependent on the latter; or in other words, a will independent of the society itself. It is no less certain than it is important, notwithstanding the contrary opinions which have been entertained, that the larger the society, provided it lie within a practicable sphere, the more duly capable will be of self government. And happily for the *republican cause,* the practicable sphere may be carried to a very great extent, by a judicious modification and mixture of the *federal principle.*

Publius

ENDNOTES

Chapter 1

1. This story was compiled from Tim Craig and Michael D. Shear, "Allen Quip Provokes Outrage, Apology," *Washington Post,* August 15, 2006, A1; Fredrick Kunkle, "Fairfax Native Says Allen's Words Stung," *Washington Post,* August 25, 2006, B1; S. R. Sidarth, "I Am Macaca," *Washington Post,* November 12, 2006, B2; and telephone and e-mail interviews with S. R. Sidarth, December 25, 28, 2009, conducted for this textbook; chapter-opening quotation from December 25, 2009, interview.

2. International Social Survey Program, as cited in Russell Dalton, *The Good Citizen* (Washington, D.C.: CQ Press, 2007), 144; Morley Winograd and Michael D. Hais, *Millennial Makeover: MySpace, YouTube and the Future of American Politics* (New Brunswick, N.J.: Rutgers University Press, 2008), 260–63. The caption for the photo on page 6 is drawn from this source.

3. Dalton, *Good Citizen,* 153.

4. Larry Bartels, *Unequal Democracy* (Princeton: Princeton University Press, 2008); David Cay Johnston, "The Gap between Rich and Poor Grows in the United States," *New York Times,* March 29, 2007. The caption for the photo on page 7 is drawn from these sources and from census data.

5. Marc Hetherington, *Why Trust Matters* (Princeton: Princeton University Press, 2005).

6. Kerem Ozan Kalkan, Geoffrey C. Layman, and Eric M. Uslaner, "Attitudes Toward Muslims in Contemporary American Society," *Journal of Politics* 69 (2009): 847–62.

7. Charles Beard, *American Government and Politics* (New York: Macmillan Company, 1915), 18.

8. Edmund Burke, *Reflections on the Revolution in France,* in *The Portable Edmund Burke,* ed. Isaac Kramnick (New York: Viking, 1999), 32.

9. John Adams to John Taylor, April 15, 1814, in *The Political Writings of John Adams: Representative Selections,* ed. George Peek Jr. (New York: Hackett Publishing, 2003), 67.

10. Quoted in David McCullough, *John Adams* (New York: Simon and Schuster, 2001), 68.

11. See Josiah Ober, *Mass and Elite in Democratic Athens* (Princeton: Princeton University Press, 1991).

12. See Larry Bartels, *Unequal Democracy* (Princeton: Princeton University Press, 2008).

13. Harold Laswell, *Politics: Who Gets What, When, How* (New York: McGraw-Hill, 1936).

14. Bryan D. Jones and Frank M. Baumgartner, *The Politics of Attention* (Chicago: University of Chicago Press, 2005).

15. Winograd and Haas, *Millennial Makeover;* Morley Winograd and Michael D. Hais, "The Boomers Had Their Day: Make Way for the Millennials," *Washington Post,* February 3, 2008, B1, B5.

16. Social Security Administration, "A Summary of the 2009 Annual Reports," http://www.ssa.gov/OACT/TRSUM/index .html. The specific numbers are as follows: in 2008, the annual cost of Social Security benefits represented 4.4 percent of gross domestic product (GDP); by 2034, it is projected to increase to 6.2 percent of GDP—nearly a 50 percent jump.

17. USA Today, "Our View on the Cost of Education: Colleges Duck Tough Cuts, Keep Hiking Pay and Tuition," March 30, 2009, *USA Today,* http://blogs.usatoday.com/.

18. Darrell West et al., "Invisible: 1.4 Percent Coverage for Education Not Enough," December 2, 2009, *Brookings Institution,* http://www.brookings.edu/.

19. U.S. Census Bureau. "State and County QuickFacts," http:// www.census.gov/.

20. See http://www.freedomhouse.org/.

Chapter 2

1. This story was compiled from *USA Today,* May 8, 1992; e-mail interview with Gregory Watson, January 29, 2010, conducted for this textbook; chapter-opening quotation from interview.

2. Gordon S. Wood, *The American Revolution* (New York: Modern Library Chronicles, 2002), 39.

3. Edmund Burke, "Edmund Burke, Speech to the Electors of Bristol," Vol.1, Chap. 13, Document 7 in *The Founders' Constitution,* ed. Philip B. Kurland and Ralph Lerner.(Chicago: University of Chicago Press, 2000), http://press-pubs.uchicago .edu/founders/documents/v1ch13s7.html.

4. Robert Middlekauff, *The Glorious Cause* (New York: Oxford University Press, 1982), 231.

5. Thomas Paine, *Common Sense* (Independence Hall Association, 1999), http://www.ushistory.org/Paine/commonsense/singlehtml.htm.

6. Articles of Confederation, Article IX, paragraph 5, http://www.usconstitution.net/articles.html.

7. University of Virginia Library, Historical Census Browser, http://fisher.lib.virginia.edu/collections/stats/histcensus/php/start.php?year=V1790.

8. Middlekauff, *Glorious Cause*, 624.

9. William Riker, "The Heresthetics of Constitution Making," *American Political Science Review* 78 (1984): 1–16.

10. William Patterson, "New Jersey Plan," http://avalon.law.yale.edu/18th_century/patexta.asp.

11. U.S. Census of Population and Housing, "1790 Census of Slave and Free Population," http://www.swivel.com/data_columns/spreadsheet/1923990.

12. Garry Wills, *Negro President: Jefferson and the Slave Power* (Boston: Houghton Mifflin, 2003).

13. See Allison M. Martens, "Reconsidering Judicial Supremacy: From the Counter-Majoritarian Difficulty to Constitutional Transformations," *Perspectives on Politics* 5 (2007): 447–59.

14. James Madison, "*Federalist* 47," in *The Federalist Papers*, http://www.constitution.org/fed/federa47.htm.

15. Madison, "*Federalist* 39," in *The Federalist Papers*, http://press-pubs.uchicago.edu/founders/documents/v1ch8s27.html.

16. Brutus, "*Anti-Federalist* 5," http://www.constitution.org/afp/brutus05.htm.

17. Brutus, http://www.constitution.org/afp/brutus01.htm.

18. Virginia ratification debates, http://www.constitution.org/rc/rat_va_08.htm

19. Brian Gaines, "Popular Myths about Popular Vote–Electoral College Splits," *Political Science and Politics* 34 (March 2001): 70–75.

20. Daryl J. Levinson and Richard H. Pildes, "Separation of Parties, Not Powers," *Harvard Law Review* 119 (2006): 2311.

21. *Furman v. Georgia*, 408 U.S. 238 (1972).

22. *Gregg v. Georgia*, 428 U.S. 153 (1976).

23. Death Penalty Information Center, "States With and Without the Death Penalty," http://www.deathpenaltyinfo.org/states-and-without-death-penalty.

24. Death Penalty Information Center, "The Federal Death Penalty," http://www.deathpenaltyinfo.org/federal-death-penalty.

25. David Baldus, Charles A. Pulaski Jr., and George Woodworth, *Equal Justice and the Death Penalty* (Boston: Northeastern University Press, 1990).

26. *McCleskey v. Kemp*, 481 U.S. 279 (1987).

27. *Roper v. Simmons*, 543 U.S. 551 (2005).

28. *Kennedy v. Louisiana*, 171 L. Ed. 2d 525 (2008).

29. The Innocence Project, "27 Years Later, Donald Gates is Declared Innocent," http://www.innocenceproject.org/Content/27_Years_Later_Donald_Gates_is_Declared_Innocent.php.

30. *District Attorney's Office v. Osborne*, 174 L. Ed. 2d 38 (2009).

31. See Alexander Keyssar, *The Right to Vote* (New York: Basic Books, 2000).

Chapter 3

1. This story was compiled from Stephanie Grace, "Bobby Goes Home," *Brown Alumni Magazine*, November/December 2003, available at http://www.brownalumnimagazine.com/content/view/883/40/; "Transcript of Gov. Jindal's GOP Response to Obama Speech," CNN, February 24, 2009, which is also the source of the chapter-opening quotation.

2. Colin Bonwick, *The American Revolution* (Charlottesville: University of Virginia Press, 1991).

3. William Riker, *Federalism: Origin, Operation, Significance* (Boston: Little, Brown, 1964), 5.

4. James Madison, *Federalist* 39, "Conformity of the Plan to Republican Principles." Available at http://www.constitution.org/fed/federa39.htm

5. *Luther v. Borden*, 7 Howard 1 (1849).

6. *Cohens v. Virginia*, 19 U.S. 264 (1821).

7. *Pennsylvania v. Nelson*, 350 U.S. 497 (1956).

8. Elinor Ostrom, *Governing the Commons: The Evolution of Institutions for Collective Action* (New York: Cambridge University Press, 1990).

9. *McCulloch v. Maryland*, 17 U.S. 316 (1819).

10. *Gibbons v. Ogden*, 22 U.S. 1 (1824).

11. *Dred Scott v. Sandford*, 19 Howard 393 (1857).

12. Andrew Johnson, "Veto of the Civil Rights Bill," in Lillian Foster, *Andrew Johnson, His Life and Speeches*, (New York: Richardson & Co., 1866). Available at http://teachingamericanhistory.org/library/index.asp?document=1944.

13. Morton Grodzins, *The American System: A New View of the Government of the United States* (New York: Rand McNally, 1966).

14. Wendy J. Schiller, "Building Careers and Courting Constituents: U.S. Senate Representation, 1889–1924," *Studies in American Political Development* 20 (2006): 1.

15. *National Labor Relations Board v. Jones & Laughlin Steel Corporation*, 301 U.S. 1 (1937).

16. *United States v. Darby Lumber Company*, 312 U.S. 100 (1941).

17. Grodzins, *American System*.

18. *Brown v. Board of Education*, 347 U.S. 484 (1954).

19. Timothy Conlon, *New Federalism: Intergovernmental Reform from Nixon to Reagan* (Washington D.C.: Brookings Institution, 1988).

20. American Rhetoric, "Ronald Reagan, First Inaugural Address," http://www.americanrhetoric.com/speeches/ronaldreagandfirstinaugural.html.

21. CBS News/*New York Times* poll, conducted February 1995.

22. President Clinton's Radio Address, "The Era of Big Government Is Over," Cable News Network transcript, 1996, http://www.cnn.com/US/9601/budget/01-27/clinton_radio/.

23. Tim Conlan and John Dinan, "Federalism, the Bush Administration, and the Transformation of American Conservatism," *Publius: The Journal of Federalism* 37 (2007): 279–303.

24. Scott F. Abernathy, *No Child Left Behind and the Public Schools* (Ann Arbor: University of Michigan Press, 2007).

25. Conlan and Dinan, "Federalism, the Bush Administration, and the Transformation of American Conservatism," 280.

26. John Schwartz, "Obama Seems to be Open to a Broader Role for States," *New York Times*, January 29, 2009, http://www.nytimes.com/2009/01/30/us/politics/30federal.html?_r=1&th&emc=th.

27. Stephen Dinan and Ben Conery, "DEA Continues Pot Raids Obama Opposes," February 5, 2009, http://www.mpp.org/news/press-releases/dea-defies-obama-pledge.html.

28. David M. Herszenhorn, "Recovery Bill Gets Final Approval," *New York Times*, February 13, 2009, http://www.nytimes.com/2009/02/14/us/politics/14web-stim.html?bl&ex=1234846800&en=6c6139da93f04ebc&ei=5087%0A.

29. *United States v. Lopez*, 514 U.S. 549 (1995).

30. *United States v. Morrison*, 529 U.S. 598 (2000).

31. *Alden v. Maine*, 527 U.S. 706 (1999).

32. *College Savings Bank Florida v. Prepaid*, 527 U.S. 627 (1999).

33. *Board of Trustees v. Garrett*, 531 U.S. 356 (2001).

34. *Gonzales v. Raich*, 545 U.S. 1 (2005).

35. Initiative Statute 1377. (09-0024. Amdt. #1S). Available at http://www.sos.ca.gov/elections/ballot-measures/qualified-ballot-measures.htm.

36. Michael Cooper, "Budget Is Job of Governor, Judges Rule," *New York Times*, December 17, 2004.

37. Charles Barrilleaux and Michael Berkman, "Do Governors Matter? Budgeting Rules and the Politics of State Policymaking," *Political Research Quarterly* 56 (2003): 409–17.

38. U.S. Department of State, "Local Government," http://www.america.gov/st/usg-english/2008/June/20080628211942eaifas0.988125.html.

39. National Conference of State Legislatures, "Initiative, Referendum, and Recall," http://www.ncsl.org/programs/legismgt/elect/initiat.htm.

40. Initiative and Referendum Institute, "Election 2008: Mixed Results," *Ballotwatch* (University of Southern California) 3 (2008), http://www.iandrinstitute.org/BW%202008-3%20Results%20v4.pdf.

41. Frances E. Lee, "Bicameralism and Geographic Politics: Allocating Funds in the House and Senate," *Legislative Studies Quarterly* 29 (2004): 185–213.

42. U.S. Census Bureau, "Federal Aid to States for Fiscal Year 2007," http://www.census.gov/prod/2008pubs/fas-07.pdf.

43. Eric Lipton, "New Rules for Giving Out Antiterror Aid," *New York Times*, January 3, 2006, http://www.nytimes.com/2006/01/03/national/nationalspecial3/03grants.html.

44. Valentino Larcinese, Leonzio Rizzo, and Cecilia Testa, "Allocating the U.S. Federal Budget to the States: The Impact of the President," *Journal of Politics* 68 (2006): 447–56.

45. *New State Ice Co. v. Liebmann*, 76 L Ed. 311 (1932), quoted in Andrew Karch, *Democratic Laboratories: Policy Diffusion among the American States* (Ann Arbor: University of Michigan Press, 2007).

46. Craig Volden, "States as Policy Laboratories: Emulating Success in the Children's Health Insurance Program," *American Journal of Political Science* 50 (2006): 294–312.

47. Michael Mintron and Sandra Vergari, "Policy Networks and Innovations Diffusion: The Case of State Education Reforms," *Journal of Politics* 60 (1998): 126–48.

48. Christopher Stream, "Health Reform in the States: A Model of State Small Group Health Insurance Market Reforms," *Political Research Quarterly* 52 (1999): 499–525.

49. Frederick J. Boehmke and Richard Witmer, "Disentangling Diffusion: The Effects of Social Learning and Economic Competition on State Policy Innovation and Expansion," *Political Research Quarterly* 57 (2004): 39–51.

50. Charles R. Shipan and Craig Volden, "Bottom-Up Federalism: The Diffusion of Antismoking Policies from U.S. Cities to States," *American Journal of Political Science* 50 (2006): 825–43.

51. Robert R. Preuhs, "State Policy Components of Interstate Migration in the United States," *Political Research Quarterly* 52 (1999): 527–47.

52. David M. Konisky, "Regulatory Competition and Environmental Enforcement: Is There a Race to the Bottom?" *American Journal of Political Science* 51 (2003): 853.

53. *Shapiro v. Thompson*, 394 U.S. 618 (1969); *Saenz v. Roe*, 526 U.S. 489 (1999).

54. Craig Volden, "The Politics of Competitive Federalism: A Race to the Bottom in Welfare Benefits?" *American Journal of Political Science* 46 (2006): 352–63.

55. U.S. Department of Education, "The Federal Role in Education," http://www.ed.gov/about/overview/fed/role.html.

56. Michael B. Berkman and Eric Plutzer, *Ten Thousand Democracies* (Washington D.C.: Georgetown University Press, 2005).

57. U.S. Department of Education, "States' Impact on Federal Education Policy: 1957–1960 Eisenhower Administration," http://www.archives.nysed.gov/edpolicy/research/res_policymakers_eisenhower2.shtml; "States' Impact on Federal Education Policy: 1965–1968 Johnson Administration," http://www.archives.nysed.gov/edpolicy/research/res_policymakers_johnson.shtml.

58. Michael W. Giles, "HEW Versus the Federal Courts: A Comparison of School Desegregation Enforcement," *American Politics Quarterly* 3 (1975): 81–90.

59. Zero to Three: National Center for Infants, Toddlers, and Families, "Federal Agencies Responsible for Implementing Programs Affecting Infants and Toddlers," http://www.zerotothree.org/site/DocServer/Federal_Agencies.pdf?docID=1689&AddInterest=1159.

60. Maria Gold, "Obama to Rebrand 'No Child Left Behind,'" *Washington Post*, June 23, 2009.

61. *Peterson's College Money Handbook* (Lawrenceville, N.J.: Nelnet, 2008).

62. Mark Kantrowitz, "Congress Passes Legislation Ending the Federally Guaranteed Student Loan Program," September 22, 2009, www.fastweb.com; The Library of Congress, http://thomas.loc.gov.

63. Statements by Dr. Jill Biden and President Obama at the signing of the Health Care and Education Reconciliation Act of 2010, March 30, 2010, http://www.whitehouse.gov. Also see "Making College More Affordable," http://www.whitehouse.gov/issues/education/higher-education.

Chapter 4

1. *Tinker v. Des Moines*, 393 U.S. 503 (1969).

2. This story was compiled from Peter Irons, *The Courage of Their Convictions* (New York: Penguin Books, 1988); John W. Johnson, "The Overlooked Litigant in *Tinker v. Des Moines*," in *Constitutionalism and American Culture*, ed. Sandra F. VanBurkleo, Kermit L. Hall, and Robert J. Kaczorowski (Lawrence: University Press of Kansas, 2002); John Tinker, "*Tinker v. Des Moines:* Frequently Asked Questions," http://schema-root.org/region/americas/north_america/usa/government/branches/judicial_branch/supreme_court/decisions/schools/tinker_v._des_moines/~jft/jft.faq.html; Diana Hadley, "Mary Beth Tinker: An 'Ordinary' Woman with Extraordinary Courage," Indiana High School Press Association, http://ihspa.blogspot.com/2009/03/ordinary-person-with-extraordinary.html; and an e-mail interview with Mary Beth Tinker, January 27, 2010, conducted for this textbook; chapter-opening quotation is from this interview.

3. *Guiles v. Marineau*, 349 F. Supp. 2d 871 (2004).

4. *Hansen v. Ann Arbor Public Schools*, 293 F. Supp. 2d 780 (2003).

5. *Lowry v. Watson Chapel School District*, 540 F. 3d 752 (2008).

6. "Brutus," *Antifederalist* 2, "To the Citizens of the State of New-York," http://www.constitution.org/afp/brutus02.htm.

7. *Schenck v. United States,* 249 U.S. 47 (1919).

8. Judith A. Baer, *Equality under the Constitution* (Ithaca, N.Y.: Cornell University Press, 1983).

9. *Gitlow v. New York*, 268 U.S. 652 (1925).

10. *Palko v. Connecticut*, 302 U.S. 319 (1937).

11. *Schenck v. United States,* 249 U.S. 47 (1919); *Debs v. United States,* 249 U.S. 211 (1919).

12. Tony Mauro, "The Quirin Ruling," *CounterPunch*, November 18, 2001, http://www.counterpunch.org/mauro1.html.

13. *Hirota v. MacArthur*, 338 U.S. 197 (1948).

14. *Hamdan v. Rumsfeld,* 548 U.S. 557 (2006).

15. Robert McMillan, "Obama Administration Defends Bush Wiretapping," *PC World,* July 15, 2009, http://www.pcworld.com/article/168502/obama_administration_defends_bush_wiretapping.html.

16. *Chaplinsky v. New Hampshire*, 315 U.S. 568 (1942).

17. David L. Hudson, Jr., "Hate Speech and Campus Speech Codes," First Amendment Center, http://www.firstamendmentcenter.org/speech/pubcollege/topic.aspx?topic=campus_speech_codes.

18. *UWM Post v. Board of Regents of the University of Wisconsin,* 774 F. Supp. 1163 (1991).

19. Kermit Hall, "Free Speech on Public College Campuses," First Amendment Center, http://www.firstamendmentcenter.org/speech/pubcollege/overview.aspx.

20. Alan Charles Kors and Harvey Silvergate, *The Shadow University: The Betrayal of Liberty on America's Campuses* (New York: Free Press, 1998).

21. *John Doe. v. University of Michigan*, 721 F. Supp. 852 (1989).

22. Ibid.

23. *UWM Post v. Board of Regents of the University of Wisconsin,* 774 F. Supp. 1163 (1991).

24. *United States v. O'Brien*, 391 U.S. 367 (1968).

25. *Virginia v. Black*, 538 U.S. 343 (2003).

26. *West Virginia Board of Education v. Barnette*, 319 U.S. 624 (1943).

27. *Texas v. Johnson*, 491 U.S. 397 (1989).

28. *Morse v. Frederick*, 551 U.S. 393 (2007).

29. *Grayned v. City of Rockford*, 408 U.S. 104 (1972).

30. *Hill v. Colorado*, 530 U.S. 703 (2000).

31. William Blackstone, *Commentaries on the Laws of England*, 1769 (Chicago: University of Chicago Press, 2002), 4:151–53.

32. *New York Times v. United States*, 403 U.S. 713 (1971).

33. *United States v. Progressive*, 467 F. Supp. 990 (1979).

34. See http://www.wikileaks.org.

35. Adam Liptak and Brad Stone, "Judge Shuts Down Web Site Specializing in Leaks," *New York Times*, February 20, 2008.

36. Anna Badkhen, "Web Can Ruin Reputation with Stroke of a Key," *San Francisco Chronicle*, May 6, 2007.

37. *Miller v. California*, 413 U.S. 15 (1973).

38. *Jenkins v. Georgia*, 418 U.S. 153 (1974).

39. *New York v. Ferber*, 458 U.S. 747 (1982).

40. *Ashcroft v. Free Speech Coalition*, 535 U.S. 234 (2002).

41. *Reno v. American Civil Liberties Union*, 521 U.S. 844 (1997).

42. *Boy Scouts v. Dale*, 530 U.S. 640 (2000).

43. *Church of Lakumi Babalu Aye v. City of Hialeah*, 508 U.S. 520 (1993).

44. *Reynolds v. United States*, 98 U.S. 145 (1878).

45. *Clay, aka, Ali v. United States*, 403 U.S. 698 (1971).

46. *Employment Division, Department of Human Resources of Oregon v. Smith*, 494 U.S. 872 (1990).

47. See "Rethinking the Incorporation of the Establishment Clause: A Federalist View," *Harvard Law Review* 105 (1992): 1700.

48. *Everson v. Board of Education*, 330 U.S. 1 (1947).

49. *Lemon v. Kurtzman*, 403 U.S. 602 (1971).

50. *Engel v. Vitale*, 370 U.S. 421 (1962); *Abington School District v. Schempp*, 374 U.S. 203 (1963).

51. *Epperson v. Arkansas*, 393 U.S. 97 (1968).

52. *Edwards v. Aguillard*, 482 U.S. 578 (1987).

53. *Lee v. Weisman*, 505 U.S. 577 (1992).

54. *Santa Fe Independent School District v. Doe*, 530 U.S. 290 (2000).

55. *Board of Education v. Allen*, 392 U.S. 236 (1968).

56. *Meek v. Pittinger*, 421 U.S. 349 (1975).

57. *District of Columbia v. Heller*, 171 L. Ed. 2d 637 (2008).

58. *McDonald v. Chicago*, 2010. http://www.supremecourtus.gov/opinions/09pdf/08-1521.pdf.

59. *Schneckloth v. Bustamonte*, 412 U.S. 218 (1973).

60. See Jeffrey A. Segal, "Predicting Supreme Court Decisions Probabilistically: The Search and Seizure Cases, 1962–1981," *American Political Science Review* 78 (1984): 801.

61. *California v. Ciraolo*, 476 U.S. 207 (1986).

62. *Kyllo v. United States*, 533 U.S. 27 (2001).

63. *Virginia v. Moore*, 553 U.S. 164 (2008).

64. *Vernonia School District 47J v. Acton*, 515 U.S. 646 (1995).

65. *National Treasury Union v. Von Raab*, 489 U.S. 656 (1989).

66. *Chandler v. Miller*, 520 U.S. 305 (1997).

67. Priscilla H. Machado Zotti, *Injustice for All: Mapp v. Ohio and the Fourth Amendment* (New York: Peter Lang, 2005).

68. *Miranda v. Arizona*, 384 U.S. 436 (1966).

69. *Dickerson v. United States*, 530 U.S. 428 (2000).

70. *Powell v. Alabama*, 287 U.S. 45 (1932).

71. *Betts v. Brady*, 316 U.S. 455 (1942).

72. *Gideon v. Wainwright*, 372 U.S. 335 (1963).

73. *Argersinger v. Hamlin*, 407 U.S. 25 (1972).

74. *Griswold v. Connecticut*, 381 U.S. 479 (1965).

75. *Eisenstadt v. Baird*, 405 U.S. 438 (1972).

76. *Roe v. Wade*, 410 U.S. 113 (1973).

77. *Planned Parenthood of Southeastern Pennsylvania v. Casey*, 505 U.S. 833 (1992).

78. Lori Ringhand, "Supreme Court Confirmation Dataset," http://www.uga.edu/.

79. *Bowers v. Hardwick*, 478 U.S. 186 (1986).

80. General Social Survey, National Opinion Research Center, University of Chicago.

81. *Lawrence v. Texas*, 539 U.S. 558 (2003).

82. *Cruzan v. Director, Missouri Department of Health*, 497 U.S. 261 (1990), at 278.

83. *Washington v. Glucksberg*, 521 U.S. 702 (1997); *Vacco v. Quill*, 521 U.S. 793 (1997).

84. *West Virginia State Board of Education v. Barnette*, 319 U.S. 624 (1943).

85. Ibid.

86. Robert Dahl, "Decision-Making in a Democracy: The Supreme Court as a National Policy-Maker," *Journal of Public Law* 6 (1957): 179–295.

87. Anthony Lewis, *Freedom for the Thought That We Hate* (New York: Basic Books, 2007).

88. John L. Sullivan, James Pierson, and George Marcus. *Political Tolerance and American Democracy* (Chicago: University of Chicago Press, 1973); James L. Gibson, "Enigmas of Intolerance: Fifty Years after Stouffer's *Communism, Conformity, and Civil Liberties*," *Perspectives on Politics* 21, no. 4 (2006): 22.

89. August 2007 Freedom Forum Survey, accessed via Roper Center for Public Opinion Research, University of Connecticut.

Chapter 5

1. This story has been compiled from Juan Williams, *Eyes on the Prize: America's Civil Rights Years, 1954–1965* (New York: Penguin Books, 1987), 130–31, also, generally, 122–61; Michael Westmoreland-White, "Diane Nash (1938–): Unsung Heroine of the Civil Rights Movement," October 20, 2002, http://www.ecapc.org/articles/WestmoW_2002.10.20.asp; Linda T. Wynn, "Diane Judith Nash (1938 –): A Mission for Equality, Justice, and Social Change," in *Tennessee Women: Their Lives and Times,* ed. Sarah Wilkerson Freeman and Beverly Greene Bond (Athens: University of Georgia Press, 2009), 281–304; interview with Diane Nash, November 12, 1985, www.teachersdomain.org; chapter-opening quotation is from this interview.

2. See Alexander Keyssar, *The Right to Vote* (New York: Basic Books, 2000).

3. Senator Lyman Trumbull, quoted in Judith Baer, *Equality under the Constitution* (Ithaca, N.Y: Cornell University Press, 1983), 96.

4. Ronald Dworkin, *Taking Rights Seriously* (Cambridge, Mass.: Harvard University Press, 1978).

5. *Dred Scott v. Sandford*, 60 U.S. 393 (1857).

6. *United States v. Cruikshank*, 92 U.S. 542 (1875).

7. Ronald Walters, "'The Association Is for the Direct Attack': The Militant Context of the NAACP Challenge to *Plessy*," *Washburn Law Journal* 43 (2003): 329.

8. *Plessy v. Ferguson,* 163 U.S. 537 (1896).

9. California Alien Land Law (1913).

10. Vicki L. Ruiz, "South by Southwest: Mexican Americans and Segregated Schooling, 1900–1950," *Magazine of History* 15 (Winter 2001), Organization of American Historians, http://www.oah.org/pubs/magazine/deseg/ruiz.html.

11. *Westminster School District v. Mendez.*, 161 F. 2d 774 (1947).

12. Ruiz, "South by Southwest."

13. Keyssar, *Right to Vote.*

14. *Minor v. Happersett*, 88 U.S. 162 (1874).

15. The Women's History Project of Lexington Area National Organization for Women, "Timeline of Women's Suffrage in the United States," http://www.dpsinfo.com/women/history/timeline.html.

16. Survey by the Office of Public Opinion Research, July 1945.

17. "The Law: Up from Coverture," *Time*, March 20, 1972, http://www.time.com/time/magazine/article/0,9171,942533,00.html.

18. *Kirchberg v. Feenstra*, 450 U.S. 455 (1981), at 456.

19. Richard Kluger, *Simple Justice* (New York: Knopf, 1975), 376.

20. Baer, *Chains of Protection.*

21. *Hoyt v. Florida*, 368 U.S. 57 (1961).

22. Peter H. Schuck and Rogers M. Smith, *Citizenship without Consent* (New Haven: Yale University Press, 1985), 1–2.

23. *Johnson v. M'Intosh*, 21 U.S. 543 (1823), at 569.

24. *Elk v. Wilkins*, 112 U.S. 94 (1884).

25. Rogers M. Smith, *Civic Ideals* (New Haven, Conn.: Yale University Press), 17.

26. "Immigration Act of 1924," Documents of American History II, http://tucnak.fsv.cuni.cz/~calda/Documents/1920s/ImmigAct1924.html.

27. *Korematsu v. United States,* 323 U.S. 214 (1944).

28. Ann McDermott, "Orphans Tell of World War II Internment," March 24, 1997, http://www.cnn.com/US/9703/24/interned.orphans/.

29. David Cole, "No More Roundups," *Washington Post*, June 16, 2004, http://www.washingtonpost.com/wp-dyn/articles/A44875-2004Jun15.html.

30. *Shelley v. Kraemer*, 334 U.S. 1 (1948).

31. *Missouri ex rel. Gaines v. Canada*, 305 U.S. 337 (1938); *Sipuel v. Board of Regents of University of Oklahoma*, 332 U.S. 631 (1948); *Sweatt v. Painter*, 339 U.S. 629 (1950).

32. *Bolling v. Sharpe*, 347 U.S. 497 (1954).

33. *Brown v. Board of Education*, 349 U.S. 294 (1955).

34. *Cooper v. Aaron*, 358 U.S. 1 (1958).

35. Gerald N. Rosenberg, *The Hollow Hope: Can Courts Bring About Social Change?* (Chicago: University of Chicago Press, 1991).

36. *Alexander v. Holmes County Board of Education*, 396 U.S. 1218 (1969).

37. *Browder v. Gayle*, 352 U.S. 903 (1956).

38. *Jackson v. Alabama*, 348 U.S. 888 (1954).

39. Quoted in Walter F. Murphy, *Elements of Judicial Strategy* (Chicago: University of Chicago Press, 1964), 193.

40. *Loving v. Virginia*, 388 U.S. 1 (1967).

41. Henry Abraham and Barbara Perry, *Freedom and the Court*, 6th ed. (New York: Oxford University Press, 1994), 380. See also David Halberstam, *The Children* (New York: Fawcett Books, 1998), 230–34. The caption for the photo on page 159 was drawn from this source.

42. Martin Luther King, Jr., "Letter from Birmingham Jail," April 16, 1963, The King Center, http://coursesa.matrix.msu.edu/~hst306/documents/letter.html.

43. Martin Luther King, Jr., "I Have a Dream," http://www.usconstitution.net/dream.html.

44. *Heart of Atlanta Motel v. United States*, 379 U.S. 241 (1964); *Katzenbach v. McClung*, 379 U.S. 294 (1964).

45. *Griggs v. Duke Power Co.*, 401 U.S. 424 (1971).

46. *Wards Cove Packing Co. v. Antonio*, 490 U.S. 642 (1989).

47. *Ricci v. DeStefano* 174 L. Ed. 2d 490 (2009).

48. *Guinn v. United States*, 238 U.S. 347 (1915).

49. *Smith v. Allwright*, 321 U.S. 649 (1944).

50. Lyndon B. Johnson, "We Shall Overcome," The History Place, http://www.historyplace.com/speeches/johnson.htm.

51. Mark Hugo Lopez and Paul Taylor, "Dissecting the 2008 Electorate: Most Diverse in U.S. History," Pew Research Center, http://pewresearch.org/pubs/1209/racial-ethnic-voters-presidential-election .

52. *Northwest Austin Municipal Utility District No. One v. Holder* 174 L. Ed. 2d 140 (2009).

53. *Bowers v. Hardwick*, 478 U.S. 186 (1986).

54. *Lawrence v. Texas,* 539 U.S. 558 (2003).

55. General Social Survey, April 2008, accessed via Roper Center for Public Opinion Research, University of Connecticut.

56. *Newsweek* poll, June 2008, accessed via Roper Center for Public Opinion Research, University of Connecticut.

57. *Bakke v. California,* 438 U.S. 265 (1978).

58. *Grutter v. Bollinger*, 539 U.S. 306 (2003).

59. *Gratz v. Bollinger*, 539 U.S. 244 (2003).

60. "Employing and Accommodating Individuals with Histories of Alcohol or Drug Abuse," National Council on Alcoholism and Drug Dependence of the San Fernando Valley, Inc., http://www.ncadd-sfv.org/profiles/disability.html.

61. David A. Harris, "Driving While Black: Racial Profiling on Our Nation's Highways," Special Report, June 1999, American Civil Liberties Union, http://www.aclu.org/racialjustice/racialprofiling/15912pub19990607.html.

62. Ibid.

63. *United States v. Travis,* 837 F. Supp. 1386 (1993); *State of New Jersey v. Patterson* 270 N. J. Super. 550 (1994); *Derricott v. State of Maryland* 611 A. 2d 592 (1992).

64. Fox News poll, April 2006, accessed from the Roper Center for Public Opinion Research, University of Connecticut.

65. *Plyler v. Doe*, 457 U.S. 202 (1982).

66. Remus Ilies, Nancy Hauserman, Susan Schwochau, and John Stibal, "Reported Incidence Rates of Work-Related Sexual Harassment in the United States," *Personnel Psychology* 56 (2003): 607–31.

67. U.S. Equal Employment Opportunity Commission, "Sexual Harassment Charges EEOC & FEPAs Combined: FY 1997–FY 2009," http://www.eeoc.gov/eeoc/statistics/enforcement/sexual_harassment.cfm.

68. *Meritor Savings Bank v. Vinson*, 477 U.S. 57 (1986).

69. National Committee on Pay Equity, "Ledbetter Bill Becomes Law," updated February 28, 2009, http://www.pay-equity.org/ (accessed May 30, 2009).

70. *Burlington Northern & Sante Fe Railway Co. v. White,* 548 U.S. 53 (2006).

71. *Ledbetter v. Goodyear Tire and Rubber Co.,* 550 U.S. 618 (2007).

72. Ibid., 645.

73. House of Representatives. Lilly Ledbetter Fair Pay Act. http://edlabor.house.gov/lilly-ledbetter-fair-pay-act/index.shtml.

74. King, "Civil Right No. 1," 26.

75. M. V. Hood, Quentin Kidd, and Irwin L. Morris, "The Key Issue: Constituency Effects and Southern Senators' Roll-Call Voting on Civil Rights," *Legislative Studies Quarterly* 26 (2001): 599-621.

76. *Dukes v. Wal-Mart Stores, Inc.* No. C-01-2252 MJJ (U.S. Court of Appeals, 9th Circuit, 2010), http://www.walmartclass.com/staticdata/En%20Banc%20Opinion.pdf.

Chapter 6

1. This story was compiled from Stephanie Clifford, "Finding Fame with a Prescient Call for Obama," *New York Times,* November 10, 2008; Adam Sternbergh, "The Spreadsheet Psychic," *New York Magazine,* October 12, 2008; James Wolcott, "The Good, the Bad, and Joe Lieberman," *Vanity Fair,* February 2009; "Will Young Voters Turn Out for Obama?" *New York Post,* August 10, 2008; opening quotation from Silver, "Will Young Voters Turn Out for Obama?"

2. Quoted in Harry Jaffa, *The Crisis of the House Divided*, 2nd ed. (Chicago: University of Chicago Press, 1959), 10.

3. The first scholar to discuss how the public rallies to support the president in time of trouble was John Mueller, *War, Presidents, and Public Opinion* (New York: Wiley, 1970).

4. Quoted in Ted Barrett and Steve Brusk, "Bush: Immigration Bill Will Enforce Borders, Workplaces," CNN, June 12, 2007, http://www.cnn.com/.

5. One CBS/*New York Times* poll, conducted October 31–November 2, 2008, indicated that only 20 percent of the public approved of Bush's job as president. Prior to that, Harry Truman (1945–53; 23 percent) and Richard Nixon (1969–74; 24 percent) had been the least popular presidents. Both Truman and Nixon rebounded a bit from that low point as they left office.

6. Brian Montopoli, "Obama Approval Rating Falls to 50 Percent," CBS News, December 9, 2009, http://www.cbsnews.com/.

7. Conducted by CBS News/*New York Times*, February 5–10, 2010, and based on 1,084 telephone interviews.

8. See Marc Hetherington, *Why Trust Matters* (Princeton, N.J.: Princeton University Press, 2005).

9. Robert Erikson and Kent Tedin, *American Public Opinion,* 6th ed. (New York: Longman, 2003), 7.

10. George Gallup, *The Pulse of Democracy* (New York: Simon and Schuster, 1940).

11. Erikson and Tedin, *American Public Opinion,* 26.

12. Alicia C. Shepard, "How They Blew It," *American Journalism Review,* January/February 2001.

13. Kathy Frankovic, "The Truth about Push Polls," CBS News, 2000, http://www.cbsnews.com/stories/2000/02/14/politics/main160398.shtml.

14. Scott Keeter, "Cell Phones and the 2008 Election: An Update," *Pew Research Center*, July 17, 2008, http://pewresearch.org/.

15. Herbert Asher, *Polling and the Public*, 7th ed. (Washington D.C.: CQ Press, 2007), 93.

16. Pew Research Center for the People & the Press, "Polls Face Growing Resistance, But Still Representative," April 20, 2004, http://people-press.org/.

17. Erikson and Tedin, *American Public Opinion,* 121.

18. John Alford and John Hibbing, "Biology and Rational Choice," *Political Economy Newsletter,* Fall 2005.

19. Amy Lavoie, "The Genes in Your Congeniality: Researchers Identify Genetic Influence in Social Networks," *Harvard Science: Culture + Society,* January 26, 2009, http://harvardscience.harvard.edu/culture-society/articles/the-genes-your-congeniality/.

20. Peter Hatemi, Nathan A Gillespie, Lindon J. Eaves, Brion S. Maher, Sarah E. Medland, David C. Smyth, Harry N. Beeby, et al., "A Genome-Wide Analysis of Liberal and Conservative Political Attitudes," *Journal of Politics* (2010): forthcoming.

21. John R. Alford, John Hibbing, and Carolyn L. Funk, "Twin Studies, Molecular Genetics, Politics, and Tolerance," *Perspectives on Politics* 6 (December 2008); John Hibbing, John R. Alford, and Carolyn L. Funk, "Beyond Liberals and Conservatives to Political Genotypes and Phenotypes," *Perspectives on Politics* 6 (June 2008): 321–28.

22. Scott Keeter, "Young Voters in the 2008 Election." *Pew Research Center*, November 12, 2008, http://pewresearch.org/.

23. Scott Keeter and Paul Taylor, "The Millennials," *Pew Research Center*, December 11, 2009, http://pewresearch.org/.

24. This theory comes out of the work of John Zaller, *Nature of Mass Beliefs* (Cambridge, U.K.: Cambridge University Press, 1992).

25. The classic book that lays out this argument about party identification is Angus Campbell, Philip Converse, Warren Miller, and Donald Stokes, *The American Voter* (New York: Wiley, 1960).

26. Conducted by CBS News/*New York Times*, September 20–23, 2001, and based on 1,216 telephone interviews.

27. See "Party Identification 7-Point Scale: 1952–-2004," *The ANES Guide to Public Opinion and Electoral Behavior*, http://www.electionstudies.org/.

28. David Brooks, "What Independents Want," *New York Times*, November 5, 2009, A31.

29. John Sides, "Three Myths about Political Independents," December 17, 2009, http://www.themonkeycage.org/.

30. Data come from a NBC News/*Wall Street Journal* poll conducted in December 2008. The same pattern exists for 2009.

31. This way of thinking about the public comes from Philip Converse, "Nature of Belief Systems in Mass Publics," in *Ideology and Discontent,* ed. David Apter (New York: Free Press, 1964).

32. Data come from William Jacoby "The Formation of Issue Concepts and Partisan Change" (paper, annual meeting of the Southern Political Science Association, New Orleans, LA, January 3–6, 2007).

33. Paul Lazarsfeld, Bernard Berelson, and Helen Gaudet, *The People's Choice* (New York: Duell, Sloane, Pearce, 1944).

34. Bernard Berelson, Paul F. Lazarsfeld, and William N. McPhee, *Voting: A Study of Opinion Formation in a Presidential Campaign* (Chicago: University of Chicago Press, 1954).

35. Converse, "Nature of Belief Systems in Mass Publics."

36. These data all come from Erikson and Tedin, *American Public Opinion,* 62.

37. See John Zaller, "Monica Lewinsky and the Mainsprings of American Politics," in *Mediated Politics: Communication in*

the *Future of Democracy,* ed. W. Lance Bennett and Robert M. Entman (Cambridge, U.K.: Cambridge University Press, 2001).

38. Stanley Kelley, *Interpreting Elections* (Princeton, N.J.: Princeton University Press, 1983).

39. Christopher Achen, "Mass Political Attitudes and the Survey Response," *American Political Science Review* 69 (1975): 1218–31.

40. Sam Popkin is most well known for this idea in his book, *The Reasoning Voter* (Chicago: University of Chicago Press, 1991).

41. Nolan McCarty, Keith Poole, and Howard Rosenthal, "Party Polarization: 1879-2009," Polarized America website, January 4, 2006, polarizedamerica.com.

42. See Morris Fiorina, *Culture War?* (New York: Longman, 2008).

43. Morris Fiorina, Samuel Abrams, and Jeremy Pope, "Polarization in the American Publics," *Journal of Politics* 70 (2008): 556–60.

44. See Alan Abramowitz, *The Disappearing Center* (New Haven, Conn.: Yale University Press, 2010).

45. These data are from the CBS/*New York Times* polls conducted during the presidential campaigns and available through the Roper Center, University of Connecticut.

46. Erikson and Tedin, *American Public Opinion,* 193.

47. Ibid., 208.

48. "Muslim Americans: Mostly Middle Class and Mostly Mainstream," *Pew Research Center,* May 22, 2007, http://pewresearch.org/.

49. Erikson and Tedin, *American Public Opinion,* 215.

50. Center for the American Woman and Politics, "The Gender Gap: Voting Choices in Presidential Elections," *Center for the American Woman and Politics,* December 2008, http://www.cawp.rutgers.edu/.

51. "Support for Abortion Slips: Issue Ranks Lower on the Agenda," *Pew Research Center,* October 1, 2009, http://pewresearch.org/.

52. Data come from the National Election Studies, http://www.electionstudies.org/.

53. Data come from the 2004 General Social Survey, conducted by the National Opinion Research Center (NORC) at the University of Chicago.

54. Carole Jean Uhlaner and F. Chris Garcia, "Latino Public Opinion," in *Understanding Public Opinion,* ed. Barbara Norrander and Clyde Wilcox (Washington, D.C.: CQ Press, 2002).

55. Rodolfo De la Garza, Louis DeSipio, F. Chris Garcia, John Garcia, and Angelo Falcon, *Latino Voices: Mexican, Puerto Rican, and Cuban Perspectives on American Politics* (Boulder, Colo.: Westview Press, 1992).

56. David Leal, "Latino Public Opinion," Texas A&M Department of Political Science, Project for Equity, Representation, and Justice, http://perg.tamu.edu/lpc/Leal.pdf.

57. Marisa Abrajano, R. Michael Alvarez, and Jonathan Nagler, "The Hispanic Vote in the 2004 Presidential Election," *Journal of Politics* 70 (2008): 368–82.

58. Ellen C. Collier, "Instances of Use of United States Forces Abroad, 1798-1993," Naval History & Heritage Command, http://www.history.navy.mil/.

59. Mueller, *War, Presidents, and Public Opinion.*

60. "Presidential Approval Ratings – Gallup Historical Statistics and Trends," Gallup website, www.gallup.com.

61. "Presidential Approval Ratings – George W. Bush," Gallup website, www.gallup.com.

62. Christian Grose and Bruce Oppenheimer, "The Iraq War, Partisanship, and Candidate Attributes: Explaining Variation in Partisan Swing in the 2006 U.S. House Elections," *Legislative Studies Quarterly* 32 (2007): 4.

63. Scott Sigmund Gartner, "The Multiple Effects of Casualties on Public Support for War: An Experimental Approach," *American Political Science Review* 102 (2008): 96–106.

64. Helene Cooper, "Fearing Another Quagmire in Afghanistan," *New York Times,* January 24, 2009.

65. Salon staff, "The Abu Ghraib Files," *Salon,* March 14, 2006, http://www.salon.com/.

66. Sarah Mendelson, "The Guantanamo Countdown," *Foreign Policy,* October 1, 2009, http://www.foreignpolicy.com/.

67. Robert S. Erikson, Michael B. MacKuen, and James A. Stimson, *The Macro Polity* (Cambridge, U.K.: Cambridge University Press, 2002).

68. See Key, *Public Opinion and American Democracy*, and Douglas Arnold, *Logic of Congressional Action* (New Haven, Conn.: Yale University Press, 1991).

Chapter 7

1. This story was compiled from the Daily Kos website, http://www.dailykos.com/special/about2#dk; Christopher Null, "The 50 Most Important People on the Web," *PC World,* March 5, 2007, http://www.pcworld.com/printable/article/id,129301/printable.html; David M. Ewalt, "The Web Celeb 25," *Forbes,* January 23, 2007, http://www.forbes.com/2007/01/23/web-celeb-25-tech-media-cx_de_06webceleb_0123top_slides_4.html; eBizMBA, "Top 25 Most Popular Blogs," http://www.ebizmba.com/articles/blogs, (accessed January 2, 2010); Markos ("Kos") Moulitsas Zúniga, foreword to Lowell Feld and Nate Wilcox, *Netroots Rising: How a Citizen Army of Bloggers and Online Activists Is Changing American Politics* (Westport, Conn: Praeger,

2008), viii, which is the source of the chapter-opening quotation.

2. Herbert Gans, *Democracy and the News* (New York: Oxford University Press, 2003), 1.

3. Pew Research Center's Project for Excellence in Journalism, "The State of the News Media 2009: The economy emerges as a major story," http://journalism.org/.

4. Thomas E. Patterson, *Out of Order* (New York: Knopf, 1993), 82.

5. Pew Research Center's Project for Excellence in Journalism, "The State of the News Media 2009: Clear Channel," http://journalism.org/.

6. Pew Research Center's Project for Excellence in Journalism, "The State of the News Media 2004: Newspapers," http://journalism.org.

7. Jeremy D. Mayer, *American Media Politics in Transition* (New York: McGraw Hill, 2007), 76.

8. Mayer, *American Media Politics in Transition*, 81.

9. Michael Schudson and Susan Tifft, "American Journalism in Historical Perspective," in *The Press,* ed. Geneva Overholser and Kathleen Hall Jamieson (New York: Oxford University Press, 2005), 19.

10. William Riker, *The Strategy of Rhetoric: Campaigning for the American Constitution* (New Haven, Conn.: Yale University Press, 1996).

11. David McCullough, *John Adams* (New York: Simon and Schuster, 2001).

12. Melvin Laracey, "Who Listened? Political Media Communications by 'Pre-Modern' Presidents" (paper presented at the annual meeting of The Midwest Political Science Association, Chicago, Ill., April 15, 2004).

13. James Hamilton, *All the News That's Fit to Sell: How the Market Transforms Information into News* (Princeton, N.J.: Princeton University Press, 2006).

14. Ibid., 53.

15. Schudson and Tifft, "American Journalism in Historical Perspective," 17–46.

16. "The ANES Guide to Public Opinion and Electoral Behavior: Watched Campaign on TV 1952-2004," American National Elections Studies, 2005, http://www.electionstudies.org/nesguide/toptable/tab6d_1.htm

17. Schudson and Tifft, "American Journalism in Historical Perspective," 26.

18. These data come from the October 2007 Current Population Survey, U.S. Census.

19. Data provided by Fenn Communications Group.

20. Pew Research Center's Project for Excellence in Journalism, "The State of the News Media 2009: Newspapers," http://journalism.org/.

21. Alex Jones, *Losing the News* (Oxford: Oxford University Press, 2009).

22. "Nielsen Online: Newspaper Websites," Newspaper Association of America, June 2009, http://www.naa.org/TrendsandNumbers/Newspaper-Websites.aspx.

23. Bill Mitchell, "Clues in the Rubble: Finding a Framework to Sustain Local News," 2010, Discussion Paper Series from the Joan Shorenstein Center, Harvard University.

24. Geoffrey Cowan, "Leading the Way to Better News," 2008, p. 7, Discussion Paper Series from the Joan Shorenstein Center., Harvard University.

25. Ibid., 7.

26. See Jones, *Losing the News*.

27. See Mitchell, "Clues in the Rubble."

28. Pew Research Center's Project for Excellence in Journalism, "The State of the News Media 2009: Audio," http://journalism.org/.

29. Pew Research Center's Project for Excellence in Journalism, "The State of the News Media 2009: Talk Radio," http://journalism.org/.

30. Lee Sigelman, "Conservative Dominance of Political Talk Radio," The Monkey Cage, February 16, 2008.

31. These data simply take the number of viewers and divide by the number of Americans at the time, which was 226 million in 1980 and 309 million in 2010.

32. Pew Research Center's Project for Excellence in Journalism, "The State of the News Media 2009: Digital Trends," http://journalism.org/.

33. Thomas Goetz, "Reinventing Television," *Wired*, September 2009.

34. Most of the data presented here came from "Journalism, Satire or Just Laughs? 'The Daily Show with Jon Stewart,' Examined," May 8, 2008, http://www.journalism.org/node/10953.

35. eBizMBA, "Top 25 Most Popular Blogs," January 2, 2010, http://www.ebizmba.com/articles/blogs.

36. Eric Lawrence, John Sides, and Henry Farrell, "Self-Segregation or Deliberation? Blog Readership, Participation, and Polarization in American Politics," *Perspectives on Politics* 8, no. 1 (2010): 146.

37. See www.huffingtonpost.com.

38. See www.drudgereport.com.

39. See http://rush-limbaugh-speaks.blogspot.com/.

40. See http://www.wired.com/epicenter/2007/05/controlled_chao/.

41. Ibid.

42. Ben Rigby, *Mobilizing Generation 2.0* (San Francisco: Jossey-Bass, 2008), 17–18.

43. Katharine Seelye, "Blogger Is Surprised by Uproar over Obama Story, but Not Bitter," *New York Times*, April 14, 2008.

44. Data collected by Peter Fenn, president of Fenn Communications Group.

45. Christine Williams and Jeff Gulati, "Social Networks in Political Campaigns: Facebook and the 2006 Midterm Elections" (paper presented at the annual meeting of the American Political Science Association, Chicago, Ill., August 30–September 2, 2007).

46. Noam Cohen, "Twitter on the Barricades: Six Lessons Learned," New York Times, June 21, 2009.

47. John Palfrey, Robert Faris, and Bruce Etling, "In Washington Post Op-Ed, Berkman Center Directors Discuss Twitter Revolution in Iran," Harvard Law School, June 22, 2009, http://www.law.harvard.edu/news/2009/06/22_iran.html.

48. Rigby, Mobilizing Generation 2.0, 130.

49. Pew Research Center's Internet and American Life Project, press release, on June 15, 2008. The findings come from a survey conducted April 8–May 11, 2008.

50. Pew Research Center, The Millennials: Confident. Connected. Open to Change, report, February 2010, http://pewsocialtrends.org/pubs/751/millennials-confident-connected-open-to-change/.

51. Data come from "Young People and News," Harvard University, July 2007.

52. Morley Winograd and Michael D. Hais, Millennial Makeover: MySpace, YouTube and the Future of American Politics (New Brunswick, N.J.: Rutgers University Press, 2008).

53. Paul Lazarsfeld, Bernard Berelson, and Hazel Gaudet, The People's Choice (New York: Columbia University Press, 1944). It is worth noting that the 1940 campaign was probably the worst campaign in American history to look at for possible media effects. This was the only election in which a sitting president was running for a third term. The stability of preference surely reflected the fact that people had opinions about Roosevelt and not much would change them one way or the other. In contrast, Senator Obama was not a well-known figure in the 2008 presidential campaign.

54. Angus Campbell et al., The American Voter (New York: Wiley, 1960).

55. Lydia Saad, "Public Support for Stimulus Package Unchanged at 52%," Gallup, February 5, 2009, http://www.gallup.com/poll/114184/public-support-stimulus-package-unchanged.aspx.

56. In political science, the most important book to reshape the field was Shanto Iyengar and Donald R. Kinder, News That Matters: Television and American Opinion (Chicago: University of Chicago Press, 1987). Also see the work of Maxwell McCombs in the area of communication.

57. Bernard Cohen, The Press and Foreign Policy (Princeton: Princeton University Press, 1963), 13.

58. Darrell West, Grover Whitehurst, and E.J. Dionne, "Invisible: 1.4 Percent Coverage for Education Is Not Enough," The Brookings Institution, December 2, 2009.

59. Shanto Iyengar and Jennifer A. McGrady, Media Politics: A Citizen's Guide (New York: W.W. Norton, 2007), 216.

60. These scholars have reshaped how we think about framing. In fact, Kahneman won a Nobel Prize for this work in 2003. See http://www-psych.stanford.edu/~knutson/bad/tversky81.pdf as one example of their scholarship.

61. Pew Research Center's Project for Excellence in Journalism, "The State of the News Media 2009: Public Attitudes," http://journalism.org/.

62. Schudson, Sociology of News, 33.

63. See the Accuracy in Media website, www.aim.org.

64. The data in this paragraph come from Gallup Polls made available through The Roper Center and their "IPOLL" search engine.

65. Thomas Patterson, "Political Roles of the Journalist," in The Politics of the News, ed. Doris Graber, Denis McQuail, and Pippa Norris (Washington, D.C.: CQ Press, 2000), 3.

66. For a thoughtful discussion of soft news, see Matthew Baum, Soft News Goes to War: Public Opinion and American Foreign Policy in the New Media Age (Princeton, NJ: Princeton University Press, 2003), 6–7.

67. Presidential Campaign Slogans, CB Presidential Research Services, 2009, http://www.presidentsusa.net/campaignslogans.html.

68. The Pew Research Center for the People and the Press, "Public Knowledge of Current Affairs Little Change by News and Information Revolutions," 2007, http://people-press.org/report/319/public-knowledge-of-current-affairs-little-changed-by-news-and-information-revolutions.

69. Pew Research Center, "High Marks for Campaign, High Bar for Obama," November 13, 2008, http://pewresearch.org/pubs/1032/high-marks-for-campaign-high-bar-for-obama/.

70. Pew Internet & American Life Project, "Home Broadband Adoption 2009," http://www.pewinternet.org/Reports/2009/10-Home-Broadband-Adoption-2009.aspx?r=1.

71. The argument presented over the next few paragraphs is inspired by the work of Markus Prior, Post Broadcast Democracy (Cambridge, U.K.: Cambridge University Press, 2007).

72. Ibid.

73. FCC v. Pacifica Foundation, 438 U.S. 726 (1978), The Oyez Project, http://www.oyez.org/ (accessed June 5, 2009).

74. FCC v. Fox Television Stations, 556 U.S. (2009), The Oyez Project, http://www.oyez.org/ (accessed June 5, 2009).

75. Matthew Lasar, "Supreme Court Remands FCC 'Nipplegate' Case to Lower Court," Ars Technica, http://arstechnica

.com/tech-policy/news/2009/05/supreme-court-remands-fcc-nipplegate-case-to-lower-court.ars/, updated May 4, 2009 (accessed June 5, 2009).

76. "Communications Decency Act," The Center for Democracy and Technology, http://cdt.org/speech/cda/ (accessed June 6, 2009); http://www.oyez.org/.

77. "Legislative History of COPA," The Center for Democracy and Technology, http://cdt.org/ (accessed June 6, 2009).

78. U.S. Court of Appeals for the 3rd Circuit, *Mukasey v. American Civil Liberties Union* http://www.cdt.org/speech/20080722COPA3rdCircuit.pdf, updated July 22, 2008 (accessed June 6, 2009).

79. "Facts for Consumers," Federal Trade Commission website, www.ftc.gov, updated September 2007 (accessed June 6, 2009).

80. Library of Congress. "An Act to prevent child abduction and the sexual exploitation of children," Thomas, S. 151. http://thomas.loc.gov/cgi-bin/bdquery/z?d108:S.151:@@@L&summ2=m&#major%20actions, updated April 30, 2003 (accessed June 6, 2009).

81. "CAN-SPAM Signed into Law," The Center for Democracy and Technology, updated December 16, 2003 (accessed June 6, 2009).

82. Federal Trade Commission. "Computers and the Internet: Privacy and Security." Federal Trade Commission website, www.ftc.gov.

83. Richard Pérez-Peña, "Group Plans to Provide Investigative Journalism," *New York Times*, October 15, 2007.

Chapter 8

1. This story was compiled from the Students for Concealed Carry on Campus website, www.concealedcampus.org; Dean A. Ferguson, "Campus Gun Ban Bill Disarmed," *Lewiston Tribune*, February 14, 2008, http://www.lmtribune.com; Suzanne Smalley, "More Guns on Campus?" *Newsweek*, February 15, 2008; and an e-mail interview with Al Baker, April 6, 2010, conducted for this textbook, which is the source of the chapter-opening quotation.

2. Alexis De Tocqueville, *Democracy in America*, trans. George Lawrence and ed. J. P. Mayer (New York: Doubleday & Company, 1969), 193.

3. Interest groups at the state level even get involved in elections for state judges. See Clive S. Thomas, Michael L. Boyer, and Ronald J. Hrebenar, "Interest Groups and State Court Elections: A New Era and Its Challenges." *Judicature* 87 (2003): 135–49.

4. For information about the National Labor Relations Act, see the National Labor Relations Board website, www.nlrb.gov.

5. U.S. Bureau of Labor Statistics, *Current Population Survey*, January 22, 2010, http://www.bls.gov/cps/.

6. The American Israel Public Affairs Committee, "About AIPAC," http://www.aipac.org.

7. Coalition to Save Darfur/ Press Releases, "Senators Frist and Clinton Sign One Millionth Postcard Urging President Bush to Advocate Multinational Peacekeeping Force to Stop Darfur Genocide," June 29, 2006, http://www.savedarfur.org.

8. Jeffrey Gettleman, "After Years of Mass Killings, Fragile Calm Holds in Darfur," *New York Times*, January 2, 2010, A1; Coalition to Save Darfur, "Sudan 365: A Beat for Peace," http://www.savedarfur.org.

9. For a broader discussion of the impact of the Internet on interest group power, see Bruce Bimber, "The Internet and Political Fragmentation," in *Domestic Perspectives on Contemporary Democracy*, ed. Peter F. Nardulli (Champaign: University of Illinois Press, 2008).

10. Carl Pope, "Not the End, Not the Beginning of the End, Perhaps the End of the Beginning," Taking the Initiative: Carl Pope's Blog, June 26, 2009, http://www.sierraclub.org.

11. Anthony J. Nownes, *Total Lobbying* (New York: Cambridge University Press, 2006).

12. Center for Responsive Politics, "Lobbying Database," http://www.opensecrets.org.

13. Center for Responsive Politics website, www.opensecrets.org.

14. Bart Jansen, 2007 "Legislative Summary. Congressional Affairs: Lobbying Practices & Disclosures," *CQ Weekly Online, January 7, 2008,* 39.

15. Gregory Koger and Jennifer N. Victor, "Polarized Agendas: Campaign Contributions by Lobbyists," *PS: Political Science and Politics* 42 (2009): 485–88.

16. Citizens for Responsibility and Ethics in Washington, "About CREW," http://www.citizensforethics.org.

17. U.S. Internal Revenue Service, "Exemption Requirements - Section 501(c)(3) Organizations," http://www.irs.gov.

18. *Buckley v. Valeo,* 424 U.S. 1 (1976).

19. See John R. Wright, *Interest Groups and Congress: Lobbying, Contributions, and Influence* (Boston: Allyn & Bacon, 1995, reprinted by Longman Classics Series 2009); Michelle L Chin, Jon R. Bond, and Nehemia Geva, "A Foot in the Door: An Experimental Study of PAC and Constituency Effects on Access," *Journal of Politics* 62 (2000): 534–49.

20. Kate Ackley, "Health Care Ads Could Pick Up After the Break," *Roll Call,* June 29, 2009.

21. Alexis de Tocqueville, *Democracy in America,* ed. Richard D. Heffner (New York: Mentor Books, 1956), 198.

22. David Truman, *The Governmental Process: Political Interests and Public Opinion* (New York: Alfred Knopf, 1971).

23. Mancur Olson, *The Logic of Collective Action* (Cambridge, Mass.: Harvard University Press, 1971).

24. Robert Dahl, *A Preface to Democratic Theory* (Chicago: University of Chicago Press, 1956). Also see Robert Dahl, *Who Governs?* 2nd ed. (New Haven, Conn.: Yale University Press, 2005).

25. C. Wright Mills, *The Power Elite* (New York: Oxford University Press, 1956).

26. Theodore J. Lowi, *The End of Liberalism: Ideology, Policy, and the End of Public Authority* (New York: Norton, 1969).

27. E. E. Schattschneider, *The Semi-Sovereign People* (New York: Holt, Rinehart, and Winston, 1960). Also see E. E. Schattschneider, *Politics, Pressures, and the Tariff* (New York: Prentice-Hall, 1935).

28. Hugh Heclo, "Issue Networks and the Executive Establishment," in *The New American Political System*, ed. Anthony King (Washington, D.C.: American Enterprise Institute, 1978).

29. Robert H. Salisbury, "An Exchange Theory of Interest Groups," *Midwest Journal of Political Science* 13 (1969): 1–32.

30. Olson, *Logic of Collective Action*.

31. Ibid.

32. DeWayne Wickham, "Group Loses Another Leader, and More Luster," *USA Today*, March 6, 2007, A13; Krissah Thompson, "100 Years Old, NAACP Debates Its Current Role," *Washington Post*, July 12, 2009.

33. *AARP Consolidated Financial Statements, December 31, 2008 and 2007*, http://www.aarp.org.

34. *AARP Summary of 2008 AARP Consolidated Financial Statements*, http://www.aarp.org.

35. The AARP's 2008 operating budget was $1.14 billion, *AARP Summary of 2008 AARP Consolidated Financial Statements*, http://www.aarp.org.

36. Staff, "The Numbers," *National Journal*, February 16, 2008, http://www.nationaljournal.com.

37. U.S. Census Bureau, "Table 3.1. Foreign-Born Population by Sex, Age, and World Region of Birth: 2008," http://www.census.gov.

38. U.S. Citizenship and Immigration Services, "About Us," http://www.uscis.gov.

39. Randall Monger and Nancy Rytina, "Annual Flow Report: U.S. Legal Permanent Residents: 2008," Washington DC: Office of Immigration Statistics, Department of Homeland Security, March 2009.

40. U.S. Department of State, "Visas," http://www.travel.state.gov.

41. U.S. Citizenship and Immigration Services, "A Guide to Naturalization," http://www.uscis.gov/natzguide.

42. South Asian Americans Leading Together website, www.saalt.org.

43. NumbersUSA: For Lower Immigration Levels, www.numbersusa.com.

44. US Immigration Support: Your Online Guide to U.S. Visas, Green Cards and Citizenship, www.usimmigrationsupport.org.

45. National Council of La Raza website, www.nclr.org.

46. Robert Pear, "A Million Faxes Later, a Little-Known Group Claims a Victory on Immigration," *New York Times*, July 14, 2007, A17.

47. U.S. Department of Health and Human Services, Administration for Children and Families, Office of Refugee Resettlement, "Who We Serve," http://www.acf.hhs.gov/programs/orr (updated September 18, 2008).

48. U.S. Department of Health and Human Services, Office of Refugee Resettlement, "Fiscal Year 2008 Refugee Arrivals," http://www.acf.hhs.gov/programs/orr.

49. U.S. Committee for Refugees and Immigrants (USCRI), "About USCRI," http://www.refugees.org.

Chapter 9

1. This story was compiled from Josh McKoon's website, www.joshmckoon.com; Larry Gierer, "Local GOP Elects New Chairman, Officers: Attorney Josh McKoon to Take Helm of Party," *Columbus Ledger-Enquirer*, March 31, 2007; Brian McDearmon, "Attorney to Run for GOP Chair: McKoon Seeks Top Post Vacated by Rob Doll," *Columbus Ledger-Enquirer*, February 26, 2007, Chuck Williams, "Republican Josh McKoon Running for Senate District 29 Seat with Abandon, Even with No Opposition Yet," *Columbus Ledger-Enquirer*, March 28, 2010; and phone interview with Josh McKoon, January 28, 2008, and e-mail interview with Josh McKoon, April 29, 2010, both conducted for this textbook. The chapter-opening quotation is from the April 29 e-mail interview.

2. V.O. Key Jr. *Politics, Parties, and Pressure Groups*, 5th ed. (New York: Thomas Y. Crowell Company, 1964).

3. Center for Responsive Politics, "Political Parties Overview," 2009, http://www.opensecrets.org.

4. Ibid.

5. For more on the informal networking that occurs among party activists, see Gregory Koger, Seth Masket, and Hans Noel, "Partisan Webs: Information Exchange and Party Networks," *British Journal of Political Science* 39 (2009): 633–53.

6. Marjorie Hershey, *Party Politics in America*, 12th ed. (New York: Pearson-Longman, 2007), 159.

7. Not all the superdelegates used their right to vote in the choice between Obama and Clinton. See www.realclearpolitics.com.

8. John M. Broder, "Show Me the Delegate Rules, and I'll Show You the Party," *New York Times*, February 17, 2008.

9. Larry M. Bartels, *Presidential Primaries and the Dynamics of Public Choice* (Princeton, N.J.: Princeton University Press, 1988).

10. Brian G. Knight and Nathan Schiff, "Momentum and Social Learning in Presidential Primaries," Working Paper W13637, National Bureau of Economic Research, November 2007.

11. George Washington, "Washington's Farewell Address," reprinted in Randall E. Adkins, *The Evolution of Political Parties, Campaigns, and Elections* (Washington, D.C.: CQ Press, 2008), 47–50.

12. John F. Bibby and Brian F. Schaffner, *Politics, Parties and Elections in America*, 6th ed. (Boston: Cengage-Wadsworth, 2008), 24.

13. United States Senate, Office of the Historian, Biographical Directory of the United States Congress, bioguide .congress.gov.

14. United States Census Bureau, www.census.gov.

15. Henry Clay, speech to the United States Senate on the Whig Party, April 14, 1834, in *Evolution of Political Parties, Campaigns, and Elections*, ed. Adkins, 73.

16. Quoted in James L. Sundquist, *Dynamics of the Party System* (Washington, D.C.: Brookings Institution Press, 1973), 65.

17. Sean M. Theriault, *The Power of the People* (Columbus: Ohio State University Press, 2005), Chapter 3.

18. Douglas W. Jones, "The Australian Paper Ballot," in "A Brief Illustrated History of Voting" (University of Iowa, Department of Computer Science, 2003), http://www.cs.uiowa .edu/~jones/voting/pictures/#australian.

19. Erik J. Engstrom and Samuel Kernell, "Manufactured Responsiveness: The Impact of State Electoral Laws on Unified Party Control of the Presidency and the House of Representatives, 1840–1940," *American Journal of Political Science* 49 (July 2005): 531–49. See p. 535.

20. Anthony Downs, *An Economic Theory of Democracy* (New York: Harper, 1957).

21. Stuart Elaine Macdonald and George Rabinowitz, "Solving the Paradox of Nonconvergence: Valence, Position, and Direction in Democratic Politics," *Electoral Studies* 17, no. 3 (1998): 281–300.

22. Maurice Duverger, "Public Opinion and Political Parties in France," *American Political Science Review* 46, no. 4 (1952): 1069–78, especially 1071.

23. Presidential Vote Statistics, 2000, "Popular Votes for Ralph Nader," http://www.statemaster.com/graph/pre_2000_pop_ vot_for_ral_nad-2000-popular-votes-ralph-nader.

24. For a detailed discussion of how interest groups interact with parties in campaigning, see Matthew J. Burbank, Ronald J. Hrebenar, and Robert C. Benedict, *Parties, Interest Groups, and Political Campaigns* (Boulder, Colo.: Paradigm Publishers, 2008).

25. Scholar Tasha Philpot pointed to underlying shifts as early as 2004. See Tasha S. Philpot, "A Party of a Different Color? Race, Campaign Communication, and Party Politics," *Political Behavior* 26 (2004): 249–70.

26. Nolan McCarty, Keith T. Poole, and Howard Rosenthal, "Party Polarization: 1879–2009," http://www.polarizedamerica .com (updated January 4, 2010).

27. The Democratic Party, "Renewing America's Promise," Democratic Party Platform 2008, http://www.democrats .org.

28. "Offering Smart Solutions: Energy," Website of Republicans in Congress, http://www.gop.gov.

29. "The Cap and Tax Fiction," *Wall Street Journal*, June 26, 2009.

30. The Library of Congress, H.R. 2454, http://thomas.loc.gov.

31. Steve Musfon, David A. Farenthold, and Paul Kane, "In Close Vote, House Passes Climate Bill," *Washington Post*, June 27, 2009.

32. "G.O.P American," Website of Republicans in Congress, http://www.gop.gov.

33. "House Vote 477-H.R.2454: On Passage American Clean Energy Act," *New York Times*, www.politics.nytimes.com

34. Ibid.

Chapter 10

1. This story was compiled from a Huffington Post poll with 10,000 respondents, reported on February 4, 2009; Aaron Schock's House of Representatives website, www.schock .house.gov; Huffington Post, "Aaron Schock in GQ: The Hill's Hottest Freshman Models Conservative Suits," September 16, 2009, http://www.huffingtonpost.com/2009/09/16/ aaron-schock-in-igqi-the_n_288888.html; and Randy James, "The First Gen Y Congressman," *Time*, January 8, 2009.

2. This claim arises from dividing the number of electoral votes by the total number of voters. Alaska had 33 electoral votes and about 317,000 voters in 2008. California had 55 electoral votes and more than 13.2 million voters.

3. CBS News polls, December 9–10, 2000.

4. CBS News polls, December 14 –16, 2000.

5. CBS News polls, January 15–17, 2001.

6. Cable News Network/USA Today poll, conducted by Gallup Organization, November 11–12, 2000.

7. These data come from surveys done by the Pew Research Center for the People & the Press.

8. These data were collected by using the iPOLL search engine from the Roper Center.

9. For a longer discussion of redistricting, see Bernard Grofman, Lisa Handley, and Richard G. Niemi, *Minority Representation and the Quest for Voting Equality* (New York: Cambridge Press, 1992).

10. Stephen Nicholson, *Voting by Agenda* (Princeton, N.J.: Princeton University Press, 2005).

11. Chris W. Bonneau and Melinda Gann Hall, *In Defense of Judicial Elections* (New York: Routledge, 2009).

12. Susan Hyde and Nikolay Marinov, "National Elections across Democracy and Autocracy" http://hyde.research .yale.edu/Hyde_Marinov_NELDA.pdf (updated July 12, 2010).

13. *Marty Cohen, David Karol, Hans Noel, and John Zaller*, The Party Decides: Presidential Nominations Before and After Reform *(Chicago: University of Chicago Press, 2008).*

14. The Federal Election Commission, "The FEC and Federal Campaign Finance Law," *Federal Election Commission*, February 2004 (updated January 2010), http://www.fec.gov/.

15. Jim Drinkard, "Let the Fundraising Begin—Again," *USA Today,* March 10, 2000, 14a.

16. The maximum an individual can contribute to a candidate in 2009–10 is $4,800, which was adjusted for inflation from the $4,600 in 2008. The $5,000 estimate for both primary and general elections reflects a guess about future inflation.

17. James G. Gimpel, Karen M. Kaufmann, and Shanna Pearson-Merkowitz, "Battleground States versus Blackout States," *Journal of Politics* 69 (2007): 786–97.

18. Taofang Huang and Daron Shaw, "Beyond Battlegrounds?" (paper presented at the University of Texas–Austin, 2009).

19. John G. Geer, *In Defense of Negativity* (Chicago: University of Chicago Press, 2006), 59–60.

20. Lynn Vavreck, *The Message Matters* (Princeton: Princeton University Press, 2009).

21. Donald Stokes, "Spatial Models of Party Competition," *American Political Science Review* 57 (1963): 368–77.

22. Sunshine Hillygus and Todd Shields, *The Persuadable Voter* (Princeton: Princeton University Press, 2008), 36.

23. Geer, *In Defense of Negativity.*

24. Anthony Downs, *An Economic Theory of Democracy* (New York: Harper, 1957).

25. Federal Election Commission, "Federal Election Campaign Laws," 2005, 56–60, http://www.fec.gov. Note that the contribution levels have been increased slightly to adjust for inflation.

26. Campaign Finance Institute, "Candidates' Money Was Up, But Party Spending Was Way Up," November 11, 2006.

27. Campaign Finance Institute, "Candidates' Money Was Up" Tables 2 and 4.

28. Albert Cover, "One Good Term Deserves Another: The Advantage of Incumbency in Congressional Elections," *American Journal of Political Science* 21, no. 3 (August 1977).

29. Gary C. Jacobson, *The Politics of Congressional Elections,* 7th ed. (Boston: Pearson Longman, 2009), 168.

30. Steve Finkel "Reciprocal Effects of Participation and Political Efficacy: A Panel Analysis," *American Journal of Political Science* 29, no. 4 (1985): 891–913; Steve Finkel, "The Effects of Participation on Political Efficacy and Political Support: Evidence from a West German Panel," *Journal of Politics* 49, no. 2 (1987): 441–64. These articles provide empirical evidence that supports the arguments of Carol Pateman, *Participation and Democratic Theory* (Cambridge: Cambridge University Press, 1970).

31. See Jan Leighley, "Attitudes, Opportunities, and Incentives," *Political Research Quarterly* 48 (1995): 184.

32. Mark Hugo Lopez and Paul Taylor, "Dissecting the Electorate: Most Diverse in U.S. History," April 30, 2009, Pew Research Center.

33. Mark Hugo Lopez, Emily Kirby, and Jared Sagoff, "The Youth Vote 2004," July 2005, *CIRCLE: The Center for Information & Research on Civic Learning and Engagement.*

34. Mark Hugo Lopez and Paul Taylor, "Dissecting the Electorate: Most Diverse in U.S. History," April 30, 2009, Pew Research Center.

35. Ibid.

36. See, for instance, Raymond Wolfinger and Steven Rosenstone, *Who Votes?* (New Haven: Yale University Press, 1980). There has been much research since the publication of this book, but this source is the best known.

37. U.S. Census Bureau report on the 2004 presidential election.

38. Cindy Kam and Carl Palmer, "Education as a Cause or Proxy? Unpacking the Effects of Education on Political Participation," *Journal of Politics* 70, no. 3 (2008): 612–31.

39. Henry Brady, Sidney Verba, and Kay Schlozman, "Beyond SES: A Resource Model of Political Participation," *American Political Science Review* 89 (June 1995): 271–94.

40. Alan Gerber, Donald Green, and David Nickerson, "Getting Out the Vote in Local Elections: Results from Six Door-to-Door Canvassing Experiments," *Journal of Politics* 65 (2003): 4.

41. Steven J. Rosenstone and Mark Hansen, *Mobilization, Participation, and Democracy in America* (New York: Macmillan Publishing Co., 1993).

42. United States Election Project, "2008 Presidential Nomination Contest Turnout Rates," http://elections.gmu.edu/ voter_turnout.htm (updated October 8, 2008).

43. International IDEA, Voter Turnout, www.idea.int/vt/.

44. G. Bingham Powell, "American Voter Turnout in Comparative Perspective," *American Political Science Review* 80 (1986): 17–37.

45. This "puzzle of participation" was first discussed in Richard Brody in *The New American Political System,* ed. Anthony King (Washington, D.C.: American Enterprise Institute for Public Policy Research, 1978).

46. Warren Miller, "Puzzle Transformed," *Political Behavior* 14 (1992): 1–43.

47. Rosenstone and Hansen, *Mobilization, Participation, and Democracy in America.*

48. Ibid.

49. Matt Bai, "Who Lost Ohio?" *New York Times Magazine,* November 21, 2004.

50. Deborah Brooks and John Geer, "Beyond Negativity," *American Journal of Political Science* 51 (2007): 1–16.

51. Steven Ansolabehere and Shanto Iyengar, *Going Negative* (New York: Free Press, 1995).

52. John G. Geer, *In Defense of Negativity* (Chicago: University of Chicago Press, 2006).

53. See, for example, Joshua Clinton and John Lapinski, "'Targeted' Advertising and Voter Turnout: An Experimental Study of the 2000 Presidential Election," *Journal of Politics* 66 (2004): 1.

54. Richard Lau, Lee Sigelman, and Ivy Brown Rovner, "A New Meta-Analysis," *Journal of Politics* 69 (2007): 1176–1209.

55. Estimate comes from the Pew Hispanic Research Center.

56. Warren et al., "One in 100: Behind Bars in America 2008," February 2008, Pew Center on the States.

57. See Larry Bartels, *Unequal Democracy* (Princeton: Princeton University Press, 2008).

58. The Task Force on American Inequality, "American Democracy in an Age of Rising Inequality," The American Political Science Association, 2004.

59. Nonprofit Voter Engagement Network, press release, October 2009.

60. Survey data available through the Roper Center's iPoll search engine.

61. Poll conducted for McClatchy, October 30–November 2, 2008.

62. Jeffrey A. Karp and Susan A. Banducci, "Party Mobilization and Political Participation in New and Old Democracies," *Party Politics* 13, no. 2 (2007): 217–34.

63. For more information on the new "Boston tea parties," see www.independentpoliticalreport.com.

64. Fox News, March 2003, available through the Roper Center.

65. These data are from a report authored by Russell Dalton, "The Myth of the Disengaged American," 2005, http://www.umich.edu/~cses/resources/results/POP_Oct2005_1.htm.

66. Dennis Johnson, in *Congress and the Internet,* ed. James Thurber and Colton Campbell (New York: Prentice Hall, 2003).

67. Sydney Jones and Susannah Fox, "Generational Differences in Online Activities," January 2009, Pew Internet and American Life Project.

68. The 20 percent comes from a Pew Center survey conducted in November 2006, about whether people were participating in blogs, online discussions, or e-mail lists about the November elections. These data are available through the Roper Center.

69. Matthew A. Mosk, "Internet Donors Fuel Obama." *Washington Post,* February 7, 2008.

70. Ibid.

71. Katherine Q. Seelye and Leslie Wayne, "The Web Takes Ron Paul for a Ride," *New York Times,* November 11, 2007.

72. The Library of Congress THOMAS, "H.R. 2," http://www.thomas.gov/cgi-bin/bdquery/z?d103:HR00002:@@@D&summ2=m&, (updated April 28, 1993; accessed June 17, 2009).

73. *Crawford v. Marion County Election Board*, 553 U.S. (2008). See also Bill Mears, "High Court Upholds Indiana's Voter ID Law," http://www.cnn.com/2008/POLITICS/04/28/scotus.voter.id/index.html, (updated April 28, 2008; accessed June 17, 2009); Linda Greenhouse, "In a 6-to-3 Vote, Justices Uphold a Voter ID Law." *New York Times,* April 29, 2008.

74. Bill Bradbury, "Vote-By-Mail: The Real Winner is Democracy." *Washington Post,* January 1, 2005.

75. The Federal Election Commission, "The FEC and Federal Campaign Finance Law: Historical Background," http://www.fec.gov/, February 2004 (updated January 2010).

76. *Buckley v. Valeo,* 424 U.S. 1 (1976); Federal Election Commission, "Court Case Abstracts: *Buckley v. Valeo,*" http://www.fec.gov/.

77. The Federal Election Commission, "Bipartisan Campaign Reform Act of 2002," http://www.fec.gov/.

78. Gerald M. Pomper, *Elections in America* (New York: Longman, 1980), 161.

79. Tracy Sulkin, "Promises Made and Promises Kept," in *Congress Reconsidered,* ed. Lawrence Dodd and Bruce Oppenheimer (Washington, D.C.: CQ Press, 2009).

80. Politifact, "The Obameter: Tracking Obama's Campaign Promises," *St. Petersburg Times,* http://www.politifact.com (updated March 5, 2010).

81. V. O. Key, *The Responsible Electorate* (Cambridge: Harvard University Press, 1966).

Chapter 11

1. This story was compiled from Answers.com, "Nydia Velázquez," http://www.answers.com; United States House of Representatives website, www.house.gov; Sally Friedman, *Dilemmas of Representation: Local Politics, National Factors, and the Home Styles of Modern U.S. Congress Members* (Albany: State University of New York Press, 2007), 164; and Congresswoman Nydia Velázquez, press release, February 25, 2009, "Velázquez: President Determined to Lay Foundation for Future Growth," http://www.house.gov/velazquez/newsroom/2009/pr-2-25-09-Obama-address-to-nation.html.

2. Mildred Amer and Jennifer E. Manning, "CRS Report for Congress, Membership of the 111th Congress: A Profile," Congressional Research Service, Washington, D.C., 2009.

3. Ibid. For a broader discussion of the careers of women legislators in the House, see Jennifer Lawless and Sean Theriault, "Will She Stay or Will She Go? Career Ceilings and Women's Retirement from the US Congress," *Legislative Studies Quarterly* 30 (2005): 581–96.

4. United States Senate website, www.senate.gov.

5. In rare cases where a senator dies or resigns, an interim replacement is chosen by the governor of the state until an election is held to fill the seat.

6. Wendy J. Schiller, *Partners and Rivals: Representation in U.S. Senate Delegations* (Princeton, N.J.: Princeton University Press, 2000).

7. U.S. Census Bureau website, www.census.gov.

8. Congress had 65 members in 1789, but after the first census of the new federal government under the Constitution, it grew to 105 members in 1792. See Brian Frederick, *Congressional Representation & Constituents: The Case for Increasing the Size of the U.S. House of Representatives* (New York: Routledge, 2010), 23–24.

9. Office of the Clerk, U.S. House of Representatives, www.clerk.house.gov.

10. For a discussion of representation by Latino members, see Jason P. Casellas, "The Institutional and Demographic Determinants of Latino Representation." *Legislative Studies Quarterly* 34, no. 3 (2009): 399-426; see also David Leal and Frederick M. Hess, "Who Chooses Experience? Examining the Use of Veteran Staff by House Freshmen," *Polity* 36 (2004).

11. See *Shaw v. Reno* (1993), *Miller v. Johnson* (1996), and *Easley v. Cromartie* (2001). *Thornburg v. Gingles* (1986) provides plaintiffs with a right to force a state to create a majority-minority district if (1) the minority community is large and concentrated enough to form a majority in the district, (2) the minority community votes cohesively, and (3) white voting prevents the minority community from electing its preferred candidate. For a longer discussion of redistricting, see Bernard Grofman, Lisa Handley, and Richard G. Niemi, *Minority Representation and the Quest for Voting Equality* (New York: Cambridge University Press, 1992).

12. Frances E. Lee and Bruce I. Oppenheimer, *Sizing up the Senate: The Unequal Consequences of Equal Representation* (Chicago: University of Chicago Press, 1999).

13. Two prominent works on this point are Richard F. Fenno, *The Power of the Purse: Appropriations Politics in Congress* (Boston: Little, Brown, 1966), and Aaron B. Wildavsky, *The New Politics of the Budgetary Process* (Boston: Addison-Wesley Educational, 1992).

14. Fiona McGillivray, "Trading Free and Opening Markets," in *International Trade and Political Institutions,* ed. Fiona McGillivray, Iain McLean, Robert Pahre, and Cheryl Schonhardt-Bailey (Cheltenham, UK: Edward Elgar, 2001), 80–98.

15. " Federal Courts' Structure," http://www.uscourts.gov.

16. Sarah A. Binder and Forrest Maltzman, "Senatorial Delay in Confirming Federal Judges, 1947–1998," *American Journal of Political Science* 46, no. 1 (2002): 190–99.

17. Sean Gailmard and Jeffery A. Jenkins, "Minority-Party Power in the Senate and the House of Representatives," in *Why Not Parties: Party Effects in the United States Senate*, ed. Nathan W. Monroe, Jason M. Roberts, and David W. Rohde (Chicago: University of Chicago Press, 2008).

18. Ibid, see pp. 79–126.

19. Barry C. Burden and Tammy M. Frisbee, "Preferences, Partisanship, and Whip Activity in the U.S. House of Representatives," *Legislative Studies Quarterly* 29 (2004): 569–90.

20. Ralph Huitt, "Democratic Party Leadership in the Senate," *American Political Science Review* 55 (1961): 333–44.

21. E. Scott Adler and John Wilkerson, "Intended Consequences: Jurisdictional Reform and Issue Control in the U.S. House of Representatives," *Legislative Studies Quarterly* 33, no. 1 (2008): 85–112.

22. Richard E. Cohen, "Dems May Repeal Term Limits for House Chairs.' *National Journal Online,* December 31, 2008, http://www.nationaljournal.com; Sara Burrows, "House Term Limits Repealed, Rangel to Retain Committee Chairmanship," Cybercast News Service, January 8, 2009, http://www.cns.com.

23. David W. Rohde, "Committee Reform in the House of Representatives and the Subcommittee Bill of Rights," *Annals of the American Academy of Political and Social Science* 411, no 1 (1974): 39–47.

24. For a list of all the current caucuses in the current session of Congress, see http://www.cha.house.gov/member_orgs.aspx.

25. Daily Digest, *Congressional Record D1675* (December 31, 2007); Daily Digest, *Congressional Record D1675* (November 17, 2008) D1277, accessed online at http://thomas.loc.gov.

26. For an extended discussion of the right of recognition and the powers it affords senators, see Floyd Riddick, *Senate Procedure*, ed. Alan Frumin (U.S. Government Printing Office: Washington D.C., 1992), 1091–99.

27. Sarah A. Binder and Steven S. Smith, *Politics or Principle: Filibustering in the U.S. Senate* (Washington DC: Brookings Institution Press, 1997). For a discussion of the use of the filibuster by retiring senators, see Martin Overby, L. Overby, and Lauren Bell, "Rational Behavior or the Norm of Cooperation? Filibustering Among Retiring Senators," *Journal of Politics* 66 (2004): 906–24.

28. Ibid.

29. Wendy J. Schiller, "Resolved the Filibuster Should Be Abolished—Con." in *Debating Reform*, ed. Richard J. Ellis and Michael Nelson (Washington D.C.: CQ Press, 2010).

30. Wendy J. Schiller, "Senators as Political Entrepreneurs: Using Bill Sponsorship to Shape Legislative Agendas," *American Journal of Political Science* 1 (1995): 186–203.

31. Glen Krutz, *Hitching a Ride: Omnibus Legislating in the U.S. Congress* (Columbus: Ohio State University Press, 2001).

32. Keith R. Krehbiel, *Information and Legislative Organization* (Ann Arbor: University of Michigan Press, 1991).

33. For a few examples of this work, see Aage Clausen, *How Congressmen Decide* (New York: St. Martin's Press, 1973); John Kingdon, *Congressmen's Voting Decisions* (New York: Harper & Row, 1989); David W. Brady, *Critical Elections and Congressional Policy Making* (Stanford, Calif.: Stanford University Press, 1988); Stanley Bach and Steven S. Smith, *Managing Uncertainty in the U.S. House of Representatives* (Washington, D.C.: Brookings Institution, 1989). For examples of the ideological examination of roll call voting, see Keith T. Poole and Howard Rosenthal, *Ideology and Congress* (New Brunswick, N.J.: Transaction Publishers, 2009).

34. "U.S. Congress Votes Database," http://projects.washingtonpost.com/congress/.

35. C. Lawrence Evans and Walter J. Oleszek, "Message Politics and Senate Procedure," in *The Contentious Senate: Partisanship, Ideology and the Myth of Cool Judgment*, ed. Colton C. Campbell and Nicol C. Rae (Lanham, Md.: Rowman & Littlefield, 2000).

36. Barbara Sinclair, *Unorthodox Lawmaking: New Legislative Processes in the U.S. Congress*, 3rd ed. (Washington, D.C.: CQ Press, 2007).

37. For the complete legislation, see the Congressional Budget and Impoundment Control Act of 1974 (Public Law 93-344). For additional background on budget history, see the Senate Committee on the Budget, www.budget.senate.gov.

38. For the complete legislation, see the Balanced Budget and Emergency Deficit Control Act of 1985 (Public Law 99-177). For historical tables on the U.S. federal budget, see Congressional Budget Office, "The Budget and Economic Outlook Fiscal Years 2010 to 2020." Issued January 26, 2010. Fiscal year 1985 budget deficit number taken from Table F-1, http://www.cbo.gov/ftpdocs/108xx/doc10871/BudgetOutlook2010_Jan.cfm.

39. See Walter J. Oleszek, *Congressional Procedures and the Policy Process*, 6th ed. (Washington, D.C: CQ Press. 2004), especially pp. 63–69. For a more comprehensive look at the history of budget politics and deficits, see Jasmine Farrier, *Passing the Buck: Congress, Budgets, and Deficits* (Lexington: University of Kentucky Press, 2004).

40. Kathleen Hunter, "GOP Readies Procedural Salvo against Reconciliation Play," *CQ Weekly Online,* March 8, 2010, p. 568.

41. Charles M. Cameron, *Veto Bargaining: Presidents and the Politics of Negative Power* (New York: Cambridge University Press, 2000).

42. Daily Digest, *Congressional Record D1675* (December 31, 2007): Daily Digest, *Congressional Record D1675* (November 17, 2008) D1277.

43. Albert D. Cover and Bruce S. Brumberg, "Baby Books and Ballots: The Impact of Congressional Mail on Constituent Opinion," *American Political Science Review* 76 (1982): 347–59.

44. Richard L. Hall, *Participation in Congress* (New Haven, Conn.: Yale University Press, 1998).

45. Tracy Sulkin, *Issue Politics in Congress* (New York: Cambridge University Press, 2005).

46. Office of the Clerk of the House of Representatives, www.clerk.house.gov

47. For a comprehensive look at this congressional activity, see Diana Evans, *Greasing the Wheels: Using Pork Barrel Projects to Build Majority Coalitions in Congress* (New York: Cambridge University Press, 2004).

48. Citizens Against Government Waste, *2009 Congressional Pig Book,* http://www.cagw.org.

49. Ibid.

50. Jennifer A. Diouhy, "Alaska 'Bridge to Nowhere' Funding Gets Nowhere; Lawmakers Delete Project after Critics Bestow Derisive Moniker," *San Francisco Chronicle*, November 17, 2005, A7.

51. Richard F. Fenno, Jr., *Home Style: Representatives in Their Districts* (Boston: Little, Brown, 1978).

52. David R. Mayhew, *Congress: The Electoral Connection.* (New Haven, Conn.: Yale University Press, 1974).

53. Center for Responsive Politics website, www.opensecrets.com.

54. For details on these programs, see the U.S. Department of Health & Human Services, Centers for Medicare & Medicaid Services (CMS) at www.cms.hhs.gov.

55. Joanna Turner, Michael Boudreaux, and Victoria Lynch, "A Preliminary Evaluation of Health Insurance Coverage in the

2008 American Community Survey,"Health Insurance Coverage Working Paper: 2008 American Community Survey, U.S. Census Bureau, issued September 22, 2008, http://www.census.gov.

56. Open Congress, "H.R. 3962—Affordable Health Care for America Act," Participatory Politics Foundation and Sunlight Foundation, http://www.opencongress.org.

57. Open Congress, "S. 1796—America's Healthy Future Act of 2009," Participatory Politics Foundation and Sunlight Foundation, http://www.opencongress.org.

58. Patricia Murphy, "Senate Passes Sweeping Health Care Reform, but Trouble Lies Ahead," *Capitolist*, December 24, 2009, http://www.politicsdaily.com.

59. Naftali Bendavid, "'Blue Dog' Democrats Hold Health-Care Overhaul at Bay," *Wall Street Journal*, July 27, 2009.

60. The Henry J. Kaiser Family Foundation, "Summary of Coverage Provisions in the Patient Protection and Affordable Care Act and the Health Care and Education Reconciliation Act of 2010," March 23, 2010, http://www.kff.org.

Chapter 12

1. This story was compiled from Meena Dev, "Alumna Hits Campaign Trail with Kerry," *Sophian* (Smith College), September 30, 2004, http://www.smithsophian.com; "Stephanie Cutter," http://www.WhoRunsGov.com; White House, Office of the Press Secretary, "President Obama Names Stephanie Cutter Assistant to the President for Special Projects, April 22, 2010. The quotation is from the article about Cutter in *Sophian*.

2. Charles Jones, *The President in a Separated System* (Washington, D.C.: Brookings Institution Press, 2005).

3. Bruce G. Peabody and Scott E. Grant, "The Twice and Future President: Constitutional Interstices and the Twenty-Second Amendment," *Minnesota Law Review* 83 (1999): 565–94.

4. Ibid.

5. Arthur Schlesinger Jr., *The Imperial Presidency*. (1973; repr., New York: Mariner Books, 2004).

6. Robert Wielaard, Associated Press, "Kosovo Recognition Irritates Russia and China," *Herald-Tribune*, February 19, 2009, A11.

7. Glenn S. Krutz, *Hitching a Ride*: Omnibus Legislating in the U.S. Congress (Columbus: Ohio State University Press, 2001). Also see Charles M. Cameron, *Veto Bargaining: Presidents and the Politics of Negative Bargaining* (New York: Cambridge University Press, 2000).

8. Wilson delivered the speech on December 2, 1913. See John Woolley and Gerhard Peters, "The American Presidency Project: Length of State of the Union Messages and Addresses (in words) Washington – Obama," http://www.presidency.ucsb.edu.

9. Ibid.

10. The chronology that follows is taken from the *Washington Post's* history of Watergate, available at http://www.washingtonpost.com/wp-srv/politics/special/watergate/index.html.

11. Ibid.

12. Douglas Linder, "The Impeachment Trial of William Clinton," Famous American Trials, 2005, http://www.law.umkc.edu.

13. "A Whitewater Chronology: What Really Happened during the Clinton Years," *Wall Street Journal*, May 28, 2003.

14. Ibid.

15. The Library of Congress, Legislative Information,, http//thomas.loc.gov.

16. William G. Howell, *Power without Persuasion: The Politics of Direct Presidential Action* (Princeton, N.J.: Princeton University Press, 2003).

17. Harold C. Relyea, "Presidential Directives: Background and Overview," Congressional Research Service Report for Congress 98-611, Washington, D.C., 2007.

18. Kenneth R. Mayer, "Executive Orders and Presidential Power," *Journal of Politics* 61 (1999): 445–66, esp. p. 448.

19. Ibid.

20. See "Press Release, Executive Order 10730, Providing for the Removal of an Obstruction of Justice within the State of Arkansas, September 24, 1957," http://www.eisenhower.archives.gov.

21. Christopher S. Kelley and Bryan W. Marshall, "The Last Word: Presidential Power and the Role of Signing Statements," *Presidential Studies Quarterly* 38 (2008): 248–67; Michael J. Berry. "Controversially Executing the Law: George W. Bush and the Constitutional Signing Statement," *Congress and the Presidency* 36 (2009): 244–71.

22. The White House, "Memorandum for the Heads of Executive Departments and Agencies: Subject: Presidential Signing Statement," March 9, 2009, http://www.whitehouse.gov.

23. Joseph A. Pika and John Anthony Maltese, *The Politics of the Presidency* (Washington, D.C.: CQ Press, 2008), 15–17.

24. C-SPAN Congressional Glossary, http://www.c-span.org.

25. George C. Edwards III, *On Deaf Ears: The Limits of the Bully Pulpit* (New Haven, Conn.: Yale University Press, 2006).

26. Also see Melvin C. Laracey, *Presidents and the People: The Partisan Story of Going Public* (College Station: Texas A&M University Press, 2002); Reed L. Welch, "Presidential Success in Communicating with the Public through Televised Addresses," *Presidential Studies Quarterly* 33 (2003): 347–65.

27. Richard E. Neustadt, *Presidential Power and the Modern Presidents* (New York: Free Press, 1990).

28. Jon R. Bond, Richard Fleisher, and B. Dan Wood, "The Marginal and Time-Varying Effect of Public Approval on Presidential Success in Congress," *Journal of Politics* 65 (2003): 92–110.

29. Emily Jane Charnock, James A. McCann, and Kathryn D. Tenpas, "Presidential Travel from Eisenhower to George W. Bush: An Electoral College Strategy," *Political Science Quarterly* 124 (2009): 323–39.

30. Joint Resolution of Congress, House Joint Resolution 1145, August 7, 1964, in *Department of State Bulletin,* August 24, 1964, repr. in *Documents of American History,* ed. Henry Steele Commager and Milton Cantor, 10th ed. (Englewood Cliffs, N.J.: Prentice Hall, 1988), vol. 2: 690.

31. Ibid., 144–51.

32. For a longer discussion of this struggle for power over the conduct of war, see William G. Howell and Jon C. Pevenhouse, *Congressional Checks on Presidential War Powers* (Princeton, N.J.: Princeton University Press, 2007).

33. For more on presidential decisions to engage in military conflicts, see James. Meernick, "Domestic Politics and the Political Use of Military Force by the United States," *Political Research Quarterly* 54 (2001): 889–904.

34. U.S. House of Representatives, House Joint Resolution, 114 Section 3 (a) 1, http://thomas.loc.gov.

35. John J. Kruzel, "Afghanistan Troop Level to Eclipse Iraq by Midyear," American Forces Press Service, United States Army. March 25, 2010, http://www.army.mil.

36. Garance Franke-Ruta, "USA Today/Gallup Poll: Majority Support Obama's Afghan Strategy," *Washington Post*, December 3, 2009, in 44: Politics and Policy in Obama's Washington, http://voices.washingtonpost.com/44/.

37. *Youngstown Sheet & Tube Co. v. Sawyer*, 343 U.S. 579 (1952).

38. *Hamdi v. United States,* 542 U.S. 507 (2004).

39. *Rasul v. Bush*, 542 U.S. 466 (2004).

40. *Hamdan v. Rumsfeld*, 548 U.S. 557 (2006).

41. *Boumediene v. Bush*, 553 U.S. 723 (2008).

42. The White House, Executive Order Nos. 13491, 13492, 13493, January 22, 2009, Washington, DC: Government Printing Office, available at http://www.docket.access.gpo.gov.

43. James P. Pfiffner, *The Modern Presidency,* 6th ed. (Boston: Wadsworth Cengage Learning, 2011), 99.

44. Stephen Skowronek, *The Politics Presidents Make: Leadership from John Adams to Bill Clinton* (Cambridge, Mass.: Harvard University Press, 1997). Also see Stephen Skowronek, *Presidential Leadership in Political Time: Reprise and Reappraisal* (Lawrence: University Press of Kansas, 2008).

45. Aaron Wildavsky, "The Two Presidencies" in *The Presidency,* ed. Aaron Wildavsky (Boston: Little, Brown, 1969), 231–43.

46. For a more recent test of this theory, see Brandes Canes-Wrone, William G. Howell, and David E. Lewis, "Toward a Broader Understanding of Presidential Power: A Reevaluation of the Two Presidencies Thesis," *Journal of Politics* 69 (2007): 1–16.

47. William W. Lammers and Michael A. Genovese, *Presidency and Domestic Policy*. See also Neustadt, *Presidential Power and the Modern Presidents*.

48. Samuel Kernell, *Going Public*, 4th ed. (Washington, D.C.: CQ Press, 2007), 131.

49. Ibid., 87–88.

50. Lammers and Genovese, *Presidency and Domestic Policy*.

51. Ronald Reagan, "The Space Shuttle 'Challenger' Tragedy Address," Top 100 Speeches, http://www.americanrhetoric.com.

52. Hank C. Jenkins-Smith, Carol L. Silva and Richard W. Waterman, "Micro- and Macrolevel Models of the Presidential Expectations Gap," *Journal of Politics* 67 (2005): 690–715.

Chapter 13

1. This story was compiled from Marilyn Adams, "Pair of Flier Advocates Fight for Airline Passengers' Rights," *USA Today,* May 19, 2008; Joan Lowy, "Government Asking Why Passengers Were Stranded," August 12, 2009, www.abcnews.go.com; Jeff Bailey, "An Air Travel Activist Is Born," *New York Times,* September 20, 2007; Matthew L. Wald, "Stiff Fines Are Set for Long Wait on the Tarmac," *New York Times,* December 21, 2009, and Coalition for an Airline Passengers' Bill of Rights, "An Early Christmas Present for the Flying Public," e-mail, December 23, 2009, www.FlyersRights.org; and an e-mail interview with Kate Hanni, January 22, 2010, conducted for this textbook, from which the quotation is taken.

2. Max Weber, *Economy and Society,* ed. Guenther Roth and Claus Wittich (Berkeley, Calif.: University of California Press, 1978).

3. Office of Management and Budget, *Analytical Perspectives, Budget of the U.S. Government, Fiscal Year 2011,* http://www.omb.gov; and United States Postal Service, "Postal Facts 2010," http://www.usps.com.

4. The White House, "The Cabinet," http://www.whitehouse.gov.

5. Office of Management and Budget, *Analytical Perspectives, Budget of the U.S. Government, Fiscal Year 2011,* "Table 26-11 Outlays by Agency in the Baseline Projection of Current Policy," p. 413, http://www.omb.gov.

6. National Council of State Legislatures, "Summary of the State Children's Health Insurance Program (SCHIP)," http://www.ncsl.org.

7. Office of Management and Budget, *Analytical Perspectives, Budget of the U.S. Government, Fiscal Year 2011* "Table 10-1 Federal Civilian Employment in the Executive Branch," p. 107, http://www.omb.gov.

8. U.S. Department of Transportation. "Budget Estimates Fiscal Year 2011, Federal Aviation Administration, Exhibit I," http://www.dot.gov.

9. Federal Aviation Administration website, www.faa.gov.

10. Department of Health and Human Services website, www.hhs.gov.

11. James Q. Wilson, *Bureaucracy* (New York: Basic Books, 1989), 91.

12. Donald F. Kettl, *System under Stress: Homeland Security and American Politics,* 2nd ed. (Washington, D.C.: CQ Press, 2007), 37–39.

13. Kettl, *System under Stress.* Also see David E. Lewis, *The Politics of Presidential Appointments: Political Control and Bureaucratic Performance* (Princeton, N.J.: Princeton University Press, 2008), pp. 141–71.

14. Wilson, *Bureaucracy,* 69–70.

15. United States Postal Service, Office of the Postmaster. *The United States Postal Service: An American History, 1775–2006* (Washington, D.C.: Office of Government Relations, United States Postal Service, 2007), pp. 6–7. Accessible online at www.usps.com.

16. Surface Transportation Board, "About STB Overview," http://www.stb.dot.gov.

17. Michael Moss, "E. Coli Path Shows Flaws in Beef Inspection," *New York Times,* October 3, 2009, A1; Michael Moss, "E. Coli Outbreak Traced to Company That Halted Testing of Ground Beef Trimmings," *New York Times,* November 12, 2009, A16.

18. U.S. Consumer Product Safety Commission website, www.cpsc.gov.

19. Barack Obama, "Remarks by the President on Consumer Financial Protection," October 9, 2009, http://www.whitehouse.gov.

20. Lewis, *Politics of Presidential Appointments,* 12–13.

21. Sean M. Theriault, *The Power of the People* (Columbus: Ohio State University Press, 2005), chapter 3.

22. Lewis, *Politics of Presidential Appointments,* 19–20; see especially Figure 2.1.

23. Office of Management and Budget, "The Budget for Fiscal Year 2011," http://www.omb.gov; United States Postal Service, "Postal Facts 2010," http://www.usps.com.

24. U.S. Office of Personnel Management, "Federal Employment Statistics: Distribution of Federal Employment by Major Geographic Area for November 2008," http://www.opm.gov.

25. Bureau of Labor Statistics, U.S. Department of Labor, *Career Guide to Industries, 2010–11 Edition,* http://www.bls.gov.

26. U.S. Office of Personnel Management, "Salaries and Wages: 2010 General Schedules (Base)," http://www.opm.gov.

27. For more on political appointees, see Jeff Gill and Richard Waterman,"Solidary and Functional Costs: Explaining the Presidential Appointment Contradiction," *Journal of Public Administration Research and Theory* 14 (2004):547-569.

28. Lewis, *Politics of Presidential Appointments,* 97; Staff, "Head Count: Tracking Obama's Appointments," *Washington Post,* http://projects.washingtonpost.com/2009/federal-appointments/.

29. Lewis, *Politics of Presidential Appointments,* 100; see Figure 4.3.

30. U.S. Office of Special Counsel, "Political Activity and the Federal Employee," 2000, http://www.osc.gov.

31. For more on the relationship between bureaucrats, members of Congress, and interest groups, see Anthony M. Bertelli and Christian R. Grose, "Secretaries of Pork? A New Theory of Distributive Public Policy,"*Journal of Politics* 71 (2009): 926–45; and Sanford C. Gordon and Catherine Hafer, "Corporate Influence and the Regulatory Mandate," *Journal of Politics* 69 (2007): 300–319.

32. OMB Watch website, www.ombwatch.org.

33. President Barack Obama, The White House, "Memorandum for the Director of the Environmental Protection Agency on State of California Request for Waiver Under 42 U.S.C. 7543(b), the Clean Air Act," issued January 26, 2009, http://www.whitehouse.gov.

34. Jack Lewis, "The Birth of the EPA," *EPA Journal* (Washington, D.C.: U.S. Environmental Protection Agency, 1985), accessed online at http://www.epa.gov.

35. OMB Watch, "Executive Order 12866," February 12, 2002, http://www.ombwatch.org.

36. Felicity Barringer, "In Reversal, Court Allows a Bush Plan on Pollution," *New York Times,* December 24, 2008, A13.

37. As quoted from the *Federal Register* 70, no. 128 (July 6, 2005): 39103–172; accessed via GPO Access, http://www.gpo.gov.

38. "A Major Setback for Clean Air," Editorial, *New York Times,* July 16, 2008.

39. Power-Gen Worldwide, "Court Tosses Out CAIR Emissions Rule," July 11, 2008, http://www.pepei.pennnet.com.

40. Deborah Zaranbeko, "Court Reinstates EPA Power Plant Pollution Rule," Reuters, December 23, 2006, http://www.reuters.com.

41. "National Emissions Standards for Hazardous Air Pollutants: Area Source Standards for Prepared Feeds Manufacturing," 40 CFR Part 63. *Federal Register* 75, no. 2 (January 5, 2010): 522–51.

42. Stephen Power and Ian Talley, "States Want Delay on Emission Rules," *Wall Street Journal,* January 11, 2010, A1.

43. For in-depth studies of congressional oversight, see Charles R. Shipan, "Regulatory Regimes, Agency Actions, and the Conditional Nature of Congressional Influence," *American Political Science Review* 9 (2004): 467–80; and Keith W. Smith, "Congressional Use of Authorization and Oversight." *Congress and the Presidency* 37 (2010): 45–63.

44. Federal Reserve Education, "History of the Federal Reserve," http://www.federalreserveeducation.org; Board of Governors of the Federal Reserve System website, www.federalreserve.gov.

45. Rebecca Christie, "Geithner Says TARP Repayments Don't Hurt Bank Lending Ability," Bloomberg.Com/News, December 19, 2009, http://www.bloomberg.com.

46. Stephen Power and Neal King Jr., "Next Challenge on Stimulus: Spending all that Money," *Wall Street Journal*, February 13, 2009, A1.

47. Daniel P. Carpenter, "Groups, the Media, Agency Waiting Costs, and FDA Drug Approval," *American Journal of Political Science* 46, no. 3 (2002): 490–505. Also see Susan L. Moffitt, "Promoting Agency Reputation through Public Advice: Advisory Committee Use in the FDA," *Journal of Politics* 72, no. 3 (2010): 1–14.

48. L. Paige Whitaker, *The Whistleblower Protection Act: An Overview*, CRS Report for Congress, 2007.

49. Gregory Zuckerman and Kara Scannell, "Madoff Misled SEC in '06, Got Off," *Wall Street Journal,* December 18, 2008.

Chapter 14

1. This story was compiled from Greg Stohr, *A Black and White Case* (Princeton, N.J.: Bloomberg Press, 2004). Documents related to the cases are available at http://supreme.lp.findlaw.com/supreme_court/docket/2002/april.html.

2. Harold J. Spaeth, *Supreme Court Policy Making* (San Francisco: W.H. Freeman, 1979), 38.

3. Administrative Office of the U.S. Courts, http://www.uscourts.gov.

4. Alexander Hamilton, *Federalist 78,* in the *Federalist Papers,* 1788, http://www.constitution.org/fed/federa78.htm.

5. *Marbury v. Madison,* 5 U.S. 137, 177 (1803).

6. *McCulloch v. Maryland,* 4 Wheaton 316 (1819); and *Gibbons v. Ogden,* 9 Wheaton 1 (1824).

7. *Cohens v. Virginia,* 6 Wheaton 264 (1821).

8. *Dred Scott v. Sandford,* 60 U.S. (19 How.) 393 (1857).

9. *United States v. E.C. Knight Co.,* 156 U.S. 1 (1895).

10. *Lochner v. New York,* 198 U.S. 45 (1905); *Adkins v. Children's Hospital,* 261 U.S. 525 (1923).

11. *Brandenburg v. Ohio,* 395 U.S. 444 (1969).

12. *New York Times v. Sullivan,* 376 U.S. 254 (1964).

13. *Memoirs v. Massachusetts,* 383 U.S. 413 (1966).

14. *Engel v. Vitale,* 370 U.S. 421 (1962); *Abington Township School District v. Schempp,* 374 U.S. 203 (1963).

15. *Brown v. Board of Education,* 347 U.S. 484 (1954).

16. *Wesberry v. Sanders,* 376 U.S. 1 (1964); *Reynolds v. Sims,* 377 U.S. 533 (1964).

17. *Griswold v. Connecticut,* 381 U.S. 479 (1965).

18. *Roe v. Wade,* 410 U.S. 113 (1973).

19. *Mapp v. Ohio,* 367 U.S. 643 (1961); *Miranda v. Arizona,* 384 U.S. 436 (1966).

20. "The Law: The Nixon Radicals," *Time,* June 5, 1972, http://www.time.com/time/magazine/article/0,9171,905984,00.html.

21. *Swann v. Charlotte-Mecklenburg Board of Education,* 402 U.S. 1 (1971), busing; *Roe v. Wade,* 410 U.S. 113 (1973), abortion; *Furman v. Georgia,* 408 U.S. 238 (1972), death penalty; *Reed v. Reed,* 404 U.S. 71 (1971), sex discrimination; and *Regents of the University of California v. Bakke* 438 U.S. 265 (1978), affirmative action.

22. *San Antonio Independent School District v. Rodriguez,* 411 U.S. 1 (1973), school funding; *United States v. Leon,* 468 U.S. 897 (1984), limiting the exclusionary rule; and *New York v. Quarles* (467 U.S. 649) (1984), limiting *Miranda.*

23. *Lawrence v. Texas,* 539 U.S. 558 (2003).

24. *Planned Parenthood v. Casey,* 505 U.S. 833 (1992); *United States v. Lopez,* 514 U.S. 549 (1995); *Gratz v. Bollinger,* 539 U.S. 244 (2003); and *Grutter v. Bollinger,* 539 U.S. 306 (2003).

25. *Bush v. Gore,* 531 U.S. 98 (2000).

26. Jeffrey A. Segal and Harold J. Spaeth, *The Supreme Court and the Attitudinal Model Revisited* (New York: Cambridge University Press, 2002), 179.

27. Lee Epstein and Jeffrey A. Segal, *Advice and Consent: The Politics of Judicial Appointments* (New York: Oxford University Press, 2006).

28. Denis Steven Rutkus, "CRS Report for Congress: Judicial Nomination Statistics, 1977-2003," http://www.senate.gov/reference/resources/pdf/RL31635.pdf, Table 2 (b).

29. David W. Rohde and Kenneth A. Shepsle, "Advising and Consenting in the 60-Vote Senate: Strategic Appointments to the Supreme Court," *Journal of Politics* 69 (2007): 664–77.

30. Denis Steven Rutkus, CRS Report for Congress: Judicial Nomination Statistics, 1977-2003, http://www.senate.gov/reference/resources/pdf/RL31635.pdf, Table 2 (b).

31. Michael A. Fletcher, "Obama Criticized as Too Cautious, Slow on Judicial Posts," *Washington Post,* October 16, 2009.

32. Bernie Becker and David Herszenhorn, "Democrats Lash Out at Secret Holds," http://thecaucusblogs.nytimes.com, May 6, 2010.

33. Information is from Democratic strategy memos obtained and reprinted by the *Wall Street Journal*. See "'He Is Latino': Why Dems Borked Estrada, in Their Own Words," http://www.opinionjournal.com/editorial/feature.html?id=110004305.

34. "Robert Bork's Position on Reproductive Rights," *New York Times*, September 13, 1987, B9.

35. Gregory Caldeira and Jack Wright, "Lobbying for Justice: Organized Interests, Supreme Court Nominations, and the United States Senate," *American Journal of Political Science* 42 (1998): 499.

36. Data here follow Jeffrey A. Segal and Albert D. Cover, "Ideological Values and the Votes of U.S. Supreme Court Justices," *American Political Science Review* 83 (1989): 557–65, updated at http://ws.cc.stonybrook.edu/polsci/jsegal/qualtable.pdf. Perceived ideology and perceived qualifications of the nominees derived from content analysis of newspaper editorials at the time of each candidate's nomination.

37. Federal litigation data can be found at http://www.uscourts.gov/Press_Releases/2009/caseload.cfm.

38. Paul M. Collins Jr., "Friends of the Court: Examining the Influence of Amicus Curiae Participation in U.S. Supreme Court Litigation," *Law & Society Review* 38 (2004): 807–32.

39. Rebecca Salokar, *The Solicitor General: The Politics of Law* (Philadelphia: Temple University Press, 1992).

40. Lisa Solowiej and Paul Collins Jr., "Counteractive Lobbying in the US Supreme Court," *American Politics Research* 37 (2009): 670–99.

41. *Regents of the University of California v. Bakke,* 438 U.S. 265 (1978).

42. Federal Bureau of Investigation, "Crime in the United States 2002," http://www.fbi.gov/ucr/cius_02/html/web/offcleared/03-NC.html.

43. United States Sentencing Commission, *2003 Sourcebook of Federal Sentencing Statistics*, 2004, 91.

44. Gregory Caldeira and John R. Wright, "Organized Interests and Agenda Setting in the U.S. Supreme Court," *American Political Science Review* 82 (1988): 1109–28.

45. *Hopwood v. Texas*, 78 F.3d 932 (1996).

46. Timothy Johnson, Paul Wahlbeck, and James Spriggs, "The Influence of Oral Arguments on the U.S. Supreme Court," *American Political Science Review* 100 (2006): 99.

47. *Gonzales v. Raich* 545 U.S. 1 (2005).

48. Segal and Spaeth, *Supreme Court and the Attitudinal Model.*

49. Lee Epstein and Jack Knight, *The Choices Justices Make* (Washington, D.C.: CQ Press, 1998); Forrest Maltzman, James F. Spriggs II, and Paul J. Wahlbeck, *Crafting Law on the Supreme Court: The Collegial Game* (New York: Cambridge University Press, 2000).

50. 58. Executive Order 10925, March 16, 1961, Equal Employment Opportunity Commission, http://www.eeoc.gov/eeoc/history/35th/thelaw/eo-10925.html.

51. 59. Charles V. Dale, "CRS Report for Congress, Federal Affirmative Action Law: A Brief History," 2005, available at http://www.policyarchive.org/handle/10207/bitstreams/4207.pdf.

52. See Lawrence Baum, *The Puzzle of Judicial Behavior* (Ann Arbor: University of Michigan Press, 1997).

53. The Supreme Court Database, http://scdb.wustl.edu/.

54. Jeffrey A. Segal and Robert M. Howard, "How Supreme Court Justices Respond to Litigant Requests to Overturn Precedent," *Judicature* 85 (2001): 148–57.

55. Jeffrey A. Segal and Robert M. Howard, "A Preference for Deference? The Supreme Court and Judicial Review," *Political Research Quarterly* 57 (2004): 131–43. See also Lori Ringhand, *The Changing Face of Judicial Activism: An Empirical Examination of Voting Behavior on the Rehnquist Natural Court, Constitutional Commentary* 24 (2007): 43.

56. Robert Dahl, "Decision Making in a Democracy: The Supreme Court as a National Policy-Maker," *Journal of Public Law* 6 (1957): 179–295.

57. *West Virginia State Board of Education v. Barnette*, 319 U.S. 624 (1943), 638.

Sources for Endpapers

Front: The United States in the Twenty-First Century

Bottled water: New York State Department of Environmental Conservation, www.nyrecycles.org; Watershed, reported in Petz Scholtus, "The U.S. Consumes 1500 Water Bottles Every Second," www.treehugger.com; Bottled Water Facts, buzzle.com.

Marriage: U.S. Census Bureau, reported in Conor Dougherty, "New Vow: I Don't Take Thee," *Wall Street Journal*, September 29, 2010, A3.

Life expectancy: U.S. Census Bureau, 2010 Statistical Abstract, www.census.gov.

Racial/ethnic groups: U.S. Census Bureau, United States Population Projections, 2000 to 2050, www.census.gov.

Schooling: UNESCO Education Statistics, www.nationmaster.com; U.S. Census Bureau, www.census.gov; National Center for Public Policy and Higher Education, www.highereducation.org;

National Center for Education Statistics, U.S. Department of Education, http://nces.ed.gov.

Population: U.S. Census Bureau, www.census.gov.

Jobs: "Business 2.0: The Next Job Boom," CNN Money, http://money.cnn.com; Gallup, "Gallup Finds U.S. Unemployment at 10.0% in Mid-October," October 18, 2010, www.gallup.com.

Work: CIA World Factbook, United States, Economy, GDP, Labor Force—By Occupation, www.cia.gov.

Gap between the rich and the poor: U.S. Census Bureau, reported in Hope Yen, "Income Gap Widens: Census Finds Record Gap between Rich and Poor," Huffington Post, September 28, 2010, http://huffingtonpost.com; U.S. Internal Revenue Service, reported in Mark Robyn and Gerald Prante, "Summary of Latest Federal Individual Income Tax Data," Fiscal Fact No. 2049, October 6, 2010, www.taxfoundation.org; U.S. Census Bureau, Current Population Survey, 1968–2010, www.census.gov.

Poverty rate: U.S. Census Bureau, People and Households, Poverty Data, www.census.gov.

Money spent on campaigns: Center for Responsive Politics, www.opensecrets.org.

Growth rate and GDP: CIA World Factbook, United States, Economy, GDP—Real Growth Rate, GDP—Per Capita, and GDP—Composition by Sector, www.cia.gov.

Back: The United States in the World

Internet connections: John D. Sutter, "Why Internet Connections Are Fastest in South Korea," March 31, 2010, CNN, www.cnn.com.

Internet users: CIA World Factbook, Country Comparison, Internet Users, www.cia.gov.

Mobile phones: CIA World Factbook, Country Comparison, Telephone—Mobile Cellular, www.cia.gov.

Warmest decade: "2009: Second Warmest Year on Record; End of Warmest Decade," January 21, 2010, National Aeronautics and Space Administration, www.nasa.gov; also National Oceanic and Atmospheric Administration, Climatic Data Center, www.noaa.gov.

World population: CIA World Factbook, World, Population, www.cia.gov; UN, Department of Economic and Social Affairs, Population Division, *World Population to 2300* (New York: United Nations, 2004).

Most populous nation: CIA World Factbook, Country Comparison—Population, www.cia.gov; UN, Department of Economic and Social Affairs, Population Division, World Population to 2300 (New York: United Nations, 2004).

Population growth rate: CIA World Factbook, Country Comparison—Population Growth Rate, www.cia.gov.

Most college degrees: College Board, reported in Jamaal Abdul-Alim, "College Board Releases 'Scorecard' Report on U.S. Degree Completion Progress," July 23, 2010, http://diverseeducation.com; Tamar Levin, "Once a Leader, U.S. Lags in College Degrees," New York Times, July 23, 2010.

Nobel Laureates: Nobel Foundation, nobelprize.org.

Carbon-monoxide emissions: Union of Concerned Scientists, "Each Country's Share of CO_2 Emissions," www.ucsusa.org.

Infant mortality: CIA World Factbook, Country Comparison—Infant Mortality Rate, www.cia.gov.

Gap between the rich and the poor: U.S. Census Bureau, reported in Hope Yen, "Census Finds Record Gap between Rich and Poor," September 28, 2010, www.salon.com.

Military expenditures: CIA World Factbook, Country Comparison—Military Expenditures, www.cia.gov.

Obesity: OECD Health Data, reported in "Fat of the Lands: The Bulging Problem of Obesity," September 23, 2010, The Economist, www.economist.com; Organisation for Economic Co-operation and Development, oecd.org.

INDEX

Note: Page numbers followed by an "f" indicate figures. Page numbers followed by a "t" indicate tables.